Copyright, 1925
BY
Augustana Book Concern

Fourth Edition

ROCK ISLAND, ILL.
Augustana Book Concern, Printers and Binders
1930

The Hymnal

and

Order of Service

Authorized by

The Evangelical Lutheran Augustana Synod

Lectionary Edition

Rock Island, Illinois
Augustana Book Concern

Preface

The need of an English hymnal specially adapted to the Augustana Synod began to be felt thirty-five or forty years ago, and in 1895 the Synod instructed the Theological Faculty to prepare such a book. Most of the members responded readily, as did also some of the college professors and not a few others, men and women, pastors and laymen.

In a few years quite a number of translations had been attempted, and in 1899 Dr. C. W. Foss was appointed to edit and revise this and other acceptable material. At the Synodical meeting in St. Paul that year a text edition of 355 hymns was therefore submitted. It was promptly adopted and a music edition ordered. This was prepared by the editor and revised by Dr. Alfred Ostrom. The completion of the work was officially reported to the Synod in 1901.

But according to the editor himself, as well as Dr. O. Olsson, reporting to the Synod in behalf of the Theological Faculty, this Hymnal was intended to serve only for the time being, until a more adequate book could be prepared. The need for such a book was felt from the beginning, and it is a tribute to the compilers of the first Hymnal that it has served its purpose as long and as well as it has. Naturally the need was most keenly felt in the exclusively English churches, and the Association of those churches kept the matter constantly before the Synod. In 1910 the Association appointed a Hymnal Committee which is still in existence (1925), though the personnel has varied considerably during the intervening years.

In 1913 the Synod elected a Hymnal Committee of its own, consisting of Dr. Adolf Hult, Dr. C. J. Södergren, and Rev. Luther Malmberg, with instructions to coöperate with the committee of the Association. In 1917 Mr. E. W. Olson was added to this Committee, in 1920 Rev. C. A. Wendell, and in 1922 Rev. E. E. Ryden. An Advisory Committee was also elected the latter year, consisting of Dr. Mauritz Stolpe and the following musicians: Per Olsson, H. Brase, Filmore Ohman, Arvid Samuelson, Gustaf Lundholm, A. D. Bodfors, Samuel Thorstenberg, and J. Victor Bergquist. In 1924 Rev. P. N. Sjogren, Rev. Victor E. Beck, Dr. S. G. Hägglund, Rev. N. E. Kron, and Rev. E. C. Bloomquist were elected as an "Advisory Committee on Criticism of the Hymnal." Dr. Adolf Hult has withdrawn, and Rev. Luther Malmberg has taken up work in another Synod.

III

For a number of years no definite progress was reported, and when the demands for a new book had become quite compelling, the Committee was reorganized. Mr. E. W. Olson was chosen to edit the work. He was released from his ordinary duties at the Augustana Book Concern and gave all his time to the Hymnal. But that was only a few months before the meeting of the Synod, in 1922, and the only thing the Committee could do was to propose a supplement to the existing Hymnal and ask for an extension of time. The Synod rejected the plan and insisted on a complete new Hymnal at the earliest date possible.

The result was a very busy year. Dr. C. W. Foss and Rev. I. O. Nothstein were chosen editors and took up the work with all possible energy, gathering material both for the text and the music. The Committee met once a month, except during the summer, often spending two days at each meeting. Thus the work on the Hymnal text was completed in time for the meeting of the Synod in Rockford, Ill., in 1923. The Synod accepted the work and instructed the Committee to publish it, at the same time authorizing such minor modifications ommittee might deem advisable.

ast amount of work remained to be done. The tunes had to be re-examined and finally passed upon, the new Liturgy adopted by the Synod had to be prepared, the Passion History (which is a mosaic of Holy Scripture) had to be revised word for word in conformity with the American Standard version of the Bible, various indexes had to be prepared, and a mass of minor details attended to. In order to facilitate the work, the Committee adopted a division of labor. Dr. Foss and Rev. Nothstein continued in the capacity of editors. The choice of tunes, the editing of the music for the Liturgy, and much other work was intrusted to Rev. E. E. Ryden, Dr. C. J. Södergren and Rev. C. A. Wendell; the revision of the Passion History and much critical work to Mr. E. W. Olson; the editing and paragraphing of the Pericopes to Rev. C. A. Wendell; the rubrics for the same, as well as the revision of the Collects, and a brief account of the Church year, to Dr. C. J. Södergren; and the preparation of the various indexes to Rev. I. O. Nothstein. One by one these undertakings were reported to the Committee and passed upon by that body. The Liturgy has been prepared by a special Committee, chosen by the Synod and consisting of the following members: Dr. E. F. Pihlblad, Dr. Abel Ahlquist, Dr. Adolf Hult, Rev. J. W. Johnson, Rev. E. E. Ryden, and Prof. I. M. Anderson. As the Hymnal Committee did not feel competent to pass on the technicalities of the music, Prof. Gerhard Alexis was elected, with the approval of the Board of Directors of Augustana Book Concern, to do this work. He was assisted by Prof. Peter Johnson. Both of them have also contributed original compositions, as have some other of our best known organists.

The list of original tunes incorporated into this Hymnal follows: Gerhard Alexis: 485, 557, 569, 609, 677, 681, 615 (harmony); J. Victor Bergquist: 432, 437, 533, 605, 656; Dr. Adolf Hult: 380 (arranged), 426; Peter Johnson: 88, 141, 189, 210, 229, 231, 318, 505, 506, 556; C. S. Malmstrom: 537; Rev. S. M.

Miller: 168, 615; Dr. August Norrbom: 564; Dr. C. J. Södergren: 263; Ralph A. Strom: 382, 399, 548, 623. The following new hymns (text) will be found in this book: Rev. Gustav Erikson: 578; Anna Hoppe: 6, 14, 15, 42, 55, 69, 73, 79, 82, 83, 87, 138, 152, 171, 176, 177, 185, 192, 193, 194, 393, 394; Rev. S. M. Miller: 140, 168, 615; E. W. Olson: 43, 323, 444, 605 (2, 3); Rev. E. E. Ryden: 141, 189, 256, 495, 556, 581, 590; Dr. George H. Trabert: 142, 247; Rev. C. A. Wendell: 496, 560, 680. In addition, this work contains translations from Swedish sources to the number of one hundred and nineteen.

To the best of its ability the Committee has tried to follow the instructions of the Synod, at the same time giving respectful attention to suggestions and criticisms offered by individual members of the Synod. At the instance of the Synod, translations from the Swedish "Psalmbok" have been solicited through the Church press, and as far as possible the results have been used. In accordance with definite instructions by the Synod, choice hymns from other sources have also been selected. Every effort has been made to find suitable tunes, not too heavy for the average congregation to sing, nor too light for becoming dignity at our public worship. Practically all the best loved chorals will be found in the Hymnal, and so will a large number of other tunes which have endeared themselves to Christian hearts.

Grateful acknowledgment is rendered in every instance where hymns and tunes are used by permission of the owners of the copyright, and the utmost care has been taken to guard against infringement of such rights. Should any case of such trespass inadvertently have occurred in this work, the publishers will be glad to make the proper amends.

It is not without regret that the Committee herewith brings its work to a close, for it has truly been a labor of love. If the wishes of the Synod have been reasonably well fulfilled; if our people will find the book serviceable; and above all, if it can serve, in some small degree, the purpose of the Lord Jesus Christ, for love of Whom we have labored, the Committee will feel abundantly satisfied.

Rock Island, Ill., April 23, 1925.

C. W. Foss,
I. O. Nothstein,
E. W. Olson,
E. E. Ryden,
C. J. Södergren,
C. A. Wendell.

Contents

Arrangement of Hymns

The Hymnal

Let the word of Christ dwell in you richly;
in all wisdom teaching and admonishing one another
with psalms and hymns and spiritual songs,
singing with grace in your hearts unto God.

Col. 3. 16.

The Hymnal

1. Prepare the Way, O Zion!

Bereden väg för Herran. 7 6, 7 6, 7 7, 6 6.   Old Swedish Melody, prior to 1560.

1. { Pre - pare the way, O Zi - on! Ye aw - ful deeps, rise high; }
   { Sink low, ye tow'r - ing moun - tains, The Lord is draw - ing nigh; }

The right-eous King of glo - ry, Fore-told in sa - cred sto - ry.

REFRAIN:

O blest is He that came In God the Fa - ther's Name. A-MEN.

2 O Zion, He approacheth,
    Thy Lord and King for aye!
Strew palms where He advanceth,
    Spread garments in His way.
God's promise faileth never,
Hosanna sound forever!

3 Fling wide thy portals, Zion,
    And hail thy glorious King;
His tidings of salvation
    To every people bring,
Who, waiting yet in sadness,
Would sing His praise in gladness.

4 He cometh not with warriors,
    And not with pomp and show,
Yet smiteth He with terror
    Sin, death, and every foe.
The Spirit's sword He wieldeth,
Not e'en to death He yieldeth.

5 Give heed, thou sinful people,
    Thy King and Saviour own:
The kingdom He hath founded
    Is not an earthly one;
No power can overthrow it,
Nor earthly wisdom know it.

6 The throne which He ascendeth
    Is fixed in heaven above:
His sanctified dominion
    Is light alone and love.
His praise be ever sounding
For grace and peace abounding.

7 Jerusalem is fallen,
    And closed its temple-door;
Its sacrifices ended;
    Its scepter is no more.
Christ's kingdom never ceaseth,
Its glory still increaseth.

Frans Mikael Franzèn, 1812.

1

2. Lift Up Your Heads, Ye Mighty Gates!

Gör porten hög. L. M. D.

Koralbok, 1697.

1. Lift up your heads, ye might-y gates! Be-hold, the King of glo-ry waits;
The King of kings is draw-ing near, The Sav-iour of the world is here;
Life and sal-va-tion He doth bring, Wherefore re-joice, and glad-ly sing:

REFRAIN:

All praise and glo-ry be to Thee, Lord Je-sus Christ, e-ter-nal-ly. A-MEN.

Or: Peterborough, No. 71.

2 The Lord is just, a Helper tried,
Mercy is ever at His side;
His kingly crown is holiness,
His scepter, pity in distress:
The end of all our woe He brings;
Wherefore the earth is glad and sings:

3 O blest the land, the city blest,
Where Christ the Ruler is confest!
O happy hearts and happy homes
To whom this King in triumph comes!
The cloudless Sun of joy He is,
Who bringeth pure delight and bliss.

4 Fling wide the portals of your heart;
Make it a temple, set apart
From earthly use for heaven's employ,
Adorned with prayer, and love, and joy:
So shall your Sovereign enter in,
And new and nobler life begin.

5 Redeemer, come! I open wide
My heart to Thee; here, Lord, abide!
Let me Thine inner presence know,
Thy grace and love on me bestow.
Thy Holy Spirit guide us on,
Until our glorious goal be won.

Georg Weissel, 1633.

3. Comfort, Comfort Ye My People.

Werde munter, mein Gemüthe. 8 7, 8 7, 7 7, 8 8.   JOHANN SCHOP, 1642.

1. Com-fort, com-fort ye my peo-ple, Speak ye peace, thus saith our God;
Com-fort those who sit in dark-ness, Mourn-ing 'neath their sor-row's load;
Speak ye to Je-ru-sa-lem Of the peace that waits for them;
Tell her that her sins I cov-er, And her war-fare now is o-ver. A-MEN.

2 For the herald's voice is crying
  In the desert far and near,
Bidding all men to repentance,
  Since the kingdom now is here.
O that warning cry obey!
Now prepare for God a way!
Let the valleys rise to meet Him,
And the hills bow down to greet Him.

3 Make ye straight what long was crooked,
  Make the rougher places plain:
Let your hearts be true and humble,
  As befits His holy reign,
For the glory of the Lord
Now o'er earth is shed abroad,
And all flesh shall see the token
That His Word is never broken.

Johannes Olearius, 1671.

4. O How Shall I Receive Thee?

O, du mitt hjärtas trängtan. 7 6, 7 6. D.   JOHAN CHRISTIAN FREDRICK HAEFFNER, 1808.

1. O how shall I re-ceive Thee, How greet Thee, Lord, a-right?
All na-tions long to see Thee, My Hope, my heart's De-light!
O kin-dle, Lord most ho-ly, Thy lamp with-in my breast,
To do in spir-it low-ly All that may please Thee best. A-MEN.

2 Thy Zion palms is strewing,
　And branches fresh and fair;
My heart, its powers renewing,
　An anthem shall prepare.
My soul puts off her sadness
　Thy glories to proclaim;
With all her strength and gladness
　She fain would serve Thy Name.

3 I lay in fetters groaning,
　Thou com'st to set me free;
I stood, my shame bemoaning,
　Thou com'st to honor me.
A glory Thou dost give me,
　A treasure safe on high,
That will not fail nor leave me
　As earthly riches fly.

4 Love caused Thine incarnation,
　Love brought Thee down to me;
Thy thirst for my salvation
　Procured my liberty.
O love beyond all telling,
　That led Thee to embrace,
In love all love excelling,
　Our lost and fallen race!

5 Rejoice then, ye sad-hearted,
　Who sit in deepest gloom,
Who mourn o'er joys departed,
　And tremble at your doom:
He who alone can cheer you,
　Is standing at the door;
He brings His pity near you,
　And bids you weep no more.

Paul Gerhardt, 1653.

5. Jerusalem, Lift Up Thy Voice!

Vom Himmel hoch da komm ich her. L. M.

VALENTIN SCHUMANN'S
Geistliche Lieder, Leipzig, 1539.

1. Je - ru - sa - lem, lift up thy voice! Daugh - ter of
Zi - on, now re - joice! Thy King is come, whose might - y
hand Hence - forth shall reign o'er ev - 'ry land. A - MEN.

2 He comes to every tribe and race,
A Messenger of truth and grace:
With peace He comes from heaven above
On earth to found His realm of love.

3 In God's eternal covenant,
He comes for our salvation sent.
The star of hope moves on before,
And hosts assemble to adore.

4 Let all the world with one accord
Now hail the coming of the Lord:
Praise to the Prince of heavenly birth
Who bringeth peace to all the earth!

Johan Olof Wallin, 1814.

6. Rise, Arise! Rise, Arise!

Fahre fort, fahre fort. 6 7, 8 7, 8 9 6.

From the German, 1704.

1. Rise, a - rise! Rise, a - rise! Zi - on, rise to greet thy King!
O - pen wide the gates be - fore Him! Let the glad ho -
san - nas ring! Haste to wor - ship and a - dore Him! Hark, the watch-man
on the moun - tain cries: "Rise, a - rise! Rise, a - rise!" A - MEN.

2 Weep no more! Weep no more!
Zion, dry thy bitter tears!
  Cast away all gloom and sadness,
For the Shiloh now appears,
  Who shall turn thy grief to gladness!
Day has dawned! Arise! The night is o'er!
Weep no more! Weep no more!

3 O rejoice! O rejoice!
Christ doth come, as long foretold!
  The Messiah long expected,
The incarnate Word behold!
  Though by kings of earth rejected,
Hail Him Lord of all with mighty voice!
O rejoice! O rejoice!

4 Crown Him King! Crown Him King!
His exalted Name confess!
  From His heavenly throne descending,
Jesus, Lord of righteousness,
  Bringeth joy and peace unending!
O let heart and tongue His praises sing!
Crown Him King! Crown Him King!

5 Worship Him! Worship Him!
Worship at His sacred feet!
  Hail the Son of God thy Saviour!
Haste, thy longed for Bridegroom greet!
  Come, receive His kingly favor!
Zion, haste, thy lamp of faith to trim!
Worship Him! Worship Him!

Anna Hoppe, 1920.

7. O Come, O Come, Immanuel.

St. Petersburg. 8 8, 8 8, 8 8.

DIMITRI BORTNIANSKY, (1752–1828).

1. O come, O come, Immanuel, And ransom captive Israel, That mourns in lonely exile here

REFRAIN:

Until the Son of God appear. Rejoice! rejoice! Immanuel Shall come to thee, O Israel! A-MEN.

2 O come, Thou Rod of Jesse, free
Thine own from Satan's tyranny;
From depths of hell Thy people save,
And give them victory o'er the grave.

3 O come, Thou Dayspring, come and cheer
Our spirits by Thine advent here:
And drive away the shades of night,
And pierce the clouds and bring us light.

4 O come, Thou Key of David, come,
And open wide our heavenly home;
Make safe the way that leads on high,
And close the path to misery.

Latin Antiphons, XI Century.
Tr. John Mason Neale, 1861.

8. Lo! He Comes, with Clouds Descending.

Kensington New. 8 7, 8 7, 4 7.

JAMES TILLEARD, 1866.
Fifth line altered.

1. Lo! He comes, with clouds de-scend-ing, Once for fa-vored sin-ners slain.
2. Ev-'ry eye shall now be-hold Him Robed in dread-ful maj-es-ty;

Thou-sand thou-sand saints at-tend-ing, Swell the tri-umph of His train:
Those who set at naught, and sold Him, Pierced, and nailed Him to the tree,

Al-le-lu-ia! God ap-pears on earth to reign.
Deep-ly wail-ing, Shall the true Mes-si-ah see. A-MEN.

3 Now redemption, long expected,
  See in solemn pomp appear,
All His saints, by man rejected,
  Now shall meet Him in the air;
    Alleluia!
  See the Day of God appear.

4 Yea, Amen, let all adore Thee,
    High on Thine eternal throne!
  Saviour, take the power and glory,
    Claim the Kingdom for Thine own;
      O come quickly,
    Alleluia! come, Lord, come!

John Cennick, 1750.

9. Jesus, Thy Church with Longing Eyes.

O Jesu Christ, meins Lebens Licht. L. M.

NÜRNBERGER GESANGBUCH, 1676.

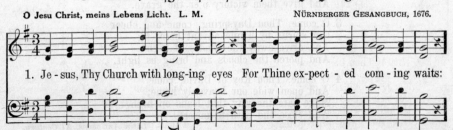

1. Je-sus, Thy Church with long-ing eyes For Thine ex-pect-ed com-ing waits:

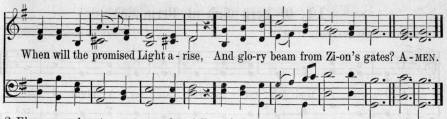

When will the promised Light a-rise, And glo-ry beam from Zi-on's gates? A-MEN.

2 E'en now, when tempests round us fall,
And wintry clouds o'ercast the sky,
Thy words with pleasure we recall,
And deem that our redemption's nigh.

3 Come, gracious Lord, our hearts renew,
Our foes repel, our wrongs redress,
Man's rooted enmity subdue,
And crown Thy gospel with success.

4 O come, and reign o'er every land;
Let Satan from his throne be hurled;
Let nations bow to Thy command,
And grace revive a dying world.

5 Teach us in watchfulness and prayer
To wait for the appointed hour;
And fit us by Thy grace to share
The triumph of Thy conquering power.

William Hiley Bathurst, 1831.

10. Once He Came in Blessing.

Gottes Sohn ist Kommen. 6 6, 6 6, 6 6. Trochaic.　　　MICHAEL WEISSE, 1531.

1. Once He came in bless-ing, All our ills re-dress-ing,
2. Still He comes with-in us, Still His voice would win us

Came in like-ness low-ly, Son of God most ho-ly;
From the sins that hurt us; Would to truth con-vert us

Bore the cross to save us, Hope and free-dom gave us.
From our fool-ish er-rors, Ere He comes in ter--rors. A-MEN.

3 Thus if Thou hast known Him,
Not ashamed to own Him,
Nor dost love Him coldly,
But will trust Him boldly,
He will now receive thee,
Heal thee, and forgive thee.

4 He who well endureth,
Bright reward secureth;
Come, then, O Lord Jesus,
From our sins release us;
Let us here confess Thee,
Till in heaven we bless Thee.

John Horn (Roh), 1544.

11. O Very God of Very God.

Nottingham (St. Magnus). C. M.   JEREMIAH CLARKE, (1670-1707).

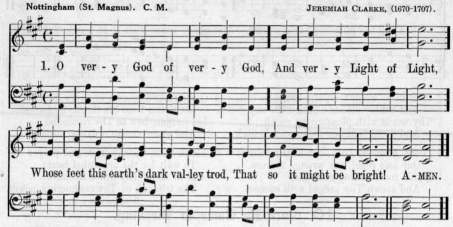

1. O ver-y God of ver-y God, And ver-y Light of Light,

Whose feet this earth's dark val-ley trod, That so it might be bright! A-MEN.

2 Our hopes are weak, our foes are strong,
   Thick darkness blinds our eyes;
Cold is the night, and O we long
   For Thee, our Sun, to rise!

3 And even now, though dull and gray,
   The east is brightening fast,
And kindling to the perfect day
   That never shall be past.

4 O guide us till our path be done,
   And we have reached the shore
Where Thou, our everlasting Sun,
   Art shining evermore!

5 We wait in faith, and turn our face
   To where the daylight springs,
Till Thou shalt come our gloom to chase,
   With healing on Thy wings.
         John Mason Neale, 1846.

12. Hark! a Thrilling Voice Is Sounding.

Lucerne. 8 7, 8 7.   T. A. WILLIS, 1876.

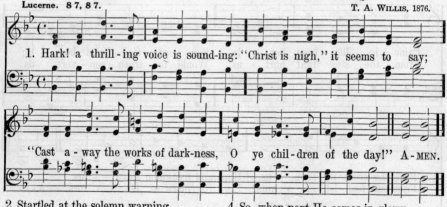

1. Hark! a thrill-ing voice is sound-ing: "Christ is nigh," it seems to say;

"Cast a-way the works of dark-ness, O ye chil-dren of the day!" A-MEN.

2 Startled at the solemn warning,
   Let the earth-bound soul arise;
Christ, our Sun, all sloth dispelling,
   Shines upon the morning skies.

3 Lo, the Lamb, so long expected,
   Comes with pardon down from heaven;
Let us haste, with tears of sorrow,
   One and all, to be forgiven.

4 So, when next He comes in glory,
   And the world is wrapped in fear,
May He then as our Defender
   On the clouds of heaven appear.

5 Honor, glory, might, and blessing
   To the Father and the Son,
With the everlasting Spirit,
   One in Three, and Three in One.
         Latin Hymn of V Century.
         Tr. Edward Caswall, 1849, a.

13. On Jordan's Banks the Herald's Cry.

Mendon. L. M. German Melody: arr. by SAMUEL DYER, 1828.

1. On Jordan's banks the herald's cry Announces that the Lord is nigh: Come then and hearken, for he brings Glad tidings from the King of kings. A-MEN.

2 Then cleansed be every breast from sin,
Make straight the way for God within,
And let us all our hearts prepare
For Christ to come and enter there.

3 For Thou art our Salvation, Lord,
Our Refuge and our great Reward.
Without Thy grace we waste away,
Like flowers that wither and decay.

4 Stretch forth Thy hand, to health restore,
And make us rise, to fall no more:
Once more upon Thy people shine,
And fill the world with love divine.

5 All praise, eternal Son, to Thee
Whose advent sets Thy people free,
Whom, with the Father, we adore,
And Holy Ghost, forevermore.

John Chandler. 1837.

14. Thou Virgin-born Incarnate Word.

Mitt hjerta, Jesu! denna dag. 8 7, 8 7, 8 8 7.   Koralbok, 1884.

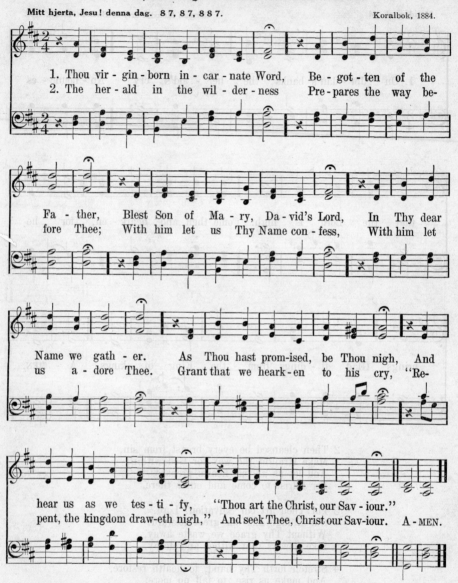

1. Thou vir-gin-born in-car-nate Word, Be-got-ten of the
2. The her-ald in the wil-der-ness Pre-pares the way be-

Fa-ther, Blest Son of Ma-ry, Da-vid's Lord, In Thy dear
fore Thee; With him let us Thy Name con-fess, With him let

Name we gath-er. As Thou hast prom-ised, be Thou nigh, And
us a-dore Thee. Grant that we heark-en to his cry, "Re-

hear us as we tes-ti-fy, "Thou art the Christ, our Sav-iour."
pent, the kingdom draw-eth nigh," And seek Thee, Christ our Sav-iour. A-MEN.

3 Thou art indeed God's holy Son,
　Beloved of Him so dearly.
The mighty works that Thou hast done
　Reveal Thy Godhead clearly:
The blind can see, the sick are healed,
The lips once dumb are now unsealed,
　All power is Thine, dear Jesus!

4 Thou art our Peace, our Righteousness,
　The Rock of our salvation.
Clothed in Thy garb of holiness,
　We fear no condemnation.
Thy blood has cleansed away our sin,
Through Thee eternal life we win,
　O crucified Redeemer!

Anna Hoppe, 1920.

15. "Repent, the Kingdom Draweth Nigh."

Breslau. L. M.   Hymnodus Sacer, Leipzig, 1625.

1. "Re - pent, the king - dom draw - eth nigh," The her - ald
of the Lord doth cry. Ye sin - ners lost through Ad - am's
fall, Will ye not heark - en to the call? A - MEN.

2 Repent! The gracious call believe,
   Haste His forgiveness to receive.
   The Prince of Life, incarnate Word,
   Life and salvation can afford.

3 Divine Redeemer, glorious King!
   Repentant hearts to Thee we bring.
   Thy holy blood for us was spilt,
   Cleanse us from all the stains of guilt.

4 Drawn by Thy Spirit, through Thy Word,
   Thine invitation we have heard.
   In answer to Thy sweet request,
   We come to Thee, O Christ, for rest.

5 Thy pardon, full, complete, and free,
   Removes sin's awful penalty.
   Our Father's love is now restored;
   Thou hast redeemed us, dearest Lord.

6 Let us Thy Name forever bless,
   On earth Thy gospel truth confess,
   Till saved by grace, through faith in Thee,
   The gates of paradise we see.

Anna Hoppe, 1921.

16. Hail to the Lord's Anointed!

Aurelia. 7 6, 7 6. D.   SAMUEL SEBASTIAN WESLEY, 1864.

1. Hail to the Lord's A - noint - ed, Great Da - vid's great - er Son!
2. He comes with suc - cor speed - y To those who suf - fer wrong;

Hail, in the time ap - point - ed, His reign on earth be - gun!
To help the poor and need - y, And bid the weak be strong:

He comes to break op - pres - sion, To set the cap - tive free;
To give them songs for sigh - ing; Their dark - ness turn to light,

To take a - way trans-gres - sion, And rule in eq - ui - ty.
Whose souls, condemned and dy - ing, Were pre-cious in His sight. A - MEN.

3 He shall come down like showers
  Upon the fruitful earth;
And love, joy, hope, like flowers,
  Spring in His path to birth.
Before Him on the mountains,
  Shall peace, the herald, go;
And righteousness in fountains
  From hill to valley flow.

4 To Him shall prayer unceasing
  And daily vows ascend;
His kingdom still increasing,
  A kingdom without end.
The tide of time shall never
  His covenant remove;
His Name shall stand forever,—
  That Name to us is Love.

James Montgomery, 1821.

17. Rejoice, All Ye Believers.

Haf trones lampa färdig.   7 6, 7 6.   D.   Swedish Folksong.

1. Re - joice, all ye be - liev - ers, And let your lights ap - pear!
2. The watch-ers on the moun - tain Pro - claim the Bride-groom near;

The eve - ning is ad - vanc - ing, And dark - er night is near.
Go meet Him as He com - eth, With hal - le - lu - jahs clear.

The Bride-groom is a - ris - ing, And soon He draw - eth nigh.
The mar - riage feast is wait - ing, The gates wide o - pen stand;

Up, watch, and pray, and wres - tle, — At mid-night comes the cry!
Up, up, ye heirs of glo - ry, The Bridegroom is at hand! A - MEN.

3 Ye saints, who here in patience
  Your cross and sufferings bore,
Shall live and reign forever,
  Where sorrow is no more.
Around the throne of glory
  The Lamb ye shall behold,
In triumph cast before Him
  Your diadems of gold!

4 Our Hope and Expectation,
  O Jesus, now appear;
Arise, Thou Sun so longèd for,
  O'er this benighted sphere!
With hearts and hands uplifted,
  We plead, O Lord, to see
The day of earth's redemption,
  That brings us unto Thee!

Laurentius Laurentii, 1700.

18. O Bride of Christ, Rejoice!

Auf meinen lieben Gott. 6 6, 7 7, 7 7.

Secular Melody.
J. REGNART, 1574.

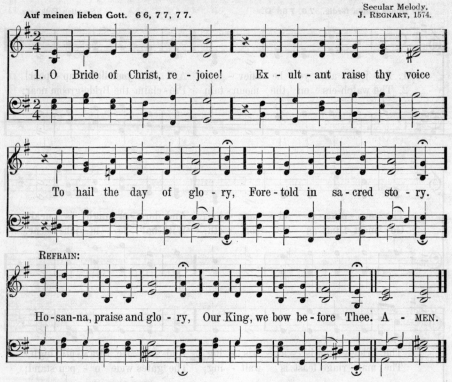

1. O Bride of Christ, re - joice! Ex - ult - ant raise thy voice

To hail the day of glo - ry, Fore - told in sa - cred sto - ry.

REFRAIN:

Ho - san - na, praise and glo - ry, Our King, we bow be - fore Thee. A - MEN.

2 Let shouts of gladness rise
Triumphant to the skies.
Here comes the King most glorious
To reign o'er all victorious.

3 He wears no kingly crown,
Yet as a king He's known;
Though not arrayed in splendor,
He still makes death surrender.

4 Thy heart now open wide,
Bid Christ with thee abide;
He graciously will hear thee,
And be forever near thee.

5 E'en babes with one accord
With thee shall praise the Lord,
And every gentile nation
Respond with exultation.

Johan Olof Wallin, 1816.

19. Hark, the Glad Sound, the Saviour Comes.

Henry. C. M.

S. B. POND, 1835.

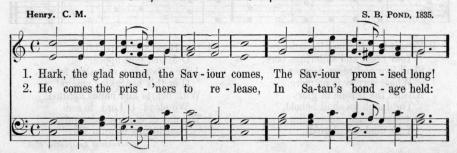

1. Hark, the glad sound, the Sav - iour comes, The Sav - iour prom - ised long!
2. He comes the pris - 'ners to re - lease, In Sa - tan's bond - age held:

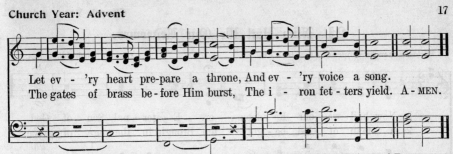

Let ev - 'ry heart pre-pare a throne, And ev - 'ry voice a song.
The gates of brass be - fore Him burst, The i - ron fet - ters yield. A - MEN.

3 He comes, the broken heart to bind,
  The bleeding soul to cure,
And, with the treasures of His grace,
  Enrich the humble poor.

4 Our glad hosannas, Prince of Peace,
  Thy welcome shall proclaim;
And heaven's eternal arches ring
  With Thy beloved Name!

Philip Doddridge, 1735.

20. Arise, the Kingdom Is at Hand.

Christmas. C. M.

GEORGE FREDERICK HÄNDEL, 1728.

1. A - rise, the king-dom is at hand, The King is draw-ing
nigh; A - rise with joy, thou faith - ful band, To
meet the Lord Most High, To meet the Lord Most High! A - MEN.

2 Look up, ye souls weighed down with care,
  The Sovereign is not far;
Look up, faint hearts, from your despair,
  Behold the Morning Star!

3 Look up, ye drooping hearts, to-day!
  The King is very near:
O cast your griefs and fears away,
  For, lo, your Help is here!

4 Hope, O ye broken hearts, at last!
  The King comes on in might;
He loved us in the ages past,
  When we lay wrapped in night.

5 Now fear and wrath to joy give place,
  Our sorrows now are o'er,
Since God hath made us, in His grace,
  His children evermore.

Johann Rist, 1651.

21. Now Hail We Our Redeemer.

Förlossningen är vunnen. 7 6, 7 6, 7 7 6.   German Enchiridion, 1524.

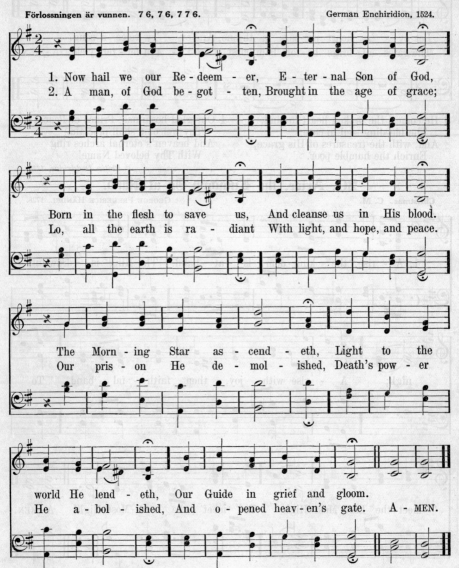

1. Now hail we our Re - deem - er, E - ter - nal Son of God,
2. A man, of God be - got - ten, Brought in the age of grace;

Born in the flesh to save us, And cleanse us in His blood.
Lo, all the earth is ra - diant With light, and hope, and peace.

The Morn - ing Star as - cend - eth, Light to the
Our pris - on He de - mol - ished, Death's pow - er

world He lend - eth, Our Guide in grief and gloom.
He a - bol - ished, And o - pened heav - en's gate. A - MEN.

3 O Jesus, grant us mercy,
  And grace on us bestow,
To walk by Thine own guidance,
  Thy saving truth to know.
For Thee our hearts are yearning,
From worldly pleasures turning
  Unto Thy righteousness.

4 Into Thy hand the Father
  Gave all, that we might be
In bonds of faith united,
  And dedicate to Thee,
A people through Thy merit
Entitled to inherit
  Thy realm eternally.

Ambrose, (340-397).
Olavus Petri, 1536.

22. Come, Thou Long Expected Jesus.

St. Hilary. 8 7, 8 7. D.

Origin uncertain.

1. Come, Thou long ex - pect - ed Je - sus, Born to set Thy peo - ple free;

From our fears and sins re - lease us, Let us find our rest in Thee.

Israel's Strength and Con-so - la - tion, Hope of all the earth Thou art;

Dear De - sire of ev - 'ry na - tion, Joy of ev - 'ry long-ing heart. A - MEN.

2 Born Thy people to deliver;
   Born a Child, and yet a King;
Born to reign in us forever,
   Now Thy gracious kingdom bring.
By Thine own eternal Spirit,
   Rule in all our hearts alone;
By Thine all-sufficient merit,
   Raise us to Thy glorious throne.

Charles Wesley, 1744.

23. Come, Thou Saviour of Our Race.

Hendon. 7 7, 7 7.   HENRI ABRAHAM CESAR MALAN, 1827.

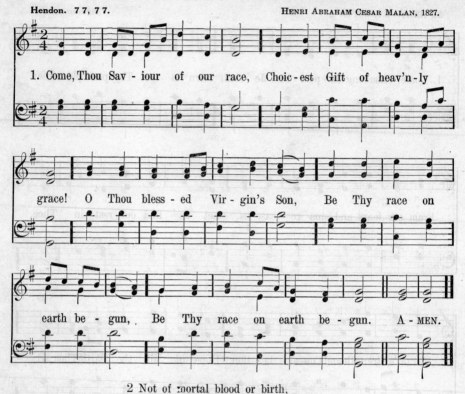

1. Come, Thou Sav-iour of our race, Choic-est Gift of heav'n-ly grace! O Thou bless-ed Vir-gin's Son, Be Thy race on earth be-gun, Be Thy race on earth be-gun. A-MEN.

2 Not of mortal blood or birth,
He descends from heaven to earth:
By the Holy Ghost conceived,
God and man by us believed.

3 Wondrous birth! O wondrous Child
Of the virgin undefiled!
Though by all the world disowned,
Still to be in heaven enthroned.

4 From the Father forth He came,
And returneth to the same;
Captive leading death and hell,—
High the song of triumph swell!

5 Equal to the Father now,
Though to dust Thou once didst bow,
Boundless shall Thy kingdom be;
When shall we its glories see?

6 Brightly doth Thy manger shine!
Glorious in its light divine:
Let not sin o'ercloud this light,
Ever be our faith thus bright.

Ambrose, (340-397).
Martin Luther, 1524.

24. Rejoice, Rejoice, Ye Christians.

Valet will ich dir geben. 7 6, 7 6. D.   MELCHIOR TESCHNER, 1613.

1. Re - joice, re - joice, ye Chris - tians, With all your heart, this morn!

O hear the bless - ed ti - dings, The Lord, the Christ, is born,

Now brought us by the an - gels That stand a - bout God's throne;

O love - ly are the voic - es That make such ti-dings known! A - MEN.

2 O hearken to their singing!
   This Child shall be your Friend;
The Father so hath willed it,
   That thus your woes should end.
The Son is freely given,
   That in Him ye may have
The Father's grace and blessing,
   And know He loves to save.

3 Nor deem the form too lowly
   That clothes Him at this hour;
For know ye what it hideth?
   'Tis God's almighty power.
Though now within the manger
   So poor and weak He lies,
He is the Lord of all things,
   He reigns above the skies.

Magdeburg Geistliche Lieder, 1540.

25. All Hail to Thee, O Blessed Morn!

Wie schön leuchtet der Morgenstern. 8 8 7, 8 8 7, 8 8 8.   PHILIPP NICOLAI, 1599.

1. All hail to thee, O bless-ed morn! To ti-dings long by prophets borne
2. 'Tis God's own Im-age and, with-al, The Son of Man, that mor-tals all

Hast thou ful-fill-ment giv-en. O sa-cred and im-mor-tal day,
May find in Him a broth-er. He comes, with peace and love to bide

When un-to earth, in glo-rious ray, De-scends the grace of heav-en!
On earth, the err-ing race to guide And help as could no oth-er;

Sing-ing, Ring-ing Sounds are blend-ing, Prais-es send-ing
Rath-er Gath-er Clos-er, fond-er, Sheep that wan-der,

Un-to heav-en For the Sav-iour to us giv-en.
Feed and fold them, Than let e-vil pow-ers hold them. A-MEN.

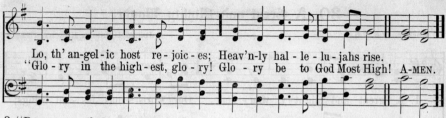

Lo, th' an-gel-ic host re-joic-es; Heav'n-ly hal-le-lu-jahs rise.
"Glo-ry in the high-est, glo-ry! Glo-ry be to God Most High! A-MEN.

3 "Peace on earth, good will from heaven,
  Reaching far as man is found;
Souls redeemed, and sins forgiven;
Loud our golden harps shall sound.

4 "Christ is born, the great Anointed;
  Heaven and earth His praises sing.
O receive whom God appointed
For your Prophet, Priest, and King.

5 "Hasten, mortals, to adore Him;
  Learn His Name, and taste His joy,
Till in heaven ye sing before Him,
'Glory be to God Most High!'".

6 Let us learn the wondrous story
Of our great Redeemer's birth;
Spread the brightness of His glory,
Till it cover all the earth!

John Cawood, 1819.

29. Immanuel, We Sing Thy Praise.

Germany. L. M.

From LUDWIG VAN BEETHOVEN. (1770-1827).
In COTTERILL'S Psalmody, 1831.

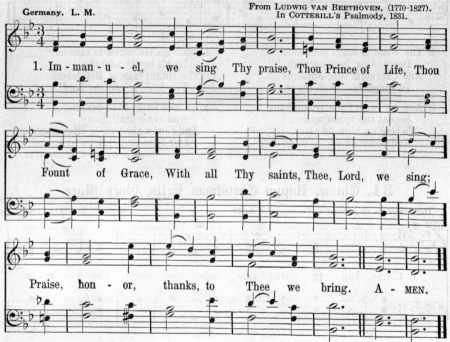

1. Im-man-u-el, we sing Thy praise, Thou Prince of Life, Thou
Fount of Grace, With all Thy saints, Thee, Lord, we sing;
Praise, hon-or, thanks, to Thee we bring. A-MEN.

2 E'er since the world began to be,
  How many a heart hath longed for Thee!
And Thou, O long expected Guest,
Hast come at last to make us blest!

3 Now art Thou here: we know Thee now:
  In lowly manger liest Thou:
A Child, yet makest all things great;
Poor, yet the earth Thy robe of state.

4 Now fearlessly I come to Thee:
  From sin and grief O set me free!
Turn wrath away, dread death destroy,
And turn my sorrow into joy.

5 Thou art my Head, my Lord divine;
  I am Thy member, wholly Thine;
And by Thy Spirit's gracious power
Will seek to serve Thee evermore.

Paul Gerhardt. 1653.

30. A Great and Mighty Wonder.

Kocher. 7 6, 7 6.   JUSTIN HEINRICH KNECHT, 1799.

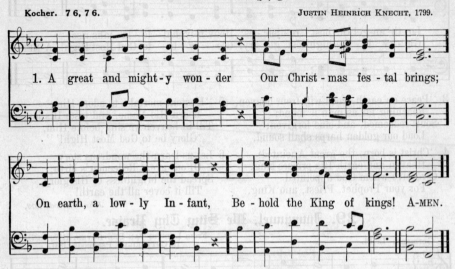

1. A great and might-y won - der   Our Christ - mas fes - tal brings;

On earth, a low - ly In - fant,   Be - hold the King of kings! A-MEN.

2 The Word is made incarnate,
   Descending from on high;
And Cherubim sing anthems
   To shepherds, from the sky.

3 And we, with them triumphant,
   Repeat the hymn again:
"To God on high be glory,
   And peace on earth, to men!"

4 Since all He comes to ransom,
   By all be He adored,
The Infant born in Bethlehem,
   The Saviour and the Lord!

5 All idol forms shall perish,
   And error shall decay,
And Christ shall wield His scepter,
   Our Lord and God for aye.

From the Greek of Anatolius.

31. Chime, Happy Christmas Bells, Once More.

Det kimer nu til julefest. (Emmanuel.) L. M.   Danish. C. BALLE, 1860.

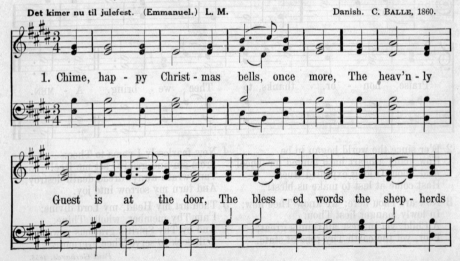

1. Chime, hap - py Christ - mas bells, once more, The heav'n - ly

Guest is at the door, The bless - ed words the shep - herds

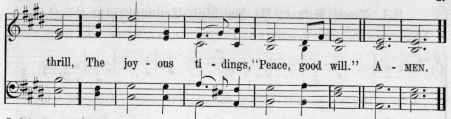

thrill, The joy-ous ti-dings, "Peace, good will." A - MEN.

2 O let us go with quiet mind,
  The gentle Babe with shepherds find,
  To gaze on Him who gladdens them,
  The loveliest flower of Jesse's stem.

3 The lowly Saviour meekly lies,
  Laid off the splendor of the skies;
  No crown bedecks His forehead fair,
  No pearl, nor gem, nor silk is there.

4 O holy Child, Thy manger gleams
  Till earth and heaven glow with its beams,
  Till midnight turns to brightest noon,
  And Jacob's Star outshines the sun.

5 Come, Jesus, glorious heavenly Guest,
  Keep Thine own Christmas in our breast,
  Then David's harp-strings, hushed so long,
  Shall swell our jubilee of song.

Nicolai Frederik Severin Grundtvig, (1783-1872).

32. Joy to the World, the Lord Is Come!

Antioch. C. M.

GEORGE FREDERICK HÄNDEL, 1742.

1. Joy to the world, the Lord is come! Let earth re-ceive her King;
2. Joy to the earth, the Sav-iour reigns! Let men their songs em-ploy;

Let ev-'ry heart pre-pare Him room, And heav'n and nature sing, And
While fields and floods, rocks, hills, and plains Re-peat the sounding joy, Re-

1. And heav'n and na-ture

heav'n and na-ture sing, And heav'n, And heav'n and na-ture sing.
peat the sound-ing joy, Re-peat, Re-peat the sound-ing joy. A - MEN.

sing, And heav'n and na-ture sing,

3 No more let sin and sorrows grow,
  Nor thorns infest the ground;
  He comes to make His blessings flow
  Where'er the curse is found.

4 He rules the world with truth and grace,
  And makes the nations prove
  The glories of His righteousness,
  And wonders of His love.

Isaac Watts, 1719.

28

Church Year: Christmas

33. Come Hither, Ye Faithful, Triumphantly Sing!

Adeste Fideles (Portuguese Hymn). 11, 11, 11, 11.   JOHN F. WADE'S Cantus Diversi, 1751.

1. Come hith-er, ye faith-ful, tri-um-phant-ly sing; Come see in the man-ger your Sav-iour and King! To Beth-le-hem has-ten with joy-ful ac-cord; ... O come ye, come hith-er; O come ye, come hith-er; O come ye, come hith-er, to wor-ship the Lord! A-MEN.

2 True Son of the Father, He comes from the skies;
The birth by a virgin He does not despise;
To Bethlehem hasten with joyful accord;
O come ye, come hither, to worship the Lord!

3 Hark, hark to the angels, all singing in heaven,
"To God in the highest all glory be given!"
To Bethlehem hasten with joyful accord;
O come ye, come hither, to worship the Lord!

4 To Thee, then, O Jesus, this day of Thy birth,
Be glory and honor through heaven and earth.
True Godhead incarnate, omnipotent Word!
O come, let us hasten to worship the Lord!

From the Latin of the XVII century.

34. Hark! the Herald Angels Sing.

Mendelssohn. 7 7, 7 7. D. With Refrain.

FELIX MENDELSSOHN-BARTHOLDY, 1840.
From a Cantata: "Gott ist Licht."

1. Hark! the her - ald an - gels sing, "Glo - ry to the new - born King!
Peace on earth, and mer - cy mild, God and sin - ners rec - on - ciled!"
Joy - ful, all ye na - tions, rise, Join the tri - umph of the skies;
U - ni - ver - sal na - ture say, "Christ the Lord is born to - day!"

REFRAIN:

Hark! the her - ald an - gels sing, "Glo - ry to the new-born King!" A-MEN.

2 Veiled in flesh the Godhead see,
Hail the incarnate Deity!
Pleased as Man with men to dwell,
Jesus, our Immanuel.
Hail, the heavenly Prince of Peace,
Hail, the Sun of Righteousness!
Light and life to all He brings,
Risen with healing in His wings.

3 Mild He lays His glory by,
Born that man no more may die;
Born to raise the sons of earth;
Born to give them second birth;
Come, Desire of nations, come,
Fix in us Thy humble home;
O to all Thyself impart,
Formed in each believing heart!

Charles Wesley, 1739.

35. All My Heart This Night Rejoices.

Warum sollt ich mich denn grämen. 8 3, 3 6. D.   JOHANN GEORG EBELING, 1666.

1. All my heart this night re - joic - es, As I hear, Far and near,

Sweet-est an - gel voic - es: "Christ is born," their choirs are sing - ing,

Till the air Ev - 'ry - where Now with joy is ring - ing. A - MEN.

2 Come and banish all your sadness,
　　One and all,
　　Great and small,
　Come with songs of gladness;
　Love Him who with love is yearning;
　　Hail the star
　　That from far
　Bright with hope is burning.

3 Hither come, ye heavy-hearted,
　　Who for sin,
　　Deep within,
　Long and sore have smarted;
　For the poisoned wounds you're feeling
　　Help is near,
　　One is here
　Mighty for their healing.

4 Hither come, ye poor and wretched,
　　Know His will
　　Is to fill
　Every hand outstretchèd;
　Here are riches without measure,
　　Here forget
　　All regret,
　Fill your hearts with treasure.

5 Faithfully Thee, Lord, I'll cherish,
　　Live to Thee,
　　And with Thee
　Dying, shall not perish,
　But shall dwell with Thee forever,
　　Far on high,
　　In the joy
　That can alter never.

Paul Gerhardt, 1656.

36. O Little Town of Bethlehem.

St. Louis. 8 6, 8 6, 7 6, 8 6.

LEWIS HENRY REDNER, 1868.

1. O lit - tle town of Beth - le - hem, How still we see thee lie;
2. For Christ is born of Ma - - ry, And gath - ered all a - bove,

A - bove thy deep and dream - less sleep The si - lent stars go by;
While mor - tals sleep, the an - gels keep Their watch of won - d'ring love.

Yet in thy dark - ness shin - eth The ev - er - last - ing Light;
O morn - ing stars, to - geth - er Pro - claim the ho - ly birth,

The hopes and fears of all the years Are met in thee to - night.
And prais - es sing to God the King, And peace to men on earth. A - MEN.

3 How silently, how silently,
　The wondrous Gift is given!
So God imparts to human hearts
　The blessings of His heaven.
No ear may hear His coming,
　But in this world of sin,
Where meek souls will receive Him still,
　The dear Christ enters in.

4 O holy Child of Bethlehem!
　Descend to us, we pray;
Cast out our sin, and enter in,
　Be born in us to-day.
We hear the Christmas angels
　The great glad tidings tell:
O come to us, abide with us,
　Our Lord Immanuel!

Phillips Brooks, 1868.

37. Triumph, Ye Heavens!

Lobe den Herren. 14 14, 4 7 8.

Stralsund Gesangbuch. 1665.
Present form since 1708.

1. Tri-umph, ye heav-ens! re-joice ye with high ad-o-ra-tion!
Sing to the Lord, to the Sav-iour, in glad ex-ul-ta-tion!
An-gels give ear! God un-to men draw-eth near,
Bring-ing to lost ones sal-va-tion. A-MEN.

2 God in man's nature! O mystery past comprehending!
 Now is the temple thrown wide and the incense ascending!
  Christ is the way!
  We who were once far away,
 Now at His footstool are bending.

3 Hast Thou, O Holy One, deigned of my need to be thinking?
 Chosen me, called me, the waters of life to be drinking?
  Shall not my mind
  Fullness of blessing here find,
 Deep in humility sinking?

4 Faithful Immanuel! let me Thy glories be telling;
 Ever, my Saviour, be Thou in mine inmost heart dwelling.
  With me abide;
  Teach me to stay at Thy side,
 Where the love-fountain is welling.

Gerhard Tersteegen, 1735.

38. Calm on the Listening Ear of Night.

Bethlehem (New). C. M. D.   GOTTFRIED WILHELM FINK, 1842.

1. Calm on the lis-t'ning ear of night Come heav'n's me-lo-dious strains,
2. The an-sw'ring hills of Pal-es-tine Send back the glad re-ply,

Where wild Ju-de-a stretch-es forth Her sil-ver-man-tled plains;
And greet from all their ho-ly heights The Day-spring from on high:

Ce-les-tial choirs from courts a-bove Shed sa-cred glo-ries there;
O'er the blue depths of Gal-i-lee There comes a ho-lier calm;

And an-gels, with their sparkling lyres, Make mu-sic on the air.
And Sharon waves in sol-emn praise Her si-lent groves of palm.   A-MEN.

3 "Glory to God!" the lofty strain
  The realm of ether fills;
How sweeps the song of solemn joy
  O'er Judah's sacred hills!
"Glory to God!" the sounding skies
  Loud with their anthems ring:
"Peace on the earth; good will to men,"
  From heaven's eternal King.

4 This day shall Christian tongues be mute,
  And Christian hearts be cold?
O catch the anthem that from heaven
  O'er Judah's mountains rolled,
When burst upon that listening night
  The high and solemn lay,
"Glory to God; on earth be peace":
  Salvation comes to-day.

Edmund Hamilton Sears, 1834.

39. It Came upon the Midnight Clear.

Carol. C. M. D.   RICHARD STORRS WILLIS, 1850.

1. It came up-on the mid-night clear, That glo-ri-ous song of old,
2. Still thro' the clo-ven skies they come, With peace-ful wings un-furled,

From an-gels bend-ing near the earth To touch their harps of gold:
And still their heav'nly mu-sic floats O'er all the wea-ry world;

"Peace on the earth, good will to men, From heaven's all-gra-cious King":
A-bove its sad and low-ly plains They bend on hov-er-ing wing,

The world in sol-emn still-ness lay, To hear the an-gels sing.
And ev-er o'er its Ba-bel sounds The bless-ed an-gels sing. A-MEN.

3 And ye, beneath life's crushing load,
   Whose forms are bending low,
Who toil along the climbing way
   With painful steps and slow,
Look now! for glad and golden hours
   Come swiftly on the wing:
O rest beside the weary road,
   And hear the angels sing.

4 For lo, the days are hastening on,
   By prophets seen of old,
When with the ever-circling years
   Shall come the time foretold,
When the new heaven and earth shall own
   The Prince of Peace their King,
And the whole world send back the song
   Which now the angels sing.

Edmund Hamilton Sears, 1850.

40. The Newborn King Who Comes To-day.

Materna. C. M. D.   SAMUEL AUGUSTUS WARD, 1882.

1. The new-born King who comes to-day Brings ti-dings of great joy, . . .
Which sin can nev-er take a-way, Nor death nor hell de-stroy. . .
Re-joice, ye Gen-tile lands, re-joice, And hail this glo-rious dawn; . . .
For God comes down, frail man to crown: The Lord of life is born! A-MEN.

2 He comes not as a king of earth,
   In pomp and pride to reign;
He seeks a poor and humble birth,
   But free from sinful stain;
Rejoice, ye Gentile lands, rejoice,
   Glad hymns of triumph sing:
The Wonderful, the Counsellor,
   He comes, your God and King!

3 For us He leaves His Father's throne,
   His sapphire throne on high,
And comes to dwell on earth alone,
   For fallen man to die.
Rejoice, ye Gentile lands, rejoice,
   All hail Messiah's dawn;
Our God comes down, earth's joy and crown:
   The King of Love is born,

4 Glad Gentiles in their eastern home
   His radiant star behold;
To God, their King, they joy to bring
   Sweet incense, myrrh, and gold.
Rejoice, ye Gentile lands, rejoice,
   In heaven your praises sing,
Before Him fall, the Lord of all,
   Your Maker and your King!

5 We join your song, celestial throng,
   Whose anthems never cease;
We tune our lyres, with angel choirs,
   To hail the Prince of Peace!
Rejoice, ye Gentile lands, rejoice,
   All hail Immanuel's morn;
For God comes down, frail man to crown:
   To us a Child is born.

Unknown.

41. The Race That Long in Darkness Pined.

St. Leonard (Smart). C. M.   HENRY SMART, 1867.

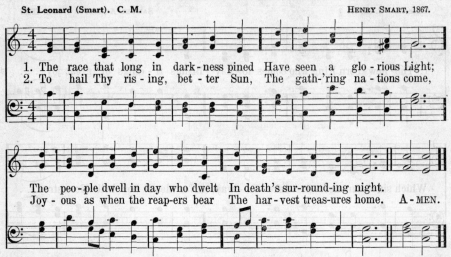

1. The race that long in dark-ness pined Have seen a glo-rious Light;
2. To hail Thy ris-ing, bet-ter Sun, The gath-'ring na-tions come,

The peo-ple dwell in day who dwelt In death's sur-round-ing night.
Joy-ous as when the reap-ers bear The har-vest treas-ures home. A-MEN.

3 For Thou our burden hast removed,
   And quelled the oppressor's sway,
Quick as the slaughtered squadrons fell
   In Midian's evil day.

4 To us a Child of Hope is born,
   To us a Son is given;
Him shall the tribes of earth obey,
   Him all the hosts of heaven.

5 His Name shall be the Prince of Peace,
   For evermore adored;
The Wonderful, the Counsellor,
   The great and mighty Lord.

6 His power increasing still shall spread,
   His reign no end shall know:
Justice shall guard His throne above,
   And peace abound below.

John Morison, 1781.

42. Precious Child, So Sweetly Sleeping.

Prescott. 8 7, 8 7, 7 7.   ROBERT PRESCOTT STEWART, 1868.

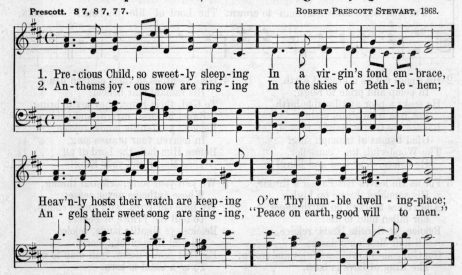

1. Pre-cious Child, so sweet-ly sleep-ing In a vir-gin's fond em-brace,
2. An-thems joy-ous now are ring-ing In the skies of Beth-le-hem;

Heav'n-ly hosts their watch are keep-ing O'er Thy hum-ble dwell-ing-place;
An-gels their sweet song are sing-ing, "Peace on earth, good will to men."

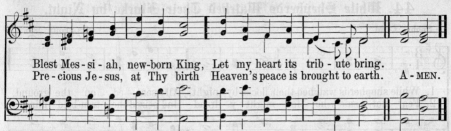

Blest Mes-si-ah, new-born King, Let my heart its trib-ute bring.
Pre-cious Je-sus, at Thy birth Heaven's peace is brought to earth. A-MEN.

3 Sweetly rest, Thou promised Saviour,
  By the prophets long foretold;
Brightly beams the Father's favor,
  Now all men His love behold.
Virgin-born Immanuel,
Let my tongue Thy praises tell!

4 Promised Saviour, I adore Thee,
  Son of David, Son of God!
What can mortals bring before Thee?
  All is Thine on earthly sod.
Take my heart and let it be
Filled with love, dear Child, to Thee.

Anna Hoppe, 1920.

43. Glorious Yuletide, Glad Bells Proclaim It.

Russian Hymn. Irregular.　　　　　　　ALEXIS THEODORE LYOFF, 1833.

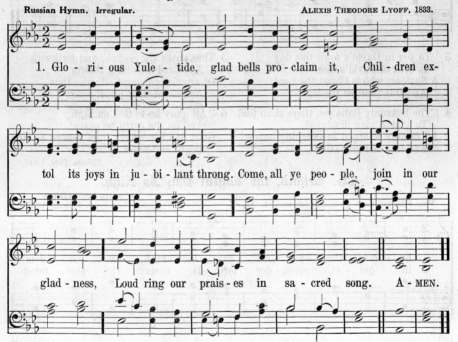

1. Glo-ri-ous Yule-tide, glad bells pro-claim it, Chil-dren ex-tol its joys in ju-bi-lant throng. Come, all ye peo-ple, join in our glad-ness, Loud ring our prais-es in sa-cred song. A-MEN.

2 Onward to Bethlehem, follow the shepherds,
  Gather around the lowly manger and stall.
Join with the angels, welcome the Saviour
Born in the flesh to be Lord of all.

3 Onward to Bethlehem, follow the wise men,
  Come from afar their gifts and homage to bring.
Sweeter than incense, prized more than jewels.
Hearts true and loyal unto the King!

Ernst William Olson, 1920.

44. While Shepherds Watched Their Flocks by Night.

Spohr. C. M.   LOUIS SPOHR, 1835.

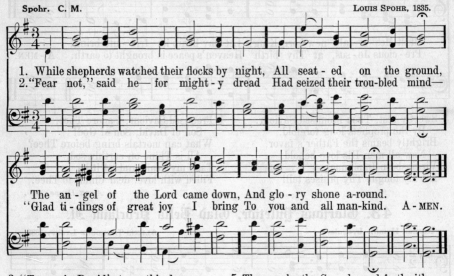

1. While shepherds watched their flocks by night, All seat-ed on the ground,
2. "Fear not," said he— for might-y dread Had seized their trou-bled mind—

The an-gel of the Lord came down, And glo-ry shone a-round.
"Glad ti-dings of great joy I bring To you and all man-kind. A-MEN.

3 "To you in David's town this day
  Is born of David's line
A Saviour, who is Christ the Lord;
  And this shall be the sign:

4 "The heavenly Babe you there shall find
  To human view displayed,
All meanly wrapped in swathing bands,
  And in a manger laid."

5 Thus spake the Seraph; and forthwith
  Appeared a shining throng
Of angels praising God, who thus
  Addressed their joyful song:

6 "All glory be to God on high,
  And on the earth be peace;
Good will henceforth from heaven to men
  Begin and never cease."

Nahum Tate, 1702.

45. Behold, the Joyful Day Is Nigh.

Vom Himmel hoch da komm ich her. L. M.

VALENTIN SCHUMANN'S
Geistliche Lieder, Leipzig, 1539.

1. Be-hold, the joy-ful day is nigh, And an-gels'
2. In qui-et splen-dor forth He comes, The scat-tered

voic-es from on high Pro-claim the news in ear-ly
sheep and ten-der lambs To gath-er, and their fold pre-

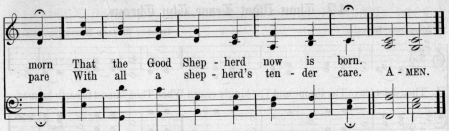

| morn | That | the | Good | Shep - herd | now | is | born. |
| pare | With | all | a | shep - herd's | ten - der | care. | A - MEN. |

3 The gentle Shepherd we behold
  Who, not with silver and with gold,
  But by His suffering and His death,
  Will save us from eternal wrath.

4 His Church, though small its seed may be,
  Shall grow into a mighty tree,
  With fruitful branches spreading o'er
  The earth till time shall be no more.

5 Arise and shine, thy Light is come,
  O humankind, O Christendom;
  Thy glory and thy peace is here;
  The Saviour of the world draws near.

6 All praise and glory be to Thee
  For wisdom, power, and majesty;
  And for Thy grace and mercy, Lord,
  Forever be Thy Name adored.

Johan Olof Wallin, 1814.

46. Silent Night! Holy Night!

Stille Nacht. Irregular.   FRANZ GRUBER, 1818.

1. Si - lent night! Ho - ly night! All is calm, all is bright,

Round yon vir - gin moth-er and Child; Ho - ly In - fant, so ten - der and mild.

Sleep in heav - en - ly peace, Sleep in heav - en - ly peace. A - MEN.

2 Silent night! Holy night!
  Shepherds quake at the sight:
  Glories stream from heaven afar;
  Heavenly hosts sing alleluia,
    Christ, the Saviour, is born!

3 Silent night! Holy night!
  Son of God, love's pure light
  Radiant beams from Thy holy face,
  With the dawn of redeeming grace,
    Jesus, Lord, at Thy birth.

Joseph Mohr, 1818.

47. Thou Didst Leave Thy Throne.

Margaret. Irregular.   TIMOTHY RICHARD MATTHEWS, 1876.

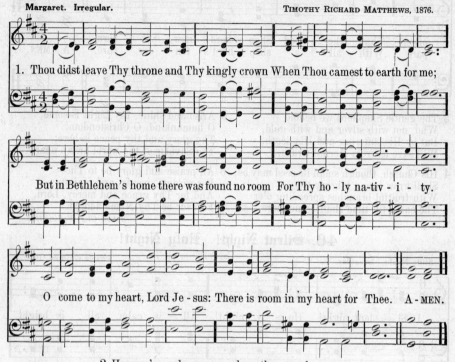

1. Thou didst leave Thy throne and Thy kingly crown When Thou camest to earth for me;

But in Bethlehem's home there was found no room For Thy ho - ly na-tiv - i - ty.

O come to my heart, Lord Je - sus: There is room in my heart for Thee. A - MEN.

2 Heaven's arches rang when the angels sang,
    Proclaiming Thy royal degree;
  But in lowly birth didst Thou come to earth,
    And in great humility.
    O come to my heart, Lord Jesus:
    There is room in my heart for Thee.

3 The foxes found rest, and the bird had its nest
    In the shade of the forest tree;
  But Thy couch was the sod, O Thou Son of God,
    In the mountains of Galilee.
    O come to my heart, Lord Jesus:
    There is room in my heart for Thee.

4 Thou camest, O Lord, with the living Word
    That should set Thy children free;
  But with mocking scorn, and with crown of thorn,
    They bore Thee to Calvary.
    O come to my heart, Lord Jesus:
    There is room in my heart for Thee.

5 When the heavens shall ring, and the angels sing
    At Thy coming to victory,
  Let Thy voice call me home, saying, "Yet there is room,
    There is room at my side for thee."
  And my heart shall rejoice, Lord Jesus,
    When Thou comest to call for me.

Emily Elizabeth Steele Elliott, 1864.

48. From All Thy Saints in Warfare.

Ewing. 7 6, 7 6. D.   ALEXANDER EWING, 1853.

1. From all Thy saints in war - fare, For all Thy saints at rest,
2. Praise for the first of mar - tyrs, Who saw Thee read - y stand

To Thee, O bless - ed Je - sus, All prais - es be ad - dressed;
To aid in midst of tor - ments, To plead at God's right hand.

Thou, Lord, didst win the bat - tle, That they might con-qu'rors be;
Share we with him, if sum - moned By death our Lord to own,

Their crowns of liv - ing glo - ry Are lit with rays from Thee.
On earth the faith-ful wit - ness, In heav'n the mar - tyr crown. A - MEN.

3 Apostles, prophets, martyrs,
   And all the sacred throng,
Who wear the spotless raiment,
   Who raise the ceaseless song,
For these, passed on before us,
   Saviour, we Thee adore,
And, walking in their footsteps,
   Would serve Thee more and more.

4 Then praise we God the Father,
   And praise we God the Son,
And God the Holy Spirit,
   Eternal Three in One;
Till all the ransomed number
   Fall down before the throne,
And honor, power, and glory
   Ascribe to God alone.

Horatio Nelson, 1864.

Other suitable hymns for this day are those for All Saints' Day. For hymns suitable for the Sunday after Christmas see Candlemas.

49. Great God, We Sing That Mighty Hand.

Hebron (Mason). L. M.

LOWELL MASON, 1830.

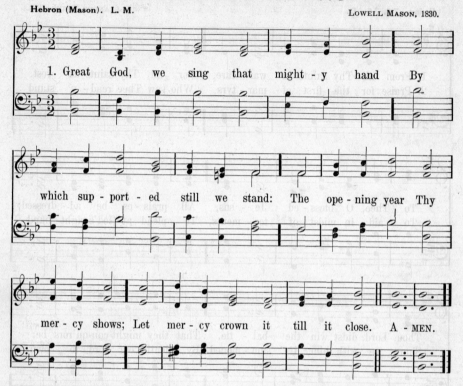

1. Great God, we sing that might-y hand By which sup-port-ed still we stand: The ope-ning year Thy mer-cy shows; Let mer-cy crown it till it close. A-MEN.

2 By day, by night, at home, abroad,
Still we are guarded by our God;
By His incessant bounty fed,
By His unerring counsel led.

3 With grateful hearts the past we own;
The future, all to us unknown,
We to Thy guardian care commit,
And, peaceful, leave before Thy feet.

4 In scenes exalted or deprest,
Be Thou our joy, and Thou our rest;
Thy goodness all our hopes shall raise,
Adored through all our changing days.

5 When death shall close our earthly songs,
And seal in silence mortal tongues,
Our Helper God, in whom we trust,
Shall keep our souls and guard our dust.

Philip Doddridge, 1755.

50. Jesus, Thy Name Hath Power to Bless.

Wenn wir in höchsten Nöthen sein. L. M.

Genevan French Psalter, 1542.

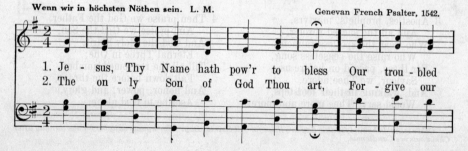

1. Je-sus, Thy Name hath pow'r to bless Our trou-bled
2. The on-ly Son of God Thou art, For-give our

souls in all dis-tress. On us, dear Lord, be-stow Thy
sins and cleanse our heart; Be-hold and help us in our

grace, And guide us safe-ly all our days.
need, Thou who art God and Man in-deed. A-MEN.

3 In Thee is all our righteousness,
In Thee all peace and blessedness.
Who trusteth in Thy holy Name
Shall be redeemed from sin and shame.

4 We praise Thee for Thy living Word,
And for Thy sacraments, O Lord.
Grant us Thy peace in all our strife,
And after death eternal life.

Basilius Förtsch, 1612.

51. Jesus, Name of Wondrous Love.

Wansted. 7 7, 7 7.   German.

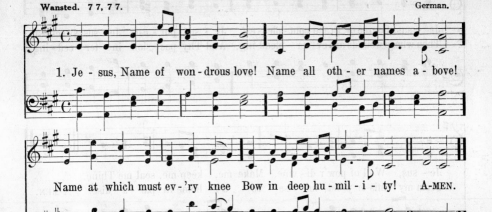

1. Je-sus, Name of won-drous love! Name all oth-er names a-bove!

Name at which must ev-'ry knee Bow in deep hu-mil-i-ty! A-MEN.

2 Jesus, Name of priceless worth
To the fallen sons of earth,
For the promise that it gave:
"Jesus shall His people save."

3 Jesus, Name of mercy mild,
Given to the holy Child,
When the cup of human woe
First He tasted here below!

4 Jesus, only Name that's given
Under all the mighty heaven
Whereby man, to sin enslaved,
Bursts his fetters, and is saved.

4 Jesus, Name of wondrous love!
Human Name of Him above!
Pleading only this, we flee
Helpless, O our God, to Thee.

William Walsham How, 1854.

52. Jesus, Name All Names Above.

Underbar en stjärna blid. 7 6, 7 6, 8 8, 7 7.   ANTON PETER BERGGREEN, d., 1880.

1. Je - sus, Name all names a - bove, Je - sus, best and dear - est,
2. Thou didst call the prod - i - gal; Thou didst par - don Ma - ry;

Je - sus, Fount of per - fect love, Ho - liest, ten - d'rest, near - est,
Thou whose words can nev - er fall, Nor Thy prom - ise va - ry:

Je - sus, Source of grace com - plet - est, Je - sus pur - est, Je - sus sweet-est,
Thou whose wounds are ev - er plead-ing, And Thy pas - sion in - ter - ced - ing,

Je - sus, Well of pow'r di - vine, Make me, keep me, seal me Thine.
From my mis-er-y let me rise To a home in par - a - dise. A-MEN.

3 Jesus, crowned with thorns for me,
    Scourged for my transgression,
Bitter was Thine agony,
    Steadfast Thy confession;
Jesus, clad in purple raiment,
For my evils making payment;
Let not all Thy woe and pain,
Let not Calvary be in vain.

4 When I reach death's bitter sea,
    And its waves roll higher,
Jesus, come, be near to me,
    As the storm draws nigher:
Jesus, leave me not to languish,
Helpless, hopeless, full of anguish!
Tell me,—"Verily, I say,
Thou shalt be with Me to-day!"

Theoctistus of the Studium (b. about 890).

53. While with Ceaseless Course the Sun.

Wells. 7 7, 7 7. D.

MARCUS MORRIS WELLS.

1. While with cease-less course the sun Hast-ed through the for-mer year,

Man-y souls their race have run, Nev-er-more to meet us here;

Fixed in an e-ter-nal state, They have done with all be-low;

We a lit-tle lon-ger wait, But how long, no one can know. A-MEN.

2 As the wingèd arrow flies
  Speedily, the mark to find;
As the lightning from the skies
  Darts, and leaves no trace behind;
Swiftly thus our fleeting days
  Bear us down life's rapid stream:
Upward, Lord, our spirits raise;
  All below is but a dream.

3 Thanks for mercies past receive,
  Pardon of our sins renew;
Teach us henceforth how to live
  With eternity in view.
Bless Thy Word to young and old,
  Fill us with a Saviour's love;
And when life's short tale is told,
  May we dwell with Thee above.

John Newton. 1774.

54. How Sweet the Name of Jesus Sounds.

St. Peter. C. M.   ALEXANDER ROBERT REINAGLE, 1826.

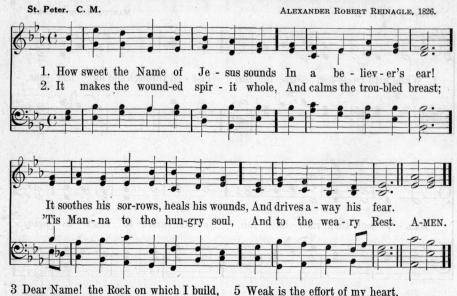

1. How sweet the Name of Je - sus sounds In a be - liev - er's ear!
2. It makes the wound-ed spir - it whole, And calms the trou-bled breast;

It soothes his sor-rows, heals his wounds, And drives a - way his fear.
'Tis Man - na to the hun-gry soul, And to the wea - ry Rest. A-MEN.

3 Dear Name! the Rock on which I build,
  My Shield and Hiding-place;
My never-failing Treasury, filled
  With boundless stores of grace.

4 By Thee my prayers acceptance gain,
  Although with sin defiled:
Satan accuses me in vain,
  And I am owned a child.

5 Weak is the effort of my heart,
  And cold my warmest thought;
But when I see Thee as Thou art,
  I'll praise Thee as I ought.

6 Till then I would Thy love proclaim
  With every fleeting breath;
And may the music of Thy Name
  Refresh my soul in death.

                                                        John Newton, 1779.

55. Jesus, O Precious Name.

O Gott, du frommer Gott. 6 7, 6 7, 6 6, 6 6.   JOHANN GEORG CHRISTIAN STÖRL, 1710.

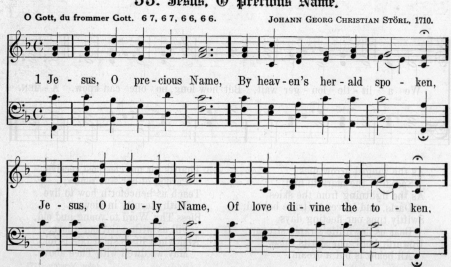

1 Je - sus, O pre - cious Name, By heav - en's her - ald spo - ken,

Je - sus, O ho - ly Name, Of love di - vine the to - ken,

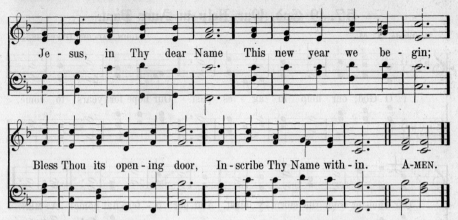

Je - sus, in Thy dear Name This new year we be - gin;

Bless Thou its open - ing door, In - scribe Thy Name with - in. A-MEN.

2 Jesus, O precious Name,
   In Thee our hopes are centered,
In Thee, O mighty Name,
   This new year we have entered.
Though seasons come and go,
   Thou, Lord, art still the same;
Immovable is still
   That solid Rock, Thy Name.

3 Jesus, O precious Name,
   Thou bringest peace and gladness,
Jesus, O worshiped Name,
   Dispelling all our sadness,
In hallowed temple halls
   Thy sacred echo rings,
While heaven's ransomed host
   Thy praise in glory sings.

Anna Hoppe, 1918.

56. Our Times Are in Thy Hand.

Glezen S. M.   E. K. GLEZEN.

1. Our times are in Thy hand. O God, we wish them there;

Our life, our friends, our souls, we leave En-tire - ly to Thy care. A-MEN.

2 Our times are in Thy hand,
   Whatever they may be,
Pleasing or painful, dark or bright,
   As best may seem to Thee.

3 Our times are in Thy hand;
   Why should we doubt or fear?
A Father's hand will never cause
   His child a needless tear.

4 Our times are in Thy hand,
   Jesus, the Crucified;
The hand our many sins have pierced
   Is now our guard and guide.

5 Our times are in Thy hand:
   We'll always trust in Thee,
Till we have left the weary land
   And all Thy glory see.

William Freeman Lloyd, 1841, a.

57. O God, Our Help in Ages Past.

Beatitudo. C. M.   JOHN BACCHUS DYKES, 1875.

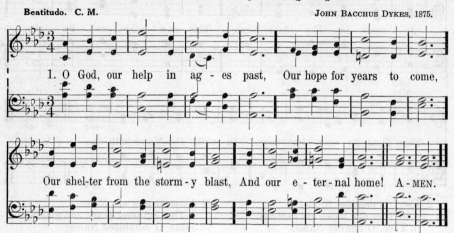

1. O God, our help in ag - es past, Our hope for years to come,

Our shel-ter from the storm - y blast, And our e - ter - nal home! A - MEN.

2 Beneath the shadow of Thy throne
  Still may we dwell secure;
Sufficient is Thine arm alone,
  And our defense is sure.

3 Before the hills in order stood,
  Or earth received her frame,
From everlasting Thou art God,
  To endless years the same.

4 A thousand ages in Thy sight
  Are like an evening gone;
Short as the watch that ends the night
  Before the rising sun.

5 The busy tribes of flesh and blood,
  With all their cares and fears,
Are carried downward by the flood,
  And lost in following years.

6 Time, like an ever-rolling stream,
  Bears all its sons away;
They fly, forgotten, as a dream
  Dies at the opening day.

7 O God, our help in ages past,
  Our hope for years to come,
Be Thou our guide while life shall last,
  And our eternal home!

Isaac Watts, 1719.

58. Help Us, O Lord, Behold, We Enter.

9 8, 9 8, 8 8.   [*Tune of No. 59.*]

1 Help us, O Lord, behold, we enter
  Upon another year to-day;
In Thee our hopes and thoughts we center,
  Renew our courage for the way:
New life, new strength, new happiness
We ask of Thee, O hear and bless!

2 May every plan and undertaking
  This year be all begun with Thee;
When I am sleeping or am waking,
  Still let me know Thou art with me;
Abroad do Thou my footsteps guide,
At home be ever at my side.

3 Be this a time of grace and pardon;
  Thy rod I take with willing mind,
But suffer naught my heart to harden,
  And let me now Thy mercy find;
In Thee alone, my God, I live,
Thou only canst my sins forgive.

4 And may this year to me be holy;
  Thy grace so fill my every thought,
That all my life be pure and lowly
  And truthful as a Christian's ought;
So make me, while yet dwelling here,
Faithful and blest from year to year.

5 Jesus, be with me and direct me;
  Jesus, my plans and hopes inspire;
Jesus, from tempting thoughts protect me;
  Jesus, be all my heart's desire;
Jesus, be in my thoughts all day,
Nor suffer me to fall away.

6 Grant, Lord, that when the year is over,
  For me in perfect peace it close.
In all things care for me, and cover
  My head in time of fear and woes;
So may I, when my years are gone,
Appear with joy before Thy throne.

Johann Rist, 1642.

59. Baptized into Thy Name Most Holy.

Wer weiss, wie nahe mir mein Ende. 9 8, 9 8, 8 8.   BRONNER'S Choral-Buch, 1715.

1. Bap - tized in - to Thy Name most ho - ly, O Fa - ther,
2. My lov - ing Fa - ther, Thou dost take me To be hence-

Son, and Ho - ly Ghost, I claim a place, though weak and low - ly,
forth Thy child and heir; My faith - ful Sav - iour, Thou dost make me

A - mong Thy seed and cho - sen host; Bur - ied with Christ, and
The fruit of all Thy sor - rows share, Thou, Ho - ly Ghost, wilt

dead to sin, Thy Spir - it now shall live with - in.
com - fort me, When dark - est clouds a - round I see. A - MEN.

3 And I have vowed to fear and love Thee,
   And to obey Thee, Lord, alone;
I felt Thy Holy Spirit move me,
   And freely pledged myself Thine own,
Renouncing sin to keep the faith,
And war with evil unto death.

4 My faithful God, Thou failest never,
   Thy covenant will e'er abide;
O cast me not away forever,
   Should I transgress it on my side;
If I have sore my soul defiled,
Yet still forgive, restore thy child.

5 Yea, all I am, and love most dearly,—
   To Thee anew I give the whole;
O let me make my vows sincerely,
   Take full possession of my soul,
Let naught within me, naught I own,
Serve any will but Thine alone.

6 And never let my purpose falter,
   O Father, Son, and Holy Ghost,
But keep me faithful to Thine altar,
   Till Thou shalt call me from my post;
To Thee I thus will live and die,
And praise Thee evermore on high.

Johann Jacob Rambach, 1734.

For other hymns suitable for this Sunday see Baptism and Trinity.

60. As with Gladness Men of Old.

Dix. 7 7, 7 7, 7 7.   CONRAD KOCHER, 1838.

1. As with glad-ness men of old Did the guid-ing star be-hold;

As with joy they hailed its light, Lead-ing on-ward, beam-ing bright:

So, most gra-cious God, may we Ev-er-more be led by Thee. A-MEN.

2 As with joyful steps they sped
To that lowly manger-bed,
There to bend the knee before
Him whom heaven and earth adore,
So may we, with willing feet,
Ever seek Thy mercy-seat.

3 As they offered gifts most rare
At that manger rude and bare,
So may we, with holy joy,
Pure, and free from sin's alloy,
All our costliest treasures bring,
Christ, to Thee, our heavenly King.

4 Holy Jesus, every day
Keep us in the narrow way;
And, when earthly things are past,
Bring our ransomed souls at last
Where they need no star to guide,
Where no clouds Thy glory hide.

5 In the heavenly country bright
Need they no created light:
Thou its Light, its Joy, its Crown,
Thou its Sun which goes not down;
There forever may we sing
Hallelujahs to our King.

William Chatterton Dix, 1860.

61. Now Israel's Hope in Triumph Ends.

Wie schön leuchtet der Morgenstern. 8 8 7, 8 8 7, 8 8 8.   PHILIPP NICOLAI, 1599.

1. { Now Is - rael's hope in tri - umph ends, With an - gels'
   O'er Beth - le - hem it shin - eth bright, All peo - ple,

glo - rious song as - cends A star of heav'n - ly splen - dor. }
guid - ed by its light, Shall come and hom - age ren - der. }

Great Light, Bright Light Now de - scend - eth, Dark - ness end - eth,

Day be - gin - neth, Light to all the world it bring - eth. A - MEN.

2 Among us dwells in truth and grace
  The hidden God, who loves our race;
    He brought us all salvation.
  The glory of the Son we see,
  The only Son's true majesty,
    And bow in adoration.
        Draw near,
        And hear,
      Every nation,
      Now salvation
        God bestoweth,
  And His love and mercy showeth.

3 Rejoice, my soul, and bless His Name
  Who to the lost and fallen came
    To open heaven's portals.
  Rejoice that God will mercy show,
  The broken covenant renew
    With us poor sinful mortals.
        Now be
        Glory
      Ever given
      God in heaven;
        Peace unending
  Be to earth from heaven descending.

Samuel Johan Hedborn, 1811.

62. Brightest and Best of the Sons of the Morning.

Morning Star. 11 10, 11 10.

J. P. HARDING, 1861.

1. Bright-est and best of the sons of the morn-ing, Dawn on our dark-ness, and lend us thine aid; Star of the East, the ho-ri-zon a-dorn-ing, Guide where our in-fant Re-deem-er is laid. A-MEN.

2 Cold on His cradle the dewdrops are shining;
   Low lies His head with the beasts of the stall:
Angels adore Him in slumber reclining,
   Maker, and Monarch, and Saviour of all!

3 Say, shall we yield Him, in costly devotion,
   Odors of Edom, and offerings divine?
Gems of the mountain, and pearls of the ocean,
   Myrrh from the forest, or gold from the mine?

4 Vainly we offer each ample oblation;
   Vainly with gifts would His favor secure:
Richer by far is the heart's adoration;
   Dearer to God are the prayers of the poor.

5 Brightest and best of the sons of the morning,
   Dawn on our darkness, and lend us thine aid;
Star of the East, the horizon adorning,
   Guide where our infant Redeemer is laid.

Reginald Heber, 1811.

63. O Thou, Who by a Star Didst Guide.

Bethlehem (New). C. M. D.					Gottfried Wilhelm Fink, 1842.

1. O Thou, who by a star didst guide The wise men on their way,

Un - til it came and stood be - side The place where Je - sus lay:

Al - though by stars Thou dost not lead Thy serv - ants now be - low,

Thy Ho - ly Spir - it, when they need, Will show them how to go. A-MEN.

Or: St. Leonard, No. 219.

2 As yet we know Thee but in part,
　But still we trust Thy Word,
That blessèd are the pure in heart,
　For they shall see the Lord.
O Saviour, give us then Thy grace
　To make us pure in heart,
That we may see Thee face to face,
　Hereafter as Thou art.

John Mason Neale, 1842.

64. Hail, Thou Source of Every Blessing.

Jesus är min vän den bäste. 8 7, 8 7. D.

GUSTAF DÜBEN. 1674.

1. Hail, Thou Source of ev-'ry bless-ing, Sov-'reign Fa-ther of man-kind!
Gen-tiles now, Thy grace pos-sess-ing, In Thy courts ad-mis-sion find.
Grate-ful now we fall be-fore Thee, In Thy Church ob-tain a place;
Now by faith be-hold Thy glo-ry, Praise Thy truth, a-dore Thy grace. A-MEN.

2 Once far off, but now invited,
　We approach Thy sacred throne;
In Thy covenant united,
　Reconciled, redeemed, made one.
Now revealed to eastern sages,
　See the star of mercy shine;
Mystery hid in former ages,
　Mystery great of love divine.

3 Hail, Thou all-inviting Saviour!
　Gentiles now their offerings bring;
In Thy temple seek Thy favor,
　Jesus Christ, our Lord and King.
May we, body, soul, and spirit,
　Live devoted to Thy praise,
Glorious realms of bliss inherit,
　Grateful anthems ever raise.

Basil Woodd, 1813.

65. Light of the Gentile Nations.

Wie soll ich dich empfangen. 76, 76. D.   JOHANN CRÜGER. 1653.

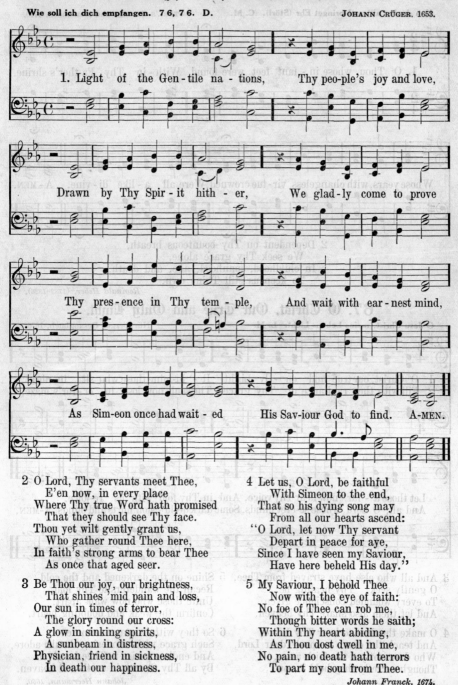

1. Light of the Gen-tile na-tions, Thy peo-ple's joy and love,

Drawn by Thy Spir-it hith-er, We glad-ly come to prove

Thy pres-ence in Thy tem-ple, And wait with ear-nest mind,

As Sim-eon once had wait-ed His Sav-iour God to find. A-MEN.

2 O Lord, Thy servants meet Thee,
    E'en now, in every place
Where Thy true Word hath promised
    That they should see Thy face.
Thou yet wilt gently grant us,
    Who gather round Thee here,
In faith's strong arms to bear Thee
    As once that aged seer.

3 Be Thou our joy, our brightness,
    That shines 'mid pain and loss,
Our sun in times of terror,
    The glory round our cross:
A glow in sinking spirits,
    A sunbeam in distress,
Physician, friend in sickness,
    In death our happiness.

4 Let us, O Lord, be faithful
    With Simeon to the end,
That so his dying song may
    From all our hearts ascend:
"O Lord, let now Thy servant
    Depart in peace for aye,
Since I have seen my Saviour,
    Have here beheld His day."

5 My Saviour, I behold Thee
    Now with the eye of faith:
No foe of Thee can rob me,
    Though bitter words he saith;
Within Thy heart abiding,
    As Thou dost dwell in me,
No pain, no death hath terrors
    To part my soul from Thee.

Johann Franck, 1674.

66. O Thou, Whose Infant Feet Were Found.

Nun danket all' und bringet Ehr (Störl). C. M.   STÖRL'S Gesang- und Notenbuch, 1710.

1. O Thou, whose in - fant feet were found With - in Thy Fa-ther's shrine,

Whose years, with changeless vir-tue crowned, Were all a - like di - vine. A - MEN.

2 Dependent on Thy bounteous breath,
   We seek Thy grace alone,
In childhood, manhood, age, and death,
   To keep us still Thine own.

Reginald Heber, (1783-1826).

67. O Christ, Our True and Only Light.

O Jesu Christ, meins Lebens Licht. L. M.   Nürnberger Gesangbuch, 1676.

1. O Christ, our true and on - ly Light, Il - lu-mine those who sit in night;
2. Fill with the ra-diance of Thy grace The souls now lost in er - ror's maze,

Let those a - far now hear Thy voice, And in Thy fold with us re-joice.
And all, O Lord, whose se-cret minds, Some dark de-lu - sion hurts and blinds. A-MEN.

3 And all who else have strayed from Thee,
  O gently seek! Thy healing be
To every wounded conscience given,
And let them also share Thy heaven.

4 O make the deaf to hear Thy Word,
  And teach the dumb to speak, dear Lord,
Who dare not yet the faith avow,
Though secretly they hold it now.

5 Shine on the darkened and the cold,
Recall the wanderers to Thy fold,
Unite those who now walk apart,
Confirm the weak and doubting heart.

6 So they with us may evermore
Such grace with wondering thanks adore,
And endless praise to Thee be given
By all Thy Church in earth and heaven.

Johann Heermann, 1630.

68. Rise, O Salem, Rise and Shine.

Jesus allt mitt goda är. 7 8, 7 8, 7 7.

JAKOB ARRHENIUS? 1694.

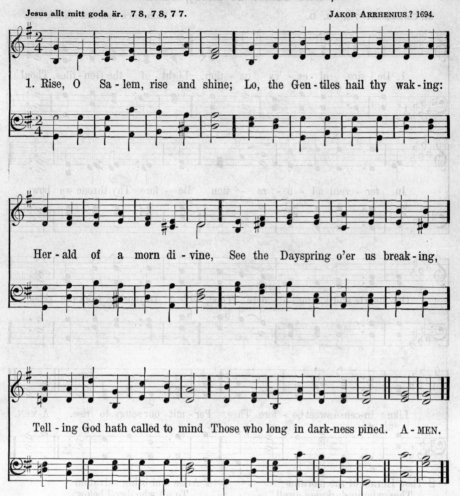

1. Rise, O Sa - lem, rise and shine; Lo, the Gen - tiles hail thy wak - ing:

Her - ald of a morn di - vine, See the Dayspring o'er us break - ing,

Tell - ing God hath called to mind Those who long in dark-ness pined. A - MEN.

2 O how blindly did we stray,
  Ere this Sun our earth had brightened;
Heaven we sought not, for no ray
  Had our wildered eyes enlightened:
All our looks were earthward bent,
All our strength on earth was spent.

3 But the Dayspring from on high
  Hath arisen with beams unclouded,
And we see before Him fly
  All the heavy gloom that shrouded
This sad earth, where sin and woe
Seemed to reign o'er all below.

4 Thine appearing, Lord, shall fill
  All my thoughts in sorrow's hour;
Thine appearing, Lord, shall still
  All my dread of death's dark power;
Whether joys or tears be mine,
Through them still Thy light shall shine.

5 Let me, when my course is run,
  Calmly leave a world of sadness
For the place that needs no sun,—
  For Thou art its light and gladness,—
For the mansions fair and bright,
Where Thy saints are crowned with light.

Johann Rist, 1655.

69. Desire of Every Nation.

St. Christopher. 7 6, 7 6. D.

FREDERICK CHARLES MAKER, 1881.

1. De - sire of ev - 'ry na - tion, Light of the Gen - tiles, Thou!

In fer - vent ad - o - ra - tion Be - fore Thy throne we bow;

Our hearts and tongues a - dore Thee, Blest Dayspring from the skies.

Like in-cense sweet be - fore Thee, Per - mit our songs to rise. A-MEN.

2 Thou Herald of the morning,
    They who in darkness dwell
Behold Thy brightness dawning
    O'er realms of Israel.
With glorious beams unclouded,
    Thy all-transcendent light
Dispels the gloom that shrouded
    Earth's dark and dismal night.

3 Arise and shine in splendor,
    Thou bright and morning Star!
The Gentiles come to render
    Their gifts from realms afar.
The word by prophets spoken
    In truth is now fulfilled,
And yearning hearts, once broken,
    With sweetest hope are filled.

4 Arise and bring salvation
    To all who dwell below,
Let earth in jubilation
    Reflect Thy radiant glow.
O long expected Saviour,
    Thou Hope of Israel,
Let Gentiles gain Thy favor,
    And of Thy glory tell.

5 Our Life and Resurrection,
    Lord Jesus Christ, Thou art;
O shed Thy light's reflection
    To earth's remotest part;
Let Gentile tongues confess Thee,
    Rejoicing in Thy light,
The ransomed thousands bless Thee,
    Thou hast dispelled the night.

Anna Hoppe, 1921.

70. Arise, O God, and Shine.

Lenox. 6 6, 6 6, 8 8 8.   LEWIS EDSON.

1. A - rise, O God, and shine In all Thy sav - ing might,
2. Bring dis - tant na - tions near To sing Thy glo - rious praise;

And pros - per each de - sign To spread Thy glo - rious light:
Let ev - 'ry peo - ple hear And learn Thy ho - ly ways:

Let heal - ing streams of mer - cy flow, That all the earth Thy
Reign, might - y God, as - sert Thy cause, And gov - ern by Thy

truth may know, That all the earth Thy truth may know.
right-eous laws, And gov - ern by Thy right - eous laws. A - MEN.

3 Pour forth Thy glorious power,
    That Gentiles all may see,
   And earth present her store
   In converts born to Thee:
   God, our own God, His Church will bless,
   And fill the world with righteousness.

4 To God, the only wise,
    The one immortal King,
   Let hallelujahs rise
   From every living thing:
   Let all that breathe, on every coast,
   Praise Father, Son, and Holy Ghost.

                                        William Hurn, 1813, a.

71. O God of God! O Light of Light!

Peterborough. L. M. D.

JOHN GOSS, 1864.

1. O God of God! O Light of light! Thou Prince of Peace, Thou King of kings,
2. Deep in the proph-ets' sa-cred page, Grand in the po - et's wing-ed word,

To Thee, where an-gels know no night, The song of praise for - ev - er rings:
Slow - ly in type, from age to age, Na - tions be - held their com - ing Lord;

To Him who sits up - on the throne, The Lamb once slain for sin - ful men,
Till through the deep Ju - de - an night Rang out the song, "Good will to men!"

Be hon - or, might, all by Him won; Glo - ry and praise! A - men, A - men!
Hymned by the first-born sons of light, Re - ech-oèd now, "Good will!" A-men! A-MEN.

3 Nations afar, in ignorance deep;
  Isles of the sea where darkness lay;
These hear Thy voice, they wake from sleep,
  And throng with joy the upward way.
They cry with us, "Send forth Thy light,
  O Lamb once slain for sinful men;
Burst Satan's bonds, O God of might;
  Set all men free! Amen, Amen!"

4 Sing to the Lord a glorious song,
  Sing to His Name, His love forthtell;
Sing on, heaven's host, His praise prolong;
  Sing, ye who now on earth do dwell:
"Worthy the Lamb for sinners slain;
  From angels, praise; and thanks from men;
Worthy the Lamb, enthroned to reign,
  Glory and power! Amen, Amen!"

John Julian, 1883.

72. Within the Father's House.

Bethlehem. S. M.   SAMUEL WESLEY, 1798.

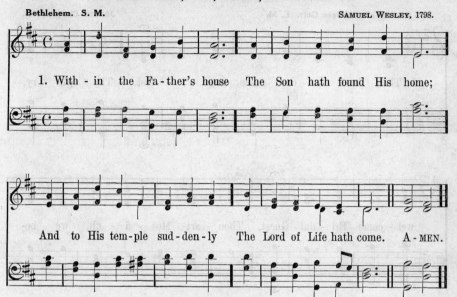

1. With - in the Fa - ther's house The Son hath found His home;

And to His tem-ple sud-den-ly The Lord of Life hath come. A - MEN.

2 Men wise in Sacred Writ
   Gaze on the wondrous Child,
And marvel at His gracious words
   Of wisdom undefiled.

3 Yet not to them is given
   The mighty truth to know,
To lift the earthly veil which hides
   Incarnate God below.

4 The secret of the Lord
   Escapes each human eye,
And faithful pondering hearts await
   The full Epiphany.

5 Lord, visit Thou our souls,
   And teach us by Thy grace
Each dim revealing of Thyself
   With loving awe to trace;

6 Till from our darkened sight
   The cloud shall pass away,
And on the cleansèd soul shall burst
   The everlasting day;

7 Till we behold Thy face,
   And know, as we are known,
Thee, Father, Son, and Holy Ghost,
   Co-equal Three in One.

James Russell Woodford, 1863, a.

73. Thou Hast Indeed Made Manifest.

Lob sei dem allmächtigen Gott. L. M.   JOHANN CRÜGER, 1640.

1. Thou hast in-deed made man-i-fest Thy glo-ry,
wel-come Bri-dal Guest, Thou art Mes-si-ah, we believe; Our ad-o-ra-tion, Lord, re-ceive. A-MEN.

2 Be Thou our constant Guest, we pray,
  O Friend of sinners, come to stay.
  Our every need do Thou supply,
  Till we become Thy guests on high.

3 O heavenly Bridegroom, haste, we pray,
  That long expected wedding day
  When trumpets sound, to call us home:
  "The bridal of the Lamb hath come."

Anna Hoppe, 1919.

74. All Praise to Thee, O Lord.

Schumann. S. M.   Arranged from ROBERT SCHUMANN, (1810–1856).

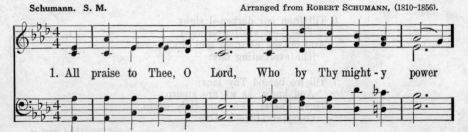

1. All praise to Thee, O Lord, Who by Thy might-y power

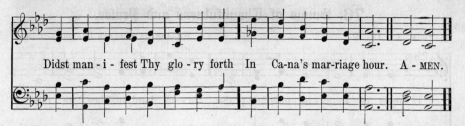

Didst man-i-fest Thy glo-ry forth In Ca-na's mar-riage hour. A-MEN.

2 Thou speakest, it is done:
   Obedient to Thy word,
The water reddening into wine
   Proclaims the present Lord.

3 Blest were the eyes which saw
   That wondrous mystery,
The great beginning of Thy works,
   That kindled faith in Thee.

4 And blessèd they who know
   Thine unseen presence true,
When in the kingdom of Thy grace
   Thou makest all things new.

5 For by Thy loving hand
   Thy people still are fed;
Thou art the cup of blessing, Lord,
   And Thou the heavenly bread.

6 O may that grace be ours,
   In Thee for aye to live,
And drink of those refreshing streams
   Which Thou alone canst give.

7 So, led from strength to strength,
   Grant us, O Lord, to see
The marriage supper of the Lamb,
   Thy great Epiphany.

Hyde Wyndham Beadon, 1863.

75. O Saviour of Our Race.

Crucis. S. M.   GEORGE MURSELL GARRETT, 1872.

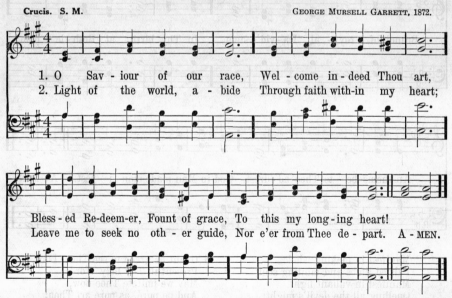

1. O Sav-iour of our race, Wel-come in-deed Thou art,
2. Light of the world, a-bide Through faith with-in my heart;

Bless-ed Re-deem-er, Fount of grace, To this my long-ing heart!
Leave me to seek no oth-er guide, Nor e'er from Thee de-part. A-MEN.

3 Thou art the Life, O Lord,
   Sole Light of life Thou art!
Let not Thy glorious rays be poured
   In vain on my dark heart.

4 Star of the East, arise!
   Drive all my clouds away;
Guide me till earth's dim twilight dies
   Into the perfect day.

Laurentius Laurentii, 1700.

64

Church Year: Epiphany

76. Songs of Thankfulness and Praise.

Viola. 7 7, 7 7. D.

WILLIAM BATCHELDER BRADBURY, 1849.

1. Songs of thank-ful-ness and praise, Je-sus, Lord, to Thee we raise,

Man-i-fest-ed by the star To the sag-es from a-far;

Branch of roy-al Da-vid's stem In Thy birth at Beth-le-hem;

An-thems be to Thee ad-drest, God in Man made man-i-fest. A-MEN.

2 Manifest in making whole
Palsied limbs and fainting soul;
Manifest in valiant fight,
Quelling all the devil's might;
Manifest in gracious will,
Ever bringing good from ill;
Anthems be to Thee addrest,
God in Man made manifest.

3 Grant us grace to see Thee, Lord,
Present in Thy holy Word;
May we imitate Thee now,
And be pure, as pure art Thou;
That we like to Thee may be
At Thy great Epiphany;
And may praise Thee, ever blest,
God in Man made manifest.

Christopher Wordsworth, 1862.

77. Fierce Was the Billow Wild.

St. Edmund. 6 4, 6 4, 6 6, 6 4.

ARTHUR SEYMOUR SULLIVAN, (1842–1900).

1. Fierce was the bil-low wild, Dark was the night;
Oars la-bored heav-i-ly, Foam glim-mered white;
Trem-bled the mar-i-ners, Per-il was draw-ing nigh;
Then said the God of God, "Peace! It is I." A-MEN.

2 Ridge of the mountain-wave,
   Lower thy crest!
Wail of the tempest fierce,
   Be thou at rest!
Sorrow can never be,
   Darkness must ever fly,
Where saith the Light of Light,
   "Peace! It is I."

3 Jesus, Deliverer,
   Come Thou to me;
Soothe Thou my voyaging
   Over life's sea:
Thou, when the storm of death
   Roars, fiercely sweeping by,
Whisper, O Truth of Truth,
   "Peace! It is I."

Ascribed to Anatolius (Greek; date unknown).

78. When Through the Torn Sail.

Dig, Jesus, min dyraste Jesus. 12 12, 12 12.   GUSTAV STOLPE, 1892.

1. When through the torn sail the wild tem-pest is stream-ing,

When o'er the dark wave the red light-ning is gleam-ing,

Nor hope lends a ray the poor sea-man to cher-ish,

We fly to our Mak-er: "Help, Lord, or we per-ish!" A-MEN.

2 O Jesus, once rocked on the breast of the billow,
Aroused by the shriek of despair from Thy pillow,
Now seated in glory, the mariner cherish,
Who cries in his anguish: "Help, Lord, or we perish!"

3 And O, when the whirlwind of passion is raging,
When sin in our hearts its wild warfare is waging,
Arise in Thy strength, Thy redeemèd to cherish;
Rebuke the destroyer: "Help, Lord, or we perish!"

Reginald Heber, 1820.

79. Heavenly Sower, Thou Hast Scattered.

Tviflan ur min själ försvinne. 8 7, 8 7, 8 8, 7 7. W. WESSNITZER, 1661.

1. Heav'n-ly Sow - er, Thou hast scat-tered Pre-cious seed up - on Thy field,

That a har-vest might be gath-ered, Rich and fruit - ful in its yield.

Gra-cious Lord, Thou hast de - fend-ed, Nur-tured, wa-tered, guarded, tend-ed

This so pre-cious seed of Thine, Spring-ing up in soil di - vine. A - MEN.

2 Lo, Thy field its fruits has yielded,
  Where Thy kingdom's seed was sown;
Gospel rain from drought has shielded,
  Pentecostal winds have blown;
Where Thy Sun of Grace in splendor
Shed its warming rays so tender,
  There Thy seed has taken root,
  There it blossomed into fruit.

3 Guard Thy gospel field, dear Master,
  Tares abound upon the soil.
Save Thy harvest from disaster,
  Let no foe Thy seed despoil.
When, upon Thy glad returning,
Tares and chaff are doomed to burning,
  Then within Thy garner, Lord,
  May the precious wheat be stored.

Anna Hoppe, 1919.

80. Hark! the Voice of Jesus Crying.

Jesus är min vän den bäste. 8 7, 8 7. D.   GUSTAF DÜBEN, 1674.

1. Hark! the voice of Jesus cry-ing, "Who will go and work to-day?
Fields are white, and har-vests wait-ing; Who will bear the sheaves a-way?"
Loud and long the Mas-ter call-eth, Rich re-ward He of-fers free;
Who will an-swer, glad-ly say-ing, "Here am I; send me, send me"? A-MEN.

2 Let none hear you idly saying,
"There is nothing I can do,"
While the souls of men are dying,
And the Master calls for you:
Gladly take the task He gives you,
Let His work your pleasure be;
Answer quickly when He calleth,
"Here am I; send me, send me."

Daniel March, 1868.

81. Almighty God, Thy Word Is Cast.

Belmont. C. M.   WILLIAM GARDINER, 1812.

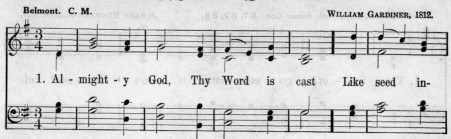

1. Al - might - y God, Thy Word is cast Like seed in -

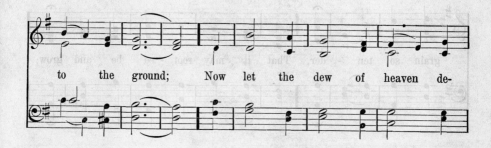

to the ground; Now let the dew of heaven de -

scend, And right - eous fruits a - bound... A - MEN.

2 Let not the foe of Christ and man
   This holy seed remove;
   But give it root in every heart,
   To bring forth fruits of love.

3 Let not the world's deceitful cares
   The rising plant destroy;
   But let it yield a hundredfold
   The fruits of peace and joy.

4 Oft as the precious seed is sown,
   Thy quickening grace bestow,
   That all whose souls the truth receive
   Its saving power may know.

John Cawood, 1819.

82. The Sower Goeth Forth to Sow.

Machs mit mir, Gott, nach deiner Güt. 8 7, 8 7, 8 8.   JOHANN HERMANN SCHEIN, 1627.

1. The Sow-er go-eth forth to sow His seed of grain so ten-der, That it may root-ed be and grow, And bring forth fruit in splen-dor. By faith He sees His har-vest field Its fruit-age in a-bun-dance yield. A-MEN.

2 Thou art the Sower, dearest Lord,
  The world Thy field so spacious,
The seed Thou sowest is the Word
Sown by Thy hand so gracious,
From heaven above, on earth below,
That it may blossom, thrive, and grow.

3 Let us not merely hearers be,
  But doers, blessèd Saviour,
Who bring forth fruit abundantly;
Grant us Thy Spirit's favor
To treasure in believing hearts
The precious truth Thy Word imparts.

Anna Hoppe, 1920.

83. Thou Goest to Jerusalem.

Du lifvets bröd. 8 7, 8 7, 8 8 7.   PETER SOHREN, 1668.

1. Thou go-est to Je-ru-sa-lem, O Son of God, to suf-fer, And for a world of sin-ful men Thy spot-less life to of-fer; Thou bear-est an-guish, pain, and loss, The mock-ers' scorn, the scourge, the cross, To win for us sal-va-tion. A-MEN.

2 Before Thee lies Gethsemane,
The scene of bitter anguish;
Thine eyes behold the Calvary
Where Thou in pain must languish;
The bleeding wounds, the bitter gall,
The crown of thorns, the judgment hall,
Thy burdened soul's affliction.

3 Thou art the Way, the Truth, the Life;
We pray Thee, Master, lead us
Away from earth's vain, restless strife;
With heavenly manna feed us.
Thou who hast died to save the lost,
Help us, dear Lord, to weigh the cost,
And follow Thee, our Saviour.

Anna Hoppe, 1921.

84. Lord, Who throughout Those Forty Days.

St. Flavian. C. M.   DAYE'S Psalter, 1562.

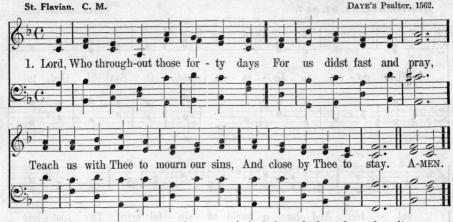

1. Lord, Who through-out those for - ty days For us didst fast and pray,

Teach us with Thee to mourn our sins, And close by Thee to stay. A-MEN.

2 As Thou with Satan didst contend,
  And didst the victory win,
O give us strength in Thee to fight,
  In Thee to conquer sin.

3 As thirst and hunger Thou didst bear,
  So teach us, gracious Lord,
To die to self, and chiefly live
  By Thy most holy Word.

4 And through these days of penitence,
  And through Thy Passiontide,
Yea, evermore, in life and death,
  Jesus, with us abide.

5 Abide with us, that so, this life
  Of suffering overpast,
An Easter of unending joy
  We may attain at last.

Claudia Frances Hernaman, 1873.

85. Forty Days and Forty Nights.

Gud, vår Gud, för världen all. 7 7, 7 7.   JOHAN FREDRIK LAGERGREN, b. 1826.

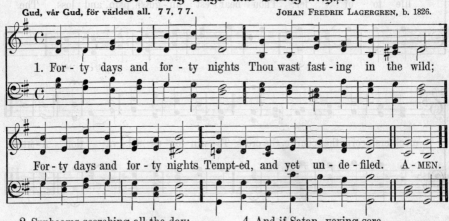

1. For - ty days and for - ty nights Thou wast fast - ing in the wild;

For - ty days and for - ty nights Tempt-ed, and yet un - de - filed. A - MEN.

2 Sunbeams scorching all the day;
  Chilly dewdrops nightly shed;
Prowling beasts about Thy way;
  Stones Thy pillow, earth Thy bed.

3 Shall we not Thy sorrow view,
  And with hearts attuned to Thine,
Yielding up our wills anew,
  Share with Thee a food divine?

4 And if Satan, vexing sore,
  Flesh or spirit should assail,
Thou, his Vanquisher before,
  Grant we may not faint nor fail.

5 So shall we have peace divine:
  Holier gladness ours shall be;
Round us, too, shall angels shine,
  Such as ministered to Thee.

George Hunt Smyttan, 1856, a.

86. Who Trusts in God a Strong Abode.

O Gud! ditt rike ingen ser. 8 7, 8 7. D.   BURKHARD WALDIS, 1553.

1. Who trusts in God a strong a-bode   In heav'n and earth pos-sess - es;

Who looks in love to Christ a-bove,   No fear his heart op-press - es;

In Thee a-lone, dear Lord, we own   Sweet hope and con-so-la - tion;

Our shield from foes, our balm for woes,   Our great and sure sal-va - tion.   A-MEN.

2 Though Satan's wrath beset our path,
 And worldly scorn assail us,
While Thou art near we will not fear;
 Thy strength shall never fail us.
Thy rod and staff shall keep us safe,
 And guide our steps forever;
Nor shades of death, nor hell beneath,
 Our souls from Thee shall sever.

3 In all the strife of mortal life
 Our feet shall stand securely;
Temptation's hour shall lose its power,
 For Thou shalt guard us surely.
O God, renew, with heavenly dew,
 Our body, soul, and spirit,
Until we stand at Thy right hand,
 Through Jesus' saving merit.

Joachim Magdeburg et al., 1527.

87. Thou Camest Down from Heaven on High.

Machs mit mir, Gott, nach deiner Güt.   8 7, 8 7, 8 8.   JOHANN HERMANN SCHEIN, 1627.

1. Thou cam-est down from heav'n on high, O Son of
2. In Thee the blind re-ceive their sight, The lame with

God the Fa-ther, For this lost world to bleed and die,
joy are leap-ing, The sor-row-ful find pure de-light,

Thy stray-ing sheep to gath-er, The works of Sa-tan
The wea-ry peace-ful sleep-ing; Thou giv-est speech un-

to de-stroy, To turn our sor-row in-to joy.
to the dumb, And vi-brant life to sens-es numb. A-MEN.

3 Thou Who hast broken Satan's power,
   Be Thou our Strength, dear Jesus!
Uphold us in the evil hour,
   And from his might release us!
His kingdom is a stronghold still,
And legions hearken to his will.

4 But O, before Thy Word, dear Lord,
   The prince of darkness trembles!
He quails before that two-edged Sword
   When Thine armed host assembles!
O mighty Word, how great thy power!
Thou art our Refuge, Shield, and Tower.

Anna Hoppe, 1920.

88. Friend of the Weary, O Refresh Us.

Norelius. 9 8, 9 8, 9 9.

PETER JOHNSON, 1922.

1. Friend of the wea-ry, O re-fresh us, And turn to
us Thy lov-ing face, With Thy sweet peace and par-don bless us,
That sin may be de-stroyed by grace; O come, Thy sweet com-
pas-sion show-ing, On our poor souls Thy grace be-stow-ing. A - MEN.

2 From Thee our only comfort cometh,
  Our strength and hope, O Lord of all;
To Thee all power still belongeth
  To save and help us in each fall;
Thy grace and pardon will deliver,
And set us free from shame forever.

3 As Thou didst help the sick and weary,
  Who once were gathered at Thy side,
'Mid earthly deserts, waste and dreary,
  In Thy sure aid we still confide;
When evils come our souls assailing,
Send us Thy Word of grace unfailing.

Ludwig Andreas Gotter (1661-1735).

89. Thy Works, Not Mine, O Christ.

Darwall's 148th. 6 6, 6 6, 4 4, 4 4.   JOHN DARWALL, 1770.

1. Thy works, not mine, O Christ, Speak glad-ness to this heart;

They tell me all is done; They bid my fear de-part. To whom, save

REFRAIN:

Thee, Who canst a-lone For sin a-tone, Lord, shall I flee? A-MEN.

2 Thy tears, not mine, O Christ,
Have wept my guilt away,
And turned this night of mine
Into a blessèd day.

3 Thy wounds, not mine, O Christ,
Can heal my bruisèd soul;
Thy stripes, not mine, contain
The balm that makes me whole.

4 Thy cross, not mine, O Christ,
Has borne the awful load
Of sins that none could bear
But the incarnate God.

5 Thy death, not mine, O Christ,
Has paid the ransom due;
Ten thousand deaths like mine
Would have been all too few.

Horatius Bonar. 1857.

90. O Lamb of God, Most Holy.

O Lamm Gottes unschuldig. 7 7, 7 7, 7 7 7. Iambic.

NICOLAUS DECIUS, 1539.

1. O Lamb of God, most ho - ly, On Cal - va - ry an of - f'ring;

De - spis - ed, meek, and low - ly, Thou in Thy death and

suf - f'ring Our sins didst bear, our an - guish; The might of

death didst van - quish; Give us Thy peace, O Je - sus! A - MEN.

Nicolaus Decius, 1526.

91. Christ, the Life of All the Living.

Jesu, meines Lebens Leben.   8 7, 8 7, 7 7, 7 7.   Darmstädter Gesangbuch, 1687.

1. Christ, the Life of all the liv-ing, Christ, the Death of death our foe,
2. Thou, O Thou, hast tak-en on Thee Bit-ter strokes, a cru-el rod;

Who, Thy-self for us once giv-ing To the dark-est depths of woe,
Pain and scorn were heaped up-on Thee, O Thou sin-less Son of God.

Pa-tient-ly didst yield Thy breath, But to save my soul from death,
Thus didst Thou our souls de-liv-er From the bonds of sin for-ev-er;

Praise and glo-ry ev-er be, Bless-ed Je-sus, un-to Thee.
Praise and glo-ry ev-er be, Bless-ed Je-sus, un-to Thee.   A-MEN.

3 Thou didst bear the smiting only,
   That it might not fall on me;
Stoodest falsely charged and lonely,
   That I might be safe and free;
Comfortless Thy soul did languish
To bring comfort in our anguish;
Praise and glory ever be,
Blessèd Jesus, unto Thee.

4 Then for all that wrought our pardon,
   For Thy sorrows deep and sore,
For Thine anguish in the garden,
   I will thank Thee evermore;
To my latest breath I'll offer
Thanks for all that Thou didst suffer,
For that last expiring sigh
Praise Thee evermore on high.

Ernst Christopher Homburg, 1659.

92. Lord, Thy Death and Passion Give.

O Liebe meiner Liebe. 7 7, 7 7. D.   Manuscript Herrnhut Choralbuch, 1735.

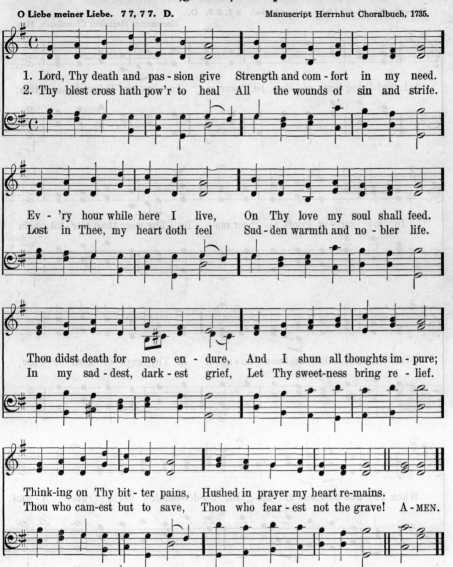

1. Lord, Thy death and pas-sion give Strength and com-fort in my need.
2. Thy blest cross hath pow'r to heal All the wounds of sin and strife.

Ev-'ry hour while here I live, On Thy love my soul shall feed.
Lost in Thee, my heart doth feel Sud-den warmth and no-bler life.

Thou didst death for me en-dure, And I shun all thoughts im-pure;
In my sad-dest, dark-est grief, Let Thy sweet-ness bring re-lief.

Think-ing on Thy bit-ter pains, Hushed in prayer my heart re-mains.
Thou who cam-est but to save, Thou who fear-est not the grave! A-MEN.

3 Lord, in Thee I place my trust,
  Thou art my Defense and Tower;
Death Thou treadest in the dust,
  O'er my soul he hath no power.
That I may have part in Thee,
Help and save and comfort me;
Give me of Thy grace and might,
Resurrection, life and light.

4 Fount of good, within me dwell,
  For the peace Thy presence sheds
Keeps us safe in conflict fell,
  Charms the pain from dying beds.
Hide me safe within Thine arm,
Where no foe can hurt or harm;
Whoso, Lord, in Thee doth rest,
He hath conquered, he is blest.

Johann Heermann, 1644.

93. Suffering Son of Man, Be Near Me.

Bohemia No. 11 (O Liebe meiner Liebe). 8 7, 8 7. D.

Manuscript Herrnhut Choralbuch, 1735.

1. Suf-f'ring Son of Man, be near me, In my suf-f'rings to sus-tain;

In my sor-er griefs to cheer me By Thy more than mor-tal pain.

Call to mind that un-known an-guish In Thy days of flesh be-low,

When Thy trou-bled soul did lan-guish Un-der-neath a world of woe. A-MEN.

2 By Thy fainting in the garden,
By Thy dreadful death, I pray,
Write upon my heart Thy pardon,
Take my sins and fears away.
By the travail of Thy Spirit,
By Thine outcry on the tree,
By Thine agonizing merit,
Gracious Lord, remember me!

Charles Wesley, 1767, a.

94. How Shall I Follow Him I Serve?

Maryton. L. M.

HENRY PERCY SMITH, 1874.

1. How shall I fol-low Him I serve? How shall I cop-y Him I love? Nor from those bless-ed foot-steps swerve, Which lead me to His seat a-bove? A - MEN.

2 Privations, sorrows, bitter scorn,
    The life of toil, the mean abode,
  The faithless kiss, the crown of thorn,—
    Are these the consecrated road?

3 'Twas thus He suffered, though a Son,
    Foreknowing, choosing, feeling all,
  Until the perfect work was done,
    And drained the bitter cup of gall.

4 Lord, should my path through suffering lie,
    Forbid that I should e'er repine;
  Still let me turn to Calvary,
    Nor heed my grief, remembering Thine.

5 O let me think how Thou didst leave
    Untasted every pure delight
  To fast, to faint, to watch, to grieve,
    The toilsome day, the homeless night:

6 To faint, to grieve, to die for me!
    Thou camest not Thyself to please:
  And, dear as earthly comforts be,
    Shall I not love Thee more than these?

7 Yes! I would count them all but loss,
    To gain the notice of Thine eye:
  Flesh shrinks and trembles at the cross,
    But Thou canst give the victory.

Josiah Conder, 1824.

95. Jesus, Refuge of the Weary.

Stilla, ja, allt mera stilla. 8 7, 8 7. D.

HAMPUS WETTERLING.

1. Jesus, Refuge of the weary, Object of the spirit's love,
Fountain in life's desert dreary, Saviour from the world above:
O how oft Thine eyes, offended, Gaze upon the sinner's fall!
Yet, upon the cross extended, Thou didst bear the pain of all. A-MEN.

2 Do we pass that cross unheeding,
  Breathing no repentant vow,
Though we see Thee wounded, bleeding,
  See Thy thorn-encircled brow?
Yet Thy sinless death has brought us
Life eternal, peace, and rest;
Only what Thy grace has taught us
Calms the sinner's stormy breast.

3 Jesus, may our hearts be burning
  With more fervent love for Thee;
May our eyes be ever turning
  To Thy cross of agony;
Till in glory parted never
  From the blessèd Saviour's side,
Graven in our hearts forever,
  Dwell the cross, the Crucified.

Girolamo Savonarola, (1454-1498).

96. Saviour, When in Dust to Thee.

Spanish Hymn. 7 7, 7 7. D.   Spanish Melody.

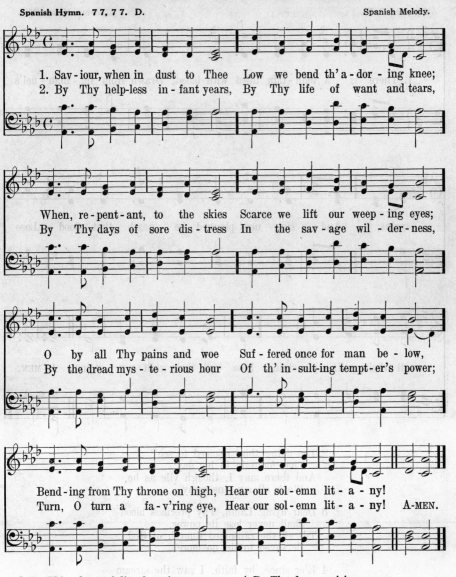

1. Sav-iour, when in dust to Thee   Low we bend th' a - dor - ing knee;
2. By Thy help-less in - fant years, By Thy life of want and tears,

When, re - pent - ant, to the skies   Scarce we lift our weep - ing eyes;
By   Thy days of sore dis - tress In   the sav - age wil - der - ness,

O by all Thy pains and woe   Suf - fered once for man be - low,
By the dread mys - te - rious hour Of th' in - sult - ing tempt - er's power;

Bend - ing from Thy throne on high, Hear our sol - emn lit - a - ny!
Turn, O turn a   fa - v'ring eye, Hear our sol - emn lit - a - ny! A-MEN.

3 By Thine hour of dire despair,
By Thine agony of prayer,
By the cross, the nail, the thorn,
Piercing spear, and torturing scorn,
By the gloom that veiled the skies
O'er the dreadful sacrifice,
Listen to our humble cry,
Hear our solemn litany!

4 By Thy deep expiring groan,
By the sad sepulchral stone,
By the vault whose dark abode
Held in vain the rising God,
O from earth to heaven restored,
Mighty, reascended Lord,
Listen, listen to the cry
Of our solemn litany!

Robert Grant, 1815.

97. There Is a Fountain Filled with Blood.

Cowper. C. M.   LOWELL MASON, 1830.

1. There is a foun-tain filled with blood, Drawn from Im-man-uel's veins; And sin-ners plunged be-neath that flood Lose all their guilt-y stains, Lose all their guilt-y stains. A-MEN.

2 The dying thief rejoiced to see
  That fountain in his day;
And there may I, though vile as he,
  Wash all my sins away.

3 Dear dying Lamb, Thy precious blood
  Shall never lose its power,
Till all the ransomed Church of God
  Be saved to sin no more.

4 E'er since, by faith, I saw the stream
  Thy flowing wounds supply,
Redeeming love has been my theme,
  And shall be till I die.

5 Then in a nobler, sweeter song,
  I'll sing Thy power to save,
When this poor lisping, stammering tongue
  Lies silent in the grave.

William Cowper, 1771, a.

98. Ride On, Ride On in Majesty!

Herr Jesu Christ, dich zu uns wend. L. M.   Cantionale Sacrum, Gotha, 1651.

1. Ride on, ride on in maj-es-ty! In low-ly pomp ride
on to die! O Christ, Thy tri-umphs now be-gin
O'er cap-tive death and con-quered sin. A-MEN.

2 Ride on, ride on in majesty!
  The angel armies of the sky
  Look down with sad and wondering eyes
  To see the approaching Sacrifice.

3 Ride on, ride on in majesty!
  Thy last and fiercest strife is nigh:
  The Father on His sapphire throne
  Expects His own anointed Son.

4 Ride on, ride on in majesty!
  In lowly pomp ride on to die!
  Bow Thy meek head to mortal pain,
  Then take, O God, Thy power, and reign!

Henry Hart Milman, 1827, a.

Other hymns suitable for Palm Sunday are those for the First Sunday in Advent.

99. O Thou, Who through This Holy Week.

Walsall. C. M.

WILKINS' Psalmody, 1699.
Attributed to HENRY PURCELL, (1658–1695).

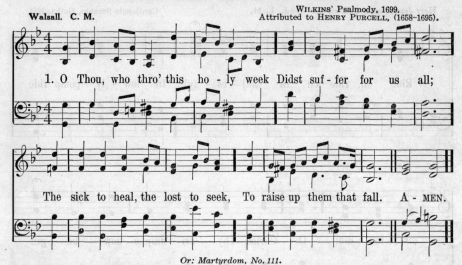

1. O Thou, who thro' this ho - ly week Didst suf - fer for us all;

The sick to heal, the lost to seek, To raise up them that fall. A - MEN.

Or: Martyrdom, No. 111.

2 We cannot understand the woe
  Thy love was pleased to bear;
  O Lamb of God, we only know
  That all our hopes are there.

3 Thy feet the path of suffering trod;
  Thy hand the victory won;
  What shall we render to our God
  For all that He hath done?

John Mason Neale, 1842.

100. 'Tis Midnight, and on Olive's Brow.

St. Cross. L. M.

JOHN BACCHUS DYKES, (1823–1876).

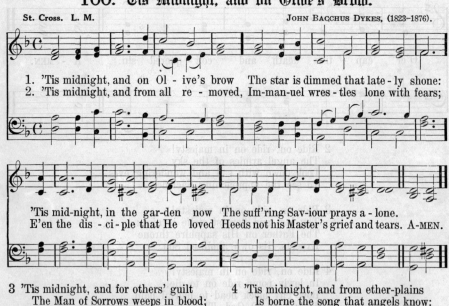

1. 'Tis midnight, and on Ol - ive's brow   The star is dimmed that late - ly shone:
2. 'Tis midnight, and from all   re - moved, Im-man-uel wres - tles lone with fears;

'Tis mid-night, in the gar-den now The suff'ring Sav-iour prays a - lone.
E'en the dis - ci - ple that He loved Heeds not his Master's grief and tears. A-MEN.

3 'Tis midnight, and for others' guilt
  The Man of Sorrows weeps in blood;
  Yet He that hath in anguish knelt
  Is not forsaken by His God.

4 'Tis midnight, and from ether-plains
  Is borne the song that angels know:
  Unheard by mortals are the strains
  That sweetly soothe the Saviour's woe.

William Bingham Tappan, 1822.

101. Over Kedron Jesus Treadeth.

Frälsta värld! i nådens under. 8 7, 8 7, 7 7, 8 8.

Koralbok, 1697.

1. O - ver Ked - ron Je - sus tread - eth To His pas - sion for us all;

Ev - 'ry hu - man eye be weep - ing, Tears of bit - ter grief let fall!

Round His Spir - it flock the foes, Place their shafts and bend their bows,

Aim - ing at the Sav - iour sole - ly, While the world forsakes Him wholly. A - MEN.

2 See Him anguish-stricken falling
  Prostrate, and with struggling breath,
Three times on His Father calling,
  Praying that the bitter death
And the cup of doom may go;
Still He cries, in all His woe:
"Not My will, but Thine, O Father,"
And the angels round Him gather.

3 See how, in that hour of darkness,
  Battling with the evil power,
Agonies untold assail Him,
  On His soul the arrows shower;
And the garden flowers are wet
With the drops of bloody sweat
From His anguished frame distilling—
Our redemption thus fulfilling.

Thomas Kingo, 1689.

102. Go to Dark Gethsemane.

Gethsemane (Redhead 76). 7 7, 7 7, 7 7.   RICHARD REDHEAD, 1853.

1. Go to dark Geth-sem-a-ne, Ye that feel the tempt-er's pow'r:
2. Fol-low to the judg-ment hall, View the Lord of life ar-raigned;

Your Re-deem-er's con-flict see; Watch with Him one bit-ter hour;
O the worm-wood and the gall! O the pangs His soul sus-tained!

Turn not from His griefs a-way; Learn of Je-sus Christ to pray.
Shun not suf-f'ring, shame, or loss; Learn of Him to bear the cross. A-MEN.

3 Calvary's mournful mountain climb;
   There, adoring at His feet,
Mark that miracle of time,
   God's own Sacrifice complete;
"It is finished," hear Him cry;
Learn of Jesus Christ to die.

4 Early hasten to the tomb,
   Where they laid His breathless clay;
All is solitude and gloom;
   Who hath taken Him away?
Christ is risen! He meets our eyes;
Saviour, teach us so to rise.

James Montgomery, 1825.

103. In the Cross of Christ I Glory.

Rathbun. 8 7, 8 7.   ITHAMAR CONKEY. 1851.

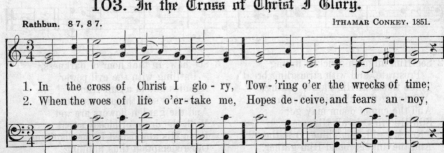

1. In the cross of Christ I glo-ry, Tow-'ring o'er the wrecks of time;
2. When the woes of life o'er-take me, Hopes de-ceive, and fears an-noy,

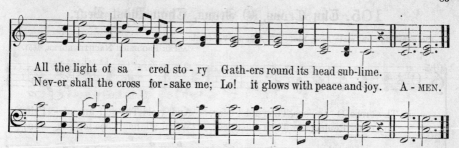

All the light of sa - cred sto - ry Gath-ers round its head sub-lime.
Nev-er shall the cross for - sake me; Lo! it glows with peace and joy. A - MEN.

3 When the sun of bliss is beaming
  Light and love upon my way,
  From the cross the radiance streaming
  Adds new luster to the day.

4 Bane and blessing, pain and pleasure,
  By the cross are sanctified;
  Peace is there that knows no measure,
  Joys that through all time abide.

John Bowring, 1825.

104. Near the Cross Was Mary Weeping.

Civitas Dei. 8 8 7, 8 8 7.   JOHN BAPTISTE CALKIN, (1827–1905).

1. Near the cross was Ma - ry weep-ing, There her mourn-ful sta - tion keep-ing,

Gaz - ing on her dy - ing Son: There in speech-less an-guish groan-ing,

Yearn-ing, trembling, sighing, moaning, Thro' her soul the sword had gone. A-MEN.

2 When no eye its pity gave us,
  When there was no arm to save us,
    He His love and power displayed:
  By His stripes He wrought our healing,
  By His death our life revealing,
    He for us the ransom paid.

3 Jesus, may Thy love constrain us,
  That from sin we may refrain us,
    In Thy griefs may deeply grieve;
  Thee our best affections giving,
  To Thy glory ever living,
    May we in Thy glory live.

Jacobus de Benedictis, 13th Century.

105. Thy Cross, O Jesus, Thou Didst Bear.

So gehst du nun, mein Jesu, hin. 8 7, 8 7, 4 4 7. Iambic.

CASPER FRIEDRICH NACHTENHÖFER, 1651.

1. Thy cross, O Je-sus, Thou didst bear,   And yield Thy-self an of-f'ring
2. Thy cross, Re-deem-er, Thou didst bear,   When all had Thee for-sak - en;

To save a sin - ful world which e'er   With scorn be-holds Thy suf-f'ring.
My sins and guilt Thou bor-est there,   Thy   love hath me o'er-tak - en!

O wondrous love From heav'n above, To bleed for Thine ac-cus - ers!
Thou callest me To   come to Thee And be Thy child for-ev - er.   A - MEN.

3 Thy cross, O Saviour, Thou didst bear:
   Thy boundless might and glory,
Forever praised by angels fair,
   And told in sacred story,
     Thou didst resign,
     O love divine
That conquereth in dying!

4 Thy cross to victory Thou didst bear;
   O grant that I, dear Saviour,
May glory in the cross and share
   Thy heavenly joy and favor!
     Then shall my soul
     Have reached its goal,
Safe in Thy loving bosom.

Erik Gustaf Geijer, 1812.

106. Come to Calvary's Holy Mountain.

Naar mit Øie, traet af Møie. 8 7, 8 7, 7 7.   LUDVIG M. LINDEMAN, (1812-1887).

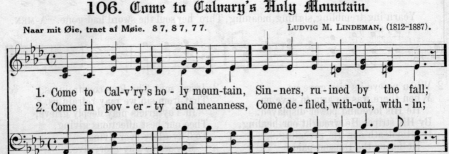

1. Come to Cal-v'ry's ho - ly moun-tain, Sin - ners, ru - ined by the fall;
2. Come in pov - er - ty and meanness, Come de - filed, with-out, with - in;

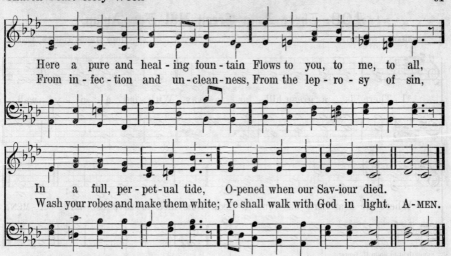

Here a pure and heal-ing foun-tain Flows to you, to me, to all,
From in-fec-tion and un-clean-ness, From the lep-ro-sy of sin,

In a full, per-pet-ual tide, O-pened when our Sav-iour died.
Wash your robes and make them white; Ye shall walk with God in light. A-MEN.

3 Come in sorrow and contrition,
   Wounded, impotent, and blind;
Here the guilty free remission,
   Here the troubled peace may find:
Health this fountain will restore;
He that drinks shall thirst no more.

4 He that drinks shall live forever;
   'Tis a soul-renewing flood:
God is faithful; God will never
   Break His covenant of blood,
Signed when our Redeemer died,
Sealed when He was glorified.

James Montgomery, 1819.

107. When I Survey the Wondrous Cross.

Vicaria. L. M.   JAMES REMINGTON FAIRLAMB, 1864.

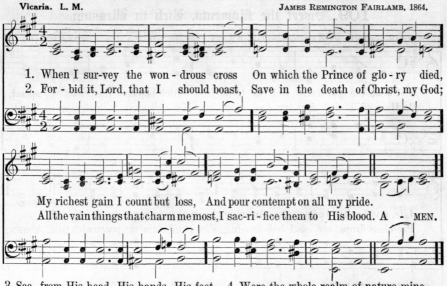

1. When I sur-vey the won-drous cross On which the Prince of glo-ry died,
2. For-bid it, Lord, that I should boast, Save in the death of Christ, my God;

My richest gain I count but loss, And pour contempt on all my pride.
All the vain things that charm me most, I sac-ri-fice them to His blood. A-MEN.

3 See, from His head, His hands, His feet,
   Sorrow and love flow mingled down!
Did e'er such love and sorrow meet,
   Or thorns compose so rich a crown?

4 Were the whole realm of nature mine,
   That were a tribute far too small;
Love so amazing, so divine,
   Demands my soul, my life, my all.

Isaac Watts, 1707, a.

108. There Is a Green Hill Far Away.

Meditation. C. M.   JOHN HENRY GOWER, 1890.

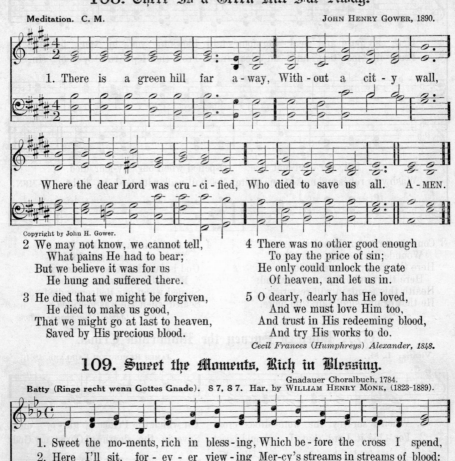

1. There is a green hill far a-way, With-out a cit-y wall,

Where the dear Lord was cru-ci-fied, Who died to save us all. A-MEN.

Copyright by John H. Gower.

2 We may not know, we cannot tell,
    What pains He had to bear;
But we believe it was for us
    He hung and suffered there.

3 He died that we might be forgiven,
    He died to make us good,
That we might go at last to heaven,
    Saved by His precious blood.

4 There was no other good enough
    To pay the price of sin;
He only could unlock the gate
    Of heaven, and let us in.

5 O dearly, dearly has He loved,
    And we must love Him too,
And trust in His redeeming blood,
    And try His works to do.

Cecil Frances (Humphreys) Alexander, 1848.

109. Sweet the Moments, Rich in Blessing.

Gnadauer Choralbuch, 1784.

Batty (Ringe recht wenn Gottes Gnade). 8 7, 8 7. Har. by WILLIAM HENRY MONK, (1823-1889).

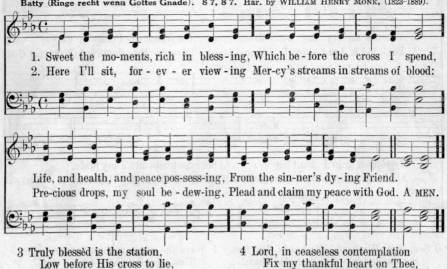

1. Sweet the mo-ments, rich in bless-ing, Which be-fore the cross I spend,
2. Here I'll sit, for-ev-er view-ing Mer-cy's streams in streams of blood:

Life, and health, and peace pos-sess-ing, From the sin-ner's dy-ing Friend.
Pre-cious drops, my soul be-dew-ing, Plead and claim my peace with God. A MEN.

3 Truly blessèd is the station,
    Low before His cross to lie,
While I see divine compassion
    Beaming in His gracious eye.

4 Lord, in ceaseless contemplation
    Fix my thankful heart on Thee,
Till I taste Thy full salvation
    And Thine unveiled glory see.

Walter Shirley, 1774, a.

110. 'Tis Finished! So the Saviour Cried.

Så är fullkomnadt. L. M.

Koralbok, 1697.

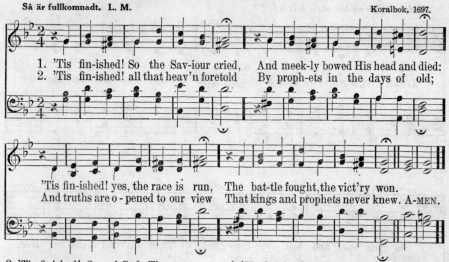

1. 'Tis fin-ished! So the Sav-iour cried, And meek-ly bowed His head and died:
2. 'Tis fin-ished! all that heav'n foretold By proph-ets in the days of old;

'Tis fin-ished! yes, the race is run, The bat-tle fought, the vict'ry won.
And truths are o-pened to our view That kings and prophets never knew. A-MEN.

3 'Tis finished! Son of God, Thy power
Hath triumphed in this awful hour;
And yet our eyes with sorrow see
That life to us was death to Thee.

4 'Tis finished! let the joyful sound
Be heard through all the nations round;
'Tis finished! let the triumph rise,
And swell the chorus of the skies.

Samuel Stennett, 1787, a.

111. Alas! and Did My Saviour Bleed?

Martyrdom. C. M.

HUGH WILSON, (1764-1824).

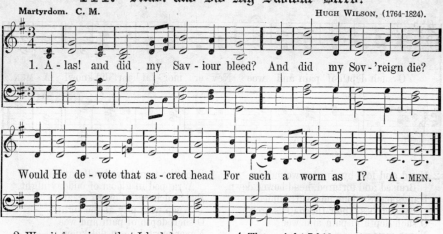

1. A-las! and did my Sav-iour bleed? And did my Sov-'reign die?

Would He de-vote that sa-cred head For such a worm as I? A-MEN.

2 Was it for crimes that I had done,
He groaned upon the tree?
Amazing pity! grace unknown!
And love beyond degree!

3 Well might the sun in darkness hide,
And shut his glories in,
When Christ the mighty Maker died
For man the creature's sin!

4 Thus might I hide my blushing face,
While His dear cross appears;
Dissolve my heart in thankfulness,
And melt mine eyes to tears.

5 But drops of grief can ne'er repay
The debt of love I owe;
Here, Lord, I give myself away,
'Tis all that I can do.

Isaac Watts, 1707, a.

112. Sinful World, Behold the Anguish.

Skåder, skåder nu här alle.   8 7, 8 7, 7 7.   Koralbok, 1697.

1. Sin-ful world, be-hold the an-guish Of our Sav-iour on the tree!

See His soul and bod-y lan-guish, Us from sin and death to free.

O such depth of pain and woe Nev-er mor-tal heart did know! A-MEN.

2 Hand and foot by sinners wounded,
   Bruised and tortured, head bowed down,
Hangs our Saviour now surrounded
   By His foes, their thorns His crown.
O such depth of pain and woe
Never mortal heart did know!

3 Hear His cry in prayer and pleading,
   "Father, to Thy hands commend
I my spirit; light and leading
   In this hour of darkness send."
O such depth of pain and woe
Never mortal heart did know!

4 Rent the temple veil, all nature
   Wrapped in gloom of midday night,
Eye and heart of every creature
   Weep with pity at the sight.
O such depth of pain and woe
Never mortal heart did know!

5 Sinful heart, in deep contrition
   Bow before the Crucified;
Contemplate His grievous passion,
   Own that for thy sins He died.
O such love as He hath shown
Never mortal heart hath known.

Johann Quirsfeld, (1642-1686), et al.

113. Now, My Soul, Thy Voice Upraising.

Requiem. 8 7, 8 7, 8 7.

WILHELM A. F. SCHULTHES, 1868.

1. Now, my soul, thy voice up - rais-ing, Tell in sweet and mourn-ful strain

How the Cru - ci - fied, en - dur - ing Grief, and wounds, and dy - ing pain,

Free - ly of His love was of - fered, Sin-less, was for sin-ners slain. A - MEN.

2 Scourged with unrelenting fury
  For the sins which we deplore,
By His livid stripes He heals us,
  Raising us to fall no more;
All our bruises gently soothing,
  Binding up the bleeding sore.

3 See! His hands and feet are fastened;
  So He makes His people free;
Not a wound whence blood is flowing
  But a fount of grace shall be:
Yea, the very nails which nail Him
  Nail us also to the tree

4 Through His heart the spear is piercing,
  Though His foes have seen Him die;
Blood and water thence are streaming
  In a tide of mystery;
Water, from our guilt to cleanse us,
  Blood, to win us crowns on high.

5 Jesus, may those precious fountains
  Drink to thirsting souls afford:
Let them be our present healing,
  And at length our full reward;
So a ransomed world shall ever
  Praise Thee, its redeeming Lord.

Claude de Santeüil, 1680.

114. My Crucified Saviour, Despised and Contemned.

Min blodige konung. 11 11, 11 11.   ANDREAS CARL RUTSTRÖM, (1721–1772).

1. My cru-ci-fied Sav-iour, de-spised and con-temned, Thou in-no-cent
Vic-tim for sin-ners con-demned, Thy gar-ments are blood-stained, Thy
spir-it doth groan, In ag-o-ny pros-trate, Thou suf-f'rest a-lone. A-MEN.

2 Thou weepest and moanest in conflict and prayer,
And writhest in agony, pain, and despair;
In thirty years' anguish our path Thou hast trod,
And diest at last to redeem us to God.

3 Our Saviour thus finished God's plan with our race,
And laid the foundation for pardon and grace.
And then rose triumphant, the conquering Lord,
Appeased the Creator and mankind restored.

4 Restored to the bliss that was lost in the fall,
Yea, greater, for Jesus prepared for us all
Eternal salvation and mansions above;
Come, poor, burdened sinners, rejoice in His love.

5 Yea, come, trembling sinner, come just as thou art,
Thy cares and thy sorrows to Jesus impart;
In Him seek salvation from death and the grave,
For Jesus is willing and mighty to save.

Andreas Carl Rutström, (1721–1772).

115. Ah, Holy Jesus, How Hast Thou Offended?

Herzliebster Jesu. 11 11, 11 5.   JOHANN CRÜGER, 1640.

1. Ah, ho-ly Je-sus, how hast Thou of-fend-ed, That man to judge Thee hath in hate pre-tend-ed? By foes de-rid-ed, by Thine own re-ject-ed, O most af-flict-ed! A-MEN.

2 Who was the guilty? Who brought this upon Thee?
Alas, my treason, Jesus, hath undone Thee!
'Twas I, Lord Jesus, I it was denied Thee:
        I crucified Thee.

3 Lo, the good Shepherd for the sheep is offered;
The slave hath sinnèd, and the Son hath suffered;
For man's atonement, while he nothing heedeth,
        God intercedeth.

4 For me, kind Jesus, was Thine incarnation,
Thy mortal sorrow, and Thy life's oblation;
Thy death of anguish and Thy bitter passion,
        For my salvation.

5 Therefore, kind Jesus, since I cannot pay Thee,
I do adore Thee, and will ever pray Thee:
Think on Thy pity and Thy love unswerving,
        Not my deserving.

Johann Heermann, 1630.
Tr. Copyright by Robert Bridges.

116. O Sacred Head, Now Wounded.

Herzlich thut mich verlangen. 76, 76. D.
HANS LEO HASSLER, 1601 and 1613.

1. O sa - cred Head, now wound - ed, With grief and shame weighed down,
   Now scorn-ful - ly sur - round - ed, With thorns Thine on - ly crown!

Once reign-ing in the high - est In light and maj - es - ty,

Dis - hon-ored now Thou di - est, Yet here I wor - ship Thee. A - MEN.

2 How art Thou pale with anguish,
   With sore abuse and scorn!
How does that visage languish,
   Which once was bright as morn!
What Thou, my Lord, hast suffered
   Was all for sinners' gain;
Mine, mine was the transgression,
   But Thine the deadly pain.

3 Lo, here I fall, my Saviour,
   'Tis I deserve Thy place:
Look on me with Thy favor,
   Vouchsafe to me Thy grace.
Receive me, my Redeemer;
   My Shepherd, make me Thine,
Of every good the Fountain,
   Thou art the Spring of mine!

4 What language shall I borrow
   To thank Thee, dearest Friend,
For this Thy dying sorrow,
   Thy pity without end!
O make me Thine forever,
   And should I fainting be,
Lord, let me never, never,
   Outlive my love to Thee.

5 Forbid that I should leave Thee;
   O Jesus, leave not me;
In faith may I receive Thee,
   When death shall set me free.
When strength and comfort languish,
   And I must hence depart,
Release me then from anguish
   By Thine own wounded heart.

Bernard of Clairvaux, (1091-1153).
Paul Gerhardt, 1653.

117. Stricken, Smitten, and Afflicted.

Wo ist Jesus, mein Verlangen. 8 7, 8 7. D.   Geistliches Volkslied, 1850.

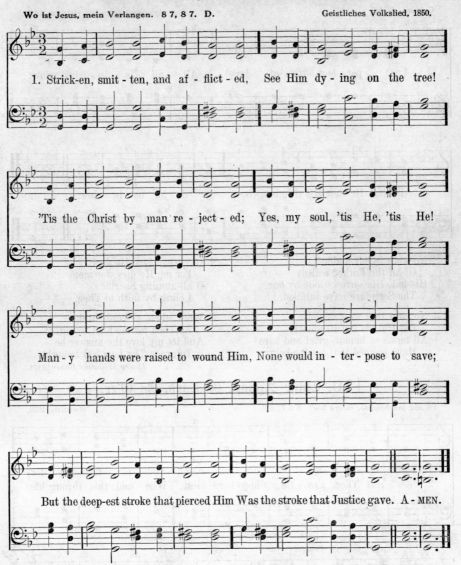

1. Strick-en, smit-ten, and af-flict-ed, See Him dy-ing on the tree!

'Tis the Christ by man re-ject-ed; Yes, my soul, 'tis He, 'tis He!

Man-y hands were raised to wound Him, None would in-ter-pose to save;

But the deep-est stroke that pierced Him Was the stroke that Justice gave. A - MEN.

2 Ye who think of sin but lightly,
  Nor suppose the evil great,
Here may view its nature rightly,
  Here its guilt may estimate.
Mark the Sacrifice appointed!
  See who bears the awful load!
'Tis the Word, the Lord's Anointed,
  Son of Man, and Son of God.

3 Here we have a firm foundation,
  Here the refuge of the lost:
Christ the Rock of our salvation:
  Christ the Name of which we boast:
Lamb of God for sinners wounded!
  Sacrifice to cancel guilt!
None shall ever be confounded
  Who on Him their hope have built.

Thomas Kelly, 1804, a.

118. O Perfect Life of Love.

Gorton. S. M.   Arranged from BEETHOVEN, 1807.

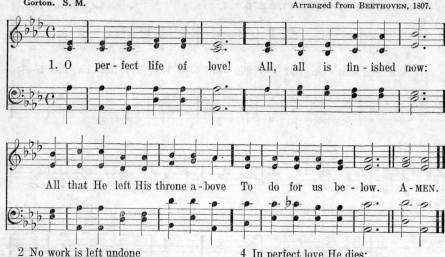

1. O per-fect life of love! All, all is fin-ished now:

All that He left His throne a-bove To do for us be-low. A-MEN.

2 No work is left undone
   Of all the Father willed;
   His toil, His sorrows, one by one,
   The Scripture have fulfilled.

3 No pain that we can share
   But He has felt its smart;
   All forms of human grief and care
   Have pierced that tender heart.

4 In perfect love He dies;
   For me He dies, for me;
   O all-atoning Sacrifice,
   I cling by faith to Thee.

5 Work, then, O Lord, in me,
   As Thou for me hast wrought;
   And let my love the answer be
   To grace Thy love has brought.

Henry Williams Baker, 1875.

119. Thine Agony, O Lord, Is O'er.

På dig jag hoppas, Herre kär! 8 8 7, 8 7.   Swedish. 1536.

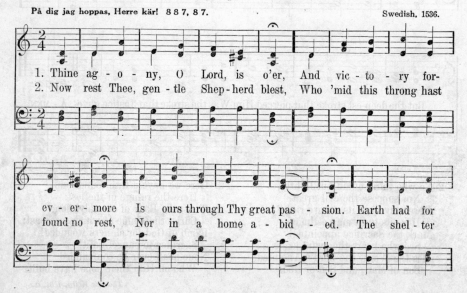

1. Thine ag-o-ny, O Lord, is o'er, And vic-to-ry for-
2. Now rest Thee, gen-tle Shep-herd blest, Who 'mid this throng hast

ev-er-more Is ours through Thy great pas-sion. Earth had for
found no rest, Nor in a home a-bid-ed. The shel-ter

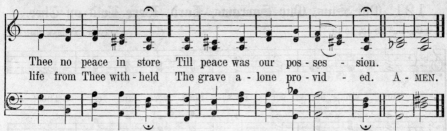

Thee no peace in store   Till peace was our pos - ses - sion.
life from Thee with - held   The grave a - lone pro - vid - ed.   A - MEN.

3 O silent grave! O blest retreat,
A refuge for my Saviour meet,
No longer dark and narrow!
Like Him, I enter thee content,
Released from toil and sorrow.

4 O sleep of death, O night profound,
My Lord hath set for thee a bound:
His promise I remember.
Like Him, triumphant I shall come
From out that peaceful chamber.

Johan Olof Wallin, 1819.

120. Mute Are the Pleading Lips of Him.

Den mun är tyst. 8 7, 8 7, 8 8, 7 7.   German, 16th Century.

1. {Mute are the plead-ing lips of Him   Who hath our cause de - fend - ed;}
   {Love drained the cup filled to the brim,   As Ho - li - ness de - mand - ed.}

The gen - tle Shep-herd here be - hold,   Slain for the sheep lost to His fold:

From la - bor, pain, and weep - ing   Now rests He with the sleep - ing.   A - MEN.

2 But not for aye, O Friend of men,
   Thou in the grave descendest;
A little while, and then again
   Thy grieving flock Thou tendest.
The corn that falls into the earth
From darkness springs in fullness forth,
In season amply giving
The life-bread to the living.

3 O Prince of Life, now to the gloom
   Of earth consigned in sorrow,
My life so guide, that in my tomb
   I wait the blessèd morrow.
When, freed from worldly strife and care,
This mortal frame reposes there,
Grant that my deathless spirit
The bliss of heaven inherit.

Johan Olof Wallin, 1819.

121. Our Sins, Our Sorrows, Lord, Were Laid on Thee.

Langran. 10 10, 10 10.   JAMES LANGRAN, 1862.

1. Our sins, our sor - rows, Lord, were laid on Thee;

Thy stripes have healed, Thy bonds have set us free;

And now Thy toil is o'er; Thy grief and pain

Have passed a - way; the veil is rent in twain. A - MEN.

2 Now hast Thou laid Thee down in perfect peace
Where all the wicked from their troubling cease,
Thy tranquil Sabbath in the grave to keep:
Thy Father giveth His Belovèd sleep.

3 Yet in Thy glory, on the throne above,
Thou wast abiding ever, Lord of love,
Eternal, filling all created things
With Thine own presence, Jesus, King of kings!

Edward William Eddis, 1864.

122. Welcome, Happy Morning! Age to Age Shall Say.

Fortunatus. 11 11, 11 11, 11.   ARTHUR SEYMOUR SULLIVAN, 1872.

1. Wel-come, hap-py morn-ing! age to age shall say, Hell to-day is van-quished, heav'n is won to-day. Lo, the Dead is liv-ing, God for ev-er-more! Him their true Cre-a-tor, all His works a-dore. Wel-come, hap-py morn-ing! age to age shall say. A-MEN.

2 Maker and Redeemer, Life and Health of all,
Thou from heaven beholding human nature's fall,
Thou of God the Father, true and only Son,
Manhood to deliver, manhood didst put on.
Hell to-day is vanquished; heaven is won to-day!

3 Thou, of life the Author, death didst undergo,
Tread the path of darkness, saving strength to show;
Come then, True and Faithful, now fulfill Thy word;
'Tis Thine own third morning: rise, O buried Lord!
Welcome, happy morning! age to age shall say.

4 Loose the souls long prisoned, bound with Satan's chain;
All that now is fallen raise to life again;
Show Thy face in brightness, bid the nations see;
Bring again our daylight; day returns with Thee!
Welcome, happy morning! Heaven is won to-day!

Venantius Fortunatus, (530-609).

123. The Saviour Is Risen.

Hvad ljus öfver griften!   6 5, 6 5, 6 5, 6 5, 6 5, 6 5, 6 4.   NIELS JESPERSÖN's Gradual, 1573.

1. {The Sav-iour is ris-en, Light bursts from the tomb; The liv-ing ful-
A-dored by the an-gels, The Vic-tor comes forth To claim for His

fill-ment Of Scrip-ture is come.}
king-dom The ran-somed on earth. } The seal has been bro-ken, The

stone rolled a-way, And fled are the watch-ers In fear and dis-

may; Hell trem-bles be-fore Him. Hal - le - lu - jah.   A - MEN.

2 Light grappled with darkness,
    Death wrestled with life;
Now light comes triumphant
    From out the dread strife.
While death lieth vanquished,
    Hope kindles again
The torch of the faithful
    To shine among men.
Ye sorrowing women
    Who hither have sped,
Why seek ye the living
    To-day 'mongst the dead?
For Jesus is risen.
    Hallelujah.

3 Now God in His heaven
    And man are at one,
The grave is a pathway,
    Through Christ, to the throne.
Ye friends that are bending
    In grief at the cross,
Now lift your heads gladly,
    Ye suffered no loss.
O flock, scattered widely,
    Return to the fold:
Thy Shepherd still liveth,
    And now as of old
He leadeth thee Godward.
    Hallelujah.

4 'Mid storms and upheavals
  His Church stands secure.
The truth of His gospel
  Shall ever endure.
Lo! unto all peoples
  His message shall speed,
Proclaiming 'mid turmoil
  The Lord's mighty deed,
Proclaiming the Saviour
  Who died for all men,
And, having arisen,
  Now liveth again,
Firstfruits of the sleeping.
  Hallelujah.

5 Then weep not, ye faithful,
  Yield not to despair:
The night soon is over,
  The day shall appear.
Though earth shall embrace you
  When death lays you low,
The seed of His sowing
  To harvests will grow;
And soon shall the Sower
  Return to His field
With angels to gather
  Its heavenly yield,
From evil tares severed.
  Hallelujah.

Frans Mikael Franzén, 1811.

124. I Know That My Redeemer Lives.

Federal Street. L. M.   HENRY KEMBLE OLIVER, 1832.

1. I know that my Re - deem - er lives! What com - fort
2. He lives to bless me with His love, He lives to

this sweet sen - tence gives! He lives, He lives, who
plead for me a - bove, He lives my hun - gry

once was dead, He lives, my ev - er - liv - ing Head.
soul to feed, He lives to help in time of need. A - MEN.

3 He lives, and grants me daily breath;
  He lives, and I shall conquer death;
  He lives my mansion to prepare;
  He lives to bring me safely there.

4 He lives, all glory to His Name!
  He lives, my Jesus, still the same;
  O the sweet joy this sentence gives,
  I know that my Redeemer lives!

Samuel Medley, 1775.

125. Blest Easter Day, What Joy Is Thine.

Lob sei dem allmächtigen Gott. L. M.   JOHANN CRÜGER, 1640.

1. Blest Eas-ter day, what joy is thine! We praise, dear
2. The tree where Thou wast of-fered up Now bears the

Lord, Thy Name di-vine, For Thou hast tri-umphed o'er the
fruit of life and hope: Thy pre-cious blood for us is

tomb; No more we need to dread its gloom.
shed, Now we may feed on heav'n-ly bread. A-MEN.

3 We thank Thee, Jesus, that Thy hand
Has freed us from sin's galling band;
No more its thralldom we need fear;
The year of liberty is here.

4 O Jesus Christ, God's Son elect,
Our Paschal Lamb without defect,
To us Thou givest strength indeed,
In all our conflicts, all our need.

5 O grant that, as Thou didst arise,
We, too, with joy may heavenward rise,
First from our sin, to love Thy way,
Then from the grave on that great Day.

6 All praise to Thee who from death's might,
From carnal lust and sin's dark plight
Redeemest me, that even I
May reach eternal life on high.

Olavus Petri, 1536.

126. Come, See the Place Where Jesus Lay.

Grace Church. L. M.   From IGNAZ JOSEF PLEYEL, 1800.

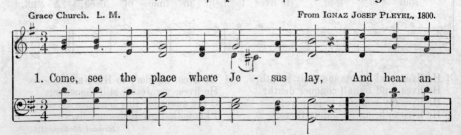

1. Come, see the place where Je-sus lay, And hear an-

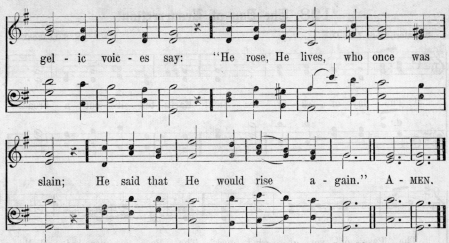

gel - ic voic - es say: "He rose, He lives, who once was

slain; He said that He would rise a - gain." A - MEN.

2 O joyful sound! O glorious hour!
 When by His own almighty power
 Our Saviour rose, and left the grave,
 And ever liveth now to save.

3 Now let our songs His triumph tell,
 Who burst the bands of death and hell;
 The First-begotten of the dead,
 For us He rose, our glorious Head.

4 No more we tremble at the grave,
 For Jesus will our spirits save.
 O risen Lord, in Thee we live,
 To Thee our ransomed souls we give.

5 All praise be Thine, O risen Lord,
 From death to endless life restored;
 All praise to God the Father be,
 And Holy Ghost eternally.

Thomas Kelly, 1804.

127. Welcome, Thou Victor in the Strife.

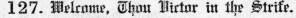

Nun danket all' und bringet Ehr (Crüger). C. M.   JOHANN CRÜGER, 1657.

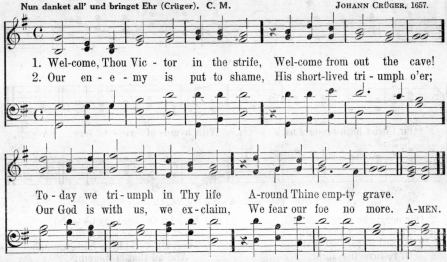

1. Wel-come, Thou Vic - tor in the strife, Wel-come from out the cave!
2. Our en - e - my is put to shame, His short-lived tri - umph o'er;

To - day we tri - umph in Thy life A-round Thine emp-ty grave.
Our God is with us, we ex-claim, We fear our foe no more. A-MEN.

3 The dwellings of the just resound
 With songs of victory;
 For in their midst Thou, Lord, art found,
 And bringest peace with Thee.

4 O let Thy conquering banner wave
 O'er hearts Thou makest free;
 And point the path that from the grave
 Leads heavenward up to Thee.

Benjamin Schmolck, 1712.

128. The Day of Resurrection!

Salvatori. 76, 76. D.   S. SALVATORI.

1. The day of res-ur-rec-tion! Earth, tell it out a-broad!

The Pass-o-ver of glad-ness, The Pass-o-ver of God!

From death to life e-ter-nal, From earth un-to the sky,

Our Christ hath brought us o-ver, With hymns of vic-to-ry. A-MEN.

Or: Valet will ich dir geben, No. 24.

2 Our hearts be pure from evil,
  That we may see aright
The Lord in rays eternal
  Of resurrection light,
And, listening to His accents,
  May hear, so calm and plain,
His own "All hail!"—and hearing,
  May raise the victor-strain.

3 Now let the heavens be joyful,
  Let earth her song begin,
The wide world keep high triumph,
  And all that is therein;
Let all things seen and unseen
  Their notes together blend,
For Christ the Lord is risen,
  Our Joy that hath no end.

John of Damascus, 8th Century.

129. Day of Wonder, Day of Gladness.

Autumn. 8 7, 8 7. D.

Spanish Melody.
FRANCOIS HIPPOLITE BARTHELEMON? (1741–1808).

1. Day of won-der, day of glad-ness, Hail thy ev-er glo-rious light!

Gone is sor-row, gone is sad-ness, End-ed is the gloom-y night.

Lis-ten to the an-gel's sto-ry, Cast a-way all fear and dread;

Give to God the Fa-ther glo-ry! Christ is ris-en from the dead! A-MEN.

Or: Jesus är min vän den bäste, No. 80.

2 In the triumph of this hour,
    Jubilant shall swell the song;
Unto Jesus, honor, power,
    Blessing, victory belong.
Scattered are the clouds of error,
    Sin and hell are captive led:
E'en the grave is free from terror,
    Christ is risen from the dead!

3 Every people, every nation
    Soon shall hear the gladsome sound;
Joyous tidings of salvation,
    Borne to earth's remotest bound.
Then shall rise, in tones excelling,
    Praise for grace so freely shed,
And the Easter hymn be swelling,
    Christ is risen from the dead!

B. H. Hall.

130. Christ the Lord Is Risen To-day.

St. George's, Windsor. 7 7, 7 7. D.   GEORGE JOB ELVEY, 1858.

1. Christ the Lord is ris'n to-day, Chris-tians, haste your vows to pay,

Of-fer ye your prais-es meet, At the Pas-chal Vic-tim's feet.

For the sheep the Lamb hath bled, Sin-less, in the sin-ner's stead;

"Christ is ris'n," to-day we cry; Now He lives, no more to die. A-MEN.

2 Christ, the Victim undefiled,
Man to God hath reconciled,
Whilst in strange and awful strife
Met together Death and Life.
Christians, on this happy day,
Haste with joy your vows to pay;
"Christ is risen," to-day we cry;
Now He lives, no more to die.

3 Christ, who once for sinners bled,
Now the First-born from the dead,
Throned in endless might and power
Lives and reigns for evermore.
Hail, eternal Hope on high!
Hail, Thou King of victory!
Hail, Thou Prince of Life adored!
Help and save us, gracious Lord.

Based on the Latin, 12th Century.

131. Come, Ye Faithful, Raise the Strain.

St. Kevin. 7 6, 7 6. D. Trochaic. ARTHUR SEYMOUR SULLIVAN, 1872.

1. Come, ye faith-ful, raise the strain Of tri-um-phant glad-ness;

God hath brought His Is-ra-el In-to joy from sad-ness;

'Tis the spring of souls to-day: Christ has burst His pris-on,

And, from three days' sleep in death, As a sun hath ris-en. A-MEN.

2 All the winter of our sins,
  Long and dark, is flying
From His light, to whom we give
  Laud and praise undying.
Neither might the gates of death,
  Nor the tomb's dark portal,
Nor the watchers, nor the seal,
  Hold Thee as a mortal.

3 But to-day amidst Thine own
  Thou didst stand, bestowing
That Thy peace which evermore
  Passeth human knowing.
Come, ye faithful, raise the strain
  Of triumphant gladness;
God hath brought His Israel
  Into joy from sadness.

John of Damascus, 8th Century.

132. Christ the Lord Is Risen To-day.

Gud, vår Gud, för världen all. 7 7, 7 7.   JOHAN FREDRIK LAGERGREN, b. 1826.

1. Christ the Lord is ris'n to-day, Sons of men and an-gels say.
2. Love's re-deem-ing work is done, Fought the fight, the bat-tle won;

Raise your joys and tri-umphs high; Sing, ye heav'ns, and earth re-ply.
Lo! the Sun's e-clipse is o'er; Lo! He sets in blood no more. A-MEN.

3 Vain the stone, the watch, the seal!
  Christ hath burst the gates of hell!
  Death in vain forbids Him rise;
  Christ hath opened paradise.

4 Lives again our glorious King;
  Where, O death, is now thy sting?
  Dying once, He all doth save;
  Where thy victory, O grave?

5 Soar we now where Christ has led,
  Following our exalted Head;
  Made like Him, like Him we rise;
  Ours the cross, the grave, the skies.

6 Hail, the Lord of earth and heaven!
  Praise to Thee by both be given:
  Thee we greet triumphant now;
  Hail, the Resurrection Thou!

Charles Wesley, 1739.

133. Morning Breaks upon the Tomb.

Pleyel's Hymn. 7 7, 7 7.   IGNAZ JOSEF PLEYEL, 1791.

1. Morn-ing breaks up-on the tomb; Je-sus scat-ters all its gloom;

Day of tri-umph, through the skies See the glo-rious Sav-iour rise. A-MEN.

2 Ye who are of death afraid,
  Triumph in the scattered shade,
  Drive your anxious fears away,
  See the place where Jesus lay!

3 Christians, dry your flowing tears,
  Chase your unbelieving fears;
  Look on His deserted grave,
  Doubt no more His power to save.

William Bengo Collyer, 1812.

134. In Death's Strong Grasp the Saviour Lay.

O Jesu Christ, du höchstes Gut. 8 7, 8 7, 8 8 7.   JOHANN CRÜGER, 1658.

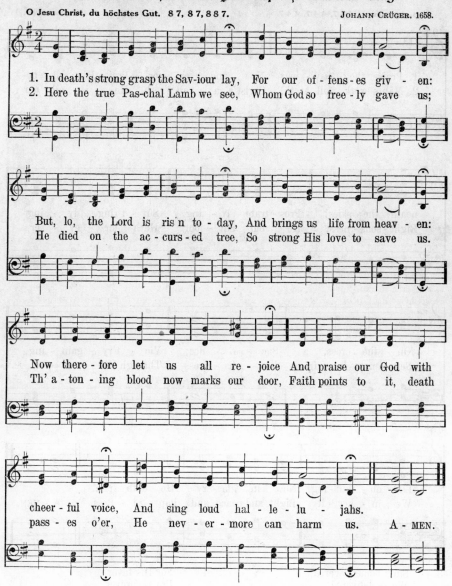

1. In death's strong grasp the Sav-iour lay, For our of-fens-es giv-en:
2. Here the true Pas-chal Lamb we see, Whom God so free-ly gave us;

But, lo, the Lord is ris'n to-day, And brings us life from heav-en:
He died on the ac-curs-ed tree, So strong His love to save us.

Now there-fore let us all re-joice And praise our God with
Th' a-ton-ing blood now marks our door, Faith points to it, death

cheer-ful voice, And sing loud hal-le-lu-jahs.
pass-es o'er, He nev-er-more can harm us. A-MEN.

3 So let us keep the festival
    Whereto the Lord invites us;
Christ is Himself the Joy of all,
    The Sun which warms and lights us:
And by His grace He doth impart
Eternal sunshine to the heart;
    The night of sin is ended.

4 Then let us feast this Easter day
    On the true Bread of heaven;
The Word of grace hath purged away
    The old and wicked leaven:
For Christ alone our souls will feed,
He is our meat and drink indeed;
    Faith lives upon no other.

Martin Luther, 1524.

135. Praise the Saviour!

Upp, min tunga, 4 4 7, 4 4 7, 4 4 7.   Koralbok, 1697.

1. Praise the Sav-iour Now and ev-er! Praise Him all be-
2. Man's work fail-eth, Christ's a-vail-eth, He is all our

neath the skies! Pros-trate ly-ing, Suf-f'ring, dy-ing
Right-eous-ness. He our Sav-iour Hath for-ev-er

On the cross, a Sac-ri-fice; Vic-t'ry gain-ing,
Set us free from dire dis-tress. Through His mer-it

Life ob-tain-ing, Now in glo-ry He doth rise.
We in-her-it Light, and peace, and hap-pi-ness. A-MEN.

3   Sin's bonds severed,
    We're delivered,
Christ hath bruised the serpent's head;
    Death no longer
    Is the stronger,
Hell itself is captive led.
    Christ hath risen
    From death's prison,
O'er the tomb He light hath shed.

4   For His favor,
    Praise forever
Unto God the Father sing;
    Praise the Saviour,
    Praise Him ever,
Son of God, our Lord and King;
    Praise the Spirit,
    Through Christ's merit,
He doth us salvation bring.

Venantius Honorius Clementianus Fortunatus, (530?-609).

136. He Lives! O Fainting Heart, Anew.

Han lefver! o min ande, känn. 8 8, 8 8, 8 8.   HAEFFNER'S Koralbok, 1819.

1. He lives! O faint-ing heart, a-new With joy thy
Lord and Sav-iour view! He from the si-lent cham-ber woke,
And speaks a-gain as e'er He spoke. A quick-'ning hand He
has to give: He lives, and thou shalt al-so live. A-MEN.

2 O hear His voice, and take His hand,
Thou traveler to a better land;
While passing through thy crucial test,
Lift up thy head,—a peaceful rest,
Thy trials over, He shall give:
He lives, and thou shalt also live.

3 Ye dead in sin, awake, arise!
The Lord is calling from the skies.
Repentant come, in faith remain,
And live in Him; from sin and pain
And death shall He salvation give:
He lives, and thou shalt also live.

4 With Him thy Guide, lies smooth and bright
Thy pathway to the realm of light;
Abiding faith, undying love,
And hope lead to the home above.
Thy life into His keeping give:
He lives, and thou shalt also live.

5 Of glory shall His raiment be;
O'er time and o'er eternity
The Sun of Righteousness shall shine;
In heaven's throne He sits divine;
A footstool earth to Him shall give:
He lives, and thou shalt also live.

Johan Olof Wallin.

137. In Triumph Our Redeemer.

Förlossningen är vunnen. 76, 76, 776.   German Enchiridion, 1524.

1. In tri-umph our Re-deem-er Is now to life returned. All praise to Him who, dy - - ing, Hath our sal-
va-tion earned! No more death's fet-ter galls us, The grave no
more ap-palls us, For Je-sus lives a-gain.

2. In glo-ry Thou ap-pear-est, And earth is filled with
light; With res-ur-rec-tion ra - - diance The ver-y
tomb is bright; There's joy in heav'n-ly plac-es When o'er all
earth-ly rac-es The dawn of mer-cy breaks. A - MEN.

3 Teach me with Thee to suffer,
    With Thee to live and die,
  In trial and temptation
    On Thy help to rely.
  To them alone who suffered
  With Thee the palm is offered
    When our last fight is won.

4 When in the morning watches
    Of that last day of dread
  Thou comest in Thy glory
    To judge both quick and dead,
  How sweet Thy promise spoken,
  Thyself the living token,
    That death shall be no more.

Erik Gustaf Geijer, 1819.

138. O Dear Redeemer Crucified.

Machs mit mir, Gott, nach deiner Güt. 8 8, 8 8, 8 8.   JOHANN HERMANN SCHEIN, 1827, a.

1. O dear Re-deem-er cru-ci-fied, Thou faith-ful
2. All we like sheep had gone a-stray From Thy blest

Shep-herd who hast died To save from death Thy help-less sheep,
fold and lost our way, Left pleas-ant pas-tures, ver-dant lands,

We pray Thee, ris-en Sav-iour, keep In Thy se-cure pro-
For bar-ren wastes and des-ert sands; But O, Thy shep-herd-

tec-tion still The sheep who heark-en to Thy will.
love so deep Sought till it found Thy err-ing sheep. A-MEN.

3 O Shepherd Saviour, we rejoice
To be Thine own, to hear Thy voice.
Bought with a price, we now are Thine,
And known of Thee, O Love divine!
By grace unto Thy fold restored,
Let us not stray again, dear Lord.

4 Dear Lord, our eyes of faith behold
In truth one Shepherd and one fold,
Kept through the Spirit's bond of peace
In unity which ne'er shall cease.
As Thou hast promised, we shall be
Thine own in all eternity.

Anna Hoppe, 1919.

139. Jesus, the Very Thought of Thee.

St. Agnes. C. M.   JOHN BACCHUS DYKES, 1866.

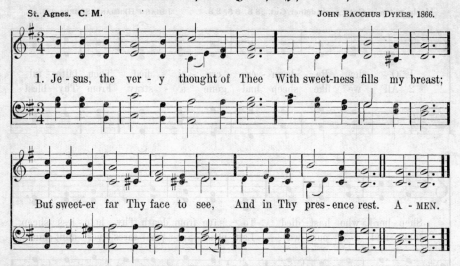

1. Je - sus, the ver - y thought of Thee With sweet-ness fills my breast;

But sweet-er far Thy face to see, And in Thy pres - ence rest. A - MEN.

2 Nor voice can sing, nor heart can frame,
   Nor can the memory find,
  A sweeter sound than Thy blest Name,
   O Saviour of mankind!

3 O Hope of every contrite heart,
   O Joy of all the meek,
  To those who fall, how kind Thou art,
   How good to those who seek!

4 But what to those who find? Ah, this
   Nor tongue nor pen can show;
  The love of Jesus, what it is,
   None but His loved ones know.

5 Jesus, our only Joy be Thou,
   As Thou our Prize wilt be;
  Jesus, be Thou our Glory now
   And through eternity!

Bernard of Clairvaux, (1091–1153).

140. In the Holy Father's Keeping.

Weston. 8 7, 8 7. D.   JOHN EDWARD ROE, (1838–1871).

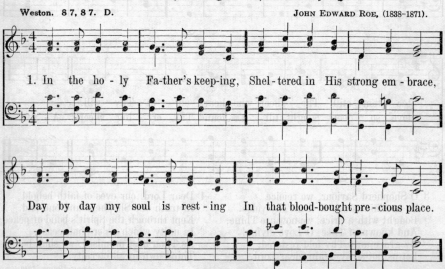

1. In the ho - ly Fa - ther's keep-ing, Shel - tered in His strong em - brace,

Day by day my soul is rest - ing In that blood-bought pre - cious place.

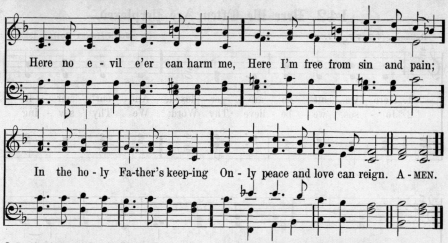

Here no e-vil e'er can harm me, Here I'm free from sin and pain;

In the ho-ly Fa-ther's keep-ing On-ly peace and love can reign. A - MEN.

2 In the holy Father's keeping
  There is joy, complete, fulfilled:
Joy which Jesus died to give me,
  Yea, His precious blood was spilled
That I might be kept securely,
  Through the Father's precious Name,
Kept for glories grand, celestial,
  Far above all earthly fame.

3 In the holy Father's keeping,
  Jesus, I will pray Thy prayer.
Holy Father, wilt Thou take me?
  Wilt Thou guard, protect me there?
By the prayer that Jesus offered,
  By His cross, His blood, His love,
Holy Father, in Thy keeping
  Take me to Thy realms above.

Samuel Martin Miller, 1922.

141. Didst Thou, Dear Jesus, Pray for Me?

Gloria Dei. C. M. PETER JOHNSON, 1923.

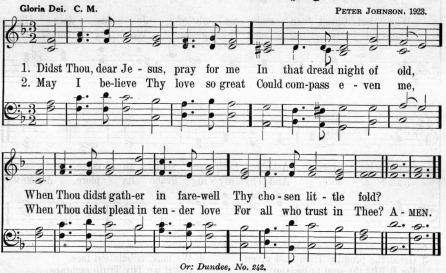

1. Didst Thou, dear Je-sus, pray for me In that dread night of old,
2. May I be-lieve Thy love so great Could com-pass e-ven me,

When Thou didst gath-er in fare-well Thy cho-sen lit-tle fold?
When Thou didst plead in ten-der love For all who trust in Thee? A - MEN.

Or: Dundee, No. 242.

3 Was there a place in Thy dear heart
    For such a one as I;
  And dost Thou still remember me
    Before the throne on high?

4 O wondrous love beyond compare,
    O mercy, full and free;
  My heart shall e'er rejoice in this,
    That Jesus prays for me!

Ernest Edwin Ryden, 1923.

142. Here We Often Are Perplexed.

Reliance. 7 7, 7 7, 7 7.   JOHN HENRY GOWER, 1895.

1. Here we oft-en are per-plexed, And our spir-it
2. Je - sus, we be - lieve Thy Word; We Thy sav-ing

oft is vexed; Sor-rows still af-flict the soul;
Truth have heard, Thou dost save when in dis-tress

Who but Christ can make us whole? Je - sus does His
Those re - ly - ing on Thy grace. We Thy ho - ly

prom-ise give, Ask in faith, ye shall re - ceive.
Name a - dore, And Thy sav-ing grace im - plore. A - MEN.

3 Great the promise Thou hast given,
For it lifts the soul to heaven;
Whatsoever we can claim—
If we ask it in Thy Name—
From the Father we receive,
If we in Thy Word believe.

4 We must tribulation face,
But if we Thy Truth embrace,
Though the world is full of sin,
Thy salvation we shall win.
Thou who didst the world o'ercome
Givest victory to Thine own.

George Henry Trabert, 1922.

143. O Jesus, Shall It Ever Be?

Brookfield. L. M.   THOMAS BISHOP SOUTHGATE, 1855.

1. O Je-sus, shall it ev-er be, A mor-tal man a-shamed of Thee? A-shamed of Thee whom an-gels praise, Whose glo-ries shine through end-less days? A-MEN.

Or: Wenn wir in höchsten Nöthen sein, No. 50.

2 Ashamed of Jesus! sooner far
Let evening blush to own a star;
He sheds the beams of light divine
O'er this benighted soul of mine.

3 Ashamed of Jesus! just as soon
Let midnight be ashamed of noon;
'Tis midnight with my soul till He,
Bright Morning Star, bid darkness flee.

4 Ashamed of Jesus! that dear Friend
On whom my hopes of heaven depend!
No; when I blush, be this my shame,
That I no more revere His Name.

5 Soon shall He come with power to bless
All who do here His Name confess;
And then may this my glory be,
That He is not ashamed of me!

Joseph Grigg, 1765, a.

144. O Christ, Our Hope, Our Heart's Desire.

St. Anne. C. M.   WILLIAM CROFT, 1708.

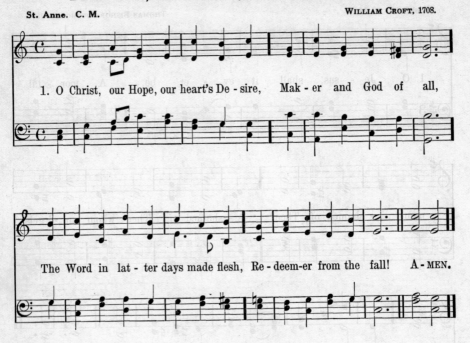

1. O Christ, our Hope, our heart's De - sire, Mak - er and God of all,

The Word in lat - ter days made flesh, Re - deem - er from the fall! A - MEN.

2 How vast the mercy and the love
   Which laid our sins on Thee,
   And led Thee to a cruel death,
   To set Thy people free!

3 But now the bands of death are burst,
   The ransom has been paid;
   And Thou art on Thy Father's throne,
   In glorious robes arrayed.

4 O may Thy mighty love prevail
   Our sinful souls to spare!
   O may we come before Thy throne,
   And find acceptance there!

5 O Christ, be Thou our present Joy,
   Our future great Reward;
   Our only glory may it be
   To glory in the Lord!

Latin, 7th or 8th Century.

145. Arise, My Soul, Arise.

St. Godric. 6 6, 6 6, 8 8.

JOHN BACCHUS DYKES, 1862.

1. A - rise, my soul, a - rise, Shake off thy guilt - y fears; The

bleed-ing Sac - ri - fice In my be - half ap-pears; Be-fore the throne my

Sure - ty stands, My name is writ - ten on His hands. A - MEN.

Or: Lenox, No. 70.

2 He ever lives above,
    For me to intercede;
His all-redeeming love,
    His precious blood to plead;
His blood atoned for all our race,
And sprinkles now the throne of grace.

3 Five bleeding wounds He bears,
    Received on Calvary;
They pour effectual prayers,
    They strongly speak for me;
"Forgive him, O forgive," they cry,
"Nor let that ransomed sinner die!"

4 The Father hears Him pray,
    His dear Anointed One;
He cannot turn away
    The presence of His Son;
His Spirit answers to the blood,
And tells me I am born of God.

5 My God is reconciled,
    His pardoning voice I hear:
He owns for me His child,
    I can no longer fear;
With confidence I now draw nigh,
And "Father, Abba, Father!" cry.

Charles Wesley, 1742.

146. To Realms of Glory I Behold.

Machs mit mir, Gott, nach deiner Güt. 8 7, 8 7, 8 8.   JOHANN HERMANN SCHEIN, 1627.

1. To realms of glo-ry I be-hold My ris-en
2. Far from my home—how long, dear Lord, Be-fore my

Lord re-turn-ing; While I, a stran-ger in the earth,
ex-ile end-eth? But far be-yond the realms of sense

For heav'n am ev-er yearn-ing. Far from my heav'n-ly
My fer-vent prayer as-cend-eth: My prayer, un-ut-tered,

Fa-ther's home, 'Mid toil and sor-row here I roam.
but a groan, Shall rend the skies and reach Thy throne. A-MEN.

3 Then visions of the goodly land
   By faith my soul obtaineth;
There I shall dwell for evermore
   Where Christ in glory reigneth,
In mansions of that blest abode,
   The city of the living God.

4 In that blest city is no night,
   Nor any pain or weeping;
There is my treasure, there my heart,
   Safe in my Saviour's keeping;
In heaven, my blessèd Lord, with Thee,
   May all my conversation be.

5 In glory He shall come again
   To earth as He ascended;
So let me wait and watch and pray,
   Until my day is ended.
That day, O Lord, is hid from me,
   But daily do I wait for Thee.

6 And blessèd shall that servant be,
   O Lord, at Thy returning,
Whose heart is waiting, Lord, for Thee,
   Whose lamp is trimmed and burning;
Him wilt Thou take to dwell with Thee
   In joy and peace eternally.

Johan Olof Wallin, 1816.

147. See, the Conqueror Mounts in Triumph.

Rex Gloriae. 8 7, 8 7. D.

HENRY SMART, 1868.

1. See, the Con-qu'ror mounts in tri - umph; See the King in roy - al state,

Rid - ing on the clouds, His char - iot, To His heav'n-ly pal - ace gate!

Hark! the choir of an - gel voic - es, Joy - ful al - le - lu - ias sing,

And the por - tals high are lift - ed To re-ceive their heav'nly King. A-MEN.

Or: Jesus är min vän den bäste, No. 155.

2 Who is this that comes in glory,
     With the trump of jubilee?
   Lord of battles, God of armies,
     He hath gained the victory!
   He who on the cross did suffer,
     He who from the grave arose,
   He hath vanquished sin and Satan,
     He by death hath spoiled His foes.

3 He hath raised our human nature
     On the clouds to God's right hand:
   There we sit in heavenly places,
     There with Him in glory stand:
   Jesus reigns adored by angels:
     Man with God is on the throne:
   Mighty Lord, in Thine ascension
     We by faith behold our own.

Christopher Wordsworth, 1862.

148. Hail the Day That Sees Him Rise.

Hendon. 7 7, 7 7.　　　　　　　　　　　　　　　　HENRI ABRAHAM CAESAR MALAN, 1827.

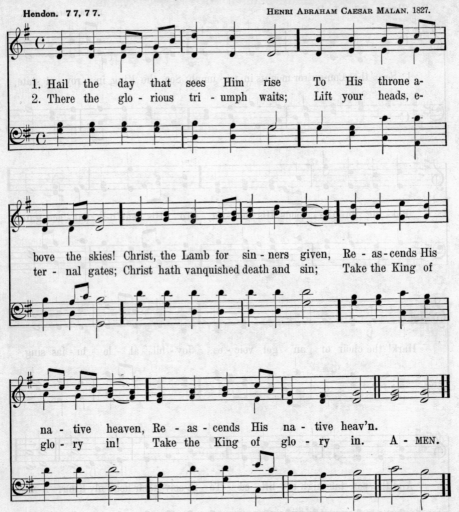

1. Hail the day that sees Him rise To His throne a-
bove the skies! Christ, the Lamb for sin-ners given, Re-as-cends His
na-tive heaven, Re-as-cends His na-tive heav'n.

2. There the glo-rious tri-umph waits; Lift your heads, e-
ter-nal gates; Christ hath vanquished death and sin; Take the King of
glo-ry in! Take the King of glo-ry in. A - MEN.

Or: Gud, vår Gud, för världen all, No. 132.

3 Him though highest heaven receives,
Still He loves the earth He leaves;
Though returning to His throne,
Still He calls mankind His own.

4 See, He lifts His hands above!
See, He shows the prints of love!
Hark! His gracious lips bestow
Blessings on His Church below!

5 Still for us His death He pleads;
Ever for us intercedes;
Near Himself prepares our place,
He the Firstfruits of our race.

6 There we shall with Thee remain,
Partners of Thine endless reign;
There Thy face unclouded see,
Find our heaven of heavens in Thee.

Charles Wesley, 1739, a.

149. Hail, Thou Once Despised Jesus.

Beecher. 8 7, 8 7, D.

JOHN ZUNDEL, 1870.

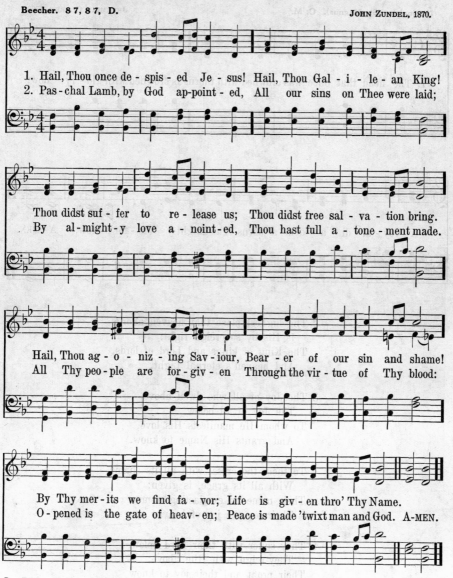

1. Hail, Thou once de - spis - ed Je - sus! Hail, Thou Gal - i - le - an King!
2. Pas - chal Lamb, by God ap-point - ed, All our sins on Thee were laid;

Thou didst suf - fer to re - lease us; Thou didst free sal - va - tion bring.
By al-might-y love a - noint-ed, Thou hast full a - tone - ment made.

Hail, Thou ag - o - niz - ing Sav - iour, Bear - er of our sin and shame!
All Thy peo - ple are for - giv - en Through the vir - tue of Thy blood:

By Thy mer - its we find fa - vor; Life is giv - en thro' Thy Name.
O - pened is the gate of heav - en; Peace is made 'twixt man and God. A-MEN.

3 Jesus, hail, enthroned in glory,
  There forever to abide!
All the heavenly hosts adore Thee,
  Seated at Thy Father's side:
There for sinners Thou art pleading,
  There Thou dost our place prepare,
Ever for us interceding,
  Till in glory we appear.

4 Worship, honor, power, and blessing,
  Thou art worthy to receive;
Loudest praises, without ceasing,
  Meet it is for us to give.
Help, ye bright angelic spirits,
  Bring your sweetest, noblest lays,
Help to sing our Saviour's merits,
  Help to chant Immanuel's praise.

John Bakewell, 1757, a.

150. The Head That Once Was Crowned with Thorns.

Nottingham (St. Magnus). C. M.   JEREMIAH CLARKE, 1709.

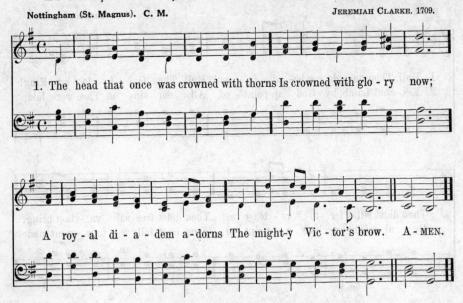

1. The head that once was crowned with thorns Is crowned with glo - ry now;

A roy - al di - a - dem a - dorns The might-y Vic - tor's brow.   A - MEN.

2 The highest place that heaven affords
   Is His by sovereign right:
   The King of kings and Lord of lords,
   And heaven's eternal Light.

3 The Joy of all who dwell above,
   The Joy of all below,
   To whom He manifests His love,
   And grants His Name to know.

4 To them the cross, with all its shame,
   With all its grace, is given;
   Their name an everlasting name,
   Their joy the joy of heaven.

5 They suffer with their Lord below,
   They reign with Him above;
   Their profit and their joy to know
   The mystery of His love.

6 The cross He bore is life and health,
   Though shame and death to Him:
   His people's hope, His people's wealth,
   Their everlasting theme.

                                      Thomas Kelly, 1820, a.

151. Hark, Ten Thousand Harps and Voices.

Prescott. 8 7, 8 7, 7 7.   ROBERT PRESCOTT STEWART, 1868.

1. Hark, ten thou - sand harps and voic - es Sound the note of
2. Je - sus, hail, whose glo - ry bright - ens All a - bove, and

praise a - bove! Je - sus reigns, and heav'n re - joic - es;
makes it fair: Lord of life, Thy smile en - light - ens,

Je - sus reigns, the God of love. See, He sits on
Cheers, and charms Thy peo - ple here. When we think of

yon - der throne; Je - sus rules the world a - lone.
love like Thine, Lord, we own it love di - vine. A - MEN.

Or: Hela världen fröjdes Herran, No. 289.

3 King of glory, reign forever;
　　Thine an everlasting crown;
Nothing from Thy love shall sever
　　Those whom Thou hast made Thine own,
Happy objects of Thy grace,
　　Destined to behold Thy face.

4 Saviour, hasten Thine appearing;
　　Bring, O bring the glorious day,
When, the awful summons hearing,
　　Heaven and earth shall pass away.
Then, with golden harps, we'll sing,
　　"Glory, glory to our King."

Thomas Kelly, 1806, a.

152. Ascend, Dear Lord!

Es ist noch Raum.   4 6, 6 10, 6 9, 9 4.   Unknown.

1. As-cend, dear Lord! Thy earth-ly toil is done, Thy pain and an-guish o'er;
Fought is the fight, the vic - to - ry is won, Thy grave's once fast-sealed door
Is o - pen. Thou hast burst its pris - on Since Thou from death to
life hast ris - en. As-cend, dear Lord! As - cend, dear Lord! A - MEN.

2 Ascend, dear Lord!
  Redemption is complete,
  For Thou hast paid the price.
  Death, sin, and hell lie vanquished at Thy
        feet,
  O Lamb, Thy sacrifice
  Grants us a blood-bought, free salvation;
  Saves us from Satan's domination;
  Ascend, dear Lord!

3 Ascend, dear Lord!
  And send Thy Spirit blest,
  Thy Comforter on high;
  Let His sweet Word now strengthen the
        oppressed
  With solace from the sky!
  Thou who hast died for our transgression,
  Grant us Thy promised intercession.
  Ascend, dear Lord!

4 Ascend, dear Lord!
  Accept Thy blood-bought crown.
  Return to that blest land
  From whence Thy Love hath caused Thee
        to come down.
  Reign at Thy Father's hand!
  Exalted Saviour, naught can sever
  Thee from the right to rule forever!
  Ascend, dear Lord!

5 Ascend, dear Lord!
  Thou Lamb for sinners slain,
  Thou blest High Priest, ascend!
  O King of kings, in righteousness e'er
        reign,
  Thy kingdom hath no end.
  Thy ransomed host on earth rejoices,
  While angels lift in song their voices.
  Ascend, dear Lord!

Anna Hoppe, 1918.

153. All Hail the Power of Jesus' Name.

Coronation. C. M.   OLIVER HOLDEN, 1793.

1. All hail the pow'r of Je-sus' Name! Let an-gels pros-trate fall;

Bring forth the roy-al di - a - dem, And crown Him Lord of all;

Bring forth the roy-al di - a - dem, And crown Him Lord of all. A-MEN.

2 Ye seed of Israel's chosen race,
  Ye ransomed from the fall,
Hail Him, who saves you by His grace,
  And crown Him Lord of all.

3 Hail Him, ye heirs of David's line,
  Whom David Lord did call;
The Lord incarnate, Man divine:
  And crown Him Lord of all.

4 Sinners, whose love can ne'er forget
  The wormwood and the gall;
Go, spread your trophies at His feet,
  And crown Him Lord of all.

5 Let every kindred, every tribe,
  On this terrestrial ball
To Him all majesty ascribe,
  And crown Him Lord of all.

6 O that with yonder sacred throng
  We at His feet may fall!
We'll join the everlasting song,
  And crown Him Lord of all.

Edward Perronet, 1780. a.

154. Come, Holy Spirit, God and Lord!

Komm, Heiliger Geist, Herre Gott. 8 8, 8 8, 8 8, 8 8 8.   JOHANN WALTHER, 1524.

1. Come, Ho - ly Spir - it, God and Lord! Be all Thy grac - es now outpoured On the be - liev - er's mind and soul, To strength-en, save, and
make us whole. Lord, by the bright-ness of Thy light, Thou in the
faith dost men u - nite Of ev - 'ry land and ev - 'ry tongue: This
to Thy praise, O Lord, be sung. Hal - le - lu - jah! Hal - le - lu - jah! A - MEN.

2 Thou strong Defense, Thou holy Light,
  Teach us to know our God aright,
And call Him Father from the heart:
The Word of life and truth impart:
That we may not love doctrines strange,
Nor e'er to other teachers range,
But Jesus for our Master own,
And put our trust in Him alone.
  Hallelujah! Hallelujah!

3 Thou sacred Ardor, Comfort sweet,
Help us to wait with ready feet
And willing heart, at Thy command,
Nor trial fright us from Thy band.
Lord, make us ready with Thy powers;
Strengthen the flesh in weaker hours,
That as good warriors we may force
Through life and death to Thee our course.
  Hallelujah! Hallelujah!

Martin Luther, 1524.

155. Holy Ghost, Dispel Our Sadness.

Jesus är min vän den bäste. 8 7, 8 7. D.   GUSTAF DÜBEN, 1674.

1. Ho - ly Ghost, dis - pel our sad - ness, Pierce the clouds of sin - ful night;

Come, Thou Source of sweet-est glad-ness, Breathe Thy life and spread Thy light!

Come, Thou best of all do - na - tions God can give, or we im - plore!

Hav-ing Thy sweet con - so - la - tions, We need wish for noth-ing more. A - MEN.

2 From that height that knows no measure,
 As a gracious shower descend,
Bringing down the richest treasure
Man can wish, or God can send.
Author of the new creation!
 Come with unction and with power;
Make our hearts Thy habitation;
 On our souls Thy graces shower.

3 Manifest Thy love forever;
 Fence us in on every side;
In distress be our Reliever,
 Guard and teach, support and guide.
Hear, O hear our supplication,
 Loving Spirit, God of peace!
Rest upon this congregation,
 With the fullness of Thy grace.

Paul Gerhardt, 1653.

156. O Holy Spirit, Enter In.

Wie schön leuchtet der Morgenstern. 8 8 7, 8 8 7, 8 4, 4 8.   PHILIPP NICOLAI, 1599.

1. { O Ho-ly Spir-it, en-ter in, And cleanse our
   Sun of the soul, Thou Light di-vine, A-round and

hearts of ev-'ry sin; Thy tem-ple deign to make us;
in us bright-ly shine; To strength and glad-ness wake us.

Where Thou shin-est, life from heav-en There is giv-en.

We be-fore Thee For that pre-cious gift im-plore Thee. A-MEN.

2 Left to ourselves we shall but stray;
O lead us on the narrow way,
    With wisest counsel guide us,
And give us steadfastness, that we
May henceforth truly follow Thee,
    Whatever woes betide us:
Heal Thou gently hearts now broken,
    Give some token
    Thou art near us,
Whom we trust to light and cheer us.

3 O mighty Rock! O Source of Life!
Let Thy dear Word, 'mid doubt and strife,
    Be so within us burning,
That we be faithful unto death,
In Thy pure love and holy faith,
    From Thee true wisdom learning!
Lord, Thy graces on us shower,
    By Thy power
    Christ confessing,
Let us win His grace and blessing.

4 O gentle Dew, from heaven now fall
With power upon the hearts of all,
  Thy tenderness instilling;
That heart to heart more closely bound,
Fruitful in kindly deeds be found,
  The law of love fulfilling;
No wrath, no strife, here shall grieve Thee,
  We receive Thee,
  Where Thou livest,
Peace and love and joy Thou givest.

5 Grant that our days, while life shall last,
  In purest holiness be past;
  Our minds so rule and strengthen
That they may rise o'er things of earth,
The hopes and joys that here have birth;
  And if our course Thou lengthen,
Keep Thou pure, Lord, from offenses,
  Heart and senses;
  Blessèd Spirit,
Bid us thus true life inherit.

Michael Schirmer, 1640.

157. Come, O Come, Thou Quickening Spirit.

Komm, o komm, du Geist des Lebens. 8 7, 8 7, 7 7.   JOHANN CHRISTOPHER BACH, 1680.

1. Come, O come, Thou quick'ning Spir-it, Thou for-ev-er art di-vine;
2. Grant my mind and my af-fec-tions Wis-dom, coun-sel, pu-ri-ty,

Let Thy pow-er nev-er fail me, Al-ways fill this heart of mine;
That I may be ev-er seek-ing Naught but that which pleas-es Thee.

Thus shall grace, and truth, and light Dis-si-pate the gloom of night.
Let Thy knowledge spread and grow, Working er-ror's o-ver-throw. A-MEN.

3 Lead me to green pastures, lead me
  By the true and living way,
Shield me from each strong temptation
  That might draw my heart astray;
And if e'er my feet should turn,
For each error let me mourn.

4 Holy Spirit, strong and mighty,
  Thou who makest all things new,
Make Thy work within me perfect,
  Help me by Thy Word so true;
Arm me with that Sword of Thine,
And the victory shall be mine.

5 In the faith, O make me steadfast;
  Let not Satan, death, or shame
Of my confidence deprive me;
  Lord, my refuge is Thy Name.
When the flesh inclines to ill,
Let Thy Word prove stronger still.

6 And when my last hour approaches,
  Let my hopes grow yet more bright;
Since I am an heir of heaven,
  In Thy glorious courts of light,
Fairer far than voice can tell,
There, redeemed by Christ, to dwell.

Heinrich Held, b. about 1659.

158. Holy Ghost, with Light Divine.

Horton. 7 7, 7 7.   C. von Wartensee, 1780.

1. Ho - ly Ghost, with light di - vine   Shine up - on   this heart of mine,
2. Let me see   my Sav-iour's face,   Let   me all   His beau-ties trace;

Chase the shades of night a - way,   Turn the dark-ness in - to day.
Show those glo-rious truths to   me   Which are on - ly known to Thee. A - men.

3 Holy Ghost, with power divine
  Cleanse this guilty heart of mine;
  In thy mercy pity me,
  From sin's bondage set me free.

4 Holy Ghost, with joy divine
  Cheer this saddened heart of mine;
  Yield a sacred, settled peace,
  Let it grow and still increase.

5 Holy Spirit, all divine,
  Dwell within this heart of mine;
  Cast down every idol throne,
  Reign supreme, and reign alone.

6 See, to Thee I yield my heart;
  Shed Thy life through every part.
  A pure temple I would be,
  Wholly dedicate to Thee.

Andrew Reed, 1817.

159. Come, Holy Spirit, from Above.

Herr Jesu Christ, dich zu uns wend. L. M.   Cantionale Sacrum, Gotha, 1651.

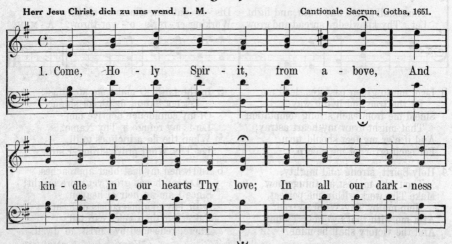

1. Come, Ho - ly   Spir - it,   from a - bove,   And

kin - dle in   our hearts Thy love;   In all   our dark - ness

on us shine, And fill us with Thy grace di-vine. A-MEN.

2 The only Comforter Thou art;
   O come and dwell within each heart,
   And give us power from above
   To keep the blessèd law of love.

3 Enlighten every darkened heart,
   And faith and hope to each impart;
   What else we need Thou well dost know,
   This let Thy love and grace bestow.

4 In Thy blest gifts on us outpoured,
   Thou art the right hand of the Lord;
   The Word of Truth Thou sendest forth
   In tongues of fire to all the earth.

5 Defend us from our wily foe,
   Upon us now Thy peace bestow;
   Keep us securely all our days
   In Thy blest covenant of grace.

6 Show us the Father's love and care,
   And of the Son Thy witness bear;
   To both Thou showest us the way,
   Spirit of both, adored for aye.

7 To God the Father, God the Son,
   For precious gifts be honor done;
   And for the Spirit's gracious power
   Be praise and glory evermore.

Martin Luther, 1524.

160. Lord God, the Holy Ghost!

Bethlehem. S. M.   SAMUEL WESLEY, 1798.

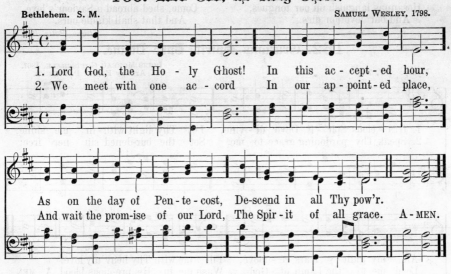

1. Lord God, the Ho-ly Ghost! In this ac-cept-ed hour,
2. We meet with one ac-cord In our ap-point-ed place,

As on the day of Pen-te-cost, De-scend in all Thy pow'r.
And wait the prom-ise of our Lord, The Spir-it of all grace. A-MEN.

3 Like mighty rushing wind
   Upon the waves beneath,
   Move with one impulse every mind,
   One soul, one feeling breathe.

4 The young, the old, inspire
   With wisdom from above;
   And give us hearts and tongues of fire,
   To pray, and praise, and love.

5 Spirit of Light, explore,
   And drive our gloom away;
   With luster shining more and more,
   Unto the perfect day!

6 Spirit of Truth, be Thou
   In life and death our Guide;
   O Spirit of adoption, now
   May we be sanctified!

James Montgomery, 1819.

161. Come, Holy Spirit, Heavenly Dove.

Belmont. C. M.   WILLIAM GARDINER, 1812.

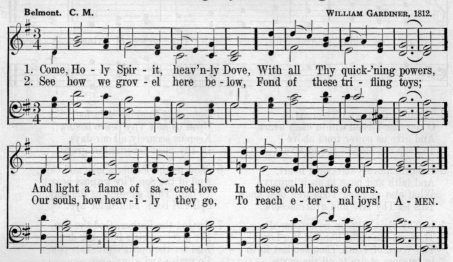

1. Come, Ho - ly Spir - it, heav'n-ly Dove, With all   Thy quick-'ning powers,
2. See how we grov - el here be - low, Fond of   these tri - fling toys;

And light a flame of sa - cred love   In these cold hearts of ours.
Our souls, how heav - i - ly   they go,   To reach e - ter - nal joys! A - MEN.

Or: Nun danket all' und bringet Ehr (Störl), No. 66.

3 In vain we tune our lifeless songs,
   In vain we strive to rise;
   Hosannas languish on our tongues,
   And our devotion dies.

4 Come, Holy Spirit, heavenly Dove,
   With all Thy quickening powers,
   Come, shed abroad a Saviour's love,
   And that shall kindle ours.

Isaac Watts, 1709.

162. Gracious Spirit, Dove Divine.

Mercy. 7 7, 7 7.   LOUIS MOREAU GOTTSCHALK, 1867.
                                                 Arr. by EDWIN P. PARKER.

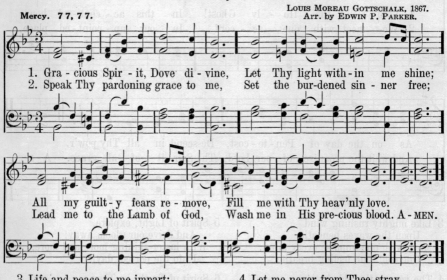

1. Gra - cious Spir - it, Dove di - vine,   Let Thy light with - in   me shine;
2. Speak Thy pardoning grace to me,   Set   the bur-dened sin - ner   free;

All   my guilt - y fears re - move,   Fill   me with Thy heav'nly love.
Lead me to   the Lamb of God,   Wash me in   His pre-cious blood. A - MEN.

3 Life and peace to me impart;
   Seal salvation on my heart;
   Breathe Thyself into my breast,
   Earnest of immortal rest.

4 Let me never from Thee stray,
   Keep me in the narrow way:
   Fill my soul with joy divine,
   Keep me, Lord, forever Thine.

John Stocker, 1777, a.

163. Holy, Holy, Holy, Lord God Almighty!

Nicaea. Irregular.

JOHN BACCHUS DYKES, 1860.

1. Ho - ly, Ho - ly, Ho - ly, Lord God Al - might - y!
Ear - ly in the morn - ing our song shall rise to Thee:
Ho - ly, Ho - ly, Ho - ly! mer - ci - ful and might - y;
God in three Per - sons, bless - ed Trin - i - ty! A - MEN.

2 Holy, Holy, Holy! all the saints adore Thee,
   Casting down their golden crowns upon the glassy sea;
Cherubim and Seraphim falling down before Thee,
   Which wert, and art, and evermore shalt be.

3 Holy, Holy, Holy! though the darkness hide Thee,
   Though the eye of sinful man Thy glory may not see,
Only Thou art holy: there is none beside Thee
   Perfect in power, in love, in purity.

4 Holy, Holy, Holy, Lord God Almighty!
   All Thy works shall praise Thy Name, in earth, and sky, and sea:
Holy, Holy, Holy! merciful and mighty;
   God in three Persons, blessèd Trinity!

Reginald Heber, 1827.

164. Come, Thou Almighty King.

Italian Hymn. 6 6 4, 6 6 6 4.   FELICE DE GIARDINI, 1769.

1. Come, Thou al - might - y King, Help us Thy Name to sing, Help us to praise! Fa - ther all - glo - ri - ous, O'er all vic - to - ri - ous, Come and reign o - ver us, An - cient of days. A - MEN.

2 Jesus, our Lord, descend;
From all our foes defend,
  Nor let us fall;
Let Thine almighty aid
Our sure defense be made,
Our souls on Thee be stayed;
  Lord, hear our call!

3 Come, Thou incarnate Word,
Gird on Thy mighty sword,
  Our prayer attend:
Come, and Thy people bless,
And give Thy Word success;
Spirit of holiness,
  On us descend.

4 Come, Holy Comforter,
Thy sacred witness bear
  In this glad hour:
Thou who almighty art,
Now rule in every heart,
And ne'er from us depart,
  Spirit of power!

5 To the great One in Three
Eternal praises be,
  Hence, evermore!
His sovereign majesty
May we in glory see,
And to eternity
  Love and adore.

Charles Wesley, 1757, a.

165. Holy, Holy, Holy Lord.

New St. Andrew. 7 7, 7 7. D.   JOHN GILL.

1. Ho - ly, Ho - ly, Ho - ly Lord God of hosts! when heav'n and earth

Out of dark - ness, at Thy word, Is - sued in - to glo - rious birth,

All Thy works be - fore Thee stood, And Thine eye be - held them good,

While they sang with sweet ac - cord, "Ho - ly, Ho - ly, Ho - ly Lord!" A - MEN.

2 Holy, Holy, Holy! Thee,
   One Jehovah evermore,
Father, Son, and Spirit, we,
   Dust and ashes, would adore;
Lightly by the world esteemed,
From that world by Thee redeemed,
Sing we here with glad accord,
   "Holy, Holy, Holy Lord!"

3 "Holy, Holy, Holy," all
   Heaven's triumphant choirs shall sing
When the ransomed nations fall
   At the footstool of their King:
Then shall saints and Seraphim,
Hearts and voices, swell one hymn
Round the throne with full accord,
   "Holy, Holy, Holy Lord!"

James Montgomery, 1832.

166. Our Father, Merciful and Good.

Es wolt uns Gott genädig sein.   8 7, 8 7, 8 7, 8 7 7.   Strassburger Kirchenampt, 1524.

1. Our Fa - ther, mer - ci - ful and good, Who dost to Thee in - vite
2. We cry to Thee with one ac - cord, 'Tis all that can a - vail

us, O cleanse us in our Sav-iour's blood, And to Thy - self u -
us; We can - not hear nor keep Thy Word, If grace di - vine doth

nite us! Send un - to us Thy ho - ly Word, And let it
fail us. Be - hold our lot, we hum - bly pray, For our dear

guide us ev - er; Then in this world of dark - ness, Lord, Shall
Sav - iour's mer - it, How Sa - tan sow - eth tares al - way, And

naught from Thee us sev - er: Grant us, O Lord, this fa - vor!
send, O Lord, Thy Spir - it, That we may life in - her - it. A - MEN.

3 O God and man, Christ Jesus blest!
  Our sorrows Thou didst carry.
Our wants and cares Thou knowest best,
  For Thou with us didst tarry.
O Jesus Christ, our Brother dear,
  To us and every nation
Thy Spirit send, let Him draw near
  With truth and consolation,
  That we may see salvation.

4 Come, Holy Ghost, Thy grace impart,
  Tear Satan's snares asunder.
The Word of God keep in our heart,
  That we its truth may ponder.
Then, sanctified, for evermore,
  In Christ alone confiding,
We'll sing His praise and Him adore,
  His precious Word us guiding
  To heavenly joys abiding.

Olavus Petri, 1530.

167. Almighty God, Eternal Lord.

O Herre Gud, oändelig. L. M.   JEAN CRESPIN, 1551.

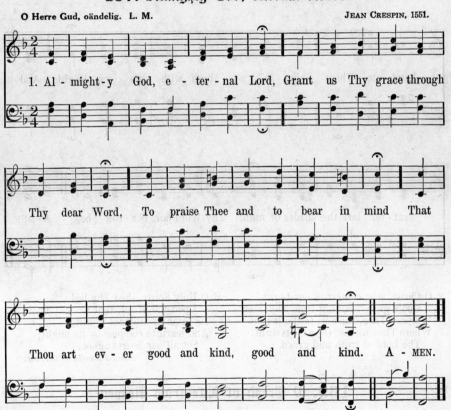

1. Al - might-y God, e - ter - nal Lord, Grant us Thy grace through
Thy dear Word, To praise Thee and to bear in mind That
Thou art ev - er good and kind, good and kind. A - MEN.

2 Lord Jesus Christ, incarnate Word,
  Thy Name be evermore adored,
For all Thine anguish, death, and pain,
  Whereby salvation we obtain.

3 O Holy Spirit, grant us grace,
  And guide us in Thy righteous ways,
That we may with the heavenly host
  Praise Father, Son, and Holy Ghost.

Johan Olof Wallin, 1816.

168. O God, Who Saidst, "Let There Be Light."

Lux Dei. 8 8, 8 8 6.   SAMUEL MARTIN MILLER, 1923.

1. O God, who saidst, "Let there be light," We lift our hearts and hands to Thee: Shine in our lives with glo - ry bright, And scat - ter far the shades of night, Thy Word our bea - con be. A - MEN.

2 O Christ, who camest as our Light,
  God's glory beaming from Thy face,
We pray Thee, raise us to the height
Where Thee we see, O precious sight,
  The Lord of truth and grace.

3 O Holy Spirit, shed Thy light
  Upon the Word, that we may know
Its saving sentences aright,
And learn to conquer by its might;
  Set all our hearts aglow.

Samuel Martin Miller, 1923.

169. O Bread of Life from Heaven.

O Welt, ich muss dich lassen. 7 7 6, 7 7 8.   HEINRICH ISAAK, about 1490.

1. O Bread of life from heav - en, To wea - ry pil - grims giv - en,

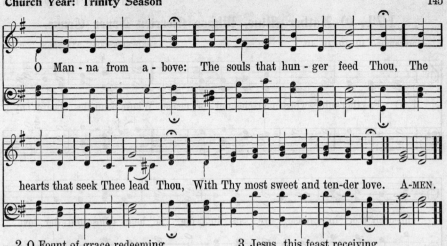

O Man - na from a - bove: The souls that hun - ger feed Thou, The

hearts that seek Thee lead Thou, With Thy most sweet and ten-der love. A-MEN.

2 O Fount of grace redeeming,
  O River ever streaming
    From Jesus' holy side:
  Come Thou, Thyself bestowing
  On thirsting souls, and flowing
    Till all their wants are satisfied.

3 Jesus, this feast receiving,
  Thy word of truth believing,
    We Thee unseen adore:
  Grant, when our race is ended,
  That we, to heaven ascended,
    May see Thy glory evermore.

Anonymous, Latin, 1661.

170. Lord, As to Thy Dear Cross We Flee.

Eventide (Smart). C. M.   HENRY SMART, 1876.

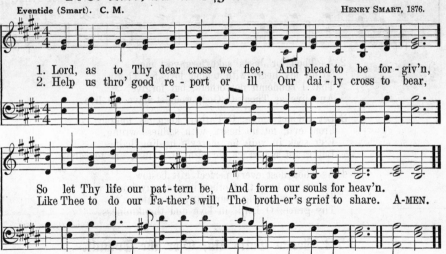

1. Lord, as to Thy dear cross we flee, And plead to be for - giv'n,
2. Help us thro' good re - port or ill Our dai - ly cross to bear,

So   let Thy life our pat - tern be, And form our souls for heav'n.
Like Thee to do our Fa - ther's will, The broth-er's grief to share. A-MEN.

3 Let grace our selfishness expel,
    Our earthliness refine,
  And kindness in our bosoms dwell
    As free and true as Thine.

4 If joy shall at Thy bidding fly,
    And grief's dark day come on,
  We in our turn would meekly cry,
    "Father, Thy will be done."

5 Should friends misjudge, or foes defame,
    Our brethren faithless prove,
  Then, like Thine own, be all our aim
    To conquer them by love.

6 Kept peaceful in the midst of strife,
    Forgiving and forgiven,
  O may we lead the pilgrim's life,
    And follow Thee to heaven.

John Hampden Gurney, 1838.

171. O Father Mine, Whose Mercies Never Cease.

Morecambe. 10 10, 10 10.   FREDERICK COOK ATKINSON, 1870.

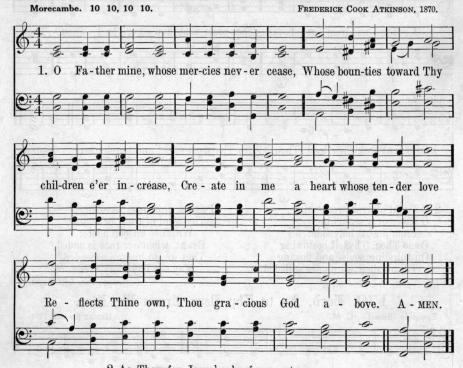

1. O Fa-ther mine, whose mer-cies nev-er cease, Whose boun-ties toward Thy
chil-dren e'er in-crease, Cre-ate in me a heart whose ten-der love
Re-flects Thine own, Thou gra-cious God a-bove. A-MEN.

2 As Thou for Jesus' sake forgavest me,
So fill my heart with tender love for Thee,
That I condemn not others, but forgive,
And live as Thou, O God, wouldst have me live.

3 Let me not judge; O Father, keep my tongue
From evil; let no heart, with sadness wrung,
E'er seek in vain for mercy's healing balm,
But grant me grace through Thee its fears to calm.

4 As Thou dost every perfect gift bestow,
So let me live, that other hearts may know
Thy never-ceasing bounties, and confess
Thy grace, O Lord, in love and thankfulness.

Anna Hoppe, 1919.

172. Jesus Calls Us; O'er the Tumult.

Galilee. 8 7, 8 7.   WILLIAM HERBERT JUDE, 1887.

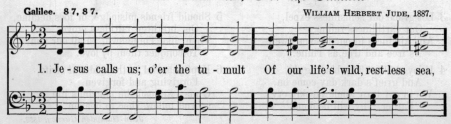

1. Je-sus calls us; o'er the tu-mult Of our life's wild, rest-less sea,

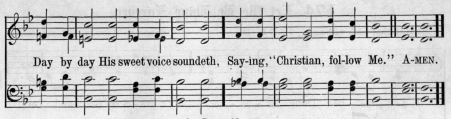

Day by day His sweet voice soundeth, Say-ing, "Christian, fol-low Me." A-MEN.

Or: Batty, No. 109.

2 As, of old, apostles heard it
  By the Galilæan lake,
 Turned from home and toil and kindred,
  Leaving all for His dear sake,

3 Jesus calls us from the worship
  Of the vain world's golden store,
 From each idol that would keep us,
  Saying, "Christian, love Me more."

4 In our joys and in our sorrows,
  Days of toil and hours of ease,
 Still He calls, in cares and pleasures,
  "Christian, love Me more than these."

5 Jesus calls us: by Thy mercies,
  Saviour, may we hear Thy call,
 Give our hearts to Thy obedience,
  Serve and love Thee best of all.

Cecil Frances (Humphreys) Alexander, 1852, a

173. Though We All in Sinful Blindness.

Dieses ist der Tag der Wonne. 8 7, 8 7, 8 8.   DRETZEL'S Musicalische Harmonie, 1731.

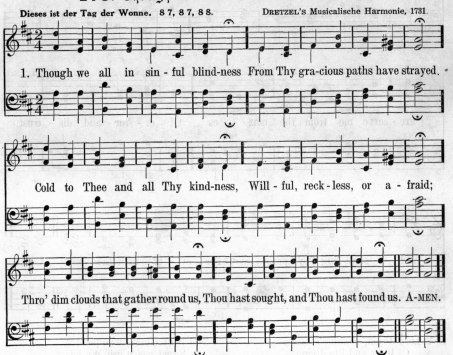

1. Though we all in sin-ful blind-ness From Thy gra-cious paths have strayed,

Cold to Thee and all Thy kind-ness, Will-ful, reck-less, or a-fraid;

Thro' dim clouds that gather round us, Thou hast sought, and Thou hast found us. A-MEN.

2 O most Merciful, most Holy,
    Light Thy wanderers on their way;
  Keep us ever Thine, Thine wholly,
    Suffer us no more to stray!
  Cloud and storm oft gather round us;
  We were lost, but Thou hast found us.

Francis Turner Palgrave, 1868.

174. Let Me Be Thine Forever.

Herzlich thut mich verlangen. 7 6, 7 6. D.   HANS LEO HASSLER, 1601 and 1613.

1. Let me be Thine for-ev-er, My gra-cious God and Lord,

May I for-sake Thee nev-er, Nor wan-der from Thy Word:

Pre-serve me from the maz-es Of er-ror and dis-trust,

And I shall sing Thy prais-es For-ev-er with the just. A-MEN.

2 Lord Jesus, bounteous Giver
  Of light and life divine,
Thou didst my soul deliver,
  To Thee I all resign:
Thou hast in mercy bought me
  With blood and bitter pain;
Let me, since Thou hast sought me,
  Eternal life obtain.

3 O Holy Ghost, who pourest
  Sweet peace into my heart,
And who my soul restorest,
  Let not Thy grace depart.
And while His Name confessing
  Whom I by faith have known,
Grant me Thy constant blessing,
  Make me for aye Thine own.

Nicolaus Selnecker, 1572, et al.

175. Not What My Hands Have Done.

Leominster. S. M. D.

GEORGE WILLIAM MARTIN, 1862.
Har. by ARTHUR SEYMOUR SULLIVAN, 1874.

1. Not what my hands have done Can save my guilt-y soul;
Not what my toil-ing flesh has borne Can make my spir-it whole.
Not what I feel or do Can give me peace with God;
Not all my prayers, and sighs, and tears Can bear my aw-ful load. A-MEN.

2 Thy grace alone, O God,
  To me can pardon speak;
Thy power alone, O Son of God,
  Can this sore bondage break.
No other work save Thine,
  No other blood will do;
No strength save that which is divine
  Can bear me safely through.

3 I bless the Christ of God;
  I rest on love divine;
And with unfaltering lip and heart
  I call this Saviour mine.
'Tis He that saveth me,
  And freely pardon gives;
I love, because He loveth me;
  I live, because He lives.

Horatius Bonar, 1862.

176. O'er Jerusalem Thou Weepest.

Frälsta verld! i nådens under. 8 7, 8 7, 7 7, 8 8.   Koralbok, 1697.

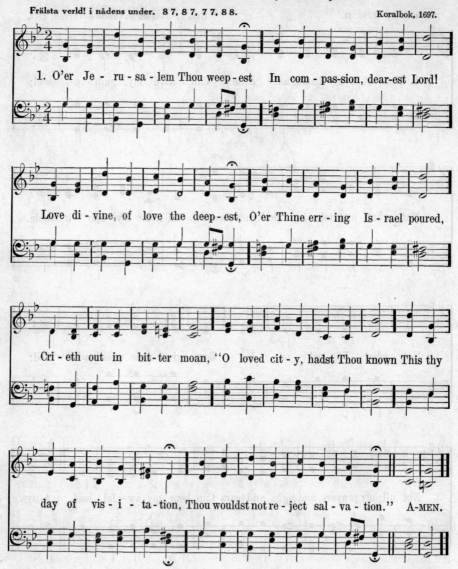

1. O'er Je - ru - sa - lem Thou weep - est In com - pas-sion, dear-est Lord!

Love di - vine, of love the deep - est, O'er Thine err - ing Is - rael poured,

Cri - eth out in bit - ter moan, "O loved cit - y, hadst Thou known This thy

day of vis - i - ta - tion, Thou wouldst not re - ject sal - va - tion." A-MEN.

2 By the love Thy tears are telling,
   O Thou Lamb for sinners slain,
Make my heart Thy temple dwelling,
   Purged from every guilty stain.
O forgive, forgive my sin!
Cleanse me, cleanse me, Lord, within!
I am Thine since Thou hast sought me,
Since Thy precious blood hath bought me.

3 O Thou Lord of my salvation,
   Grant my soul Thy blood-bought peace.
By the tears of lamentation
   Bid my faith and love increase.
Grant me grace to love Thy Word,
Grace to keep the message heard,
Grace to own Thee as my Treasure,
Grace to love Thee without measure.

Anna Hoppe, 1919.

177. By Nature Deaf to Things Divine.

Wie schön leuchtet der Morgenstern. 8 8 7, 8 8 7, 8 4, 4 8.   PHILIPP NICOLAI, 1599.

1. By na-ture deaf to things di-vine, My ears hear
   By na-ture dumb to speak Thy praise, My car-nal

not this Word of Thine, The gos-pel of sal-va - tion.
tongue doth fail to raise A song of ad-o-ra - tion.

Heal Thou me now, blest Phy-si-cian, In con-tri-tion

I be-seech Thee, Let my prayer and plead-ing reach Thee. A-MEN.

2 I thank Thee, dear Redeemer mine,
  That Thou in love and power divine
    Thy healing word hast spoken.
  Thy Word indeed doth balm afford,
  And Thy forgiveness, dearest Lord,
    The power of sin hath broken.
  Thy Word, dear Lord, still endureth,
    And assureth
      Me, O Saviour,
  Of Thy everlasting favor.

3 Indeed Thou doest all things well,
  Incarnate God, Immanuel,
    Thou promised Saviour, Jesus.
  My ears can hear Thy Word divine.
  My lips can praise that power of Thine
    Which healeth all diseases.
  Till I sing Thy praise in glory,
    Let the story
      Of salvation
  Be my theme of adoration.

Anna Hoppe, 1919.

178. O Would, My God, That I Could Praise Thee.

Wer weiss, wie nahe mir mein Ende. 9 8, 9 8, 8 8.   BRONNER'S Choral-Buch, 1715.

1. O would, my God, that I could praise Thee With thou-sand tongues by day and night! How man-y a song my lips should raise Thee, Who or-der'st all things here a-right! My thank-ful heart would ev-er be Tell-ing what God hath done for me. A-MEN.

2 O all ye powers that He implanted,
   Arise, keep silence thus no more,
   Put forth the strength that He hath granted,
   Your noblest work is to adore;
   O soul and body, be ye meet
   With heartfelt praise your Lord to greet.

3 O Father, deign Thou, I beseech Thee,
   To listen to my earthly lays;
   A nobler strain in heaven shall reach Thee,
   When I with angels hymn Thy praise,
   And learn amid their choirs to sing
   Loud hallelujahs to my King.

Johann Mentzer, 1704.

179. In Holy Contemplation.

Valet will ich dir geben. 7 6, 7 6. D.   MELCHIOR TESCHNER, 1613.

1. In ho - ly con - tem - pla - tion We sweet - ly now pur - sue

The theme of God's sal - va - tion, And find it ev - er new.

Set free from pres - ent sor - row, We cheer - ful - ly can say,

Let the un - known to - mor - row Bring with it what it may. A-MEN.

2 It can bring with it nothing
  But He will bear us through;
Who gives the lilies clothing
  Will clothe His people too.
Beneath the spreading heavens
  No creature but is fed;
And He who feeds the ravens
  Will give His children bread.

3 Though vine or fig tree neither
  Their wonted fruit should bear,
Though all the field should wither,
  Nor flocks nor herds be there,
God still the same abiding,
  His praise shall tune my voice;
For while in Him confiding,
  I cannot but rejoice.

William Cowper, 1779.

180. O That the Lord Would Guide My Ways.

Evan. C. M.   WILLIAM HENRY HAVERGAL, 1846.

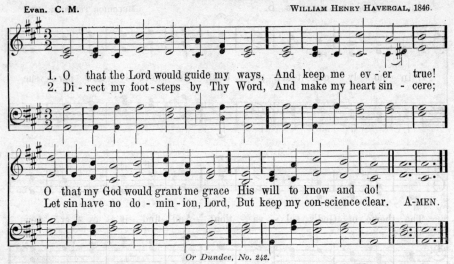

1. O   that the Lord would guide my ways, And keep me ev - er   true!
2. Di - rect my foot - steps by Thy Word, And make my heart sin - cere;

O that my God would grant me grace His will to know and do!
Let sin have no do - min - ion, Lord, But keep my con-science clear. A-MEN.

Or Dundee, No. 242.

3 Assist my soul, too apt to stray,
  A stricter watch to keep;
And should I e'er forget Thy way,
  Restore Thy wandering sheep.

4 Make me to walk in Thy commands;
  'Tis a delightful road:
Nor let my head, or heart, or hands,
  Offend against my God.

Isaac Watts, 1719, a.

181. O God of Mercy, God of Might.

Just As I Am. 8 8, 8 6.   JOSEPH BARNBY, 1893.

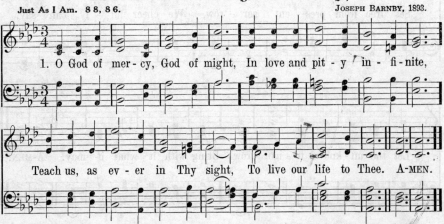

1. O God of mer - cy, God of might, In love and pit - y in - fi - nite,

Teach us, as ev - er in Thy sight, To live our life to Thee. A-MEN.

2 Teach us the lesson Thou hast taught,
  To feel for those Thy blood hath bought,
  That every word, and deed, and thought,
    May work a work for Thee.

3 For all are brethren, far and wide,
  Since Thou, O Lord, for all hast died;
  Then teach us, whatsoe'er betide,
    To love them all in Thee.

4 In sickness, sorrow, want, or care,
  Whatever it be ours to share,
  May we, where help is needed, there
    Give help as unto Thee.

5 And may Thy Holy Spirit move
  All those who live, to live for love,
  Till Thou shalt greet in heaven above
    All those who live to Thee,

Godfrey Thring. 1877.

182. We Give Thee But Thine Own.

Trentham. S. M.   ROBERT JACKSON, 1894.

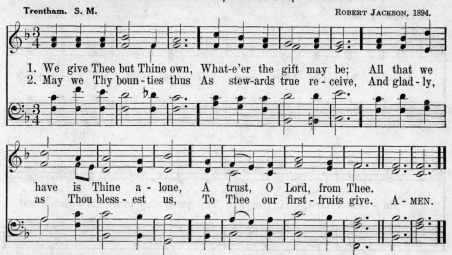

1. We give Thee but Thine own, What-e'er the gift may be;   All that we
2. May we Thy boun-ties thus As stew-ards true re-ceive, And glad-ly,

have is Thine a-lone, A trust, O Lord, from Thee.
as Thou bless-est us, To Thee our first-fruits give. A-MEN.

3 O hearts are bruised and dead,
   And homes are bare and cold,
   And lambs for whom the Shepherd bled
   Are straying from the fold.

4 To comfort and to bless,
   To find a balm for woe,
   To tend the lone and fatherless,
   Is angels' work below.

5 The captive to release,
   The lost to God to bring,
   To teach the way of life and peace,—
   It is a Christlike thing.

6 And we believe Thy Word,
   Though dim our faith may be;
   Whate'er for Thine we do, O Lord,
   We do it unto Thee.

William Walsham How, 1858.

183. Long Hast Thou Wept and Sorrowed.

Ach bleib mit deiner Gnade. (Christus der ist mein Leben.) 7 6, 7 6.
                                              MELCHIOR VULPIUS, 1609.

1. Long hast thou wept and sor-rowed, Poor mourn-er, dry thy tears;

Be-hold, with light and com-fort, The Lord Him-self ap-pears. A-MEN.

2 "Trust in My mercy ever,
   My people!" saith the Lord.
   Hold fast, in deepest sorrow,
   That soul-sustaining Word.

3 Then rest, sad heart, in patience,
   With this petition still,
   "Lord, all these vacant places
   With Thine own fullness fill!"

Meta Heusser-Schweizer, 1837.

184. With Broken Heart and Contrite Sigh.

St. Crispin. L. M.   GEORGE JOB ELVEY, (1816–1893).

1. With bro-ken heart and con-trite sigh, A trem-bling
sin-ner, Lord, I cry: Thy par-d'ning grace is rich and
free: O God, be mer-ci-ful to me. A-MEN.

Or: Erhalt uns, Herr, bei deinem Wort, No. 220.

2 I smite upon my troubled breast,
With deep and conscious guilt oppressed;
Christ and His cross my only plea;
O God, be merciful to me.

3 Far off I stand with tearful eyes,
Nor dare uplift them to the skies;
But Thou dost all my anguish see:
O God, be merciful to me.

4 Nor alms, nor deeds that I have done,
Can for a single sin atone;
To Calvary alone I flee:
O God, be merciful to me.

5 And when, redeemed from sin and hell,
With all the ransomed throng I dwell,
My raptured song shall ever be,
God has been merciful to me.

Cornelius Elven, 1852.

185. O Friend of Sinners, Son of God.

Purleigh. 8 8 6. D.   ARTHUR HENRY BROWN, 1856.

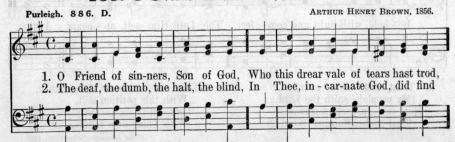

1. O Friend of sin-ners, Son of God, Who this drear vale of tears hast trod,
2. The deaf, the dumb, the halt, the blind, In Thee, in-car-nate God, did find

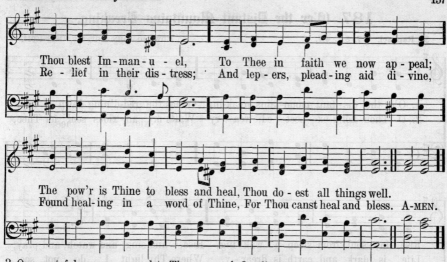

Thou blest Im-man-u - el, To Thee in faith we now ap-peal;
Re - lief in their dis - tress; And lep - ers, plead-ing aid di - vine,

The pow'r is Thine to bless and heal, Thou do - est all things well.
Found heal-ing in a word of Thine, For Thou canst heal and bless. A-MEN.

3 Our grateful prayers ascend to Thee,
For Thou hast healed sin's leprosy,
And cleansed us from its stain.
O blest Physician, Thou hast still
A cure for every mortal ill,
A balm for every pain.

4 Our lives we consecrate to Thee,
Thou spotless Lamb of Calvary,
Let us be wholly Thine. [Thee,
Cleansed, pardoned, ransomed, healed by
O grant us grace eternally
To praise Thy love divine.

Anna Hoppe, 1919.

186. O Gracious Hand That Freely Gives.

Wenn wir in höchsten Nöthen sein. L. M.

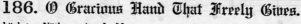

Genevan French Psalter, 1542.

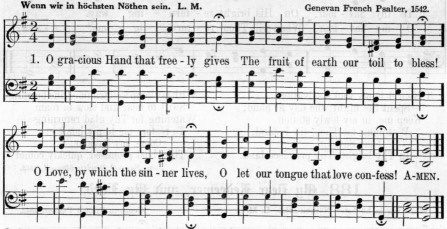

1. O gra-cious Hand that free - ly gives The fruit of earth our toil to bless!

O Love, by which the sin - ner lives, O let our tongue that love con-fess! A-MEN.

2 Our God for all our need provides;
His sun alike o'er all doth shine;
From none His glorious beams He hides;
So rich, so free, His love divine.

3 Again this love our garners fills;
This love again let all adore;
The cry of want this bounty stills,
Who biddeth all His Name implore.

4 O may our lives through grace abound
In holy fruits, and Thee proclaim!
Let all Thy courts with praises sound
Thy gracious hand, Thy wondrous Name.

5 Lord, when Thou shalt descend from heaven,
Thy ransomed harvest here to reap,
May in that day Thy joy be given
To those who now go forth and weep.

Arthur Tozer Russell, 1851.

187. O'er the Distant Mountains Breaking.

St. Raphael. 8 7, 8 7, 4 7.   EDWARD JOHN HOPKINS, (1818–1901).

1. O'er the dis-tant moun-tains break-ing, Comes the red-d'ning dawn of day;
2. O Thou Long-ex-pect-ed, wea-ry Waits my an-xious soul for Thee,

Rise, my soul, from sleep a-wak-ing, Rise, and sing, and watch, and pray;
Life is dark, and earth is drear-y, Where Thy light I do not see;

'Tis thy Sav-iour, On His bright re-turn-ing way.
O my Sav-iour, When wilt Thou re-turn to me? A-MEN.

3 Nearer is my soul's salvation,
  Spent the night, the day at hand;
Keep me, in my lowly station,
  Watching for Thee, till I stand,
    O my Saviour,
  In Thy bright, Thy promised land.

4 With my lamp well trimmed and burning,
  Swift to hear and slow to roam,
Watching for Thy glad returning
  To restore me to my home—
    Come, my Saviour,
  Thou hast promised, quickly come!
        John Samuel Bewley Monsell, 1863.

188. My Dear Redeemer, and My Lord.

Wenn wir in höchsten Nöthen sein. L. M.   Genevan French Psalter, 1542.

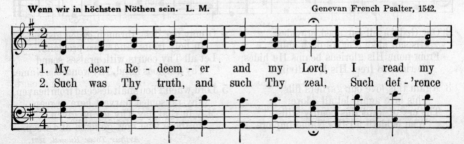

1. My dear Re-deem-er and my Lord, I read my
2. Such was Thy truth, and such Thy zeal, Such def-'rence

du - ty in Thy Word; But in Thy life the law ap-
to Thy Fa - ther's will, Such love, and meek - ness so di-

pears, Drawn out in liv - ing char - ac - ters.
vine, I would tran - scribe and make them mine. A - MEN.

3 Cold mountains and the midnight air
Witnessed the fervor of Thy prayer;
The desert Thy temptations knew,
Thy conflict and Thy victory too.

4 Be Thou my Pattern; make me bear
More of Thy gracious image here:
Then God the Judge shall own my name
Among the followers of the Lamb.

Isaac Watts, 1709.

189. Behold What Love, That God Should Give.

St. Paul. C. M. PETER JOHNSON, 1924.

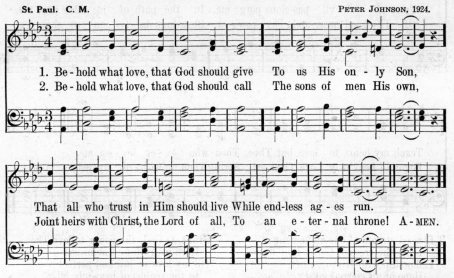

1. Be - hold what love, that God should give   To us His on - ly Son,
2. Be - hold what love, that God should call   The sons of men His own,

That all who trust in Him should live While end-less ag - es run.
Joint heirs with Christ, the Lord of all, To an e - ter - nal throne! A - MEN.

3 Behold what things He hath prepared
For those who love Him here;
No eye hath seen, no ear hath shared
The glories of that sphere.

4 Thy love, O God, transcends all thought,
How faint and weak is mine!
Help me to love Thee as I ought,
O give me love like Thine!

Ernest Edwin Ryden, 1924.

190. Lord! Thou Source of All Perfection.

Tviflan ur min själ försvinne. 8 7, 8 7, 8 8, 7 7.   W. WESSNITZER, 1661.

1. Lord! Thou Source of all per - fec - tion, Foun-tain of e - ter - nal love,
2. Lord, in Thee I have my be - ing, All I am to Thee I owe,

Fill the fam - ished soul that thirst-eth For the wa - ters from a - bove.
Ev - 'ry heav'n-ward as - pi - ra - tion, Ev-'ry thought from Thee doth flow;

From all e - vil pas-sions purge me, In the path of jus - tice urge me,
Of Thy good - ness and Thy pow - er Bless-ings dai - ly on us show - er;

Teach my heart to love but Thee, Thou who ev - er lov - est me.
Fount of heav'n-ly Love Thou art, Spring Thou up with - in my heart. A-MEN.

3 Blessed stream of our atonement
    From the cross of Christ that flowed,
Fellowship with Him in glory,
    Hope of all eternal good,
On my path His light and leading,
And His grace, all grace exceeding,—
All the blessings from above
Prompt me to return Thy love.

4 Grant, O God, the power to love Thee
    Here in truth and holiness,
Till my love be full and perfect
    In the realms of heavenly bliss,
When, translated into glory,
    With Thy countenance shining o'er me,
I shall drink with saints above
From the well-spring of Thy love.

Balthazar Muenter, 1773.

191. O Jesus, Our Salvation.

Old 130th Psalm. 7 6, 7 6. D.   Genevan Psalter, 1556.

1. O Je - sus, our Sal - va - tion, Low at Thy cross we lie:
2. O gra - cious In - ter - ces - sor! O Priest with - in the veil,

Lord, in Thy great com - pas - sion, Hear our be - wail - ing cry.
Plead for each lost trans - gress - or The blood that can - not fail.

We come to Thee with mourn - ing, We come to Thee in woe;
We lay our sins be - fore Thee, We tell them one by one:

With con-trite hearts re - turn - ing, And tears that o - ver - flow.
O for Thy Name's great glo - ry For - give all we have done. A-MEN.

3 O by Thy cross and passion,
  Thy tears and agony,
And crown of cruel fashion,
  And death on Calvary;
By all that untold suffering,
  Endured by Thee alone,
O Priest, O spotless Offering,
  Plead, for Thou didst atone!

4 And in these hearts now broken
  Reënter Thou and reign,
And say, by that dear token,
  We are absolved again.
And build us up, and guide us,
  And guard us day by day;
And in Thy presence hide us,
  And take our sins away.

James Hamilton, 1867.

192. Have Ye Heard the Invitation?

Love Divine No. 2. 8 7, 8 7. D.   GEORGE FITZ-CURWOOD LE JEUNE, 1872.

1. Have ye heard the in - vi - ta - tion, Sin - ners ruin - ed by the fall?

Fam - ished souls who seek sal - va - tion, Have ye heard the lov - ing call?

Hark! a her - ald of the Fa - ther Bids you of His sup - per taste.

Round the sa - cred ta - ble gath - er. All is read - y; sin - ners, haste! A - MEN.

2 O ye chosen, have ye slighted
    This sweet call to you proclaimed?
Lo! the King hath now invited
    All the halt, the blind, the maimed:
"Come, ye poor from out the highways,
    Come, a feast awaits you, come!"
Leave the hedges and the byways,
    Hasten to the Father's home.

3 We have heard Thee call, dear Father,
    In Thy Word and sacrament;
Round Thy festal board we'll gather
    Till our life's last day is spent.
Ours the risen Saviour's merit,
    Ours the bounties of Thy love,
Ours Thy peace, till we inherit
    Endless life in heaven above.

                                                Anna Hoppe, 1919.

193. O God of Mercies, Father Mine.

Komm, Heiliger Geist, Herre Gott. 8 8, 8 8, 8 8, 8 8 8.   JOHANN WALTHER, 1524.

1. O God of mer-cies, Fa-ther mine, Drawn by Thy bound-less love di-
2. My blest Re-deem-er, Thy dear Son, On Cal-va-ry my ran-som

vine, I come to Thee, a way-ward child, Bowed down by guilt, with
won. The Friend of sin-ners died for me, To rec-on-cile me

sin de - filed. Re - lieve my bur - dened heart, I pray, Dear Fa - ther,
un - to Thee. The curse of Law for me He bore. For His dear

cast me not a - way. In deep con - tri - tion I im - plore, Re - mem - ber
sake, my God, re - store Sal - va - tion's ho - ly joy to me. Hark to a

Thou my sin no more. Have mer - cy, Lord! Have mer - cy, Lord!
con - trite sin - ner's plea: For - give me, Lord! For - give me, Lord! A - MEN.

3 Thy Holy Spirit, through Thy word,
Assures me of Thy grace, dear Lord.
My risen High Priest intercedes,
His holy blood for pardon pleads.
Wash Thou me in that crimson flow,
And I shall be as white as snow.
Remove my sin-stained carnal dress,
Grant me Christ's robe of righteousness.
O cleanse me, Lord! O cleanse me, Lord!

4 Thy loving-kindness I shall praise,
O gracious Lord, through all my days.
Grant Thou me grace, while here I live,
In true compassion to forgive,
And unto erring brethren show
The love Thou didst on me bestow
Till, glorified by grace, my God,
In realms on high Thy Name I laud
Forevermore! Forevermore!

Anna Hoppe, 1923.

194. How Blest Are They Who through the Power.

Ortonville. C. M.   Thomas Hastings, 1837.

1. How blest are they who through the pow'r Of heav - en - kin - dled
2. Grant us a firm - er, stron - ger faith In Thee, O Cru - ci -

faith Con - fide in Thee each day and hour, O
fied; In joy and pain, in life and death, With

Christ of Naz - a - reth! O Christ of Naz - a - reth!
Thy re-deemed a - bide, With Thy re-deemed a - bide. A - MEN.

Or: St. Anne, No. 144.

3 Thy pardon, full, complete, bestow
   Upon Thy ransomed own,
   That all the Father's love may know,
   And trust Thy grace alone.

4 What joy, when faith is changed to sight,
   And heaven's gates we see,
   To laud Thy Name in mansions bright,
   Through all eternity!

Anna Hoppe, 1920.

195. Father, Who on Man Dost Shower.

Quem pastores laudavere. 8 8, 8 7.   German, 15th Century.

1. Fa - ther, who on man dost show - er Gifts of
2. Give pure hap - pi - ness in leis - ure, Tem - per -

plen-ty from Thy dow-er, To Thy peo-ple give the
ance in ev-'ry pleas-ure, Ho-ly use of earth-ly

pow-er All Thy gifts to use a-right.
treas-ure, Bod-ies clear and spir-its bright. A-MEN.

3 Lift from this and every nation
  All that brings us degradation;
  Quell the forces of temptation;
  Put Thine enemies to flight.

4 Father, who hast sought and found us,
  Son of God, whose love hath bound us,
  Holy Ghost, within us, round us,
  Hear us, Godhead infinite.

Percy Dearmer, 1906.

196. We Need Not Climb the Heavenly Steeps.

Serenity. C. M.   WILLIAM VINCENT WALLACE, 1856.

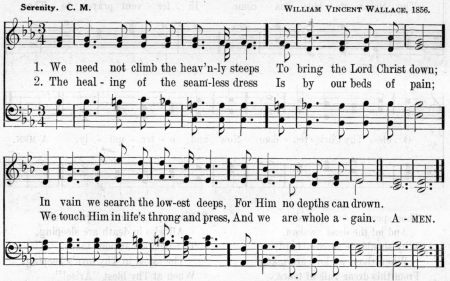

1. We need not climb the heav'n-ly steeps To bring the Lord Christ down;
2. The heal-ing of the seam-less dress Is by our beds of pain;

In vain we search the low-est deeps, For Him no depths can drown.
We touch Him in life's throng and press, And we are whole a-gain. A-MEN.

3 Through Him the first fond prayers are said
  Our lips of childhood frame;
  The last low whispers of our dead
  Are burdened with His Name.

4 O Lord and Master of us all,
  Whate'er our name or sign,
  We own Thy sway and hear Thy call,
  We test our lives by Thine!

John Greenleaf Whittier, (1802–1892).

197. Thou Lord of Life and Death.

O Gott, du frommer Gott. 6 7, 6 7, 6 6, 6 6.   JOHANN GEORG CHRISTIAN STÖRL, 1710.

1. Thou Lord of life and death, Blest Son of God the Fa - ther,

Je - sus, in hum - ble faith Be - fore Thy throne we gath - er;

Thy Spir - it bids us come In fer - vent prayer to Thee,

O bless Thy Chris - ten - dom Now and e - ter - nal - ly. A-MEN.

2 Thou speakest but a word,
  And lo! the dead awaken.
Why should we sorrow, Lord,
  When those we love are taken
From this drear vale of tears
  To realms of bliss above?
Hush Thou our griefs and fears,
  Thou Fount of boundless love.

3 When judgment trumpets wake
  All who in death are sleeping,
To Salem's mansions take
  The saved in Thy love's keeping.
When at Thy blest "Arise!"
  We greet Thee, risen King,
The realms beyond the skies
  With endless praise shall ring.

Anna Hoppe, 1920.

198. O Son of God, We Wait for Thee.

O Jesu Christ, du höchstes Gut. 8 7, 8 7, 8 7 7.

JOHANN CRÜGER. 1658.

1. O Son of God, we wait for Thee, We long for Thine ap-
2. We wait for Thee, 'mid toil and pain, In wea - ri - ness and

pear - ing; We know Thou sit - test on the throne, And we Thy
sigh - ing; But glad that Thou our guilt hast borne, And can-celled

Name are bear - ing. Who trusts in Thee may joy - ful be, And
it by dy - ing. Hence, cheer-ful - ly may we with Thee Take

see Thee, Lord, de - scend - ing To bring us bliss un - end - ing.
up our cross and bear it, Till we the crown in - her - it. A-MEN.

3 We wait for Thee; here Thou hast won
 Our hearts to hope and duty;
But while our spirits feel Thee near,
 Our eyes would see Thy beauty;
We fain would be at rest with Thee
 In peace and joy supernal,
 In glorious life eternal.

4 We wait for Thee; soon Thou wilt come,
 The time is swiftly nearing;
In this we also do rejoice,
 And long for Thine appearing.
O bliss 'twill be when Thee we see,
 Homeward Thy people bringing,
 With ecstasy and singing!

Philipp Friedrich Hiller, 1767.

199. Wake, Awake, for Night Is Flying.

Wachet auf.   8 9 8, 8 9 8, 6 6 4, 8 8.   PHILIPP NICOLAI, 1599.

1. { Wake, a-wake, for night is fly-ing: The watch-men on the heights are
Mid-night's sol-emn hour is toll-ing, His char-iot wheels are near-er

cry-ing, A-wake, Je-ru-sa-lem, a-rise! }
roll-ing; He comes; pre-pare, ye vir-gins wise! } Rise up with will-ing

feet, Go forth, the Bride-groom meet: Al-le-lu-ia! Bear through the

night your well trimmed light, Speed forth to join the mar-riage rite. A-MEN.

2 Zion hears the watchmen singing,
And all her heart with joy is springing,
  She wakes, she rises from her gloom;
Forth her Bridegroom comes, all-glorious,
The strong in grace, in truth victorious;
  Her Star is risen, her Light is come!
All hail, Thou precious One!
Lord Jesus, God's dear Son!
    Alleluia!
The joyful call we answer all,
And follow to the nuptial hall.

3 Lamb of God, the heavens adore Thee,
And men and angels sing before Thee,
  With harp and cymbal's clearest tone.
By the pearly gates in wonder
We stand, and swell the voice of thunder,
  That echoes round Thy dazzling throne.
To mortal eyes and ears
What glory now appears!
    Alleluia!
We raise the song, we swell the throng,
To praise Thee ages all along.

Philipp Nicolai, 1599.

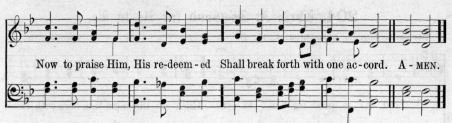

Now to praise Him, His re-deem-ed Shall break forth with one ac-cord. A-MEN.

2 In the arms of her who bore Him,
   Virgin pure, behold Him lie,
   While His agèd saints adore Him,
   Ere in perfect faith they die.
   Hallelujah! Hallelujah!
   Lo, the incarnate God Most High!

3 Jesus, by Thy presentation,
   Thou Who didst for us endure,
   Make us see Thy great salvation,
   Seal us with Thy promise sure;
   And present us in Thy glory
   To Thy Father, cleansed and pure.

Henry John Pye, about 1851, a.

203. O Wondrous Type! O Vision Fair.

Lob sei dem allmächtigen Gott. L. M.   JOHANN CRÜGER, 1640.

1. O won-drous type! O vi-sion fair Of glo-ry that the Church shall share, Which Christ up-on the moun-tain shows, Where bright-er than the sun He glows! A-MEN.

2 From age to age the tale declare,
   How with the three disciples there,
   Where Moses and Elijah meet,
   The Lord holds converse high and sweet.

3 With shining face and bright array,
   Christ deigns to manifest to-day
   What glory shall be theirs above
   Who joy in God with perfect love.

4 And faithful hearts are raised on high
   By this great vision's mystery,
   For which in joyful strains we raise
   The voice of prayer, the hymn of praise.

5 O Father, with the eternal Son,
   And Holy Spirit, ever One,
   Vouchsafe to bring us by Thy grace
   To see Thy glory face to face.

Latin: Sacrum Brev., Venice, 1495, a.

204. Lord, It Is Good for Us to Be.

Gör porten hög, gör dörren bred. L. M. D.   Koralbok, 1697.

1. Lord, it is good for us to be High on the moun-tain here with Thee,

Where stand re-vealed to mor-tal gaze Those glo-rious saints of oth-er days,

Who once re-ceived on Hor-eb's height Th'e-ter-nal laws of truth and right,

Or caught the still small whisper, higher Than storm, than earthquake, or than fire. A-MEN.

2 Lord, it is good for us to be
Entranced, enwrapt, alone with Thee;
And watch Thy glistening raiment glow
Whiter than Hermon's whitest snow,
The human lineaments that shine
Irradiant with a light divine:
Till we too change from grace to grace,
Gazing on that transfigured face.

3 Lord, it is good for us to be
Here on the holy mount with Thee;
When darkling in the depths of night,
When dazzled with excess of light,
We bow before the heavenly voice
That bids bewildered souls rejoice,
Though love wax cold and faith be dim:
"This is my Son; O hear ye Him!"

Arthur Penrhyn Stanley, 1870.

205. Lord Jesus, on the Holy Mount.

Serenity. C. M.

WILLIAM VINCENT WALLACE, 1856.

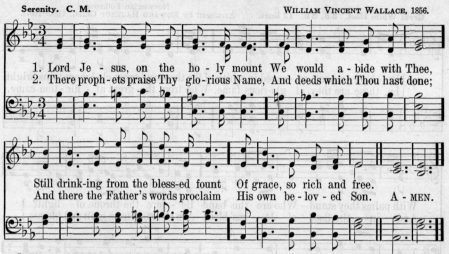

1. Lord Je - sus, on the ho - ly mount We would a - bide with Thee,
2. There proph - ets praise Thy glo - rious Name, And deeds which Thou hast done;

Still drink-ing from the bless-ed fount Of grace, so rich and free.
And there the Father's words proclaim His own be - lov - ed Son. A - MEN.

3 The rays of Thy transfigured face
   Beam with such golden light
That we would never leave the place,
   Nor lose the heavenly sight.

4 But there is work on earth to do,
   The suffering souls to heal;
The harvest great, the laborers few
   Thy kingdom to reveal.

5 We may not linger on the mount,
   Where bright Thy glories shine;
We may not taste the sacred fount
   Of blessedness divine.

6 But let some beams of heavenly light
   Make bright our earthly way;
Then grant the beatific sight
   Of heaven and endless day.

John Anketell, 1889.

206. For All Thy Saints, O Lord.

Ferguson. S. M.

GEORGE KINGSLEY, 1843.

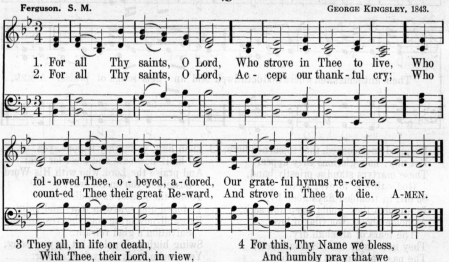

1. For all Thy saints, O Lord, Who strove in Thee to live, Who
2. For all Thy saints, O Lord, Ac - cept our thank - ful cry; Who

fol - lowed Thee, o - beyed, a - dored, Our grate - ful hymns re - ceive.
count-ed Thee their great Re-ward, And strove in Thee to die. A - MEN.

3 They all, in life or death,
   With Thee, their Lord, in view,
Learned from Thy Holy Spirit's breath
   To suffer and to do,

4 For this, Thy Name we bless,
   And humbly pray that we
May follow them in holiness,
   And live and die in Thee.

Richard Mant, 1837.

207. Behold a Host, Arrayed in White.

Norwegian Folksong.

Great White Host. 8 8, 8 6. 12 lines.   Arranged by Edward Hagerup Grieg, (1843–1907).

1. { Be - hold a host, ar - rayed in white, Like thousand snow-clad mountains bright,
   { Lo, these are they, of glo - rious fame, Who from the great af - flic - tion came,

With palms they stand—Who are this band Be - fore the throne of light? }
And in the flood of Je - sus' blood Are cleansed from guilt and blame; }

Now gath-ered in the ho - ly place Their voic - es they in wor-ship raise,

Their anthems swell where God doth dwell 'Mid an - gels' songs of praise. A-MEN.

2 Despised and scorned, they sojourned here,
But now, how glorious they appear!
These martyrs stand a priestly band,
    God's throne forever near.
So oft, in troubled days gone by,
In anguish they would weep and sigh;
At home above, the God of love
    The tears of all shall dry.
They now enjoy their Sabbath rest,
The paschal banquet of the blest;
The Lamb, their Lord, at festal board
    Himself is host and guest.

3 Then hail, ye mighty legions, yea,
All hail! now safe and blest for aye;
And praise the Lord, who with His Word
    Sustained you on the way.
Ye did the joys of earth disdain,
Ye toiled and sowed in tears and pain;
Farewell, now bring your sheaves, and sing
    Salvation's glad refrain.
Swing high your palms, lift up your song,
Yea, make it myriad voices strong:
Eternally shall praise to Thee,
    God, and the Lamb, belong!

Hans Adolph Brorson, about 1760.

208. Stars of the Morning, So Gloriously Bright.

Regnator orbis (O quanta qualia). 10 10, 10 10.   Adapted from a Melody in LA FEILLÉE.
Plain Chant, 1782.

1. Stars of the morn-ing, so glo-rious-ly bright,

Filled with ce-les-tial re-splen-dence and light,

These that, where night nev-er fol-low-eth day,

Raise the "Thrice Ho-ly, Lord!" ev-er and aye.   A-MEN.

2 These are Thy ministers, these dost Thou own,
  Lord God of Sabaoth! nearest Thy throne;
  These are Thy messengers, these dost Thou send,
  Help of the helpless ones, man to defend.

3 Still let them succor us; still let them fight,
  Lord of angelic hosts! battling for right,
  Till, where their anthems they ceaselessly pour,
  We with the angels may bow and adore.

Joseph the Hymnographer, about 850.

209. Who Are These in Bright Array?

St. George's, Windsor. 7 7, 7 7. D.

GEORGE JOB ELVEY, 1858.

1. Who are these in bright ar - ray, This in - nu - mer - a - ble throng,

Round the al - tar, night and day, Hymn-ing one tri - um-phant song?

"Wor - thy is the Lamb, once slain, Bless - ing, hon - or, glo - ry, pow'r,

Wis-dom, rich - es to ob - tain, New do-min - ion ev - 'ry hour." A-MEN.

2 These through fiery trials trod,
These from great affliction came;
Now, before the throne of God,
Sealed with His almighty Name,
Clad in raiment pure and white,
Victor-palms in every hand,
Through their great Redeemer's might,
More than conquerors they stand.

3 Hunger, thirst, disease unknown,
On immortal fruits they feed;
Then the Lamb amidst the throne
Shall to living fountains lead;
Joy and gladness banish sighs;
Perfect love dispels all fears;
And forever from their eyes
God shall wipe away the tears.

James Montgomery, 1819.

210. Come, Let Us Join Our Friends Above.

Carolina. C. M.   PETER JOHNSON, 1922.

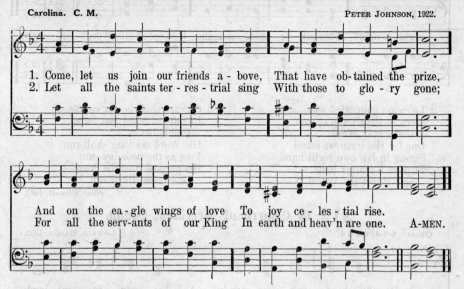

1. Come, let us join our friends a-bove, That have ob-tained the prize,
2. Let all the saints ter-res-trial sing With those to glo-ry gone;

And on the ea-gle wings of love To joy ce-les-tial rise.
For all the serv-ants of our King In earth and heav'n are one. A-MEN.

3 One family, we dwell in Him.
   One Church above, beneath;
   Though now divided by the stream,
   The narrow stream of death.

4 One army of the living God,
   To His command we bow;
   Part of His host has crossed the flood,
   And part is crossing now.

5 E'en now by faith we join our hands
   With those that went before,
   And greet the blood-besprinkled bands
   On the eternal shore.

6 Lord Jesus, be our constant Guide,
   And when the word is given,
   Bid the cold waves of death divide,
   And land us all in heaven.

Charles Wesley, 1759, a.

211. Lord of All Power and Might.

Dort. 6 6 4, 6 6 6 4.   LOWELL MASON, 1832.

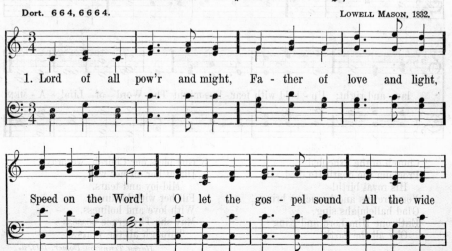

1. Lord of all pow'r and might, Fa-ther of love and light,

Speed on the Word! O let the gos-pel sound All the wide

world a-round, Wher-ev-er man is found! God speed His Word! A-MEN.

2 Lo! what embattled foes,
   Stern in their hate, oppose
      God's holy Word;
   One for His truth we stand,
   Strong in His own right hand,
   Firm as a martyr band:—
      God shield His Word!

3 Onward shall be our course,
   In spite of fraud and force;
      God is before:
   His Word ere long shall run
   Free as the noonday sun;
   His purpose must be done:—
      God bless His Word!

Hugh Stowell, 1853.

212. O Church of Freedom, Stand.

Olivet. 6 6 4, 6 6 6 4.   LOWELL MASON. 1832.

1. O Church of free-dom, stand, A bea-con to our land, In storm and strife! In-spire us with thy light, With love of law and right; Up-hold with fear-less might The Word of Life! A-MEN.

2 Church of the Crucified,
   Proclaim the death He died,
      His royal birth!
   Your crowns and branches bring,
   Glad hallelujahs sing,
   Enthrone Him Lord and King
      O'er all the earth!

3 God bless our Church, we pray,
   Direct her on her way,
      'Mid joy and tears.
   Fill her with lowliness,
   With love and holiness,
   May she Thy grace possess
      Through all the years.

Harry Tennyson Domer, 1919. a.

213. We Hail Thee, Lord, Thy Church's Rock.

O Gud! ditt rike ingen ser. 8 7, 8 7. D.

BURKHARD WALDIS, 1553.

1. We hail Thee, Lord, Thy Church's Rock, With joy-ful ac-cla-ma-tion!

Thou guar-dian Shep-herd of Thy flock, Come, feed Thy con-gre-ga - tion.

We own the doc-trine of Thy cross To be our sole foun-da - tion:

Ac-cept from ev-'ry one of us The deep-est ad-o-ra-tion. A-MEN.

2 O Thou, who always dost abide
    Thy Church's Head and Saviour,
  Be still Thy servants' constant guide,
    Direct our whole behavior.
  Thy statutes to Thy Church declare,
    Still watch o'er its salvation:
  Each member make Thy special care,
    And aid him in his station.

3 Jesus, the Church's Head and Lord,
    Who as a shepherd leadest,
  And with Thy Sacrament and Word
    Thy people richly feedest:
  For mercies in such countless throng
    We bow our hearts before Thee,
  And hope we shall in heaven ere long
    More worthily adore Thee.

Nicolaus Ludwig Zinzendorf, 1741.

214. Faith of Our Fathers, Living Still.

St. Catherine. 8 8, 8 8, 8 8.

HENRI FREDRICK HEMY, 1865.
Alt. by JAMES GEORGE WALTON, 1871.

1. Faith of our fa - thers! liv - ing still In spite of dun - geon, fire, and sword, O how our hearts beat high with joy When-e'er we hear that glo - rious word: Faith of our fa - thers, ho - ly faith! We will be true to thee till death. A - MEN.

2 Our fathers, chained in prisons dark,
    Were still in heart and conscience free;
  How sweet would be their children's fate,
    If they, like them, could die for thee!
  Faith of our fathers, holy faith!
  We will be true to thee till death.

3 Faith of our fathers! we will love
    Both friend and foe in all our strife:
  And preach thee, too, as love knows how,
    By kindly words and virtuous life:
  Faith of our fathers, holy faith!
  We will be true to thee till death.

Frederick William Faber, 1840.

215. Thy Sacred Word, O Lord, of Old.

O Gud! ditt rike ingen ser. 8 7, 8 7. D.

BURKHARD WALDIS, 1553.

1. Thy sa - cred Word, O Lord, of old Was veiled a - bout and dark - ened,

And in its stead were leg - ends told, To which the peo - ple hark - ened;

Thy Word, for which the faith - ful yearned, The world-lings kept in hid - ing,

And in - to hu - man fa - bles turned Thy truth, the all - a - bid - ing. A-MEN.

2 Now thanks and praise be to our Lord,
Who boundless grace bestoweth,
And daily through the sacred Word
His precious gifts forthshoweth.
His Word is come to light again,
A trusty lamp to guide us;
No strange and divers teachings then
Bewilder and divide us.

Olavus Petri, (1497-1552).

216. O Word of God Incarnate.

Everts. 7 6, 7 6. D.

From the German.
LOWELL MASON, 1841.

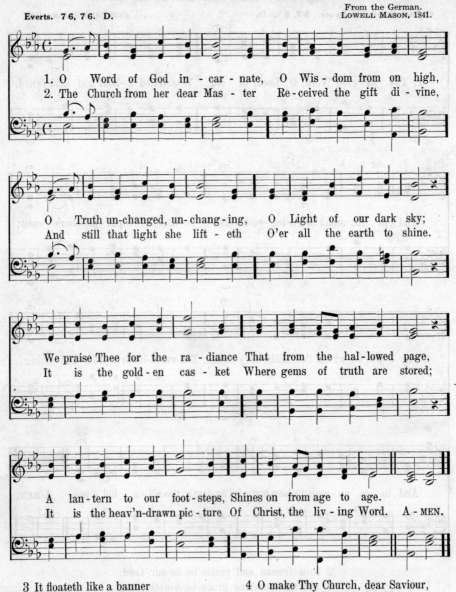

1. O Word of God in - car - nate, O Wis - dom from on high,
2. The Church from her dear Mas - ter Re - ceived the gift di - vine,

O Truth un-changed, un- chang - ing, O Light of our dark sky;
And still that light she lift - eth O'er all the earth to shine.

We praise Thee for the ra - diance That from the hal-lowed page,
It is the gold - en cas - ket Where gems of truth are stored;

A lan-tern to our foot - steps, Shines on from age to age.
It is the heav'n-drawn pic - ture Of Christ, the liv - ing Word. A - MEN.

3 It floateth like a banner
  Before God's hosts unfurled;
It shineth like a beacon
  Above the darkling world:
It is the chart and compass
  That o'er life's surging sea,
'Mid mists, and rocks, and quicksands,
  Still guides, O Christ, to Thee.

4 O make Thy Church, dear Saviour,
  A lamp of burnished gold
To bear before the nations
  Thy true light as of old:
O teach Thy wandering pilgrims
  By this their path to trace,
Till, clouds and darkness ended,
  They see Thee face to face.

William Walsham How, 1867.

217. How Precious Is the Book Divine.

St. Peter. C. M.   ALEXANDER ROBERT REINAGLE, 1826.

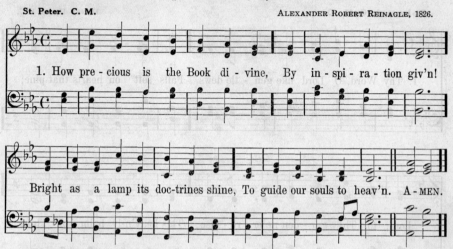

1. How pre-cious is the Book di-vine, By in-spi-ra-tion giv'n!

Bright as a lamp its doc-trines shine, To guide our souls to heav'n. A-MEN.

2 It sweetly cheers our drooping hearts
  In this dark vale of tears;
  Life, light, and joy it still imparts,
  And quells our rising fears.

3 This lamp through all the tedious night
  Of life shall guide our way,
  Till we behold the clearer light
  Of an eternal day.

John Fawcett, 1782.

218. Father of Mercies, in Thy Word.

St. Agnes. C. M.   JOHN BACCHUS DYKES, 1866.

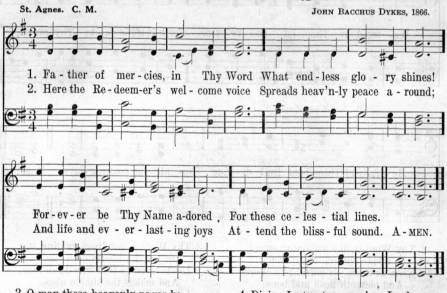

1. Fa-ther of mer-cies, in Thy Word What end-less glo-ry shines!
2. Here the Re-deem-er's wel-come voice Spreads heav'n-ly peace a-round;

For-ev-er be Thy Name a-dored For these ce-les-tial lines.
And life and ev-er-last-ing joys At-tend the bliss-ful sound. A-MEN.

3 O may these heavenly pages be
  My ever dear delight;
  And still new beauties may I see,
  And still increasing light.

4 Divine Instructor, gracious Lord,
  Be Thou forever near;
  Teach me to love Thy sacred Word,
  And view my Saviour there.

Anne Steele, 1760.

219. Thy Word, O Lord, Like Gentle Dews.

St. Leonard. C. M. D.   HENRY HILES, 1867.

1. Thy Word, O Lord like gen - tle dews, Falls soft on hearts that pine;

Lord, to Thy gar - den ne'er re - fuse This heav'n-ly balm of Thine.

Wa - tered by Thee, let ev - 'ry tree Forth - blos - som to Thy praise,

By grace of Thine bear fruit di - vine, Thro' all the com-ing days. A-MEN.

2 Thy Word is like a flaming sword,
  A wedge that cleaveth stone;
Keen as a fire, so burns Thy Word,
  And pierceth flesh and bone.
Let it go forth o'er all the earth
  To cleanse our hearts within,
To show Thy power in Satan's hour,
  And break the might of sin.

3 Thy Word a wondrous guiding star
  On pilgrim hearts doth rise,
Leads those to God who dwell afar,
  And makes the simple wise.
Let not its light e'er sink in night;
  In every spirit shine,
That none may miss heaven's final bliss,
  Led by Thy light divine.

Carl Bernard Garve, 1825.

220. Lord, Keep Us Steadfast in Thy Word.

Erhalt uns, Herr, bei deinem Wort. L. M.   JOSEPH KLUG'S Geistliche Lieder, 1543.

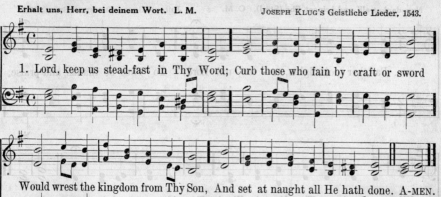

1. Lord, keep us stead-fast in Thy Word; Curb those who fain by craft or sword

Would wrest the kingdom from Thy Son, And set at naught all He hath done. A-MEN.

Or: Mendon, No. 280.

2 Lord Jesus Christ, Thy power make known,
For Thou art Lord of lords alone;
Defend Thy Christendom, that we
May evermore sing praise to Thee.

3 O Comforter, of priceless worth,
Send peace and unity on earth;
Support us in our final strife,
And lead us out of death to life.

Martin Luther, 1541.

221. Lamp of Our Feet, Whereby We Trace.

Evan. C. M.   WILLIAM HENRY HAVERGAL, 1846.

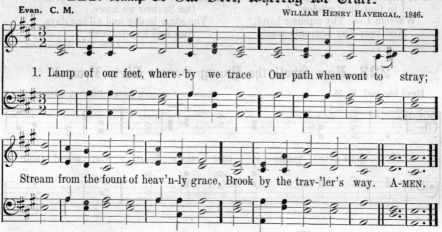

1. Lamp of our feet, where-by we trace   Our path when wont to   stray;

Stream from the fount of heav'n-ly grace, Brook by the trav-'ler's way. A-MEN.

2 Bread of our souls, whereon we feed,
True manna from on high;
Our guide and chart, wherein we read
Of realms beyond the sky;

3 Pillar of fire through watches dark,
Or radiant cloud by day;
When waves o'erwhelm our tossing bark,
Our anchor and our stay:

4 Word of the ever-living God,
Will of His glorious Son;
Without Thee, how could earth be trod,
Or heaven itself be won?

5 Lord, grant us all aright to learn
The wisdom it imparts;
And to its heavenly teaching turn
With simple, childlike hearts.

Bernard Barton, 1826.

222. Father of Lights, Eternal Lord.

Nun danket all' und bringet Ehr (Störl).   C. M.   JOHANN GEORG CHRISTIAN STÖRL, 1710.

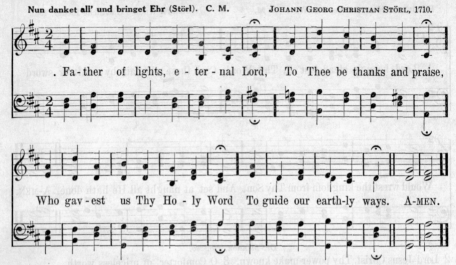

Fa-ther of lights, e-ter-nal Lord, To Thee be thanks and praise,

Who gav-est us Thy Ho-ly Word To guide our earth-ly ways. A-MEN.

2 How gently in this precious Word
   Thy Spirit speaks to mine!
   O Father, there Thy voice is heard
   By every child of Thine.

3 A pilgrim in this far-off land,
   I in that light rejoice,
   Wherein I see Thy guiding hand,
   And hear Thy heavenly voice.

4 True faith in Thee and in Thy Word,
   With deeds of Christian love,
   And peace with heaven and earth, O Lord,
   Shall me Thy servant prove.

5 In Thee our Father's will we praise,
   Our Saviour we adore,
   The same to-day and all our days,
   Now and for evermore.
                              Johan Olof Wallin, 1816.

223. How Shall the Young Secure Their Hearts?

Hvad hör jag?   C. M.   JOHANN ABRAHAM PETER SCHULZ, (1747–1800).

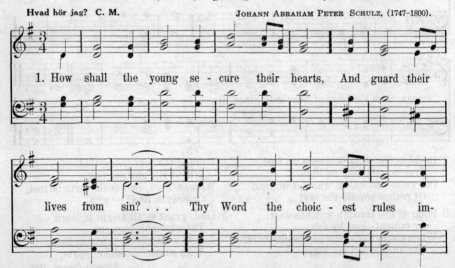

1. How shall the young se-cure their hearts, And guard their

lives from sin? . . . Thy Word the choic-est rules im-

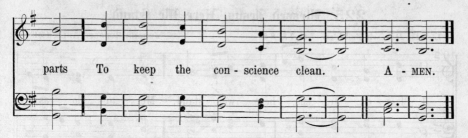

parts   To   keep   the   con - science   clean.   A - MEN.

2 'Tis like the sun, a heavenly light,
  That guides us all the day;
  And through the dangers of the night
  A lamp to lead our way.

3 The starry heavens Thy rule obey,
  The earth maintains her place;
  And these Thy servants, night and day,
  Thy skill and power express.

4 But still Thy law and gospel, Lord,
  Have lessons more divine;
  Not earth stands firmer than Thy Word,
  No stars so nobly shine.

5 Thy Word is everlasting truth:
  How pure is every page!
  That holy Book shall guide our youth,
  And well support our age.

                              Isaac Watts, 1719.

224. Lord, Thy Word Abideth.

St. Cyprian.   6 6, 6 6.   Trochaic.   RICHARD ROBERT CHOPE, 1862.

1. Lord, Thy Word a - bid - eth,   And our foot - steps guid - eth;
2. When our foes are near   us,   Then Thy Word doth cheer   us,

Who its truth be - liev - eth   Light and joy re - ceiv - eth.
Word of con - so - la - tion,   Mes - sage of sal - va - tion.   A-MEN.

3 When the storms are o'er us,
  And dark clouds before us,
  Then its light directeth,
  And our way protecteth.

4 Who can tell the pleasure,
  Who recount the treasure
  By Thy Word imparted
  To the simple-hearted?

5 Word of mercy, giving
  Succor to the living;
  Word of life, supplying
  Comfort to the dying!

6 O that we, discerning
  Its most holy learning,
  Lord, may love and fear Thee,
  Evermore be near Thee!

                              Henry Williams Baker, 1861.

225. Blessed Jesus, Here We Stand.

Liebster Jesu, wir sind hier. 7 8, 7 8, 8 8.   JOHANN RUDOLPH AHLE, 1664.

1. Bless - ed Je - sus, here we stand, Met to do as
Thou hast spo - ken; And this child, at Thy com - mand,
Now we bring to Thee in to - ken That to Thee it
here is giv - en; For of such shall be Thy heav - en. A-MEN.

2 Yes, Thy warning voice is plain,
    And we fain would keep it duly;
He who is not born again,
    Heart and life renewing truly,
Born of water and the Spirit,
Shall the kingdom ne'er inherit.

3 Therefore hasten we to Thee;
    Take the pledge we bring, O take it!
Let us here Thy glory see,
    And in tender pity make it
Now Thy child, and leave it never,
Thine on earth and Thine forever.

4 Make it, Lord, Thy member now;
    Shepherd, take Thy lamb, and feed it,
Prince of Peace, its peace be Thou;
    Way of life, to heaven lead it,
Vine, this branch may nothing sever,
Grafted firm in Thee forever.

5 Now upon Thy heart it lies,
    What our hearts so dearly treasure:
Heavenward lead our burdened sighs,
    Pour Thy blessing without measure;
Write the name we now have given—
Write it in the book of heaven.

Benjamin Schmolck, 1707.

226. God in Human Flesh Appearing.

Jesus är min vän den bäste. 8 7, 8 7. D.

GUSTAF DÜBEN, 1674.

1. God, in hu-man flesh ap-pear-ing, Took the chil-dren to His breast,

Lambs with His green pas-tures cheer-ing, Fit-ting for His heav'n-ly rest;

This is gen-tle-ness un-bound-ed, This is low-li-ness of heart;

All are by His love sur-round-ed, None are ev-er bid de-part. A-MEN.

2 Lord, I bless Thy mercy endless,
   For Thy pleasure is to bless;
Me, too, when my soul was friendless,
   Thou didst to Thy bosom press:
For I, too, to Thee was given
   In the pure baptismal wave,
Thou hast made me heir of heaven,
   Who hast died my soul to save.

3 Feeble is the love of mother,
   Father's blessings are as naught,
When compared, my King and Brother,
   With the wonders Thou hast wrought;
Thus it pleased Thy heavenly meekness;
   Pleasing also be my praise,
Till my songs of earthly weakness
   Burst into celestial lays.

Philipp Friedrich Hiller, 1762.

227. Father, Who Hast Created All.

Resignation. 8 6, 8 6, 8 8, or C. H. M.   Adapted by J. SIEBOTH.

1. Father, who hast created all In wisest love, we pray, Look on this babe, who at Thy call Is en-t'ring on life's way. Bend o'er it now with bless-ing fraught, And make Thou some-thing out of naught.

2. O Son, who diedst for us, be-hold, We bring our child to Thee! Great Shep-herd, take it to Thy fold, Thine own for aye to be: De-fend it through this earth-ly strife, And lead it in the path of life. A-MEN.

3 O Spirit, brooding o'er the wave,
  Descend upon this child:
Give endless life, its spirit lave
  With waters undefiled:
Grant it a child of God to be,
A holy temple unto Thee.

4 O God, Thine own command is done:
  We speak, but Thine the might:
This child, which scarce hath seen the sun,
  O pour on it Thy light,
In faith and hope, in joy and love,
Thou Sun of all, below, above!

Albert Knapp, 1841.

228. O Lord, Our Little Ones to Thee.

Djupt sjunker året i sin gång. C. M.

LUDWIG VAN BEETHOVEN, (1770–1827).

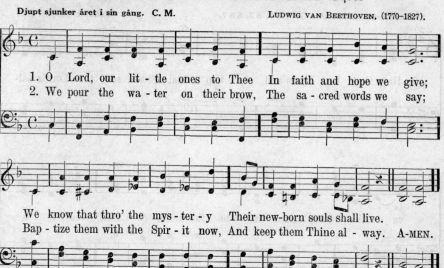

1. O Lord, our lit - tle ones to Thee In faith and hope we give;
2. We pour the wa - ter on their brow, The sa - cred words we say;

We know that thro' the mys - ter - y Their new-born souls shall live.
Bap - tize them with the Spir - it now, And keep them Thine al - way. A-MEN.

3 Help them to go from strength to strength, 4 And then, with all the heavenly host,
  Until, full-grown in Thee,   In everlasting songs,
They come before Thy face at length,   Praise Father, Son, and Holy Ghost,
  And all Thy glory see.   To whom all praise belongs.

William Whiting, 1872.

229. Arise, and Be Baptized.

Mildred. S. M.

PETER JOHNSON, 1923.

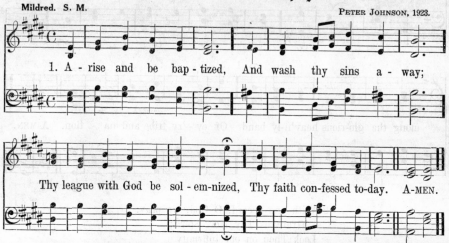

1. A - rise and be bap - tized, And wash thy sins a - way;

Thy league with God be sol - em-nized, Thy faith con-fessed to-day. A-MEN.

2 No more thine own, but Christ's;   3 O bright the conqueror's crown,
  With all the saints of old,   The song of triumph sweet,
Apostles, seers, evangelists,   When faith casts every trophy down
  And martyr throngs enrolled.   At our Redeemer's feet.

Edward Henry Bickersteth, 1870.

230. He That Believes and Is Baptized.

O Jesu Christ, du höchstes Gut. 8 7, 8 7, 8 8 7.   JOHANN CRÜGER. 1658.

1. He that be - lieves and is bap - tized Shall see the Lord's sal-
va - tion; Bap - tized in - to the death of Christ, He is a
new cre - a - tion; Thro' Christ's re - demp - tion he shall stand A-
mong the glo-rious heav'n-ly band Of ev-'ry tribe and na - tion. A-MEN.

2 With one accord, O God, we pray:
    Grant us Thy Holy Spirit;
Look Thou on our infirmity
    Through Jesus' blood and merit!
Grant us to grow in grace each day
By holy baptism, that we may
    Eternal life inherit!

Thomas Kingo, 1689.

231. O Father, Bless the Children.

Gustavus Adolphus. 7 6, 7 6. D.   PETER JOHNSON, 1923.

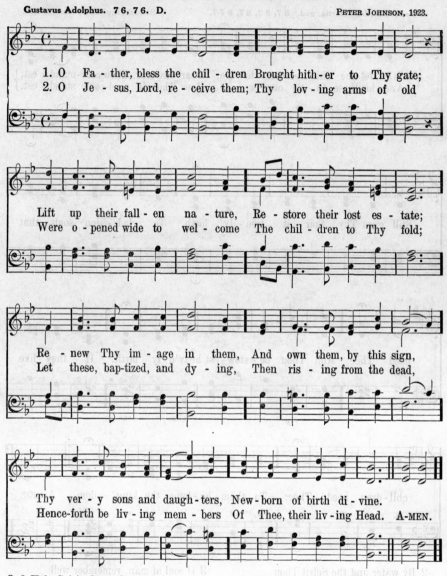

1. O Fa - ther, bless the chil - dren Brought hith - er to Thy gate;
2. O Je - sus, Lord, re - ceive them; Thy lov - ing arms of old

Lift up their fall - en na - ture, Re - store their lost es - tate;
Were o - pened wide to wel - come The chil - dren to Thy fold;

Re - new Thy im - age in them, And own them, by this sign,
Let these, bap-tized, and dy - ing, Then ris - ing from the dead,

Thy ver - y sons and daugh - ters, New - born of birth di - vine.
Hence-forth be liv - ing mem - bers Of Thee, their liv - ing Head. A-MEN.

3 O Holy Spirit, keep them;
   Dwell with them to the last,
Till all the fight is ended,
   And all the storms are past.
Renew the gift baptismal,
   From strength to strength, till each,
The troublous waves o'ercoming,
   The land of life shall reach.

4 O Father, Son, and Spirit,
   O Wisdom, Love, and Power,
We wait the promised blessing
   In this accepted hour.
We name upon the children
   The threefold Name divine;
Receive them, cleanse them, own them,
   And keep them ever Thine.

John Ellerton, 1888.

232. O Let the Children Come to Me.

O Fader vår, barmhertig, god. 8 7, 8 7, 8 7, 8 7 7.   Strassburger Kirchenampt, 1525.

1. {"O let the chil-dren come to Me," Dear Sav-iour, Thou com-mand-est;}
   {And for these lit-tle ones we see How Thou in wel-come stand-est.}

Still goes Thy Spir-it free-ly forth, To glad-den souls that need Thee, And Thou be-stow-est heav'n-ly birth, If they like chil-dren heed Thee: To them be-longs the king-dom. A-MEN.

2 By water and the Spirit Thou
    Our sinful nature cleansest;
Thy Word doth show the path to go,
    And daily grace Thou sendest.
O may Thy sanctifying love
    Surround us all with blessing;
And may we all Thy favor prove
    In daily Thee confessing,
And close to Thee abiding.

3 O soul of man, remember well
    The holy Name thou bearest:
Of everything that tongue can tell
    That Name is still the dearest.
O child of God, His voice attend,
    Live worthy of His choosing;
For He is thy eternal Friend:
    Beware lest thou be losing
His grace so freely given.

Johan Olof Wallin. (1773-1839).

233. Jesus Took the Lambs and Blessed Them.

Orient Morning. 8 7, 8 7, 4 7.   ARTHUR HENRY MANN, 1885.

1. Je - sus took the lambs and blessed them, When they came to Him of old,

Fond - ly in His arms ca - ressed them, Bade them wel - come in His fold,

Warm - ly wel-comed, When dis - ci - ples' hearts were cold. A - MEN.

2 Jesus calls them still with kindness
Passing every mortal thought,
Bids them come, while human blindness
Still would chide when they are brought,
Takes and blesses
Whom He hath so dearly bought.

3 Jesus, we would not forbid them,
We would have them brought to Thee;
Thou of all their guilt dost rid them,
From the curse dost set them free,
Thine dost make them—
Thine let them forever be!

Matthias Loy, 1880.

Other hymns on Baptism:
Baptized into Thy Name most holy.
Saviour, who Thy flock art feeding.

234. The Death of Jesus Christ, Our Lord.

Mein Seel, o Herr, muss loben dich. L. M.   BARTHOLOMÄUS GESIUS, 1601.

1. The death of Je-sus Christ, our Lord, We cel-e-
2. He blot-ted out with His own blood The judg-ment

brate with one ac-cord; It is our com-fort in dis-
that a-gainst us stood; He full a-tone-ment for us

tress, Our heart's sweet joy and hap-pi-ness.
made, And all our debt He ful-ly paid. A-MEN.

3 That this is so and ever true
He gives an earnest, ever new,
In this His holy Supper, here
We taste His love, so sweet, so near.

4 For His true body, as He said,
And His true blood, for sinners shed,
In this communion we receive:
His sacred Word we do believe.

5 A precious food is this indeed,
It never faileth; such we need,
A heavenly manna for our soul,
Until we safely reach our goal.

6 Then blest is every worthy guest
Who in this promise findeth rest,
For Jesus will in love abide
With those who do in Him confide.

7 O sinner, come with true intent
To turn to God and to repent,
To live for Christ, to die to sin,
And thus a holy life begin.

8 Who does unworthy here appear,
Does not believe, nor is sincere,
Salvation here can never find.
May we this warning bear in mind.

9 O Jesus Christ, our Brother dear,
Unto Thy cross we now draw near;
Thy sacred wounds indeed make whole
A wounded and afflicted soul.

10 Help us sincerely to believe
That we Thy mercy do receive,
And in Thy grace do find our rest,
Amen. He who believes is blest.

Haquin Spegel, 1686.

235. Thine Own, O Loving Saviour.

O Jesu! än de dina. 7 6, 7 6, 8 7 6.   HANS THOMISSÖNS PSALMEBOG, 1569.

1. Thine own, O lov-ing Sav-iour, Thou bid-dest come to Thee,
2. To us on earth still dwell-ing Thou dost de-scend to give,

Thy pas-sion's fruits, Thy fa-vor, Thy grace, Thou giv-est free
In love all love ex-cel-ling, Thy-self that we may live,

To them who by Thy grace and love Are mem-bers
And say-est, ev-er kind and good: "Take, eat, this

of Thy king-dom, Now here, and then a-bove.
is My bod-y, Take, drink, this is My blood." A-MEN.

3 We hear Thine invitation;
  We hear, O Lord, Thy call,
The word of consolation,
  It is for us, for all;
It draws us to Thy loving heart,
It brings to us Thy blessing,
It does Thy peace impart.

4 Thy heart is in all anguish
  A refuge to the poor,
Thy heart for us did languish,
  And bitter death endure.
Thy heart, yet filled with peace and rest,
With comfort and salvation,
Draws near to every breast.

5 Thou still in loving favor
  To us, Thine own, art near,
To lead us as our Saviour
  Unto a Father dear,
A Father willing to forgive
The children Thou didst ransom,
And who through Thee shall live.

6 We are Thine own forever;
  Until our latest breath
Will we be true, and never
  In joy, in grief, in death,
Depart from Thee, for Thou always
Art present with Thy people,
As Thine own promise says.

Frans Mikael Franzén, 1814.

236. O Living Bread from Heaven.

Herzlich thut mich verlangen. 7 6, 7 6. D.   HANS LEO HASSLER, 1601 and 1613.

1. O Liv-ing Bread from heav-en, How hast Thou fed Thy guest!
2. My Lord, Thou here hast led me With-in Thy ho-liest place,

The gifts Thou now hast giv-en Have filled my heart with rest.
And there Thy-self hast fed me With treas-ures of Thy grace;

O won-drous food of bless-ing, O cup that heals our woes!
And Thou hast free-ly giv-en What earth could nev-er buy,

My heart, this gift pos-sess-ing, In thank-ful song o'er-flows.
The Bread of Life from heav-en, That now I shall not die! A-MEN.

3 Thou givest all I wanted;
　Let praise my tongue employ,
For Thou hast freely granted
　The Cup of endless joy.
Ah, Lord, I do not merit
　The favor Thou hast shown,
With all my soul and spirit
　I bow before Thy throne.

4 Lord, grant me that, thus strengthened
　With heavenly food, while here
My course on earth is lengthened,
　I serve with holy fear:
And when Thou call'st my spirit
　To leave this world below,
I enter, through Thy merit,
　Where joys unmingled flow.

Johann Rist, 1651.

237. Crushed by My Sin, O Lord, to Thee.

Du lifvets bröd. 8 7, 8 7, 8 8 7.

PETER SOHREN, 1668.

1. Crushed by my sin, O Lord, to Thee I come in my af-
flic - tion: O full of pit - y, look on me, Im - part Thy
ben - e - dic - tion. My sins are great, where shall I flee? The
blood of Je - sus speaks for me; For all my sins He car - ried.

2. Re - pent - ant at Thy feet I fall, To Thy cross hum - bly
cling - ing, O Je - sus, hear me when I call, My wants be -
fore Thee bring - ing. My trust is in Thy grace and pow'r; For
all was fin-ished in that hour When Thou didst make a - tone - ment. A-MEN.

3 When I approach Thine altar, Lord,
　　May I this comfort cherish,
　　That on the cross Thy blood was poured
　　　For me, lest I should perish.
　　Thou didst for me God's law fulfill,
　　That holy joy my heart might thrill,
　　　When on Thy love I'm feasting.

4 Shield me against the tempter's power,
　　Whene'er he would assail me;
　　Confirm my faith in death's dark hour,
　　　O let it never fail me!
　　Lord Jesus, who hast died for me,
　　My life I would devote to Thee,
　　　To praise Thy Name forever.

Christian Fürchtegott Gellert, 1767.

238. A Voice, a Heavenly Voice I Hear.

Hvad röst, hvad ljuflig röst jag hör! 8 8 6, 8 8.   OLOF ÅHLSTRÖM, 1825.

1. A voice, a heav'n-ly voice I hear! A - rise, O soul, come
and draw near To hal - low and re - vere The day the Lord thy
God doth make, And of the bread of life par - take. A-MEN.

2 I come, dear Jesus, at Thy word,
A guest unworthy to Thy board,
My Saviour and my Lord,
O clothe me with Thy righteouness,
My soul with Thy salvation bless!

Johan Olof Wallin, 1814.

239. According to Thy Gracious Word.

Naomi. C. M.   Arr. from JOHANN GEORG NÄGELI by
LOWELL MASON, 1836.

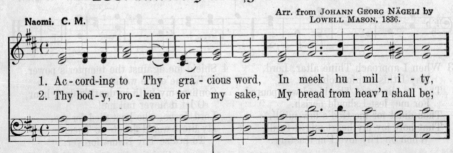

1. Ac - cord-ing to Thy gra - cious word, In meek hu - mil - i - ty,
2. Thy bod - y, bro - ken for my sake, My bread from heav'n shall be;

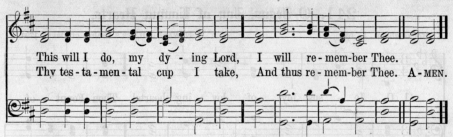

This will I do, my dy - ing Lord, I will re - mem - ber Thee.
Thy tes - ta - men - tal cup I take, And thus re - mem - ber Thee. A - MEN.

3 Gethsemane can I forget,
  Or there Thy conflict see,
Thine agony and bloody sweat,
  And not remember Thee?

4 When to the cross I turn mine eyes,
  And rest on Calvary,
O Lamb of God, my Sacrifice!
  I must remember Thee.

5 Remember Thee and all Thy pains,
  And all Thy love to me;
Yea, while a breath, a pulse remains,
  Will I remember Thee.

6 And when these failing lips grow dumb,
  And mind and memory flee,
When Thou shalt in Thy kingdom come,
  O Lord, remember me!

James Montgomery, 1825.

240. Lord Jesus Christ, to Thee We Pray.

Ack, blif hos oss, o Jesu Krist   L. M.   Swedish Melody, 1697.

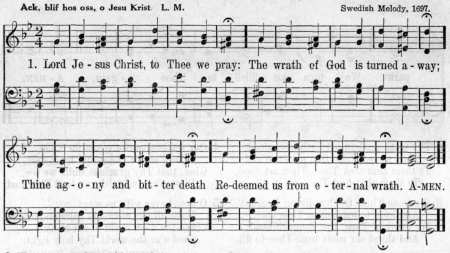

1. Lord Je - sus Christ, to Thee we pray: The wrath of God is turned a - way;

Thine ag - o - ny and bit - ter death Re-deemed us from e - ter - nal wrath. A - MEN.

2 That we may keep this truth in mind,
Thy broken body here we find;
Here we receive Thy precious blood,
A cleansing, sacrificial flood.

3 Then praise the Father, by whose love
The Son descended from above,
Became the Bread of Life to thee,
And bore thy sins upon the tree.

4 Most firmly this we do believe,
That here the sick their food receive,
Which heals them from the wounds of sin,
Creating heavenly health within.

5 Our Saviour saith: Come unto Me,
All ye who feel your poverty:
My mercy I will freely give,
Your anguished conscience to relieve.

6 If in thy heart this faith doth rest,
Which thou hast here in words confessed,
A welcome guest thou here shalt be,
And Christ Himself shall banquet thee.

7 But fruits must still thy faith approve,
Thy neighbor thou must truly love;
That love let him from thee receive
Which here to thee thy God doth give.

Martin Luther, 1524.

241. O Jesus, Joy of Loving Hearts.

Rockingham. L. M.   EDWARD MILLER'S Psalms of David, 1790.

1. O Je - sus, Joy of lov - ing hearts! Thou Fount of life! Thou Light of men! From full - est bliss that earth im - parts, We turn un - filled to Thee a - gain. A - MEN.

2 Thy truth unchanged hath ever stood,
   Thou savest those that on Thee call;
   To them that seek Thee, Thou art good,
   To them that find Thee, all in all.

3 We taste Thee, O Thou living Bread,
   And long to feast upon Thee still;
   We drink of Thee, the Fountainhead,
   And thirst our souls from Thee to fill.

4 Our restless spirits yearn for Thee,
   Where'er our changeful lot is cast,
   Glad, that Thy gracious smile we see,
   Blest, that our faith can hold Thee fast.

5 O Jesus, ever with us stay!
   Make all our moments calm and bright;
   Chase the dark night of sin away,
   Shed o'er the world Thy holy light.

                                    Bernard of Clairvaux, (1091-1153).

242. Here at Thy Table, Lord, We Meet.

Dundee. C. M.   HART'S Psalter, 1615.

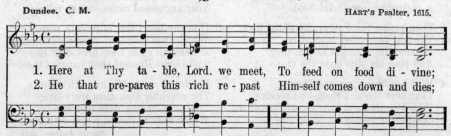

1. Here at Thy ta - ble, Lord, we meet, To feed on food di - vine;
2. He that pre-pares this rich re - past Him-self comes down and dies;

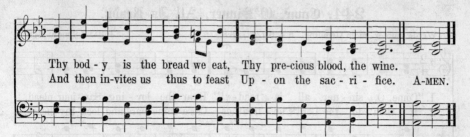

Thy bod-y is the bread we eat, Thy pre-cious blood, the wine.
And then in-vites us thus to feast Up-on the sac-ri-fice. A-MEN.

3 O was there ever love so free,
   Dear Saviour, so divine!
   Well Thou may'st claim that heart of me
   Which owes so much to Thine.

4 Yea, surely Thou shalt have my heart,
   My soul, my strength, my all;
   With life itself I'll freely part,
   My Jesus, at Thy call.

Samuel Stennett, 1777.

243. With Holy Joy My Heart Doth Beat.

Mein Seel, o Herr, muss loben dich. L. M.   BARTHOLOMÄUS GESIUS, 1601.

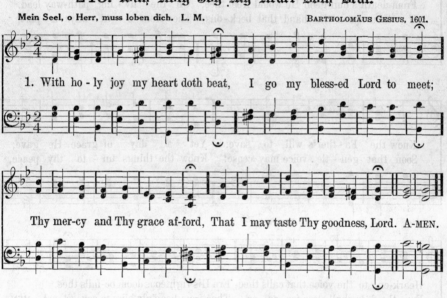

1. With ho-ly joy my heart doth beat, I go my bless-ed Lord to meet;

Thy mer-cy and Thy grace af-ford, That I may taste Thy goodness, Lord. A-MEN.

2 O Lord, forgive my sin, I pray,
  Turn not from my distress away;
  Thou bearest all our sin and woe,
  On me Thy saving grace bestow.

3 Though I have done this evil, Lord,
  And sinned against Thy holy Word,
  Yet do I now draw near to Thee;
  Extend Thy mercy, Lord, to me.

4 O let me all my sorrows see
  Turned into joy and peace by Thee;
  When at Thy table, Lord, I kneel,
  Let me Thy loving presence feel.

5 A heavenly food I there receive,
  Which doth my hungry soul relieve;
  What care I now for want or need?
  Thy precious love is wealth indeed.

6 O come, dear Saviour, then, to me,
  Deign to prepare a place for Thee
  Within my heart and there remain,
  And faith, and hope, and love maintain.

7 Thine let me be, whate'er befall,
  Thou art my Life, my Joy, mine All;
  Thou Light and Comfort of my heart,
  In life, in death, my Hope Thou art.

Samuel Johan Hedborn, 1814.

244. Come, O Sinner, All Is Ready.

Werde munter, mein Gemüthe. 8 7, 8 7, 7 7, 8 8.   JOHANN SCHOP, 1642.

1. "Come, O sin-ner, all is read-y!" Hear the lov-ing Sav-iour plead.
2. If thou to the Lord's en-treat-ies Close thine ears and lock thy heart,

From death's dun-geon He would free thee, On the liv-ing path-way lead.
If thou spurn the hand that beck-ons Thee from e-vil ways a-part,

Know the Fa-ther's will to save: Yet a day of grace He gave;
Soon that gen-tle voice may cease: Know the things un-to thy peace,

Heark-en to the voice that calls thee, Ere His righteous doom be-falls thee.
Ere the door shall close for-ev-er, Thee from heav'nly bliss to sev-er. A-MEN.

3 But if thou in deep contrition
   Ownest to thy helplessness,
 Trusting solely in His merit
   Who achieved thy righteousness,
 Hearken, then, unto His call,
 At His table humbly fall,
 There receive the food from heaven
 For thy faith's sustention given.

4 Lord and Saviour, keep and guide me
   By Thy gospel light, I pray,
 That the world by her seductions
   Draw me not from Thee away.
 In Thy body and Thy blood
 Give me now that precious food
 Which Thy witness here shall make me,
 Till to Thine abode Thou take me.

Christopher Dahl, 1814.

245. Come, O Jesus, and Prepare Me.

Jesus är min vän den bäste. 8 7, 8 7. D.   GUSTAF DÜBEN, 1674.

1. Come, O Je-sus, and pre-pare me Now to be Thy wor-thy guest.

Like Thy well be-lov'd dis-ci-ple, Let me lean up-on Thy breast

At Thy ta-ble, where Thou giv-est Of Thy bod-y and Thy blood,

Seal-ing in this blest com-mun-ion My bap-tis-mal vow to God. A-MEN.

First Communion of Catechumens.

2 Take my heart and make it holy
  By Thy Spirit and Thy grace;
Back into Thy footsteps guide me,
  If I stray in evil ways.
Thou who lovèdst me from childhood,
  Be my Refuge in my youth;
In a world where error lures me,
  Lead me in Thy paths of truth.

3 Let me heed Thy voice entreating,
  "Come, my child, abide with Me;
Wouldst thou spurn the loving-kindness
  Of the Friend who died for thee?"
Grant that, at Thy sacred altar,
  Through Thy sacrament of grace,
With the faithful I be numbered,
  And Thy saving love embrace.

Frans Mikael Franzén, 1814.

246. Deck Thyself, My Soul, with Gladness.

Schmücke dich, o liebe Seele. L. M. D.   JOHANN CRÜGER, 1649.

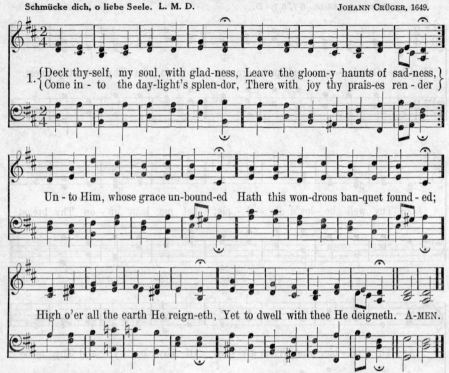

1. {Deck thy-self, my soul, with glad-ness, Leave the gloom-y haunts of sad-ness,}
   {Come in - to the day-light's splen-dor, There with joy thy prais-es ren - der}

Un - to Him, whose grace un-bound-ed Hath this won-drous ban-quet found - ed;

High o'er all the earth He reign-eth, Yet to dwell with thee He deigneth. A-MEN.

2 Hasten as a bride to meet Him,
And with loving reverence greet Him,
For with words of life immortal
Now He knocketh at thy portal;
Open wide the gates before Him,
Saying, while thou dost adore Him,
"Suffer, Lord, that I receive Thee,
And I nevermore will leave Thee."

3 He who costly goods desireth
To obtain, much gold requireth;
But to freely give the treasure
Of Thy love is Thy good pleasure,
For on earth there is no coffer
Which as payment we might offer
For this cup Thy blood containing,
And this manna on us raining.

4 Ah! how hungers all my spirit
For the love I do not merit!
Oft have I, with sighs fast thronging,
Thought upon this food with longing;
In the battle, well-nigh worsted,
For this cup of life have thirsted,
For the Friend who here invites us,
And to God Himself unites us.

5 Sun, who all my life dost brighten,
Light, who dost my soul enlighten,
Joy, the sweetest man e'er knoweth,
Fount, whence all my being floweth,
At Thy feet I cry, my Maker,
Let me be a fit partaker
Of this blessèd food from heaven,
For our good, Thy glory, given.

6 Lord, Thy fervent love hath driven
Thee to leave Thy throne in heaven,
For us on the cross to languish,
And to die in bitter anguish,
To forego all joy and gladness,
And to shed Thy blood in sadness,
Which we drink now; grant that never
We forget Thy love, dear Saviour!

7 Jesus, Bread of Life, I pray Thee,
Let me gladly here obey Thee;
By Thy love I am invited,
Be Thy love with love requited;
From this banquet let me measure,
Lord, how vast and deep love's treasure;
Through the gifts Thou here dost give me
As Thy guest in heaven receive me.

Benjamin Schmolck, 1653.

247. With Deep Humility, O Lord.

Belmont. C. M.

WILLIAM GARDINER, 1812.

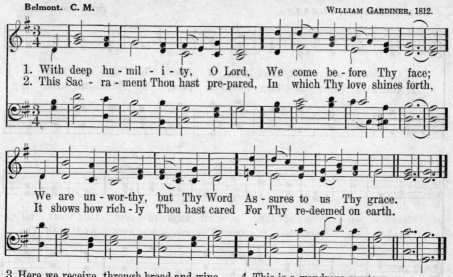

1. With deep hu-mil-i-ty, O Lord, We come be-fore Thy face;
2. This Sac-ra-ment Thou hast pre-pared, In which Thy love shines forth,

We are un-wor-thy, but Thy Word As-sures to us Thy grace.
It shows how rich-ly Thou hast cared For Thy re-deemed on earth.

3 Here we receive, through bread and wine,
Thy body and Thy blood,
We are refreshed by grace divine
With this most precious food.

4 This is a wondrous mystery,
But we believe Thy Word;
All who confess their sins will see
How Thou dost life afford.

George Henry Trabert, 1922.

248. I Am Not Worthy, Holy Lord.

Crowle. C. M.

JAMES GREEN's Book of Psalm Tunes, 1724.
Arranged by EDWARD JOHN HOPKINS.

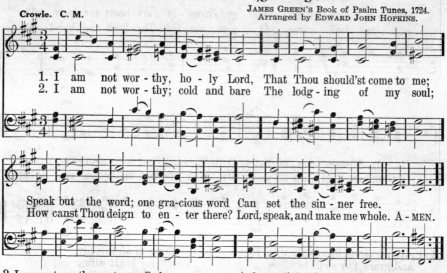

1. I am not wor-thy, ho-ly Lord, That Thou should'st come to me;
2. I am not wor-thy; cold and bare The lodg-ing of my soul;

Speak but the word; one gra-cious word Can set the sin-ner free.
How canst Thou deign to en-ter there? Lord, speak, and make me whole. A-MEN.

3 I am not worthy; yet, my God,
How can I say Thee nay,
Thee who didst give Thy flesh and blood
My ransom-price to pay?

4 O come! in this sweet morning hour
Feed me with food divine,
And fill with all Thy love and power
This worthless heart of mine,

Henry Williams Baker. (1821-1877).

249. O Jesus Christ, Thou Bread of Life.

Du lifvets bröd. 8 7, 8 7, 8 8 7.   PETER SOHREN, 1668.

1. O Je - sus Christ, Thou Bread of Life, To sin - ners free - ly
2. Deign to Thine al - tar, bless - ed Lord, By Thine own hand to

giv - en Who of their e - vil ways re - pent, Cast out all
lead me, There to re - new Thy cov - e - nant, And with Thy

earth - ly leav - en, And gra - cious - ly my heart pre - pare The
gifts to feed me; O give me, in Thy flesh and blood, To

Ho - ly Sup - per now to share, With Thee in blest com - mun - ion.
taste and see that Thou art good; My soul re - fresh and quick - en. A - MEN.

3 O give me strength to walk with Thee,
  And grace Thy steps to follow,
Thus to fulfill the law of God,
  To Him my service hallow.
Bless now Thy sacramental guest,
Take Thine abode within my breast,
  And nevermore forsake me.

4 Cleanse me of all iniquity,
  Renew my heart within me;
My soul so fully occupy
  That evil shall not win me.
As Thou didst suffer on the cross,
So teach Thy child to suffer loss,
  Through faith in Thee, my Saviour.

5 Thy grace, O God, I merit less
  Than stripes of Thy chastising;
In all my sins and dire distress
  I yet were agonizing,
Save for the willing sacrifice
Of Christ, who bought us with a price,
  And earned our full salvation.

6 Sore stricken, unto Thee I come,
  For grace and succor pleading.
Mine eyes are blind; to Thee I turn
  For light and gentle leading.
Whene'er I stumble, raise me up;
When faint and famished, from Thy cup,
  Lord, tender me Thy healing!

7 Come, Saviour dear, with me abide,
  Thy love in me upwelling;
O Holy Spirit, be my Guide,
  And make my heart Thy dwelling.
In all my griefs my comfort be,
Grant me that unity with Thee
  Which life nor death can sever.

8 Before Thy sacred table, Lord,
  My prayers grow faint and falter;
Now make me worthy to partake
  The bounties of Thine altar.
If one with Thee Thou make me there,
I know that also I shall share
  With Thee the joy of heaven.

Johann Rist, 1654.

250. O Jesus, Saviour Dear.

O Gott, du frommer Gott (Meiningen). 6 7, 6 7, 6 6, 6 6.   JOHANN GEORG CHRISTIAN STÖRL, 1710.

1. {O Je - sus, Sav - iour dear, How shall Thy Name be prais - ed!}
   {Thy sa - cred ta - ble now Is spread with gifts most bless - ed.}

With - in that ho - ly cup Is heal - ing for my soul;

Thou art the Bread of Life, Bro - ken to make me whole. A - MEN.

2 The burden of my sins
  Hast Thou in mercy taken;
Thou touchest but my heart,
  And Christian graces waken.
The feeble flame of faith
  Is quickened by Thy grace;
My soul to peace restored,
  With Thee at hand to bless.

3 My Treasure, Lord, Thou art,
  The Fount of every blessing;
If Thou be in my heart,
  All else am I possessing.
Be and abide with me,
  A constant Eucharist,
Then death to me is life
  With Thee, O Jesus Christ.

Johann Heermann, (1585-1647).

251. Blessed Saviour, Who Hast Taught Me.

Ripley. 8 7, 8 7. D.

From a Gregorian Chant,
by LOWELL MASON, 1839.

1. Bless-ed Sav-iour, Thou hast taught me I should live to Thee a-lone,
All these years Thy hand hath brought me, Since I first was made Thine own.
At the font my vows were spok-en By my par-ents in the Lord;
That my vows shall be un-bro-ken, At the al-tar I re-cord. A-MEN.

2 I would trust in Thy protecting,
Wholly rest upon Thine arm;
Follow wholly Thy directing,
O my only Guard from harm!
Meet me now with Thy salvation,
In the Church's ordered way;
Let me feel Thy confirmation
In Thy truth and fear to-day:

3 So that, faith and firmness gaining,
Hope in danger, joy in grief,
Now and evermore remaining
Steadfast in the true belief,
Resting in my Saviour's merit,
Strengthened with the Spirit's strength,
With Thy Church I may inherit
All my Father's joy at length.

John Mason Neale, 1842.

252. Thine Forever! God of Love.

Mercy. 7 7, 7 7. Arranged from LOUIS M. GOTTSCHALK, 1867.

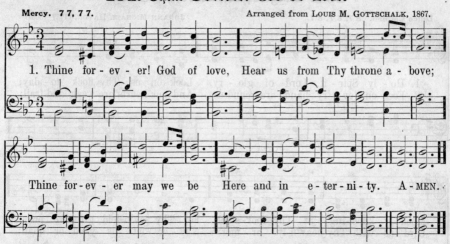

1. Thine for-ev-er! God of love, Hear us from Thy throne a-bove;

Thine for-ev-er may we be Here and in e-ter-ni-ty. A-MEN.

2 Thine forever! Lord of Life,
Shield us through our earthly strife;
Thou, the Life, the Truth, the Way,
Guide us to the realms of day.

3 Thine forever! O how blest
They who find in Thee their rest!
Saviour, Guardian, heavenly Friend,
O defend us to the end.

4 Thine forever! Shepherd, keep
These, Thy frail and trembling sheep,
Safe alone beneath Thy care,
Let us all Thy goodness share.

5 Thine forever! Thou our Guide,
All our wants by Thee supplied,
All our sins by Thee forgiven,
Lead us, Lord, from earth to heaven.

Mary Fawler Maude (Hooper), 1847.

253. O God, Accept My Heart This Day.

Eventide (Smart). C. M. HENRY SMART, 1876.

1. O God, ac-cept my heart this day, And make it al-ways Thine,
2. Be-fore the cross of Him who died, Be-hold, I pros-trate fall;

That I from Thee no more may stray, No more from Thee de-cline.
Let ev-'ry sin be cru-ci-fied, Let Christ be all in all! A-MEN.

3 Anoint me with Thy heavenly grace,
Adopt me for Thine own,
That I may see Thy glorious face,
And worship at Thy throne.

4 Let every thought, and work, and word
To Thee be ever given;
Then life shall be Thy service, Lord,
And death the gate of heaven.

Matthew Bridges, 1848.

254. Holy Spirit, Lord of Glory.

Dulce Carmen. 8 7, 8 7, 8 7.   JOHANN MICHAEL HAYDN, (1737–1806)?

1. Ho-ly Spir-it, Lord of glo-ry, Look on us Thy flock to-day;
2. Foes on ev-'ry hand are round us, And our hearts are weak and frail;

Meek-ly kneel-ing at Thy foot-stool, For Thy sev'n-fold gifts we pray;
Gird us with Thy heav'n-ly ar-mor; Nev-er let us yield or quail;

Guide us all our earth-ly jour-ney In the true and nar-row way.
Give us vic-t'ry in the strug-gle When the hosts of sin as-sail. A-MEN.

3 Lead us by Thy guiding presence
      Through the waste, with danger rife;
   Feed us with the heavenly manna,
      That we faint not in the strife;
   Slake the thirst of weary spirits
      From the living well of life.

4 Looking ever unto Jesus,
      Leaning on His staff and rod,
   May we follow in His footsteps,
      Tread the path that He has trod,
   Till we dwell with Him forever
      In the Paradise with God.

Robert Hall Baynes, 1864.

255. O Happy Day, That Stays My Choice.

Hamburg. L. M.   From a Gregorian Chant,
                    by LOWELL MASON, 1825.

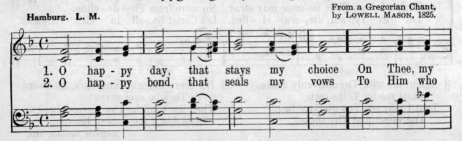

1. O hap-py day, that stays my choice On Thee, my
2. O hap-py bond, that seals my vows To Him who

Sav - iour and my God! Well may this glow - ing heart re-
mer - its all my love! Let cheer - ful an - thems fill His

joice, And tell its rap - tures all a - broad.
house, While to that sa - cred shrine I move. A - MEN.

3 'Tis done, the great transaction's done;
    I am my Lord's, and He is mine:
  He drew me, and I followed on,
    Glad to obey the voice divine.

4 High heav'n, that heard the solemn vow,
    That vow renewed shall daily hear,
  Till in life's latest hour I bow,
    And bless in death a bond so dear.

Philip Doddridge, 1755.

256. With Solemn Joy We Come, Dear Lord.

St. Peter. C. M.   ALEXANDER ROBERT REINAGLE, 1826.

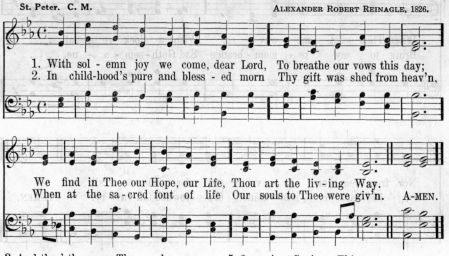

1. With sol - emn joy we come, dear Lord, To breathe our vows this day;
2. In child-hood's pure and bless - ed morn Thy gift was shed from heav'n,

We find in Thee our Hope, our Life, Thou art the liv - ing Way.
When at the sa - cred font of life Our souls to Thee were giv'n. A - MEN.

3 And thro' the years Thy wondrous grace
    Has followed all the way;
  Thy love has never let us go,
    Though we are prone to stray.

4 Forgive, dear Lord, each fault and stain,
    And cleanse our hearts from sin;
  Help us to walk in humble faith,
    And keep us pure within.

5 O precious Saviour, Thine we are,
    Thy Name we would confess;
  Thy Spirit pour into our hearts,
    Our youthful lives to bless.

6 O keep us faithful, keep us true,
    And seal us for Thine own,
  That we may stand at last with joy
    Before Thy great white throne!

Ernest Edwin Ryden, 1923.

257. In the Hour of Trial.

Penitence (Lane). 6 5, 6 5. D.

SPENCER LANE, 1879.

1. In the hour of tri - al, Je - sus, plead for me,
2. With for - bid - den pleas - ures Would this vain world charm,

Lest by base de - ni - al I de - part from Thee;
Or its sor - did treas - ures Spread to work me harm;

When Thou seest me wav - er, With a look re - call, . . .
Bring to my re - mem - brance Sad Geth - sem - a - ne, . . .

Nor from fear or fa - vor Suf - fer me to fall.
Or, in dark - er sem - blance, Cross-crowned Cal-va - ry.   A-MEN.

3 Should Thy mercy send me
    Sorrow, toil, and woe;
Or should pain attend me
    On my path below,
Grant that I may never
    Fail Thy hand to see;
Grant that I may ever
    Cast my care on Thee.

4 When my last hour cometh,
    Fraught with strife and pain,
When my dust returneth
    To the dust again,
On Thy truth relying,
    Through that mortal strife,
Jesus, take me, dying,
    To eternal life.

James Montgomery, 1834, a.

258. O Lord, Our Strength in Weakness.

Need. 7 6, 7 6. D.　　　　　　　　　　　　　　Composer Unknown.

1. O Lord, our strength in weak - ness, We pray to Thee for grace;
2. We then were sealed and hal - lowed By Thy life - giv - ing Word,

For pow'r to fight the bat - tle, For speed to run the race;
Were made the Spir - it's tem - ples, And mem - bers of the Lord;

When Thy bap - tis - mal wa - ters Were poured up - on our brow,
With His own blood He bought us, And made the pur - chase sure;

We then were made Thy chil - dren, And pledged our ear - liest vow.
His are we: may He keep us For - ev - er chaste and pure. A-MEN.

Or: Aurelia, No. 16.

3 Conformed to His own likeness,
　　May we so live and die,
　That in the grave our bodies
　　In holy peace may lie,
　And at the resurrection
　　Forth from those graves may spring
　Like to the glorious body
　　Of Christ, our Lord and King.

4 The pure in heart are blessèd,
　　For they shall see the Lord
　Forever and forever
　　By Seraphim adored;
　And they shall drink the pleasures,
　　Such as no tongue can tell,
　From heaven's crystal river,
　　And life's eternal well.

Christopher Wordsworth, (1807-1885), a.

259. O Jesus, I Have Promised.

Angel's Story (Norwich). 7 6, 7 6. D.   ARTHUR HENRY MANN, 1881.

1. O Je - sus I have prom - ised   To serve Thee to the end;
2. O let me feel Thee near me,   The world is ev - er near;

Be Thou for - ev - er near me,   My Mas - ter and my Friend:
I see the sights that daz - zle,   The tempt - ing sounds I hear:

I shall not fear the bat - tle   If Thou art by my side,
My foes are ev - er near me,   A - round me and with - in;

Nor wan - der from the path - way   If Thou wilt be my Guide.
But, Je - sus, draw Thou near - er,   And shield my soul from sin.   A-MEN.

3 O let me hear Thee speaking
    In accents clear and still,
Above the storms of passion,
    The murmurs of self-will:
O speak to reassure me,
    To hasten or control;
O speak, and make me listen,
    Thou Guardian of my soul.

4 O Jesus, Thou hast promised
    To all who follow Thee
That where Thou art in glory
    There shall Thy servant be;
And, Jesus, I have promised
    To serve Thee to the end;
O give me grace to follow
    My Master and my Friend.

John Ernest Bode, 1868.

260. Take the Name of Jesus with You.

Take the Name. 8 7, 8 7. With Refrain.

WILLIAM HOWARD DOANE, 1871.

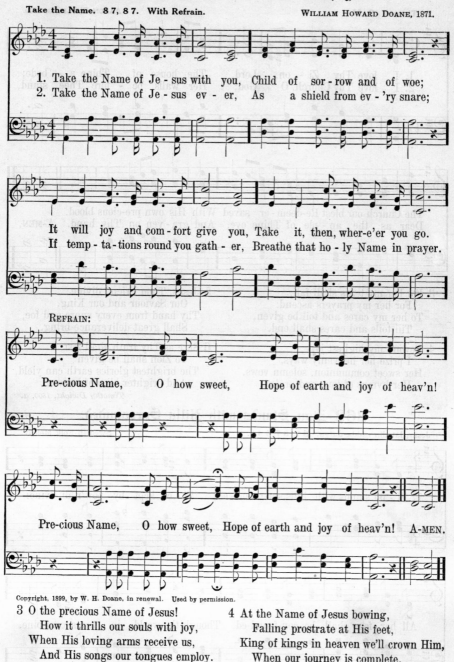

1. Take the Name of Je - sus with you, Child of sor - row and of woe;
2. Take the Name of Je - sus ev - er, As a shield from ev - 'ry snare;

It will joy and com - fort give you, Take it, then, wher-e'er you go.
If temp - ta - tions round you gath - er, Breathe that ho - ly Name in prayer.

REFRAIN:

Pre-cious Name, O how sweet, Hope of earth and joy of heav'n!

Pre-cious Name, O how sweet, Hope of earth and joy of heav'n! A-MEN.

3 O the precious Name of Jesus!
  How it thrills our souls with joy,
When His loving arms receive us,
  And His songs our tongues employ.

4 At the Name of Jesus bowing,
  Falling prostrate at His feet,
King of kings in heaven we'll crown Him,
  When our journey is complete.

Lydia Baxter, 1871.

261. I Love Thy Zion, Lord.

St. Thomas. S. M.   AARON WILLIAMS, 1770.

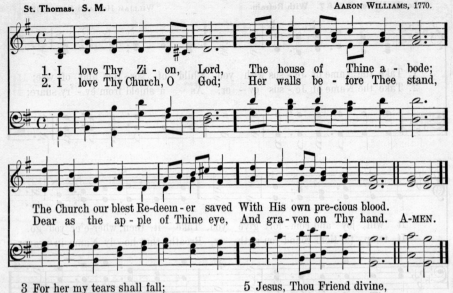

1. I love Thy Zi-on, Lord, The house of Thine a-bode;
2. I love Thy Church, O God; Her walls be-fore Thee stand,

The Church our blest Re-deem-er saved With His own pre-cious blood.
Dear as the ap-ple of Thine eye, And gra-ven on Thy hand. A-MEN.

3 For her my tears shall fall;
   For her my prayers ascend:
To her my cares and toil be given,
   Till toils and cares shall end.

4 Beyond my highest joy
   I prize her heavenly ways,
Her sweet communion, solemn vows,
   Her hymns of love and praise.

5 Jesus, Thou Friend divine,
   Our Saviour and our King,
Thy hand from every snare and foe,
   Shall great deliverance bring.

6 Sure as Thy truth shall last,
   To Zion shall be given
The brightest glories earth can yield,
   And brighter bliss of heaven.

Timothy Dwight, 1800, a.

262 Zion Stands with Hills Surrounded.

Jesus, låt din rädda dufva. 8 7, 8 7, 4 4 7.   Swedish Folk Melody.

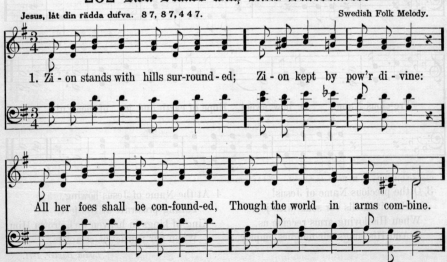

1. Zi-on stands with hills sur-round-ed; Zi-on kept by pow'r di-vine:

All her foes shall be con-found-ed, Though the world in arms com-bine.

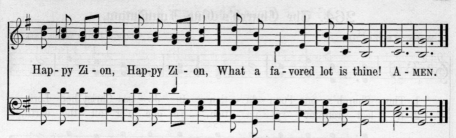

Hap-py Zi-on, Hap-py Zi-on, What a fa-vored lot is thine! A-MEN.

2 Every human tie may perish;
    Friend to friend unfaithful prove;
  Mothers cease their own to cherish;
    Heaven and earth at last remove:
      But no changes
    Can attend Jehovah's love.

3 In the furnace God may prove thee,
    Thence to bring thee forth more bright,
  But can never cease to love thee;
    Thou art precious in His sight:
      God is with thee,
    God, thine everlasting Light.

Thomas Kelly, 1806.

263. Be Not Dismayed, Thou Little Flock.

Agatha. 8 8 7, 8 8 7.   CARL JOHANNES SÖDERGREN, 1924.

1. Be not dis-mayed, thou lit-tle flock, Al-though the foe's fierce bat-tle shock

Loud on all sides as-sail thee. Though o'er thy fall they laugh se-cure,

Their tri-umph can-not long en-dure, Let not thy cour-age fail thee. A-MEN.

2 Thy cause is God's—go at His call,
  And to His hand commit thine all;
    Fear thou no ill impending;
  His Gideon shall arise for thee,
  God's Word and people manfully
    In God's own time defending.

3 Our hope is sure in Jesus' might;
  Against themselves the godless fight,
    Themselves, not us, distressing;
  Shame and contempt their lot shall be;
  God is with us, with Him are we;
    To us belongs His blessing.

Johann Michael Altenburg, 1632.

264. The Church's One Foundation.

Webb. 76, 76. D.

GEORGE JAMES WEBB, 1830.

1. The Church's one Foun-da-tion Is Je-sus Christ her Lord:
2. E-lect from ev-'ry na-tion, Yet one o'er all the earth,

She is His new cre-a-tion By wa-ter and the Word;
Her char-ter of sal-va-tion One Lord, one faith, one birth,

From heav'n He came and sought her To be His ho-ly Bride,
One ho-ly Name she bless-es, Par-takes one ho-ly food,

With His own blood He bought her, And for her life He died.
And to one hope she press-es, With ev-'ry grace en-dued. A-MEN.

3 Though with a scornful wonder
  Men see her sore opprest,
By conflicts rent asunder,
  By heresies distrest,
Yet saints their watch are keeping,
  Their cry goes up, "How long?"
And soon the night of weeping
  Shall be the morn of song.

4 'Mid toil, and tribulation,
  And tumult of her war,
She waits for consummation
  Of peace forevermore;
Till with the vision glorious
  Her longing eyes are blest,
And the great Church victorious
  Shall be the Church at rest.

Samuel John Stone, 1866.

265. Thy Scepter, Jesus, Shall Extend.

Es ist gewisslich an der Zeit. 8 7, 8 7, 8 8 7.   Wittenberg Gesangbuch, 1535.

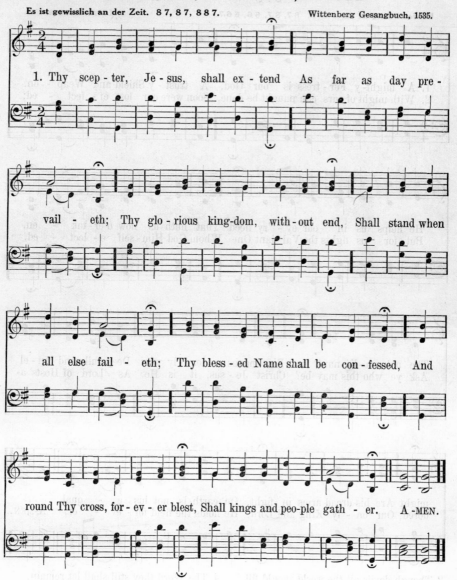

1. Thy scep - ter, Je - sus, shall ex - tend As far as day prevail - eth; Thy glo - rious king-dom, with-out end, Shall stand when
all else fail - eth; Thy bless - ed Name shall be con - fessed, And
round Thy cross, for - ev - er blest, Shall kings and peo-ple gath - er. A -MEN.

2 The child when born to Thee we take,
  To Thee in death we hasten;
In joy we often Thee forsake,
  But not when sorrows chasten.
Where truth and virtue are oppressed,
Where sorrow dwells, pain and unrest,
  Thy help alone availeth.

3 Come, Jesus, then, in weal and woe,
  In life and death be near us;
Thy grace upon our hearts bestow,
  And let Thy Spirit cheer us,
For every conflict strength afford,
And gather us in peace, O Lord,
  When all the world Thou judgest.

Frans Mikael Franzén, 1816.

266. A Mighty Fortress Is Our God.

Ein feste Burg ist unser Gott.   8 7, 8 7, 6 6, 6 6 7.   MARTIN LUTHER, 1529.

1. A might-y For-tress is our God, A trust-y Shield and Weap - on,
2. With might of ours can naught be done, Soon were our loss ef - fect - ed;

He helps us in   our ev - 'ry need That hath us now o'er-tak - en.
But for   us fights the Val-iant One Whom God Him-self e - lect - ed.

The old ma-lig-nant foe E'er means us dead-ly woe: Deep guile and cru - el
Ask ye who this may be? Christ Je - sus, it is He, As   Lord of Hosts a -

might Are his dread arms in fight, On earth is not his e - qual.
dored, Our on - ly King and Lord, He holds the field for - ev - er. A-MEN.

3 Though devils all the world should fill,
  All watching to devour us,
We tremble not, we fear no ill,
  They cannot overpower us.
    For this world's prince may still
    Scowl fiercely as he will,
      We need not be alarmed,
      For he is now disarmed;
  One little word o'erthrows him.

4 The Word they still shall let remain,
  Nor any thanks have for it;
He's by our side upon the plain,
  With His good gifts and Spirit
    Take they, then, what they will,
    Life, goods, yea, all; and still,
      E'en when their worst is done,
      They yet have nothing won,
  The kingdom ours remaineth,

Martin Luther, 1529.

267. Chosen Seed and Zion's Children.

Love Divine No. 2. 8 7, 8 7. D.

GEORGE FITZ-CURWOOD LE JEUNE, 1872.

1. Cho - sen seed and Zi - on's chil - dren, Ran - somed from e - ter - nal wrath,
2. Still re - joice a - mid thy tri - als, Nor re - gard thy lot a - miss;

Trav - 'ling to the heav'n-ly Ca - naan On a rough and thorn - y path;
For the kind and lov - ing Sav - iour Is the source of all our bliss.

Church of God in Christ e - lect - ed, Thou to God art rec - on - ciled,
May He ev - er be thy por - tion, He who gave thee life and breath:

But on earth thou art a stran-ger, Per - se - cu - ted and re - viled.
In His keep-ing fear no e - vil Now or in the hour of death. A - MEN.

Or: Jesus är min vän den bäste, No. 245.

3 Pleasantly thy lines have fallen
    Underneath the tree of life;
For the Lord is thy salvation,
    And thy shield in all thy strife:
Here the sparrow finds a shelter,
    Here the swallow finds a nest,
Trembling fugitive a refuge,
    And the weary pilgrim rest.

4 And upon this blest foundation,
    Lord, our Lord, and Saviour King,
May Thy Spirit e'er unite us,
    To it may we ever cling.
May we, members of one body,
    Grow into a perfect whole;
Grant, O Lord, that in Thy people
    There may be one heart and soul.

Andreas Carl Rutström, (1721-1772).

268. Abide with Us, O Saviour Dear.

Brookfield. L. M.   THOMAS BISHOP SOUTHGATE, 1855.

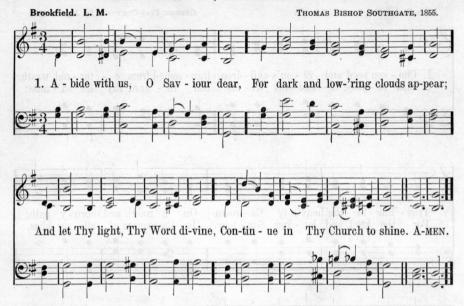

1. A - bide with us,   O Sav - iour dear,   For dark and low-'ring clouds ap-pear;

And let Thy light, Thy Word di-vine, Con-tin - ue in   Thy Church to shine. A-MEN.

2 This is a dark and evil day,
  Forsake us not, O Lord, we pray;
  And let us in our grief and pain
  Thy Word and sacraments retain.

3 Lord Jesus, help, Thy Church uphold,
  For we are weak, indifferent, cold;
  Give us Thy Spirit and Thy grace,
  And spread Thy truth in every place.

4 And keep us steadfast in Thy Word,
  Stay Satan's fatal wiles, O Lord;
  To us Thy grace and power reveal,
  And let Thy Church Thy presence feel.

5 And since the cause is Thine, we pray,
  Do Thou the arm of evil stay;
  And grace and power and wisdom lend
  To those who would Thy Word defend.

6 Thy Word is in distress and need
  Our comfort and defense indeed;
  By it Thy Church keep pure within
  And free from error, shame, and sin.

7 Grant that Thy Word may light our way,
  That we in darkness may not stray,
  But, through this vale of sin and woe,
  May to the heavenly mansions go.

Nicolaus Selnecker, 1611.

269. On the Mountain's Top Appearing.

Orient Morning. 8 7, 8 7, 4 7.   ARTHUR HENRY MANN, 1885.

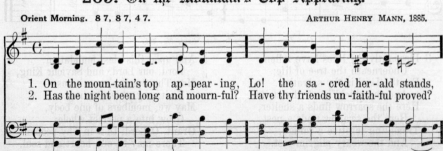

1. On the moun-tain's top   ap - pear - ing, Lo!   the sa - cred her - ald stands,
2. Has the night been long and mourn-ful? Have thy friends un -faith-ful proved?

Wel-come news to Zi - on bear - ing, Zi - on long in hos - tile lands.
Have thy foes been proud and scorn - ful, By thy sighs and tears un - moved?

Mourn - ing cap - tive, God Him - self will loose thy bands.
Cease thy mourn-ing, Zi - on still is well be - loved. A-MEN.

3 God, thy God, will now restore thee;
   He Himself appears thy Friend;
   All thy foes shall flee before thee;
     Here their boasts and triumphs end:
       Great deliverance
   Zion's King will surely send.

4 Enemies no more shall trouble;
   All thy wrongs shall be redressed:
   For thy loss thou shalt have double,
     In thy Maker's favor blest:
       All thy conflicts
   End in everlasting rest.

Thomas Kelly, 1802, a.

270. O Where Are Kings and Empires Now?

Wiltshire. C. M.   GEORGE THOMAS SMART, (1776-1867).

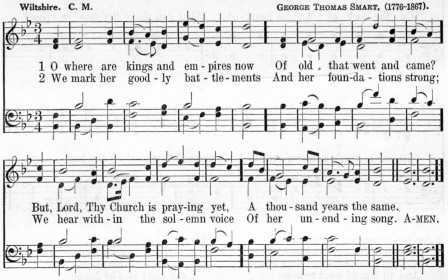

1 O where are kings and em - pires now Of old , that went and came?
2 We mark her good - ly bat - tle - ments And her foun-da - tions strong;

But, Lord, Thy Church is pray-ing yet, A thou - sand years the same.
We hear with - in the sol - emn voice Of her un - end - ing song. A-MEN.

3 For not like kingdoms of the world
     Thy holy Church, O God!   [her,
   Though earthquake shocks are threatening
     And tempests are abroad.

4 Unshaken as eternal hills,
     Immovable she stands,
   A mountain that shall fill the earth,
     A house not made by hands.

Arthur Cleveland Coxe, 1839.

271. Glorious Things of Thee Are Spoken.

Harwell. 8 7, 8 7. D.   LOWELL MASON, 1840.

1. Glo-rious things of thee are spo-ken, Zi-on, cit-y of our God;

He, whose Word can not be bro-ken, Formed thee for His own a-bode.

On the Rock of A-ges found-ed, What can shake thy sure re-pose?

With sal-va-tion's walls sur-round-ed, Thou may'st smile at all thy foes. A-MEN.

2 See the streams of living waters,
    Springing from eternal love,
Well supply thy sons and daughters,
    And all fear of want remove.
Who can faint while such a river
    Ever flows their thirst to assuage;
Grace, which, like the Lord, the Giver,
    Never fails from age to age?

3 Saviour, if of Zion's city
    I, through grace, a member am,
Let the world deride or pity,
    I will glory in Thy Name.
Fading is the worldling's pleasure,
    All his boasted pomp and show;
Solid joys and lasting treasure
    None but Zion's children know.

John Newton, 1779.

272. With God and His Mercy, His Spirit, and Word.

Ack, saliga stunder. 11 11 11, 6 6 11.   OSKAR AHNFELT, (1813–1882).

1. With God and His mer-cy, His Spir-it, and Word, And lov-ing com-mun-ion at al-tar and board, We meet with as-sur-ance the dawn of each day: The Shep-herd is with us, The Shep-herd is with us, To lead and pro-tect us, and teach us the way. A-MEN.

2 In perilous times, amid tempests and night,
A band presses on through the gloom
    toward light;
Though humble, and meek, and disowned
    by the world,
They follow the Saviour,
And march on to glory, with banners
    unfurled.

3 While groveling worldlings with dross
    are content,
And ever on sin and transgression are
    bent,
I follow, victorious hosts, at your word,
    And march on to glory,
We march on to glory, our captain the Lord.

4 The sign of the cross I triumphantly bear,
Though none of my kindred that emblem
    may wear;
I joyfully follow the champions of right,
    Who march on to glory,
Who march on to glory, with weapons of
    might.

5 O Shepherd, abide with us, care for us still,
And feed us and lead us and teach us
    Thy will;
And when in Thy heavenly fold we shall
    be,
    Our thanks and our praises,
Our thanks and our praises we'll render
    to Thee.

Carl Olof Rosenius, (1816–1868).

273. Christ, Thou Art the Sure Foundation.

Regent Square.   8 7, 8 7, 8 7.   HENRY SMART, 1867.

1. Christ, Thou art the sure Foun-da - tion, Thou the Head and Cor - ner-stone;
2. To   this tem - ple, where we call Thee, Come, O Lord of Hosts, to - day!

Cho - sen of   the Lord, and pre-cious, Bind - ing all   the Church in one;
With Thy wont - ed   lov - ing-kind-ness Hear Thy serv - ants as they pray,

Thou Thy Zi-on's help for - ev - er, And her con - fi - dence a - lone.
And Thy full-est ben - e - dic - tion Shed with-in these walls al - way.   A-MEN.

3 Here vouchsafe to all Thy servants
  What they ask of Thee to gain,
What they gain from Thee forever
  With the blessèd to retain,
And hereafter in Thy glory
  Evermore with Thee to reign.

4 Praise and honor to the Father,
  Praise and honor to the Son,
Praise and honor to the Spirit,
  Ever Three and ever One;
One in might and one in glory,
  While eternal ages run.

Latin, 6th or 7th Century.

274. On This Stone Now Laid with Prayer.

Gud, vår Gud, för världen all.   7 7, 7 7.   JOHAN FREDRIK LAGERGREN, b. 1826.

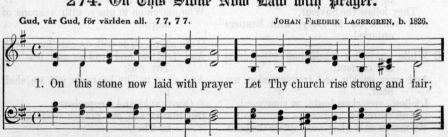

1. On this stone now laid with prayer Let Thy church rise strong and fair;

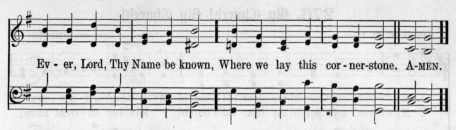

Ev - er, Lord, Thy Name be known, Where we lay this cor-ner-stone. A-MEN.

2 Let Thy holy Child, who came
Man from error to reclaim,
And for sinners to atone,
Bless, with Thee, this corner-stone.

3 May Thy Spirit here give rest
To the heart by sin oppressed,
And the seeds of truth be sown,
Where we lay this corner-stone.

4 Open wide, O God, Thy door
For the outcast and the poor,
Who can call no house their own,
Where we lay this corner-stone.

5 By wise master-builders squared,
Here be living stones prepared
For the temple near Thy throne,
Jesus Christ its Corner-stone.

John Pierpont, 1839.

275. O Lord of Hosts, Whose Glory Fills.

Old Hundredth. L. M.

LOUIS BOURGEOIS,
The Genevan Psalter, 1551.

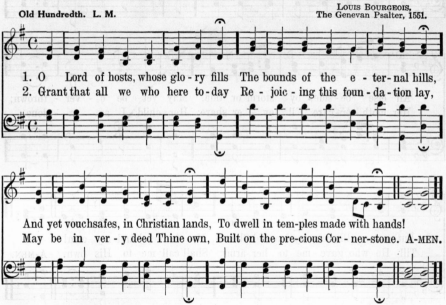

1. O Lord of hosts, whose glo-ry fills The bounds of the e-ter-nal hills,
2. Grant that all we who here to-day Re-joic-ing this foun-da-tion lay,

And yet vouchsafes, in Christian lands, To dwell in tem-ples made with hands!
May be in ver-y deed Thine own, Built on the pre-cious Cor-ner-stone. A-MEN.

3 Endue the creatures with Thy grace,
That shall adorn Thy dwelling-place;
The beauty of the oak and pine,
The gold and silver, make them Thine.

4 To Thee they all belong; to Thee
The treasures of the earth and sea;
And when we bring them to Thy throne,
We but present Thee with Thine own.

5 The minds that guide, endue with skill;
The hands that work, preserve from ill;
That we, who these foundations lay,
May raise the top-stone in its day.

6 Both now and ever, Lord, protect
The temple of Thine own elect;
Be Thou in them, and they in Thee,
O ever blessèd Trinity!

John Mason Neale, 1844.

276. My Church! My Church!

Athens. C. M. D.   FELICE DE GIARDINI, (1716–1796).

1. My Church! my Church! my dear old Church! My fa-thers' and my own!
2. My Church! my Church! my dear old Church! I love her an-cient name;

On proph-ets and a-pos-tles built, And Christ the cor-ner-stone!
And God for-bid, a child of hers Should ev-er cause her shame!

All else be-side, by storm or tide, May yet be o-ver-thrown;
Her moth-er-care I'll ev-er share; Her child I am a-lone,

But not my Church, my dear old Church, My fa-thers' and my own!
Till He who gave me to her arms Shall call me to His own. A-MEN.

3 My Church! my Church! I love my Church,
   For she doth lead me on
To Zion's palace beautiful,
   Where Christ my Lord hath gone.
From all below she bids me go
   To Him, the Life, the Way,
The Truth to guide my erring feet
   From darkness into day.

4 Then here, my Church! my dear old Church!
   Thy child would add a vow,
To that whose token once was signed
   Upon his infant brow:—
Assault who may, kiss and betray,
   Dishonor and disown,
My Church shall yet be dear to me,
   My fathers' and my own!

Anonymous.

277. Here, in Thy Name, Eternal God.

Vom Himmel hoch da komm ich her. L. M.

VALENTIN SCHUMANN'S
Geistliche Lieder, Leipzig, 1539.

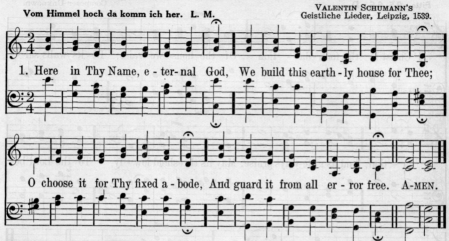

1. Here in Thy Name, e-ter-nal God, We build this earth-ly house for Thee;

O choose it for Thy fixed a-bode, And guard it from all er-ror free. A-MEN.

2 Here, when Thy people seek Thy face,
  And dying sinners pray to live,
Hear Thou in heaven, Thy dwelling-place,
  And when Thou hearest, Lord, forgive.

3 Here, when Thy messengers proclaim
  The blessèd gospel of Thy Son,
Still, by the power of Thy great Name,
  Be mighty signs and wonders done.

4 When children's voices raise the song,
  Hosanna to the heavenly King,
Let heaven, with earth, the strain prolong;
  Hosanna let the angels sing.

5 Thy glory never hence depart;
  Yet choose not, Lord, this house alone;
Thy kingdom come to every heart;
  In every bosom fix Thy throne.

James Montgomery, 1817.

278. Thou, Whose Unmeasured Temple Stands.

Lambeth. C. M.

WILHELM A. F. SCHULTHES, 1871.

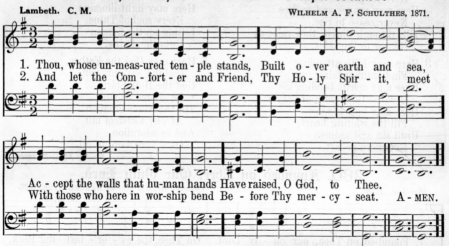

1. Thou, whose un-meas-ured tem-ple stands, Built o-ver earth and sea,
2. And let the Com-fort-er and Friend, Thy Ho-ly Spir-it, meet

Ac-cept the walls that hu-man hands Have raised, O God, to Thee.
With those who here in wor-ship bend Be-fore Thy mer-cy-seat. A-MEN.

3 May they who err be guided here
  To find the better way;
And they who mourn and they who fear
  Be strengthened as they pray.

4 May faith grow firm, and love grow warm,
  And hallowed wishes rise,
While round these peaceful walls the storm
  Of earth-born passion dies.

William Cullen Bryant, 1820.

279. Christ Is the Foundation.

Pitts. 6 5, 6 5. D.   Composer Unknown.

1 Christ is the foun-da - tion Of the house we raise; Be its walls sal-
va - tion, And its gate-ways praise. May its threshold low - ly To the Lord be
dear, May the hearts be ho - ly That shall wor - ship here. A - MEN.

Or: Urswicke, No. 200.

2 On the Rock of Ages
　Resting broad and deep,
When life's tempest rages
　Here let passion sleep:
Here may prayer and praises
　Never cease to rise,
Till, through Christ, they raise us
　Nearer to the skies.

3 Here may faith attending
　Find fruition fair;
Here may spirits bending
　Breathe the breath of prayer:
Here may holy gladness
　Fill the waiting heart,
Until sin and sadness
　Evermore depart.

4 Here may every token
　Of thy presence be,
Here may chains be broken,
　Prisoners here set free:
Here may light illumine
　Every soul of Thine,
Lifting up the human
　Unto the divine.

5 Here may God the Father,
　God the Saviour, Son,
God the Holy Spirit,
　Be adored as One;
Till the whole creation
　At Thy footstool fall,
And in adoration
　Own Thee Lord of all.

John Samuel Bewley Monsell, 1866.

280. Founded on Thee, Our Only Lord.

Mendon. L. M.   German Melody: arr. by SAMUEL DYER, 1828.

1. Found-ed on Thee, our on - ly Lord, On Thee, the ev - er - last-ing Rock,
2. For Thee our wait - ing spir - its yearn, For Thee this house of praise we rear;

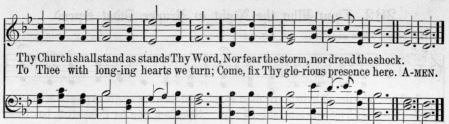

Thy Church shall stand as stands Thy Word, Nor fear the storm, nor dread the shock.
To Thee with long-ing hearts we turn; Come, fix Thy glo-rious presence here. A-MEN.

3 Come, with Thy Spirit and Thy power,
 The Conqueror, once the Crucified;
Our God, our Strength, our King, our Tower,
 Here plant Thy throne, and here abide.

4 Accept the work our hands have wrought;
 Accept, O God, this earthly shrine;
Be Thou our Rock, our Life, our Thought,
 And we, as living temples, Thine.

Samuel Francis Smith, 1894.

281. Jehovah, God, Who Dwelt of Old.

Coronation. C. M.   OLIVER HOLDEN, 1793.

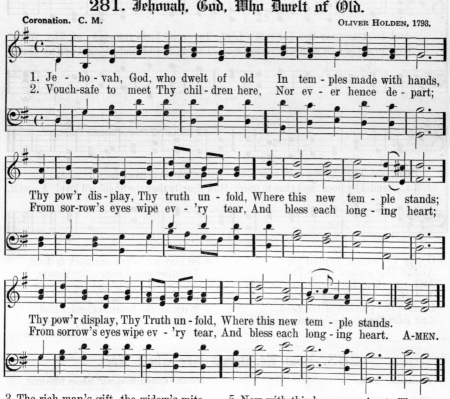

1. Je - ho - vah, God, who dwelt of old   In tem - ples made with hands,
2. Vouch-safe to meet Thy chil - dren here, Nor ev - er hence de - part;

Thy pow'r dis - play, Thy truth un - fold, Where this new tem - ple stands;
From sor-row's eyes wipe ev - 'ry tear, And bless each long - ing heart;

Thy pow'r display, Thy Truth un - fold, Where this new tem - ple stands.
From sorrow's eyes wipe ev - 'ry tear, And bless each long - ing heart. A-MEN.

3 The rich man's gift, the widow's mite
 Are blended in these walls;
These altars welcome all alike
 Who heed God's gracious calls.

4 From things unholy and unclean
 We separate this place;
May naught here ever come between
 This people and Thy face.

5 Now with this house we give to Thee
 Ourselves, our hearts, our all,
The pledge of faith and loyalty,
 Held subject to Thy call.

6 And when at last the blood-washed throng
 Is gathered from all lands,
We'll enter with triumphant song
 The house not made with hands.

Lewis R. Amis, (1856-1904).

282. Thou Who the Night in Prayer Didst Spend.

Han lefver! o min ande känn. 8 8, 8 8, 8 8.   HAEFFNER'S Koralbok, 1819.

1. Thou Who the night in prayer didst spend, And then the twelve to preach didst send;
2. O   may Thy pas - tors faith-ful   be,   Not   la-b'ring for themselves, but Thee;

And bidst us pray the har-vest's Lord   To   send forth sow - ers   of Thy Word,
Give grace to feed with wholesome food   The sheep and lambs bought by Thy blood;

Hear, and Thy cho-sen serv-ants bless With sev'nfold gifts of ho - li - ness.
To   tend Thy flock, and thus to prove How dear-ly they the Shepherd love! A - MEN.

3 O may Thy people faithful be,
   And in Thy pastors honor Thee,
   And with them work, and for them pray,
   And gladly Thee in them obey;
   Receive the prophet of the Lord,
   And gain the prophet's own reward!

4 So may we, when our work is done,
   Together stand before the throne,
   And joyful hearts and voices raise
   In one united song of praise,
   With all the bright celestial host,
   To Father, Son, and Holy Ghost.

Anonymous.

283. How Beauteous Are Their Feet.

Franconia. S. M.   JOHANN GEORG EBELING? (about 1620-1676).

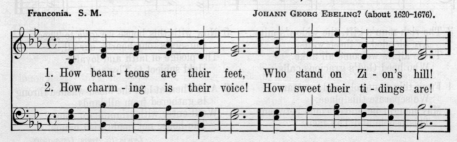

1. How beau - teous   are   their   feet,   Who stand on   Zi - on's   hill!
2. How charm - ing   is   their   voice!   How sweet their ti - dings are!

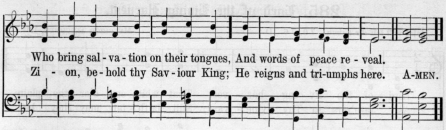

Who bring sal - va - tion on their tongues, And words of peace re - veal.
Zi - on, be - hold thy Sav - iour King; He reigns and tri - umphs here. A-MEN.

3 How happy are our ears,
   That hear this joyful sound,
Which kings and prophets waited for,
   And sought, but never found!

4 How blessèd are our eyes,
   That see this heavenly light!
Thy saints of old desired it long,
   But died without the sight.

5 The watchmen join their voice,
   And tuneful notes employ;
Jerusalem breaks forth in songs,
   And deserts learn the joy.

6 The Lord makes bare His arm
   Through all the earth abroad;
Let all the nations now behold
   Their Saviour and their God.

Isaac Watts, 1707.

284. Lord of the Church, We Humbly Pray.

Purleigh. 8 8 6. D.   ARTHUR HENRY BROWN, 1856.

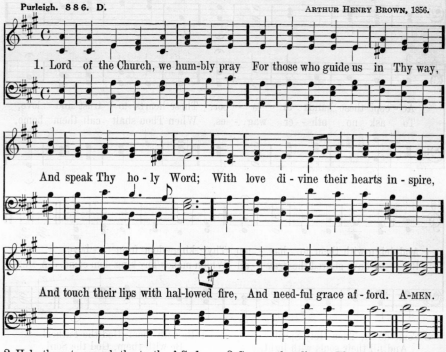

1. Lord of the Church, we hum-bly pray For those who guide us in Thy way,

And speak Thy ho - ly Word; With love di - vine their hearts in - spire,

And touch their lips with hal-lowed fire, And need-ful grace af - ford. A-MEN.

2 Help them to preach the truth of God,
   Redemption through the Saviour's blood;
   Nor let the Spirit cease
On all the Church His gifts to shower;
   To them a Messenger of power,
     To us, of life and peace.

3 So may they live to Thee alone,
   Then hear the welcome word, "Well done!"
   And take their crown above;
Enter into their Master's joy,
   And all eternity employ
     In praise, and bliss, and love.

Edward Osler, 1836.

285. Lord of the Living Harvest.

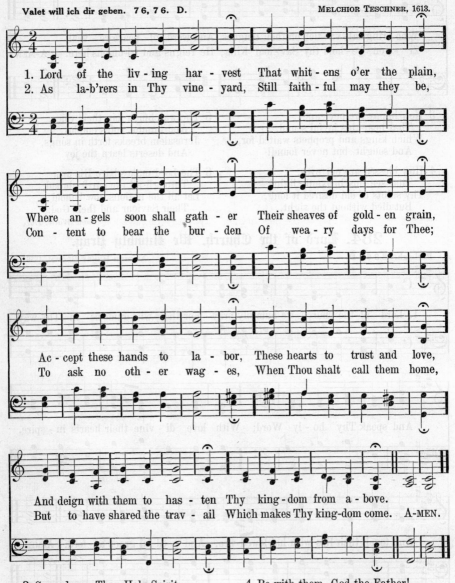

Valet will ich dir geben. 7 6, 7 6. D.   MELCHIOR TESCHNER, 1613.

1. Lord of the liv-ing har-vest That whit-ens o'er the plain,
2. As la-b'rers in Thy vine-yard, Still faith-ful may they be,

Where an-gels soon shall gath-er Their sheaves of gold-en grain,
Con-tent to bear the bur-den Of wea-ry days for Thee;

Ac-cept these hands to la-bor, These hearts to trust and love,
To ask no oth-er wag-es, When Thou shalt call them home,

And deign with them to has-ten Thy king-dom from a-bove.
But to have shared the trav-ail Which makes Thy king-dom come. A-MEN.

3 Come down, Thou Holy Spirit,
  And fill their souls with light,
Clothe them in spotless raiment,
  In vesture clean and white;
Within Thy sacred temple
  Be with them where they stand,
To guide and teach Thy people
  In this and every land.

4 Be with them, God the Father!
  Be with them, God the Son!
And God the Holy Spirit!
  Most blessèd Three in One!
Make them Thy chosen heralds,
  On them the Spirit pour,
And fill them with Thy fullness
  Both now and evermore!

John Samuel Bewley Monsell, 1866.

286. Father, Be Thy Blessing Shed.

Schwing dich auf zu deinem Gott. 7 7, 7 7. D.　　　　　　JOHANN CRÜGER. 1653.

1. Fa - ther, be Thy bless - ing shed　On Thy cho - sen serv - ant's head;
2. Seal this day the vows that hold　Flock and shep - herd in one fold.

Sav - iour, need - ed grace im - part　To sus - tain and keep his heart;
May he Je - sus' man - date keep,　"Feed My lambs," and "Feed My sheep!"

Ho - ly Spir - it, with Thy fire　Touch his lips, his soul in - spire,
By Thee to Thy peo - ple sent　With Thy Word and Sac - ra - ment,

That Thy truth thro' him be told Fear - less - ly to young and old.
May he so pro - claim the Word That who hear him hear Thee, Lord. A-MEN.

3 In Thy vineyard called to toil,
　Wisely may he search the soil;
　Sinners may he love and win,
　While he hates and brands the sin.
　Give him boldness for the right,
　Give him meekness in the fight,
　Teach him zeal and care to blend,
　Give him patience to the end.

4 Grant him in his charge to find
　Listening ear and fervent mind,
　Helpful counsel, deepening peace,
　Earnest life and glad increase;
　May they, by each other led,
　Grow to one in Christ, their Head,
　And at last together be
　Ripe for heaven and meet for Thee.

Samuel Gilman, 1869.

287. Heavenly Shepherd, Thee We Pray.

O Liebe meiner Liebe. 7 7, 7 7. D.   Manuscript Herrnhut Choralbuch, 1735.

1. Heav'n-ly Shep-herd, Thee we pray For Thy serv-ant here to - day:
2. From the si - lent pow'r of sin Lurk-ing se - cret-ly with - in,

By the charge he tak - eth now, By his or - di - na - tion vow,
May the grace that flows from Thee, Heav'n-ly Shep-herd, set him free;

By the prayers which we have prayed For the Ho - ly Spir - it's aid,
Thou, the Way, the Truth, the Life, Gird him for the sa - cred strife,

Grant him faith-ful watch to keep, Tend Thy lambs, and feed Thy sheep.
Aye his faith-ful watch to keep, Tend Thy lambs, and feed Thy sheep. A-MEN.

See also hymns under "Christian Service."

3 Speed him on his life-long way,
Speed him whom we speed to-day,
Till he win the promised crown,
When he lays his burden down
Humbly at his Saviour's feet,
Low before the mercy-seat:
Give him, Lord, Thy grace to keep,
Tend Thy lambs, and feed Thy sheep.

4 To the blessèd Trinity
Now let praise and glory be,
In whose Name we meet to-day
For our guidance, as we pray
That we may, in all we do,
Pastor, and his flock, be true.
Till we, sheep and shepherd, meet,
Ransomed at Thy judgment seat.

Charles Goddard Woodhouse, (1835-1876).

288. Sing Praise to God Who Reigns Above.

Af himlens här den högstes makt. 8 7, 8 7, 8 8 7.   Swedish, 1697.

1. Sing praise to God who reigns a-bove, The God of all cre-a-tion,
2. The an-gel host, O King of kings, Thy praise for-ev-er tell-ing,

The God of pow'r, the God of love, The God of our sal-
In earth and sky all liv-ing things Be-neath Thy shad-ow

va-tion. With heal-ing balm my soul He fills, And ev-'ry
dwell-ing A-dore the wis-dom that could span, And pow'r which

faith-less mur-mur stills; To God all praise and glo-ry!
formed cre-a-tion's plan; To God all praise and glo-ry! A-MEN.

3 I cried to God in my distress,
  His mercy heard me calling;
My Saviour saw my helplessness,
  And kept my feet from falling;
For this, Lord, praise and thanks to Thee!
Praise God Most High, praise God with me!
  To God all praise and glory!

4 Thus all my gladsome way along,
  I'll sing aloud Thy praises,
That men may hear the grateful song
  My voice unwearied raises:
Be joyful in the Lord, my heart!
Both soul and body, bear your part!
  To God all praise and glory!

Johann Jakob Schütz, 1675.

289. Praise the Lord, Each Tribe and Nation.

Hela världen fröjdes Herran! 8 7, 8 7, 7 7.   Swedish, 1689.

1. Praise the Lord, each tribe and na-tion, Praise Him with a joy-ous heart;

Ye who know His full sal-va-tion, Gath-er now from ev-'ry part;

Let your voic-es glo-ri-fy In His tem-ple God on high. A-MEN.

2 He's our God and our Creator,
   We, His flock and chosen seed:
He, our Lord and Liberator,
   Us from sin and peril freed;
And at last His flock shall rest
In the mansions of the blest.

3 Magnify Him in His portals;
   In His courts His deeds proclaim;
Hither come, ye ransomed mortals,
   Glorify our Saviour's Name.
Ever kind and loving, He
Keeps His faith eternally.

Johann Franck, 1650.

290. Before Jehovah's Awful Throne.

Old Hundredth. L. M.   LOUIS BOURGEOIS.
                                            Genevan Psalter, 1551.

1. Be-fore Je-ho-vah's aw-ful throne, Ye na-tions, bow with sa-cred joy;

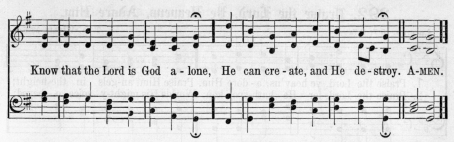

Know that the Lord is God a - lone, He can cre - ate, and He de - stroy. A-MEN.

2 His sovereign power, without our aid,
  Made us of clay, and formed us men;
  And when like wandering sheep we strayed,
  He brought us to His fold again.

3 We are His people, we His care,
  Our souls and all our mortal frame:
  What lasting honors shall we rear,
  Almighty Maker, to Thy Name?

4 We'll crowd Thy gates with thankful songs,
  High as the heavens our voices raise;
  And earth, with her ten thousand tongues,
  Shall fill Thy courts with sounding praise.

5 Wide as the world is Thy command,
  Vast as eternity Thy love;
  Firm as a rock Thy truth must stand,
  When rolling years shall cease to move.

Isaac Watts, 1719.

291. O Bless the Lord, My Soul!

St. Thomas. S. M.   AARON WILLIAMS, 1770.

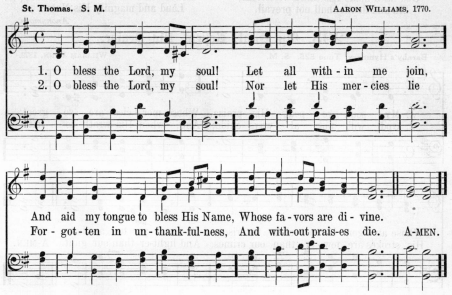

1. O bless the Lord, my soul! Let all with - in me join,
2. O bless the Lord, my soul! Nor let His mer - cies lie

And aid my tongue to bless His Name, Whose fa - vors are di - vine.
For - got - ten in un - thank - ful - ness, And with - out prais - es die. A-MEN.

3 'Tis He forgives thy sins;
  'Tis He relieves thy pain;
  'Tis He that heals thy sicknesses,
  And gives thee strength again.

4 He crowns thy life with love,
  When ransomed from the grave.
  He that redeemed my soul from death
  Hath sovereign power to save.

5 He fills the poor with good;
  He gives the sufferers rest;
  The Lord hath judgments for the proud,
  And justice for the opprest.

6 His wondrous works and ways
  He made by Moses known,
  But sent the world His truth and grace
  By His belovèd Son.

Isaac Watts, 1719.

292. Praise the Lord, Ye Heavens, Adore Him.

Lucerne. 8 7, 8 7.

T. A. WILLIS, 1876.

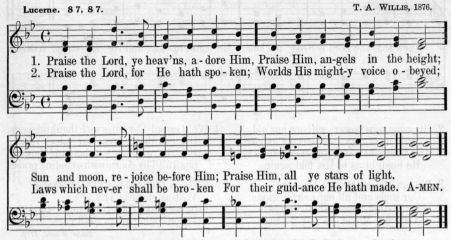

1. Praise the Lord, ye heav'ns, a-dore Him, Praise Him, an-gels in the height;
2. Praise the Lord, for He hath spo-ken; Worlds His might-y voice o-beyed;

Sun and moon, re-joice be-fore Him; Praise Him, all ye stars of light.
Laws which nev-er shall be bro-ken For their guid-ance He hath made. A-MEN.

3 Praise the Lord, for He is glorious;
   Never shall His promise fail;
God hath made His saints victorious,
   Sin and death shall not prevail.

4 Praise the God of our salvation,
   Hosts on high, His power proclaim;
Heaven and earth, and all creation,
   Laud and magnify His Name.

Anonymous.

293. My Soul, Repeat His Praise.

Barnby's Hymnary, Tune 525. S. M.

WILLIAM WINN, 1872.

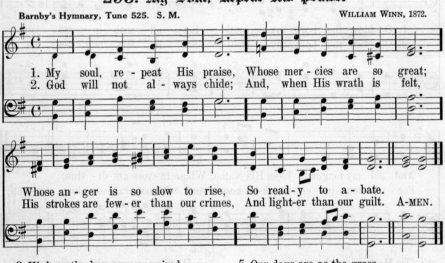

1. My soul, re-peat His praise, Whose mer-cies are so great;
2. God will not al-ways chide; And, when His wrath is felt,

Whose an-ger is so slow to rise, So read-y to a-bate.
His strokes are few-er than our crimes, And light-er than our guilt. A-MEN.

3 High as the heavens are raised
   Above the ground we tread,
So far the riches of His grace
   Our highest thoughts exceed.

4 His power subdues our sins;
   And His forgiving love,
Far as the east is from the west,
   Doth all our guilt remove.

5 Our days are as the grass,
   Or like the morning flower;
If one sharp blast sweep o'er the field,
   It withers in an hour.

6 But Thy compassions, Lord,
   To endless years endure,
And children's children ever find
   Thy words of promise sure.

Isaac Watts, 1719

294. Come, Sound His Praise Abroad.

Dennis. S. M.   Arr. from JOHANN GEORG NÄGELI, by LOWELL MASON, 1845.

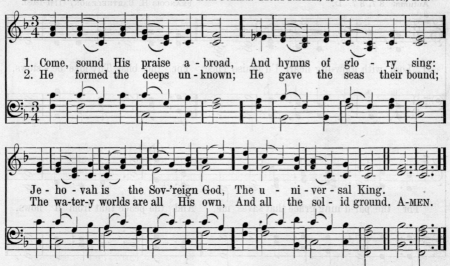

1. Come, sound His praise a - broad, And hymns of glo - ry sing:
2. He formed the deeps un - known; He gave the seas their bound;

Je - ho - vah is the Sov-'reign God, The u - ni - ver - sal King.
The wa-ter-y worlds are all His own, And all the sol - id ground. A-MEN.

3 Come, worship at His throne;
  Come, bow before the Lord.
We are His work, and not our own:
  He formed us by His Word.

4 To-day attend His voice,
  Nor dare provoke His rod;
Come, like the people of His choice,
  And own your gracious God.

Isaac Watts, 1719.

295. God Is Love: His Mercy Brightens.

Brocklesbury. 8 7, 8 7.   CHARLOTTE A. BARNARD, 1868.

1. God is Love: His mer - cy bright-ens All the path in which we rove;
2. Time and change are bus - y ev - er; Man de - cays, and ag - es move;

Bliss He wakes, and woe He light-ens: God is Wis-dom, God is Love.
But His mer - cy wan-eth nev - er; God is Wis-dom, God is Love. A-MEN.

3 E'en the hour that darkest seemeth
  Will His changeless goodness prove;
From the gloom His brightness streameth:
  God is Wisdom, God is Love.

4 He with earthly cares entwineth
  Hope and comfort from above:
Everywhere His glory shineth;
  God is Wisdom, God is Love.

John Bowring, 1825, a.

296. Lord, with Glowing Heart I'd Praise Thee.

Autumn. 8 7, 8 7. D.

Spanish Melody.
FRANCOIS H. BARTHELEMON? (1741-1808).

1. Lord, with glow-ing heart I'd praise Thee For the bliss Thy love be - stows,

For the par-d'ning grace that saves me, And the peace that from it flows.

Help, O God, my weak en - deav - or; This dull soul to rap-ture raise:

Thou must light the flame, or nev - er Can my love be warmed to praise. A - MEN.

2 Praise, my soul, the God that sought thee,
  Wretched wanderer, far astray;
Found thee lost, and kindly brought thee
  From the paths of death away.
Praise, with love's devoutest feeling,
  Him who saw thy guilt-born fear,
And, the light of hope revealing,
  Bade the bloodstained cross appear.

3 Lord, this bosom's ardent feeling
  Vainly would my lips express;
Low before Thy footstool kneeling,
  Deign Thy suppliant's prayer to bless.
Let Thy grace, my soul's chief treasure,
  Love's pure flame within me raise:
And, since words can never measure,
  Let my life show forth Thy praise.

Francis Scott Key, 1823.

297. Love Divine, All Love Excelling.

Beecher. 8 7, 8 7. D.   JOHN ZUNDEL, 1870.

1. Love di-vine, all love ex-cel-ling, Joy of heav'n, to earth come down!

Fix in us Thy hum-ble dwell-ing, All Thy faith-ful mer-cies crown.

Je-sus, Thou art all com-pas-sion, Pure, un-bound-ed love Thou art;

Vis-it us with Thy sal-va-tion; En-ter ev-'ry trem-bling heart. A-MEN.

2 Breathe, O breathe Thy loving Spirit
  Into every troubled breast;
Let us all in Thee inherit,
  Let us find Thy promised rest.
Take away the love of sinning,
  Alpha and Omega be;
End of faith, as its beginning,
  Set our hearts at liberty.

3 Finish then Thy new creation,
  Pure and spotless let us be;
Let us see Thy great salvation
  Perfectly restored in Thee:
Changed from glory unto glory,
  Till in heaven we take our place,
Till we cast our crowns before Thee,
  Lost in wonder, love, and praise.

Charles Wesley, 1747.

298. Come, Saviour Dear, with Us Abide.

Kom, huldaste förbarmare. 8 7, 8 7, 8 8 7.   FREDRIK GABRIEL HEDBERG, (1811–1893).

1 Come, Sav-iour dear, with us a-bide, We need Thy kind com-pas-sion;

Thy flock to liv-ing wa-ters guide, Which are Thy wounds and pas-sion;

And lead us in-to pas-tures green, Where faith-ful souls are

ev-er seen In peace and bliss-ful un-ion. A-MEN.

2. O Sea of love, pour out Thy flood
O'er all in blessèd showers;
The fiery darts quench with Thy blood,
And crush hell's evil powers.
Thou, of the world the Mercy-Seat,
Let of Thy love the gentle heat
Set all our hearts aglowing.

Andreas Carl Rutström, (1721–1772).

299. Now Thank We All Our God.

Nun danket alle Gott. 6 7, 6 7, 6 6, 6 6.   JOHANN CRÜGER, 1648.

1. Now thank we all our God With heart and hands and voic - es,
Who won - drous things hath done, In whom His earth re - joic - es;
Who from our moth - er's arms Hath blessed us on our way
With count-less gifts of love, And still is ours to - day. A - MEN.

2 O may this bounteous God
  Through all our life be near us,
With ever joyful hearts
  And blessèd peace to cheer us;
And keep us in His grace,
  And guide us when perplexed,
And free us from all ills
  In this world and the next.

3 All praise and thanks to God
  The Father now be given,
The Son, and Him who reigns
  With them in highest heaven:
The One eternal God,
  Whom earth and heaven adore;
For thus it was, is now,
  And shall be evermore.

Martin Rinkart, 1630.

300. All Glory Be to Thee, Most High.

Allein Gott in der Höh sei Ehr. 8 7, 8 7, 8 8 7.

VALENTIN SCHUMANN'S Geistliche Lieder, 1539.
NICOLAUS DECIUS? 1539.

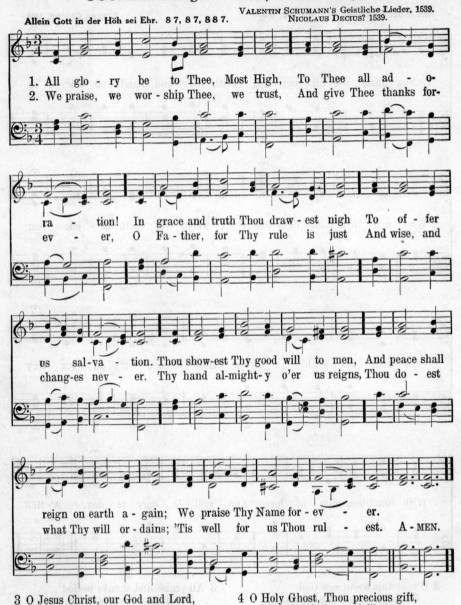

1. All glo - ry be to Thee, Most High, To Thee all ad - o-
2. We praise, we wor - ship Thee, we trust, And give Thee thanks for-

ra - tion! In grace and truth Thou draw - est nigh To of - fer
ev - er, O Fa - ther, for Thy rule is just And wise, and

us sal-va - tion. Thou show-est Thy good will to men, And peace shall
chang-es nev - er. Thy hand al-might-y o'er us reigns, Thou do - est

reign on earth a - gain; We praise Thy Name for - ev - er.
what Thy will or - dains; 'Tis well for us Thou rul - est. A - MEN.

3 O Jesus Christ, our God and Lord,
   Son of the Heavenly Father,
O Thou, who hast our peace restored,
   The straying sheep dost gather,
Thou Lamb of God, to Thee on high
Out of the depths we sinners cry:
   Have mercy on us, Jesus!

4 O Holy Ghost, Thou precious gift,
   Thou Comforter, unfailing,
From Satan's snares our souls uplift,
   And let Thy power, availing,
Avert our woes and calm our dread;
For us the Saviour's blood was shed,
   We trust in Thee to save us!

Nicolaus Decius, 1526, 1539.

301. O Fount of Truth and Mercy.

Valet will ich dir geben. 7 6, 7 6. D.

MELCHIOR TESCHNER, 1613.

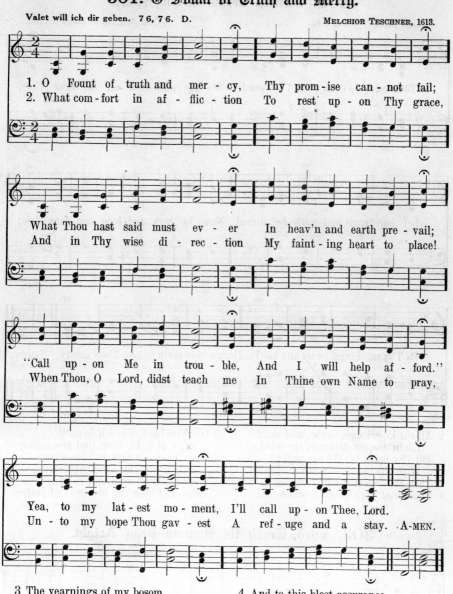

1. O Fount of truth and mer - cy, Thy prom - ise can - not fail;
2. What com - fort in af - flic - tion To rest up - on Thy grace,

What Thou hast said must ev - er In heav'n and earth pre - vail;
And in Thy wise di - rec - tion My faint - ing heart to place!

"Call up - on Me in trou - ble, And I will help af - ford."
When Thou, O Lord, didst teach me In Thine own Name to pray,

Yea, to my lat - est mo - ment, I'll call up - on Thee, Lord.
Un - to my hope Thou gav - est A ref - uge and a stay. A-MEN.

3 The yearnings of my bosom
  Thou hearest, Lord, I know;
What to my weal pertaineth
  I know Thou wilt bestow.
In times of deepest anguish
  Thy helping hand is near,
And on Thy loving bosom
  My sorrows Thou wilt bear.

4 And to this blest assurance
  I'll cling for evermore;
And never shall I weary
  A Father to implore.
Depart, despair and anguish
  That oft my soul oppress;
I'll cling unto my Saviour
  Till He my soul shall bless.

Per Olof Nyström, 1816.

302. Blessed Jesus, at Thy Word.

Liebster Jesu. 7 8, 7 8, 8 8.   CARL WOLFGANG BRIEGEL, 1687.

1. Bless-ed Je-sus, at Thy word We are gath-ered all to hear Thee;

Let our hearts and souls be stirred Now to seek and love and fear Thee;

By Thy teachings, sweet and ho-ly, Drawn from earth to love Thee sole-ly. A-MEN.

2 All our knowledge, sense, and sight
    Lie in deepest darkness shrouded,
Till Thy Spirit breaks our night
    With the beams of truth unclouded.
Thou alone to God canst win us;
Thou must work all good within us.

3 Glorious Lord, Thyself impart!
    Light of light, from God proceeding,
Open Thou our ears and heart,
    Help us by Thy Spirit's pleading;
Hear the cry Thy people raises,
Hear, and bless our prayers and praises.

Tobias Clausnitzer, 1663.

303. Lord, Teach Us How to Pray Aright.

Manoah. C. M.   From GIOACHINO A. ROSSINI, (1792-1868).

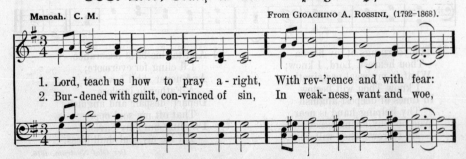

1. Lord, teach us how to pray a-right, With rev-'rence and with fear:
2. Bur-dened with guilt, con-vinced of sin, In weak-ness, want and woe,

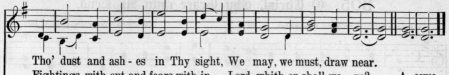

Tho' dust and ash - es in Thy sight, We may, we must, draw near.
Fightings with-out and fears with-in, Lord, whith-er shall we go? A-MEN.

3 God of all grace, we come to Thee
   With broken, contrite hearts;
   Give what Thine eye delights to see,
   Truth in the inward parts.

4 Give deep humility; the sense
   Of godly sorrow give;
   A strong desire, with confidence,
   To hear Thy voice and live:

5 Faith in the only Sacrifice
   That can for sin atone;
   To cast our hopes, to fix our eyes,
   On Christ, on Christ alone.

6 Give these, and then Thy will be done;
   Thus strengthened with all might,
   We, through Thy Spirit and Thy Son,
   Shall pray, and pray aright.

James Montgomery, 1818.

304. Come, My Soul, Thy Suit Prepare.

Horton. 7 7, 7 7.   C. VON WARTENSEE, 1780.

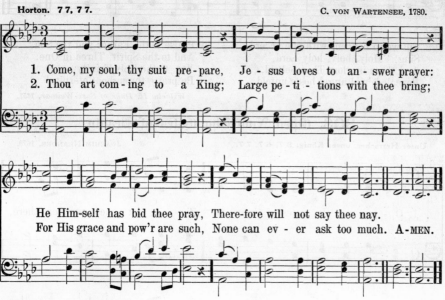

1. Come, my soul, thy suit pre - pare, Je - sus loves to an - swer prayer:
2. Thou art com - ing to a King; Large pe - ti - tions with thee bring;

He Him-self has bid thee pray, There-fore will not say thee nay.
For His grace and pow'r are such, None can ev - er ask too much. A-MEN.

3 With my burden I begin;
   Lord, remove this load of sin;
   Let Thy blood for sinners spilt
   Set my conscience free from guilt.

4 Lord, I come to Thee for rest;
   Take possession of my breast;
   There Thy blood-bought right maintain,
   And without a rival reign.

5 While I am a pilgrim here,
   Let Thy love my spirit cheer:
   Be my Guide, my Guard, my Friend,
   Lead me to my journey's end.

6 Show me what I have to do,
   Every hour my strength renew;
   Let me live a life of faith,
   Let me die Thy people's death.

John Newton, 1779.

305. O Christ, Thy Grace unto Us Lend.

Herr Jesu Christ, dich zu uns wend. L. M.   Cantionale Sacrum, Gotha, 1651.

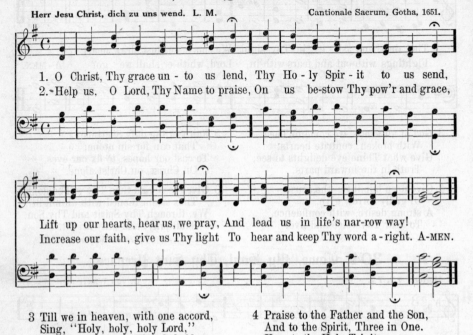

1. O Christ, Thy grace un-to us lend, Thy Ho-ly Spir-it to us send,
2. Help us, O Lord, Thy Name to praise, On us be-stow Thy pow'r and grace,

Lift up our hearts, hear us, we pray, And lead us in life's nar-row way!
Increase our faith, give us Thy light To hear and keep Thy word a-right. A-MEN.

3 Till we in heaven, with one accord,
Sing, "Holy, holy, holy Lord,"
And there in glory Thee behold,
Revealed 'mid angel hosts untold.

4 Praise to the Father and the Son,
And to the Spirit, Three in One.
Yea, to the Holy Trinity
Be praise throughout eternity!

Wilhelm II, Duke of Saxe-Weimar, 1651.

306. Open Now Thy Gates of Beauty.

Unser Herrscher, unser König. 8 7, 8 7, 7 7.   JOACHIM NEANDER, 1679.

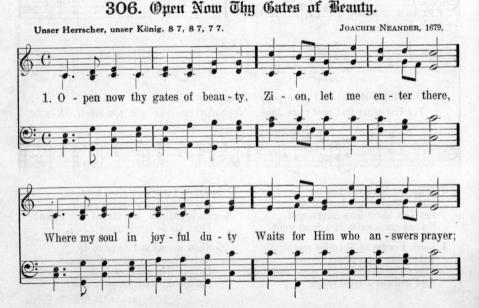

1. O-pen now thy gates of beau-ty, Zi-on, let me en-ter there,

Where my soul in joy-ful du-ty Waits for Him who an-swers prayer;

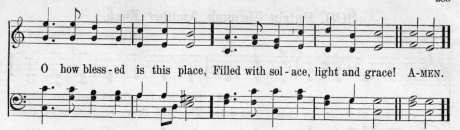

O how bless-ed is this place, Filled with sol-ace, light and grace! A-MEN.

2 Gracious God, I come before Thee,
  Come Thou also down to me;
 Where we find Thee and adore Thee,
  There a heaven on earth must be.
 To my heart O enter Thou,
 Let it be Thy temple now.

3 Here Thy praise is gladly chanted,
  Here Thy seed is duly sown:
 Let my soul, where it is planted,
  Bring forth precious sheaves alone,
 So that all I hear may be
 Fruitful unto life in me.

4 Thou my faith increase and quicken,
  Let me keep Thy gift divine;
 Howsoe'er temptations thicken,
  May Thy Word still o'er me shine
 As my guiding star through life,
 As my comfort in all strife.

5 Speak, O God, and I will hear Thee,
  Let Thy will be done indeed;
 May I undisturbed draw near Thee
  While Thy people Thou dost feed:
 Here of life the fountain flows,
 Here is balm for all our woes.

Benjamin Schmolck, 1734.

307. Prayer Is the Soul's Sincere Desire.

Lambeth. C. M.   WILHELM A. F. SCHULTHES, 1871.

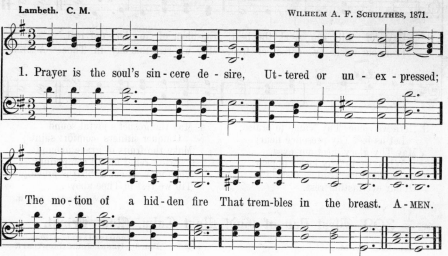

1. Prayer is the soul's sin-cere de - sire, Ut-tered or un - ex - pressed;

The mo-tion of a hid-den fire That trem-bles in the breast. A-MEN.

2 Prayer is the simplest form of speech
  That infant lips can try;
 Prayer the sublimest strains that reach
  The Majesty on high.

3 Prayer is the contrite sinner's voice,
  Returning from his ways;
 While angels in their songs rejoice
  And cry, "Behold, he prays!"

4 Prayer is the Christian's vital breath,
  The Christian's native air;
 His watchword at the gates of death;
  He enters heaven with prayer.

5 O Thou, by whom we come to God,
  The Life, the Truth, the Way,
 The paths of prayer Thyself hast trod:
  Lord, teach us how to pray!

James Montgomery, 1818.

308. Safely Through Another Week.

Dix. 7 7, 7 7, 7 7.   CONRAD KOCHER, 1838.

1. Safe - ly thro' an - oth - er week God has brought us on our way;
2. While we pray for par-d'ning grace Thro' the dear Re-deem-er's Name,

Let us now a bless - ing seek, Wait - ing in His courts to - day:
Show Thy rec - on - cil - èd face, Take a - way our sin and shame:

Day of all the week the best, Em-blem of e - ter - nal rest.
From our world - ly cares set free, May we rest this day in Thee. A-MEN.

3 Here we come, Thy Name to praise;
   Let us feel Thy presence near;
May Thy glory meet our eyes,
   While we in Thy house appear:
Here afford us, Lord, a taste
Of our everlasting rest.

4 May the gospel's joyful sound
   Conquer sinners, comfort saints;
Make the fruits of grace abound,
   Bring relief for all complaints:
Thus may all our Sabbaths prove,
Till we rest in Thee above.

John Newton, 1774, a.

309. Blest Day of God! Most Calm, Most Bright.

THOMAS HAWEIS, 1780.
Chesterfield. C. M.   Har. by HENRY JOHN GAUNTLETT.

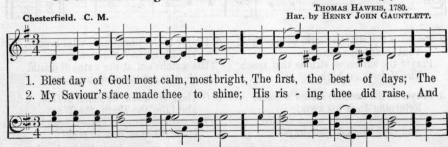

1. Blest day of God! most calm, most bright, The first, the best of days; The
2. My Saviour's face made thee to shine; His ris - ing thee did raise, And

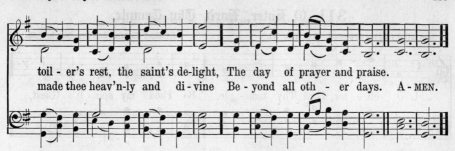

toil - er's rest, the saint's de-light, The day of prayer and praise.
made thee heav'n-ly and di - vine Be - yond all oth - er days. A - MEN.

3 The firstfruits oft a blessing prove
   To all the sheaves behind;
And they the day of Christ who love
   A happy week shall find.

4 This day I must with God appear;
   For, Lord, the day is Thine;
Help me to spend it in Thy fear,
   And thus to make it mine.

John Mason, 1683.

310. In Thy Name, O Lord, Assembling.

Dulce Carmen. 8 7, 8 7, 8 7.   JOHANN MICHAEL HAYDN, (1737-1806)?

1. In Thy Name, O Lord, as - sem-bling, We, Thy peo - ple, now draw near:

Teach us to re - joice with trem-bling, Speak, and let Thy serv - ants hear;

Hear with meekness, Hear with meekness, Hear Thy Word with god - ly fear. A-MEN.

2 While our days on earth are lengthened,
   May we give them, Lord, to Thee;
Cheered by hope, and daily strengthened,
   May we run, nor weary be,
      Till the glory
Without cloud in heaven we see.

3 There, in worship, purer, sweeter,
   Thee Thy people shall adore,
Tasting of enjoyment greater
   Than they could conceive before;
      Full enjoyment,
Full and pure for evermore.

Thomas Kelly, 1815.

311. O Enter, Lord, Thy Temple.

Mig kläd i helig prydnad. 7 6, 7 6. D.   ALBERT ESAIAS LINDSTRÖM, b. 1853.

1. O en-ter, Lord, Thy tem-ple, Be Thou my spir-it's Guest,

Who at my birth didst give me A sec-ond birth more blest.

Though here to dwell Thou deign-est, Thou in the God-head, Lord,

For-ev-er e-qual reign-est, Art e-qual-ly a-dored. A-MEN.

2 O enter, let me know Thee,
    And feel Thy power within,
The power that breaks our fetters,
    And rescues us from sin.
That I may serve Thee truly,
    O wash and cleanse Thou me,
To render honor duly
    With perfect heart to Thee.

3 'Tis Thou, O Spirit, teachest
    The soul to pray aright;
Thy songs are sweetest music,
    Thy prayers have wondrous might.
They pierce the highest heaven,
    Unheard they cannot fall,
Till He His help hath given
    Who surely helpeth all.

4 The whole wide world, O Spirit,
    Upon Thy hands doth rest;
Our wayward hearts Thou turnest
    As to Thee seemeth best.
As Thou hast done so often,
    Once more Thy power make known,
Convert the wicked, soften
    To tears the heart of stone.

5 Our path in all things order
    According to Thy mind;
And when this life is over,
    And all must be resigned,
With calm and fearless spirit
    O grant us then to die,
And after death inherit
    Eternal life on high.

Paul Gerhardt, 1653.

312. O Day of Rest and Gladness!

Lausanne. 7 6, 7 6. D.   Lausanne Psalter.

1. O day of rest and glad-ness! O day of joy and light!
O balm for care and sad-ness, Most beau-ti-ful and bright!
On thee the high and low-ly, Through ag-es joined in tune,
Sing, ho-ly, ho-ly, ho-ly, To God, the great Tri-une.

2. On thee, at the cre-a-tion, The light first had its birth;
On thee, for our sal-va-tion, Christ rose from depths of earth;
On thee our Lord vic-to-rious, The Spir-it sent from heav'n;
And thus on thee, most glo-rious, A three-fold light was giv'n. A-MEN.

3 To-day on weary nations
 The heavenly manna falls;
To holy convocations
 The silver trumpet calls,
Where gospel light is glowing
 With pure and radiant beams,
And living water flowing
 With soul-refreshing streams.

4 New graces ever gaining
 From this one day of rest,
We reach the rest remaining
 To spirits of the blest;
To Holy Ghost be praises,
 To Father and to Son,
The Church her voice upraises
 To Thee, blest Three in One.

Christopher Wordsworth, 1862, a.

313. Guardian of Pure Hearts, and Hearer.

Werde munter, mein Gemüthe. 8 7, 8 7, 7 7, 8 8.   JOHANN SCHOP, 1642.

1. Guard-ian of pure hearts, and Hear-er, Lord, of ev - 'ry faith-ful prayer,
2. With the right-eous oft it far - eth Here as if his deeds were ill;

In Thy courts one day is dear - er Than a thou-sand days else - where.
Blight fair vir - tue's flow'rs im - pair - eth, Weeds of vice do flour - ish still;

Worn with earth's un - rest, how sweet In Thy tem - ple fair to meet!
Joy and for - tune haste a - way, Friends with friends—how short their stay!

There to sing a - way each sor-row That from life and toil we bor - row!
Rach - el still her children mourneth, And her soul from comfort turn-eth.   A-MEN.

3 But when here devoutly soareth
   High the temple-anthem sweet,
Grief grows calm, no plaint outpoureth,
Hearts with holy rapture beat:
Free from earthly clouds, the soul
Presses toward a higher goal,
Takes from hope the comfort given,
Speaks e'en now the tongue of heaven.

4 O my soul, on wings ascending,
   Thou on Salem's mount shalt rest;
There where cherub-harps are blending
   With the singing of the blest;
Let thy note of praise and prayer
To thy God precede thee there,
While e'en yet a careworn mortal,
Still without thy Father's portal.

5 Christians, while on earth abiding,
   Let us ever praise and pray,
Firmly in our God confiding,
   As our fathers in their day;
Be the children's voices raised
To the God their fathers praised.
Let His bounty, failing never,
Be on us and all forever.

6 Bless us, Father, and protect us,
   Be our souls' sure hiding-place,
Let Thy wisdom still direct us,
   Light our darkness with Thy grace!
Let Thy countenance on us shine,
Fill us all with peace divine.
Praise the Father, Son, and Spirit,
Praise Him all that life inherit.

Johan Olof Wallin, 1816.

314. Unto the Lord of All Creation.

Wer weiss, wie nahe mir mein Ende. 9 8, 9 8, 8 8.   BRONNER'S Choral-Buch, 1715.

1. Un - to the Lord of all cre - a - tion Thy voice, my soul, in an - thems raise. Let ev - 'ry heart a fit ob - la - tion Bring un - to Him with songs of praise. O con - tem - plate in hum - ble - ness The pow'r and rich - es of His grace.

2. In Him we live and have our be - ing; And all the hosts of heav'n and earth The liv - ing God, all - wise, all - see - ing, Thro' His own Spir - it brought to birth. His ho - ly Name, writ in His Word, Thro' all the u - ni - verse is heard. A - MEN.

3 The Lord who laid the earth's foundation,
   And for the stars their course decreed,
Whose hand hath ordered all creation,
   Provideth for our every need;
For God is Love: the Father's care
His smallest child shall duly share.

4 From out the gloom mine eye descrieth
   The Maker's footprints in the sky;
The starry chorus testifieth
   To His eternal majesty;
While on my path each tiny flower
Proclaims His glory and His power.

5 Into Thy hand, O God Almighty,
   My weal and woe I will entrust;
My need Thou seest who takest pity
   On every worm that crawls the dust.
In pleasure's path or sorrow's way
Be Thou my Guide, O Lord, I pray.

6 And when the morning star appeareth,
   Thy grace, Thy glory we proclaim;
When falls the dew, and evening neareth,
   O Lord, we call upon Thy Name.
Upon Thy mercy we rely,
Father, Creator, God on high.

Arvid August Afzelius, 1814.

315. Holy Majesty, Before Thee.

Wachet auf. 8 9 8, 8 9 8, 6 6 4, 8 8.   PHILIPP NICOLAI, 1599.

1. Ho - ly Maj - es - ty, be - fore Thee   We bow to wor-ship and a - dore Thee;
2. God of light, ex - alt - ed, ho - ly!   Thy ten - der care pro-tects the low - ly,

With grate-ful hearts to Thee we   sing.   Earth and heav-en   tell the sto - ry
Nor leaves Thy chil-dren to their fate.   Gra-cious art Thou, God our Fa - ther,

Of   Thine e - ter-nal might and glo - ry,   And all Thy works their in-cense bring.
Thy cho - sen peo-ple Thou dost gath - er   With - in Thine arms com-pas-sion-ate.

Lo, hosts of Cher - u - bim   And count-less Ser - a - phim   Sing, Ho - san - na,
Thou gav-est us Thy Son,   Thro' whom Thy grace is won,   And Thy Spir - it

Ho - ly is God, al-might-y God,   All-mer - ci - ful and all-wise God!
Dwelleth with-in   to cleanse from sin   Whom Thine own Son hath died to win. A - MEN.

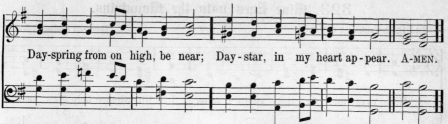

Day-spring from on high, be near; Day-star, in my heart ap-pear. A-MEN.

2 Dark and cheerless is the morn,
  Unaccompanied by Thee;
Joyless is the day's return
  Till Thy mercy's beams I see,
Till Thou inward light impart,
Cheer my soul, and warm my heart.

3 Visit then this soul of mine;
  Pierce the gloom of sin and grief;
Fill me, Radiance divine;
  Scatter all my unbelief:
More and more Thyself display,
Shining to the perfect day.

Charles Wesley, 1740.

322. Lord of the Worlds Above.

Darwall's 148th. 6 6, 6 6, 4 4, 4 4. JOHN DARWALL, 1770.

1. Lord of the worlds a-bove, How pleas-ant and how fair The
dwell-ings of Thy love, Thine earth-ly tem-ples are! To Thine a-bode
My heart a-spires With warm de-sires To see my God. A-MEN.

2 O happy souls that pray
    Where God appoints to hear!
  O happy men that pay
    Their constant service there!
      They praise Thee still;
      And happy they
      That love the way
    To Zion's hill.

3 They go from strength to strength
    Through this dark vale of tears,
  Till each arrives at length,
    Till each in heaven appears.
      O glorious seat
      Of God our King!
      Lord, thither bring
    Our willing feet!

Isaac Watts, 1719.

323. Mine Eyes unto the Mountains.

Old 130th Psalm. 7 6, 7 6. D. **Genevan Psalter, 1556.**

1. Mine eyes un - to the moun - tains I lift, whence help goes forth;
My help comes from Je - ho - vah, Mak - er of heav'n and earth.
Thy foot shall nev - er fal - ter; Thy ev - 'ry step He keeps;
The Lord who keep - eth Is - rael, He slum - bers not, nor sleeps. A - MEN.

2 The shade of the Almighty
  Shields thee upon the right.
The sunlight shall not smite thee,
  Nor shall the moon by night.
Thy coming in He blesseth,
  And from the temple door
Thy going out He guideth
  Now and forevermore.

Ernst William Olson, 1922.

324. Praise to the Lord, the Almighty.

Lobe den Herren. 14 14, 4 7 8.

Stralsund Gesangbuch, 1665.
Present form since 1708.

1. Praise to the Lord, the Al-might-y, the King of cre-a - - tion!
O my soul, praise Him, for He is thy health and sal - va - - tion!
All ye who hear, Now to His tem - ple draw near,
Join me in glad ad - o - ra - - tion. A - MEN.

2 Praise to the Lord, who o'er all things so wondrously reigneth,
Shelters thee under His wings, yea, so gently sustaineth!
Hast thou not seen
How thy desires e'er have been
Granted in what He ordaineth?

3 Praise to the Lord, who doth prosper thy work and defend thee!
Surely His goodness and mercy here daily attend thee;
Ponder anew
What the Almighty can do,
If with His love He befriend thee!

4 Praise thou the Lord, who with marvelous wisdom hath made thee,
Decked thee with health, and with loving hand guided and stayed thee.
How oft in grief
Hath not He brought thee relief,
Spreading His wings to o'ershade thee!

5 Praise to the Lord! O let all that is in me adore Him!
All that hath life and breath, come now with praises before Him!
Let the Amen
Sound from His people again;
Gladly for aye we adore Him.

Joachim Neander, 1680.

325. Heavenly Light, Benignly Beaming.

Jesus! du dig själf uppväckte. 8 7, 8 7, 8 7 7.   Swedish, 1675.

1. Heav'n-ly Light, be-nign-ly beam-ing, Break-eth o'er the hope-less earth.
2. All un-known to world-ly sag-es, Who were to His glo-ry blind,

From the Sun e-ter-nal stream-ing, Spring the rays of prom-ise forth.
Je-sus came, O light of ag-es, Day of grace to all man-kind!

Light su-per-nal, O how glo-rious To our eyes is
Truth He brought to ev-'ry seek-er, Grace to ev-'ry

Thy ad-vance, Giv-ing us to see God's plans!
trou-bled breast, Man with peace and mer-cy blest.   A - MEN.

3 In a world where lusts contended,
    Crimes were bred and bitterness,
  Christ appeared; with Him descended
    Love divine and holiness.
  Hearts were filled with His pure Spirit,
    Love bade warring passions cease;
    Earth was blest with joy and peace.

4 Blessèd they who ever ready
    Hear the heavenly Teacher's Word,
  They who walk with purpose steady
    In the footsteps of the Lord;
  Guided by His Holy Spirit,
    Led by faith, and not by sight,
    They shall gain the realms of light.

5 Lo, their faith and love shall conquer
    Vanity and unbelief,
  Shedding o'er a word of rancor
    Kindly light, to solace grief.
  In life's turmoil, in death's shadow
    Anchor they their hope secure
    On the Rock that shall endure.

6 Radiance of the Father's glory,
    Send Thy beams in splendor forth.
  Break upon the ages hoary,
    Dawn of faith and peace on earth!
  Let this world be as the pathway
    To that heaven where shall be
    Gathered they who walked with Thee.

Johan Olof Wallin, 1816.

326. Pleasant Are Thy Courts Above.

Maidstone. 7 7, 7 7. D.   WALTER BOND GILBERT, 1862.

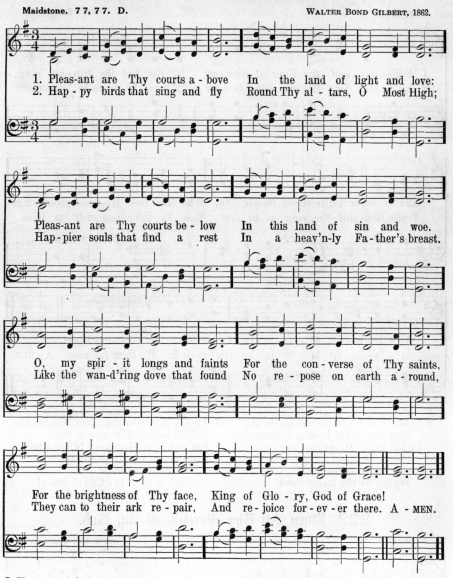

1. Pleas-ant are Thy courts a - bove   In   the land of light and love:
2. Hap - py birds that sing and fly   Round Thy al - tars, O   Most High;

Pleas-ant are Thy courts be - low   In   this land of   sin and woe.
Hap - pier souls that find a rest   In   a heav'n-ly Fa-ther's breast.

O, my spir - it longs and faints   For the con - verse of Thy saints,
Like the wan-d'ring dove that found   No re - pose on earth a - round,

For the brightness of Thy face,   King of Glo - ry, God of Grace!
They can to their ark re - pair,   And re - joice for - ev - er there. A - MEN.

3 Happy souls! their praises flow
Even in this vale of woe;
Waters in the desert rise,
Manna feeds them from the skies;
On they go from strength to strength,
Till they reach Thy throne at length,
At Thy feet adoring fall,
Who hast led them safe through all.

4 Lord, be mine this prize to win;
Guide me through a world of sin;
Keep me by Thy saving grace;
Give me at Thy side a place.
Sun and shield alike Thou art;
Guide and guard my erring heart.
Grace and glory flow from Thee;
Shower, O shower them, Lord, on me!

Henry Francis Lyte, 1834, a.

327. Praise, My Soul, the King of Heaven.

Regent Square. 8 7, 8 7, 8 7.   HENRY SMART, 1867.

1. Praise, my soul, the King of heav-en; To His feet thy trib-ute bring;
2. Praise Him for His grace and fa-vor To our fa-thers in dis-tress;

Ran-somed, healed, re-stored, for-giv-en, Who like thee His praise should sing?
Praise Him, still the same as ev-er, Slow to chide, and swift to bless:

Al - le - lu - ia! Al - le - lu - ia! Praise the ev - er - last-ing King!
Al - le - lu - ia! Al - le - lu - ia! Glo-rious in His faith-ful-ness! A - MEN.

3 Father-like He tends and spares us,
   Well our feeble frame He knows;
In His hands He gently bears us,
   Rescues us from all our foes:
      Alleluia! Alleluia!
   Widely as His mercy flows!

4 Angels in the height adore Him,
   Who behold Him face to face;
Sun and moon bow down before Him;
   Dwellers in all time and space:
      Alleluia! Alleluia!
   Praise with us the God of grace!

Henry Francis Lyte, 1834, a.

328. When All Thy Mercies, O My God.

Warwick. C. M.   SAMUEL STANLEY, 1800.

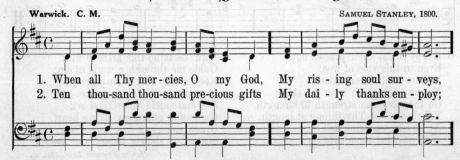

1. When all Thy mer-cies, O my God, My ris-ing soul sur-veys,
2. Ten thou-sand thou-sand pre-cious gifts My dai-ly thanks em-ploy;

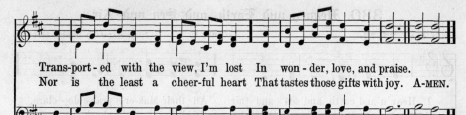

Trans-port-ed with the view, I'm lost In won-der, love, and praise.
Nor is the least a cheer-ful heart That tastes those gifts with joy. A-MEN.

3 Through every period of my life
  Thy goodness I'll pursue;
And after death, in distant worlds,
  The glorious theme renew.

4 Through all eternity to Thee
  A joyful song I'll raise:
But O, eternity's too short
  To utter all Thy praise!

Joseph Addison, 1712.

329. God of Merry, God of Grace.

Demmin. 7 7, 7 7, 7 7.

JOHANN SCHOP (D. 1664).
Harm. by SAMUEL SEBASTIAN WESLEY, (1810-1876).

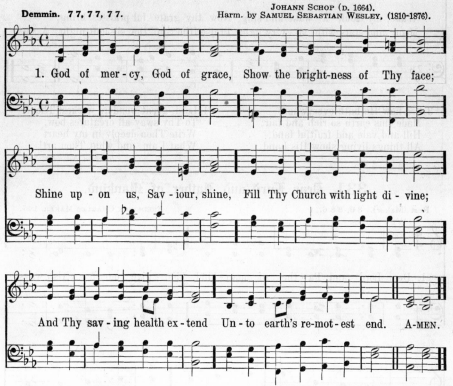

1. God of mer-cy, God of grace, Show the bright-ness of Thy face;

Shine up-on us, Sav-iour, shine, Fill Thy Church with light di-vine;

And Thy sav-ing health ex-tend Un-to earth's re-mot-est end. A-MEN.

2 Let the people praise Thee, Lord;
  Be by all that live adored:
Let the nations shout and sing
  Glory to their Saviour King;
At Thy feet their tributes pay,
  And Thy holy will obey.

3 Let the people praise Thee, Lord;
  Earth shall then her fruits afford,
God to man His blessing give,
  Man to God devoted live;
All below, and all above,
  One in joy, and light, and love.

Henry Francis Lyte, 1834.

330. Heaven and Earth, and Sea and Air.

St. Bees. 7 7, 7 7.   JOHN BACCHUS DYKES, 1874.

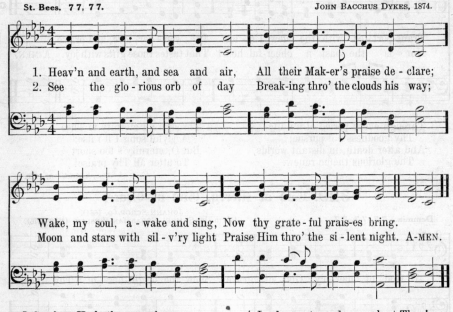

1. Heav'n and earth, and sea and air,   All their Mak-er's praise de-clare;
2. See the glo-rious orb of day   Break-ing thro' the clouds his way;

Wake, my soul, a-wake and sing, Now thy grate-ful prais-es bring.
Moon and stars with sil-v'ry light Praise Him thro' the si-lent night. A-MEN.

3 See how He hath everywhere
Made this earth so rich and fair;
Hill and vale and fruitful land,
All things living show His hand.

4 Lord, great wonders workest Thou!
To Thy sway all creatures bow.
Write Thou deeply in my heart
What I am, and what Thou art!

Joachim Neander, 1680.

331. Dear Lord and Father of Mankind.

Rest (Maker). 8 6, 8 8 6.   FREDERICK CHARLES MAKER, 1887.

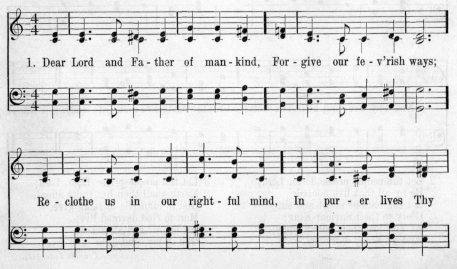

1. Dear Lord and Fa-ther of man-kind, For-give our fe-v'rish ways;

Re-clothe us in our right-ful mind, In pur-er lives Thy

serv - ice find, In deep - er rev - 'rence, praise. A - MEN.

2 In simple trust like theirs who heard,
   Beside the Syrian sea,
The gracious calling of the Lord,
Let us, like them, without a word
   Rise up and follow Thee.

3 O Sabbath rest by Galilee!
   O calm of hills above,
Where Jesus knelt to share with Thee
The silence of eternity
   Interpreted by love!

4 Drop Thy still dews of quietness,
   Till all our strivings cease;
Take from our souls the strain and stress,
And let our ordered lives confess
   The beauty of Thy peace.

5 Breathe through the heat of our desire
   Thy coolness and Thy balm;
Let sense be dumb, let flesh retire;
Speak thro' the earthquake, wind, and fire,
   O still, small voice of calm.

John Greenleaf Whittier, 1872

332. Children of the Heavenly King.

Händel. 7 7, 7 7.   GEORGE FREDERICK HÄNDEL, (1685–1759).

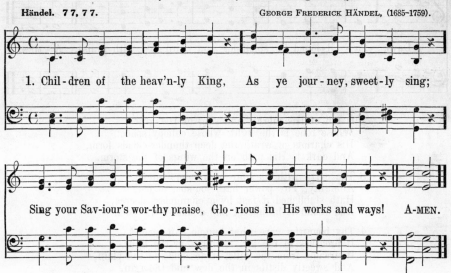

1. Chil - dren of the heav'n - ly King, As ye jour - ney, sweet - ly sing;

Sing your Sav - iour's wor - thy praise, Glo - rious in His works and ways! A-MEN.

2 Ye are traveling home to God
   In the way the fathers trod;
They are happy now, and ye
Soon their happiness shall see.

3 O ye banished seed, be glad!
   Christ our Advocate is made;
Us to save, our flesh assumes,
Brother to our souls becomes.

4 Sing, ye little flock and blest;
   You on Jesus' throne shall rest;
There your seat is now prepared,
There your kingdom and reward.

5 Lord, obediently we go,
   Gladly leaving all below;
Only Thou our Leader be,
And we still will follow Thee.

John Cennick, 1742.

333. O Worship the King, All-glorious Above.

Lyons. 10 10, 11 11.   Arr. from JOHANN MICHAEL HAYDN, (1737-1806).

1. O wor-ship the King, all - glo-rious a - bove, And grate-ful - ly

sing His won-der-ful love; Our Shield and De - fend-er, the An-cient of

Days,   Pa - vil-ioned in splen-dor and gird - ed with praise. A - MEN.

2 O tell of His might, and sing of His grace,
   Whose robe is the light, whose canopy space;
   His chariots of wrath the deep thunder-clouds form,
   And dark is His path on the wings of the storm.

3 The earth with its store of wonders untold,
   Almighty, Thy power hath founded of old;
   Hath stablished it fast by a changeless decree,
   And round it hath cast like a mantle the sea.

4 Thy bountiful care what tongue can recite?
   It breathes in the air, it shines in the light,
   It streams from the hills, it descends to the plain,
   And sweetly distils in the dew and the rain.

5 Frail children of dust, and feeble as frail,
   In Thee do we trust, nor find Thee to fail;
   Thy mercies how tender, how firm to the end
   Our Maker, Defender, Redeemer, and Friend.

6 O measureless Might! ineffable Love!
   While angels delight to hymn Thee above,
   The humble creation, though feeble its lays,
   With true adoration shall sing to Thy praise.

Robert Grant, 1833, a.

334. What Shall I Render to My God?

Devereux. C. M.

L. DEVEREUX.
Arranged by G. KINGSLEY, 1839.

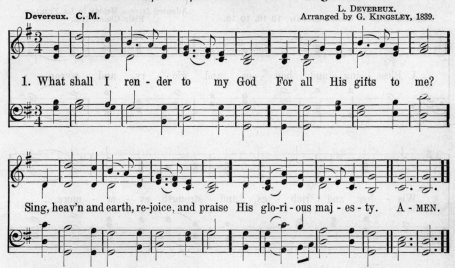

1. What shall I ren-der to my God For all His gifts to me?

Sing, heav'n and earth, re-joice, and praise His glo-ri-ous maj-es-ty. A-MEN.

2 O let me praise Thee while I live,
    And praise Thee when I die,
    And praise Thee when I rise again,
    And to eternity.

3 Mysterious depths of endless love
    Our admiration raise;
    My God, Thy Name exalted is
    Above our highest praise.

John Mason, 1683, a.

335. Name of Jesus, Softly Stealing.

Beatrice. 8 7, 8 7.

WILLIAM WALLACE COE, 1895.

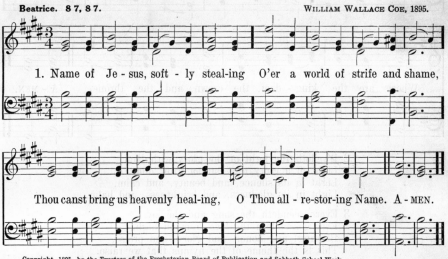

1. Name of Je-sus, soft-ly steal-ing O'er a world of strife and shame,

Thou canst bring us heavenly heal-ing, O Thou all-re-stor-ing Name. A-MEN.

2 Name of Jesus, Heaven of gladness,
    Cause our doubts and fears to cease;
    Soothe away the aching sadness;
    Name of Jesus, give us peace.

Unknown.

336. Blessing, and Honor, and Glory, and Power.

Regnator orbis (O quanta qualia). 10 10, 10 10.   Adapted from a Melody in LA FEILLEE.
                                                              Plain Chant. 1782.

1. Bless - ing, and hon - or, and glo - ry, and power,

Wis - dom, and rich - es, and strength ev - er - more, . .

Give ye to Him who our bat - tle hath won, . .

Whose are the king - dom, the crown, and the throne.   A - MEN.

2 Dwelleth the light of the glory with Him,
  Light of a glory that cannot grow dim,
  Light in its silence, and beauty, and calm,
  Light in its gladness, and brightness, and balm.

3 Ever ascendeth the song and the joy,
  Ever descendeth the love from on high,
  Blessing, and honor, and glory, and praise,
  This is the theme of the hymns that we raise.

4 Life of all life, and true Light of all light,
  Star of the dawning, unchangingly bright,
  Sing we the song of the Lamb that was slain,
  Dying in weakness, but rising to reign.

Horatius Bonar, 1866.

337. Holy, Holy, Holy, Blessed Lord.

Helig, helig, helig Herre Gud. 9 10, 9 10, 10.

GUSTAF STOLPE, 1892.

1. Ho - ly, ho - ly, ho - ly, bless - ed Lord! All the choirs of heav - en now a - dore Thee; O that I might join that great white host, Cast - ing down their gold - en crowns be - fore Thee, Cast - ing down their gold - en crowns be - fore Thee. A - MEN.

2 Look on me, a creature of the dust,
    Pity me, though I have naught of merit;
  Let me bring to Thee for Jesus' sake
    Humble praises of a contrite spirit.

3 Bend Thine ear, dear Lord, and hear my prayer;
    Cleanse me in Thy blood for sinners given;
  Deck me in the robe of spotless white
    Thou hast promised to Thy bride in heaven.

Friedrich Karl von Gerok, (1815–1890).

338. For the Beauty of the Earth.

God of Hosts. 7 7, 7 7, 7 7.   EDWARD JOHN HOPKINS, (1818–1901).

1. For the beau-ty of the earth, For the beau-ty of the skies,
2. For the beau-ty of each hour Of the day and of the night,

For the love which from our birth O-ver and a-round us lies:
Hill and vale, and tree and flow'r, Sun and moon and stars of light,

Christ our God, to Thee we raise This our sac-ri-fice of praise.
Christ our God, to Thee we raise This our sac-ri-fice of praise. A-MEN.

3 For the joy of ear and eye,
   For the heart and mind's delight,
For the mystic harmony
   Linking sense to sound and sight,
Christ our God, to Thee we raise
This our sacrifice of praise.

4 For Thyself, best Gift divine!
   To our race so freely given,
For that great, great love of Thine,
   Peace on earth and joy in heaven,
Christ our God, to Thee we raise
This our sacrifice of praise.

Folliott Sandford Pierpoint, 1864.

339. O God! How Wonderful Thou Art.

Beatitudo. C. M.   JOHN BACCHUS DYKES, 1875.

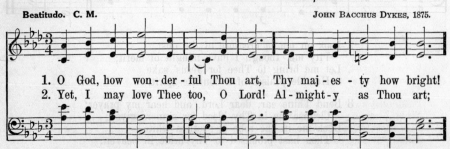

1. O God, how won-der-ful Thou art, Thy maj-es-ty how bright!
2. Yet, I may love Thee too, O Lord! Al-might-y as Thou art;

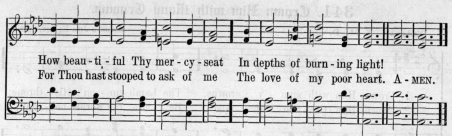

How beau-ti-ful Thy mer-cy-seat   In depths of burn-ing light!
For Thou hast stooped to ask of me   The love of my poor heart. A-MEN.

3 No earthly father loves like Thee,
   No mother e'er so mild
Bears and forbears as Thou hast done
   With me, Thy sinful child.

4 O God, how wonderful Thou art,
   Thou everlasting Friend!
On Thee I stay my trusting heart
   Till faith and vision end.

Frederick William Faber, 1849.

340. Jesus, Saviour, Pilot Me.

Pilot. 7 7, 7 7, 7 7.

JOHN EDGAR GOULD, 1871.

1. Je-sus, Sav-iour, pi-lot me   O-ver life's tem-pes-tuous sea;

Un-known waves be-fore me roll,   Hid-ing rock and treach'rous shoal;

Chart and com-pass came from Thee: Je-sus, Sav-iour, pi-lot me.   A-MEN.

2 As a mother stills her child,
   Thou canst hush the ocean wild;
Boisterous waves obey Thy will
When Thou say'st to them, "Be still."
Wondrous Sovereign of the sea,
Jesus, Saviour, pilot me.

3 When at last I near the shore,
   And the fearful breakers roar
'Twixt me and the peaceful rest,
Then, while leaning on Thy breast,
May I hear Thee say to me,
"Fear not, I will pilot thee."

Edward Hopper, 1871.

341. Crown Him with Many Crowns.

Diademata. S. M. D.   GEORGE JOB ELVEY, 1868.

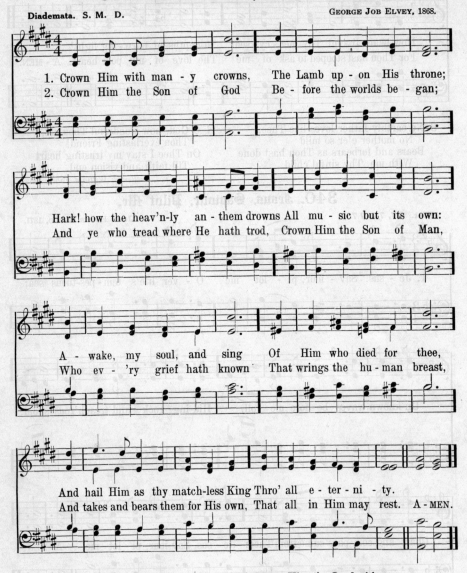

1. Crown Him with man - y crowns, The Lamb up - on His throne;
2. Crown Him the Son of God Be - fore the worlds be - gan;

Hark! how the heav'n-ly an - them drowns All mu - sic but its own:
And ye who tread where He hath trod, Crown Him the Son of Man,

A - wake, my soul, and sing Of Him who died for thee,
Who ev - 'ry grief hath known That wrings the hu - man breast,

And hail Him as thy match-less King Thro' all e - ter - ni - ty.
And takes and bears them for His own, That all in Him may rest. A - MEN.

3 Crown Him the Lord of life,
  Who triumphed o'er the grave,
And rose victorious in the strife
  For those He came to save;
His glories now we sing,
  Who died, and rose on high,
Who died eternal life to bring,
  And lives, that death may die.

4 Crown Him the Lord of heaven,
  Enthroned in worlds above,
Crown Him the King to whom is given
  The wondrous name of Love.
Crown Him with many crowns
  As thrones before Him fall,
Crown Him, ye kings, with many crowns,
  For He is King of all.

Stanza 1, Matthew Bridges, 1851.
Stanzas 2-4, Godfrey Thring, 1882.

342. All Blessing, Honor, Thanks, and Praise.

Es ist gewisslich an der Zeit. 8 7, 8 7, 8 8 7.

Wittenberg Gesangbuch, 1535.

1. All bless-ing, hon-or, thanks, and praise To Fa-ther, Son, and Spir-it, The God who saved us by His grace, All glo-ry to His mer-it: O Fa-ther in the heav'ns a-bove, Thy glo-rious works show forth Thy love, Thy wor-thy Name be hal-lowed. A-MEN.

2 Thy kingdom come, Thy will be done
In earth, as 'tis in heaven:
Keep us in life, by grace led on,
Forgiving and forgiven;
Save Thou us in temptation's hour,
And from all ills; Thine is the power,
And all the glory, Amen!

Paul Speratus, 1523.

343. What a Friend We Have in Jesus.

What a friend. 8 7, 8 7. D.

CHARLES CROZAT CONVERSE, 1868.

1. What a friend we have in Je - sus, All our sins and griefs to bear!
What a priv - i - lege to car - ry Ev - 'ry-thing to God in prayer!
O what peace we oft - en for - feit! O what need-less pain we bear!
All be-cause we do not car - ry Ev - 'ry-thing to God in prayer. A-MEN.

2 Have we trials and temptations?
　Is there trouble anywhere?
We should never be discouraged,
　Take it to the Lord in prayer.
Can we find a friend so faithful,
　Who will all our sorrows share?
Jesus knows our every weakness,
　Take it to the Lord in prayer.

3 Are we weak and heavy laden,
　Cumbered with a load of care?
Precious Saviour, still our refuge,—
　Take it to the Lord in prayer.
Do thy friends despise, forsake thee?
　Take it to the Lord in prayer;
In His arms He'll take and shield thee,
　Thou wilt find a solace there.

Joseph Scriven, 1855.

344. Lead, Kindly Light.

Lux Benigna. 10 4, 10 4, 10 10.

JOHN BACCHUS DYKES, 1867.

1. Lead, kind-ly Light, a - mid th' en - cir - cling gloom, Lead Thou me on; The night is dark, and I am far from home; Lead Thou me on: Keep Thou my feet; I do not ask to see . . . The dis - tant scene,—one step e - nough for me. A - MEN.

2 I was not ever thus, nor prayed that Thou
    Shouldst lead me on;
I loved to choose and see my path; but now
    Lead Thou me on;
I loved the garish day, and, spite of fears,
Pride ruled my will. Remember not past years.

3 So long Thy power hath blest me, sure it still
    Will lead me on
O'er moor and fen, o'er crag and torrent, till
    The night is gone;
And with the morn those angel faces smile
Which I have loved long since, and lost awhile.

John Henry Newman, 1833.

345. Strike Up, O Harp and Psaltery!

Upp, psaltare och harpa! 7 8, 7 8, 7 6, 7 6, 7 6, 7 8.   Johan Kugelmann, about 1540.

1. {Strike up, O harp and psal-ter-y! O Word of might, two-edg-ed sword,
A-rise and smite the na-tions, That they may know and fear the Lord!}

O gos-pel voice from heav-en, A-wake the hearts of men,

That un-to them be giv-en To turn to God a-gain.

All ye who dwell in Zi-on, Hark to your Shep-herd Lord,

Who leads you to green pas-tures, And feeds you with His liv-ing Word! A-men.

2 Adorn thyself to meet Him,
  O Shulamite, O bride of Christ!
Go gladly forth to greet Him,
  When of His coming now apprised!
He for thy sin was given,
  And thou art sanctified.
Behold, the Son of heaven
  Hath claimed thee for His bride!
Give Him thy heart forever,
  Whose love shall never cease;
Let no affliction sever
  The bonds of unity and peace!

3 O Lord, Thy Zion, thronging
  Thy holy temple, e'er shall raise,
With hearts and tongues in rapture,
  To Thee their solemn prayer and praise!
O let Thy Word in clearness
  A day-star o'er us shine,
That we may feel Thy nearness,
  And bring forth fruit divine.
Like sands from out the ocean,
  So let Thy people be,
To voice our heart's devotion,
  And praise Thee through eternity.

Johan Olof Wallin, 1816.

346. Light of Light, Enlighten Me.

Meinhold. 7 8, 7 8, 7 7. From JOHANN SEBASTIAN BACH, (1685–1750).

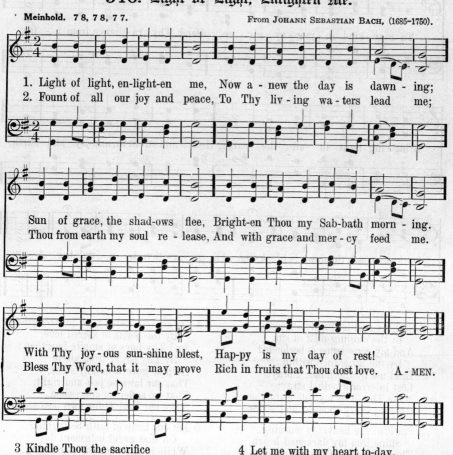

1. Light of light, en-light-en me, Now a-new the day is dawn-ing;
2. Fount of all our joy and peace, To Thy liv-ing wa-ters lead me;

Sun of grace, the shad-ows flee, Bright-en Thou my Sab-bath morn-ing.
Thou from earth my soul re-lease, And with grace and mer-cy feed me.

With Thy joy-ous sun-shine blest, Hap-py is my day of rest!
Bless Thy Word, that it may prove Rich in fruits that Thou dost love. A-MEN.

3 Kindle Thou the sacrifice
  That upon my lips is lying;
Clear the shadows from mine eyes,
  That, from every error flying,
No strange fire may in me glow
That Thine altar doth not know.

4 Let me with my heart to-day,
  Holy, holy, holy, singing,
Rapt awhile from earth away,
  All my soul to Thee upspringing,
Have a foretaste inly given,
How they worship Thee in heaven.

Benjamin Schmolck, 1715.

347. Light of Light, O Sun of Heaven.

Freu dich sehr, o meine Seele. 8 7, 8 7, 7 7, 8 8.

French Psalter, 1555.

1. Light of light, O Sun of heav-en, O Thou bright and morn-ing Star,
To man-kind in mer-cy giv-en, Send Thy ra-diance from a - far,
Bring-ing light to all the earth, Health and strength, and joy and mirth;
Dark-ness past, the dawn is break-ing, All cre - a - tion is a - wak-ing. A - MEN.

2 Still my soul is thickly shrouded
  In the chilling mist of sin,
And my conscience is beclouded
  By the ignorance within.
Lead me by the hand, I pray,
Lest in error's path I stray;
Make Thy light my sole attraction,
Guiding every thought and action.

3 Spirit of the heavenly morning,
  Shine into my darkened heart,
That, the way of life discerning,
  I may choose the better part.
Make my erring walk secure,
Every thought and action pure;
Wheresoe'er my feet be turning,
Keep Thy zeal within me burning.

4 Deign Thy feeble flock to strengthen
  By the bonds of sacred love,
And Thy lines of empire lengthen
  By Thy power from above.
Help us govern in Thy sight,
That our laws be just and right;
That we suffer no oppression,
Make our land Thine own possession.

5 Let our lamp of faith be burning
  On that awful judgment day.
While in sin's domain sojourning,
  Guide us in the heavenward way:
Then their praise and thanks to Thee,
Lord, in all eternity
Shall Thy happy children render,
For Thy mercies, kind and tender.

Martin Opitz (1597-1639).

348. O Lord, Give Heed unto Our Plea.

Af himlens här den högstes makt. 8 7, 8 7, 8 8 7.

Swedish, 1697.

1. O Lord, give heed un - to our plea, O Spir - it, grant Thy grac - es,
That we who put our trust in Thee May right - ly sing Thy prais - es. Thy Word, O Christ, un - to us give, That grace and pow'r we may re - ceive To fol - low Thee, our Mas - ter. A - MEN.

2 Touch Thou the shepherd's lips, O Lord,
  That in this blessèd hour
He may proclaim Thy sacred Word
  With unction and with power.
What Thou wouldst have Thy servant say,
Put Thou into his heart, we pray,
  With grace and strength to say it.

3 Let heart and ear be opened wide
  Unto Thy Word and pleading;
Our minds, O Holy Spirit, guide
  By Thine own light and leading.
The law of Christ we would fulfill,
And walk according to His will,
  His Word our rule of living.

Jesper Swedberg.

349. In the Temple Where Our Fathers.

Werde munter, mein Gemüthe. 8 7, 8 7, 7 7, 8 8.   JOHANN SCHOP, 1642.

1. In the tem-ple where our fa-thers Ren-dered praise to Thee, O Lord,
2. Lord, Thy ho-ly tem-ple of-fers Hal-lowed ref-uge, per-fect peace,

Now Thy flock for wor-ship gath-ers, Hun-g'ring for Thy pre-cious Word,
Ref-uge from all foes and scof-fers, Peace that bids all strife to cease.

By Thy guid-ance and Thy grace Drawn un-to this ho-ly place
Like the swal-low in her nest, In Thy house shall I find rest;

Where the heav'nly bread is ten-dered, And true life in Christ en-gen-dered.
Who in Christ his faith re-pos-es He with-in His fold en-clos-es. A-MEN.

3 Not the peace of false assurance
　In Thy house, O Father, dwells;
There the strength for our endurance
　From Thy sacred altar wells.
　　To Thy presence we draw nigh,
　　Grant us power from on high;
With Thy sword and helmet arm us,
That no worldly foes alarm us.

4 Let Thy Church, O heavenly Father,
　Be to us the open way
To that temple where we gather
　Round Thy throne some blessèd day.
　　Gentle Shepherd, as of old,
　　Feed us, tend us, in Thy fold,
And at last Thy flock deliver,
In Thy heaven to dwell forever.

Erik Natanael Söderberg, (b. 1869).

350. Sweet Hour of Prayer.

Sweet hour of prayer. L. M. D.

WILLIAM BATCHELDER BRADBURY, (1816–1868).

1. Sweet hour of prayer, sweet hour of prayer, That calls me from a world of care,

And bids me at my Fa-ther's throne Make all my wants and wish-es known;

In sea-sons of dis-tress and grief, My soul has oft-en found re-lief,

And oft es-caped the tempter's snare By thy re-turn, sweet hour of prayer. A-MEN.

Used by permission of the Biglow & Main Co., owners of the copyright.

2 Sweet hour of prayer, sweet hour of prayer,
Thy wings shall my petitions bear
To Him whose truth and faithfulness
Engage the waiting soul to bless;
And since He bids me seek His face,
Believe His Word, and trust His grace,
I'll cast on Him my every care,
And wait for thee, sweet hour of prayer.

3 Sweet hour of prayer, sweet hour of prayer,
May I thy consolation share,
Till from Mount Pisgah's lofty height
I view my home and take my flight;
This robe of flesh I'll drop, and rise
To seize the everlasting prize;
And shout, while passing through the air,
Farewell, farewell, sweet hour of prayer.

Frances Jane (Crosby) Van Alstyne, 1861.

351. Tell Me the Old, Old Story.

Evangel. 7 6, 7 6. D. With Refrain.   WILLIAM HOWARD DOANE, 1869.

1. Tell me the old, old sto - ry Of un - seen things a - bove;
2. Tell me the sto - ry slow - ly, That I may take it in—

Of Je - sus and His glo - ry, Of Je - sus and His love.
That won - der - ful re - demp - tion, God's rem - e - dy for sin.

Tell me the sto - ry sim - ply, As to a lit - tle child;
Tell me the sto - ry oft - en, For I for - get so soon;

For I am weak and wea - ry, And help - less and de - filed.
The ear - ly dew of morn - ing Has passed a - way at noon.

REFRAIN:

Tell me the old, old sto - ry; Tell me the old, old. sto - ry,

Tell me the old, old sto - ry, Of Je - sus and His love. A-MEN.

Used by permission of W. H. Doane.

3 Tell me the story softly,
   With earnest tones and grave;
Remember, I'm the sinner
   Whom Jesus came to save.
Tell me that story always,
   If you would really be,
In any time of trouble,
   A comforter to me.

4 Tell me the same old story,
   When you have cause to fear
That this world's empty glory
   Is costing me too dear;
And when the light of heaven
   Is dawning on my soul,
Tell me the old, old story:
   "Christ Jesus makes thee whole."
                          Katherine Hankey, 1866.

352. Here Behold Me, As I Cast Me.

Sieh, hier bin ich, Ehrenkönig. 8 7, 8 7, 4 4 7.   Darmstädter Gesangbuch, 1698.

1. Here be - hold me, as I cast me 'Neath Thy throne, O glo-rious King!

Sor - rows throng-ing, child-like long - ing, Son of Man, to Thee I bring.

Let me find Thee! Let me find Thee! Me, a poor and worth-less thing. A-MEN.

2 Look upon me, Lord, I pray Thee,
   Let Thy Spirit dwell in mine;
Thou hast sought me, Thou hast bought me,
   Only Thee to know I pine.
   Let me find Thee!
   Take my heart, and own me Thine!

3 Naught I ask for, naught I strive for,
   But Thy grace, so rich and free,
That Thou givest whom Thou lovest,
   And who truly cleave to Thee.
   Let me find Thee!
   He hath all things who hath Thee.
                          Joachim Neander. 1680.

353. Lead Us, Heavenly Father, Lead Us.

Guide me. 8 7, 8 7, 4 4 7.   WILLIAM LETTON VINER, (1790–1867).

1. Lead us, heav'n-ly Fa-ther, lead us O'er the world's tem-pes-tuous sea; Guard us, guide us, keep us, feed us, For we have no help but Thee; Yet pos-sess-ing Ev-'ry bless-ing, If our God our Fa-ther be. A-MEN.

2 Saviour, breathe forgiveness o'er us;
  All our weakness Thou dost know;
Thou didst tread this earth before us,
  Thou didst feel its keenest woe;
      Lone and dreary,
      Faint and weary,
Through the desert Thou didst go.

3 Spirit of our God, descending,
  Fill our hearts with heavenly joy,
Love, all other love transcending,
  Pleasure that can never cloy;
      Thus provided,
      Pardoned, guided,
Nothing can our peace destroy.

See also Morning and Evening Hymns.   *James Edmeston, 1821, a.*

354. Lord, Dismiss Us with Thy Blessing.

Sicilian Mariners' Hymn. 8 7, 8 7, 4 4 7.

Old Latin Hymn, "O Sanctissima."
MACANTOINE PORTOGALLO.

1. Lord, dis-miss us with Thy bless-ing, Fill our hearts with
joy and peace! Let us each, Thy love pos-sess-ing,
Tri-umph in re-deem-ing grace. O re-fresh us,
O re-fresh us, Trav-'ling through this wil-der-ness. A-MEN.

2 Thanks we give and adoration
For Thy gospel's joyful sound.
May the fruits of Thy salvation
In our hearts and lives abound:
May Thy presence
With us evermore be found.

3 So, whene'er the signal's given
Us from earth to call away,
Borne on angels' wings to heaven,
Glad the summons to obey,
May we, ready,
Rise and reign in endless day.

John Fawcett, 1773, a.

355. On What Has Now Been Sown.

St. Godric. 6 6, 6 6, 8 8.   JOHN BACCHUS DYKES, 1862.

1. On what has now been sown, Thy bless-ing, Lord, be-stow; The
pow'r is Thine a-lone To make it spring and grow: Do Thou the gra-cious
har-vest raise, And Thou a-lone shalt have the praise. A-MEN.

2 To Thee our wants are known,
   From Thee are all our powers,
Accept what is Thine own,
   And pardon what is ours:
Our praises, Lord, and prayers receive,
And to Thy Word a blessing give.

3 O grant that each of us,
   Who meet before Thee here,
May meet together thus,
   When Thou and Thine appear,
And follow Thee to heaven, our home;
E'en so, Amen, Lord Jesus, come!

John Newton, 1779.

356. Blest Be the Tie That Binds.

Dennis. S. M.   Arr. from JOHANN GEORG NÄGELI, by LOWELL MASON, 1845.

1. Blest be the tie that binds Our hearts in Chris-tian love:
2. Be-fore our Fa-ther's throne We pour our ar-dent prayers;

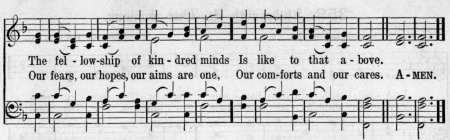

The fel - low-ship of kin - dred minds Is like to that a - bove.
Our fears, our hopes, our aims are one, Our com-forts and our cares. A - MEN.

3 We share our mutual woes,
  Our mutual burdens bear;
And often for each other flows
  The sympathizing tear.

4 From sorrow, toil, and pain,
  And sin we shall be free;
And perfect love and friendship reign
  Through all eternity.

John Fawcett, 1772.

357. Now Our Worship Sweet Is O'er.

Liebster Jesu, wir sind hier. 7 8, 7 8, 8 8.   JOHANN RUDOLPH AHLE, 1664.

1. Now our wor - ship sweet is o'er—Sing-ing, pray-ing, teach-ing, hear - ing:

Let us glad-ly God a-dore For His gra - cious strength and cheer-ing:

Bless His Name, who fain would save us, For the rich re-past He gave us. A - MEN.

2 Now the blessing cheers our heart,
  And the service all is ended,
Let us joyfully depart,
  Be our souls to God commended:
His good Spirit ever guide us,
And with all things well provide us.

3 Let our going out be blest,
  Bless our entrance in like measure;
Bless, O Lord, our toil and rest,
  Bless our bread, our grief, and pleasure;
Be in death Thy blessing given;
Make us blessèd heirs of heaven!

Hartmann Schenk, (1634-1681).

358. Abide with Us, Our Saviour.

Christus der ist mein Leben. 7 6, 7 6.   MELCHIOR VULPIUS, 1609.

1. A - bide with us, our Sav - iour, Nor let Thy mer - cy cease;
2. A - bide with us, our Sav - iour, Sus - tain us by Thy Word;

From Sa - tan's might de - fend us, And grant our souls re - lease.
That we with all Thy peo - ple To life may be re - stored. A-MEN.

3 Abide with us, our Saviour,
  Thou Light of endless light;
Increase to us Thy blessings,
  And save us by Thy might.

4 To Father, Son, and Spirit,
  Eternal One in Three,
As was, and is forever,
  All praise and glory be.

Joshua Stegmann, 1628.

359. For a Season Called to Part.

Solitude. 7 7, 7 7.   LEWIS THOMAS DOWNES, 1851.

1. For a sea - son called to part, Let us now our - selves com-mend
2. Je - sus, hear our hum - ble prayer, Ten - der Shep - herd of Thy sheep,

To the gra - cious eye and heart Of our ev - er - pres-ent Friend.
Let Thy mer - cy and Thy care All our souls in safe - ty keep. A-MEN.

3 What we each have now been taught,
  Let our memories retain.
May we, if we live, be brought
  Here to meet in peace again.

4 Then, if Thou instruction bless,
  Songs of praises shall be given;
We'll our thankfulness express,
  Here on earth, and then in heaven.

John Newton, 1779.

360. Heavenly Father, We Beseech Thee.

Heavenly Father. 8 7, 8 7. With Refrain.

ROBERT LOWRY, (1826–1899).

1. Heav'n-ly Fa-ther, we be-seech Thee, Grant Thy bless-ing ere we part;
2. Lov-ing Sav-iour, go Thou with us, Be our com-fort and our stay;

Take us in Thy care and keep-ing, Guard from e-vil ev-'ry heart.
Grate-ful praise to Thee we ren-der For the joy we feel to-day.

REFRAIN:

Bless the words we here have spo-ken, Of-fered prayer, and cheer-ful strain;

If Thy will, O Lord, we pray Thee, Grant we all may meet a-gain. A-MEN.

3 Holy Spirit, dwell within us,
May our souls Thy temple be;
May we tread the path to glory,
Led and guided still by Thee.

4 Heavenly Father, loving Saviour,
Holy Spirit, Three in One,
As among Thy saints and angels,
So on earth Thy will be done.

Frances Jane (Crosby) Van Alstyne, (1820–1915).

361. O Saviour, Bless Us Ere We Go.

St. Petersburg. 8 8, 8 8, 8 8.   DIMITRI BORTNIANSKY, (1752–1828).

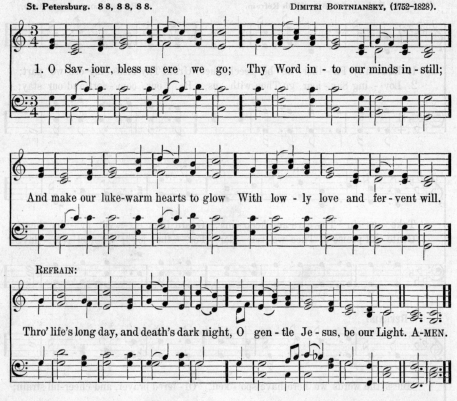

1. O Sav-iour, bless us ere we go; Thy Word in-to our minds in-still;

And make our luke-warm hearts to glow With low-ly love and fer-vent will.

REFRAIN:

Thro' life's long day, and death's dark night, O gen-tle Je-sus, be our Light. A-MEN.

2 Grant us, O Lord, from evil ways
  True absolution and release;
And bless us more than in past days
  With purity and inward peace.

3 Do more than pardon: give us joy,
  Sweet fear and sober liberty,
And loving hearts without alloy,
  That only long to be like Thee.

4 Our tasks are sweet, for Thou hast toiled;
  And care is light, for Thou hast cared;
Ah, never let our works be soiled
  With self, or by deceit ensnared.

5 For all we love, the poor, the sad,
  The sinful, unto Thee we call;
O let Thy mercy make us glad;
  Thou art our Jesus and our All.

Frederick William Faber, 1849.

362. May the Grace of Christ Our Saviour.

Gnadauer Choralbuch, 1784.
Batty (Ringe recht wenn Gottes Gnade). 8 7, 8 7. Har. by WILLIAM HENRY MONK, (1823–1889).

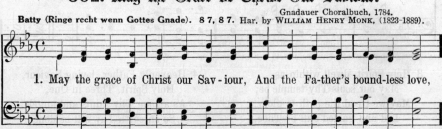

1. May the grace of Christ our Sav-iour, And the Fa-ther's bound-less love,

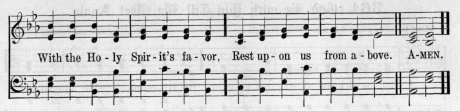

With the Ho - ly Spir - it's fa - vor, Rest up - on us from a - bove. A-MEN.

> 2 Thus may we abide in union
> With each other and the Lord;
> And possess, in sweet communion,
> Joys which earth cannot afford.
>
> *John Newton, 1779.*

363. Saviour, Again to Thy Dear Name We Raise.

Ellers. 10 10, 10 10.   EDWARD JOHN HOPKINS, 1869.

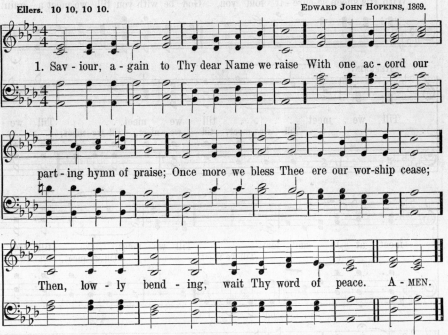

1. Sav - iour, a - gain to Thy dear Name we raise With one ac - cord our part - ing hymn of praise; Once more we bless Thee ere our wor-ship cease; Then, low - ly bend - ing, wait Thy word of peace. A - MEN.

> 2 Grant us Thy peace upon our homeward way;
> With Thee began, with Thee shall end the day:
> Guard Thou the lips from sin, the hearts from shame,
> That in this house have called upon Thy Name.
>
> 3 Grant us Thy peace, Lord, through the coming night;
> Turn Thou for us its darkness into light;
> From harm and danger keep Thy children free,
> For dark and light are both alike to Thee.
>
> 4 Grant us Thy peace throughout our earthly life,
> Our balm in sorrow, and our stay in strife;
> Then, when Thy voice shall bid our conflict cease,
> Call us, O Lord, to Thine eternal peace.
>
> *John Ellerton, 1866. (Text of 1868.)*

364. God Be with You Till We Meet Again.

God be with you. 9 8, 8 9. With Refrain.

WILLIAM GOULD TOMER, 1882.

1. God be with you till we meet a-gain, By His coun-sels guide, up-hold you,

With His sheep se-cure-ly fold you, God be with you till we meet a-gain.

REFRAIN:

Till we meet, ... till we meet, .. Till we
Till we meet, till we meet, till we meet,

meet at Je-sus' feet; Till we meet, ... till we
Till we meet; Till we meet, till we

meet, God be with you till we meet a-gain. A-MEN.
meet, till we meet,

2 God be with you till we meet again,
'Neath His wings protecting hide you,
Daily manna still divide you,
God be with you till we meet again.

See also Evening Hymns.

Jeremiah Eames Rankin, 1882.

365. Saviour, Sprinkle Many Nations.

Greenville. 8 7, 8 7. D.   JEAN JACQUES ROUSSEAU, (1712-1778).

1. Sav - iour, sprin - kle man - y na - tions, Fruit-ful let Thy sor - rows be;
By Thy pains and con - so - la - tions Draw the Gen - tiles un - to Thee.
Of Thy cross the won - drous sto - ry, Be it to the na - tions told;
Let them see Thee in Thy glo - ry, And Thy mer - cy man - i - fold.   A-MEN.

2 Far and wide, though all unknowing,
   Pants for Thee each mortal breast:
Human tears for Thee are flowing,
   Human hearts in Thee would rest.
Thirsting as for dews of even,
   As the new-mown grass for rain,
Thee they seek, as God of heaven,
   Thee as Man, for sinners slain.

3 Saviour, lo, the isles are waiting,
   Stretched the hand, and strained the
For Thy Spirit, new-creating,   [sight,
   Love's pure flame, and wisdom's light.
Give the word, and of the preacher
   Speed the foot, and touch the tongue,
Till on earth by every creature,
   Glory to the Lamb be sung.

Arthur Cleveland Coxe, 1851.

366. The Morning Light Is Breaking.

Webb. 7 6, 7 6. D.

GEORGE JAMES WEBB, 1830.

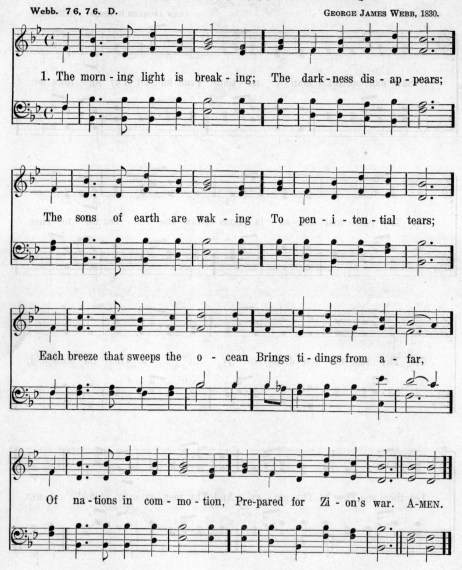

1. The morn - ing light is break - ing; The dark - ness dis - ap - pears;
The sons of earth are wak - ing To pen - i - ten - tial tears;
Each breeze that sweeps the o - cean Brings ti - dings from a - far,
Of na - tions in com - mo - tion, Pre-pared for Zi - on's war. A-MEN.

2 See heathen nations bending
    Before the God we love,
And thousand hearts ascending
    In gratitude above;
While sinners, now confessing,
    The gospel call obey,
And seek the Saviour's blessing,
    A nation in a day.

3 Blest river of salvation,
    Pursue thine onward way;
Flow thou to every nation,
    Nor in thy richness stay;
Stay not till all the lowly
    Triumphant reach their home:
Stay not till all the holy
    Proclaim, "The Lord is come!"

Samuel Francis Smith, 1832.

367. From Greenland's Icy Mountains.

Missionary Hymn. 76, 76. D.   LOWELL MASON, 1823.

1. From Green-land's i - cy moun - tains, From In - dia's cor - al strand;
2. What though the spi - cy breez - es Blow soft o'er Cey - lon's isle;

Where Af - ric's sun - ny foun - tains Roll down their gold - en sand;
Though ev - 'ry pros - pect pleas - es, And on - ly man is vile:

From many an an - cient riv - er, From many a palm - y plain,
In vain with lav - ish kind - ness The gifts of God are strown:

They call us to de - liv - er Their land from er - ror's chain.
The hea-then, in his blind-ness, Bows down to wood and stone. A-MEN.

3 Shall we, whose souls are lighted
  With wisdom from on high,
Shall we to men benighted
  The lamp of life deny?
Salvation, O, salvation!
  The joyful sound proclaim,
Till each remotest nation
  Has learned Messiah's Name.

4 Waft, waft, ye winds, His story,
  And you, ye waters, roll,
Till, like a sea of glory,
  It spreads from pole to pole;
Till o'er our ransomed nature
  The Lamb for sinners slain,
Redeemer, King, Creator,
  In bliss returns to reign.

Reginald Heber, 1819.

368. Jesus Shall Reign Where'er the Sun.

Duke Street. L. M.   JOHN HATTON, 1790.

1. Je - sus shall reign wher - e'er the sun Does his suc-
2. To Him shall end - less prayer be made, And end - less

ces - sive jour - neys run; His king - dom stretch from shore to
prais - es crown His head; His Name, like in - cense, shall a-

shore Till moons shall wax . . . and wane no more.
rise With ev - 'ry morn - ing sac - ri - fice. A - MEN.

3 People and realms of every tongue
Dwell on His love with sweetest song;
And infant voices shall proclaim
Their early blessings on His Name.

4 Blessings abound where'er He reigns;
The prisoner leaps to lose his chains;
The weary find eternal rest,
And all the sons of want are blest.

5 Where He displays His healing power,
Death and the curse are known no more;
In Him the tribes of Adam boast
More blessings than their father lost.

6 Let every creature rise and bring
Peculiar honors to our King;
Angels descend with songs again,
And earth repeat the loud Amen.

Isaac Watts, 1719. Abridged.

369. Lord of the Harvest, Hear.

Schumann. S. M.   Arranged from ROBERT SCHUMANN, (1810-1856).

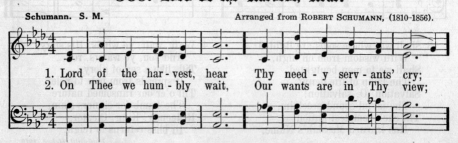

1. Lord of the har - vest, hear Thy need - y serv - ants' cry;
2. On Thee we hum - bly wait, Our wants are in Thy view;

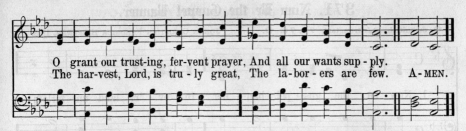

O grant our trust-ing, fer-vent prayer, And all our wants sup-ply.
The har-vest, Lord, is tru-ly great, The la-bor-ers are few. A-MEN.

3 Anoint and send forth more
  Into Thy Church abroad,
And let them speak Thy Word of power,
  As workers with their God.

4 O let them spread Thy Name,
  Their mission fully prove;
Thy universal grace proclaim,
  Thine all-redeeming love.

Charles Wesley, 1742.

370. Thou, Whose Almighty Word.

Italian Hymn. 6 6 4, 6 6, 6 4.   FELICE DE GIARDINI, 1769.

1. Thou, whose al-might-y word Cha-os and dark-ness heard,
2. Thou, who didst come to bring, On Thy re-deem-ing wing,

And took their flight, Hear us, we hum-bly pray; And where the
Heal-ing and sight, Health to the sick in mind, Sight to the

gos-pel day Sheds not its glo-rious ray, Let there be light.
in-ly blind, Now un-to all man-kind Let there be light! A-MEN.

3 Spirit of truth and love,
  Life-giving, holy Dove,
    Speed forth Thy flight;
  Move on the waters' face,
  Bearing the light of grace,
  And in earth's darkest place
    Let there be light!

4 Holy and blessèd Three,
  Glorious Trinity,
    Love, Wisdom, Might!
  Boundless as ocean's tide,
  Rolling in fullest pride,
  Through the earth, far and wide,
    Let there be light!

John Marriott, 1818.

371. Now Be the Gospel Banner.

O, du mitt hjärtas trängtan. 7 6, 7 6. D. JOHAN CHRISTIAN FREDRICK HÆFFNER, 1808.

1. Now be the gos-pel ban-ner In ev-'ry land un-furled;
And be the shout, Ho-san-na! Re-ech-oed through the world;
Till ev-'ry isle and na-tion, Till ev-'ry tribe and tongue,
Re-ceive the great sal-va-tion, And join the hap-py throng. A-MEN.

2 Yes, Thou shalt reign forever,
O Jesus, King of kings!
Thy light, Thy love, Thy favor,
Each ransomed captive sings:
The isles for Thee are waiting,
The deserts learn Thy praise,
The hills and valleys, greeting,
The song responsive raise.

Thomas Hastings, 1831.

372. How Wondrous and Great Thy Works, God of Praise!

Lyons. 10 10, 11 11.   Arr. from JOHANN MICHAEL HAYDN, (1737–1806).

1. How won-drous and great Thy works, God of praise!

How just, King of saints, and true are Thy ways!

O who shall not fear Thee, and hon-or Thy Name?

Thou on-ly art ho-ly, Thou on-ly su-preme. A-MEN.

2 To nations long dark Thy light shall be shown;
  Their worship and vows shall come to Thy throne:
  Thy truth and Thy judgments shall spread all abroad,
  Till earth's every people confess Thee their God.

Henry Ustic Onderdonk, 1826.

373. Speed Thy Servants, Saviour, Speed Them.

Regent Square. 8 7, 8 7, 8 7.

HENRY SMART, 1867.

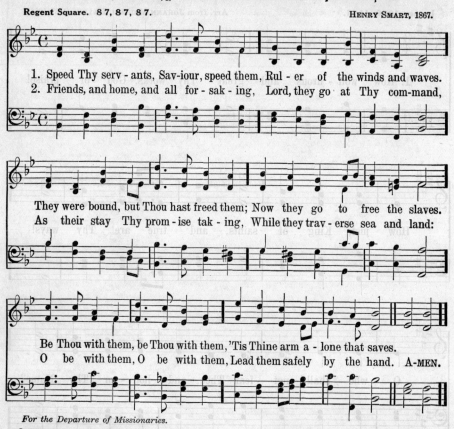

1. Speed Thy serv - ants, Sav-iour, speed them, Rul - er   of the winds and waves.
2. Friends, and home, and all for - sak - ing, Lord, they go at Thy com-mand,

They were bound, but Thou hast freed them; Now they go   to   free the slaves.
As   their stay Thy prom - ise tak - ing, While they trav - erse sea and land:

Be Thou with them, be Thou with them, 'Tis Thine arm a - lone that saves.
O be with them, O be with them, Lead them safely by the hand. A-MEN.

For the Departure of Missionaries.

3 When no fruit appears to cheer them,
　And they seem to toil in vain,
Then in mercy, Lord, draw near them,
Then their sinking hopes sustain.
　　Thus supported,
　Let their zeal revive again.

4 In the midst of opposition
　Let them trust, O Lord, in Thee;
When success attends their mission,
Let Thy servants humble be;
　　Never leave them,
　Till Thy face in heaven they see!

Thomas Kelly, 1820.

374. O Lord Our God, Arise.

Thatcher. S. M.

Arr. from GEORGE FREDERICK HÄNDEL, 1732.

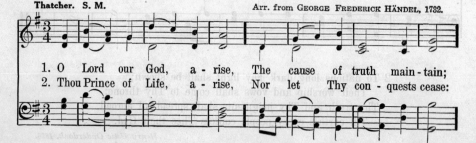

1. O Lord our God, a - rise, The cause of truth main - tain;
2. Thou Prince of Life, a - rise, Nor let   Thy con - quests cease:

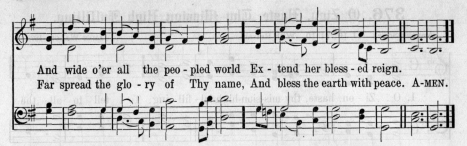

And wide o'er all the peo - pled world Ex - tend her bless - ed reign.
Far spread the glo - ry of Thy name, And bless the earth with peace. A-MEN.

3 Thou, Holy Ghost, arise,
   Exert Thy quickening power,
And o'er a dark and ruined world
   Thy light and peace outpour.

4 All men on earth, arise,
   To God the Saviour sing;
From shore to shore, from earth to heaven,
   Let His high praises ring.

Ralph Wardlaw, 1800.

375. Mighty Lord, Extend Thy Kingdom.

Coronæ. 8 7, 8 7, 4 7.   WILLIAM HENRY MONK, 1871.

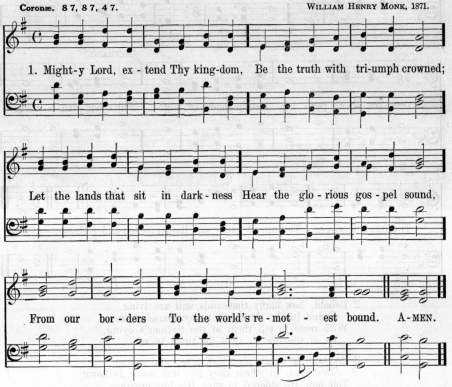

1. Might-y Lord, ex - tend Thy king-dom, Be the truth with tri-umph crowned;

Let the lands that sit in dark - ness Hear the glo - rious gos - pel sound,

From our bor - ders To the world's re - mot - est bound. A-MEN.

2 By Thine arm, eternal Father,
   Scatter far the shades of night;
Let the great Immanuel's Kingdom
   Open like the morning light:
      Let all barriers
   Yield before Thy heavenly might.

3 Come in all Thy Spirit's power;
   Come, Thy reign on earth restore;
In Thy strength ride forth and conquer,
   Still advancing more and more,
      Till all people
   Shall Thy holy Name adore.

Joseph Cottle, 1828, a.

376. O Zion, Haste, Thy Mission High Fulfilling.

Angelic Songs. 11 10, 11 10. With Refrain.

JAMES WALCH, 1875.

1. O Zi-on, haste, thy mis-sion high ful-fill-ing, To tell to all the
world that God is Light; That He who made all na-tions is not will-ing
One soul should per-ish, lost in shades of night. Pub-lish glad ti-dings;
REFRAIN:
Ti-dings of peace; Ti-dings of Je-sus, Re-demp-tion and re-lease. A-MEN.

2 Behold, how many thousands still are lying
    Bound in the darksome prison-house of sin,
With none to tell them of the Saviour's dying,
    Or of the life He died for them to win.

3 Proclaim to every people, tongue, and nation
    That God, in whom they live and move, is Love:
Tell how He stooped to save His lost creation,
    And died on earth that man might live above.

4 Give of thy sons to bear the message glorious;
    Give of thy wealth to speed them on their way;
Pour out thy soul for them in prayer victorious,
    And haste the coming of the glorious day.

Mary Ann Thomson, 1870.

377. Winter Reigns o'er Many a Region.

Theodoret. 8 7, 8 7. D.

JEREMIAH FRANKLIN OHL, 1887.

1. Win - ter reigns o'er man-y a re - gion, Man - y a seed - field fal - low lies;
2. Lord, Thy Church is ev - er pray - ing: Now her anx - ious yearnings hear;

When, O Lord, shall come the springtime, With its quick-'ning en - er - gies?
Speed the tri - umphs of Thy King-dom; Spread its vic - t'ries far and near.

When shall this long night be end - ed? When the morn - ing dawn ap - pear?
Own the work, Thy grace at - tend it, Which we un - der - take for Thee;

When shall drought give place to freshness? When these deserts bloom with cheer?
Let a ho - ly love in-flame us; Kin - dle zeal and fer - ven - cy. A-MEN.

From "School and Parish Hymnal." by permission.

3 That Thy fields be rightly cultured,
    Send the laborers that we need,
Men to light the heavy darkness,
    Sow the wastes with precious seed.
Then send down the gentle showers,
    Make Thy gracious sunlight shine,
That each field may joy with blessing,
    Bringing forth the fruits divine.

4 By the breezes of Thy Spirit,
    Fan all deadness into life;
Bless the seeds to Thee upspringing,
    Keep each plant from blast and strife.
And, ye toilers in this seeding,
    Know the promise God hath given:
Glorious crowns await the faithful,
    And eternal gains in heaven.

Leonhard Meisser, 1840 (?).

378. Go Forth, Ye Heralds, in My Name.

Wenn wir in höchsten Nöthen sein. L. M.   Genevan French Psalter, 1542.

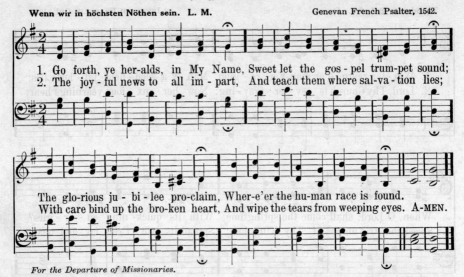

1. Go forth, ye her-alds, in My Name, Sweet let the gos-pel trum-pet sound;
2. The joy-ful news to all im-part, And teach them where sal-va-tion lies;

The glo-rious ju-bi-lee pro-claim, Wher-e'er the hu-man race is found.
With care bind up the bro-ken heart, And wipe the tears from weeping eyes. A-MEN.

For the Departure of Missionaries.

3 Be wise as serpents where you go,
  But harmless as the peaceful dove;
  And let your heaven-taught conduct show
  Ye are commissioned from above.

4 Freely from Me ye have received,
  Freely, in love, to others give;
  Thus shall your doctrines be believed,
  And, by your labors, sinners live.

James Maxwell, 1789.

379. Hasten, Lord, the Glorious Time.

Weber (Seymour). 7 7, 7 7.   CARL MARIA VON WEBER, 1826.

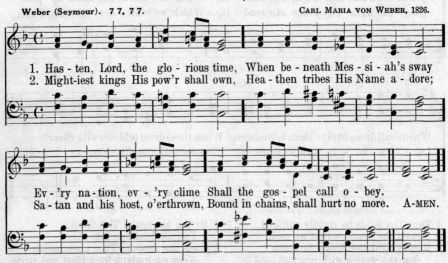

1. Has-ten, Lord, the glo-rious time, When be-neath Mes-si-ah's sway
2. Might-iest kings His pow'r shall own, Hea-then tribes His Name a-dore;

Ev-'ry na-tion, ev-'ry clime Shall the gos-pel call o-bey.
Sa-tan and his host, o'erthrown, Bound in chains, shall hurt no more. A-MEN.

3 Then shall war and tumult cease,
  Then be banished grief and pain;
  Righteousness and joy and peace
  Undisturbed shall ever reign.

4 Bless we, then, our gracious Lord;
  Ever praise His glorious Name;
  All His mighty acts record,
  All His wondrous love proclaim.

Harriet Auber, 1829.

380. Awake, Thou Spirit, Who Didst Fire.

Ich will dich lieben. 8 8, 8 8, 8 8.

König's Harmonischer Liederschatz, 1731.
Arr. by ADOLF HULT, 1923.

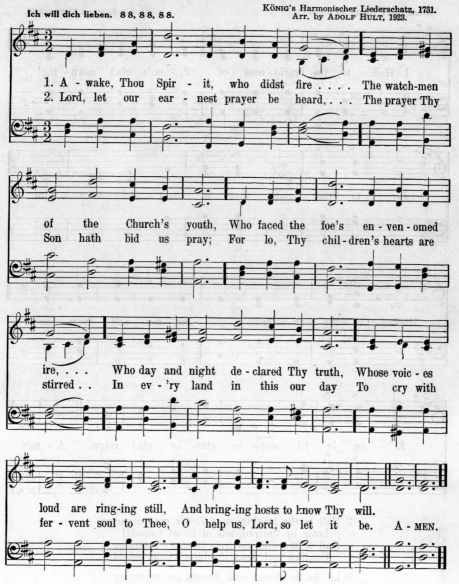

1. A - wake, Thou Spir - it, who didst fire .... The watch-men
of the Church's youth, Who faced the foe's en - ven - omed
ire, ... Who day and night de - clared Thy truth, Whose voic - es
loud are ring-ing still, And bring-ing hosts to know Thy will.

2. Lord, let our ear - nest prayer be heard, ... The prayer Thy
Son hath bid us pray; For lo, Thy chil - dren's hearts are
stirred .. In ev - 'ry land in this our day To cry with
fer - vent soul to Thee, O help us, Lord, so let it be. A - MEN.

Or: St. Catherine, No. 214.

3 O haste to help, ere we are lost!
Send preachers forth, in spirit strong,
Armed with Thy Word, a dauntless host,
Bold to attack the rule of wrong;
Let them the earth for Thee reclaim,
Thy heritage, to know Thy Name.

4 O let Thy Word have speedy course,
Through every land be glorified,
Till all the heathen know its force,
And fill Thy churches far and wide;
Wake Israel from her sleep, O Lord,
And spread the conquests of Thy Word!

Karl Heinrich von Bogatzky, 1750.

381. Hail to the Brightness of Zion's Glad Morning!

Wesley. 11 10, 11 10.   LOWELL MASON, 1833.

1. Hail to the bright-ness of Zi-on's glad morn-ing!

Joy to the lands that in dark-ness have lain!

Hushed be the ac-cents of sor-row and mourn-ing;

Zi-on in tri-umph be-gins her glad reign. A-MEN.

2 Hail to the brightness of Zion's glad morning,
   Long by the prophets of Israel foretold!
Hail to the millions from bondage returning!
   Gentiles and Jews the blest vision behold.

3 Lo, in the desert rich flowers are springing,
   Streams ever copious are gliding along;
Loud from the mountain-tops echoes are ringing,
   Wastes rise in verdure, and mingle in song.

4 Hark, from all lands, from the isles of the ocean,
   Praise to Jehovah ascending on high;
Fallen the engines of war and commotion,
   Shouts of salvation are rending the sky.

Thomas Hastings, 1832.

382. Our Country's Voice Is Pleading.

Beaumont. 7 6, 7 6. D.   RALPH ALVIN STROM, 1924.

1. Our coun - try's voice is plead - ing, Ye men of God, a - rise!
His prov - i - dence is lead - ing, The land be - fore you lies;
O'er it the day has bright-ened, And prom - ise clothes the soil;
Wide fields, for har - vest whit - ened, In - vite the reap-er's toil. A-MEN.

2 The love of Christ unfolding,
    Speed on from east to west,
Till all, His cross beholding,
    In Him are fully blest.
Great Author of salvation,
    Haste, haste the glorious day
When we, a ransomed nation,
    Thy scepter shall obey.

Maria Frances Anderson, 1848.

383. O That the Lord's Salvation.

Christus der ist mein Leben.   7 6, 7 6.   MELCHIOR VULPIUS, 1609.

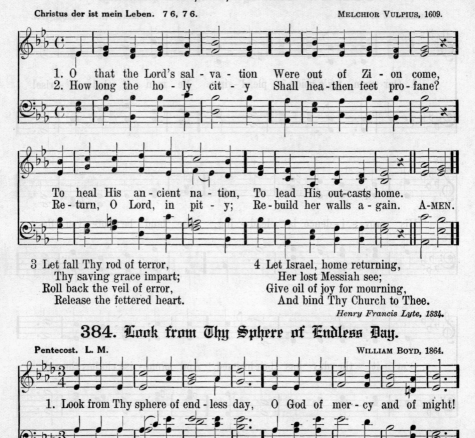

1. O that the Lord's sal - va - tion Were out of Zi - on come,
2. How long the ho - ly cit - y Shall hea - then feet pro - fane?

To heal His an - cient na - tion, To lead His out-casts home.
Re - turn, O Lord, in pit - y; Re - build her walls a - gain.   A-MEN.

3 Let fall Thy rod of terror,
    Thy saving grace impart;
  Roll back the veil of error,
    Release the fettered heart.

4 Let Israel, home returning,
    Her lost Messiah see;
  Give oil of joy for mourning,
    And bind Thy Church to Thee.

Henry Francis Lyte, 1834.

384. Look from Thy Sphere of Endless Day.

Pentecost. L. M.   WILLIAM BOYD, 1864.

1. Look from Thy sphere of end - less day, O God of mer - cy and of might!

In pit - y look on those who stray, Benighted in this land of light.   A-MEN.

2 In peopled vale, in lonely glen,
    In crowded mart, by stream or sea,
  How many of the sons of men
    Hear not the message sent from Thee!

3 Send forth Thy heralds, Lord, to call
    The thoughtless young, the hardened old,
  A scattered, homeless flock, till all
    Be gathered to Thy peaceful fold.

4 Send them Thy mighty Word, to speak
    Till faith shall dawn, and doubt depart,
  To awe the bold, to stay the weak,
    And bind and heal the broken heart.

5 Then all these wastes,— a dreary scene,
    That fills with sadness as we gaze,—
  Shall grow with living waters green,
    And lift to heaven the voice of praise.

William Cullen Bryant, 1840, a.

385. Thine Arm, O Lord, in Days of Old.

St. Matthew. C. M. D.   WILLIAM CROFT, (1678-1727).

1. Thine arm, O Lord, in days of old Was strong to heal and save;
It tri-umphed o'er dis-ease and death, O'er dark-ness and the grave;
To Thee they went, the blind, the dumb, The pal-sied and the lame,
The lep-er with His taint-ed life, The sick with fe-vered frame. A-MEN.

2 And lo, Thy touch brought life and health,
  Gave speech, and strength, and sight;
And youth renewed and frenzy calmed
  Owned Thee the Lord of light.
And now, O Lord, be near to bless,
  Almighty as of yore,
In crowded street, by restless couch,
  As by Gennes'ret's shore.

3 Be Thou our great Deliverer still,
  Thou Lord of life and death;
Restore and quicken, soothe and bless,
  With Thine almighty breath.
To hands that work and eyes that see
  Give wisdom's heavenly lore,
That whole and sick, and weak and strong,
  May praise Thee evermore.

Edward Hayes Plumptre, 1864.

386. Blessed Fount of Heavenly Gladness.

Stuttgart. 8 7, 8 7.   Psalmodia Sacra, Gotha, 1715.

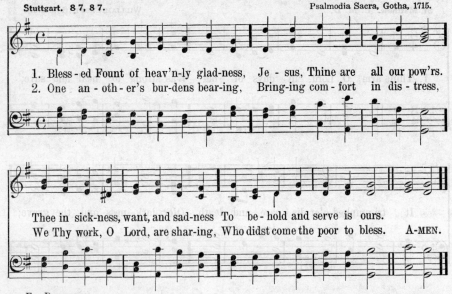

1. Bless - ed Fount of heav'n-ly glad-ness, Je - sus, Thine are all our pow'rs.
2. One an - oth - er's bur-dens bear-ing, Bring-ing com - fort in dis - tress,

Thee in sick-ness, want, and sad-ness To be - hold and serve is ours.
We Thy work, O Lord, are shar-ing, Who didst come the poor to bless. A-MEN.

For Deaconesses.

3 Where a child with love is tended,
    Where the hungry are supplied,
  Where the prisoner is befriended,
    Thou art our Reward and Guide.

4 Send Thy love with fire from heaven,
    Love that longs to help and bless;
  Be it in the world a leaven
    Unto peace and righteousness.

Theodor Fliedner, (1800–1864).

387. Where Cross the Crowded Ways of Life.

En främling klappar på din dörr. L. M.   German.

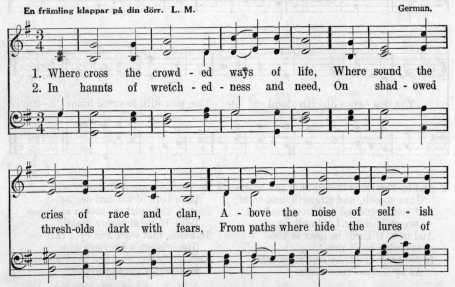

1. Where cross the crowd - ed ways of life, Where sound the
2. In haunts of wretch - ed - ness and need, On shad - owed

cries of race and clan, A - bove the noise of self - ish
thresh-olds dark with fears, From paths where hide the lures of

strife, We hear Thy voice, O Son of Man.
greed, We catch the vi - sion of Thy tears. A - MEN.

3 From tender childhood's helplessness,
   From woman's grief, man's burdened toil,
From famished souls, from sorrow's stress,
   Thy heart has never known recoil.

4 The cup of water given for Thee
   Still holds the freshness of Thy grace;
Yet long these multitudes to see
   The sweet compassion of Thy face.

5 O Master, from the mountain side
   Make haste to hear these hearts of pain;
Among these restless throngs abide,
   O tread the city's streets again,

6 Till sons of men shall learn Thy love,
   And follow where Thy feet have trod;
Till glorious from Thy heaven above
   Shall come the City of our God.

Frank Mason North, 1905.

388. O Fount of Good, to Own Thy Love.

Nun danket all' und bringet Ehr (Störl). C. M.   JOHANN GEORG CHRISTIAN STÖRL, 1710.

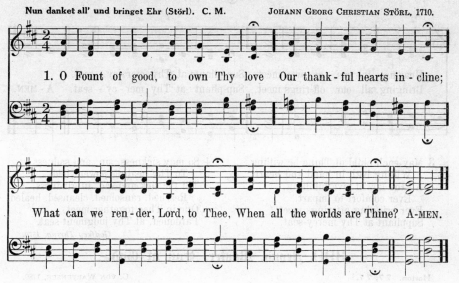

1. O Fount of good, to own Thy love Our thank - ful hearts in - cline;

What can we ren - der, Lord, to Thee, When all the worlds are Thine? A-MEN.

2 But Thou hast needy brethren here,
   Partakers of Thy grace,
Whose humble names Thou wilt confess
   Before Thy Father's face.

3 In their sad accents of distress
   Thy pleading voice is heard;
In them Thou mayst be clothed and fed,
   And visited, and cheered.

4 Then help us, Lord, Thy yoke to wear,
   And joy to do Thy will,
Each other's burdens gladly bear,
   And love's sweet law fulfill.

5 To Thee our all devoted be,
   In whom we move and live;
Freely we have received of Thee,
   As freely may we give.

Philip Doddridge, (1702-1751).

389. Thou to Whom the Sick and Dying.

Jesu meine Lust und Wonne. 8 7, 8 7, 7 7.   Lüneburgisches Gesangbuch, 1686.

1. Thou to whom the sick and dy - ing   Ev - er came, nor came in vain,
2. Still the wea - ry, sick and dy - ing   Need a broth - er's, sis-ter's care;

Still with heal-ing words re - ply-ing   To the wea-ried cry of pain,
On Thy high-er help re - ly-ing,   May we now their bur-den share,

Hear us, Je-sus, as we meet, Sup-pliants at Thy mer-cy - seat.
Bringing all our off'rings meet, Sup-pliant at Thy mer-cy - seat.   A - MEN.

3 May each child of Thine be willing,
   Willing both in hand and heart,
All the law of love fulfilling,
   Ever comfort to impart,
Ever bringing offerings meet,
Suppliant at Thy mercy-seat.

4 So may sickness, sin, and sadness
   To Thy healing power yield,
Till the sick and sad, in gladness,
   Rescued, ransomed, cleansèd, healed,
One in Thee together meet,
Pardoned, at Thy judgment-seat.
        Godfrey Thring, 1870.

390. Jesus, Master, Son of God.

Horton. 7 7, 7 7.   C. VON WARTENSEE, 1780.

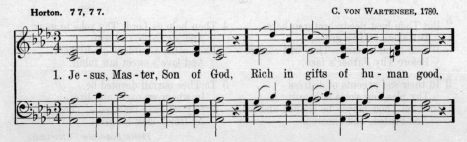

1. Je - sus, Mas - ter, Son of God,   Rich in gifts of hu - man good,

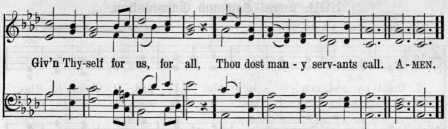

Giv'n Thy-self for us, for all, Thou dost man-y serv-ants call. A-MEN.

For Deaconesses

2 By Thy mercy and Thy love,
Through Thy Spirit from above,
Plenteous grace to each is given,
Grace to serve the Lord of heaven.

3 Thanks for those devoted bands
Who, with earnest hearts and hands,
Wait and work the sick to cheer,
Spreading mercies far and near.

4 While the sacred cross they bear,
Grant them Thy rewards to share;
Be their Help where'er they go,
Bearing balm for human woe.

5 Guide and bless them on their way;
Let Thy Spirit be their stay;
May their numbers, Lord, increase,
Bring them to Thy heavenly peace.

Joseph Augustus Seiss, 1899.

391. O God of Mercy! Hearken Now.

Quebec (Hesperus). L. M.

HENRY BAKER, 1866.
Modified by JAMES PEARCE, 1868.

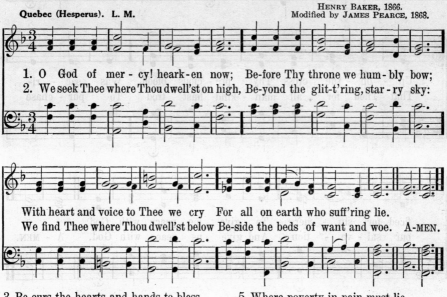

1. O God of mer-cy! heark-en now; Be-fore Thy throne we hum-bly bow;
2. We seek Thee where Thou dwell'st on high, Be-yond the glit-t'ring, star-ry sky:

With heart and voice to Thee we cry For all on earth who suff'ring lie.
We find Thee where Thou dwell'st below Be-side the beds of want and woe. A-MEN.

3 Be ours the hearts and hands to bless
The sorrowing sons of wretchedness;
Send Thou the help we cannot give;
Bid dying souls arise and live.

4 O let the healing waters spring,
Touched by Thy pitying angel's wing;
With quickening power new strength impart
To palsied will, to withered heart.

5 Where poverty in pain must lie,
Where little suffering children cry,
Bid us haste forth as called by Thee,
And in Thy poor Thyself to see.

6 Be Thou, O God eternal, blest,
Thy holy Name on earth confest!
Echo Thy praise from every shore
For ever and for evermore.

Miss E. S. Clark.

392. Great Joy and Consolation.

O Jesu! än de dina. 7 6, 7 6, 8 7 6.   HANS THOMISSÖNS Psalmebog, 1569.

1. Great joy and con - so - la - tion   I   find, O Christ, in Thee,
2. Be - neath Thy cross I   tar - ry,   O teach me   in Thy death

For Thou art   my Sal - va - tion, Thy pas - sion sets me free;
Hum - bly my own to   car - ry   A - long the hal - lowed path

Up - on   the   cross Thy   pre - cious blood Was   sac - ri -
That Thou for   all man - kind hast   trod   To   pur - chase

ficed for sin - ners   To   give   me peace with God.
our   sal - va - tion And give   us peace with God. A - MEN.

3 I see Thee serve and labor
   In love to save mankind;
So may I help my neighbor
   Whom needy I may find;
And though ungrateful he may **prove**,
   O let me not grow weary
In Christlike deeds of love.

4 And when my days are ended,
   And all my struggles cease,
Thine arms I see extended
   To give eternal peace.
Whoever here confesses Thee
   Shalt Thou confess in glory
Where we shall dwell with Thee.

Johan Olof Wallin, 1816.

393. O Precious Saviour, Heal and Bless.

Af himlens här den högstes makt. 8 7, 8 7, 8 8 7.

Swedish, 1697.

1. O pre-cious Sav-iour, heal and bless The suf-f'rers in af-flic-tion. Thou know-est, Lord, their help-less-ness; Look down in ben-e-dic-tion Up-on the sick who seek Thine aid, Let them in faith, all un-a-fraid, Rest in Thy ten-der mer-cy. A-MEN.

2 "Remember them that are in bonds,"
Thy Word so gently pleadeth,
Thy mercy to our prayers responds,
Thy kindness intercedeth.
Fill us with love, Thou Love divine,
Toward all who in affliction pine,
Let us reflect Thy patience.

3 O dearest Lord, remember those
In bonds of dread diseases;
Incarnate God, Thy wisdom knows
The balsam that releases.
Thou Sufferer of Calvary,
Let these afflicted hide in Thee,
And in Thy wounds find healing.

Anna Hoppe, 1922.

394. Lord Jesus Christ, the Children's Friend.

Saxby. L. M.   TIMOTHY RICHARD MATTHEWS, 1883.

1. Lord Jesus Christ, the children's Friend, To Thee the
or-phans we com-mend; Do Thou their ev-'ry need supply Un-til they reach their home on high. A-MEN.

2 Thou pleadest still so tenderly,
"Let little ones come unto Me."
O grant us grace to do Thy will,
Our hearts with love and mercy fill.

3 Bless Thou the fatherless, we pray,
Abide with them from day to day,
Feed Thou Thy lambs, O dearest Lord,
In verdant pastures of Thy Word.

4 Grant that we heed Thy Word's commands,
And give us willing hearts and hands;
Let us our gifts of love bestow,
That they Thy boundless love may know.

5 Bless all who in the parents' stead
Provide these little ones with bread;
Bless all who shield with loving arms
These helpless ones from all alarms.

6 O precious Saviour, hear our prayers!
Protect Thy lambs from earthly snares;
Be Thou their Guide, O heavenly Friend,
Until they reach their journey's end.

Anna Hoppe, 1921.

395. Awake! the Watchman Crieth.

Old 130th Psalm. 7 6, 7 6. D.   Genevan Psalter, 1556.

1. A - wake! the watch-man cri - eth On Zi - on's ram-parts still!
The Lord His grace sup - pli - eth, Re - pent, and heed His will.
Life's jour - ney fast is near - ing The ev - er - last - ing shore;
The hour of death ap - pear - ing, When time shall be no more.

2. Too late the sin - ners wak - en Where day hath ceased to dawn;
Where grace that was for - sak - en Is ev - er - more with-drawn;
Where's heard no pray - ing sen - tence God's mer - cy to im - plore;
For there is no re - pent-ance, When time shall be no more. A - MEN.

3 O souls who spurn salvation!
  See this eternity
Of darkness, desolation,
  And constant agony.
The torments none can banish,
  Nor aught can peace restore;
And hope itself shall vanish,
  When time shall be no more!

4 Awake! the voice still soundeth,
  'Tis now the accepted hour;
The grace of God aboundeth
  To save from sin's dread power.
Make haste, implore Christ's favor,
  Thy sins confess, and bow
Before Thy Lord and Saviour;
  The accepted time is now.

Frans Mikael Franzén, 1814.

396. Behold a Stranger at the Door.

Holley. L. M.

GEORGE HEWS, 1835.

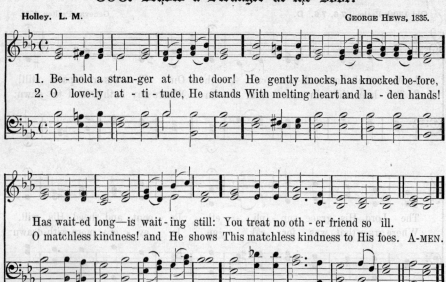

1. Be - hold a stran-ger at the door! He gently knocks, has knocked be-fore,
2. O love-ly at - ti - tude, He stands With melting heart and la - den hands!

Has wait-ed long—is wait - ing still: You treat no oth - er friend so ill.
O matchless kindness! and He shows This matchless kindness to His foes. A-MEN.

3 But will He prove a friend indeed?
He will; the very friend you need;
The Friend of sinners—yes, 'tis He,
With garments dyed on Calvary.

4 Admit Him, lest His anger burn,
And He, departing, ne'er return;
Admit Him, or the hour's at hand
You'll at His door rejected stand.

Joseph Grigg, 1756.

397. Jesus Sinners Doth Receive.

Meinhold. 7 8, 7 8, 7 7.

From JOHANN SEBASTIAN BACH, (1685-1750).

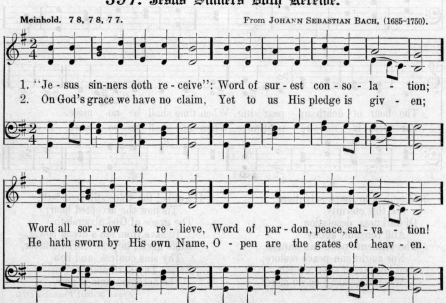

1. "Je - sus sin-ners doth re - ceive": Word of sur - est con - so - la - tion;
2. On God's grace we have no claim, Yet to us His pledge is giv - en;

Word all sor - row to re - lieve, Word of par - don, peace, sal - va - tion!
He hath sworn by His own Name, O - pen are the gates of heav - en.

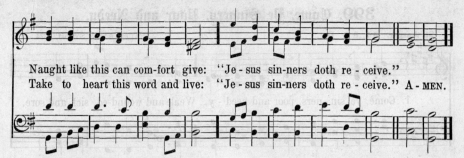

Naught like this can com-fort give: "Je-sus sin-ners doth re-ceive."
Take to heart this word and live: "Je-sus sin-ners doth re-ceive." A-MEN.

3 When a helpless lamb doth stray,
  After it, the Shepherd, pressing
Through each dark and dangerous way,
  Brings it back, His own possessing.
Jesus seeks thee, O believe:
"Jesus sinners doth receive."

4 Sorrowing, Lord, I yield to Thee,
  Weary of sin's heavy burden;
Let Thy grace my portion be,
  All I crave for is Thy pardon.
This Thy promise I believe:
"Jesus sinners doth receive."

Erdmann Neumeister, 1718.

398. Just As Thou Art, without One Trace.

Woodworth. L. M.   WILLIAM BATCHELDER BRADBURY, 1849.

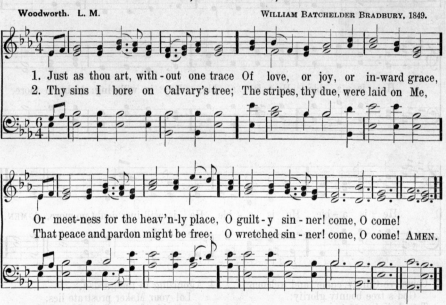

1. Just as thou art, with-out one trace Of love, or joy, or in-ward grace,
2. Thy sins I bore on Calvary's tree; The stripes, thy due, were laid on Me,

Or meet-ness for the heav'n-ly place, O guilt-y sin-ner! come, O come!
That peace and pardon might be free; O wretched sin-ner! come, O come! AMEN.

3 Burdened with guilt, would'st thou be
    blessed?
Trust not the world; it gives no rest;
I bring relief to hearts oppressed;
    O weary sinner! come, O come!

4 Come, leave thy burden at the cross,
Count all thy gains but worthless dross:
My grace repays all earthly loss;
    O needy sinner! come, O come!

5 Come, hither bring thy boding fears,
Thine aching heart, thy bursting tears;
'Tis mercy's voice salutes thine ears;
    O trembling sinner! come, O come!

6 "The Spirit and the bride say, Come!"
Rejoicing saints reëcho, "Come!"
Who faints, who thirsts, who will, may
    come;
Thy Saviour bids thee come, O come!

Russell Sturgis Cook, 1850.

399. Come, Ye Sinners, Poor and Needy.

St. Ansgar. 8 7, 8 7. D.   RALPH ALVIN STROM, 1924.

1. Come, ye sin-ners, poor and need-y, Weak and wound-ed, sick and sore,

Je-sus read-y stands to save you, Full of pit-y, love, and pow'r.

He is a-ble, He is a-ble, He is will-ing: doubt no more,

He is a-ble, He is a-ble, He is will-ing: doubt no more. A-MEN.

2 Come, ye thirsty, come. and welcome.
    God's free bounty glorify:
True belief, and true repentance,
    Every grace that brings us nigh,
       Without money,
    Come to Jesus Christ, and buy.

3 Let not conscience make you linger,
    Nor of fitness fondly dream;
All the fitness He requireth
    Is to feel your need of Him;
       This He gives you;
    'Tis His Spirit's rising beam.

4 Agonizing in the garden,
    Lo! your Maker prostrate lies;
On the bloodstained tree behold Him;
    Hear Him cry. before He dies.
       "It is finished!"
    Sinner, will not this suffice?

5 Lo! the incarnate God, ascended,
    Pleads the merit of His blood:
Venture to Him, venture wholly,
    Let no other trust intrude:
       None but Jesus
    Can do helpless sinners good.

Joseph Hart, 1759.

400. Shun, My Heart, the Thought Forever.

Freu dich sehr, o meine Seele. 8 7, 8 7, 7 7, 8 8.

French Psalter, 1555.

1. Shun, my heart, the thought for - ev - er That thou hast been cast a - way,
2. Thou art, as is ev - 'ry oth - er, Taint - ed with the bane of sin

Rest up - on God's Word and fa - vor, Nev - er cease to watch and pray.
That the ser - pent through our fa - ther A - dam, by the fall, brought in.

E'en though thou un - right - eous art, True and faith - ful is God's heart;
But if thou God's voice dost hear, With a con - trite heart draw near

Hast thou death deserved for - ev - er? God's appeased, despond thou nev - er!
Un - to God, He will re - ceive thee, All thy sins He will for - give thee. A-MEN.

3 Thou wilt find in Him a Father
    Who is patient, kind, and true,
  He doth love thee as no brother
    And no other friend can do.
  E'en our smallest cares He knows,
  He is touched by all our woes;
  Our most secret prayers He heareth,
  And our saddened hearts He cheereth.

4 Hear His word, "As I am living,
    I the death of none would see,
  But that every sinner, giving
    Up his heart, would turn to Me.
  How my heart with rapture burns
  When a prodigal returns!
  My own child I love to call him,
  And no evil shall befall him."

5 Never shepherd's heart so yearneth
    For the sheep that go astray
  As God's loving bosom burneth
    For His erring child alway.
  How He thirsts, and longs, and yearns
  For the soul that from Him turns!
  Couldst thou know His love so tender,
  Thou wouldst praise unto Him render.

6 Of such wondrous love and favor
    Open wide the door to me,
  And Thy goodness, precious Saviour,
    Let me ever taste and see.
  Love me, Lord, and let me be
  Ever nearer drawn to Thee;
  Let Thy Spirit lead and guide me,
  In Thy loving bosom hide me.

Paul Gerhardt, 1648.

401. O Jesus, Thou Art Standing.

St. Edith. 76, 76. D.

JUSTIN HEINRICH KNECHT, 1799.
Adapted by EDWARD HUSBAND, 1871.

1. O Jesus, Thou art stand-ing Out-side the fast-closed door, In low-ly pa-tience wait-ing To pass the thresh-old o'er: Shame on us, Chris-tian broth-ers, His Name and sign who bear: O shame, thrice shame up-on us, To keep Him stand-ing there! A-MEN.

2 O Jesus, Thou art knocking;
And lo, that hand is scarred,
And thorns Thy brow encircle,
And tears Thy face have marred:
O love that passeth knowledge,
So patiently to wait!
O sin that hath no equal,
So fast to bar the gate!

3 O Jesus, Thou art pleading
In accents meek and low,
"I died for you, My children,
And will ye treat Me so?"
O Lord, with shame and sorrow
We open now the door;
Dear Saviour, enter, enter,
And leave us nevermore.

William Walsham How, 1867.

402. Ajar the Temple Gates Are Swinging.

Wer weiss, wie nahe mir mein Ende. 9 8, 9 8, 8 8.   BRONNER'S Choral-Buch, 1715.

1. A - jar the tem - ple gates are swing - ing, Lo! still the grace of God is free. Per - haps when next the bells are ring - ing The grave shall o - pen un - to thee, And thou art laid be - neath the sod No more to see this house of God. A - MEN.

2 But if to-day the Lord thou seekest,
  His blessèd gospel to embrace,
He who gives strength unto the weakest
  Shall fill thy heart with truth and grace.
In life He will thy footsteps guide,
In death He still is at thy side.

3 O come to-day, and do not reckon
  Upon the day that is not thine.
The Lord in mercy still doth beckon:
  Accept to-day His grace divine.
Then shall thy prayers and praises rise
A sacred incense to the skies.

Frans Mikael Franzén, 1814.

403. God Calling Yet.

Federal Street. L. M.   HENRY KEMBLE OLIVER, 1832.

1. God call - ing yet! shall I not hear? Earth's pleas - ures
shall I still hold dear? Shall life's swift pass - ing
years all fly, And still my soul in slum - ber lie? A - MEN.

2 God calling yet! shall I not rise?
Can I His loving voice despise,
And basely His kind care repay?
He calls me still, can I delay?

3 God calling yet! and shall He knock,
And I my heart the closer lock?
He still is waiting to receive,
And shall I dare His Spirit grieve?

4 God calling yet! and shall I give
No heed, but still in bondage live?
I wait, but He does not forsake;
He calls me still: my heart, awake!

5 Ah, yield Him all: in Him confide.
Where but with Him doth peace abide?
Break loose, let earthly bonds be riven,
And let the spirit rise to heaven!

6 God calling yet! I cannot stay,
My heart I yield without delay:
Vain world, farewell! from thee I part;
The voice of God hath reached my heart!

Gerhard Tersteegen, 1735.

404. Weary of Earth, and Laden with My Sin.

Langran. 10 10, 10 10.   JAMES LANGRAN, 1862.

1. Wea-ry of earth, and la-den with my sin, I look at heav'n and long to en-ter in; But there no e-vil thing may find a home; And yet I hear a voice that bids me come. A-MEN.

2 It is the voice of Jesus that I hear;
His are the hands stretched out to draw me near,
And His the blood that can for all atone,
And set me faultless there before the throne.

3 'Twas He who found me on the deathly wild,
And made me heir of heaven, the Father's child,
And day by day, whereby my soul may live,
Gives me His grace of pardon, and will give.

4 O great Absolver, grant my soul may wear
The lowliest garb of penitence and prayer,
That in Thy Father's courts my glorious dress
May be the garment of Thy righteousness.

5 Yea, Thou wilt answer for me, righteous Lord;
Thine all the merits, mine the great reward;
Thine the sharp thorns, and mine the golden crown,
Mine the life won, through Thine, the life laid down.

Samuel John Stone, 1866.

405. Lord, to Thee I Make Confession.

Herr, ich habe missgehandelt.   8 7, 8 7, 8 8.   Trochaic.   JOHANN CRÜGER, 1649.

1. Lord, to Thee I make con - fes - sion, I have sinned and gone a-
2. Though my conscience doth ap - pall me, Fa - ther, I will seek Thy

stray, I have mul - ti - plied trans - gres - sion, Cho - sen
face; Though Thy child I dare not call me, Yet re-

for my - self the way. Forced at last to see my er - rors,
ceive me to Thy grace; For my sins do not for - sake me,

Lord, I trem - ble at Thy ter - rors.
O let not Thy wrath o'er - take me. A - MEN.

3 For Thy Son hath suffered for me,
  And the blood He shed for sin
Can to life and faith restore me,
  Quench this burning fire within;
'Tis alone His cross can vanquish
These dark fears, and soothe this anguish.

4 Then on Him I cast my burden,
  Sink it in the depths below;
Let me feel Thy gracious pardon,
  Wash me, make me white as snow.
Let Thy Spirit leave me never,
Make me Thine alone forever!

Johann Franck, 1649.

406. Out of the Depths I Cry to Thee.

O Jesu, när jag hädan skall. 8 7, 8 7, 8 8 7.   Geistliche Lieder, 1535.

1. Out of the depths I cry to Thee; Lord, hear me, I im - plore Thee!
Bend down Thy gra-cious ear to me, My prayer let come be - fore Thee!
If Thou re - mem - ber each mis - deed, If each should have its
right - ful meed, Who may a - bide Thy pres - ence? A - MEN.

2 Our pardon is Thy gift; Thy love
  And grace alone avail us.
Our works could ne'er our guilt remove,
  The strictest life would fail us.
That none may boast himself of aught,
But own in fear Thy grace hath wrought
  What in him seemeth righteous.

3 And thus, my hope is in the Lord,
  And not in mine own merit;
I rest upon His faithful word
  To them of contrite spirit.
That He is merciful and just,—
This is my comfort and my trust,
  His help I wait with patience.

4 And though it tarry till the night,
  And round till morning waken,
My heart shall ne'er mistrust Thy might,
  Nor count itself forsaken.
Do thus, O ye of Israel's seed,
Ye of the Spirit born indeed,
  Wait for your God's appearing.

5 Though great our sins and sore our woes,
  His grace much more aboundeth;
His helping love no limit knows,
  Our utmost need it soundeth;
Our kind and faithful Shepherd He,
Who shall at last set Israel free
  From all their sin and sorrow.

Martin Luther, 1524.

407. Lord, I Hear of Showers of Blessing.

Even Me. 8 7, 8 7. With Refrain.   WILLIAM BATCHELDER BRADBURY, 1862.

1. Lord, I hear of show'rs of bless-ing Thou art scat-t'ring full and free;
2. Pass me not, O gra-cious Fa-ther, Sin-ful though my heart may be;

Show'rs, the thirst-y land re-fresh-ing; Let some drops de-scend on me,
Thou mightst leave me, but the rath-er Let Thy mer-cy light on me,

E - ven me, e - ven me, Let some drops de-scend on me.
E - ven me, e - ven me, Let Thy mer-cy light on me. A - MEN.

3 Pass me not, O tender Saviour,
Let me love and cling to Thee,
I am longing for Thy favor;
When Thou comest, call for me,
Even me, even me,
When Thou comest, call for me.

4 Pass me not, O mighty Spirit,
Thou canst make the blind to see;
Witnesser of Jesus' merit,
Speak the word of power to me,
Even me, even me,
Speak the word of power to me.

Elizabeth Conder, 1860.

408. Approach, My Soul, the Mercy-Seat.

London New. C. M.   PLAYFORD'S Psalter, 1671.
Altered from the Scotch Psalter, 1635.

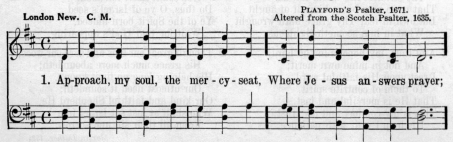

1. Ap-proach, my soul, the mer-cy-seat, Where Je-sus an-swers prayer;

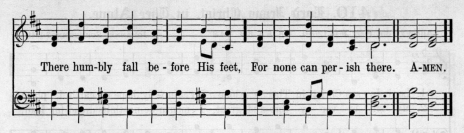

There hum-bly fall be-fore His feet, For none can per-ish there. A-MEN.

2 Thy promise is my only plea,
   With this I venture nigh:
   Thou callest burdened souls to Thee,
   And such, O Lord, am I.

3 Bowed down beneath a load of sin,
   By Satan sorely pressed,
   By wars without and fears within,
   I come to Thee for rest.

4 Be Thou my Shield and Hiding-place,
   That, sheltered near Thy side,
   I may my fierce accuser face,
   And tell him Thou hast died.

5 O wondrous Love, to bleed and die,
   To bear the cross and shame,
   That guilty sinners such as I
   Might plead Thy gracious Name.

John Newton, 1779.

409. Lord, We Confess Our Numerous Faults.

Meditation. C. M. JOHN HENRY GOWER, 1890.

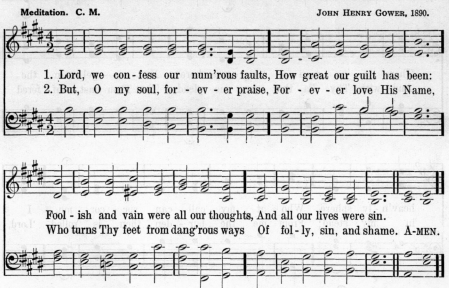

1. Lord, we con-fess our num'rous faults, How great our guilt has been:
2. But, O my soul, for-ev-er praise, For-ev-er love His Name,

Fool-ish and vain were all our thoughts, And all our lives were sin.
Who turns Thy feet from dang'rous ways Of fol-ly, sin, and shame. A-MEN.

3 'Tis not by works of righteousness
   Which our own hands have done;
   But we are saved by sovereign grace
   Abounding through His Son.

4 'Tis from the mercy of our God
   That all our hopes begin;
   'Tis by the water and the blood
   Our souls are washed from sin.

5 'Tis through the purchase of His death
   Who hung upon the tree
   The Spirit is sent down to breathe
   On such dry bones as we.

6 Raised from the dead, we live anew,
   And, justified by grace,
   We shall appear in glory too,
   And see our Father's face.

Isaac Watts, 1709.

410. Lord Jesus Christ, in Thee Alone.

Allein zu dir, Herr Jesu Christ. 8 8, 8 8, 8 8, 8 4 8.   JOHANNES SCHNEESING? 1541.

1. Lord Je-sus Christ, in Thee a-lone My on-ly hope on earth I place,
2. My sin is ver-y sore and great, I mourn be-neath its dread-ful load;

For oth-er com-fort-er is none, No help have I but in Thy grace.
O free me from this heav-y weight, My Sav-iour, thro' Thy pre-cious blood;

There is no man or crea-ture here, No an-gel in the
And with Thy Fa-ther for me plead That Thou hast suf-fered

heav'n-ly sphere, Who at my call can suc-cor me. I
in my stead; From me the bur-den then is rolled. Lord,

cry to Thee, In Thee I trust im-plic-it-ly.
I lay hold On Thy dear prom-is-es of old. A-MEN.

3 And in Thy mercy now bestow
 True Christian faith on me, O Lord,
That all the sweetness I may know
 Which in Thy holy cross is stored,
Love Thee o'er earthly pride and pelf,
And love my neighbor as myself;
And when at last is come my end,
Be Thou my friend,
From Satan's wiles my soul defend.

4 Glory to God in highest heaven,
 The Father of eternal love;
For His dear Son, for sinners given,
 Whose watchful grace we daily prove;
To God the Holy Ghost on high,
O ever be His comfort nigh,
And teach us, in His love and fear,
To please Him here,
And serve Him in the heavenly sphere.

Johannes Schneesing, about 1540.

411. Alas, My God! My Sins Are Great.

Ach Gott und Herr. 8 7, 8 7. Iambic. SCHEIN's Cantional, 1627.

1. A - las, my God! my sins are great, My con-science
doth up - braid me; And now I find that in my
strait No man hath pow'r to aid me. A - MEN.

2 And fled I hence in my despair,
 In some lone spot to hide me,
My griefs would still be with me there,
 And peace be still denied me.

3 Lord, Thee I seek; I merit naught,
 Yet pity and restore me;
Be not Thy wrath, just God, my lot:
 Thy Son hath suffered for me.

4 If pain and woe must follow sin,
 Then be my path still rougher;
Here spare me not: if heaven I win,
 On earth I gladly suffer.

5 But curb my heart, forgive my guilt,
 Make Thou my patience firmer,
For they must miss the good Thou wilt,
 Who at Thy chastenings murmur.

6 Then deal with me as pleaseth Thee,
 Thy grace will help me bear it,
If but at last I see Thy rest,
 And with my Saviour share it.

7 O Father, Son, upon one throne,
 And Holy Ghost together,
Receive my prayer, and let me share
 Thy grace and truth forever.

Martin Rutilius, 1613.

412. How Helpless Guilty Nature Lies.

St. Anne. C. M.   WILLIAM CROFT, 1708.

1. How help - less guilt - y na - ture lies, Un - con-scious of its load!

The heart unchanged can nev - er rise To hap - pi - ness and God. A - MEN.

2 Can aught beneath a power divine
The stubborn will subdue?
'Tis Thine, Almighty Saviour, Thine
To form the heart anew.

3 'Tis Thine the passions to recall,
And bid them upward rise;
And make the scales of error fall
From reason's darkened eyes.

4 To chase the shades of death away,
And bid the sinner live,
A beam of heaven, a vital ray,
'Tis Thine alone to give.

5 O change these wretched hearts of ours,
And give them life divine!
Then shall our passions and our powers,
Almighty Lord, be Thine.

Anne Steele, 1769.

413. God of Mercy! God of Grace!

Weber (Seymour). 7 7, 7 7.   CARL MARIA VON WEBER, 1826.

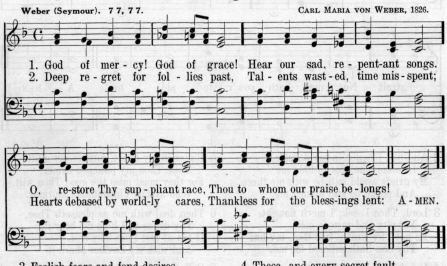

1. God of mer - cy! God of grace! Hear our sad, re - pent-ant songs.
2. Deep re - gret for fol - lies past, Tal - ents wast - ed, time mis - spent;

O, re-store Thy sup - pliant race, Thou to whom our praise be - longs!
Hearts debased by world-ly cares, Thankless for the bless-ings lent: A - MEN.

3 Foolish fears and fond desires,
Vain regrets for things as vain:
Lips too seldom taught to praise,
Oft to murmur and complain;

4 These, and every secret fault,
Filled with grief and shame, we own.
Humbled at Thy feet we lie,
Seeking pardon from Thy throne.

John Taylor, 1795.

414. I Bow My Forehead to the Dust.

Amesbury. C. M. D.

Uzziah Christopher Burnap, 1895.

1. I bow my fore-head to the dust, I veil mine eyes for shame,
2. I dim-ly guess, from bless-ings known, Of great-er out of sight;

And urge, in trem-bling self-dis-trust, A prayer with-out a claim.
And, with the chas-tened Psalm-ist, own His judg-ments too are right.

No of-f'ring of my own I have, Nor works my faith to prove;
And if my heart and flesh are weak To bear an un-tried pain,

I can but give the gifts He gave, And plead His love for love.
The bruis-ed reed He will not break, But strengthen and sus-tain. A-MEN.

3 I know not what the future hath
   Of marvel or surprise,
Assured alone that life and death
   His mercy underlies.
And so beside the silent sea
   I wait the muffled oar:
No harm from Him can come to me
   On ocean or on shore.

4 I know not where His islands lift
   Their fronded palms in air;
I only know I cannot drift
   Beyond His love and care.
And Thou, O Lord, by whom are seen
   Thy creatures as they be,
Forgive me if too close I lean
   My human heart on Thee.

John Greenleaf Whittier, 1867, a.

415. Lord, Disperse the Mists of Error.

Jesus! du dig själf uppväckte. 8 7, 8 7, 8 7 7.   Swedish, 1695.

1. Lord, dis - perse the mists of er - ror, In Thy light let me see light;

Give Thou me that faith and vi - sion Where-by I may walk a - right,

In my Sav -iour's path dis - cern - ing, Through this vale of

doubt and strife, Foot -steps to e - ter - nal life. A - MEN.

2 Shed Thy light upon my pathway,
    Be my light in death's dark hour.
Let me, freed from sin's dread burden,
    From the Law's accusing power,
Nearer draw, and ever nearer,
    To that land with glory bright,
Where Thou art Eternal Light.

Johan Åström, 1816.

416. Pass Me Not, O Gentle Saviour.

Pass me not. 8 5, 8 5.   With Refrain.   WILLIAM HOWARD DOANE, 1870.

1. Pass me not, O gen - tle Sav - iour,   Hear my hum - ble cry;
2. Let me at the throne of mer - cy   Find a sweet re - lief,

While on oth - ers Thou art call - ing,   Do not pass me by.
Kneel - ing there in deep con - tri - tion,   Help my un - be - lief.

REFRAIN:

Sav - iour,   Sav - iour,   hear my hum - ble cry,

While on oth - ers Thou art call - ing,   Do not pass me by.   A - MEN.

3 Trusting only in Thy merit,
  Would I seek Thy face:
  Heal my wounded, broken spirit,
  Save me by Thy grace.

4 Thou the spring of all my comfort,
  More than life to me,
  Whom have I on earth beside Thee?
  Whom in heaven but Thee?

Frances Jane (Crosby) Van Alstyne, 1870.

417. Blessed, Blessed He Who Knoweth.

Schmücke dich, o liebe Seele. L. M. D.   JOHANN CRÜGER, 1649.

Bless-ed, bless-ed he who know-eth That His faith on Thee is found-ed, Whom the Fa-ther's love be-stow-eth Of e-ter-nal grace un-bound-ed, Je-sus Christ, to ev-'ry na-tion A Re-deem-er free-ly giv-en, In whose Name is our sal-va-tion, And none else in earth or heav-en. A-MEN.

Johan Olof Wallin, 1816.

418. I Lay My Sins on Jesus.

Crucifix. 7 6, 7 6. D.

Greek Melody.

1. I lay my sins on Je - sus, The spot-less Lamb of God;

He bears them all, and frees us From the ac-curs-ed load.

I bring my guilt to Je - sus, To wash my crim - son stains

White in His blood most pre - cious, Till not a spot re - mains. A-MEN.

2 I lay my wants on Jesus,
  All fullness dwells in Him;
He heals all my diseases,
  He doth my soul redeem.
I lay my griefs on Jesus,
  My burdens and my cares;
He from them all releases,
  He all my sorrows shares.

3 I long to be like Jesus,
  Meek, loving, lowly, mild;
I long to be like Jesus,
  The Father's holy child.
I long to be with Jesus,
  Amid the heavenly throng,
To sing with saints His praises,
  To learn the angels' song.

Horatius Bonar, 1843. Abridged.

419. Jesus, Lover of My Soul.

Martyn. 7 7, 7 7. D.

SIMEON BUTLER MARSH, 1834.

1. Je - sus, Lov - er of my soul, Let me to Thy bos - om fly,
2. Oth - er ref - uge have I none; Hangs my help-less soul on Thee;

While the near - er wa - ters roll, While the tem - pest still is high!
Leave, ah, leave me not a - lone, Still sup-port and com - fort me!

Hide me, O my Sav - iour, hide, Till the storm of life is past;
All my trust in Thee is stayed, All my help from Thee I bring:

Safe in - to the ha - ven guide: O re-ceive my soul at last!
Cov - er my de-fense-less head With the shad-ow of Thy wing. A-MEN.

3 Thou, O Christ, art all I want;
  More than all in Thee I find.
Raise the fallen, cheer the faint,
  Heal the sick, and lead the blind.
Just and holy is Thy name,
  I am all unrighteousness;
False and full of sin I am,
  Thou art full of truth and grace.

4 Plenteous grace with Thee is found,
  Grace to cover all my sin;
Let the healing streams abound,
  Make and keep me pure within.
Thou of life the Fountain art,
  Freely let me take of Thee:
Spring Thou up within my heart,
  Rise to all eternity.

Charles Wesley, 1740.

420. In Vain We Seek for Peace with God.

Martyrdom. C. M.

HUGH WILSON, (1764-1824).

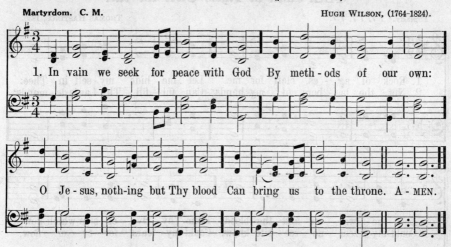

1. In vain we seek for peace with God By meth-ods of our own:

O Je-sus, noth-ing but Thy blood Can bring us to the throne. A-MEN.

2 'Tis Thine atoning sacrifice
  Hath answered all demands;
And peace and pardon from the skies
  Are blessings from Thy hands.

3 'Tis by Thy death we live, O Lord;
  'Tis on Thy cross we rest;
Forever be Thy love adored,
  Thy Name forever blest.

Isaac Watts, 1721.

421. Chief of Sinners Though I Be.

Jesus för världen gifvit sitt lif. 7 7, 7 7.

A. EKSTRÖM. Altered.

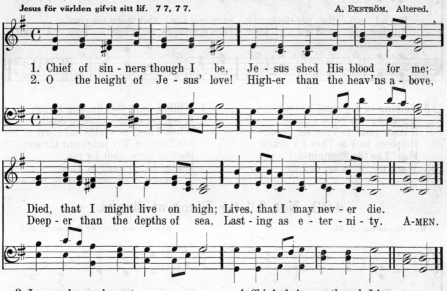

1. Chief of sin-ners though I be, Je-sus shed His blood for me;
2. O the height of Je-sus' love! High-er than the heav'ns a-bove,

Died, that I might live on high; Lives, that I may nev-er die.
Deep-er than the depths of sea, Last-ing as e-ter-ni-ty. A-MEN.

3 Jesus only can impart
Balm to heal the smitten heart;
Peace that flows from sins forgiven,
Joy that lifts the soul to heaven.

4 Chief of sinners though I be,
Christ is all in all to me;
All my wants to Him are known,
All my sorrows are His own.

William McComb, 1848.

422. Rock of Ages, Cleft for Me.

Toplady. 7 7, 7 7, 7 7.   THOMAS HASTINGS, 1830.

1. Rock of ag - es, cleft for me, Let me hide my - self in Thee:
2. Not the la - bors of my hands Can ful - fill Thy Law's de - mands;

Let the wa - ter and the blood From Thy riv - en side which flowed,
Could my zeal no res - pite know, Could my tears for - ev - er flow,

Be of sin the per - fect cure, Save me, Lord, and make me pure.
All for sin could not a - tone; Thou must save, and Thou a - lone. A - MEN.

3 Nothing in my hand I bring,
  Simply to Thy cross I cling;
  Naked, come to Thee for dress;
  Helpless. look to Thee for grace;
  Foul, I to the fountain fly:
  Wash me, Saviour, or I die!

4 While I draw this fleeting breath,
  When my eyelids close in death,
  When I soar to worlds unknown,
  See Thee on Thy judgment throne;
  Rock of ages, cleft for me,
  Let me hide myself in Thee.

Augustus Montague Toplady, 1776, a.

423. Not All the Blood of Beasts.

Ben Rhydding. S. M.   ALEXANDER ROBERT REINAGLE, 1865.

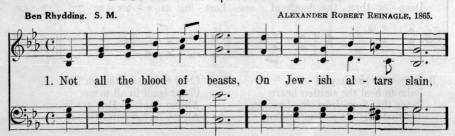

1. Not all the blood of beasts, On Jew - ish al - tars slain,

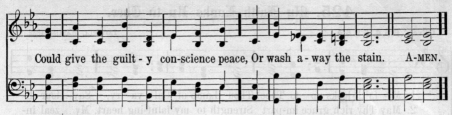

Could give the guilt - y con-science peace, Or wash a - way the stain.   A-MEN.

2 But Christ, the heavenly Lamb,
Takes all our sins away;
A Sacrifice of nobler name,
And richer blood than they.

3 My faith would lay her hand
On that dear head of Thine,
While like a penitent I stand,
And there confess my sin.

4 My soul looks back to see
The burden Thou didst bear,
When hanging on the cursèd tree,
And knows her guilt was there.

5 Believing, we rejoice
To see the curse remove;
We bless the Lamb with cheerful voice,
And sing His bleeding love.

Isaac Watts, 1709.

424. My Hope Is Built on Nothing Less.

HENRI FREDRICK HEMY, 1865.
Altered by JAMES GEORGE WALTON, 1871.

St. Catherine. 8 8, 8 8, 8 8.

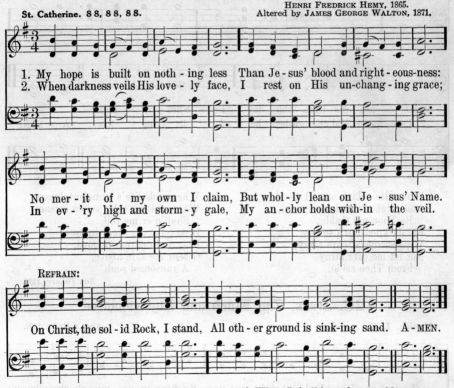

1. My hope is built on noth - ing less Than Je - sus' blood and right - eous-ness:
2. When darkness veils His love - ly face, I rest on His un-chang - ing grace;

No mer - it of my own I claim, But whol - ly lean on Je - sus' Name.
In ev - 'ry high and storm - y gale, My an - chor holds with-in the veil.

REFRAIN:

On Christ, the sol - id Rock, I stand, All oth - er ground is sink-ing sand.   A - MEN.

3 His oath, His covenant and blood,
Support me in the sinking flood;
When every earthly prop gives way,
He then is all my hope and stay.

4 When I shall launch to worlds unseen,
O may I then be found in Him!
Dressed in His righteousness alone,
Faultless to stand before the throne.

Edward Mote, 1836.

425. My Faith Looks Up to Thee.

Olivet. 6 6 4, 6 6 6 4.   LOWELL MASON, 1832.

1. My faith looks up to Thee, Thou Lamb of Cal - va - ry, Sav - iour di -
2. May Thy rich grace im-part Strength to my faint-ing heart, My zeal in -

vine! Now hear me while I pray; Take all my guilt a - way;
spire; As Thou hast died for me, O may my love to Thee

O let me from this day Be whol - ly Thine.
Pure, warm, and change-less be, A liv - ing fire. A - MEN.

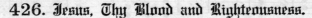

3 When life's dark maze I tread,
And griefs around me spread,
  Be Thou my Guide;
Bid darkness turn to day,
Wipe sorrow's tears away,
Nor let me ever stray
  From Thee aside.

4 When ends life's transient dream,
When death's cold, sullen stream
  Shall o'er me roll,
Blest Saviour, then, in love,
Fear and distrust remove;
O bear me safe above,
  A ransomed soul.

Ray Palmer, 1830.

426. Jesus, Thy Blood and Righteousness.

Messiah. L. M.   ADOLF HULT, 1899.

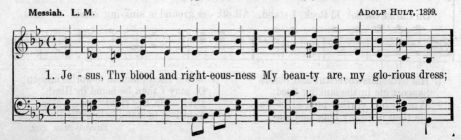

1. Je - sus, Thy blood and right-eous-ness My beau-ty are, my glo-rious dress;

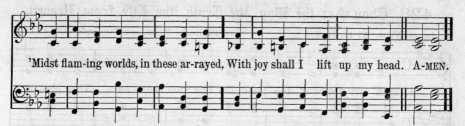

'Midst flam-ing worlds, in these ar-rayed, With joy shall I lift up my head. A-MEN.

2 Bold shall I stand in Thy great day,
For who aught to my charge shall lay?
Fully through these absolved I am
From sin and fear, from guilt and shame.

3 This spotless robe the same appears,
When ruined nature sinks in years:
No age can change its constant hue;
Thy blood preserves it ever new.

4 O let the dead now hear Thy voice;
Now bid Thy banished ones rejoice!
Their beauty this, their glorious dress,
Jesus, Thy blood and righteousness!

5 When from the dust of death I rise,
To claim my mansion in the skies,
Then this shall be my only plea:
"Jesus hath lived and died for me."

Nicolaus Ludwig Zinzendorf, 1739.

427. Just As I Am, without One Plea.

Woodworth. L. M.   WILLIAM BATCHELDER BRADBURY, 1849.

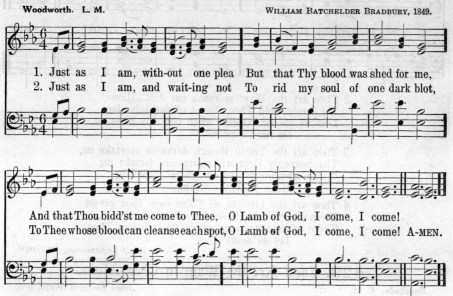

1. Just as I am, with-out one plea But that Thy blood was shed for me,
2. Just as I am, and wait-ing not To rid my soul of one dark blot,

And that Thou bidd'st me come to Thee, O Lamb of God, I come, I come!
To Thee whose blood can cleanse each spot, O Lamb of God, I come, I come! A-MEN.

3 Just as I am, though tossed about
With many a conflict, many a doubt,
Fightings and fears within, without,
O Lamb of God, I come, I come!

4 Just as I am, poor, wretched, blind;
Sight, riches, healing of the mind,
Yea, all I need in Thee I find,
O Lamb of God, I come, I come!

5 Just as I am; Thou wilt receive,
Wilt welcome, pardon, cleanse, relieve,
Because Thy promise I believe;
O Lamb of God, I come, I come!

6 Just as I am; Thy love unknown
Hath broken every barrier down;
Now to be Thine, yea, Thine alone,
O Lamb of God, I come, I come!

Charlotte Elliott, 1836.

428. Thou Art the Way, the Truth, the Life from Heaven.

Integer Vitae. 11 11, 11 5.   FRIEDRICH FERDINAND FLEMMING, (1778–1813).

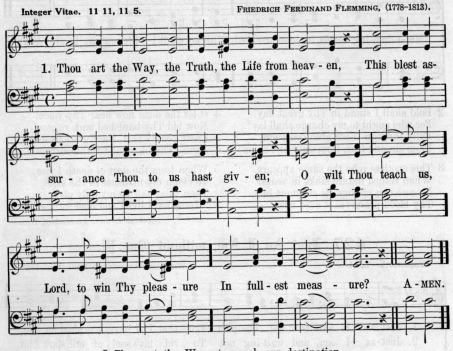

1. Thou art the Way, the Truth, the Life from heav - en, This blest as-
sur - ance Thou to us hast giv - en; O wilt Thou teach us,
Lord, to win Thy pleas - ure In full - est meas - ure? A - MEN.

2 Thou art the Way: to reach our destination
We sorely need Thee, Fount of our salvation;
Lest we should stumble when our sins beset us,
  Do not forget us.

3 Thou art the Truth: though darkness overtake us,
Thy heavenly light will nevermore forsake us;
O shine within us, all our gloom dispelling,
  Make us Thy dwelling.

4 Thou art the Life: to all Thine own Thou givest
Eternal life where Thou forever livest;
There without ceasing, as we stand before Thee,
  Let us adore Thee.

                                    Friedrich Adolf Krummacher, (1767–1845).

429. Thou Art the Way: to Thee Alone.

Beatitudo. C. M.   JOHN BACCHUS DYKES, 1875.

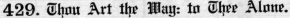

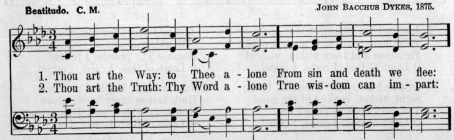

1. Thou art the Way: to Thee a - lone From sin and death we flee:
2. Thou art the Truth: Thy Word a - lone True wis - dom can im - part:

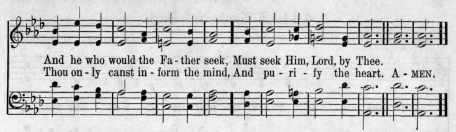

And he who would the Fa-ther seek, Must seek Him, Lord, by Thee.
Thou on-ly canst in-form the mind, And pu-ri-fy the heart. A-MEN.

3 Thou art the Life: the rending tomb
  Proclaims Thy conquering arm:
  And those who put their trust in Thee,
  Nor death nor hell shall harm.

4 Thou art the Way, the Truth, the Life:
  Grant us that Way to know,
  That Truth to keep, that Life to win
  Whose joys eternal flow.

George Washington Doane, 1824.

430. One There Is above All Others.

Amen sjunge hvarje tunga. 8 7, 8 7, 7 7.

ANTON PETER BERGGREN, (1801–1880).

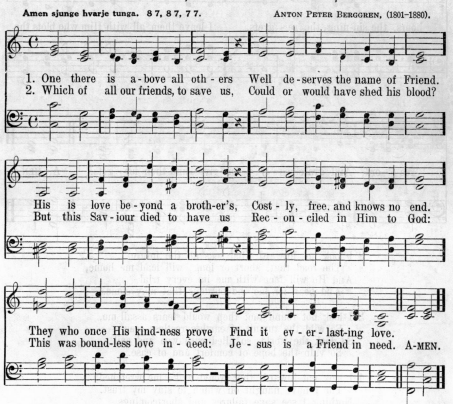

1. One there is a-bove all oth-ers   Well de-serves the name of Friend.
2. Which of all our friends, to save us,   Could or would have shed his blood?

His is love be-yond a broth-er's,   Cost-ly, free, and knows no end.
But this Sav-iour died to have us   Rec-on-ciled in Him to God:

They who once His kind-ness prove   Find it ev-er-last-ing love.
This was bound-less love in-deed: Je-sus is a Friend in need. A-MEN.

3 When He lived on earth abasèd,
  Friend of sinners was His Name:
  Now, above all glory raisèd,
  He rejoices in the same:
  Still He calls them brethren, friends,
  And to all their wants attends.

4 O for grace our hearts to soften!
  Teach us, Lord, at length to love.
  We, alas, forget too often
  What a Friend we have above:
  But when home our souls are brought,
  We will love Thee as we ought.

John Newton, 1799.

431. I Look Not Back.

O sälla land. 11 10, 11 10.   OSKAR AHNFELT, (1813–1882).

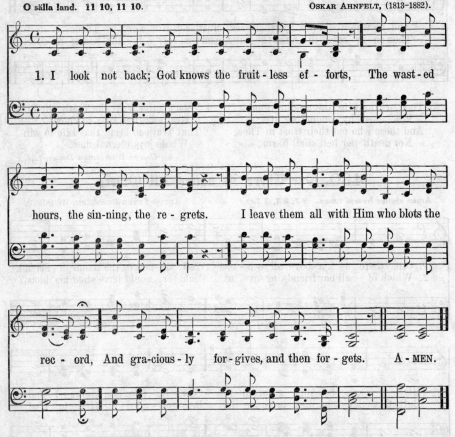

1. I look not back; God knows the fruit - less ef - forts, The wast - ed
hours, the sin - ning, the re - grets. I leave them all with Him who blots the
rec - ord, And gra - cious - ly for - gives, and then for - gets. A - MEN.

2 I look not forward; God sees all the future,
    The road that, short or long, will lead me home,
  And He will face with me its every trial,
    And bear for me the burdens that may come.

3 I look not round me; then would fears assail me,
    So wild the tumult of earth's restless seas,
  So dark the world, so filled with woe and evil,
    So vain the hope of comfort and of ease.

4 I look not inward; that would make me wretched;
    For I have naught on which to stay my trust.
  Nothing I see save failures and shortcomings,
    And weak endeavors, crumbling into dust.

5 But I look up—into the face of Jesus,
    For there my heart can rest, my fears are stilled;
  And there is joy, and love, and light for darkness,
    And perfect peace, and every hope fulfilled.

                                                                Unknown.

432. I Heard the Voice of Jesus Say.

Muriel. C. M. D.   JOHN VICTOR BERGQUIST, 1924.

1. I heard the voice of Je - sus say, "Come un - to Me and rest;

Lay down, thou wea - ry one, lay down Thy head up - on My breast."

I came to Je - sus as I was, Wea - ry, and worn, and sad;

I found in Him a rest-ing-place, And He has made me glad. A-MEN.

2 I heard the voice of Jesus say,
    "Behold, I freely give
The living water; thirsty one,
    Stoop down and drink, and live."
I came to Jesus and I drank
    Of that life-giving stream;
My thirst was quenched, my soul revived,
    And now I live in Him.

3 I heard the voice of Jesus say,
    "I am this dark world's Light;
Look unto Me, thy morn shall rise,
    And all thy day be bright."
I looked to Jesus, and I found
    In Him my Star, my Sun;
And in that Light of life I'll walk,
    Till traveling days are done.

Horatius Bonar, 1846.

433. Dear Christians, One and All, Rejoice.

Es ist gewisslich an der Zeit. 8 7, 8 7, 8 8 7.   Wittenberg Gesangbuch, 1535.

1. Dear Chris-tians, one and all, re - joice, With ex - ul - ta - tion spring-ing,
2. Fast bound in Sa-tan's chains I lay, Death brood-ed dark - ly o'er me,

And, with u - nit - ed heart and voice And ho - ly rap - ture sing - ing,
Sin was my tor-ment night and day, In sin my moth - er bore me;

Pro - claim the won - ders God hath done, How His right arm the
Still deep - er in de - spair I fell, Life had be - come a

vic - t'ry won; Right dear - ly it hath cost Him.
liv - ing hell, So firm - ly sin pos - sessed me. A - MEN.

3 Then God beheld my wretched state
  With deep commiseration;
He thought upon His mercy great,
  And willed my soul's salvation;
He turned to me a Father's heart;
Not small the cost! to heal my smart,
  He gave His best and dearest.

4 He spoke to His belovèd Son:
  "'Tis time to take compassion:
Then go, bright Jewel of My crown,
  And bring to man salvation;
From sin and sorrow set him free,
Slay bitter death for him, that he
  May live with Thee forever."

5 The Son obeyed Him cheerfully,
  And, born of virgin mother,
Came down upon the earth to me,
  That He might be my brother:
His mighty power doth work unseen,
He came in fashion poor and mean,
  And took the devil captive.

6 We thank Thee, Lord, for boundless grace,
  And sing Thy praise forever,
For granting us in dire distress
  Thine everlasting favor.
Both death and hell were stricken down,
When Thou didst for our sins atone,
  O Jesus, blessèd Saviour.

Martin Luther, 1523.

434. I Know in Whom I Trust.

Ach Jesu, dessen Treu. 6 7, 6 7, 6 6, 6 6.   Lüneburg Gesangbuch, 1648.

1. I know in Whom I trust When guilt of sin op-press-es,
2. I know in Whom I trust When, troub-led and de-ject-ed,

When an-guish and re-morse My bur-dened soul dis-tress-es;
I lack the strength to go The way of God se-lect-ed;

I come be-fore Thy throne, O God, in Je-sus' Name;
To Je-sus then I pray With a re-pent-ant mind,

Thy mer-cy, love, and truth For-ev-er are the same.
And strength of ho-li-ness I through His Spir-it find. A-MEN.

3 I know in Whom I trust
　　When worldly pomp and splendor
Would lure my heart away,
　　For He is my Defender.
I hear His warning voice,
　　I feel His loving hand;
Temptations and deceits
　　With Him I thus withstand.

4 I know in Whom I trust
　　When peace and joy forsake me,
When fain my heart would break,
　　And sorrows overtake me.
The suffering of my Lord,
　　His anguish, pain, and woe
Remind me of the way
　　We after Him must go.

5 I know in Whom I trust
　　When evening shadows lengthen,
When death stands at the door,—
　　For Christ is there to strengthen.
He died upon the cross
　　To conquer death and hell;
A Conqueror He rose,
　　And all with us is well.

6 I know in Whom I trust;
　　I praise Him and adore Him;
By works I show my faith;
　　My heart I lay before Him;
Not only crying, "Lord!"
　　I take Him as my Guide,
And thus in life and death
　　In Him alone abide.

Johan Olof Wallin, 1816.

435. There's a Wideness in God's Mercy.

Cross of Jesus. 8 7, 8 7.   JOHN STAINER, 1887.

1. There's a wide-ness in God's mer-cy, Like the wide-ness of the sea:
2. There is wel-come for the sin-ner, And more grac-es for the good;

There's a kind-ness in His jus-tice, Which is more than lib-er-ty.
There is mer-cy with the Sav-iour; There is heal-ing in His blood. A-MEN.

3 For the love of God is broader
   Than the measure of man's mind;
   And the heart of the Eternal
   Is most wonderfully kind.

4 If our faith were but more simple,
  We should take Him at His Word;
  And our lives would be all sunshine
  In the presence of our Lord.

Frederick William Faber, (1814-1863), a.

436. God Loved Our Erring Mortal Race.

Old Hundredth. L. M.   LOUIS BOURGEOIS.
                                                             Genevan Psalter, 1551.

1. God loved our err-ing mor-tal race, And thro' His Son be-stowed His grace,
2. Christ Je-sus is the ground of faith, Who was made flesh and suf-fered death;

That all who will in Him be-lieve May ev-er-last-ing life re-ceive.
All who con-fide in Him a-lone Have built on this chief Cor-ner-stone. A-MEN.

3 God would not have the sinner die;
  His Son with saving grace is nigh,
  His Spirit in the Word doth teach
  How man the blessèd goal may reach.

4 Glory to God the Father, Son,
  And Holy Spirit, Three in One!
  To Thee, O blessèd Trinity,
  Be praise throughout eternity!

Johannes Olearius, 1671.

437. From Every Stormy Wind That Blows.

Emilia. L. M. JOHN VICTOR BERGQUIST, 1924.

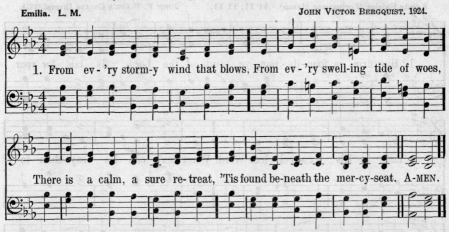

1. From ev-'ry storm-y wind that blows, From ev-'ry swell-ing tide of woes,
There is a calm, a sure re-treat, 'Tis found be-neath the mer-cy-seat. A-MEN.

2 There is a place where Jesus sheds
The oil of gladness on our heads;
A place than all besides more sweet;
It is the blood-bought mercy-seat.

3 There is a scene where spirits blend,
Where friend holds fellowship with friend;
Though sundered far, by faith they meet
Around one common mercy-seat.

4 Ah! whither could we flee for aid,
When tempted, desolate, dismayed;
Or how the host of hell defeat,
Had suffering saints no mercy-seat?

5 There, there on eagle wing we soar,
And sin and sense seem all no more,
And heaven comes down our souls to greet,
And glory crowns the mercy-seat.

Hugh Stowell, 1828.

438. My Spirit on Thy Care.

St. Michael. S. M. DAYE'S Psalter, 1562.

1. My spir-it on Thy care, Blest Sav-iour, I re-cline;
2. In Thee I place my trust, On Thee I calm-ly rest;

Thou wilt not leave me to de-spair, For Thou art Love di-vine.
I know Thee good, I know Thee just, And count Thy choice the best. A-MEN.

3 Whate'er events betide,
Thy will they all perform;
Safe in Thy breast my head I hide,
Nor fear the coming storm.

4 Let good or ill befall,
It must be good for me,
Secure of having Thee in all,
Of having all in Thee.

Henry Francis Lyte, 1834.

439. How Firm a Foundation, Ye Saints of the Lord.

Adeste Fideles (Portuguese Hymn). 11 11, 11 11.   JOHN F. WADE'S Cantus Diversi, 1751.

1. How firm a foun-da-tion, ye saints of the Lord, Is laid for your faith in His ex-cel-lent Word! What more can He say than to you He hath said, Who un-to the Sav-iour for ref-uge have fled, Who un-to the Sav-iour for ref-uge have fled? A-MEN.

2 "Fear not, I am with thee; O be not dismayed;
For I am thy God, and will still give thee aid;
I'll strengthen thee, help thee, and cause thee to stand
Upheld by My righteous, omnipotent hand.

3 "When through the deep waters I call thee to go,
The rivers of sorrow shall not overflow;
For I will be with thee, thy troubles to bless,
And sanctify to thee thy deepest distress.

4 "When through fiery trials thy pathway shall lie,
My grace, all-sufficient, shall be thy supply;
The flame shall not hurt thee; I only design
Thy dross to consume, and thy gold to refine.

5 "E'en down to old age, all My people shall prove
My sovereign, eternal, unchangeable love;
And then, when gray hairs shall their temples adorn
Like lambs they shall still in My bosom be borne.

6 "The soul that on Jesus hath leaned for repose,
I will not, I cannot desert to His foes:
That soul, though all hell should endeavor to shake,
I'll never—no, never—no, never forsake!"

"K," in Rippon's Selection, 1787.

440. Vanish Doubt and Hesitation!

Tviflan ur min själ försvinne. 8 7, 8 7, 8 8, 7 7.   W. WESSNITZER, 1661.

1. Van-ish doubt and hes-i-ta-tion! My Re-deem-er is the Lord.
2. He will pit-y and re-lieve me, Who can then con-demn my soul?

Heark-en to His in-vi-ta-tion By the Spir-it and the Word.
Sa-tan and the world de-ceive me, Je-sus Christ will make me whole.

Clear-ly He per-ceives thy an-guish; O my soul, why lon-ger lan-guish?
Why, then, should my heart ac-cuse me, Or my con-science still con-fuse me?

Al-though I am weak and ill, God re-mains my Fa-ther still.
God the Fa-ther makes me free, And His Spir-it com-forts me. A-MEN.

3 Jesus Christ for me has suffered,
   And by faith He is my own.
Satisfaction He has offered,
   And the way to heaven shown.
Through His full propitiation
I have free and full salvation.
He has conquered death and hell;
He has thus made all things well.

4 In His merit now confiding,
   I look up to Him with joy;
For His promise is abiding—
   Who can now my peace destroy?
Weal nor woe shall e'er deprive me
Of the portion that He gave me.
My Redeemer, Lord divine,
I am Thine, forever Thine.

Johann Adolf Schlegel, 1722.

441. Now I Have Found the Ground Wherein.

Colchester. 8 8, 8 8, 8 8.   SAMUEL SEBASTIAN WESLEY, (1810–1876).

1. Now I have found the ground wherein My soul's sure an-chor may re-main:

The wounds of Je-sus, for my sin Be-fore the world's foun-da-tion slain;

Whose mer-cy shall un-shak-en stay When heav'n and earth are fled a-way. A-MEN.

Or: St. Catherine, No. 424.

2 O Father, Thine eternal grace
  Our scanty thought surpasses far;
Thy heart still melts with tenderness,
  Thine arms of love still open are,
Returning sinners to receive,
That mercy they may taste, and live.

3 O love, so great, so bottomless!
  My sins are swallowed up in Thee;
And covered my unrighteousness,
  No spot of guilt remains in me;
While Jesus' blood, through earth and skies,
For mercy, boundless mercy, cries!

Johann Andreas Rothe, 1727.

442. All That I Was, My Sin, My Guilt.

Dundee. C. M.   HART'S Psalter, 1615.

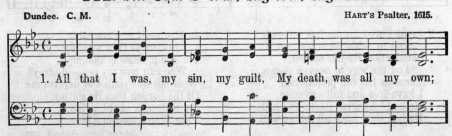

1. All that I was, my sin, my guilt, My death, was all my own;

All that I am, I owe to Thee, My gra-cious God, a - lone. A-MEN.

2 The evil of my former state
   Was mine, and only mine;
   The good in which I now rejoice
   Is Thine, and only Thine.

3 The darkness of my former state,
   The bondage, all was mine;
   The light of life in which I walk,
   The liberty, is Thine.

4 Thy grace first made me feel my sin,
   It taught me to believe;
   Then, in believing, peace I found,
   And now I live, I live.

5 All that I am, e'en here on earth,
   All that I hope to be
   When Jesus comes, and glory dawns,
   I owe it, Lord, to Thee.

Horatius Bonar, 1845.

443. O for a Faith That Will Not Shrink.

Lambeth. C. M.   WILHELM A. F. SCHULTHES, 1871.

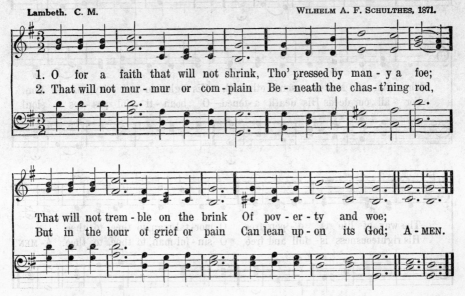

1. O for a faith that will not shrink, Tho' pressed by man - y a foe;
2. That will not mur - mur or com - plain Be - neath the chas - t'ning rod,

That will not trem - ble on the brink Of pov - er - ty and woe;
But in the hour of grief or pain Can lean up - on its God; A - MEN.

3 A faith that shines more bright and clear
   When tempests rage without;
   That when in danger knows no fear,
   In darkness feels no doubt;

4 That bears unmoved the world's dread
      frown,
   Nor heeds its scornful smile;
   That sin's wild ocean cannot drown,
   Nor Satan's arts beguile;

5 A faith that keeps the narrow way
   Till life's last hour is fled,
   And with a pure and heavenly ray
   Lights up a dying bed.

6 Lord, give us such a faith as this,
   And then whate'er may come,
   We'll taste e'en here the hallowed
      bliss
   Of an eternal home.

William Hiley Bathurst, 1831.

444. Behold, by Sovereign Grace Alone.

Wach auf, mein Geist! erhebe dich. 8 8 7, 8 8 7, 8 8.

JOHANN SCHOP, 1642.
JOHANN CRÜGER, 1653.

1. Be - hold, by sov'reign grace a - lone Hath God the Fa - ther from His throne
2. Thro' love a - lone His Son was sent To bear the law's dread pun-ish-ment

Or-dained our full sal - va - tion. Un - to the ut- most ends of earth
For all our dire trans-gres - sion. Our sins He bore, our guilt He owned,

The Sun of Mer - cy send-eth forth His light to ev - 'ry na - tion.
For all our deeds His death a -toned—O boun - ti - ful pos - ses - sion!

The way of life is o - pen, free, O mor - tal man, to thee, to thee.
His righteousness is full and free, O sin - ful man, to thee, to thee. A - MEN.

3 For this o'erwhelming sacrifice
  The Lord will nevermore despise
    A contrite heart and spirit.
By Jesus' death, by Jesus' blood,
Full pleasing in the sight of God,
    His mercy we inherit.
The fount of grace flows full and free,
O pardoned soul, for thee, for thee.

4 By faith alone, for Jesus' sake,
  Each ransomed sinner may partake
    Of His abounding merit.
If in His promise ye abide,
By faith shall ye be justified,
    And blest with His free Spirit.
His righteousness the just shall own
By faith alone, by faith alone.

Ernst William Olson, 1917.

445. We Christians Should Ever Consider.

Oss kristna bör tro och besinna. 9 8. 9 8, 9 9 8.

Swedish Melody, known 1540.

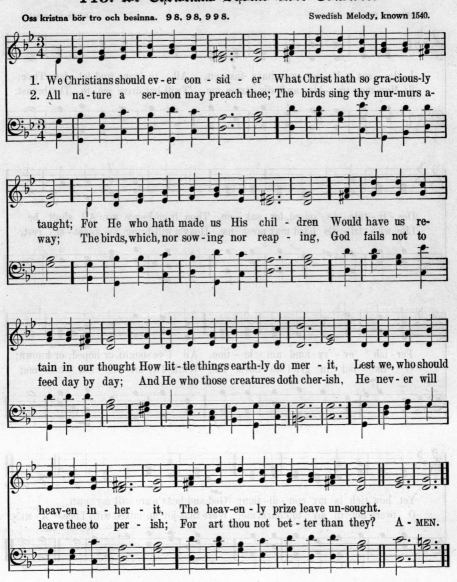

1. We Christians should ev-er con-sid-er What Christ hath so gra-cious-ly taught; For He who hath made us His chil-dren Would have us re-tain in our thought How lit-tle things earth-ly do mer-it, Lest we, who should heav-en in-her-it, The heav-en-ly prize leave un-sought.

2. All na-ture a ser-mon may preach thee; The birds sing thy mur-murs a-way; The birds, which, nor sow-ing nor reap-ing, God fails not to feed day by day; And He who those creatures doth cher-ish, He nev-er will leave thee to per-ish; For art thou not bet-ter than they? A - MEN.

3 The lilies, nor toiling nor spinning,
  Their clothing how gorgeous and fair!
What tints in their tiny robes woven,
  What wondrous devices are there!
All Solomon's stores could not render
One festival robe of such splendor
  As modest field lilies do wear.

4 If God o'er the grass and the flowers
  Such delicate beauty hath spread,—
The flowers which to-day are so fragrant,
  To-morrow are faded and dead,—
O why, then, should earthly cares fret thee?
Thy Father will never forget thee,
  Nor fail to provide thee with bread.

Haquin Spegel, 1686.

446. Jesus, I My Cross Have Taken.

St. Hilary. 8 7, 8 7. D.   Origin uncertain.

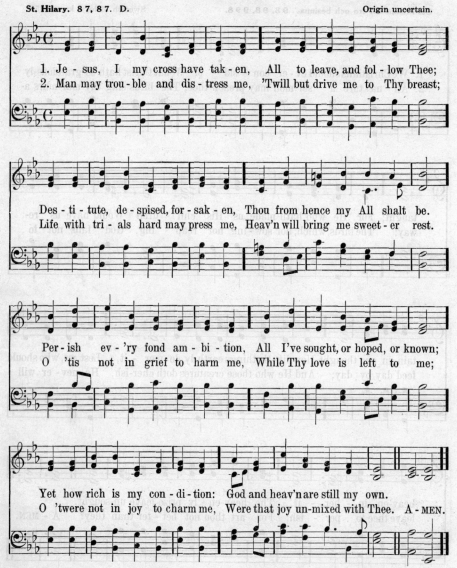

1. Je - sus, I my cross have tak - en, All to leave, and fol - low Thee;
2. Man may trou - ble and dis - tress me, 'Twill but drive me to Thy breast;

Des - ti - tute, de - spised, for - sak - en, Thou from hence my All shalt be.
Life with tri - als hard may press me, Heav'n will bring me sweet - er rest.

Per - ish ev - 'ry fond am - bi - tion, All I've sought, or hoped, or known;
O 'tis not in grief to harm me, While Thy love is left to me;

Yet how rich is my con - di - tion: God and heav'n are still my own.
O 'twere not in joy to charm me, Were that joy un-mixed with Thee. A - MEN.

3 Take, my soul, thy full salvation,
    Rise o'er sin, and fear, and care;
Joy to find in every station
    Something still to do or bear.
Think what Spirit dwells within thee,
    What a Father's smile is thine,
What a Saviour died to win thee;
    Child of heaven, shouldst thou repine?

4 Haste, then, on from grace to glory,
    Armed by faith and winged by prayer;
Heaven's eternal day's before thee,
    God's own hand shall guide thee there.
Soon shall close thine earthly mission,
    Swift shall pass thy pilgrim days;
Hope shall change to glad fruition,
    Faith to sight, and prayer to praise.

Henry Francis Lyte, 1824.

447. Stand Up, Stand Up for Jesus.

Webb. 7 6, 7 6. D.   GEORGE JAMES WEBB, 1830.

1. Stand up, stand up for Je - sus, Ye sol - diers of the cross;
2. Stand up, stand up for Je - sus, The trump - et call o - bey;

Lift high His roy - al ban - ner, It must not suf - fer loss:
Forth to the might - y con - flict In this His glo - rious day:

From vic - t'ry un - to vic - t'ry His ar - my He shall lead,
Ye that are men, now serve Him A - gainst un - num - bered foes;

Till ev - 'ry foe is van - quished, And Christ is Lord in - deed.
Your cour - age rise with dan - ger, And strength to strength op - pose. A - MEN.

3 Stand up, stand up for Jesus,
    Stand in His strength alone;
The arm of flesh will fail you,
    Ye dare not trust your own;
Put on the gospel armor,
    And, watching unto prayer,
Where duty calls or danger,
    Be never wanting there.

4 Stand up, stand up for Jesus,
    The strife will not be long;
This day the noise of battle,
    The next the victor's song:
To him that overcometh,
    A crown of life shall be;
He with the King of glory
    Shall reign eternally.

George Duffield, 1858.

448. Nearer, My God, to Thee.

Bethany. 6 4, 6 4, 6 6, 6 4.   LOWELL MASON, 1856.

1. Near - er, my God, to Thee! Near - er to Thee!
E'en though it be a cross That rais - eth me,
Still all my song shall be, Near - er, my God, to Thee,
Near - er, my God, to Thee, Near - er to Thee!   A - MEN.

2 Though, like the wanderer,
    The sun gone down,
  Darkness be over me,
    My rest a stone,
  Yet in my dreams I'd be
  Nearer, my God, to Thee
    Nearer to Thee!

3 There let my way appear
    Steps unto heaven;
  All that Thou sendest me
    In mercy given;
  Angels to beckon me
  Nearer, my God, to Thee,
    Nearer to Thee!

4 Then with my waking thoughts,
    Bright with Thy praise,
  Out of my stony griefs
    Bethel I'll raise,
  So by my woes to be
  Nearer, my God, to Thee,
    Nearer to Thee!

5 Or if on joyful wing,
    Cleaving the sky,
  Sun, moon, and stars forgot,
    Upwards I fly;
  Still all my song shall be,
  Nearer, my God, to Thee,
    Nearer to Thee!

Sarah (Flower) Adams, 1841.

449. Draw Me, O Lord, to Thee!

Kedron. 6 4, 6 4, 6 6 4.

ANN BAIRD SPRATT.

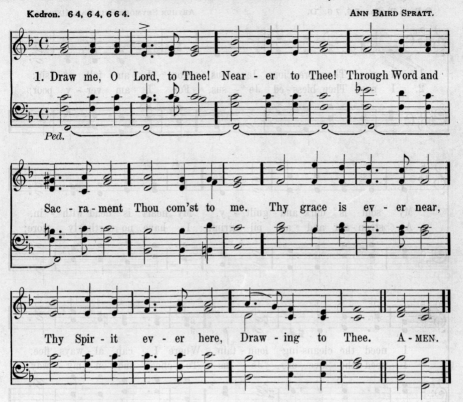

1. Draw me, O Lord, to Thee! Near - er to Thee! Through Word and Sac - ra - ment Thou com'st to me. Thy grace is ev - er near, Thy Spir - it ev - er here, Draw - ing to Thee. A - MEN.

2 Ages on ages rolled,
  Ere earth appeared,
  Yet Thine unmeasured love
  The way prepared,
  Long hast Thou yearned for me
  That I might nearer be,
  Nearer to Thee!

3 Thou, Christ, hast come to earth,
  My sin to bear,
  My every wound to heal,
  My pain to share.
  "God in the flesh" for me
  Now brings me nearer Thee,
  Nearer to Thee!

4 Lo! all my debt is paid,
  My guilt is gone.
  See! He has risen for me,
  My throne is won.
  Thanks, O my God, to Thee!
  None now can nearer be,
  Nearer to Thee!

5 Welcome, then, to Thy home,
  Blest One in Three!
  As Thou hast promised, come!
  Come, Lord, to me!
  Work, Thou, O God, through me,
  Live Thou, O God, in me,
  Even in me!

6 By the baptismal stream
  Which made me Thine,
  By the dear flesh and blood
  Thy love made mine,
  Purge Thou all sin from me,
  That I may nearer be,
  Nearer to Thee!

7 Surely it matters not
  What earth may bring;
  Death is of no account,
  Grace will I sing.
  Nothing remains for me
  Save to be nearer Thee,
  Nearer to Thee!

Henry Eyster Jacobs, 1887. a.

450. I Need Thee, Precious Jesus.

O Bona Patria. 7 6, 7 6. D.   ARTHUR SEYMOUR SULLIVAN, (1842-1900).

1. I need Thee, pre-cious Je - sus, For I am full of sin:
2. I need Thee, bless-ed Je - sus, For I am ver-y poor;

My soul is dark and guilt-y, My heart is dead with - in.
A stran-ger and a pil-grim, I have no earth-ly store;

I need the cleans-ing foun-tain Where I can al-ways flee,
I need the love of Je - sus To cheer me on my way,

The blood of Christ most pre-cious, The sin-ner's per-fect plea.
To guide my doubt-ing foot-steps, To be my strength and stay. A-MEN.

Or: St. Christopher, No. 69.

3 I need Thee, blessèd Jesus,
   I need a friend like Thee,
A friend to soothe and pity,
   A friend to care for me:
I need the heart of Jesus
   To feel each anxious care,
To tell my every trouble,
   And all my sorrows share.

4 I need Thee, blessèd Jesus,
   I need Thee day by day,
To fill me with Thy fullness,
   To lead me on my way:
I need Thy Holy Spirit
   To teach me what I am,
To show me more of Jesus,
   To point me to the Lamb.

Frederick Whitfield, 1855.

451. Beneath the Cross of Jesus.

St. Christopher. 7 6, 8 6, 8 6, 8 6.   FREDERICK CHARLES MAKER, 1881.

1. Be - neath the cross of Je - sus I fain would take my stand, —

The shad - ow of a might - y Rock With - in a wea - ry land;

A home with - in the wil - der - ness, A rest up - on the way,

From burn - ing of the noon-tide heat, And bur - dens of the day. A-MEN.

2 Upon the cross of Jesus
  Mine eye at times can see
The very dying form of One
  Who suffered there for me:
And from my stricken heart with tears
  Two wonders I confess, —
The wonders of redeeming love,
  And my own worthlessness.

3 I take, O cross, thy shadow
  For my abiding-place:
I ask no other sunshine than
  The sunshine of His face;
Content to let the world go by,
  To know no gain nor loss;
My sinful self my only shame,
  My glory all, the cross.

Elizabeth Cecilia Clephane, 1872.

452. Guide Me, O Thou Great Jehovah.

Guide me.   8 7, 8 7, 8 7.   WILLIAM LETTON VINER, (1790-1867).

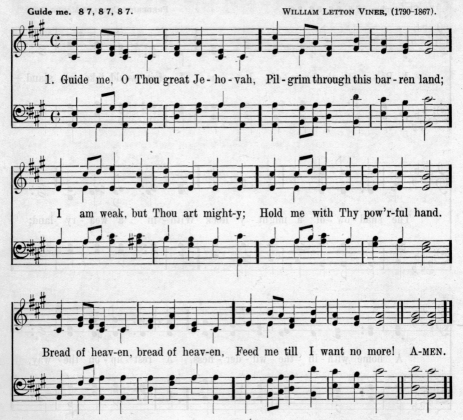

1. Guide me, O Thou great Je - ho - vah, Pil - grim through this bar - ren land;

I am weak, but Thou art might-y; Hold me with Thy pow'r-ful hand.

Bread of heav-en, bread of heav-en, Feed me till I want no more! A-MEN.

2 Open now the crystal fountain,
    Whence the healing streams do flow;
  Let the fiery, cloudy pillar
    Lead me all my journey through;
      Strong Deliverer,
  Be Thou still my Strength and Shield!

3 When I tread the verge of Jordan,
    Bid my anxious fears subside;
  Bear me through the swelling current,
    Land me safe on Canaan's side:
      Songs of praises
  I will ever give to Thee.

                                  William Williams, 1745, a.

453. O for a Heart to Praise My God.

Beatitudo.   C. M.   JOHN BACCHUS DYKES, 1875.

1. O   for a heart to praise my God, A heart from sin set free,

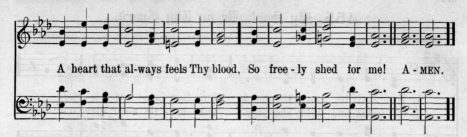

A heart that al-ways feels Thy blood, So free-ly shed for me! A-MEN.

2 A heart resigned, submissive, meek,
  My great Redeemer's throne;
Where only Christ is heard to speak,
  Where Jesus reigns alone.

3 An humble, lowly, contrite heart,
  Believing, true, and clean;
Which neither life nor death can part
From Him that dwells within.

4 A heart in every thought renewed,
  And full of love divine;
Devout, and right, and pure, and good,
  A copy, Lord, of Thine!

5 Thy nature, gracious Lord, impart,
  Come quickly, from above;
Write Thy new Name upon my heart,
  Thy new, best Name of Love.

Charles Wesley, 1772, a.

454. Am I a Soldier of the Cross?

Arlington. C. M.   THOMAS AUGUSTINE ARNE, 1762.

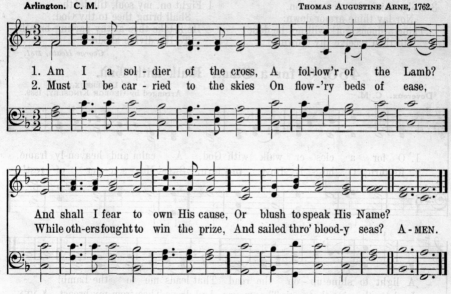

1. Am I a sol-dier of the cross, A fol-low'r of the Lamb?
2. Must I be car-ried to the skies On flow-'ry beds of ease,

And shall I fear to own His cause, Or blush to speak His Name?
While oth-ers fought to win the prize, And sailed thro' blood-y seas? A-MEN.

3 Are there no foes for me to face?
  Must I not stem the flood?
Is this vain world a friend to grace,
  To help me on to God?

4 Nay, I must fight, if I would reign:
  Increase my courage, Lord;
I'll bear the toil, endure the pain,
  Supported by Thy Word.

5 Thy saints, in all this glorious war,
  Shall conquer, though they die;
They see the triumph from afar,
  By faith they bring it nigh.

6 When that illustrious day shall rise,
  And all Thine armies shine
In robes of victory through the skies,
  The glory shall be Thine.

Isaac Watts, 1724.

455. My Soul, Be on Thy Guard.

Heath. S. M.   Arr. from Robert Alexander Schumann, (1810-1856).

1. My soul, be on thy guard; Ten thou-sand foes a-rise,
2. O watch, and fight, and pray, The bat-tle ne'er give o'er;

And hosts of sin are press-ing hard To draw thee from the skies.
Re-new it bold-ly ev-'ry day, And help di-vine im-plore. A-MEN.

3 Ne'er think the victory won,
   Nor lay thine armor down;
Thine arduous work will not be done
   Till thou receive thy crown.

4 Fight on, my soul, till death
   Shall bring thee to thy God;
He'll take thee at thy parting breath
   To His divine abode.

George Heath, 1781.

456. O for a Closer Walk with God.

L. Devereux.
Devereux. C. M.   Arranged by George Kingsley, 1839.

1. O for a clos-er walk with God, A calm and heaven-ly frame,
2. Re-turn, O ho-ly Dove, re-turn, Sweet Mes-sen-ger of rest!

A light to shine up-on the road That leads me to the Lamb!
I hate the sins that made Thee mourn, And drove Thee from my breast. A-MEN.

3 The dearest idol I have known,
   Whate'er that idol be,
Help me to tear it from Thy throne,
   And worship only Thee.

4 So shall my walk be close to God,
   Calm and serene my frame;
And purer light shall mark the road
   That leads me to the Lamb.

William Cowper, 1772, a.

457. The Little While I Linger Here.

Wo Gott der Herr nicht bei uns hält. 8 7, 8 7, 8 8 7.   JOSEPH KLUG's Geistliche Lieder, 1543.

1. The lit-tle while I lin-ger here Should fear and sor-row fret me?
2. I hear Him speak, I know His voice, I go wher-e'er He beck-ons.

No; Je-sus is my Shep-herd dear, He nev-er will for-get me.
His own He knows, they are His choice, Their num-bers, too, He reck-ons.

He gave His life His flock to save, His Spir-it and His
And He will seek the stray-ing sheep, The fee-ble in His

Word He gave. With these He's ev-er with us.
bos-om keep, And gen-tly raise the fall-en. A - MEN.

3 He strengthens me with living bread,
  With waters sweet and gracious,
Which flow from life's great Fountain-head,
  With peace and joy most precious.
Though rough and thorny is my way,
If from His path I do not stray,
  I shall not be forsaken.

4 How vain the worldling's pomp and show,
  How brief his joys and pleasures!
The night approaches now, and lo!
  We leave all earthly treasures.
Then, what are all things here below
To Jesus' promise, "Where I go,
  I will receive you also."

Frans Mikael Franzén, 1814.

458. Jesus, Still Lead On.

Seelenbräutigam. 5 5, 8 8, 5 5.   ADAM DRESE, 1698.

1. Je - sus, still lead on, Till our rest be won, And al-
2. If the way be drear, If the foe be near, Let not

though the way be cheer - less, We will fol - low, calm and fear - less.
faith - less fears o'er - take us, Let not faith and hope for - sake us;

Guide us by Thy hand To our Fa - ther - land!
For through man - y a foe To our home we go! A - MEN.

3 When we seek relief
From a long-felt grief,
When temptations come alluring,
Make us patient and enduring,
Show us that bright shore
Where we weep no more!

4 Jesus, still lead on,
Till our rest be won;
Heavenly Leader, still direct us,
Still support, console, protect us,
Till we safely stand
In our Fatherland!

Nicolaus Ludwig Zinzendorf, 1721.

459. So Let Our Lips and Lives Express.

Min ljufva tröst. L. M.   ALBERT ESAIAS LINDSTRÖM, 1853—

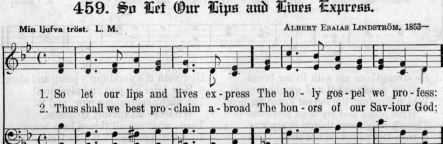

1. So let our lips and lives ex - press The ho - ly gos - pel we pro - fess:
2. Thus shall we best pro - claim a - broad The hon - ors of our Sav-iour God;

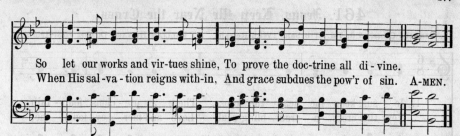

So let our works and vir-tues shine, To prove the doc-trine all di-vine.
When His sal-va-tion reigns with-in, And grace subdues the pow'r of sin. A-MEN.

3 Our flesh and sense must be denied,
And passion, envy, lust, and pride;
While justice, temperance, truth, and love
Our inward piety approve.

4 His promise bears our spirits up,
While we expect that blessèd hope,
The bright appearance of the Lord,
And faith stands leaning on His Word.

Isaac Watts, 1709, a.

460. Merciful Saviour, Come and Be My Comfort.

Integer Vitae. 11 11, 11 5.   FRIEDRICH FERDINAND FLEMMING, (1778-1813).

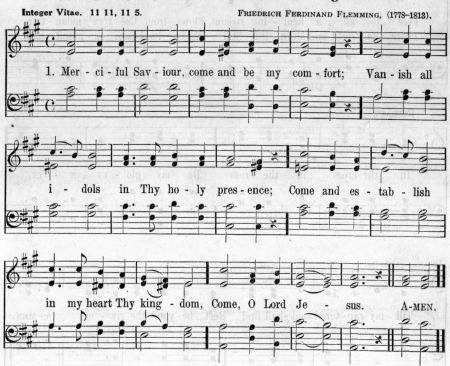

1. Mer-ci-ful Sav-iour, come and be my com-fort; Van-ish all i-dols in Thy ho-ly pres-ence; Come and es-tab-lish in my heart Thy king-dom, Come, O Lord Je-sus. A-MEN.

2 Come as the Bridegroom to the bride belovèd,
    Come Thou to strengthen faith and love and patience;
    Be Thou a very present help in danger;
        Come, O Lord Jesus.

3 Come in my pleasures, come to me in sorrow,
    Come in the anguished hour of dire temptation,
    Come and deliver me from sin and evil,
        Come, O Lord Jesus.

Katarina Elisabet Posse, (1818-1880).

461. Jesus, Keep Me Near the Cross.

Near the Cross. 7 6, 7 6. Trochaic. With Refrain.   WILLIAM HOWARD DOANE, (1831-1915).

1. Je - sus, keep me near the cross, There a pre - cious foun - tain,
2. Near the cross, a trem - bling soul, Love and mer - cy found me;

Free to all, a heal - ing stream, Flows from Cal - v'ry's moun - tain.
There the Bright and Morn - ing Star Sheds its beams a - round me.

REFRAIN:

In the cross, in the cross Be my glo - ry ev - er,

Till my rap - tured soul shall find Rest be - yond the riv - er.   A - MEN.

Used by permission of W. H. Doane, owner of the Copyright.

3 Near the cross! O Lamb of God,
    Bring its scenes before me;
Help me walk from day to day
    With its shadows o'er me.

4 Near the cross I'll watch and wait,
    Hoping, trusting ever,
Till I reach the golden strand
    Just beyond the river.

Frances Jane (Crosby) Van Alstyne, 1869.

462. I Need Thee Every Hour.

I need Thee. 6 4, 6 4. With Refrain.   ROBERT LOWRY, 1872.

1. I need Thee ev - 'ry hour, Most gra - cious Lord,

No ten - der voice like Thine Can peace af - ford.

REFRAIN:

I need Thee, O I need Thee, Ev - 'ry hour I need Thee:

O bless me now, my Sav - iour, I come to Thee. A - MEN.

2 I need Thee every hour,
  Stay Thou near by;
Temptations lose their power
  When Thou art nigh.

3 I need Thee every hour,
  In joy or pain;
Come quickly and abide,
  Or life is vain.

4 I need Thee every hour,
  Teach me Thy will;
And Thy rich promises
  In me fulfill.

5 I need Thee every hour,
  Most Holy One,
O make me Thine indeed,
  Thou blessèd Son.

Annie Sherwood Hawks, 1872.

463. How Blest Are the Moments That Jesus Bestows.

Ack, saliga stunder. 11 11 11, 6 6 11.   OSKAR AHNFELT, (1813–1882).

1. How blest are the moments that Je - sus bestows, When won-ders of grace to the
spir - it He shows! His Word lights the way to the heav - en - ly goal,
His Spir - it is near us, His Spir - it is near us,
To teach us, and cheer us, and com - fort our soul! A - MEN

2 Lord Jesus, our Saviour, A Pentecost give
To quicken, and strengthen, and cause us to live;
Grant faith and give love, and in mercy bestow
    Whatever is needed,
To exercise faith in our hearts here below.

3 Our hearts are as cold and as hard as a stone;
Such are they by nature, and Thou art alone,
On earth and in heaven, the Saviour who can,
    A new heart creating,
A new heart creating, make each a new man.

4 From sorrows of earth Thou wilt now turn our mind,
For days that are coming, O help us to find
Our joy and our comfort in what Thou hast wrought;
    For we are Thy people,
With blood and with anguish so preciously bought.

5 Lord, therefore remember, in mercy and love,
Thy people, and grant us Thy help from above;
Thy law cause to wake us, Thy grace give us cheer,
    And send us Thy Spirit,
And give us to know that Thy presence is near.

Ahnfelts Sånger.

464. All the Way My Saviour Leads Me.

All the way. 8 7, 8 7. D.

ROBERT LOWRY, (1826-1899).

1. All the way my Sav-iour leads me; What have I to ask be-side?
Can I doubt His ten-der mer-cy, Who thro' life has been my Guide?
Heav'n-ly peace, di-vin-est com-fort, Here by faith in Him to dwell!
For I know, what-e'er be-fall me, Je-sus do-eth all things well;
For I know what-e'er be-fall me, Je-sus do-eth all things well. A-MEN.

2 All the way my Saviour leads me,
　Cheers each winding path I tread,
Gives me grace for every trial,
　Feeds me with the living bread.
Though my weary steps may falter,
　And my soul athirst may be,
Gushing from the Rock before me,
　Lo! a spring of joy I see.

3 All the way my Saviour leads me;
　O the fullness of His love!
Perfect rest to me is promised
　In my Father's house above.
When my spirit, clothed immortal,
　Wings its flight to realms of day,
This my song through endless ages:
　Jesus led me all the way.

Frances Jane (Crosby) Van Alstyne, (1820-1915).

465. O Lord, Devoutly Love I Thee.

Herzlich lieb hab ich dich, o Herr. 8 8 7, 8 8 7, 8 8, 8 8, 4 8 8.   MATTHIAS GASTRITZ, 1571.

1. O Lord, de-vout-ly love I Thee; Come, Je-sus, and a-bide with me,
   In this wide world of anx-ious care, Vain-glo-ry find I ev-'ry-where,

And grant me e'er Thy fa - vor.
But peace with Thee, my Sav - iour. E'en though, in woe-ful ag-o-ny,

My soul and bod-y pine a-way, Thou art my Com-fort, ev-er blest,

I safe-ly on Thy bos-om rest. Lord Je-sus Christ, My Sav-iour

dear, My Sav-iour dear, Thy sav-ing hand is ev-er near. A - MEN.

2 Almighty God, for what I own,
Receive, and am, to Thee alone
  I ought my thanks to render.
Teach me to use Thy gifts, I pray,
To aid the poor, and never stay,
  O Lord, Thy mercies tender.
Make known to me, O God, Thy will,
And purge my soul of every ill;
Yea, make me patient and content,
Nor let my soul to earth be bent,
Lord Jesus Christ, for Thy death's sake
The bonds of my affliction break.

3 Send, Lord, Thine angels forth at last
To bear my soul, when life is past,
  Where heavenly joy aboundeth;
And let my weary body rest
In peace, where'er Thou seest best,
  Until Thy voice resoundeth.
Then lo! in holy raiment clad,
I shall behold my Lord and God;
His grace and glory then shall be
My joy in all eternity.
Lord Jesus Christ, my prayer fulfill;
In life, in death, Thine am I still.

Martin Mikael Schalling, 1571.
Johan Olof Wallin, 1819.

466. What Our Father Does Is Well.

Lux Prima. 7 7, 7 7, 7 7. CHARLES FRANCOIS GOUNOD, 1872.

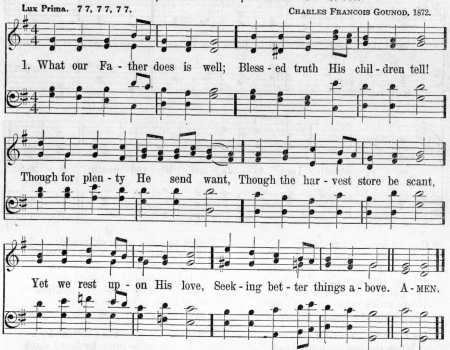

2 What our Father does is well;
Shall the wilful heart rebel
If a blessing He withold
In the field, or in the fold?
Is He not Himself to be
All our store eternally?

3 What our Father does is well:
Though He sadden hill and dell,
Upward yet our praises rise
For the strength His Word supplies.
He has called us sons of God;
Can we murmur at His rod?

4 What our Father does is well;
May the thought within us dwell.
Though nor milk nor honey flow
In our barren Canaan now,
God can save us in our need,
God can bless us, God can feed.

5 Therefore unto Him we raise
Hymns of glory, songs of praise;
To the Father and the Son
And the Spirit, Three in One,
Honor, might, and glory be,
Now and through eternity.

Benjamin Schmolck, 1720.

467. Look to Jesus Christ Thy Saviour.

Jesus! du dig själf uppväckte.   8 7, 8 7, 8 7 7.   Swedish, 1695.

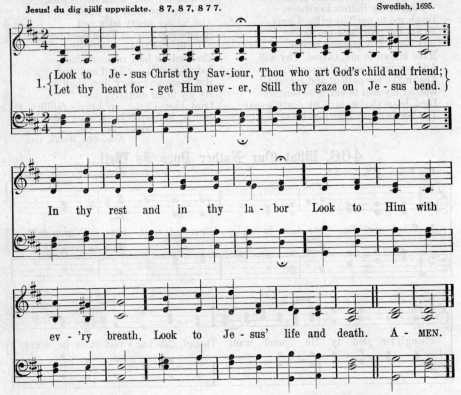

1. { Look to Je-sus Christ thy Sav-iour, Thou who art God's child and friend;
Let thy heart for-get Him nev-er, Still thy gaze on Je-sus bend. }

In thy rest and in thy la-bor Look to Him with

ev-'ry breath, Look to Je-sus' life and death. A - MEN.

2 Look to Jesus, till reviving
  Faith and love thy bosom swell;
Strength for all things good deriving
  From Him who did all things well;
Work as He did, in thy season,
Works which shall not fade away,
Work while it is called To-day.

3 Look to Jesus, praying, waking,
  When thy feet on roses tread;
Follow, worldly pomp forsaking,
  With thy cross where He hath led.
Look to Jesus in temptation;
Baffled shall the tempter flee,
And God's angels come to thee.

4 Look to Jesus, when dark lowering
  Perils thy horizon dim;
Unlike His disciples cowering,
  Calm 'mid tempests look on Him.
Trust in Him who still rebuketh
Wind and billow, fire and flood;
Forward! then, and trust in God.

5 Look to Jesus when distressèd,
  See what He, the Sinless, bore;
Is thy heart with conflict pressèd?
  Is thy soul still harassed sore?
See His bloody sweat, His conflict,
Watch His agony increase,
Hear His prayer, and taste His peace!

6 Art thou by sore want surrounded?
  Do thy pains press forth thy sighs?
Art thou wronged and deeply wounded?
  Does a scornful world despise?
Friends forsake thee or deny thee?
See what Jesus must endure,
He who as the light was pure!

7 Look to Jesus still to shield thee,
  When this dwelling thou must leave;
In that last need He will yield thee
  Peace the world can never give.
Look to Him, thy head low bending;
He, who finished all for thee,
Takes thee then with Him to be.

Frans Mikael Franzén, 1816.

468. I Have a Friend So Patient, Kind, Forbearing.

Jag har en vän. 11 10, 11 10. Iambic.

Swedish Folksong.

1. I have a Friend so pa-tient, kind, for-bear-ing,
Of all my friends this Friend doth love me best;
Though I am weak and sin-ful, yet, when shar-ing
His love and mer-cy, I am ev-er blest. A - MEN.

Or: Aline, No. 533.

2 He is my Lord, my Friend, my loving Brother,
   And Jesus Christ is His most blessèd Name.
   He loves more tenderly than any mother:
   To rest in Him is more than wealth and fame.

3 My poor and wretched soul He liberated
   From sin and condemnation, death and hell;
   The serpent's head is bruised, his might defeated,
   Rejoice, my ransomed soul, for all is well!

4 I am redeemed; no more the law prevaileth,
   And Christ, the Lord, is my Redeemer's Name;
   His precious blood more than my sin availeth;
   His merit covers all my guilt and shame.

5 With hallelujahs here I'll tell the story,
   My Lord to praise, to laud and magnify,
   And praise His Name for evermore in glory,
   Before His throne, with all the saints on high.

Carl Olof Rosenius, (1816–1868).

469. Thee Will I Love, My Strength, My Tower.

Pater Omnium. 8 8, 8 8, 8 8.   HENRY J. E. HOLMES, 1875.

1. Thee will I love, my Strength, my Tow'r, Thee will I love, my
2. I thank Thee, un - cre - at - ed Sun, That Thy bright beams on

Joy, my Crown; Thee will I love with all my pow'r,
me have shined; I thank Thee, who hast o - ver - thrown

In all Thy works, and Thee a - lone; Thee will I love, till
My foes, and healed my wound - ed mind; I thank Thee, whose en-

Thy pure fire Fill all my soul with chaste de - sire.
liv-en-ing voice Bids my freed heart in Thee re - joice. A - MEN.

Or: St. Catherine, No. 486.

3 Uphold me in the doubtful race,
  Nor suffer me again to stray;
Strengthen my feet with steady pace
  Still to press forward in Thy way;
That all my powers, with all their might,
  In Thy sole glory may unite.

4 Thee will I love, my Joy, my Crown;
  Thee will I love, my Lord, my God;
Thee love beneath Thy smile or frown,
  Beneath Thy scepter or Thy rod.
What though my flesh and heart decay?
  Thee shall I love in endless day.

Johann Scheffler, 1657.

470. Jesus Is My Friend Most Precious.

Jesus är min vän den bäste. 8 7, 8 7. D.

GUSTAF DÜBEN, 1674.

1. Je - sus is my Friend most pre-cious, Nev - er friend did love as He;

Can I leave this Friend so gra-cious, Spurn His won-drous love for me?

No! nor friend nor foe shall sev - er Me from Him who loves me so;

His shall be my will for - ev - er, There a-bove, and here be - low. A-MEN.

2 Bitter death for me He suffered;
  From all guilt He set me free;
To His Father He hath offered
  Everlasting prayers for me.
Who is he that would condemn me?
  Christ hath saved me by His grace;
Who can from my Saviour draw me?
  I am safe in His embrace.

3 Now I am convinced that never
  Life or death can sever me
From my blessèd Lord and Saviour;
  Present things, nor things to be,
Height nor depth, nor fear nor favor,
  Naught that heaven or earth affords
Makes the sacred promise waver:
  "Ye are Christ's, and He's the Lord's."

Jacob Arrhenius, 1691.

471. Shine on Our Souls, Eternal God.

Nun danket all' und bringet Ehr (Störl). C. M.   JOHANN GEORG CHRISTIAN STÖRL, 1710.

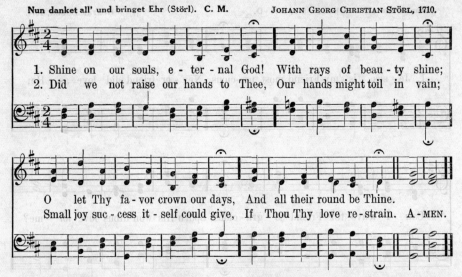

1. Shine on our souls, e-ter-nal God! With rays of beau-ty shine;
2. Did we not raise our hands to Thee, Our hands might toil in vain;

O let Thy fa-vor crown our days, And all their round be Thine.
Small joy suc-cess it-self could give, If Thou Thy love re-strain. A-MEN.

3 With Thee let every week begin,
   With Thee each day be spent,
   For Thee each fleeting hour improved,
   Since each by Thee is lent.

4 Thus cheer us through this toilsome road,
   Till all our labors cease;
   And heaven refresh our weary souls
   With everlasting peace.

Philip Doddridge, 1755, a.

472. Must Jesus Bear the Cross Alone?

Maitland. C. M.   GEORGE NELSON ALLEN, (1812-1877.)

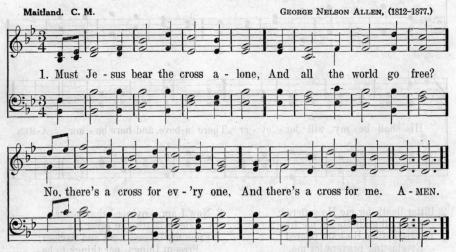

1. Must Je-sus bear the cross a-lone, And all the world go free?

No, there's a cross for ev-'ry one, And there's a cross for me. A-MEN.

2 How happy are the saints above,
   Who once were sorrowing here!
   For now they taste unmingled love,
   And joy without a tear.

3 The consecrated cross I'll bear,
   Till death shall set me free;
   And then go home, my crown to wear,
   For there's a crown for me.

Unknown.

473. If God Himself Be for Me.

Old 130th Psalm. 76, 76. D.   Genevan Psalter, 1556.

1. If God Him-self be for me, I may a host de-fy;
2. I build on this foun-da-tion, That Je-sus and His blood

For when I pray, be-fore me My foes con-found-ed fly.
A-lone are my Sal-va-tion, The true E-ter-nal Good;

If Christ, the Head, be-friend me, If God be my sup-port,
With-out Him, all that pleas-es Is val-ue-less on earth;

The mis-chief they in-tend me Shall quick-ly come to naught.
The gifts I owe to Je-sus A-lone my love are worth. A-MEN.

3 His Holy Spirit dwelleth
  Within my willing heart,
Tames it when it rebelleth,
  And soothes the keenest smart.
He crowns His work with blessing,
  And helpeth me to cry,
"My Father," without ceasing,
  To Him who reigns on high.

4 To mine His Spirit speaketh
  Sweet words of soothing power,
How God for him that seeketh
  For rest hath rest in store;
How God Himself prepareth
  My heritage and lot,
And, though my body weareth,
  My heaven shall fail me not.

Paul Gerhardt, 1656.

474. Commit Thou All Thy Griefs.

Kane. S. M. D.

LOWELL MASON, (1792-1872).
Har. by HENRY EDWARD DIBDIN, (1813-1866).

1. Com - mit thou all thy griefs And ways in - to His hands,
2. Thou on the Lord re - ly, So safe shalt thou go on;

To His sure truth and ten - der care Who earth and heav'n com-mands:
Fix on His work thy stead - fast eye, So shall thy work be done.

Who points the clouds their course, Whom winds and seas o - bey,
No prof - it canst Thou gain By self - con - sum - ing care;

He shall di - rect thy wan-d'ring feet, He shall pre-pare thy way.
To Him com-mend thy cause; His ear At - tends the soft - est prayer. A-MEN.

3 Thy everlasting truth,
   Father, Thy ceaseless love,
Sees all Thy children's wants, and knows
   What best for each will prove.
And whatsoe'er Thou will'st,
   Thou dost, O King of kings!
What Thine unerring wisdom chose,
   Thy power to being brings.

4 Thou everywhere hast sway,
   And all things serve Thy might;
Thy every act pure blessing is,
   Thy path unsullied light.
When Thou arisest, Lord,
   What shall Thy work withstand?
When what Thy children want Thou giv'st,
   Who, who shall stay Thy hand?

Paul Gerhardt, 1656.

475. Jesus, in My Walk and Living.

Freu dich sehr, o meine Seele. 8 7, 8 7, 7 7, 8 8.   French Psalter, 1555.

1. Je - sus, in my walk and liv - ing, Let me ev - er fol - low Thine;
2. Let Thy pre - cepts be my guid-ance, Shin-ing on my gloom - y way;

Bear - er of the cross, O teach me Pa - tient - ly to take up mine.
Hold - ing to Thy blest ex - am - ple, Who can err or go a - stray?

If by fel - low men de - spised, Make me like to Thee, O Christ,
Thou who ful - ly didst ful - fill For our sake Thy Fa - ther's will,

O'er their sins and er-rors griev-ing, And all in - jur - ies for - giv-ing.
Help me so to live that nev - er Aught from Thee my soul shall sev-er. A-MEN.

3 In my joys and in my sorrows,
    Teach Thou me that perfect faith
Which, in trustful prayer persistent,
    Wavers not in life or death.
My will unto Thine I yield;
With Thy Word and Spirit filled,
Let my life to Thee be given:
Service here, and praise in heaven.

4 For my task, O Lord, equip me
    From Thy store of rich supply,
That the world and all its evils
    I may in Thy strength defy.
Willing, yet in body weak,
I Thy safe protection seek;
Perfect strength in weakness give me,
In Thy saving arms receive me.

Johan Hjertén, 1816.

476. Though Troubles Assail Us, and Dangers Affright.

På jorden är allting föränderligt. **11 11, 11 11.**   WOLFGANG AMADEUS MOZART, (1756-1791).

1. Though trou-bles as-sail us, and dan-gers af-fright,

Though friends should all fail us, and foes all u-nite,

Yet one thing se-cures us, what-ev-er be-tide,

The prom-ise as-sures us—"The Lord will pro-vide." A-MEN.

2 The birds, without garner or storehouse, are fed;
From them let us learn to trust God for our bread:
His saints what is fitting shall ne'er be denied
So long as 'tis written, "The Lord will provide."

3 When Satan assails us to stop up our path,
And courage all fails us, we triumph by faith.
He cannot take from us, though oft he has tried,
This heart-cheering promise, "The Lord will provide."

4 No strength of our own, and no goodness we claim;
Yet, since we have known of the Saviour's great Name,
In this our strong tower for safety we hide:
The Lord is our power, "The Lord will provide."

John Newton, 1779, a.

477. Come, Ye Disconsolate, Where'er Ye Languish.

Consolation. 11 10, 11 10.   SAMUEL WEBBE, 1792.

1. Come, ye dis - con - so - late, wher - e'er ye lan - guish;
Come to the mer - cy - seat, fer - vent - ly kneel:
Here bring your wound - ed hearts, here tell your an - guish;
Earth has no sor - row that Heav'n can - not heal. A - MEN.

2 Joy of the desolate, light of the straying,
  Hope of the penitent, fadeless and pure!
  Here speaks the Comforter, tenderly saying,
  "Earth has no sorrow that Heaven cannot cure."

3 Here see the Bread of Life; see waters flowing
  Forth from the throne of God, pure from above;
  Come to the feast of love; come, ever knowing
  Earth has no sorrow but Heaven can remove.

St. 1, 2, Thomas Moore, 1816.
St. 3, Thomas Hastings, 1831.

478. God Moves in a Mysterious Way.

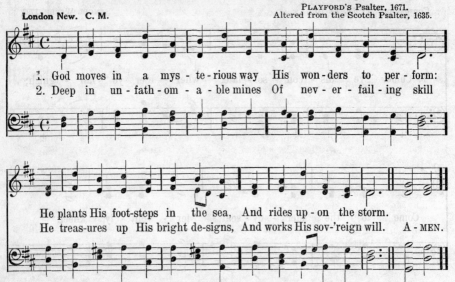

PLAYFORD'S Psalter, 1671.
Altered from the Scotch Psalter, 1635.

London New. C. M.

1. God moves in a mys-te-rious way His won-ders to per-form:
2. Deep in un-fath-om-a-ble mines Of nev-er-fail-ing skill

He plants His foot-steps in the sea, And rides up-on the storm.
He treas-ures up His bright de-signs, And works His sov-'reign will. A-MEN.

3 Ye fearful saints, fresh courage take:
　The clouds ye so much dread
Are big with mercy, and shall break
　In blessings on your head.

4 Judge not the Lord by feeble sense,
　But trust Him for His grace;
Behind a frowning Providence
　He hides a smiling face.

5 His purposes will ripen fast,
　Unfolding every hour;
The bud may have a bitter taste,
　But sweet will be the flower.

6 Blind unbelief is sure to err,
　And scan His works in vain;
God is His own interpreter,
　And He will make it plain.

William Cowper, 1774.

479. Watch, My Soul, and Pray.

Seelenbräutigam. 5 5, 8 8, 5 5.   ADAM DRESE, 1698.

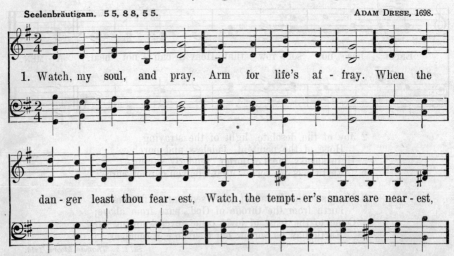

1. Watch, my soul, and pray, Arm for life's af-fray. When the

dan-ger least thou fear-est, Watch, the tempt-er's snares are near-est,

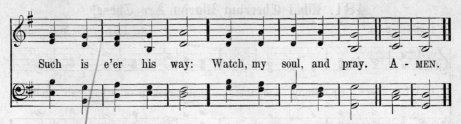

Such is e'er his way: Watch, my soul, and pray. A-MEN.

2 Watch and pray, my soul,
  Flesh and blood control;
When the world, in tempting story,
Tells of pleasure, wealth, and glory,
  Be not led astray:
  Watch, my soul, and pray.

3 See the goodly land
  On the heavenly strand;
See God's people, thither tending,
Through the sea and desert wending,
  Led by Joshua's hand:
  Seek the goodly land.

4 Through thy pilgrimage
  Guard thy heritage:
Pray and fight, on Christ relying,
Live to Him, thyself denying;
  Onward to the goal,
  Win the crown, my soul!

5 Watch, and fight, and pray
  Through this mortal day;
Soon thy Canaan thou attainest,
Soon the crown and palm thou gainest,
  Peace is won for aye:
  Watch, my soul, and pray.

Johan Olof Wallin, 1816.

480. The Lord My Shepherd Is.

Dennis. S. M.   Arr. from JOHANN GEORG NÄGELI, by LOWELL MASON, 1845.

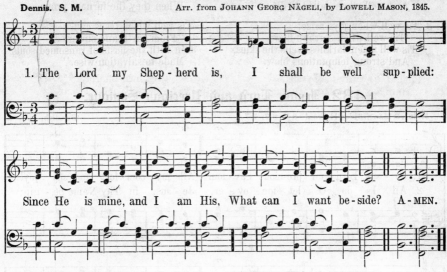

1. The Lord my Shep-herd is, I shall be well sup-plied:
Since He is mine, and I am His, What can I want be-side? A-MEN.

2 He leads me to the place
  Where heavenly pasture grows,
Where living waters gently pass,
  And full salvation flows.

3 If e'er I go astray,
  He doth my soul reclaim,
And guides me in His own right way,
  For His most holy Name.

4 While He affords His aid,
  I cannot yield to fear: [shade,
Though I should walk through death's dark
  My Shepherd's with me there.

5 The bounties of Thy love
  Shall crown my coming days;
Nor from Thy house will I remove,
  Nor cease to speak Thy praise.

Isaac Watts, 1719.

481. What Cheering Words Are These!

Holborn. S. M.   ST. ALBAN'S Tune Book, 1865.

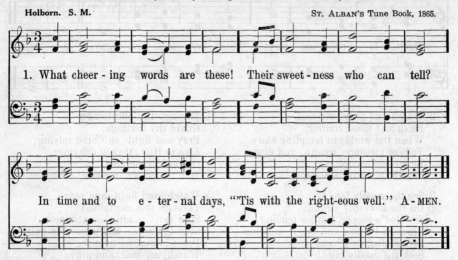

1. What cheer - ing words are these! Their sweet-ness who can tell?

In time and to e - ter - nal days, "'Tis with the right-eous well." A - MEN.

2 In every state secure,
　　Kept by Jehovah's eye,
　'Tis well with them while life endure,
　　And well when called to die.

3 'Tis well when joys arise;
　　'Tis well when sorrows flow;
　'Tis well when darkness veils the skies,
　　And strong temptations blow.

4 'Tis well when on the mount
　　They feast on dying love,
　And 'tis as well in God's account,
　　When they the furnace prove.

5 'Tis well when Jesus calls,
　　"From earth and sin arise,
　Join with the hosts of ransomed souls,
　　Made to salvation wise."

John Kent, 1803, a.

482. Jesus, Lord and Precious Saviour.

Hela världen fröjdes Herran! 8 7, 8 7, 7 7.   Swedish, 1689.

1. Je - sus, Lord and pre-cious Sav - iour, All my com-fort and my joy!
2. All I do, O let me ev - er, Je - sus, in Thy Name be - gin;

Gra-cious-ly ex-tend Thy fa - vor, Let Thy Word my soul em-ploy.
Give suc-cess to my en-deav - or, Fi - nal vic-to - ry there-in.

REFRAIN:

Je-sus, come, a-bide with me, Let me ev-er be with Thee. A-MEN.

3 Let my words and thoughts, O Saviour,
To Thy praise and glory tend;
Help me, Lord, that I may gather
Treasures that shall never end.

4 When my days on earth are over,
Let me enter into rest.
Bear me home, O blessèd Saviour,
When to Thee it seemeth best.

Johan Olof Wallin, 1819.

483. How Happy Is the Man Who Hears.

Devizes. C. M.   I. TUCKER, 1800.

1. How hap-py is the man who hears In-struc-tion's warn-ing voice,
2. For she has treas-ures great-er far Than East or West un-fold;

And who ce-les-tial wis-dom makes His ear-ly,
And her re-wards more pre-cious are Than all their

on-ly choice! His ear-ly, on-ly choice!
stores of gold, Than all their stores of gold. A-MEN.

3 She guides the young with innocence
In happy paths to tread;
A crown of glory she bestows
Upon the hoary head.

4 According as her labors rise,
So her rewards increase;
Her ways are ways of pleasantness,
And all her paths are peace.

Michael Bruce, 1770.

484. Let, O My Soul, Thy God Direct Thee.

Neumark. 9 8, 9 8, 8 8.   GEORG NEUMARK, 1657.

1. Let, O my soul, thy God di-rect thee, And trust in Him through all thy days; In ev-'ry dan-ger He'll pro-tect thee, And crown thy years with peace and grace. He doth not build up-on the sand Who trusts in God's al-might-y hand. A - MEN.

Or: Wer weiss, wie nahe mir mein Ende, No. 402.

2 Of what avail is all our sorrow?
   What profit all our sighs and tears?
Why should we grieve for each to-morrow?
   Why thus begin and end our years?
Our sighs and sorrows but increase
Our burdens, and disturb our peace.

3 Be still, in faith and hope abiding,
   Trust in thy God and be content;
In His unfailing love confiding,
   Take what His gracious hand hath sent;
'To God who chose thee as His own
Thy every need and care is known.

4 The time to comfort thee He knoweth,
   He giveth thee whate'er is best;
The prayer that from thy bosom goeth
   He heareth ere it is expressed.
With gifts He cometh unawares
In answer to thy fervent prayers.

5 Think not when tried and tempest-driven,
   Thou art forsaken by thy God;
For those who are the heirs of heaven
   Must pass beneath the chastening rod.
The night of weeping may ere long
Be changed into the morn of song.

6 What does it cost the Lord Almighty
   To raise the humble and the low?
Or to abase the high and mighty,
   And cause their utter overthrow?
For He whose wonders none can trace,
He lifteth up, He doth abase.

7 Walk in His truth, be firm and fearless,
   And do thy duty day by day;
Trust in His Word when sad and cheerless,
   Make it thy comfort and thy stay.
The Lord thy God thy refuge make,
And He will never thee forsake.

Georg Neumark, 1657.
Johan Olof Wallin, 1819.

485. Thou Hidden Love of God, Whose Height.

Ingrid. 8 8, 8 8, 8 8.

GERHARD THEODORE ALEXIS, 1924.

1. Thou hid-den love of God, whose height, Whose depth un-
fath-omed no man knows, I see from far Thy beau-teous light,
In-ly I sigh for Thy re-pose: My heart is pained, nor
can it be At rest, till it find rest in Thee.

2. Is there a thing be-neath the sun That strives with
Thee my heart to share? Ah! tear it thence, and reign a-lone,
The Lord of ev-'ry mo-tion there. Then shall my heart from
earth be free, When it hath found re-pose in Thee. A-MEN.

Or: St. Petersburg, No. 7.

3 O hide this self from me, that I
No more, but Christ in me, may live!
My base affections crucify,
Nor let one favorite sin survive;
In all things nothing may I see,
Nothing desire, or seek, but Thee.

4 Each moment draw from earth away
My heart that lowly waits Thy call!
Speak to my inmost soul, and say:
"I am thy Love, thy God, thy All!"
To feel Thy power, to hear Thy voice,
To taste Thy love, be all my choice!

Gerhard Tersteegen, 1729.

486. O Jesus, Source of Calm Repose.

St. Catherine. 8 8, 8 8, 8 8.

HENRI FREDRICK HEMY, 1865.
Alt. by JAMES GEORGE WALTON, 1871.

1. O Je - sus, Source of calm re - pose, Thy like no man nor an - gel knows,

Fair-est a - mong ten thou-sand fair! E'en those whom death's sad fet - ters bound,

Whom thickest darkness compassed round, Find light and life, if Thou ap-pear.   A - MEN.

2 Renew Thine image, Lord, in me,
  Lowly and gentle may I be;
    No charms but these to Thee are dear;
  No anger may'st Thou ever find,
  No pride, in my unruffled mind,   [there.
    But faith, and heaven-born peace, be

3 A patient, a victorious mind,
  That life and all things casts behind,
    Springs forth obedient to Thy call,
  A heart that no desire can move,
  But still to praise, believe, and love,
    Give me, my Lord, my Life, my All!

Johann Anastasius Freylinghausen, 1704.

487. Children of the Heavenly Father.

Tryggare kan ingen vara. L. M.

Swedish Folksong.

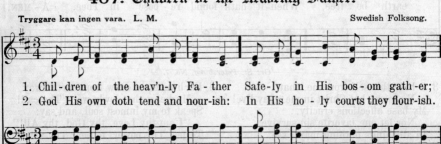

1. Chil - dren of   the heav'n-ly Fa - ther   Safe-ly   in   His bos - om gath -er;
2. God His own doth tend and nour-ish: In   His ho - ly courts they flour-ish.

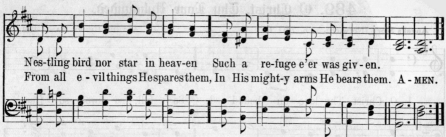

Nes-tling bird nor star in heav-en Such a re-fuge e'er was giv-en.
From all e - vil things He spares them, In His might-y arms He bears them. A - MEN.

3 Neither life nor death shall ever
From the Lord His children sever;
Unto them His grace He showeth,
And their sorrows all He knoweth.

4 Lo, their very hairs He numbers,
And no daily care encumbers
Them that share His every blessing,
And His help in woes distressing.

5 Praise the Lord in joyful numbers:
Your Protector never slumbers.
At the will of your Defender
Every foeman must surrender.

6 Though He giveth or He taketh,
God His children ne'er forsaketh,
His the loving purpose solely
To preserve them pure and holy.

Carolina Vilhelmina (Sandell) Berg, (1832-1903).

488. O Thou Who Hast Thy Servants Taught.

Ortonville. C. M.   THOMAS HASTINGS, 1837.

1. O Thou who hast Thy serv - ants taught That not by words a-
lone, But by the fruits of ho - li - ness, The
life of God is shown, The life of God is shown! A - MEN.

Or: St. Anne, No. 412.

2 While in Thy house of prayer we meet,
And call Thee God and Lord,
Give us a heart to follow Thee,
Obedient to Thy Word!

3 Through all the dangerous paths of life,
Uphold us as we go;
That with our lips, and in our lives,
Thy glory we may show.

Henry Alford, 1844.

489. O Christ, Thy Love Unbounded.

(Norwich). 7 6, 7 6. D.   ARTHUR HENRY MANN, 1881.

1. O Christ, Thy love un - bound - ed, So full, so sweet, so free,

Leaves all our thoughts con - found - ed, When - e'er we think of Thee.

For us Thou cam'st from heav - en, For us didst bleed and die,

That, ran-somed and for - giv - en, We might as - cend on high. A-MEN.

2 We know that Thou hast bought us,
   And washed us in Thy blood:
We know Thy grace hath brought us
   As kings and priests to God.
We know the blessèd morning,
   Long looked for, draweth near,
When we, at Thy returning,
   In glory shall appear.

3 O let Thy love constrain us
   To give our hearts to Thee;
Let nothing please or pain us,
   Apart, O Lord, from Thee;
Our joy, our one endeavor,
   Through suffering, conflict, shame,
To serve Thee, gracious Saviour,
   And magnify Thy Name.

Bosworth's Church Hymns, 1865.

490. My Jesus, As Thou Wilt!

Denby. 6 6, 6 6. D.

CHARLES J. DALE, 1904.

1. My Jesus, as Thou wilt! O may Thy will be mine!
Into Thy hand of love I would my all re-sign;
Thro' sor-row, or thro' joy, Con-duct me as Thine own,
And help me still to say, "My Lord, Thy will be done!" A-MEN.

2 My Jesus, as Thou wilt!
  If needy here and poor,
Give me Thy people's bread,
  Their portion rich and sure.
The manna of Thy Word
  Let my soul feed upon;
And if all else should fail,
  My Lord, Thy will be done.

3 My Jesus, as Thou wilt!
  Though seen through many a tear,
Let not my star of hope
  Grow dim or disappear:
Since Thou on earth hast wept
  And sorrowed oft alone,
If I must weep with Thee,
  My Lord, Thy will be done.

4 My Jesus, as Thou wilt!
  When death itself draws nigh,
To Thy dear wounded side
  I would for refuge fly,
And, leaning on Thee, go
  Where Thou before hast gone,—
The rest as Thou shalt please:
  My Lord, Thy will be done.

5 My Jesus, as Thou wilt!
  All shall be well for me:
Each changing future scene
  I gladly trust with Thee.
Thus to my home above
  I travel calmly on,
And sing, in life or death,
  My Lord, Thy will be done.

Benjamin Schmolck, (1672–1737).

491. Jesus Is My Joy, My All.

Jesus allt mitt goda är. 7 8, 7 8, 7 7.   JAKOB ARRHENIUS? 1694.

1. Je - sus is my Joy, my All, He for me His life hath giv - en;
2. Rich-es, pomp, and earth-ly joy Can-not tempt my soul from heav-en;

I am His, I hear His call; He hath writ my name in heav-en.
Gold is min-gled with al - loy, Bit - ter - ness with sweet-ness giv - en,

Earth-ly treas-ures pass a - way; Je - sus I will love for aye.
Rich - es flee and hopes de - cay; Je - sus' grace a - bides al - way. A- MEN.

3 In my Jesus I am blest,
   He to pleasant pastures leads me,
Stills my soul and gives it rest,
   And with heavenly manna feeds me.
Earthly things must fade and fall;
Jesus is my Life, my All.

4 Then away, O world! thy joy
   Leads the soul to grief and sorrow;
Death is found in sin's employ,
   Fears to-day, regrets to-morrow.
Jesus only satisfies;
Jesus points me to the skies!

Ahasuerus Fritsch. Johan Olof Wallin, 1814.

492. Blest Are the Pure in Heart.

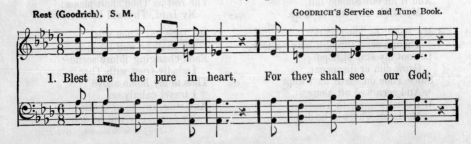

Rest (Goodrich). S. M.   GOODRICH'S Service and Tune Book.

1. Blest are the pure in heart, For they shall see our God;

The se-cret of the Lord is theirs, Their soul is Christ's a-bode. A-MEN.

2 Still to the lowly soul
    He will Himself impart;
  And for His temple and His throne
    Doth choose the pure in heart.

3 Lord, we Thy presence seek,
    May ours this blessing be;
  O give the pure and lowly heart
    A temple meet for Thee!

John Keble, 1827, a.

493. More Love to Thee, O Christ.

More love to Thee. 6 4, 6 4, 6 6, 4 4.   WILLIAM HOWARD DOANE, (1832–1915).

1. More love to Thee, O Christ, More love to Thee; Hear Thou the

prayer I make On bend-ed knee; This is my ear-nest plea,

More love, O Christ, to Thee, More love to Thee; More love to Thee. A-MEN.

2 Once earthly joy I craved,
    Sought peace and rest;
  Now Thee alone I seek,
    Give what is best;
  This all my prayer shall be,
  More love, O Christ, to Thee,
    More love to Thee.

3 Then shall my latest breath
    Whisper Thy praise;
  This be the parting cry
    My heart shall raise;
  This still its prayer shall be,
  More love, O Christ, to Thee,
    More love to Thee.

Elizabeth Prenti

494. Nearer, Still Nearer, Close to Thy Heart.

Nearer, still nearer. 9 10, 9 10, 10.   MRS. C. H. MORRIS.

1. Near - er, still near - er, close to Thy heart, Draw me, my
2. Near - er, still near - er, noth - ing I bring, Naught as an

Sav - iour, so pre - cious Thou art;   Fold me, O fold me
of - f'ring to Je - sus my King;   On - ly my sin - ful,

close to Thy breast, Shel - ter me safe in that ha - ven of rest,
now con - trite heart, Grant me the cleans - ing Thy blood doth im - part,

Shel - ter me safe in that ha - ven of rest.
Grant me the cleans - ing Thy blood doth im - part.   A - MEN.

3 Nearer, still nearer, Lord, to be Thine,
  Sin, with its follies, I gladly resign;
  All of its pleasures, pomp, and its pride,
  Give me but Jesus, my Lord crucified.

4 Nearer, still nearer, while life shall last,
  Till safe in glory my anchor is cast;
  Through endless ages ever to be,
  Nearer, my Saviour, still nearer to Thee.

C. H. Morris.

495. O Blessed Is the Man Who Stays.

Säll du, som dig åt Gud betror.   8 7, 8 7, 8 7, 8 7, 4 8.

BURKHARD WALDIS, 1553.

1. {O bless-ed is the man who stays His trust in God for - ev - er;}
   {He dwells with-in the se-cret place Where foes may en - ter nev - er.}

God is my Ref-uge and my Stay, My God who e'er di-rects me,

In dan-gers, fears, and plagues that slay, His wings shall still pro-tect me.

I will not fear When God, my Shield, is ev - er near. A - MEN.

2 Though thousands at my side may fall,
  Ten thousand near me stumble,
On Thee, my Saviour, will I call,
  Thou carest for the humble.
I will not fear the arrow's flight,
  Nor yet the dark night's terror:
Thy saints are precious in Thy sight,
  Thou keepest them from error,
For Thou hast sent
Thine angels bright to guard my tent.

3 "He loveth Me," thus saith the Lord,
  "Therefore will I uphold him;
Because he waits upon My Word,
  With love will I enfold him.
His enemies shall rage in vain,
  No evil shall come near him;
His prayers with Me acceptance gain,
  Before he calls, I'll hear him.
His days I'll bless
With joy, and peace, and righteousness."

91st Psalm, paraphrased by Ernest Edwin Ryden, 1924.
Based on Johan Olof Wallin's version.

496. Search Me, God, and Know My Heart.

Wennerberg. 7 6, 7 6. D.   GUNNAR WENNERBERG, (1817–1901).

1. Search me, God, and know my heart,   Lord of truth and mer - cy;

Try me, Thou who from a - far   Know - est all my se - crets;

And if an - y wick - ed way   Should be found with - in   me,

Bless - ed Sav - iour, lead Thou me   In the way e - ter - nal.   A - MEN.

Ps. 139. 23, 24, paraphrased by Claus August Wendell, 1924.

497. He Leadeth Me! O Blessed Thought!

Aughton. L. M. With Refrain.

WILLIAM BATCHELDER BRADBURY, 1860.

1. He lead-eth me! O bless-ed thought! O words with heav'n-ly com-fort fraught!
2. Sometimes 'mid scenes of deep-est gloom, Sometimes where E-den's bow-ers bloom,

What-e'er I do, wher-e'er I be, Still 'tis God's hand that lead-eth me.
By wa-ters calm, o'er troubled sea, Still 'tis His hand that lead-eth me.

REFRAIN:

He lead-eth me! He lead-eth me! By His own hand He lead-eth me!

His faith-ful fol-l'wer I would be, For by His hand He lead-eth me. A-MEN.

3 Lord, I would clasp Thy hand in mine,
Nor ever murmur nor repine;
Content, whatever lot I see,
Since 'tis my God that leadeth me.

4 And when my task on earth is done,
When by Thy grace the vict'ry's won,
E'en death's cold wave I will not flee,
Since God through Jordan leadeth me.

Joseph Henry Gilmore, 1859.

498. In My Quiet Contemplation.

Stilla jag på dig vill akta. 8 7, 8 7, 8 8. Trochaic.   German, 18th Century.

1. In my qui-et con-tem-pla-tion I look up to Thee, O Lord.

Guid-ed by Thy rev-e-la-tion, Light-ed by Thy liv-ing Word,

Touched by Thy great love and pas-sion, I draw near to Thy sal-va-tion. A-MEN.

Or: Herr, ich habe missgehandelt, No. 405.

2 In the quiet path of duty
  I my earthly span may fill,
Pressing onward in the beauty
  Of performing but Thy will,
Well content with all Thou sendest,
If Thy grace to me Thou lendest.

3 Let me live in peace and stillness,
  Giving to no soul offense;
Pain or pleasure. health or illness
  Take I from Thy providence,
Never wounding. ever healing,
Thus a Christly life revealing.

4 Here my cross with patience bearing,
  I will go where Jesus leads,
All enduring, all forbearing,
  For His sake who knows my needs.
O how swift the hours of trial,
Spent in Christian self-denial!

5 Keep me quietly expecting
  Thine appearance, Saviour dear;
In my life, Thy life reflecting,
  Let Thy sacred love appear,
Till on earth my last day closes,
And my soul in Thee reposes.

6 Gracious Saviour, deign to number
  Me with saints in glory there,
Calm and peaceful then my slumber
  After my last evening prayer;
When from dust my spirit rises,
All my tears shall change to praises.

7 Let my body then be hidden
  In a humble, nameless tomb;
When at last I shall be bidden
  To forsake that narrow room,
Jesus knows where they are sleeping
Who were given in His keeping.

Johan Olof Wallin, 1818.

499. Saviour, Thy Dying Love.

Something for Thee. 6 4, 6 4, 6 6, 6 4.   ROBERT LOWRY, (1826–1899).

1. Sav - iour, Thy dy - ing love Thou gav - est me,
Nor should I aught with - hold, Dear Lord, from Thee:
In love my soul would bow, My heart ful - fill its vow,
Some of - f'ring bring Thee now, Some - thing for Thee. A - MEN.

2 At the blest mercy-seat,
   Pleading for me,
  My feeble faith looks up,
   Jesus, to Thee:
  Help me the cross to bear,
  Thy wondrous love declare,
  Some song to raise, or prayer,
   Something for Thee.

3 Give me a faithful heart,—
   Likeness to Thee,—
  That each departing day
   Henceforth may see
  Some work of love begun,
  Some deed of kindness done,
  Some wanderer sought and won,
   Something for Thee.

Sylvanus Dryden Phelps, 1862.

500. Our God Is Love, and All His Saints.

Lambeth. C. M.   WILHELM A. F. SCHULTHES, 1871.

1. Our God is love, and all His saints His im-age bear be-low;
2. Teach us to love each oth-er, Lord, As we are loved by Thee;

The heart with love to God in-spired With love to man will glow.
None who are tru-ly born of God Can live in en-mi-ty. A-MEN.

3 Heirs of the same immortal bliss,
   Our hopes and fears the same,
With bonds of love our hearts unite,
   With mutual love inflame.

4 So may the unbelieving world
   See how true Christians love;
And glorify our Saviour's grace,
   And seek that grace to prove.

Thomas Cotterill, (1779–1823).

501. A Charge to Keep I Have.

Boylston. S. M.   LOWELL MASON, 1832.

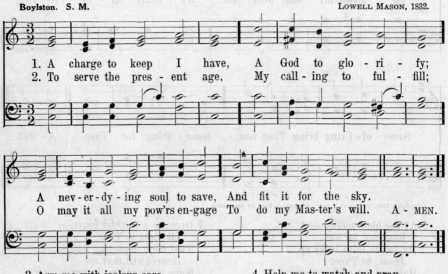

1. A charge to keep I have, A God to glo-ri-fy;
2. To serve the pres-ent age, My call-ing to ful-fill;

A nev-er-dy-ing soul to save, And fit it for the sky.
O may it all my pow'rs en-gage To do my Mas-ter's will. A-MEN.

3 Arm me with jealous care,
   As in Thy sight to live;
And O, Thy servant, Lord, prepare
   A strict account to give.

4 Help me to watch and pray,
   On Thee alone rely,
Assured, if Thee I trust alway,
   That I shall never die.

Charles Wesley, 1762. c.

502. Forth in Thy Name, O Lord, I Go.

Canonbury. L. M.   Arr. from ROBERT ALEXANDER SCHUMANN, 1839.

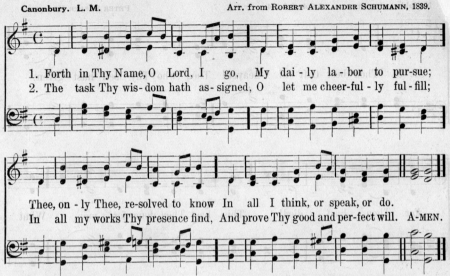

1. Forth in Thy Name, O Lord, I go, My dai-ly la-bor to pur-sue;
2. The task Thy wis-dom hath as-signed, O let me cheer-ful-ly ful-fill;

Thee, on-ly Thee, re-solved to know In all I think, or speak, or do.
In all my works Thy presence find, And prove Thy good and per-fect will. A-MEN.

3 Give me to bear Thy easy yoke.
  And every moment watch and pray;
And still to things eternal look,
  And hasten to Thy glorious day.

4 Fain would I still for Thee employ
  Whate'er Thy bounteous grace hath given;
Would run my even course with joy,
  And closely walk with Thee to heaven.

Charles Wesley, 1762.

503. Teach Me, My God and King.

Woolwich. S. M.   C. E. KETTLE.

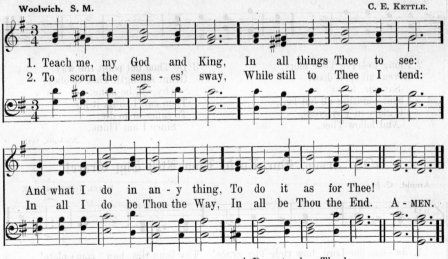

1. Teach me, my God and King, In all things Thee to see:
2. To scorn the sens-es' sway, While still to Thee I tend:

And what I do in an-y thing, To do it as for Thee!
In all I do be Thou the Way, In all be Thou the End. A-MEN.

3 All may of Thee partake:
  Nothing so small can be,
But draws, when acted for Thy sake,
  Greatness and worth from Thee.

4 Done to obey Thy laws,
  E'en servile labors shine:
Hallowed is toil, if this the cause,
  The meanest work divine.

John Wesley, 1739.

504. O Thou Best Gift of Heaven!

Nu lukker sig mit oege. 6 6 4, 6 6 4 4.   PETER CASPER KROSSING.

1. O Thou best Gift of heaven! Thou who Thy-self hast given,—
For Thou hast died! This hast Thou done for me: What
have I done for Thee, Thou Cru - ci - fied, Thou Cru - ci - fied? A - MEN.

2 I long to serve Thee more:
Reveal an open door,
  Saviour, to me;
Then, counting all but loss,
I'll glory in Thy cross,
  And follow Thee.

3 Do Thou but point the way,
Grant strength Thee to obey;
  Thy will be mine:
Then can I think it joy
To suffer or to die,
  Since I am Thine.

Nicholls, 1837.

505. Jesus, Our Lord, How Rich Thy Grace!

Arnold. C. M.   PETER JOHNSON, 1923.

1. Je - sus, our Lord, how rich Thy grace! Thy boun-ties how com - plete!

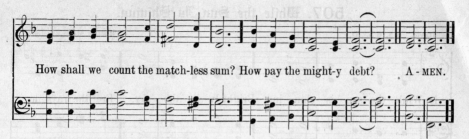

How shall we count the match-less sum? How pay the might-y debt? A - MEN.

2 High on a throne of radiant light
  Dost Thou exalted shine;
  What can our poverty bestow,
  When all the worlds are Thine?

3 But Thou hast brethren here below,
  The partners of Thy grace,
  And wilt confess their humble names
  Before Thy Father's face.

4 In them Thou may'st be clothed and fed,
  And visited and cheered;
  And in their accents of distress
  Our Saviour's voice is heard.

5 Thy face, with reverence and with love,
  We in Thy poor would see;
  O may we minister to them,
  And in them, Lord, to Thee.

Philip Doddridge, (1702–1751), a.

506. Awake, My Soul, Stretch Every Nerve.

Richard. C. M.   PETER JOHNSON, 1923.

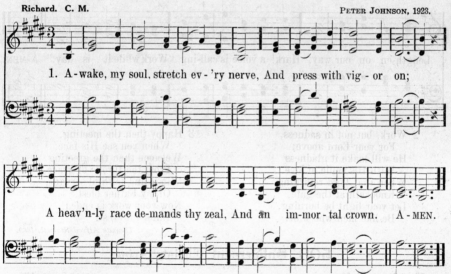

1. A-wake, my soul, stretch ev-'ry nerve, And press with vig-or on;

A heav'n-ly race de-mands thy zeal, And an im-mor-tal crown. A - MEN.

2 A cloud of witnesses around
  Hold thee in full survey;
  Forget the steps already trod,
  And onward urge thy way.

3 'Tis God's all-animating voice
  That calls thee from on high;
  'Tis His own hand presents the prize
  To thine aspiring eye.

4 That prize with peerless glories bright
  Which shall new luster boast,
  When victors' wreaths and monarchs' gems
  Shall blend in common dust.

5 Blest Saviour, introduced by Thee,
  Have I my race begun;
  And, crowned with vict'ry, at Thy feet
  I'll lay my honors down.

Philip Doddridge, 1755.

507. While the Sun Is Shining.

David. 6 5, 6 5. D.   THOMAS MORLEY, 1867.

1. While the sun is shin-ing Bright-ly in the sky, Ere the rays de-

clin-ing Tell that night is nigh; Ere the shad-ows fall-ing,

Length-en on our way, Hark! a voice is call-ing, "Work while it is day." A-MEN.

2 Work, but not in sadness,
   For your Lord above;
   He will make it gladness
   With His smile of love.
   When that Lord returning
   Knocketh at the gate,
   Let your light be burning,
   Be like men who wait.

3 Happy then the meeting,
   When you see His face;
   Welcome then the greeting
   From the throne of grace,
   "Good and faithful servant,
   Of my Father blest,
   Now your work is ended,
   Enter into rest."

Thomas Alfred Stowell, 1869.

508. Soldiers of Christ, Arise.

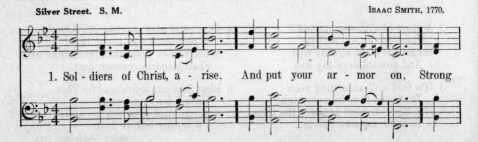

Silver Street. S. M.   ISAAC SMITH, 1770.

1. Sol-diers of Christ, a-rise, And put your ar-mor on, Strong

in the strength which God sup - plies, Through His e - ter - nal Son. A-MEN.

2 Strong in the Lord of Hosts,
   And in His mighty power,
Who in the strength of Jesus trusts
   Is more than conqueror.

3 Stand, then, in His great might,
   With all His strength endued;
But take, to arm you for the fight,
   The panoply of God.

4 From strength to strength go on,
   Wrestle, and fight, and pray:
Tread all the powers of darkness down,
   And win the well-fought day.

5 Thus having all things done,
   And all your conflicts past,
May ye o'ercome through Christ alone,
   And stand entire at last.

Charles Wesley, 1749.

509. Go, Labor On! Spend and Be Spent.

Waltham. L. M. JOHN BAPTISTE CALKIN, 1872.

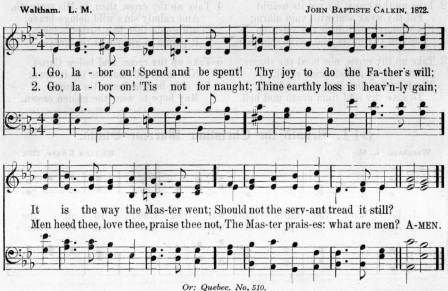

1. Go, la - bor on! Spend and be spent! Thy joy to do the Fa-ther's will;
2. Go, la - bor on! 'Tis not for naught; Thine earthly loss is heav'n-ly gain;

It is the way the Mas-ter went; Should not the serv-ant tread it still?
Men heed thee, love thee, praise thee not, The Mas-ter prais-es: what are men? A-MEN.

Or: Quebec. No. 510.

3 Go, labor on! Enough, while here,
   If He shall praise thee, if He deign
The willing heart to mark and cheer:
   No toil for Him shall be in vain.

4 Go, labor on, while it is day!
   The world's dark night is hastening
      on:
Speed, speed thy work! Cast sloth away!
   It is not thus that souls are won.

5 Toil on, faint not! Keep watch, and pray!
   Be wise the erring soul to win!
Go forth, into the world's highway!
   Compel the wanderer to come in!

6 Toil on, and in thy toil rejoice!
   For toil comes rest, for exile, home;
Soon shalt thou hear the Bridegroom's
      voice,
   The midnight peal, "Behold, I come!"

Horatius Bonar, 1843.

510. "Take Up Thy Cross," the Saviour Said.

Quebec (Hesperus). L. M.

HENRY BAKER, 1866.
Modified by JAMES PEARCE, 1868.

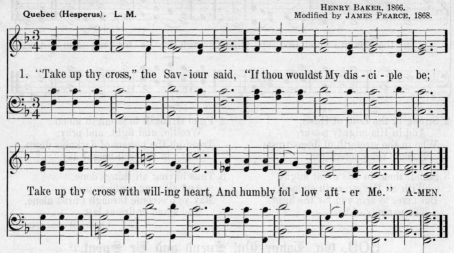

1. "Take up thy cross," the Sav-iour said, "If thou wouldst My dis-ci-ple be;

Take up thy cross with will-ing heart, And humbly fol-low aft-er Me." A-MEN.

2 Take up thy cross; let not its weight
  Fill thy weak soul with vain alarm;
His strength shall bear thy spirit up,
  Sustain thy heart, and nerve thine arm.

3 Take up thy cross, nor heed the shame,
  Nor let thy foolish pride rebel;
The Lord for thee the cross endured,
  To save thy soul from death and hell.

4 Take up thy cross, then, in His strength,
  And calmly sin's wild deluge brave;
'Twill guide thee to a better home,
  It points to glory o'er the grave.

5 Take up thy cross, and follow Christ,
  Nor think till death to lay it down;
For only he who bears the cross
  May hope to wear the golden crown.

Charles William Everest, 1835.

511. Behold the Christian Warrior Stand.

Wareham. L. M.

WILLIAM KNAPP, 1738.

1. Be-hold   the   Chris-tian   war-rior   stand   In   all   the
2. In   pan-o-ply   of   truth   com-plete,   Sal-va-tion's

ar-mor   of   his God;   The   Spir-it's   sword   is   in   his
hel-met   on   his head,   With   right-eous-ness   a   breast-plate

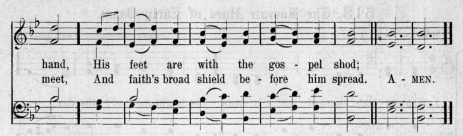

hand,   His   feet   are   with   the   gos - pel shod;
meet,   And   faith's broad shield   be - fore   him spread.   A - MEN.

3 Undaunted to the field he goes;
   Yet vain were skill and valor there,
   Unless, to foil his legion foes,
   He takes the trusted weapon, prayer.

4 Thus, strong in his Redeemer's strength,
   Sin, death, and hell he tramples down;
   Fights the good fight, and wins at length,
   Through mercy, an immortal crown.

James Montgomery, 1825.

512. I Gave My Life for Thee.

I gave My life for thee.   6 6, 6 6, 8 6.   PHILIP PAUL BLISS, 1874.

1. I   gave   My   life   for   thee,   My   pre - cious blood   I   shed,
2. My   Fa-ther's house of   light,   My   glo - ry - cir - cled   throne

That thou might'st ran-somed be,   And quick - ened   from the   dead;
I   left for earth - ly   night,   For   wan-d'rings sad   and   lone;

I gave, I gave My life for thee, What hast thou given for Me?
I left, I left   it   all for thee, Hast thou left aught for Me?   A - MEN.

3 I suffered much for thee,
   More than thy tongue can tell,
   Of bitterest agony,
   To rescue thee from hell;
   I've borne, I've borne it all for thee,
   What hast thou borne for Me?

4 And I have brought to thee,
   Down from My home above,
   Salvation full and free,
   My pardon and My love;
   I bring, I bring rich gifts to thee,
   What hast thou brought to Me?

Frances Ridley Havergal, 1858.

513. The Roseate Hues of Early Dawn.

Materna. C. M. D.   SAMUEL AUGUSTUS WARD, 1882.

1. The roseate hues of early dawn, The brightness of the day,
The crimson of the sunset sky, How fast they fade away!
O for the pearl-y gates of heav'n! O for the gold-en floor!
O for the Sun of Right-eous-ness That set-teth nev-er-more! A-MEN.

2 The highest hopes we cherish here,
   How fast they tire and faint!
How many a spot defiles the robe
   That wraps an earthly saint!
O for a heart that never sins!
   O for a soul washed white!
O for a voice to praise our King,
   Nor weary day or night!

3 Here faith is ours, and heavenly hopes,
   And grace to lead us higher:
But there are perfectness and peace
   Beyond our best desire.
O by Thy love and anguish, Lord,
   O by Thy life laid down,
Grant that we fall not from Thy grace,
   Nor cast away our crown!

Cecil Frances (Humphreys) Alexander, 1853.

514. Rise, My Soul, and Stretch Thy Wings.

Amsterdam. 7 6, 7 6, 7 7, 7 6.   The Foundery Collection, 1742.

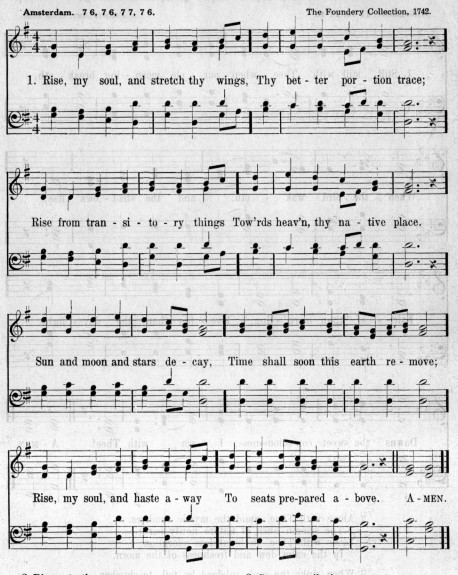

1. Rise, my soul, and stretch thy wings, Thy bet-ter por-tion trace;

Rise from tran-si-to-ry things Tow'rds heav'n, thy na-tive place.

Sun and moon and stars de-cay, Time shall soon this earth re-move;

Rise, my soul, and haste a-way To seats pre-pared a-bove. A-MEN.

2 Rivers to the ocean run,
　　Nor stay in all their course;
　Fire ascending seeks the sun;
　　Both speed them to their source:
　So my soul that came from God
　Longs to view His glorious face,
　Forward tends to His abode,
　　To rest in His embrace.

3 Cease, ye pilgrims, cease to mourn,
　　Press onward to the prize;
　Soon our Saviour will return
　　Triumphant in the skies:
　Yet a season, and you know
　Happy entrance will be given,
　All our sorrows left below,
　　And earth exchanged for heaven!

Robert Seagrave, 1742.

515. Still, Still with Thee, When Purple Morning Breaketh.

Willingham. 11 10, 11 10.   FRANTZ ABT, (1819–1885).

1. Still, still with Thee, when pur - ple morn - ing break - eth,

When the bird wak - eth, and the shad - ows flee;

Fair - er than morn - ing, love - lier than the day - light,

Dawns the sweet con-scious-ness, I am with Thee! A - MEN.

2 Alone with Thee, amid the mystic shadows,
    The solemn hush of nature newly born;
Alone with Thee, in breathless adoration,
    In the calm dew and freshness of the morn.

3 When sinks the soul, subdued by toil, to slumber,
    Its closing eye looks up to Thee in prayer;
Sweet the repose beneath Thy wings o'ershading,
    But sweeter still to wake and find Thee there.

4 So shall it be at last, in that bright morning,
    When the soul waketh, and life's shadows flee;
O for that hour when fairer than the dawning
    Shall rise the glorious thought, I am with Thee!

Harriet Elizabeth (Beecher) Stowe, 1855.

516. My Heart Is Yearning Ever.

I djupet af mitt hjärta. 7 6, 4 4, 7 6, 7 6.   OSKAR AHNFELT, (1813–1882).

1. My heart is yearn-ing ev - er To reach a place of rest,

Je - ru - sa - lem, My hap - py home, In Thee my heart shall

nev - er By sin or grief be pressed. My heart is yearn-ing

ev - er To reach that cit - y blest. A - MEN.

2 Within its radiant portals
  None ever sheds a tear.
    God's city bright
    Gives all delight;
  No grief nor wail of mortals
  Is heard where He is near.
  Within its radiant portals
  None ever sheds a tear.

3 Their blessèd Lord and Saviour
  Doth rule and govern them
    In peace and joy,
    Without alloy,
  For sin can enter never
  The new Jerusalem.
  Their blessèd Lord and Saviour
  Doth rule and govern them.

4 Behold the goal in glory,
  Now shining from afar;
    O city of
    The God of love,
  Where no more earthly worry
  My happiness shall mar!
  Behold the goal in glory,
  Now shining from afar!

5 And even I shall conquer
  In Jesus' Name and might.
    Though weak and faint,
    Yet as a saint,
  I'll in the haven anchor,
  Sweet haven of delight.
  Yea, even I shall conquer,
  In Jesus' Name and might.

From Ahnfelts Sånger, 1850.

517. Where Is the Friend for Whom I'm Ever Yearning?

O du Guds Lam. 11 11, 11 5.   Th. Söderberg.

1. Where is the Friend for whom I'm ev - er yearn - ing?
My long-ing grows when night to day is turn - ing; And though I
find Him not as day re - ced - eth, My heart still plead - eth.   A - MEN.

2 His hand I see in every force and power,
  Where waves the harvest and where blooms the flower;
  In every breath I draw, my spirit burneth:
          His love discerneth.

3 When summer winds blow gently, then I hear Him;
  Where sing the birds, where rush the streams, I'm near Him;
  But nearer still when in my heart He blesses
          Me with caresses.

4 And yet, to hide Him, oft a cloud prevaileth;
  My prayer can reach Him, but my vision faileth.
  Would I could see His face and heart so loving,
          And cease my roving.

5 O where such beauty is itself revealing
  In all that lives, through all creation stealing,
  What must the Source be whence it comes, the Giver?
          Beauty forever.

6 Be strong, my soul; hope, pray, await His favor,
  And thou shalt know the sweetness of thy Saviour;
  When in His gentle arms secure He holds thee,
          His love enfolds thee.

7 Soon on that shore where stormy wave ne'er breaketh
  The weary dove its final refuge taketh;
  The timorous lamb shall by the Shepherd's favor
          Find rest forever.

Johan Olof Wallin, 1818.

518. O Precious Thought! Some Day the Mist Shall Vanish.

O sälla land. 11 10, 11 10.   OSKAR AHNFELT, (1813-1882).

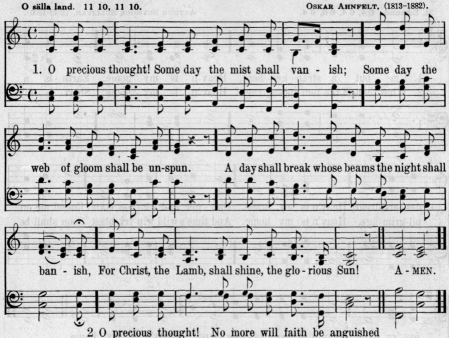

1. O precious thought! Some day the mist shall van-ish; Some day the
web of gloom shall be un-spun. A day shall break whose beams the night shall
ban-ish, For Christ, the Lamb, shall shine, the glo-rious Sun!   A - MEN.

2 O precious thought! No more will faith be anguished
   By doubt's uncertainties, by trembling fears.
   The pangs that wound the heart shall all be vanquished,
   And light shall flood the gloom of bygone years.

3 Some day each mystery shall find solution,
   Each troublous question an undimmed reply.
   The hidden deeps that now seem all confusion
   My God will open up and clarify.

4 O precious thought! With vision all unclouded,
   The One whom I believed shall I behold.
   Now from my sight His hallowed form is shrouded,
   Then He shall fill my soul with bliss untold.

5 Some day I'll see my ever-faithful Saviour,
   Who pardoned all my sin in boundless grace.
   Here clouds of trial oft obscure His favor,
   There I'll behold the brightness of His face.

6 O precious thought! All sinless, pure. and holy,
   By flesh and Satan nevermore oppressed,
   My thoughts and deeds shall glorify Him solely,
   Who brought my soul unto His perfect rest.

7 The saints of God, all clad in spotless raiment,
   Before the Lamb shall wave victorious palms.
   For bliss eternal Christ has rendered payment,
   Earth's tearful strains give way to joyous psalms.

8 I pray Thee, O my precious Saviour, waken
   These hallowed thoughts of Paradise in me,
   And let them solace me. till I am taken
   To dwell in Salem evermore with Thee.

Carl Olof Rosenius, (1816-1868).

519. I'm But a Stranger Here.

St. Edmund. 6 4, 6 4, 6 6, 6 4.   ARTHUR SEYMOUR SULLIVAN, (1842–1900).

1. I'm but a stran-ger here, Heav'n is my home; Earth is a
2. What though the tem-pests rage? Heav'n is my home; Short is my

des-ert drear, Heav'n is my home. Dan-ger and sor-row stand Round me on
pil-grim-age, Heav'n is my home. And time's wild win-try blast Soon shall be

ev-'ry hand, Heav'n is my fa-ther-land, Heav'n is my home.
o-ver-past, I shall reach home at last; Heav'n is my home. A-MEN.

3 There at my Saviour's side,
  Heaven is my home;
May I be glorified;
  Heaven is my home:
There are the good and blest,
Those I love most and best,
Grant me with them to rest;
  Heaven is my home.

4 Grant me to murmur not,
  Heaven is my home;
Whate'er my earthly lot,
  Heaven is my home.
Grant me at last to stand,
Jesus, at Thy right hand,
There in my fatherland:
  Heaven is my home!

Thomas Rawson Taylor, 1836.

520. Forever with the Lord!

Thatcher. S. M.   Arr. from GEORG FREDERICK HÄNDEL, 1732.

1. For-ev-er with the Lord! A-men; so let it be;
2. Here in the bod-y pent, Ab-sent from Him I roam,

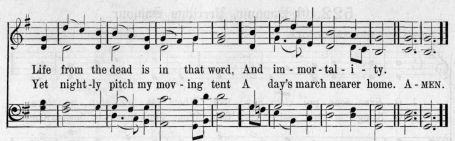

Life from the dead is in that word, And im - mor - tal - i - ty.
Yet night-ly pitch my mov - ing tent A day's march nearer home. A - MEN.

3 My Father's house on high,
　Home of my soul, how near,
At times, to faith's foreseeing eye,
　Thy golden gates appear!

4 And when my latest breath
　Shall rend the veil in twain,
By death I shall escape from death,
　And life eternal gain.

James Montgomery, (1771-1854).

521. O Love That Wilt Not Let Me Go.

St. Margaret. 8 8, 8 8 6.　　　　　　　　ALBERT LISTER PEACE, 1885.

1. O Love that wilt not let me go, I rest my wea - ry soul in
2. O Light that fol-low'st all my way, I yield my flick'ring torch to

Thee; I give Thee back the life I owe, That
Thee; My heart re - stores its bor - rowed ray, That

in Thine o-cean depths its flow May rich - er, full - er be.
in Thy sunshine's glow its day May brighter, fair - er be. A - MEN.

3 O Joy that seekest me through pain,
　I cannot close my heart to Thee;
I trace the rainbow through the rain,
　And feel the promise is not vain
　That morn shall tearless be.

4 O Cross that liftest up my head,
　I dare not ask to hide from Thee;
I lay in dust life's glory dead,
　And from the ground there blossoms red
　Life that shall endless be.

George Matheson, 1882, a.

522. O Saviour, Precious Saviour.

Angel's Story (Norwich). 7 6, 7 6. D.   ARTHUR HENRY MANN, 1881.

1. O Sav - iour, pre - cious Sav - iour, Whom, yet un - seen, we love;
2. O Bring - er of sal - va - tion, Who won - drous - ly hast wrought,

O Name of might and fa - vor, All oth - er names a - bove:
Thy-self the rev - e - la - tion Of Love be - yond our thought;

We wor - ship Thee, we bless Thee, To Thee a - lone we sing;
We wor - ship Thee, we bless Thee, To Thee a - lone we sing;

We praise Thee and con - fess Thee, Our ho - ly Lord and King.
We praise Thee and con - fess Thee, Our gra - cious Lord and King. A - MEN.

3 In Thee all fullness dwelleth,
   All grace and power divine;
The glory that excelleth,
   O Son of God, is Thine.
We worship Thee, we bless Thee,
   To Thee alone we sing;
We praise Thee and confess Thee,
   Our glorious Lord and King.

4 O grant the consummation
   Of this our song above,
In endless adoration
   And everlasting love;
Then shall we praise and bless Thee
   Where perfect praises ring,
And evermore confess Thee,
   Our Saviour and our King.

Frances Ridley Havergal, 1870.

523. Come unto Me, When Shadows Darkly Gather.

Consolation (Mendelssohn). 11 10, 11 10.   FELIX MENDELSSOHN-BARTHOLDY, (1809-1847).

1. Come un-to Me, when shad-ows dark-ly gath - er,
When the sad heart is wea - ry and dis - tressed;
Seek - ing for com - fort from your heav'n - ly Fa - ther,
Come un - to Me, and I will give you rest. A - MEN.

2 Ye who have mourned when tender flowers were taken,
When the ripe fruit fell richly to the ground,
When the loved slept, in brighter homes to waken,
Where their pale brows with spirit-wreaths are crowned.

3 Large are the mansions in thy Father's dwelling,
Glad are the homes that sorrows never dim;
Sweet are the harps in holy music swelling,
Soft are the tones which raise the heavenly hymn.

4 There like an Eden blossoming in gladness,
Bloom the fair flowers the earth too rudely pressed:
Come unto Me, all ye who droop in sadness,
Come unto Me, and I will give you rest.

Catherine H. Esling, 1839.

524. We Would See Jesus.

Windsor. 11 10, 11 10.   JOSEPH BARNBY, (1838–1896).

1. We would see Jesus, for the shadows lengthen

A-cross this little landscape of our life;

We would see Jesus, our weak faith to strengthen

For the last weariness, the final strife. A-MEN.

2 We would see Jesus, the great Rock-foundation
Whereon our feet were set by sovereign grace:
Nor life nor death, with all their agitation,
Can thence remove us, if we see His face.

3 We would see Jesus: other lights are paling,
Which for long years we have rejoiced to see;
The blessings of our pilgrimage are failing:
We would not mourn them, for we go to Thee.

4 We would see Jesus: this is all we're needing;
Strength, joy, and willingness come with the sight;
We would see Jesus, dying, risen, pleading;
Then welcome, day, and farewell, mortal night.

Anna Bartlett Warner, (1821–1915).

525. When Peace Like a River Attendeth My Way.

It is well with my soul. 11 8, 11 9.   H. G. SPAFFORD, 1876.

1. When peace like a river attendeth my way,
When sorrows like sea billows roll; What-
ever my lot, Thou hast taught me to say,
It is well, it is well with my soul. A - MEN.

2 Though Satan should buffet, though trials should come,
  Let this blest assurance control,
That Christ hath regarded my helpless estate,
  And hath shed His own blood for my soul.

3 He lives, O the bliss of this glorious thought;
  My sin, not in part, but the whole,
Is nailed to His cross and I bear it no more,
  Praise the Lord, praise the Lord, O my soul.

4 And, Lord, haste the day when our faith shall be sight,
  The clouds be rolled back as a scroll,
The trumpet shall sound and the Lord shall descend;
  Even so—it is well with my soul.

Philip Paul Bliss, 1876.

526. I'm a Pilgrim, and I'm a Stranger.

Jag är främling. 9 11, 10 10, 9 11.   OSKAR AHNFELT, (1813-1882).

1. I'm a pil-grim, and I'm a stran-ger, I can tar-ry, I can tar-ry but a night; Do not de-tain me, for I am go-ing To where the fountains are ev-er flow-ing: I'm a pil-grim, and I'm a stran-ger, I can tar-ry, I can tar-ry but a night. A-MEN.

2 There the glory is ever shining;
O my longing heart, my longing heart is there:
Here in this country so dark and dreary
I long have wandered, forlorn and weary:
I'm a pilgrim, and I'm a stranger,
I can tarry, I can tarry but a night.

3 Of the city to which I'm going
My Redeemer, my Redeemer is the light;
There is no sorrow, nor any sighing,
Nor any sinning, nor any dying:
Of the city to which I'm going
My Redeemer, my Redeemer is the light.

Mary S. B. Shindler, 1841.

527. Lord, Who at Cana's Wedding Feast.

St. Leonard. C. M. D.

HENRY HILES, 1867.

1. Lord, who at Ca-na's wed-ding feast Didst as a guest ap-pear,
Thou dear-er far than earth-ly guest, Vouch-safe Thy pres-ence here;
For ho-ly Thou in-deed dost prove The mar-riage vow to be,
Pro-claim-ing it a type of love Be-tween the Church and Thee. A-MEN.

2 The holiest vow that man can make,
  The golden thread in life,
The bond that none may dare to break,
  That bindeth man and wife;
Which, blest by Thee, whate'er betides,
  No evil shall destroy,
Through care-worn days each care divides,
  And doubles every joy.

3 On those who at Thine altar kneel,
  O Lord, Thy blessing pour,
That each may wake the other's zeal
  To love Thee more and more:
O grant them here in peace to live
  In purity and love,
And, this world leaving, to receive
  A crown of life above.

Adelaide Thrupp, 1853.
St. 2, Godfrey Thring, 1882.

528. O Perfect Love, All Human Thought Transcending.

Perfect Love. 11 10, 11 10.　　　　　　　　　　　　　　　　JOSEPH BARNBY, 1889.

1. O per-fect Love, all hu-man thought tran-scend-ing, Low-ly we

kneel in prayer be-fore Thy throne, That theirs may be the love which knows no

end-ing, Whom Thou for ev-er-more dost join in one. A-MEN.

2 O perfect Life, be Thou their full assurance
Of tender charity and steadfast faith,
Of patient hope, and quiet, brave endurance,
With childlike trust that fears nor pain nor death.

3 Grant them the joy which brightens earthly sorrow;
Grant them the peace which calms all earthly strife,
And to life's day the glorious unknown morrow
That dawns upon eternal love and life.

Dorothy Frances (Blomfield) Gurney, 1883.

529. Saviour, Let Thy Sanction Rest.

Lux Prima. 7 7, 7 7, 7 7.　　　　　　　　　　　　CHARLES FRANCOIS GOUNOD, 1872.

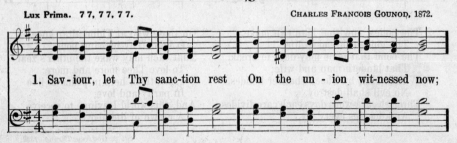

1. Sav-iour, let Thy sanc-tion rest On the un-ion wit-nessed now;

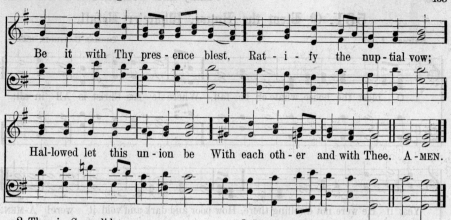

Be it with Thy pres-ence blest, Rat-i-fy the nup-tial vow;

Hal-lowed let this un-ion be With each oth-er and with Thee. A-MEN.

2 Thou in Cana didst appear
    At a marriage feast like this;
Deign to meet us, Saviour, here,
    Fountain of unmingled bliss!
Send Thine influence from above,
Consecrating earthly love.

3 Let the path these friends pursue,
    From this hour together trod,
Many though their days or few,
    Be a pilgrimage to God,
To the land where rest is given,
To our Father's house in heaven.

Thomas Raffles, 1812.

530. The Voice That Breathed o'er Eden.

St. Alphege. 7 6, 7 6.   HENRY JOHN GAUNTLETT, (1806–1876).

1. The voice that breathed o'er E-den That ear-liest wed-ding day,

The pri-mal mar-riage bless-ing, It hath not passed a-way. A-MEN.

2 Still in the pure espousal
    Of Christian man and maid,
The Holy Three are with us,
    The threefold grace is said.

3 Be present, Heavenly Father,
    To give away this bride,
As Eve Thou gav'st to Adam
    Out of his own pierced side:

4 Be present, Son of Mary,
    To join their loving hands,
As Thou didst bind two natures
    In Thine eternal bands:

5 Be present, Holy Spirit,
    To bless them as they kneel,
As Thou for Christ the Bridegroom
    The heavenly Spouse dost seal.

6 O spread Thy pure wings o'er them,
    Let no ill power find place,
When onward to Thine altar
    Their hallowed path they trace

7 To lay their hearts before Thee
    In perfect sacrifice,
Till to the home of gladness
    With Christ's own Bride they rise.

John Keble, 1857.

531. O Blest the House, Whate'er Befall.

Retreat. L. M.   THOMAS HASTINGS, 1840.

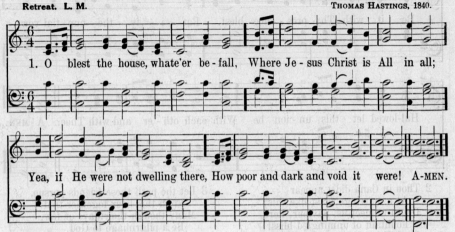

1. O blest the house, whate'er be-fall, Where Je-sus Christ is All in all;

Yea, if He were not dwelling there, How poor and dark and void it were! A-MEN.

2 O blest the house where faith ye find,
And all within have set their mind
To trust their God and serve Him still,
And do in all His holy will.

3 O blest the parents who give heed
Unto their children's foremost need,
And weary not of care or cost:
To them and heaven shall none be lost.

4 Blest such a house, it prospers well,
In peace and joy the parents dwell,
And in their children's lot is shown
How richly God can bless His own.

5 Then here will I and mine to-day
A solemn covenant make and say:
Though all the world forsake Thy Word,
I and my house will serve the Lord.

Christoph Carl Ludwig von Pfeil, 1782.

532. Father of All, Thy Care We Bless.

Maryton. L. M.   HENRY PERCY SMITH, 1874.

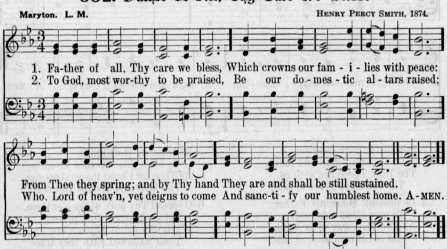

1. Fa-ther of all, Thy care we bless, Which crowns our fam - i - lies with peace:
2. To God, most wor-thy to be praised, Be our do-mes-tic al-tars raised;

From Thee they spring; and by Thy hand They are and shall be still sustained.
Who, Lord of heav'n, yet deigns to come And sanc-ti-fy our humblest home. A-MEN.

3 To Thee may each united house
Morning and night present its vows;
Our children these, the rising race,
Be taught Thy precepts and Thy grace.

4 So may each future age proclaim
The honors of Thy glorious Name,
And each succeeding race remove
To join the family above.

Philip Doddridge, 1755.

533. O Happy Home, Where Thou Art Loved the Dearest.

Aline. 11 10, 11 10.   JOHN VICTOR BERGQUIST, 1924.

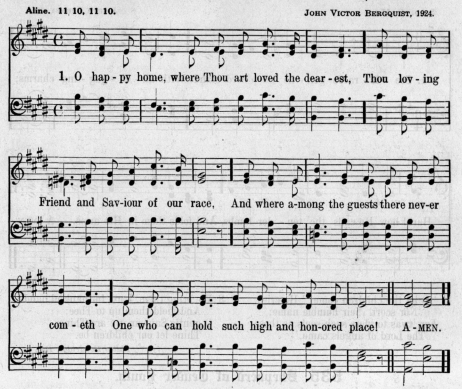

1. O hap-py home, where Thou art loved the dear-est, Thou lov-ing Friend and Sav-iour of our race, And where a-mong the guests there nev-er com-eth One who can hold such high and hon-ored place! A-MEN.

2 O happy home, where two, in heart united,
  In holy faith and blessèd hope are one,
Whom death a little while alone divideth,
  And cannot end the union here begun!

3 O happy home, whose little ones are given
  Early to Thee in humble faith and prayer,
To Thee, their Friend, who from the heights of heaven
  Guides them, and guards with more than mother's care!

4 O happy home, where each one serves Thee lowly,
  Whatever his appointed work may be,
Till every common task seems great and holy,
  When it is done, O Lord, as unto Thee!

5 O happy home, where Thou art not forgotten
  When joy is overflowing, full and free,
O happy home, where every wounded spirit
  Is brought, Physician, Comforter, to Thee.

6 And when at last all earthly toil is ended,
  All meet Thee in the blessèd home above,
From whence Thou camest, where Thou hast ascended,—
  Thine everlasting home of peace and love.

Carl Johann Philipp Spitta. 1833.

534. See Israel's Gentle Shepherd Stand.

Soho. C. M.   JOSEPH BARNBY, 1881.

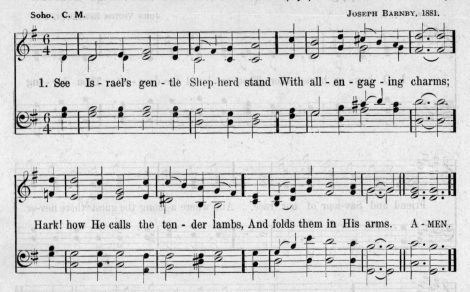

1. See Is-rael's gen-tle Shep-herd stand With all-en-gag-ing charms;

Hark! how He calls the ten-der lambs, And folds them in His arms.   A-MEN.

2 "O let the children come," He cries,
   "Nor scorn their humble name;
For 'twas to bless such souls as these
   The Lord of angels came."

3 We bring them, Lord, in thankful hands,
   And yield them up to Thee;
O gentle Saviour, we are Thine,
   Thine let our children be.

Philip Doddridge, 1755, a.

535. Shepherd of Tender Youth.

Hemans. 6 6 4, 6 6 6 4.   Composer Unknown.

1. Shep-herd of   ten-der youth, Guid-ing in   love and truth Thro' de-vious
2. Thou art our ho-ly Lord, O   all-sub-du-ing Word, Heal-er of

ways;   Christ, our tri-um-phant King, We come Thy Name to sing,
strife: Thou didst Thy-self a-base, That from sin's deep dis-grace

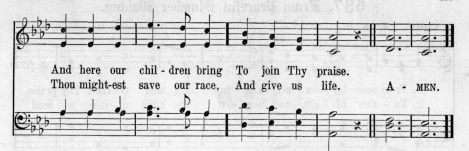

And here our chil-dren bring To join Thy praise.
Thou might-est save our race, And give us life. A - MEN.

3 Ever be near our side,
  Our Shepherd and our Guide,
    Our staff and song:
  Jesus, Thou Christ of God,
  By Thine enduring Word,
  Lead us where Thou hast trod;
    Our faith make strong.

4 So now, and till we die,
  Sound we Thy praises high,
    And joyful sing:
  Let all the holy throng
  Who to Thy Church belong
  Unite to swell the song
    To Christ our King!

From Clement of Alexandria, about 200.
Hunter's Select Melodies, 1851, a.

536. Thou Who a Tender Father Art.

Naomi. C. M.

Arr. from JOHANN GEORG NÄGELI by
LOWELL MASON, 1836.

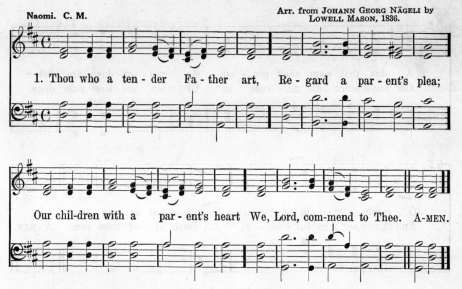

1. Thou who a ten - der Fa - ther art, Re - gard a par - ent's plea;
Our chil-dren with a par - ent's heart We, Lord, com-mend to Thee. A-MEN.

2 Our children are our greatest care,
    A charge which Thou hast given;
  In all Thy graces let them share,
    And all the joys of heaven.

3 If a centurion could succeed,
    Who for his servant cried,
  O grant us faith like his to plead
    For those more near allied.

4 On us Thou hast bestowed Thy grace,
    And ours, as Father kind,
  And heaven is our dwelling place;
    O leave not one behind!

5 Vouchsafe Thy blessing here below
    For our remaining days,
  And when to brighter worlds we go,
    We'll give Thee endless praise.

Unknown.

537. From Peaceful Slumber Waking.

Chisago. 7 6, 7 6. D.   CARL SIGURD MALMSTROM, 1924.

1. From peace-ful slum - ber wak - ing, We sing, O Lord, Thy praise.
When o'er the world is break - ing An - oth - er day of grace—
A day that soon shall per - ish, As yes - ter - days are past—
O, teach us, then, to cher - ish Each mo-ment as our last.

2. Fa - ther of light and beau - ty, The light di - vine us send
To see and do our du - ty, Lest when this day shall end
Our con-science doth ac - cuse us Of sin and tres-pass done,
And shame our face suf - fus - es At blush of set - ting sun. A-MEN.

Or: Aurelia, No. 16.

3 Give God thy heart, thy labor,
    Walk in thy Saviour's grace,
And be unto thy neighbor
    A present help always:
The Name of Christ we hallow
    Not by our faith alone;
If we His path would follow,
    His will through us be done.

4 Blest be each faithful servant,
    Whene'er the Lord shall come;
The dutiful and fervent
    He taketh to His home,
To share with Him in glory
    What eye hath not beheld,
Nor tongue hath told in story,
    Nor mortal heart hath held.

Johan Olof Wallin, 1814.

538. Now That the Daylight Fills the Sky.

Canonbury. L. M.   Arr. from ROBERT ALEXANDER SCHUMANN, 1839.

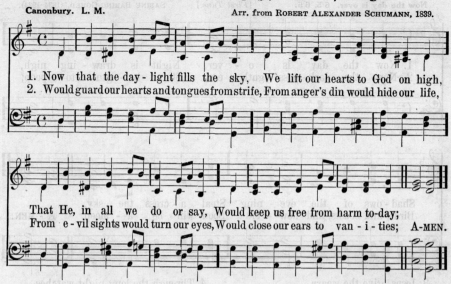

1. Now that the day-light fills the sky, We lift our hearts to God on high,
2. Would guard our hearts and tongues from strife, From anger's din would hide our life,

That He, in all we do or say, Would keep us free from harm to-day;
From e-vil sights would turn our eyes, Would close our ears to van-i-ties; A-MEN.

3 Would keep our inmost conscience pure,
Our souls from folly would secure,
Would bid us check the pride of sense
With due and holy abstinence;
See also Morning Hymns.

4 So we, when this new day is gone,
And night in turn is drawing on,
With conscience by the world unstained
Shall praise His Name for victory gained.
From the Latin, 5th Century.

539. Softly Now the Light of Day.

Weber (Seymour). 7 7, 7 7.   CARL MARIA VON WEBER, 1826.

1. Soft-ly now the light of day Fades up-on my sight a-way;

Free from care, from la-bor free, Lord, I would commune with Thee. A-MEN.

2 Thou whose all-pervading eye
Naught escapes, without, within,
Pardon each infirmity,
Open fault, and secret sin.

3 When for me the light of day
Shall forever pass away,
Then, from sin and sorrow free,
Take me, Lord, to dwell with Thee.

George Washington Doane, 1824.

540. Now the Day Is Over.

Now the day is over. 6 5, 6 5.   [*First Tune.*]   SABINE BARING-GOULD, (1834-1924).

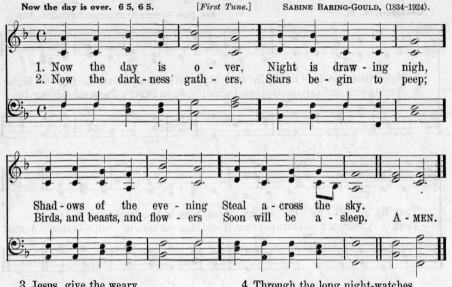

1. Now the day is o - ver, Night is draw-ing nigh,
2. Now the dark - ness gath - ers, Stars be - gin to peep;

Shad - ows of the eve - ning Steal a - cross the sky.
Birds, and beasts, and flow - ers Soon will be a - sleep. A - MEN.

3 Jesus, give the weary
   Calm and sweet repose;
With Thy tenderest blessing
   May my eyelids close.

4 Through the long night-watches
   May Thine angels spread
Their white wings above me,
   Watching round my bed.

Sabine Baring-Gould, 1865.

540. Now the Day Is Over.

Merrial. 6 5, 6 5.   [*Second Tune.*]   JOSEPH BARNBY, 1868.

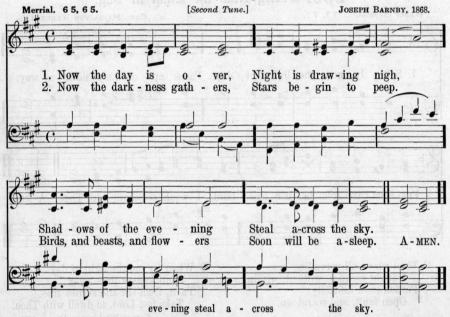

1. Now the day is o - ver, Night is draw-ing nigh,
2. Now the dark - ness gath - ers, Stars be - gin to peep.

Shad - ows of the eve - ning Steal a-cross the sky.
Birds, and beasts, and flow - ers Soon will be a-sleep. A - MEN.

eve - ning steal a - cross the sky.

541. Great God, We Praise Thy Gracious Care.

Old Hundredth. L. M.

LOUIS BOURGEOIS,
The Genevan Psalter, 1551.

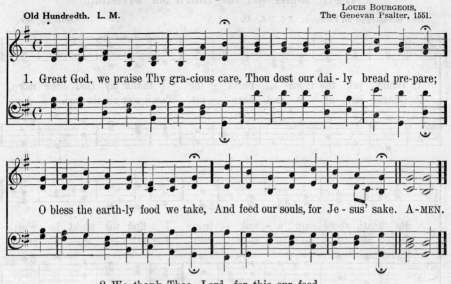

1. Great God, we praise Thy gra-cious care, Thou dost our dai-ly bread pre-pare;

O bless the earth-ly food we take, And feed our souls, for Je-sus' sake. A-MEN.

2 We thank Thee, Lord, for this our food,
   For life and health, and every good:
   Let manna to our souls be given,
   The Bread of life, sent down from heaven.

John Cennick, 1741.

542. Our Table Now with Food Is Spread.

Hebron (Mason). L. M.

LOWELL MASON, 1830.

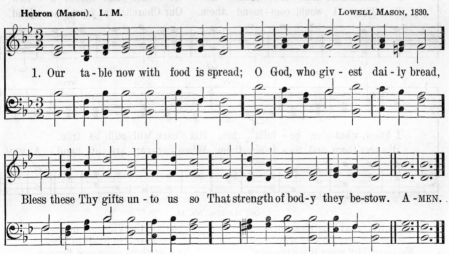

1. Our ta-ble now with food is spread; O God, who giv-est dai-ly bread,

Bless these Thy gifts un-to us so That strength of bod-y they be-stow. A-MEN.

2 O feed the hungry, God of love,
   Who sigh for bread to Heaven above;
   Give to our land prosperity,
   And bless the earth, the sky, the sea!

3 O may this day for Thee be spent,
   And give us all a mind content!
   O grant our souls the heavenly food
   Which Jesus purchased with His blood.

Thomas Kingo, 1689.

543. While Yet the Morn Is Breaking.

Den blomstertid nu kommer. 76, 76. D.

Swedish, 1695.

1. While yet the morn is break-ing, I thank my God once more,
2. Guard-ian of Is-rael, hear me, Watch o'er me through the day,

Be-neath whose care a-wak-ing, I find the night is o'er;
In all I do be near me: For oth-ers too I pray;

I thank Him that He calls me To life and health a-new,
To Thee I would com-mend them, Our Church, our youth, our land,

I know, what-e'er be-falls me, His care will still be true.
Di-rect them and de-fend them, When dan-gers are at hand. A-MEN.

Or: Aurelia, No. 16.

3 O gently grant Thy blessing,
That we may do Thy will,
No more Thy ways transgressing,
Our proper task fulfill;
With Peter's full affiance
Let down our nets again;
If Thou art our reliance,
Our toil will not be vain.

4 Thou art the Vine—O nourish
The branches graft in Thee,
And let them grow and flourish,
A fair and fruitful tree;
The Spirit put within us,
And let His gifts of grace
To all good actions win us
That best may show His praise.

Johannes Mühlmann, 1610.

544. My Inmost Heart Now Raises.

Valet will ich dir geben. 7 6, 7 6. D.

MELCHIOR TESCHNER, 1613.

1. My in-most heart now rais-es, In this fair morn-ing hour,
2. For Thou from me hast ward-ed All per-ils of the night;

A song of thank-ful prais-es To Thine al-might-y pow'r,
From ev-'ry harm hast guard-ed My soul till morn-ing light.

To hon-or and a-dore Thee, O God, up-on Thy throne,
O Sav-iour, have com-pas-sion, Hum-bly to Thee I cry:

I bring my praise be-fore Thee, Thro' Christ, Thine on-ly Son.
And par-don my trans-gres-sion: Have mer-cy, Lord Most High! A-MEN.

3 And shield me from all evil,
   O gracious God, this day,
From sin, and from the devil,
   From shame and from dismay,
From water's devastation,
   From fire's consuming breath,
From need and consternation,
   From evil, sudden death.

4 Amen! I say, not fearing
   That God rejects my prayer;
I doubt not He is hearing
   And granting me His care.
I look not long behind me,
   But I put forth my hands
And ply the task assigned me
   By God, as He commands.

Johannes Mathesius, 1592.

545. Again Thy Glorious Sun Doth Rise.

Nun danket all' und bringet Ehr (Störl). C. M.   JOHANN GEORG CHRISTIAN STÖRL, 1710.

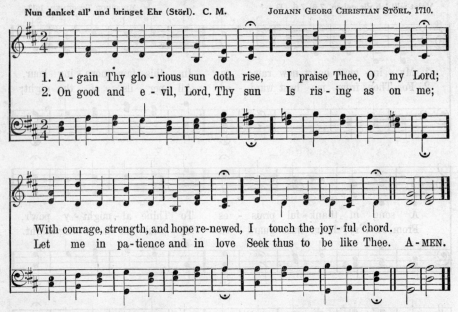

1. A - gain Thy glo - rious sun doth rise,   I praise Thee, O my Lord;
2. On good and e - vil, Lord, Thy sun   Is ris - ing as on me;

With courage, strength, and hope re-newed, I   touch the joy - ful chord.
Let   me in pa - tience and in love Seek thus to be like Thee. A - MEN.

3 May I in virtue and in faith,
   And with Thy gifts content,
Rejoice beneath Thy covering wings,
   Each day in mercy sent.

4 Safe with Thy counsel in my work,
   Thee, Lord, I'll keep in view,
And feel that still Thy bounteous grace
   Is every morning new.

Johan Olof Wallin, 1816.

546. Awake, My Soul, and with the Sun.

Morning Hymn. L. M.   FRANCOIS HIPPOLITE BARTHELEMON, 1780.

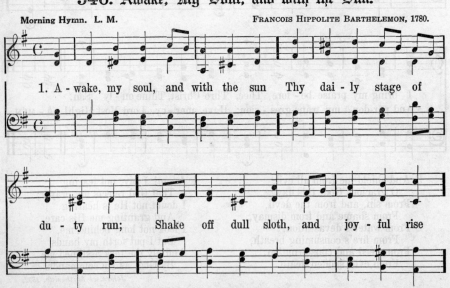

1. A - wake, my soul, and with the sun Thy dai - ly stage of

du - ty run; Shake off dull sloth, and joy - ful rise

To pay thy morn - ing sac - ri - fice. A - MEN.

2 Wake and lift up thyself, my heart,
And with the angels bear thy part,
Who all night long unwearied sing
High praise to the eternal King.

3 All praise to Thee, who safe hast kept,
And hast refreshed me while I slept:
Grant, Lord, when I from death shall wake,
I may of endless life partake.

4 Lord, I my vows to Thee renew;
Disperse my sins as morning dew;
Guard my first springs of thought and will,
And with Thyself my spirit fill.

5 Direct, control, suggest, this day,
All I design, or do, or say;
That all my powers, with all their might,
In Thy sole glory may unite.

Thomas Ken, 1695, a.

547. Now That the Sun Is Beaming Bright.

Belmont. C. M. WILLIAM GARDINER, 1812.

1. Now that the sun is beam-ing bright, Once more to God we pray,
2. No sin - ful word, no deed of wrong, Nor thoughts that i - dly rove,

That He, the un - cre - a - ted Light, May guide our souls this day.
But sim - ple truth be on our tongue, And in our hearts be love. A - MEN.

3 And while the hours in order flow,
O Christ, securely fence
Our gates beleaguered by the foe,
The gate of every sense.

4 And grant that to Thine honor, Lord,
Our daily toil may tend:
That we begin it at Thy word,
And in Thy favor end.

From the Latin.

548. Dayspring of Eternity.

Elmie. 7 8, 7 8, 7 3.

RALPH ALVIN STROM, 1924.

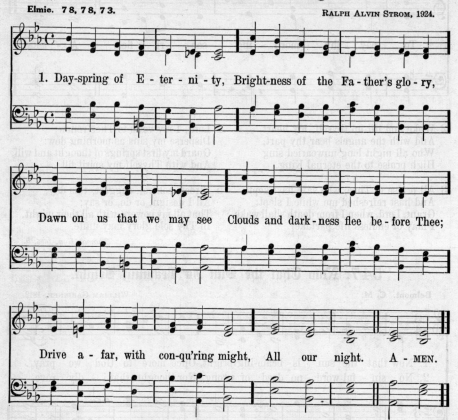

1. Day-spring of E - ter - ni - ty, Bright-ness of the Fa - ther's glo - ry,

Dawn on us that we may see Clouds and dark - ness flee be - fore Thee;

Drive a - far, with con-qu'ring might, All our night. A - MEN.

2 As the soft, refreshing dew
    Falls upon the drooping flower,
  So our fainting hearts renew
    By Thy Spirit's quickening power;
  Ne'er Thy bounteous grace withhold
      From Thy fold.

3 Let the glow of Thy pure love
    All our icy coldness banish;
  In the radiance from above
    May our doubts and fears all vanish,
  That ere dying we may be
      Found in Thee.

4 Light us to the golden shore,
    O Thou rising Sun of morning!
  Lead where tears shall flow no more,
    Where all sighs to songs are turning,
  Where Thy glory sheds alway
      Perfect day.

Christian Knorr von Rosenroth, 1684.

549. When, Streaming from the Eastern Skies.

Brownwell. 8 8, 8 8, 8 8.   FRANZ JOSEPH HAYDN, (1732-1809).

1. When, stream-ing from the east-ern skies, The morn-ing light sa-lutes mine eyes, O Sun of right-eous-ness di-vine, On me with beams of mer-cy shine; Chase all dark clouds of guilt a-way, And turn my dark-ness in-to day.

2. When un-to heav-en's glo-rious King My morn-ing sac-ri-fice I bring; And, griev-ing o'er my guilt and shame, Ask mer-cy, Sav-iour, in Thy Name: My con-science sprin-kle with Thy blood, And be my Ad-vo-cate with God. A-MEN.

Or: St. Catherine, No. 486.

3 When each day's scenes and labors close,
And wearied nature seeks repose,
With pardoning mercy richly blest,
Guard me, my Saviour, while I rest:
And as each rising sun I see,
O draw me nearer unto Thee.

4 And at my life's last setting sun,
My conflict o'er, my labors done,
Jesus, Thy heavenly radiance shed,
To cheer and bless my dying bed;
And from death's gloom my spirit raise,
To see Thy face and sing Thy praise.

William Shrubsole, 1813, a.

550. Abide with Me! Fast Falls the Eventide.

Eventide (Monk). 10 10, 10 10.   WILLIAM HENRY MONK, 1861.

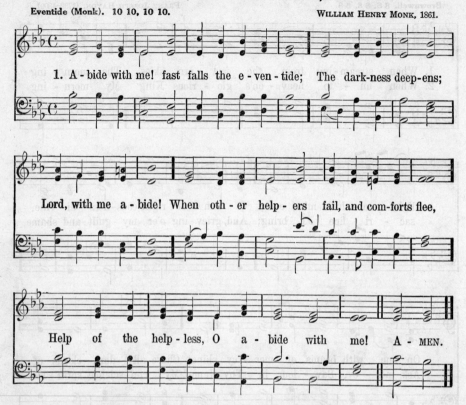

1. A-bide with me! fast falls the e-ven-tide; The dark-ness deep-ens;
Lord, with me a-bide! When oth-er help-ers fail, and com-forts flee,
Help of the help-less, O a-bide with me! A-MEN.

2 Swift to its close ebbs out life's little day;
Earth's joys grow dim, its glories pass away;
Change and decay in all around I see;
O Thou who changest not, abide with me!

3 Not a brief glance I beg, a passing word,
But as Thou dwell'st with Thy disciples, Lord,
Familiar, condescending, patient, free,
Come not to sojourn, but abide with me!

4 I need Thy presence every passing hour:
What but Thy grace can foil the tempter's power?
Who like Thyself my guide and stay can be?
Through cloud and sunshine, O abide with me!

5 I fear no foe, with Thee at hand to bless:
Ills have no weight, and tears no bitterness.
Where is death's sting? where, grave, thy victory?
I triumph still, if Thou abide with me!

6 Hold Thou Thy cross before my closing eyes,
Shine through the gloom, and point me to the skies:
Heaven's morning breaks, and earth's vain shadows flee;
In life, in death, O Lord, abide with me!

Henry Francis Lyte, 1847.

551. Now God Be with Us, for the Night Is Closing.

Nightfall. 11 11, 11 5.   JOSEPH BARNBY, 1872.

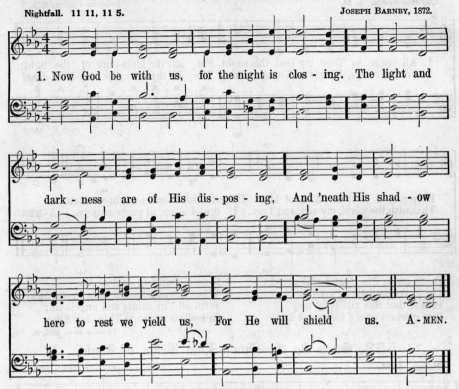

1. Now God be with us, for the night is clos-ing. The light and
dark-ness are of His dis-pos-ing, And 'neath His shad-ow
here to rest we yield us, For He will shield us. A-MEN.

Or: Integer Vitae, No. 460.

2 Let evil thoughts and spirits flee before us;
  Till morning cometh, watch, O Master, o'er us,
  In soul and body Thou from harm defend us,
  Thine angels send us.

3 Let pious thoughts be ours when sleep o'ertakes us;
  Our earliest thoughts be Thine when morning wakes us;
  Thee let us serve in all that we are doing,
  Thy praise pursuing.

4 Through Thy Belovèd soothe the sick and weeping,
  And bid the captive lose his griefs in sleeping;
  Widows and orphans, we to Thee commend them;
  Do Thou befriend them.

5 We have no refuge, none on earth to aid us,
  Save Thee, O Father, who Thine own hast made us;
  But Thy dear presence will not leave them lonely
  Who seek Thee only.

6 Father, Thy Name be praised, Thy kingdom given,
  Thy will be done on earth as 'tis in heaven,
  Give daily bread, forgive our sins, deliver
  Us now and ever.

Bohemian Brethren, 1566, a.

552. All Praise to Thee, My God, This Night.

Old Hundredth. L. M.

LOUIS BOURGEOIS.
Genevan Psalter, 1551.

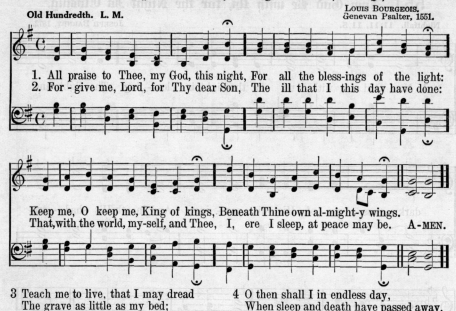

1. All praise to Thee, my God, this night, For all the bless-ings of the light:
2. For - give me, Lord, for Thy dear Son, The ill that I this day have done:

Keep me, O keep me, King of kings, Beneath Thine own al-might-y wings.
That, with the world, my-self, and Thee, I, ere I sleep, at peace may be. A-MEN.

3 Teach me to live, that I may dread
The grave as little as my bed;
To die, that this vile body may
Rise glorious at the judgment day.

4 O then shall I in endless day,
When sleep and death have passed away,
With all Thy saints and angels sing
In endless praise to Thee, my King.

Thomas Ken, 1695. a.

553. Sunk Is the Sun's Last Beam of Light.

Holley. L. M.

GEORGE HEWS, 1835.

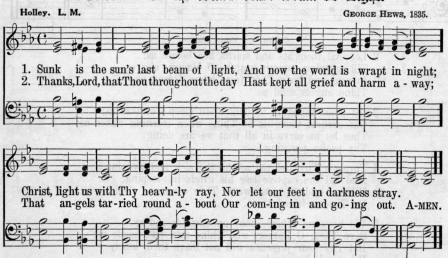

1. Sunk is the sun's last beam of light, And now the world is wrapt in night;
2. Thanks, Lord, that Thou throughout the day Hast kept all grief and harm a-way;

Christ, light us with Thy heav'n-ly ray, Nor let our feet in darkness stray.
That an-gels tar-ried round a-bout Our com-ing in and go-ing out. A-MEN.

3 Whatever wrong we've done or said,
Let not the charge on us be laid;
That through Thy free forgiveness blest,
In peaceful slumber we may rest.

4 Thy guardian angels round us place,
All evil from our couch to chase;
Our soul and body, while we sleep,
In safety, gracious Father, keep.

Nicholas Hermann, 1560.

554. Saviour, Breathe an Evening Blessing.

Evening Prayer (Stebbins). 8 7, 8 7.   GEORGE COLES STEBBINS, 1878.

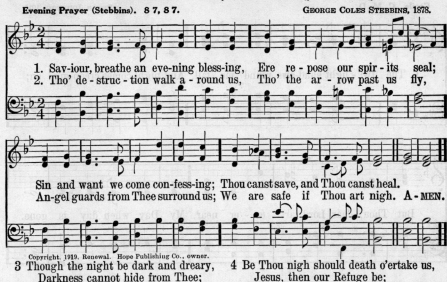

1. Sav-iour, breathe an eve-ning bless-ing, Ere re-pose our spir-its seal;
2. Tho' de-struc-tion walk a-round us, Tho' the ar-row past us fly,

Sin and want we come con-fess-ing; Thou canst save, and Thou canst heal.
An-gel guards from Thee surround us; We are safe if Thou art nigh. A-MEN.

Copyright. 1919. Renewal. Hope Publishing Co., owner.

3 Though the night be dark and dreary,
Darkness cannot hide from Thee;
Thou art He, who, never weary,
Watchest where Thy people be.

4 Be Thou nigh should death o'ertake us,
Jesus, then our Refuge be;
And in Paradise awake us,
There to rest in peace with Thee.

James Edmeston, 1820.
St. 4, Godfrey Thring, 1882.

555. I Love to Steal Awhile Away.

St. Agnes. C. M.   JOHN BACCHUS DYKES, 1866.

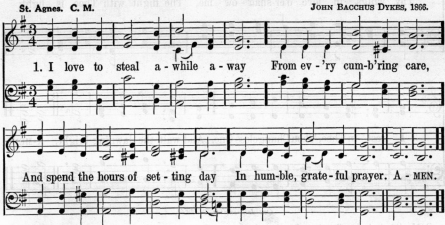

1. I love to steal a-while a-way From ev-'ry cum-b'ring care,

And spend the hours of set-ting day In hum-ble, grate-ful prayer. A-MEN.

2 I love in solitude to shed
The penitential tear,
And all His promises to plead
Where none but God can hear.

3 I love to think of mercies past,
And future good implore,
And all my cares and sorrows cast
On Him whom I adore.

4 I love by faith to take a view
Of brighter scenes in heaven;
The prospect doth my strength renew,
While here by tempests driven.

5 Thus when life's toilsome day is o'er,
May its departing ray
Be calm as this impressive hour,
And lead to endless day.

Phoebe (Hinsdale) Brown, 1824.

556. The Twilight Shadows Round Me Fall.

Cecile. C. M. D.   PETER JOHNSON, 1915.

1. The twi-light shad-ows round me fall, And night comes creep-ing on;

But Thou, dear Lord, art ev-er near, My Day when day is gone.

Thy wings in love o'er-shad-ow me, The night with Thee is light;

I rest in Thee, Thou Changeless One, And wait the dawning bright. A-MEN.

Or: Ishpeming, No. 557.

2 My life is but a fleeting day,
    My race, how quickly run!
The dawn and noonday glory fade
    Into the setting sun.
A stranger and a pilgrim here,
    With faltering feet I roam;
Lord, let Thy glory light the way
    That leads me to my home.

3 By faith I see the better land,
    Where falls no earthly night,
Where Thou dost shine, a radiant Sun,
    The Everlasting Light.
Then help me, Lord, to walk with Thee,
    And keep me Thine alway,
That when I sleep, I may awake
    Unto the perfect day.

                              Ernest Edwin Ryden, 1924.

557. Another Day Is at Its Close.

Ishpeming. C. M. D.   GERHARD THEODORE ALEXIS, 1924.

1. An-oth-er day is at its close, Its joys and sor-rows spent;

An-oth-er night with sweet re-pose Un-to the earth is sent.

In Thee, O Lord, my trust I place, No change can Thee be-fall;

My days and nights, filled with Thy grace, By Thee are num-bered all. A-MEN.

2 Safe in Thy keeping let me be
  When daylight fades away;
And gladly will I worship Thee
  When dawns another day.
If death this night should summon me,
  O Jesus, be Thou nigh;
Grant that I rest secure in Thee
  Whether I live or die.

Johann Friedrich Herzog, 1670.
Johan Olof Wallin, 1816.

558. Father, Merciful and Holy.

Werde munter, mein Gemüthe. 8 7, 8 7, 7 7, 8 8.   JOHANN SCHOP, 1642.

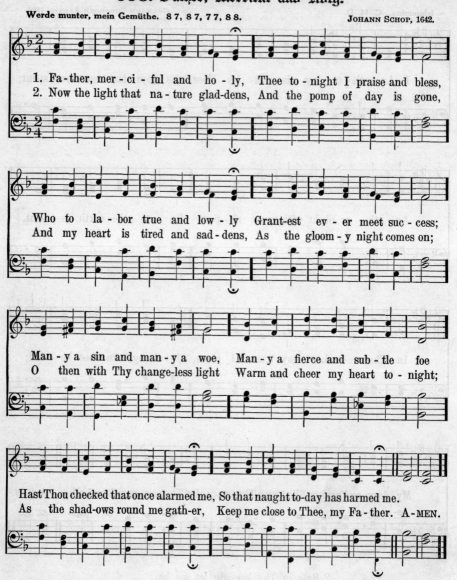

1. Fa-ther, mer-ci-ful and ho-ly, Thee to-night I praise and bless,
2. Now the light that na-ture glad-dens, And the pomp of day is gone,

Who to la-bor true and low-ly Grant-est ev-er meet suc-cess;
And my heart is tired and sad-dens, As the gloom-y night comes on;

Man-y a sin and man-y a woe, Man-y a fierce and sub-tle foe
O then with Thy change-less light Warm and cheer my heart to-night;

Hast Thou checked that once alarmed me, So that naught to-day has harmed me.
As the shad-ows round me gath-er, Keep me close to Thee, my Fa-ther. A-MEN.

3 Lord, the daylight now has vanished,
  Send Thy blessing on my sleep,
Every sin and terror banished,
  Let my rest be calm and deep.
Soul and body, mind and health,
All my loved ones, house and wealth,
Friend and foe, the sick, the stranger,
Keep Thou safe from harm and danger.

4 O Thou mighty God, now hearken
  To the prayer Thy child hath made;
Jesus, while the night hours darken,
  Be Thou still my hope, my aid;
Holy Ghost, on Thee I call,
Friend and Comforter of all,
Hear my earnest prayer, O hear me!
Yea, Thou hearest, Thou art near me.

Johann Rist, 1642.

559. Day Is Dying in the West.

(Written for the Chautauqua Vesper Hour.)

Evening Praise. 7 7, 7 7 4. With Refrain.

WILLIAM FISK SHERWIN, 1877.

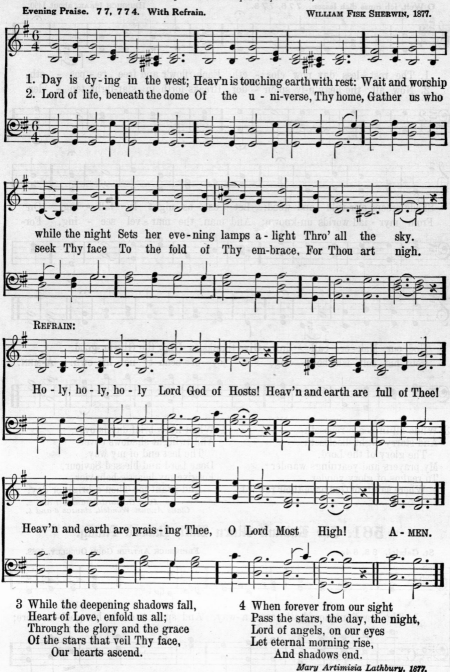

1. Day is dy-ing in the west; Heav'n is touching earth with rest: Wait and worship
2. Lord of life, beneath the dome Of the u-ni-verse, Thy home, Gather us who

while the night Sets her eve-ning lamps a-light Thro' all the sky.
seek Thy face To the fold of Thy em-brace, For Thou art nigh.

REFRAIN:

Ho-ly, ho-ly, ho-ly Lord God of Hosts! Heav'n and earth are full of Thee!

Heav'n and earth are prais-ing Thee, O Lord Most High! A-MEN.

3 While the deepening shadows fall,
    Heart of Love, enfold us all;
  Through the glory and the grace
  Of the stars that veil Thy face,
    Our hearts ascend.

4 When forever from our sight
    Pass the stars, the day, the **night**,
  Lord of angels, on our eyes
  Let eternal morning rise,
    And shadows end.

Mary Artimisia Lathbury, 1877.

560. The Restless Day Now Closeth.

O Welt, ich muss dich lassen. 7 7 6, 7 7 8.   HEINRICH ISAAK. about 1490.

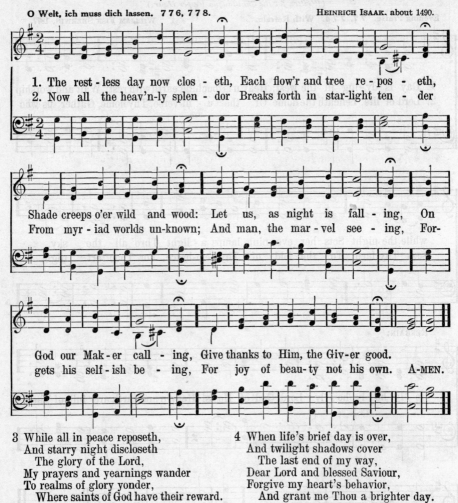

1. The rest-less day now clos-eth, Each flow'r and tree re-pos-eth,
2. Now all the heav'n-ly splen-dor Breaks forth in star-light ten-der

Shade creeps o'er wild and wood: Let us, as night is fall-ing, On
From myr-iad worlds un-known; And man, the mar-vel see-ing, For-

God our Mak-er call-ing, Give thanks to Him, the Giv-er good.
gets his self-ish be-ing, For joy of beau-ty not his own. A-MEN.

3 While all in peace reposeth,
   And starry night discloseth
      The glory of the Lord,
   My prayers and yearnings wander
   To realms of glory yonder,
      Where saints of God have their reward.

4 When life's brief day is over,
   And twilight shadows cover
      The last end of my way,
   Dear Lord and blessed Saviour,
   Forgive my heart's behavior,
      And grant me Thou a brighter day.

Paul Gerhardt, stanzas 1 and 2.
Claus August Wendell, stanzas 3 and 4.

561. The Radiant Morn Hath Passed Away.

St. Gabriel. 8 8, 8 4.   FREDERICK ARTHUR GORE OUSELEY, 1868.

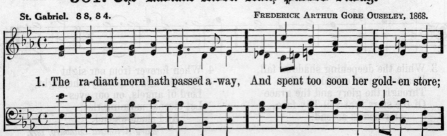

1. The ra-diant morn hath passed a-way, And spent too soon her gold-en store;

The shad-ows of de-part-ing day Creep on once more. A-MEN.

2 Our life is but an autumn sun,
Its glorious noon how quickly past;
Lead us, O Christ, our life-work done,
Safe home at last.

3 O by Thy soul-inspiring grace
Uplift our hearts to realms on high;
Help us to look to that bright place
Beyond the sky,

4 Where light, and life, and joy, and peace
In undivided empire reign,
And thronging angels never cease
Their deathless strain;

5 Where saints are clothed in spotless white,
And evening shadows never fall,
Where Thou, eternal Light of Light,
Art Lord of all.

Godfrey Thring, 1864, 1899.

562. Through the Day Thy Love Has Spared Us.

Amen sjunge hvarje tunga. 8 7, 8 7, 7 7.　　　　ANTON PETER BERGGREN, (1801–1880).

1. Through the day Thy love has spared us, Now we lay us down to rest;

Through the si-lent watch-es guard us, Let no foe our peace mo-lest;

Je-sus, Thou our Guard-ian be; Sweet it is to trust in Thee. A-MEN.

2 Pilgrims here on earth, and strangers,
Dwelling in the midst of foes,
Us and ours preserve from dangers;
In Thine arms may we repose;
And when life's brief day is past,
Rest with Thee in heaven at last.

Thomas Kelly, 1806.

563. Sun of My Soul, Thou Saviour Dear.

Hursley. L. M.   Attributed to PETER RITTER, 1792.

1. Sun of my soul, Thou Sav-iour dear,   It is not night if Thou be near;
2. When the soft dews of kind-ly sleep   My wea-ried eye-lids gen-tly steep,

O may no earth-born cloud a-rise   To hide Thee from Thy servant's eyes.
Be my last thought, how sweet to rest For-ev-er on my Sav-iour's breast. A-MEN.

3 Abide with me from morn till eve,
For without Thee I cannot live;
Abide with me when night is nigh,
For without Thee I dare not die.

4 If some poor wandering child of Thine
Have spurned to-day the voice divine,
Now, Lord, the gracious work begin;
Let him no more lie down in sin.

5 Watch by the sick; enrich the poor
With blessings from Thy boundless store;
Be every mourner's sleep to-night,
Like infant's slumber, pure and light.

6 Come near and bless us when we wake,
Ere through the world our way we take;
Till in the ocean of Thy love
We lose ourselves in heaven above.

John Keble, 1827. a.

564. The Day Departs, Yet Thou Art Near.

Augustana. L. M.   AUGUST NORRBOM, 1924.

1. The day departs, yet Thou art near;   With Thee at hand, we have no fear.

By night Thine eyes their vigil keep,   When our faint eyes are closed in sleep. A-MEN.

2 We rest secure beneath Thy hand,
Protector of our home and land.
To guard Thy children's peaceful rest,
Around them stand Thine angels blest.

3 They sweetly sleep who fear the Lord,
And walk obedient to His Word;
They wake again in joyous mood
To praise the Lord, their Father good.

Frans Mikael Franzén, 1847.

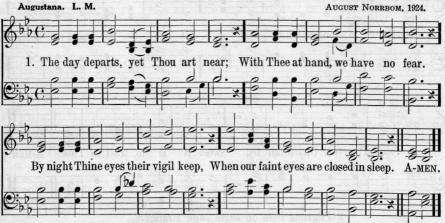

565. When Vesper Bells Are Calling.

Old 130th Psalm. 76, 76. D.   Genevan Psalter, 1556.

1. When ves-per bells are call-ing The hour of rest and prayer,
When eve-ning shades are fall-ing, And I must hence re-pair,
I seek my cham-ber nar-row, Nor my brief day de-plore,
For I shall see the mor-row Where night shall be no more. A-MEN.

2 O take me in Thy keeping,
    Dear Father, good and just;
Let not my soul be sleeping
    In sin, and pride, and lust.
If in my life Thou guide me
    According to Thy will,
I may in death confide me
    Into Thy keeping still.

Frans Mikael Franzén, 1814.

566. God Bless Our Native Land.

America. 6 6 4, 6 6, 6 4.   Harmonia Anglicana, about 1742.

1. God bless our na - tive land, Firm may she ev - er stand, Thro' storm and night;
2. For her our prayer shall rise To God a - bove the skies; On Him we wait:

When the wild tem - pests rave, Rul - er of wind and wave,
Thou who art ev - er nigh, Guard-ing with watch - ful eye,

Do Thou our coun - try save By Thy great might.
To Thee a - lone we cry, God save the State! A - MEN.

John Sullivan Dwight, 1844.

567. My Country, 'Tis of Thee.

1 My country, 'tis of thee,
Sweet land of liberty,
Of thee I sing;
Land where my fathers died,
Land of the pilgrim's pride,
From every mountain side
Let freedom ring.

2 My native country, thee,
Land of the noble free,
Thy name I love;
I love thy rocks and rills,
Thy woods and templed hills;
My heart with rapture thrills
Like that above.

3 Let music swell the breeze,
And ring from all the trees
Sweet freedom's song:
Let mortal tongues awake;
Let all that breathe partake;
Let rocks their silence break,
The sound prolong.

4 Our fathers' God, to Thee,
Author of liberty,
To Thee we sing:
Long may our land be bright
With freedom's holy light;
Protect us by Thy might,
Great God, our King.

Samuel Francis Smith, 1832.

568. Before the Lord We Bow.

St. Godric. 6 6, 6 6, 8 8.   JOHN BACCHUS DYKES, 1862.

1. Be-fore the Lord we bow, The God who reigns a-bove, And rules the world be-low, Bound-less in pow'r and love. Our thanks we bring In joy and praise, Our hearts we raise To heav-en's King. A-MEN.

2 May every mountain height,
    Each vale and forest green
Shine in Thy Word's pure light,
    And its rich fruits be seen!
        May every tongue
        Be turned to praise,
        And join to raise
        A grateful song.

3 Earth! hear thy Maker's voice,
    Thy great Redeemer own;
Believe, obey, rejoice,
    And worship Him alone.
        Cast down thy pride,
        Thy sin deplore,
        And bow before
        The Crucified.

Francis Scott Key, 1832. a.

569. We Plow the Fields, and Scatter.

Maria. 7 6, 7 6. D.   GERHARD THEODORE ALEXIS, 1924.

1. We plow the fields, and scat - ter The good seed on the land,
But it is fed and wa - tered By God's al - might - y hand;
He sends the snow in win - ter, The warmth to swell the grain,
The breez - es and the sun - shine, And soft, re - fresh - ing rain. A - MEN.

2 He only is the Maker
   Of all things near and far;
He paints the wayside flower,
   He lights the evening star;
The winds and waves obey Him,
   By Him the birds are fed;
Much more to us, His children,
   He gives our daily bread.

3 We thank Thee, then, O Father,
   For all things bright and good,
The seedtime and the harvest,
   Our life, our health, our food;
No gifts have we to offer
   For all Thy love imparts,
But that which Thou desirest,
   Our humble, thankful hearts.

Matthias Claudius, 1782.

570. To Thee, O Lord, Our Hearts We Raise.

Golden Sheaves. 8 7, 8 7. D.

ARTHUR SEYMOUR SULLIVAN, 1874.

1. To Thee, O Lord, our hearts we raise In hymns of ad - o - ra - tion,
2. And now, on this our fes - tal day, Thy boun-teous hand con - fess - ing,

To Thee bring sac - ri - fice of praise With shouts of ex - ul - ta - tion:
Up - on Thine al - tar, Lord, we lay The first-fruits of Thy bless - ing:

Bright robes of gold the fields a - dorn, The hills with joy are ring - ing,
By Thee the souls of men are fed With gifts of grace su - per - nal;

The val-leys stand so thick with corn That e - ven they are sing - ing.
Thou who dost give us dai - ly bread, Give us the Bread e - ter - nal.   A - MEN.

3 We bear the burden of the day,
   And often toil seems dreary;
But labor ends with sunset ray,
   And rest is for the weary;
May we, the angel-reaping o'er,
   Stand at the last accepted,
Christ's golden sheaves for evermore
   To garners bright elected.

4 O blessèd is that land of God
   Where saints abide for ever,
Where golden fields spread fair and broad,
   Where flows the crystal river:
The strains of all its holy throng
   With ours to-day are blending;
Thrice blessèd is that harvest-song
   Which never hath an ending.

William Chatterton Dix, 1864.

571. Sing to the Lord of Harvest.

Greenland. 7 6, 7 6. D.   Arranged from JOHANN MICHAEL HAYDN, 1819.

1. Sing to the Lord of har - vest, Sing songs of love and praise; With joyful hearts and voic - es Your al - le - lu - ias raise: By Him the roll - ing sea - sons In fruit-ful or-der move; Sing to the Lord of har-vest A song of hap-py love. A-MEN.

2 By Him the clouds drop fatness,
　The deserts bloom and spring,
　The hills leap up in gladness,
　The valleys laugh and sing:
He filleth with His fullness
　All things with large increase,
He crowns the year with goodness,
　With plenty, and with peace.

3 Heap on His sacred altar
　The gifts His goodness gave,
　The golden sheaves of harvest,
　The souls He died to save:
Your hearts lay down before Him,
　When at His feet ye fall,
And with your lives adore Him,
　Who gave His life for all.

John Samuel Bewley Monsell, 1866.

572. Praise to God, Immortal Praise.

Mercy. 7 7, 7 7.   Arranged from LOUIS MOREAU GOTTSCHALK, 1867.

1. Praise to God, im - mor - tal praise, For the love that crowns our days!
2. For the bless-ings of the field, For the stores the gar - dens yield;

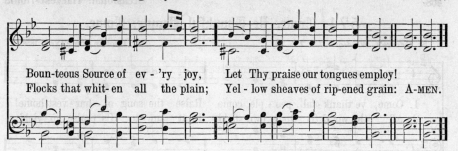

Boun-teous Source of ev - 'ry joy, Let Thy praise our tongues employ!
Flocks that whit-en all the plain; Yel - low sheaves of rip-ened grain: A-MEN.

3 All that spring, with bounteous hand,
Scatters o'er the smiling land;
All that autumn freely pours
From her overflowing stores:

4 These to Thee, our God, we owe,
Source whence all our blessings flow.
And for these our souls shall raise
Grateful vows and solemn praise.

Anna Lætitia (Aikin) Barbauld, 1773.

573. O Lord of Heaven and Earth and Sea.

Almsgiving. 8 8, 8 4. JOHN BACCHUS DYKES, 1865.

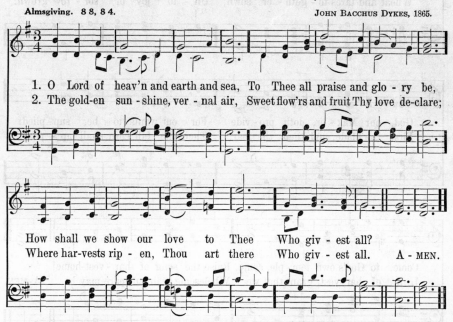

1. O Lord of heav'n and earth and sea, To Thee all praise and glo - ry be,
2. The gold-en sun - shine, ver - nal air, Sweet flow'rs and fruit Thy love de-clare;

How shall we show our love to Thee Who giv - est all?
Where har-vests rip - en, Thou art there Who giv - est all. A - MEN.

3 For peaceful homes and healthful days,
For all the blessings earth displays,
We owe Thee thankfulness and praise
Who givest all.

4 Thou didst not spare Thine only Son,
But gav'st Him for a world undone,
And freely with that Blessèd One
Thou givest all.

5 For souls redeemed, for sins forgiven,
For means of grace and hopes of heaven,
Father, what can to Thee be given
Who givest all?

6 To Thee, from Whom we all derive
Our life, our gifts, our power to give;
O may we ever with Thee live
Who givest all.

Christopher Wordsworth, 1863, a.

574. Come, Ye Thankful People, Come.

St. George's, Windsor. 7 7, 7 7. D.   GEORGE JOB ELVEY, 1858.

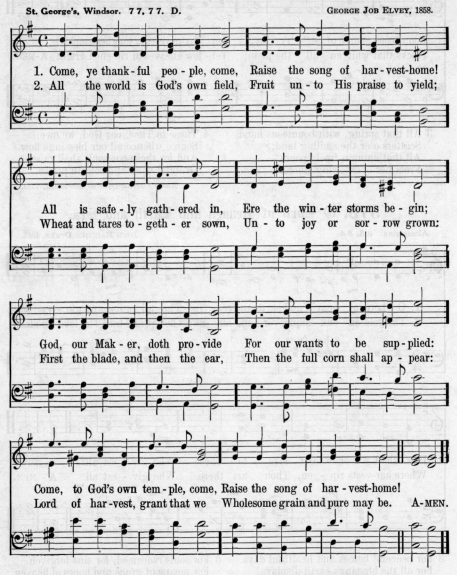

1. Come, ye thank-ful peo-ple, come, Raise the song of har-vest-home!
2. All the world is God's own field, Fruit un-to His praise to yield;

All is safe-ly gath-ered in, Ere the win-ter storms be-gin;
Wheat and tares to-geth-er sown, Un-to joy or sor-row grown:

God, our Mak-er, doth pro-vide For our wants to be sup-plied:
First the blade, and then the ear, Then the full corn shall ap-pear:

Come, to God's own tem-ple, come, Raise the song of har-vest-home!
Lord of har-vest, grant that we Wholesome grain and pure may be.   A-MEN.

3 For the Lord our God shall come,
  And shall take His harvest home;
  From His field shall in that day
  All offenses purge away;
  Give His angels charge at last
  In the fire the tares to cast,
  But the fruitful ears to store
  In His garner evermore.

4 Even so, Lord, quickly come
  To Thy final harvest-home;
  Gather Thou Thy people in,
  Free from sorrow, free from sin;
  There forever purified,
  In Thy presence to abide:
  Come, with all Thine angels, come,
  Raise the glorious harvest-home!

                                        Henry Alford, 1844.

575. When in the Hour of Utmost Need.

Erhalt uns, Herr, bei deinem Wort. L. M.   Joseph Klug's Geistliche Lieder, 1543.

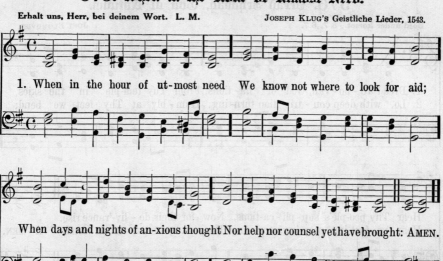

1. When in the hour of ut-most need We know not where to look for aid;

When days and nights of an-xious thought Nor help nor counsel yet have brought: Amen.

2 Then this our comfort is alone,
  That we may meet before Thy throne,
  And cry, O faithful God, to Thee
  For rescue from our misery:

3 To Thee may raise our hearts and eyes,
  Repenting sore with bitter sighs,
  And seek Thy pardon for our sin,
  And respite from our griefs within.

4 For Thou hast promised graciously
  To hear all those who cry to Thee,
  Through Him whose Name alone is great,
  Our Saviour and our Advocate.

5 And thus we come, O God, to-day,
  And all our woes before Thee lay;
  For tried, afflicted, lo! we stand,
  Peril and foes on every hand.

6 Ah, hide not for our sins Thy face;
  Absolve us through Thy boundless grace;
  Be with us in our anguish still,
  Free us at last from every ill

7 That so with all our hearts we may
  Once more our glad thanksgiving pay,
  And walk obedient to Thy Word,
  And now and ever praise Thee, Lord.

Paul Eber, 1560.

576. Dread Jehovah, God of Nations.

Böjd under korset. 8 7, 8 7.   JOEL BLOMQVIST.

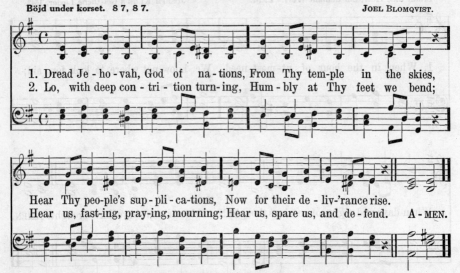

1. Dread Je-ho-vah, God of na-tions, From Thy tem-ple in the skies,
2. Lo, with deep con-tri-tion turn-ing, Hum-bly at Thy feet we bend;

Hear Thy peo-ple's sup-pli-ca-tions, Now for their de-liv-'rance rise.
Hear us, fast-ing, pray-ing, mourning; Hear us, spare us, and de-fend.   A-MEN.

3 Though our sins, our hearts confounding, 4 Let that love veil our transgression,
  Long and loud for vengeance call,   Let that blood our guilt efface:
Thou hast mercy more abounding,   Save Thy people from oppression,
Jesus' blood can cleanse from all.   Save from spoil Thy holy place.

Unknown, 1804.

577. O God of Love, O King of Peace.

Ack, blif hos oss, o Jesu Krist. L. M.   Swedish, 1697.

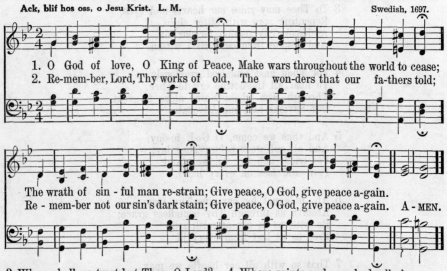

1. O God of love, O King of Peace, Make wars throughout the world to cease;
2. Re-mem-ber, Lord, Thy works of old, The won-ders that our fa-thers told;

The wrath of sin-ful man re-strain; Give peace, O God, give peace a-gain.
Re-mem-ber not our sin's dark stain; Give peace, O God, give peace a-gain.   A-MEN.

3 Whom shall we trust but Thee, O Lord? 4 Where saints and angels dwell above,
Where rest but on Thy faithful Word?   All hearts are knit in holy love;
None ever called on Thee in vain;   O bind us in that heavenly chain;
Give peace, O God, give peace again.   Give peace, O God, give peace again.

See also Hymns of Repentance.   *Henry Williams Baker, 1861.*

578. This Solemn Hour O Let Us Be.

St. Catherine. 8 8, 8 8, 8 8.

HENRI FREDRICK HEMY, 1865.
Altered by JAMES GEORGE WALTON, 1871.

1. This so-lemn hour O let us be, Dear Heav'n-ly Fa-ther, close to Thee. It pass-es now, the dy-ing year, E-ter-ni-ty is draw-ing near. Bless us this night, O Lord, we pray: Help us to fol-low Thee al-way. A-MEN.

2 We pray to-night: O Saviour dear,
If we should live another year,
Give grace and faith that it may be
A year of service unto Thee.
Bless us this night, O Lord, we pray:
Help us to follow Thee alway.

Gustaf Erikson, 1923.

579. Now Rest, Ye Pilgrim Host.

Chalvey. S. M. D.   Leighton George Hayne, 1868.

1. Now rest, ye pil-grim host,   Look back up-on your way,
2. How man-y, at His call,   Have part-ed from our throng!

The mountains climbed, the tor-rents crossed, Through man-y a wea-ry day.
They watch us from the crys-tal wall, And ech-o back our song.

From this vic-to-rious height,   How fair the past ap-pears,
They rest, be-yond com-plaints,   Be-yond all sighs and tears:

God's grace and glo-ry shin-ing bright On all the by-gone years.
Praise be to God for all His saints Who wrought in by-gone years. A-men.

3 The banners they upbore
　　Our hands still lift on high;
The Lord they followed evermore
　　To us is also nigh.
Arise, arise, and tread
　　The future without fears;
He leadeth still Whose hand hath led
Through all the bygone years.

4 When we have reached the home
　　We seek with weary feet,
Our children's children still shall come
　　To keep these ranks complete;
And He Whose host is one
　　Throughout the countless spheres
Will guide His marching servants on
Through everlasting years.

See also:
"Now thank we all our God."
"God is Love."

Rossiter Worthington Raymond, 1879.

580. Lord of Life, of Love, of Light.

Spanish Hymn. 7 7, 7 7. D.

Spanish Melody.

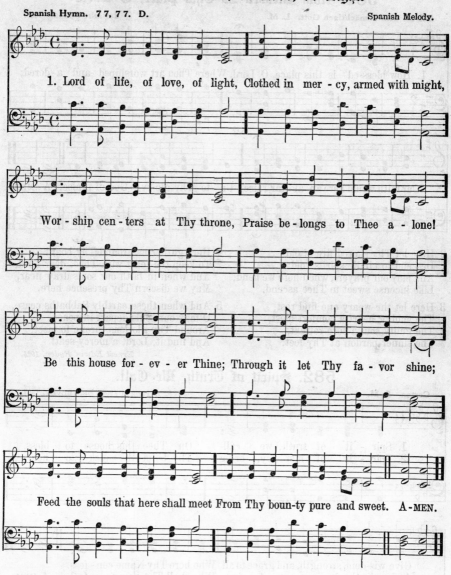

1. Lord of life, of love, of light, Clothed in mer - cy, armed with might,

Wor - ship cen - ters at Thy throne, Praise be - longs to Thee a - lone!

Be this house for - ev - er Thine; Through it let Thy fa - vor shine;

Feed the souls that here shall meet From Thy boun-ty pure and sweet. A - MEN.

2 Write salvation on these walls;
Succor those whom sin enthralls;
Lightened with celestial rays,
Let these gates reflect Thy praise.
Thou who dwell'st where'er is sung
Praise to Thee by human tongue,
With the presence of Thy grace
Dwell henceforth within this place.

3 On Thine agèd servants pour
Richest mercies from Thy store,
And till life's brief hour shall end,
Be their Guardian, Saviour, Friend.
Father holy! Christ most blest!
Evermore within us rest!
Spirit pure, illume our ways
With Thy bright, celestial rays!

Benjamin H. Hall, 1881.

581. How Blessed Is This Place, O Lord.

Lob sei dem allmächtigen Gott. L. M.   JOHANN CRÜGER, 1640.

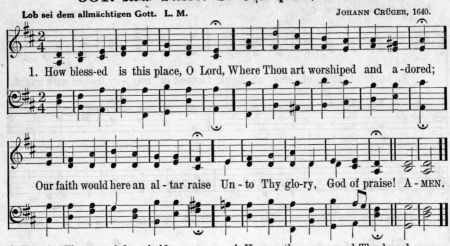

1. How bless-ed is this place, O Lord, Where Thou art worshiped and a-dored;

Our faith would here an al-tar raise Un-to Thy glo-ry, God of praise! A-MEN.

2 Here let Thy sacred fire of old
Descend to kindle spirits cold;
And may our prayers, when here we bend,
Like incense sweet to Thee ascend.

3 Here let the weary one find rest,
The aching heart a comfort blest,
The guilty soul a sure retreat,
The sinner pardon at Thy feet.

4 Here gather us around Thy board
To keep the feast with Thee, dear Lord,
And when in faith our souls draw near,
May we discern Thy presence here.

5 And when these earthly Sabbaths cease,
O may our souls depart in peace,
Around Thy glorious throne to meet,
And find it, Lord, a mercy-seat!

Ernest Edwin Ryden, 1924.

582. Spirit of Truth, We Call.

Gorton. S. M.   Arranged from BEETHOVEN, 1807.

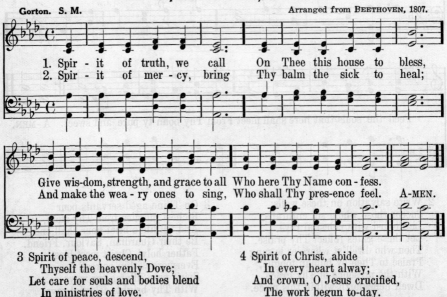

1. Spir-it of truth, we call On Thee this house to bless,
2. Spir-it of mer-cy, bring Thy balm the sick to heal;

Give wis-dom, strength, and grace to all Who here Thy Name con-fess.
And make the wea-ry ones to sing, Who shall Thy pres-ence feel. A-MEN.

3 Spirit of peace, descend,
Thyself the heavenly Dove;
Let care for souls and bodies blend
In ministries of love.

4 Spirit of Christ, abide
In every heart alway;
And crown, O Jesus crucified,
The work begun to-day.

W. A. White, 1890.

583. Raised between the Earth and Heaven.

Beecher. 8 7, 8 7. D.   JOHN ZUNDEL, 1870.

1. Raised be-tween the earth and heav-en, Now our bell is set on high,

In the Name of Him Who giv - eth Skill, and strength, and in - dus - try.

For His praise we meek - ly place it As a gift be - neath His throne;

All its sweet and no - blest mu - sic Shall resound for Him a - lone. A-MEN.

2 Faithful men afar shall listen,
  'Mid their daily toil or rest,
While the melody shall bid them
  Love the Church where all are blest.
They who languish, sick and lonely,
  Shall be minded, as they sigh,
Of the Church's one communion,
  God's true home and family.

3 When the spirits of the faithful
  Pass away to light and peace;
Solemn tones shall then forewarn us,
  Soon our life and work must cease.
May these loud reverberations,
  Pealing forth in grand accord,
Lift our hearts through joy and sorrow
  To Thy throne, most gracious Lord.

Wharton Buchanan Smith, 1882.

584. Angel Voices Ever Singing.

Angel Voices. 8 5, 8 5, 8 4 3.   ARTHUR SEYMOUR SULLIVAN, 1872.

1. An - gel voic - es ev - er sing - ing Round Thy throne of light,

An - gel harps, for - ev - er ring - ing, Rest not day nor night;

Thousands on - ly live to bless Thee, And con-fess Thee Lord of might. A-MEN.

2 Thou, who art beyond the farthest
    Mortal eye can scan,
Can it be that Thou regardest
    Songs of sinful man?
Can we know that Thou art near us,
    And wilt hear us?
      Yea, we can.

3 Yea, we know that Thou rejoicest
    O'er each work of Thine;
Thou didst ears and hands and voices
    For Thy praise combine;
Craftsman's art and music's measure
    For Thy pleasure
      Didst design.

4 Here, great God, to-day we offer
    Of Thine own to Thee,
And for Thine acceptance proffer,
    All unworthily,
Hearts and minds and hands and voices
    In our choicest
      Melody.

5 Honor, glory, might, and merit
    Thine shall ever be,
Father, Son, and Holy Spirit,
    Blessèd Trinity:
Of the best that Thou hast given
    Earth and heaven
      Render Thee.

Francis Pott, 1861.

585. O Thou in Whom Thy Saints Repose.

Han lefver! o min ande, känn. 8 8, 8 8, 8 8.　　　HAEFFNER'S Koralbok, 1819.

1. O Thou in Whom Thy saints re - pose, When life's brief con - flict finds its close, Be - hold us met be - fore Thy face To hal - low this their rest - ing - place: Safe are the souls whom Thou dost keep; And safe - ly here their dust shall sleep.

2. Thou know - est, Lord,—for Thou hast wept Be - side the tomb where Lazarus slept,—What tears must flow, what hearts must bleed, When here we sow the pre - cious seed: Thou still re - mem-b'rest, on Thy throne, Thy gar - den grave and seal - ed stone. A - MEN.

3 Bid then Thy hosts encamp around
This chosen spot of holy ground:
Let here calm hope with memory dwell,
And faith of heavenly comfort tell:
No thought of ill, no footstep rude
Profane the sacred solitude.

4 When here Thy mourners shall repair
In lonely grief and trembling prayer,
Lift Thou sad hearts and streaming eyes
To those fair glades of Paradise,
Where safe within the guarded gate
Thy ransomed souls in patience wait.

John Ellerton, 1870.

586. Holy Father, in Thy Mercy.

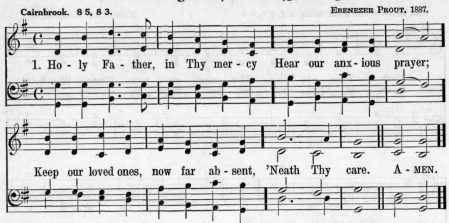

Cairnbrook. 8 5, 8 3.   Ebenezer Prout, 1887.

1. Ho - ly Fa - ther, in Thy mer - cy Hear our anx - ious prayer;

Keep our loved ones, now far ab - sent, 'Neath Thy care. A - MEN.

2 Jesus, Saviour, let Thy presence
  Be their light and guide;
Keep, O keep them, in their weakness,
  At Thy side.

3 When in sorrow, when in danger,
  When in loneliness,
In Thy love look down and comfort
  Their distress.

4 Holy Spirit, let Thy teaching
  Be their strength and stay;
May they love and may they praise Thee
  Day by day.

5 Father, Son, and Holy Spirit,
  God the One in Three,
Bless them, guide them, save them, keep [them
  Near to Thee.

Isabella S. Stephenson, 1889.

587. O Lord, Be with Us When We Sail.

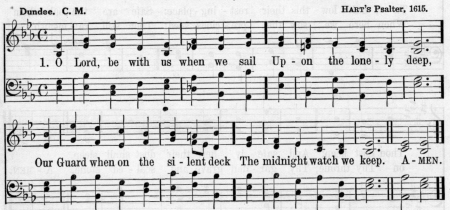

Dundee. C. M.   Hart's Psalter, 1615.

1. O Lord, be with us when we sail Up - on the lone - ly deep,

Our Guard when on the si - lent deck The midnight watch we keep. A - MEN.

2 We need not fear, though all around
  'Mid rising winds we hear
The multitude of waters surge,
  For Thou, O God, art near.

3 The calm, the breeze, the gale, the storm
  That pass from land to land,
All, all are Thine, are held within
  The hollow of Thy hand.

4 Across this troubled tide of life
  Our Pilot Thou abide
Until we reach that better land
  Beyond both time and tide.

5 To Thee the Father, Thee the Son,
  Whom earth and sky adore,
And Spirit, moving on the deep,
  Be praise for evermore.

Edward Arthur Dayman, 1865.

588. Rejoice, Ye Pure in Heart.

Marion. S. M. with Refrain.

ARTHUR HENRY MESSITER, 1885.

1. Re - joice, ye pure in heart, Re - joice, give thanks, and sing:

Your fes - tal ban - ner wave on high, The cross of Christ your King.

REFRAIN:

Re - joice, re - joice, Re - joice, give thanks, and sing. A - MEN.

Re - joice, re - joice,

2 Bright youth and snow-crowned age,
   Strong men and maidens meek,
Raise high your free, exulting song,
   God's wondrous praises speak.

3 Yes, on through life's long path,
   Still chanting as ye go,
From youth to age, by night and day,
   In gladness and in woe.

4 At last the march shall end,
   The wearied ones shall rest,
The pilgrims find their Father's house,
   Jerusalem the blest.

5 Then on, ye pure in heart,
   Rejoice, give thanks, and sing;
Your glorious banner wave on high,
   The cross of Christ your King.

Edward Hayes Plumptre, 1865.

589. Onward, Christian Soldiers.

St. Gertrude. 6 5, 6 5. D. With Refrain.   ARTHUR SEYMOUR SULLIVAN, 1872.

1. On-ward, Chris-tian sol - diers, March-ing as to war, With the Cross of
2. At the sign of tri - umph, Sa - tan's ar-mies flee; On, then, Christian

Je - sus Go - ing on be - fore. Christ, the roy - al Mas - ter,
sol - diers, On to vic - to - ry. Hell's foun - da - tions quiv - er,

Leads a-gainst the foe; For-ward in - to bat - tle See His ban-ners go.
At the shout of praise: Brothers, lift your voic - es, Loud your an-thems raise.

REFRAIN:

On - ward, Chris - tian sol - diers, March - ing as to war,

With the Cross of Je - sus Go - ing on be - fore. A - MEN.

3 Crowns and thrones may perish,
   Kingdoms rise and wane,
But the Church of Jesus
   Constant shall remain.
Gates of hell can never
   'Gainst that Church prevail:
We have Christ's own promise,
   And that cannot fail.

4 Onward, then, ye faithful,
   Join our happy throng,
Blend with ours your voices
   In the triumph-song:
Glory, laud, and honor
   Unto Christ the King:
This through countless ages
   Men and angels sing.

Sabine Baring-Gould, 1865.

590. O Lord, Now Let Thy Servant.

Lancashire. 7 6, 7 6. D.   HENRY SMART, 1836.

1. O Lord, now let Thy serv-ant De-part with heav'n-ly peace,
For I have seen the glo-ry Of Thy re-deem-ing grace:
A Light to lead the Gen-tiles Un-to Thy ho-ly hill,
The glo-ry of Thy peo-ple, Thy cho-sen Is-ra-el. A-MEN.

2 How blessèd is the vision
   E'en here of Thy great love,
But still my spirit yearneth
   To see Thy face above,
Where in Thy holy image
   I, too, shall join the throng
Of ransomed souls in glory,
   And sing the Lamb's new song.

3 Then grant that I may follow
   Thy gleam, O glorious Light,
Till earthly shadows scatter,
   And faith is changed to sight;
Till raptured saints shall gather
   Upon that shining shore,
Where Christ, the blessèd Daystar,
   Shall light them evermore.

Ernest Edwin Ryden, 1924.

591. Sunset and Evening Star.

Crossing the bar. Irregular.   JOSEPH BARNBY, 1892.

Sun - set and eve - ning star,   And one clear call   for me!

And may there be   no moan - ing of the bar   When I   put out to

sea, . . .   But such a   tide   as   mov - ing seems a - sleep,   Too

full for sound and foam, When that which drew from out the bound-less deep

Turns a-gain home. Twi-light and eve-ning bell, And

Twi - - light and eve-ning bell,

aft-er that the dark! And may there be no sad-ness of fare-well

cres - - cen - -

When I em-bark; For, though from out our bourne of time and

- - - do rit. *f*

place The flood may bear me far, . . . I hope to see my

Pi-lot face to face When I have crossed the bar. A - MEN.

For Choir or Quartette.   *Alfred Tennyson, 1889.*

592. A Few More Years Shall Roll.

Chalvey. S. M. D.   LEIGHTON GEORGE HAYNE, 1868.

1. A few more years shall roll, A few more sea-sons come,

And we shall be with those that rest, A-sleep with-in the tomb:

Then, O my Lord, pre-pare My soul for that great day;

O wash me in Thy pre-cious blood, And take my sins a-way! A-MEN.

2 A few more storms shall beat
    On this wild, rocky shore,
And we shall be where tempests cease,
    And surges swell no more.
A few more struggles here,
    A few more partings o'er,
A few more toils, a few more tears,
    And we shall weep no more.

3 'Tis but a little while
    And He shall come again,
Who died that we might live, who lives
    That we with Him may reign:
Then, O my Lord, prepare
    My soul for that glad day;
O wash me in Thy precious blood,
    And take my sins away!

Horatius Bonar, 1844.

593. My God, I Know That I Must Die.

Vater unser im Himmelreich. 88, 88, 88.   Strassburger Gesangbuch, 1537.

1. My God, I know that I must die: My mor - tal
life is pass - ing hence; On earth I nei - ther hope nor try
To find a last - ing res - i - dence. Then teach me by Thy
heav'n-ly grace With joy and peace my death to face. A - MEN.

2 My God, I know not when I die;
   What is the moment or the hour,
How soon the clay may broken lie,
   How quickly pass away the flower:
Then may Thy child prepared be
Through time to meet eternity.

3 My God, I know not how I die;
   For death in many ways doth come,
In dark, mysterious agony,
   Or gently as a sleep to some.
Just as Thou wilt, if but it be
To bring me, blessèd Lord, to Thee!

4 My God, I know not where I die,
   Where is my grave, upon what strand;
Yet from its gloom I do rely
   To be delivered by Thy hand.
Content, I take what spot is mine,
Since all the earth, my Lord, is Thine.

5 My gracious God, when I must die,
   O bear my happy soul above,
With Christ, my Lord, eternally
   To share Thy glory and Thy love:
Then all is right and well with me,
When, where, and how my death shall be.

Benjamin Schmolck, 1700.

594. Lord Jesus Christ, True Man and God.

Misströsta ej att Gud är god. 8 8, 8 8, 8 8.

Swedish, 1695.
ISRAEL KOLMODIN? (1643-1709).

1. Lord Je - sus Christ, true man and God, Who hast the
path of suf - f'ring trod, And died at last up - on the tree,
To bring Thy Fa - ther's grace to me: I pray Thee, through that
bit - ter woe, Let me, a sin - ner, mer - cy know. A - MEN.

Or: "Vater unser im Himmelreich," No. 593.

2 When comes the hour of failing breath,
  And I must wrestle, Lord, with death,
  Then come, Lord Jesus, come with speed,
  And help me in my hour of need;
  Lead me from this dark vale beneath,
  And shorten Thou the pangs of death.

Paul Eber, 1565.

595. Sleep Thy Last Sleep.

Requiem (Barnby). 4 6, 4 6. D.   JOSEPH BARNBY, 1869.

1. Sleep thy last sleep, Free from care and sor - row;

Rest where none weep, Till th' e - ter - nal mor - row;

Though dark waves roll O'er the si - lent riv - er,

Thy faint - ing soul Je - sus can de - liv - er. A - MEN.

2 Life's dream is past,
    All its sin and sadness;
Brightly at last
    Dawns a day of gladness:
    Under the sod,
      Earth, receive our treasure,
To rest in God,
    Waiting all His pleasure.

3 Though we may mourn
    Those in life the dearest,
They shall return,
    Christ, when Thou appearest:
    Soon shall Thy voice
      Comfort those now weeping,
Bidding rejoice
    All in Jesus sleeping.

Edward Arthur Dayman, 1868.

596. In Thy Dear Wounds I Fall Asleep.

I Kristi sår jag somnar in. L. M.   Swedish, 1689.

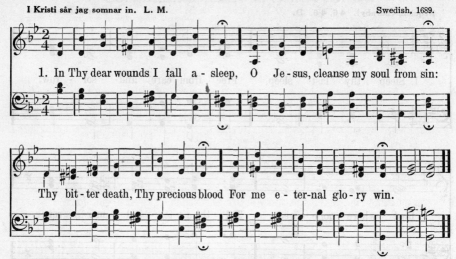

1. In Thy dear wounds I fall a-sleep, O Je-sus, cleanse my soul from sin:

Thy bit-ter death, Thy precious blood For me e-ter-nal glo-ry win.

2 By Thee redeemed, I have no fear,
  When now I leave this mortal clay,
  With joy before Thy throne I come;
  God's own must die, yet live alway.

3 Welcome, O death! thou bringest me
  To dwell with God eternally;
  Through Christ my soul from sin is free,
  O take me now, dear Lord, to Thee!

Paul Eber, 1538.

597. How Blest the Righteous When He Dies!

Herr Jesu Christ, dich zu uns wend. L. M.   Cantionale Sacrum, Gotha, 1651.

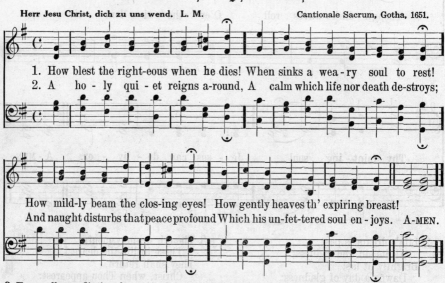

1. How blest the right-eous when he dies! When sinks a wea-ry soul to rest!
2. A ho-ly qui-et reigns a-round, A calm which life nor death de-stroys;

How mild-ly beam the clos-ing eyes! How gently heaves th' expiring breast!
And naught disturbs that peace profound Which his un-fet-tered soul en-joys. A-MEN.

3 Farewell, conflicting hopes and fears,
  Where lights and shades alternate dwell;
  How bright th' unchanging morn appears!
  Farewell, inconstant world, farewell!

4 Life's labor done, as sinks the clay,
  Light from its load the spirit flies,
  While heaven and earth combine to say,
  "How blest the righteous when he dies!"

Anna Lætitia (Aikin) Barbauld, 1792.

598. Asleep in Jesus! Blessed Sleep.

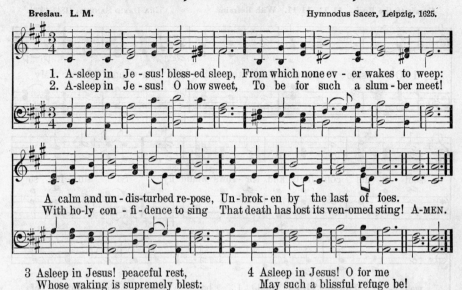

Breslau. L. M.   Hymnodus Sacer, Leipzig, 1625.

1. A-sleep in Je - sus! bless-ed sleep, From which none ev - er wakes to weep:
2. A-sleep in Je - sus! O how sweet, To be for such a slum - ber meet!

A calm and un - dis-turbed re-pose, Un-brok-en by the last of foes.
With ho-ly con - fi-dence to sing That death has lost its ven-omed sting! A-MEN.

3 Asleep in Jesus! peaceful rest,
  Whose waking is supremely blest:
  No fear, no woe, shall dim that hour
  That manifests the Saviour's power.

4 Asleep in Jesus! O for me
  May such a blissful refuge be!
  Securely shall my ashes lie,
  And wait the summons from on high.

Margaret (MacKay) Mackay, 1832, a.

599. Jesus, While Our Hearts Are Bleeding.

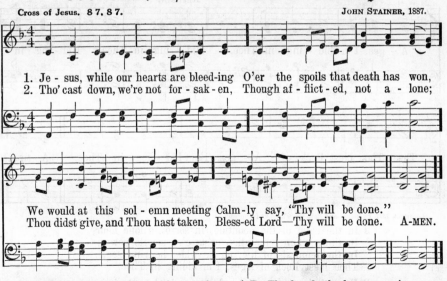

Cross of Jesus. 8 7, 8 7.   JOHN STAINER, 1887.

1. Je - sus, while our hearts are bleed-ing O'er the spoils that death has won,
2. Tho' cast down, we're not for - sak - en, Though af - flict - ed, not a - lone;

We would at this sol - emn meeting Calm-ly say, "Thy will be done."
Thou didst give, and Thou hast taken, Bless-ed Lord—Thy will be done.   A-MEN.

3 Though to-day we're filled with mourning,
  Mercy still is on the throne;
  With Thy smiles of love returning,
  We can sing, "Thy will be done."

4 By Thy hands the boon was given,
  Thou hast taken but Thine own:
  Lord of earth, and God of heaven,
  Evermore Thy will be done.

Thomas Hastings, 1834.

600. O Safe to the Rock That Is Higher Than I.

'O safe to the Rock. 11 11, 11 11. With Refrain.   IRA DAVID SANKEY, (1840–1908).

1. O safe to the Rock that is high - er than I, My

soul in its con - flicts and sor - rows would fly; So sin - ful, so

wea - ry, Thine, Thine would I be; Thou blest Rock of

REFRAIN:

A - ges, I'm hid - ing in Thee. Hid - ing in Thee, Hid - ing in

Thee, Thou blest Rock of A - ges, I'm hid - ing in Thee. A - MEN.

2 In the calm of the noontide, in sorrow's lone hour,
In times when temptation casts o'er me its power;
In the tempests of life, on its wide, heaving sea,
Thou blest Rock of Ages, I'm hiding in Thee.

3 How oft in the conflict, when pressed by the foe,
I have fled to my Refuge and breathed out my woe;
How often, when trials like sea billows roll,
Have I hidden in Thee, O Thou Rock of my soul.

William Orcutt Cushing, (1823–).

601. Fade, Fade, Each Earthly Joy.

Fade, fade, each earthly joy. 6 4, 6 4, 6 6 6 4.   WILLIAM BATCHELDER BRADBURY. (1816-1868).

1. Fade, fade, each earth-ly joy; Je-sus is mine.
2. Tempt not my soul a-way; Je-sus is mine.

Break, ev-'ry ten-der tie; Je-sus is mine.
Here would I ev-er stay; Je-sus is mine.

Dark is the wil-der-ness, Earth has no rest-ing-place,
Per-ish-ing things of clay, Born but for one brief day,

Je-sus a-lone can bless; Je-sus is mine.
Pass from my heart a-way; Je-sus is mine.   A-MEN.

3 Farewell, ye dreams of night;
   Jesus is mine.
Lost in this dawning bright
   Jesus is mine.
All that my soul has tried
Left but a dismal void;
Jesus has satisfied;
   Jesus is mine.

4 Farewell, mortality;
   Jesus is mine.
Welcome, eternity;
   Jesus is mine.
Welcome, O loved and blest,
Welcome, sweet scenes of rest,
Welcome, my Saviour's breast:
   Jesus is mine.

Jane Catharine (Lundie) Bonar, 1844.

602. In Hope My Soul, Redeemed to Bliss Unending.

I hoppet sig min frälsta själ förnöjer.   11 11, 5 5 11.   Northern Melody from 16th Century.

1. { In hope my soul, re-deemed to bliss un-end - ing,
     To heav-en's glo-rious height by faith as-cend - ing, }

Is mind - ful ev - er That Christ did sev - er

The bonds of death, that I might live for - ev - er. A - MEN.

2 In Him I have salvation's way discovered,
The heritage for me He hath recovered.
　　Though death o'ertakes me,
　　Christ ne'er forsakes me,
To everlasting life He surely wakes me.

3 More radiant there than sun e'er shone in brightness,
My soul shall shine before God's throne in whiteness.
　　My God, who knows me,
　　In glory clothes me,
As He declared when for His own He chose me.

4 O may I come where strife and grief are ended,
Where all Thy saints shall meet, with peace attended!
　　Lord, grant Thy favor
　　And mercy ever,
And turn my sorrow into joy forever.

5 Lord Jesus Christ, keep me prepared and waking,
Till from the vale of tears Thy bride Thou'rt taking
　　To dwell in heaven,
　　Where joy is given,
And clouds of darkness are forever riven.

Elle Andersdatter, 1645?

603. I Near the Grave, Where'er I Go.

Jag går mot döden, hvar jag går. 8 7, 8 7, 6 6, 8 8.   Cantional Gotha, 1726.

1. I near the grave, wher-e'er I go, Wher-e'er my path-way tend - eth;

If rough or pleas-ant here be - low, My way at death's gate end - eth.

I have no oth - er choice; Be - tween my griefs and joys My mor - tal

life is or-dered so: I near the grave, wher-e'er I go. A - MEN.

2 I go to heaven, where'er I go,
  If Jesus' steps I follow;
The crown of life He will bestow,
  When earth this frame shall swallow.
    If through this tearful vale
    I in that course prevail,
And walk with Jesus here below,
I go to heaven, where'er I go.

Hans Adolph Brorson, 1334.

604. We Shall Sleep, But Not Forever.

We shall sleep, but not forever. 8 7, 8 7. D. With Refrain.   SILAS JONES VAIL, (1818–1883).

1. We shall sleep, but not for - ev - er, There will be a glo-rious dawn;

We shall meet to part—no, nev - er, On the res - ur - rec - tion morn!

From the deep - est caves of o - cean, From the des - ert and the plain,

From the val - ley and the moun-tain, Count-less throngs shall rise a - gain.

REFRAIN:

We shall sleep, but not for - ev - er, There will be a glo-rious dawn;

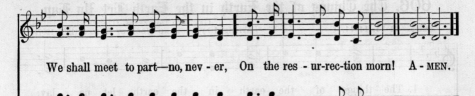

We shall meet to part—no, nev - er, On the res - ur-rec-tion morn! A - MEN.

2 When we see a precious blossom
  That we tended with such care
Rudely taken from our bosom,
  How our aching hearts despair!
Round its little grave we linger,
  Till the setting sun is low,
Feeling all our hopes have perished
  With the flower we cherished so.

3 We shall sleep, but not forever,
  In the lone and silent grave;
Blessèd be the Lord that taketh,
  Blessèd be the Lord that gave.
In the bright, eternal city
  Death can never, never come!
In His own good time He'll call us
  From our rest to home, sweet home.

Mary Ann Kidder, 1878.

605. Jesus, Let My Final Rest.

Final Rest. 7 8, 8 7. JOHN VICTOR BERGQUIST, 1903.

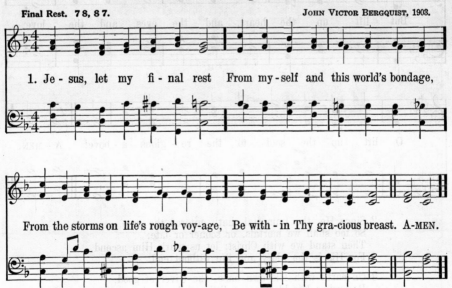

1. Je - sus, let my fi - nal rest From my - self and this world's bondage,

From the storms on life's rough voy-age, Be with - in Thy gra-cious breast. A-MEN.

2 From a world of stress and strife
  Hide me, O my Saviour, hide me;
  Through the narrow gateway guide me,
Leading to eternal life.

3 To Thy bosom gently prest,
  I am ready when Thou take me,
  So a humble place Thou make me
In the mansions of the blest.

Ernst William Olson, 1924.
Stanza 1, source unknown.

606. The Things of the Earth in the Earth Let Us Lay.

Paulina. 11 11, 11 11.   GAETANO DONIZETTI, (1797–1848).
                                          Arranged by LEONARD WOOLSEY BACON, (1830–1907).

1. The things of the earth in the earth let us lay;

The ash-es with ash-es, the dust with the clay;

But lift up the heart, and the eyes, and the love,

O lift up the soul to the re-gions a-bove! A-MEN.

2 Since He, the Immortal, hath entered the gate,
So too shall we mortals, or sooner or late:
Then stand we with Christ; let us mark Him ascend,
For His is the glory and life without end.

3 On earth with His own once the Giver of good,
Bestowing His blessing, a little while stood;
Now nothing can part us, nor distance, nor foes,
For lo! He is with us, and who can oppose?

4 So, Lord, we commit this our loved one to Thee,
Whose body is dead, but whose spirit is free:
We know that through grace, when our life here is o'er,
In bliss we shall be with the Lord evermore.

From the Greek, by John Mason Neale, 1864. a.

607. Safely, Safely Gathered In.

Wells. 7 7, 7 7. D.   MARCUS MORRIS WELLS, (1815—).

1. Safe - ly, safe - ly gath - ered in, Far from sor - row, far from sin,

No more child - ish griefs or fears, No more sad - ness, no more tears;

For the life so young and fair Now hath passed from earth - ly care;

God Him-self the soul will keep, Giv - ing His be - lov - ed sleep. A - MEN.

2 Safely, safely gathered in,
   Far from sorrow, far from sin;
   Passed beyond all grief and pain,
   Death for thee is truest gain;
   For our loss we may not weep,
   Nor our loved ones long to keep
   From the home of rest and peace,
   Where all sin and sorrow cease.

3 Safely, safely gathered in,
   Far from sorrow, far from sin;
   God has saved from weary strife,
   In its dawn, this fresh young life;
   Now it waits for us above,
   Resting in the Saviour's love;
   Jesus, grant that we may meet
   There, adoring, at Thy feet.

Henrietta O. de Lisle Dobree, 1881.

608. Safe in the Arms of Jesus.

Safe in the arms of Jesus. 7 6, 7 6. D. With Refrain.   WILLIAM HOWARD DOANE, 1870.

1. Safe in the arms of Je - sus, Safe on His gen - tle breast,

There by His love o'er - shad - ed, Sweet - ly my soul shall rest.

Hark! 'tis the voice of an - gels, Borne in a song to me,

O - ver the fields of glo - ry, O - ver the jas - per sea......

REFRAIN:

Safe in the arms of Je - sus, Safe on His gen - tle breast,

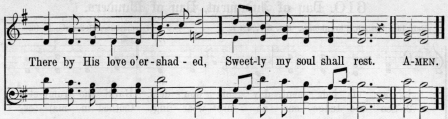

There by His love o'er - shad - ed, Sweet-ly my soul shall rest. A-MEN.

2 Safe in the arms of Jesus,
  Safe from corroding care,
Safe from the world's temptations,
  Sin cannot harm me there.
Free from the blight of sorrow,
  Free from my doubts and fears;
Only a few more trials,
  Only a few more tears!

3 Jesus, my heart's dear refuge,
  Jesus has died for me;
Firm on the Rock of Ages
  Ever my trust shall be.
Here let me wait with patience,
  Wait till the night is o'er;
Wait till I see the morning
  Break on the golden shore.

Frances Jane (Crosby) Van Alstyne, 1869.

609. Saviour, for the Little One.

Blessed Hope. 7 7, 7 7, 7 7.   GERHARD THEODORE ALEXIS, 1924.

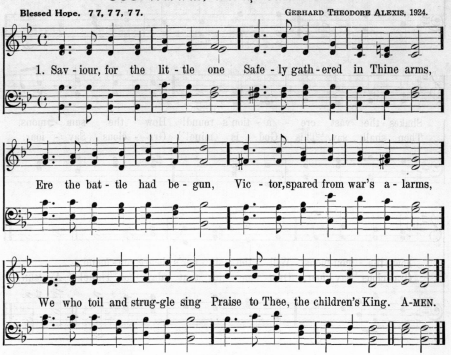

1. Sav - iour, for the lit - tle one Safe - ly gath - ered in Thine arms,

Ere the bat - tle had be - gun, Vic - tor, spared from war's a - larms,

We who toil and strug-gle sing Praise to Thee, the children's King. A-MEN.

2 Thou dost give and take away,
  Full of love in all Thy ways:
Be each mourner's heart to-day
  Full of loving trust and praise,
In the midst of grief to bring
Thanks to Thee, the children's King.

Mary Ann Thomson, 1872.

610. Day of Judgment, Day of Wonders.

Sieh, hier bin ich, Ehrenkönig. 8 7, 8 7, 4 4 7.   Darmstädter Gesangbuch, 1698.

1. Day of judg-ment, day of won-ders, Hark! the trump-et's
2. See the Judge our na-ture wear-ing, Clothed in maj-es-

aw-ful sound, Loud-er than a thou-sand thun-ders,
ty di-vine! Ye who long for His ap-pear-ing

Shakes the vast cre-a-tion's round! How the sum-mons,
Then shall say, "This God is mine!" Gra-cious Sav-iour,

how the sum-mons, Will the sin-ner's heart con-found.
Gra-cious Sav-iour, Own me in that day for Thine! A-MEN.

3 At His call the dead awaken,
   Rise to life from earth and sea;
All the powers of nature, shaken
   By His looks, prepare to flee:
     Careless sinner,
   What will then become of thee?

4 But to those who have confessèd,
   Loved, and served the Lord below,
He will say, "Come near, ye blessèd!
   See the kingdom I bestow!
     You forever
   Shall my love and glory know."

John Newton, 1779.

611. Great God, What Do I See and Hear!

Es ist gewisslich an der Zeit. 8 7, 8 7, 8 8 7.   Wittenberg Gesangbuch, 1535.

1. Great God, what do I see and hear! The end of things cre - at - ed!
2. The dead in Christ shall first a - rise, At the last trump-et's sound-ing,

The Judge of man I see ap - pear, On clouds of glo - ry seat - ed.
Caught up to meet Him in the skies, With joy their Lord sur - round-ing;

The trump - et sounds: the graves re - store The dead which they con -
No gloom - y fears their souls dis - may; His pres - ence sheds e -

tained be - fore; Pre - pare, my soul, to meet Him.
ter - nal day On those pre - pared to meet Him. A - MEN.

3 But sinners, filled with guilty fears,
    Behold His wrath prevailing,
For they shall rise, and find their tears
    And sighs are unavailing;
The day of grace is past and gone;
They trembling stand before the throne,
    All unprepared to meet Him.

4 Thou who hast died and yet dost live,
    To me impart Thy merit;
My pardon seal, my sins forgive,
    And cleanse me by Thy Spirit.
Beneath Thy cross I view the day
When heaven and earth shall pass away,
    And thus prepare to meet Thee.

William Bengo Collyer, 1812.

612. Wake, Arise! a Voice Appalling.

Wachet auf. 8 9 8, 8 9 8, 6 6 4, 4 4 8.   PHILIPP NICOLAI, 1599.

1. Wake, a-rise! a voice ap-pall-ing   In sol-emn maj-es-ty is call-ing

To all the deeps of earth and sea. Wake, a-rise, ye dead un-num-bered,

That in your si-lent graves have slumbered, Re-leased from toil and ag-o-ny.

God's voice is heard at last; The night of death is past, Day is dawn-ing,

The Lord's great day, That dreadful day, When judgment shall be passed for aye. A-MEN.

2 Earth and sea and sky shall tremble,
The angels of the Lord assemble,
When Christ in glory comes again.
Mountains fall, and deeps are yawning
When in eternity's dread dawning
He comes to judge the sons of men.
There shall be joy and tears,
And hope shall blend with fears,
But the faithful
Shall enter bold
The Shepherd's fold,
And all receive their crowns of gold.

3 Christ, Thy coming all shall gladden
Who in Thy footsteps here have trodden
Upon Thy thorny path below.
Palms for thorns shall then be given;
And, waiting for the joys of heaven,
Contented to my grave I go.
The little while I sleep,
Thy angels vigil keep,
Till Thou comest
My soul to wake
And, for Thy sake,
My spirit into bliss to take.

Philipp Nicolai, 1599.
Johan Olof Wallin, 1817.

613. That Day of Wrath, That Dreadful Day.

St. Cross. L. M.

JOHN BACCHUS DYKES, (1823-1876).

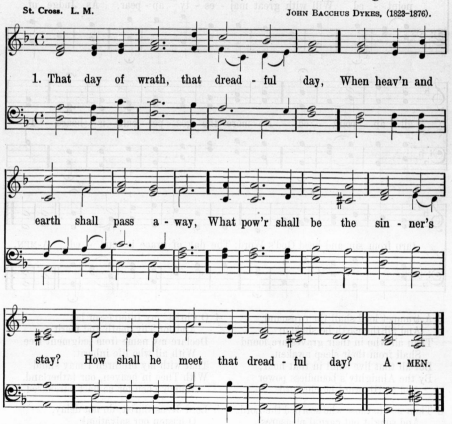

1. That day of wrath, that dread - ful day, When heav'n and earth shall pass a - way, What pow'r shall be the sin - ner's stay? How shall he meet that dread - ful day? A - MEN.

2 When, shriveling like a parchèd scroll,
The flaming heavens together roll;
When louder yet, and yet more dread,
Swells the high trump that wakes the dead:

3 Lord, on that day, that wrathful day,
When man to judgment wakes from clay,
Be Thou the trembling sinner's stay,
Though heaven and earth shall pass away.

Thomas of Celano, 13th Century.

614. The Day Is Surely Drawing Near.

Du lifvets bröd. 8 7, 8 7, 8 8 7.   PETER SOHREN, 1668.

1. The day is sure-ly draw-ing near, When He, the Lord's A-
noint-ed, Will with great maj-es-ty ap-pear, As Judge of
all ap-point-ed. No more the gos-pel call is heard To
turn from sin and heed God's Word: The day of grace is end-ed. A-MEN.

2 A trumpet loud shall then resound,
  And all the earth be shaken;
Then all who in their graves are found
  Shall from their sleep awaken.
But all that live shall in that hour,
By the Almighty's boundless power
  And at His word be changèd.

3 Then woe to those who scorned the Lord,
  And sought but carnal pleasures,
Who here despised His precious Word,
  And loved their earthly treasures,
With shame and trembling they shall stand,
And at the Judge's stern command
  Depart from Him forever.

4 O Christ, my Intercessor be,
  And for Thy death and merit
Declare my name from judgment free,
  With all who life inherit;
That with my brethren I may stand
With Thee in heaven, our fatherland,
  Which Thou for us hast purchased.

5 Lord Jesus Christ, do not delay,
  O hasten our salvation!
We often tremble on our way,
  In fear and tribulation.
Then hear us when we cry to Thee:
Come, mighty Judge, come, make us free
  From every evil. Amen!

Bartholomäus Ringwaldt, about 1565, a.

615. When Jesus Comes in Glory.

Daystar. 76, 76. D.

SAMUEL MARTIN MILLER, 1922.
Harmonized by GERHARD THEODORE ALEXIS, 1925.

1. When Je-sus comes in glo-ry, As Lord and King of kings,
2. His voice like rush-ing wa-ters Will reach with might-y sound

O what a won-drous sto-ry The bless-ed Bi-ble brings:
In-to the deep-est quar-ters Of all cre-a-tion round;

His face will shine like sun-light, His head be white as snow,
And at this won-drous greet-ing The dead in Christ shall rise,

His eyes like flam-ing fire-light, His feet like brass a-glow.
Their Lord and Sav-iour meet-ing In glo-ry in the skies. A-MEN.

3 And we who are believing,
  And His appearing love,
Shall know we are receiving
  His glory from above;
His resurrection power
  Will raise us to the place
Where we that wondrous hour
  Shall see Him face to face.

4 O hasten Thine appearing,
  Thou Bright and Morning Star!
Lord, may we soon be hearing
  The trumpet sound afar;
Thy people all are yearning
  To be Thy raptured bride,
And at Thine own returning
  Be caught up to Thy side.

Samuel Martin Miller, 1922.

616. There Is a Gate That Stands Ajar.

Gates Ajar. 8 7, 8 7. With Refrain.   SILAS JONES VAIL, (1818–1883).

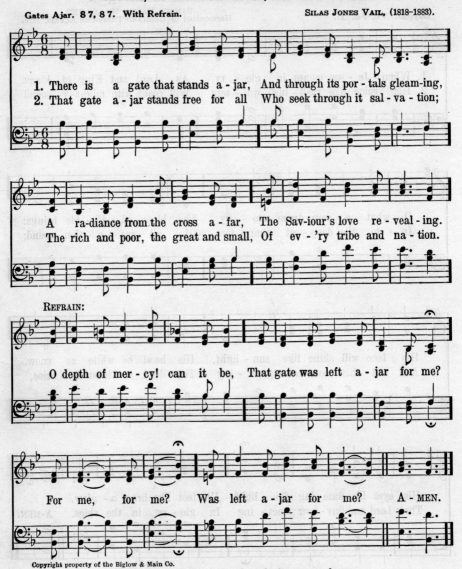

1. There is a gate that stands a - jar, And through its por - tals gleam-ing,
2. That gate a - jar stands free for all Who seek through it sal - va - tion;

A ra-diance from the cross a - far, The Sav-iour's love re - veal - ing.
The rich and poor, the great and small, Of ev - 'ry tribe and na - tion.

REFRAIN:

O depth of mer - cy! can it be, That gate was left a - jar for me?

For me, for me? Was left a - jar for me? A - MEN.

Copyright property of the Biglow & Main Co.

3 Press onward, then, though foes may frown,
    While mercy's gate is open;
Accept the cross and win the crown,
    Love's everlasting token.

4 Beyond the river's brink we'll lay
    The cross that here is given,
And bear the crown of life away,
    And love Him more in heaven.

Lydia Baxter, 1874.

617. Ten Thousand Times Ten Thousand.

Alford. 7 6, 8 6. D.

JOHN BACCHUS DYKES, 1875.

1. Ten thou - sand times ten thou - sand   In spar - kling rai - ment bright,
2. What rush of al - le - lu - ias   Fills all the earth and sky!

The ar - mies of the ran-somed saints Throng up the steeps of light:
What ring-ing of a thou - sand harps Be - speaks the tri - umph nigh!

'Tis fin - ished, all is fin - ished, Their fight with death and sin:
O day, for which cre - a - tion And all its tribes were made;

Fling o - pen wide the gold - en gates, And let the vic - tors in.
O joy, for all its for - mer woes A thou-sand-fold re - paid!   A-MEN.

3 O then what raptured greetings
    On Caanan's happy shore;
What knitting severed friendships up
    Where partings are no more!
Then eyes with joy shall sparkle,
    That brimmed with tears of late;
Orphans no longer fatherless,
    Nor widows desolate.

4 Bring near Thy great salvation,
    Thou Lamb for sinners slain;
Fill up the roll of Thine elect,
    Then take Thy power, and reign:
Appear, Desire of nations,
    Thine exiles long for home;
Show in the heaven Thy promised sign;
    Thou Prince and Saviour, come.

Henry Alford, 1867.

618. When I Can Read My Title Clear.

Ortonville. C. M.   THOMAS HASTINGS, 1837.

1. When I can read my ti-tle clear To man-sions in the
2. Should earth a-gainst my soul en-gage, And hell-ish darts be

skies, I bid fare-well to ev-'ry fear, And
hurled, Then I can smile at Sa-tan's rage, And

wipe my weep-ing eyes, And wipe my weep-ing eyes.
face a frown-ing world, And face a frown-ing world. A-MEN.

3 Let cares like some wild deluge come,
   And storms of sorrow fall,
May I but safely reach my home,
   My God, my heaven, my all!

4 There shall I bathe my weary soul
   In seas of heavenly rest,
And not a wave of trouble roll
   Across my peaceful breast.

Isaac Watts, 1707.

619. We Speak of the Realms of the Blest.

Devotion. 8 8, 8 8. Dactylic.   J. A. JOHNSON, 1846.

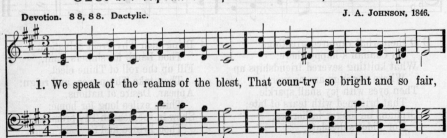

1. We speak of the realms of the blest, That coun-try so bright and so fair,

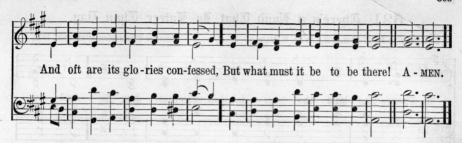

And oft are its glo-ries con-fessed, But what must it be to be there! A - MEN.

2 We speak of its pathways of gold,
  Its walls decked with jewels so rare,
Its wonders and pleasures untold,
  But what must it be to be there!

3 We speak of its freedom from sin,
  From sorrow, temptation, and care,
From trials without and within,
  But what must it be to be there!

4 We speak of its service of love,
  The robes which the glorified wear,
The Church of the first-born above,
  But what must it be to be there!

5 Do Thou, Lord, 'mid sorrow and woe,
  For heaven my spirit prepare,
And shortly I also shall know
  And feel what it is to be there.

Elizabeth (King) Mills, 1829.

620. There Is a Land of Pure Delight.

St. Peter. C. M.

ALEXANDER ROBERT REINAGLE, 1826.

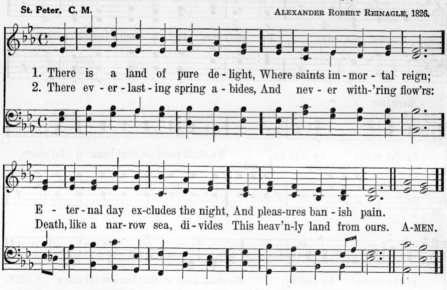

1. There is a land of pure de - light, Where saints im - mor - tal reign;
2. There ev - er - last - ing spring a - bides, And nev - er with-'ring flow'rs:

E - ter - nal day ex-cludes the night, And pleas-ures ban - ish pain.
Death, like a nar-row sea, di - vides This heav'n-ly land from ours. A-MEN.

3 Sweet fields, beyond the swelling flood,
  Stand dressed in living green:
So to the Jews old Canaan stood,
  While Jordan rolled between.

4 But timorous mortals start and shrink
  To cross this narrow sea,
And linger, shivering on the brink,
  And fear to launch away.

5 O could we make our doubts remove,
  Those gloomy doubts that rise,
And view the Canaan that we love
  With unbeclouded eyes!

6 Could we but climb where Moses stood,
  And view the landscape o'er,
Not Jordan's stream, nor death's cold flood,
  Should fright us from the shore.

Isaac Watts, 1707.

621. There's a Land That Is Fairer Than Day.

Sweet by and by. 9 9, 9 9. With Refrain.   JOSEPH PHILBRICK WEBSTER, 1868.

1. There's a land that is fair-er than day, And by faith we can see it a-far; For the Fa-ther waits o-ver the way To pre-pare us a dwell-ing-place there.

REFRAIN:

In the sweet by and by,
In the sweet by and by,
We shall meet on that beau-ti-ful shore,
In the sweet by and by,
In the sweet by and by,
We shall meet on that beau-ti-ful shore. A-MEN.

By permission of Oliver Ditson Co., owners of copyright.

2 We shall sing on that beautiful shore
The melodious songs of the blest,
And our spirits shall sorrow no more,
Not a sigh for the blessing of rest.

3 To our bountiful Father above
We will offer our tribute of praise
For the glorious gift of His love,
And the blessings that hallow our days.
S. Fillmore Bennett.

622. Jerusalem the Golden.

Ewing. 7 6, 7 6. D. ALEXANDER EWING, 1853.

1. Je - ru - sa - lem the gold - en, With milk and hon - ey blest,

Be - neath thy con - tem - pla - tion Sink heart and voice op - prest:

I know not, O I know not, What joys a - wait us there!

What ra - dian-cy of glo - ry, What light be - yond com-pare! A - MEN.

2 And when I fain would sing them,
  My spirit fails and faints,
And vainly would it image
  The assembly of the saints,
They stand, those halls of Zion,
  Conjubilant with song,
And bright with many an angel,
  And all the martyr throng:

3 There is the throne of David;
  And there, from care released,
The song of them that triumph,
  The shout of them that feast;
And they who, with their Leader,
  Have conquered in the fight
Forever and forever
  Are clad in robes of white!

Bernard de Morlaix, 12th Century.

623. Jerusalem, My Happy Home.

Mathilda. C. M. D.   RALPH ALVIN STROM, 1924.

1. Je - ru - sa - lem, my hap - py home, Name ev - er dear to me!

When shall my la - bors have an end In joy, and peace, and thee?

O when, thou cit - y of my God, Shall I thy courts as - cend,

Where ev - er-more the an-gels sing, Where Sabbaths have no end?   A-MEN.

2 There happier bowers than Eden's bloom,
  Nor sin nor sorrow know:
Blest seats! through rude and stormy scenes
  I onward press to you.
Why should I shrink from pain and woe,
  Or feel at death dismay?
I've Canaan's goodly land in view,
  And realms of endless day.

3 Apostles, martyrs, prophets there
  Around my Saviour stand;
And soon my friends in Christ below
  Will join the glorious band.
Jerusalem, my happy home!
  My soul still longs for thee;
Then shall my labors have an end,
  When I thy joys shall see.

James Montgomery, (1771-1854).

624. Abode of Peace, My Father's Home Forever.

Till fridens hem. 11 10, 11 10, 8 8, 7 7.   PRINCE GUSTAF, (1827-1852).

1. { A - bode of peace, my Fa-ther's home for - ev - er! My wea - ry
   I home-ward look to Thee, my Lord and Sav - iour, To Thine a-

soul in faith doth yearn for thee. }
bode of peace, e - ter - nal - ly. } There is on earth no peace-ful

rest; Our faith is weak, our souls op - pressed, Our vi - sion

dim and fail - ing, Our vi - sion dim and fail - ing. A-MEN.

2 The Lord be praised that time so swiftly flieth;
   God's promise is fulfilled for evermore.
Who on God's Word and promises relieth
   Shall find at last the choicest wine in store.
Forgotten then is all distress,
Eternal peace and happiness
   Shall then be ours forever.

3 Then, keep my heart forever, O my Saviour,
   And let me never, Lord, from Thee depart.
In joy, in pain, in sorrow, now and ever,
   Thou only givest solace to my heart.
For when, O Lord, I am with Thee,
All other comforts well may flee;
   With Thee I'm blest forever.

Agata Rosenius.

625. Jerusalem, Jerusalem.

Jerusalem. C. M. D.   CHARLES HENRY PURDAY, (1799–1885).

1. Je - ru - sa - lem, Je - ru - sa - lem, Thou cit - y ev - er blest,

With - in thy por - tals first I find My safe - ty, peace, and rest.

Here dan - gers al - ways threat - en me, My days in strife are spent,

And la - bor, sor - row, wor - ry, grief, I find at best their strength. A-MEN.

2 No wonder, then, that I do long,
  O blessèd home, for thee,
Where I shall find a resting-place,
  From sin and sorrow free;
Where tears and weeping are no more,
  Nor death, nor pain, nor night,
For former things are passed away,
  And darkness turned to light.

3 Now all for me has lost its charm
  Which by the world is praised,
Since on the cross, through faith, I saw
  My Saviour Jesus raised;
My goal is fixed, one thing I ask,
  Whate'er the cost may be,
Jerusalem, Jerusalem,
  Soon to arrive in thee.

Carolina Vilhelmina (Sandell) Berg, (1832-1903).

626. Jerusalem, Thou City Fair and High.

Jerusalem, du Herrens nya stad. 10 6, 10 6, 7 6, 7 6.

English Melody.

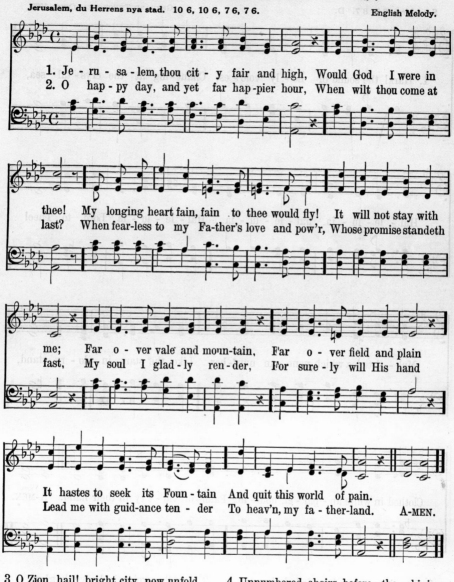

1. Je - ru - sa - lem, thou cit - y fair and high, Would God I were in
2. O hap - py day, and yet far hap-pier hour, When wilt thou come at

thee! My longing heart fain, fain to thee would fly! It will not stay with
last? When fear-less to my Fa-ther's love and pow'r, Whose promise standeth

me; Far o - ver vale and moun-tain, Far o - ver field and plain
fast, My soul I glad - ly ren - der, For sure - ly will His hand

It hastes to seek its Foun - tain And quit this world of pain.
Lead me with guid-ance ten - der To heav'n, my fa - ther-land.   A-MEN.

3 O Zion, hail! bright city, now unfold
   The gates of grace to me
How many a time I longed for thee of old,
   Ere yet I was set free
From yon dark life of sadness,
   Yon world of shadowy naught,
And God had given the gladness,
   The heritage I sought.

4 Unnumbered choirs before the shining
   Their joyful anthems raise,   [throne
The heavenly halls re-echo with the tone
   Of that great hymn of praise,
And all its host rejoices,
   And all its blessèd throng
Unite their myriad voices
   In one eternal song.

Johann Matthäus Meyfart, 1626.

627. Hark! the Sound of Holy Voices.

Seraphim. 8 7, 8 7. D.   GERHARD THEODORE ALEXIS, 1923.

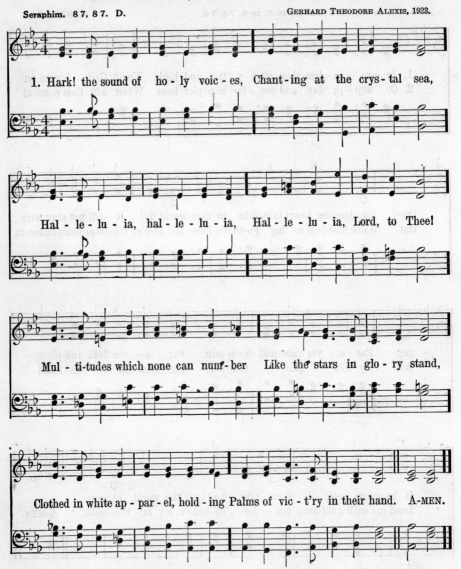

1. Hark! the sound of ho - ly voic - es, Chant - ing at the crys - tal sea,
Hal - le - lu - ia, hal - le - lu - ia, Hal - le - lu - ia, Lord, to Thee!
Mul - ti-tudes which none can num - ber Like the stars in glo - ry stand,
Clothed in white ap - par - el, hold - ing Palms of vic - t'ry in their hand. A-MEN.

2 They have come from tribulation,
    And have washed their robes in blood,
Washed them in the blood of Jesus;
    Tried they were, and firm they stood;
Mocked, imprisoned, stoned, tormented,
    Sawn asunder, slain with sword,
They have conquered death and Satan
    By the might of Christ the Lord.

3 Now they reign in heavenly glory,
    Now they walk in golden light,
Now they drink, as from a river,
    Holy bliss and infinite:
Love and peace they taste forever,
    And all truth and knowledge see
In the beatific vision
    Of the blessèd Trinity.

Christopher Wordsworth, 1862, a.

628. In Heaven Above, in Heaven Above.

I himmelen, i himmelen. 86, 86, 886. Koralbok, 1697.

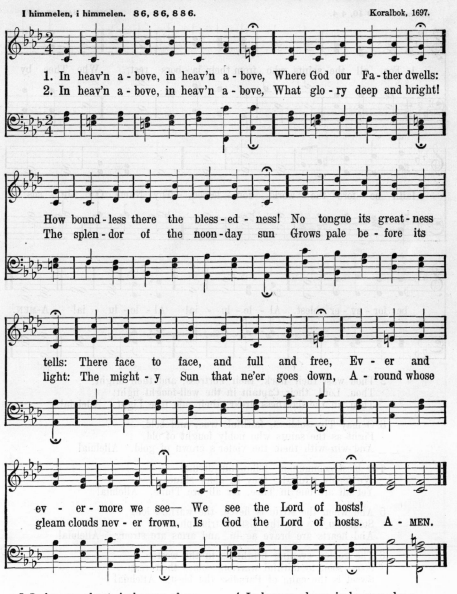

1. In heav'n a - bove, in heav'n a - bove, Where God our Fa - ther dwells:
2. In heav'n a - bove, in heav'n a - bove, What glo - ry deep and bright!

How bound - less there the bless - ed - ness! No tongue its great - ness
The splen - dor of the noon - day sun Grows pale be - fore its

tells: There face to face, and full and free, Ev - er and
light: The might - y Sun that ne'er goes down, A - round whose

ev - er - more we see— We see the Lord of hosts!
gleam clouds nev - er frown, Is God the Lord of hosts. A - MEN.

3 In heaven above, in heaven above,
  No tears of pain are shed:
There nothing e'er shall fade or die;
Life's fullness round is spread,
And, like an ocean, joy o'erflows,
And with immortal mercy glows
  Our God the Lord of hosts.

4 In heaven above, in heaven above,
  God hath a joy prepared,
Which mortal ear hath never heard,
  Nor mortal vision shared,
Which never entered mortal breast,
By mortal lips was ne'er expressed,
  O God the Lord of hosts!

Johan Åström, 1819.

629. For All the Saints Who from Their Labors Rest.

Sarum. 10 10 10, 4 4.   JOSEPH BARNBY, 1869.

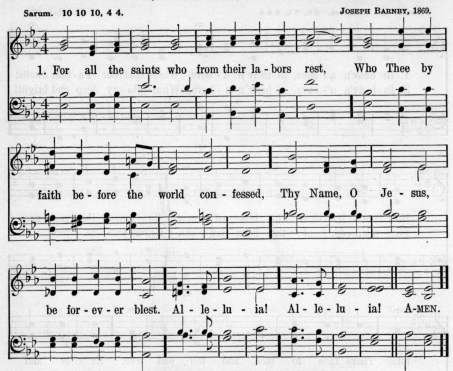

1. For all the saints who from their la-bors rest, Who Thee by
faith be-fore the world con-fessed, Thy Name, O Je-sus,
be for-ev-er blest. Al-le-lu-ia! Al-le-lu-ia! A-MEN.

2 Thou wast their Rock, their Fortress, and their Might;
Thou, Lord, their Captain in the well-fought fight;
Thou, in the darkness drear, their one true Light. Alleluia!

3 O may Thy soldiers, faithful, true, and bold,
Fight as the saints who nobly fought of old,
And win with them the victor's crown of gold. Alleluia!

4 O blest communion, fellowship divine!
We feebly struggle, they in glory shine;
Yet all are one in Thee, for all are Thine. Alleluia!

5 And when the strife is fierce, the warfare long,
Steals on the ear the distant triumph-song,
And hearts are brave again, and arms are strong. Alleluia!

6 The golden evening brightens in the west;
Soon, soon to faithful warriors comes their rest;
Sweet is the calm of Paradise the blest. Alleluia!

7 But lo! there breaks a yet more glorious day;
The saints triumphant rise in bright array;
The King of Glory passes on His way. Alleluia!

8 From earth's wide bounds, from ocean's farthest coast,
Through gates of pearl streams in the countless host,
Singing to Father, Son, and Holy Ghost. Alleluia!

William Walsham How, 1864, (Text of 1875).

630. Who Are These, Like Stars Appearing?

All Saints (Old). 8 7, 8 7, 7 7.   Darmstädter Gesangbuch, 1698.

1. Who are these, like stars ap-pear-ing, These be-fore God's throne who stand?

Each a gold-en crown is wear-ing; Who are all this glo-rious band?

Al-le-lu-ia! hark they sing, Prais-ing loud their heav'n-ly King. A-MEN.

2 Who are these of dazzling brightness,
   These in God's own truth arrayed,
Clad in robes of purest whiteness,
   Robes whose luster ne'er shall fade,
      Ne'er be touched by time's rude hand?
      Whence comes all this glorious band?

3 These are they who have contended
   For their Saviour's honor long,
Wrestling on till life was ended,
   Following not the sinful throng:
      These, who well the fight sustained,
      Triumph through the Lamb have gained.

4 These are they whose hearts were riven,
   Sore with woe and anguish tried,
Who in prayer full oft have striven
   With the God they glorified:
      Now, their painful conflict o'er,
      God has bid them weep no more.

5 These, like priests, have watched and waited,
   Offering up to Christ their will,
Soul and body consecrated,
   Day and night they serve Him still.
      Now in God's most holy place,
      Blest they stand before His face.

Heinrich Theobald Schenk, 1719.

631. Strait Is the Gate to All That Come.

Ortonville. C. M.   THOMAS HASTINGS, 1837.

1. Strait is the gate to all that come, And nar-row is the
way Which leads un-to the heav'n-ly home, Where
yet is room for thee, Where yet is room for thee. A-MEN.

2 In heaven, where God His own shall take,
　　There's also room for thee.
　In Jesus' Name, for Jesus' sake,
　　The gates shall opened be.

3 Where thousands stand arrayed in white,
　　Whom God His own declared,
　There yet is room and life and light,
　　By grace for thee prepared.

4 In Jesus' heart there's room, I know,
　　And in His heaven of bliss.
　He in His gospel tells me so,
　　Thanks be to God for this!

5 Thanks be to God, that even I
　　May in that city dwell,
　Where peace shall reign eternally,
　　And all with me be well!

Carolina Vilhelmina (Sandell) Berg, (1832-1903).

632. I Love to Hear the Story.

Hos Gud är idel glädje. 7 6, 7 6. D.   AHNFELTS Sånger.

1. I love to hear the sto - ry Which an - gel voic - es tell,

How once the King of glo - ry Came down on earth to dwell.

I am both weak and sin - ful, But this I sure - ly know,

The Lord came down to save me, Be-cause He loved me so. A-MEN.

Christmas.

2 I'm glad my blessèd Saviour
  Was once a child like me,
  To show how pure and holy
  His little ones should be;
  And if I try to follow
  His footsteps here below,
  He never will forget me,
  Because He loves me so.

3 To sing His love and mercy
  My sweetest songs I'll raise;
  And though I cannot see Him,
  I know He hears my praise;
  For He has kindly promised
  That even I may go
  To sing among His angels,
  Because He loves me so.

Emily (Huntington) Miller, 1867.

633. Once in Royal David's City.

Irby. 8 7, 8 7, 7 7.   HENRY JOHN GAUNTLETT, 1849.

1. Once in roy-al Da-vid's cit-y Stood a low-ly cat-tle-shed,

Where a moth-er laid her Ba-by In a man-ger for His bed;

Ma-ry was that moth-er mild, Je-sus Christ her lit-tle Child. A-MEN.

Christmas.

2 He came down to earth from heaven,
   Who is God and Lord of all,
And His shelter was a stable,
   And His cradle was a stall;
With the poorest of the earth
Was our holy Saviour's birth.

3 Not in that poor lowly stable,
   With the oxen standing by,
We shall see Him, but in heaven,
   Set at God's right hand on high;
When like stars His children, crowned,
All in white shall wait around.

Cecil Frances (Humphreys) Alexander, 1848, a.

634. As Each Happy Christmas.

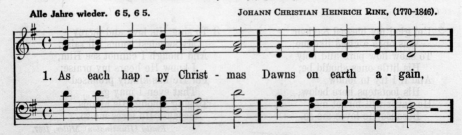

Alle Jahre wieder. 6 5, 6 5.   JOHANN CHRISTIAN HEINRICH RINK, (1770-1846).

1. As each hap-py Christ-mas Dawns on earth a-gain,

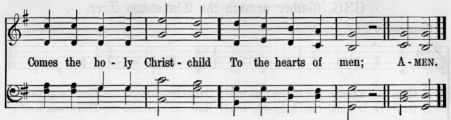

Comes the ho - ly Christ - child To the hearts of men; A - MEN.

Christmas.

2 Enters with His blessing
Into every home,
Guides and guards our footsteps,
As we go and come.

3 All unknown, beside me
He will ever stand,
And will safely lead me
With His own right hand.

Johann Wilhelm Hey, 1837.

635. When Christmas Morn Is Dawning.

När juldagsmorgon glimmar. 7 6, 7 6. German Folksong.

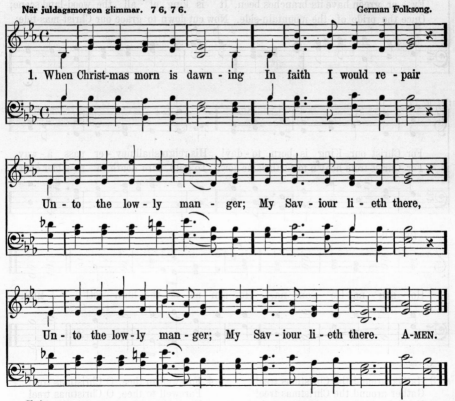

1. When Christ-mas morn is dawn - ing In faith I would re - pair

Un - to the low - ly man - ger; My Sav - iour li - eth there,

Un - to the low - ly man - ger; My Sav - iour li - eth there. A - MEN.

Christmas.

2 How kind, O loving Saviour,
To come from heaven above!
From sin and evil save us,
And keep us in Thy love.

3 We need Thee, blessèd Jesus,
Our dearest friend Thou art;
Forbid that we by sinning
Should grieve Thy loving heart.

Hemlandssånger.

636. Gather around the Christmas Tree.

Evergreen. 8 8, 8 9, 8 8. With Refrain.   Composer Unknown.

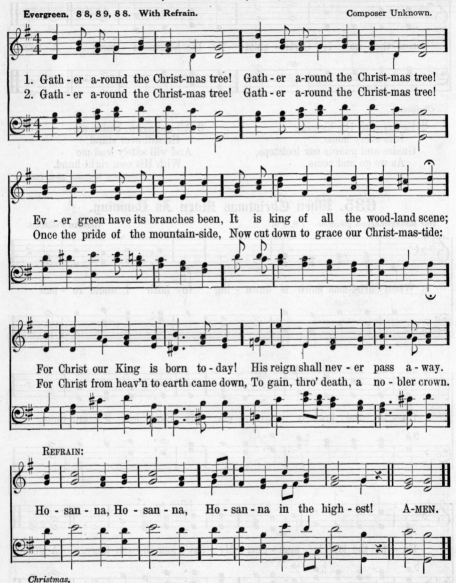

1. Gath - er a-round the Christ-mas tree! Gath - er a-round the Christ-mas tree!
2. Gath - er a-round the Christ-mas tree! Gath - er a-round the Christ-mas tree!

Ev - er green have its branches been, It is king of all the wood-land scene;
Once the pride of the mountain-side, Now cut down to grace our Christ-mas-tide:

For Christ our King is born to - day! His reign shall nev - er pass a - way.
For Christ from heav'n to earth came down, To gain, thro' death, a no - bler crown.

REFRAIN:

Ho - san - na, Ho - san - na, Ho - san - na in the high - est! A-MEN.

Christmas.

3 Gather around the Christmas tree!
Gather around the Christmas tree!
Every bough bears a burden now,—
They are gifts of love for us, we
trow;
For Christ is born, His love to show,
And give good gifts to men below.

4 Farewell to thee, O Christmas tree!
Farewell to thee, O Christmas tree!
Twelve months o'er, we shall meet once
more,
Merry welcome singing, as of yore:
For Christ now reigns, our Saviour dear,
And gives us Christmas every year!

Unknown.

637. Away in a Manger, No Crib for His Bed.

Away in a manger. 11 11, 11 11. **Composer Unknown.**

1. A - way in a man - ger, no crib for His bed,

The lit - tle Lord Je - sus laid down His sweet head;

The stars in the sky looked down where He lay,—

The lit - tle Lord Je - sus, a - sleep on the hay. A - MEN.

Christmas.

2 The cattle are lowing, the poor Baby wakes,
　But little Lord Jesus no crying He makes;
　I love Thee, Lord Jesus, look down from the sky,
　And stay by my cradle till morning is nigh.

Unknown.

638. When, His Salvation Bringing.

JOHAN ABRAHAM PETER SCHULZ, (1747-1800).
Adapted by HARRIET REYNOLDS SPAETH, (1845—).

Palm Sunday. 7 6, 7 6. D. With Refrain.

1. When, His sal-va-tion bring-ing, To Zi-on Je-sus came, The
chil-dren all stood sing-ing Ho-san-na to His Name. Nor did their
zeal of-fend Him, But as He rode a-long, He let them still attend Him, And smiled to hear their song. Ho-san-na, Ho-san-na, To
David's roy-al Son, Ho-san-na, Ho-san-na, Ho-san-na. A-MEN.

Palm Sunday.

2 And since the Lord retaineth
   His love for children still,
Though now as King He reigneth
   On Zion's heavenly hill;
We'll flock around His banner,
   Who sits upon the throne,
And cry aloud, hosanna
   To David's royal Son.

3 For should we fail proclaiming
   Our great Redeemer's praise,
The stones, our silence shaming,
   Would their hosannas raise.
But shall we only render
   The tribute of our words?
No! while our hearts are tender,
   They, too, shall be the Lord's.

Joshua King, 1830.

639. Glory Be to Jesus.

Caswall. 6 5, 6 5.   FRIEDRICH FILITZ, 1847.

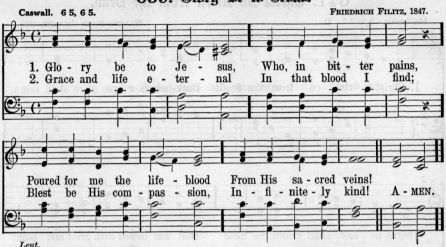

1. Glo - ry be to Je - sus, Who, in bit - ter pains,
2. Grace and life e - ter - nal In that blood I find;

Poured for me the life - blood From His sa - cred veins!
Blest be His com - pas - sion, In - fi - nite - ly kind! A - MEN.

Lent.

3 Blest through endless ages
  Be the precious stream
  Which from endless torments
  Doth the world redeem!

4 Abel's blood for vengeance
  Pleaded to the skies;
  But the blood of Jesus
  For our pardon cries!

5 Oft as earth exulting
  Wafts its praise on high,
  Angel-hosts rejoicing
  Make their glad reply.

6 Lift we then our voices,
  Swell the mighty flood;
  Louder still, and louder
  Praise the precious blood!

From the Italian.

640. Glory to the Father Give.

Sabbatsdag, hur skön du är. 7 7, 7 7.   JOEL BLOMQVIST.

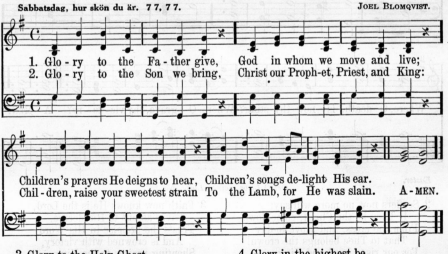

1. Glo - ry to the Fa - ther give, God in whom we move and live;
2. Glo - ry to the Son we bring, Christ our Proph-et, Priest, and King:

Children's prayers He deigns to hear, Children's songs de-light His ear.
Chil - dren, raise your sweetest strain To the Lamb, for He was slain. A - MEN.

3 Glory to the Holy Ghost,
  Who reclaims the sinner lost;
  Children's minds may He inspire,
  Touch their tongues with holy fire.

4 Glory in the highest be
  To the blessèd Trinity,
  For the gospel from above,
  For the word that God is love.

James Montgomery, 1825.

641. Christ Is Risen from the Dead.

Maidstone. 7 7, 7 7. D.   WALTER BOND GILBERT, 1862.

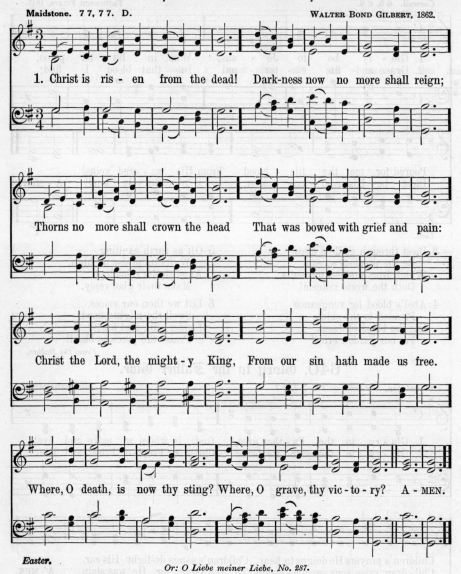

1. Christ is ris - en from the dead! Dark-ness now no more shall reign;

Thorns no more shall crown the head That was bowed with grief and pain:

Christ the Lord, the might - y King, From our sin hath made us free.

Where, O death, is now thy sting? Where, O grave, thy vic - to - ry? A - MEN.

Easter.

Or: O Liebe meiner Liebe, No. 287.

2 Scoffers now no more will say:
  If Thou be the Christ, come down
From the cross, and prove to-day
  That to Thee belongs the crown!
For our risen Lord and King
  From our sin hath made us free.
Where, O death, is now thy sting?
  Where, O grave, thy victory?

3 Faith now knows He is the Lord,
  Gives assent to His decree,
Trusts the promise in His Word,
  And is crowned with victory,
Shouting praises to the King,
  Who from sin hath made us free.
Where, O death, is now thy sting?
  Where, O grave, thy victory?

Henry Albert Becker, 1880.

642. Jesus, King of Glory.

St. Alban. 6 5, 6 5. D. With Refrain.   From FRANZ JOSEPH HAYDN, 1775.

1. Je-sus, King of glo - ry, Throned a-bove the sky, Jesus, ten-der Sav - iour,

Hear Thy chil-dren cry. Par-don our trans-gres-sions, Cleanse us from our sin,

REFRAIN:

By Thy Spir - it help us Heav'n-ly life to win. Je - sus, King of glo - ry,

Throned a-bove the sky, Je-sus, ten-der Sav-iour, Hear Thy children cry. A-MEN.

2 Help us ever steadfast
   In the faith to be:
In Thy Church's conflicts
   Fighting valiantly.
Loving Saviour, strengthen
   These weak hearts of ours,
Through Thy cross to conquer
   Crafty evil powers.

3 When the shadows lengthen,
   Show us, Lord, Thy way;
Through the darkness lead us
   To the heavenly day;
When our course is finished,
   Ended all the strife,
Grant us, with the faithful,
   Palms and crowns of life.

W. Hope Davison, 1887.

643. Humble Praises, Holy Jesus.

Vesper Hymn. 8 7, 8 7. With Refrain.   DIMITRI BORTNIANSKY, (1752-1828).

1. Hum-ble prais-es, ho-ly Je-sus, In-fant voic-es raise to Thee:

In Thy mer-cy, O re-ceive us! Suf-fer us Thy lambs to be.

REFRAIN:

Hal-le-lu-jah, sweet-ly sing-ing, Joy-ful trib-ute now we bring.

Hal-le-lu-jah, Hal-le-lu-jah! Hal-le-lu-jah, to our King! A-MEN.

2 Gracious Saviour, be Thou with us;
    Let Thy mercy richly flow:
Give Thy Spirit, blessèd Jesus,
    Light and life on us bestow.

Composite.

644. Saviour, Like a Shepherd Lead Us.

Shepherd. 8 7, 8 7. D.   WILLIAM BATCHELDER BRADBURY, (1816–1868).

1. Sav-iour, like a shep-herd lead us, Much we need Thy tend'rest care;

In Thy pleas-ant pas-tures feed us, For our use Thy fold pre-pare.

Bless-ed Je-sus, bless-ed Je-sus, Thou hast bought us, Thine we are;

Bless-ed Je-sus, bless-ed Je-sus, Thou hast bought us, Thine we are. A-MEN.

2 Thou hast promised to receive us,
  Poor and sinful though we be;
Thou hast mercy to relieve us,
  Grace to cleanse, and power to free.
Blessèd Jesus, blessèd Jesus,
  Let us early turn to Thee.

3 Early let us seek Thy favor,
  Early let us do Thy will;
Blessèd Lord and only Saviour,
  With Thy love our bosom fill.
Blessèd Jesus, blessèd Jesus,
  Thou hast loved us, love us still.

Unknown.

645. O What Praises Shall We Render?

Ripley. 8 7, 8 7. D.

From a Gregorian Chant,
by LOWELL MASON, 1839.

1. O what prais-es shall we ren-der To the Lord who reigns a-bove,

For His mer-cies, con-stant, ten-der, For His con-de-scend-ing love?

Though we oft-en have of-fend-ed, And transgressed His ho-ly will,

Still has He our souls be-friend-ed; We may call Him Fa-ther still. A-MEN.

2 Heavenly Father, Thou hast taught us
  Thus to seek Thee in our youth;
Hitherto Thy grace hath brought us,
  Lead us onward in Thy truth.
We are weak, do Thou uphold us,
  And from every snare defend;
Let Thy mighty arms enfold us,
  Save us, keep us, to the end.

3 O our Father, great and glorious!
  Draw our youthful hearts to Thee;
Let Thy grace be there victorious,
  Let Thy love our portion be.
May we know Thy great salvation,
  Serve and love Thee all our days;
Then in heaven, Thy habitation,
  Join to sing Thine endless praise.

John Burton, Jr., (1803-1877).

646. Saviour, Who Thy Flock Art Feeding.

Weston. 8 7, 8 7. D.   JOHN EDWARD ROE, (1838–1871).

1. Sav - iour, who Thy flock art feed - ing, With a shep-herd's kind-est care,

All the fee - ble gen - tly lead - ing, While the lambs Thy bos - om share,

Now, these lit - tle ones re - ceiv - ing, Fold them in Thy gra-cious arm;

There, we know, Thy Word be-liev-ing, On - ly there se-cure from harm. A-MEN.

Baptism.

2 Never, from Thy pasture roving,
  Let them be the lion's prey;
Let Thy tenderness, so loving,
  Keep them through life's dangerous way.
Then within Thy fold eternal
  Let them find a resting-place:
Feed in pastures ever vernal,
  Drink the rivers of Thy grace.

William Augustus Muhlenberg, 1826.

647. Come to the Saviour, Make No Delay.

Come to the Saviour. 9 9, 9 6. With Refrain.   GEORGE FREDERICK ROOT, 1870.

1. Come to the Sav-iour, make no de-lay; Here in His Word He's
shown us the way; Here in our midst He's stand-ing to-day,

REFRAIN:

Ten-der-ly say-ing, "Come!" Joy-ful, joy-ful will the meet-ing be,
When from sin our hearts are pure and free; And we shall gath-er,
Sav-iour, with Thee In our e-ter-nal home. A-MEN.

2 "Suffer the children!" O hear His voice,
Let every heart leap forth and rejoice,
And let us freely make Him our choice;
Do not delay, but come!

3 Think once again He's with us to-day;
Heed now His blest commands, and obey;
Hear now His accents tenderly say,
"Will you, My children, come?"

George Frederick Root, 1870.

648. Yield Not to Temptation.

Yield not to temptation. 6 5, 6 5. D. With Refrain.   HORATIO RICHMOND PALMER, 1868.

1. Yield not to temp-ta-tion, For yield-ing is sin; Each vic-t'ry will
help you Some oth-er to win. Fight man-ful-ly on-ward,
Dark pas-sions sub-due; Look ev-er to Je-sus, He'll car-ry you through.

REFRAIN:

Ask the Sav-iour to help you, Com-fort, strengthen, and keep you;
He is will-ing to aid you, He will car-ry you through. A-MEN.

Copyright. 1868. by H. R. Palmer.

2 Shun evil companions;
   Bad language disdain;
God's Name hold in reverence,
   Nor take it in vain.
Be thoughtful and earnest,
   Kind-hearted and true;
Look ever to Jesus,
   He'll carry you through.

3 To him that o'ercometh,
   God giveth a crown;
Through faith we shall conquer,
   Though often cast down.
He who is our Saviour
   Our strength will renew;
Look ever to Jesus,
   He'll carry you through.

Horatio Richmond Palmer, 1868.

649. I Think, When I Read That Sweet Story of Old.

Sweet Story. 12 10, 12 10. D.   English Melody.

1. I think, when I read that sweet sto - ry of old, When Je - sus was here a-mong men, How He called lit - tle chil-dren as lambs to His fold, I should like to have been with them then. I wish that His hand had been placed on my head, That His arm had been thrown around me, And that I might have seen His kind look when He said, "Let the lit-tle ones come un - to Me." A-MEN.

2 Yet still to His footstool in prayer I may go,
  And ask for a share in His love;
  And if only I earnestly seek Him below,
  I shall see Him and hear Him above,
  In that beautiful place He has gone to prepare
  For all who are washed and forgiven;
  Full many dear children are gathering there,
  "For of such is the kingdom of heaven."

3 But thousands and thousands who wander and fall
  Never heard of that heavenly home:
  I should like them to know there is room for them all,
  And that Jesus has bid them to come.
  And O how I long for that glorious time,
  The sweetest and brightest and best,
  When the dear little children of every clime
  Shall crowd to His arms and be blest!

Jemima Thompson Luke, 1853.

650. I Am Jesus' Little Lamb.

Weil ich Jesu Schäflein bin. 7 7, 8 8, 7 7.　　　　　　　　　　　　　　German.

1. I am Je-sus' lit-tle lamb, There-fore glad at heart I am;
Je-sus loves me, Je-sus knows me, All that's good and fair He shows me,
Tends me ev'-ry day the same, E-ven calls me by my name. A-MEN.

2 Out and in I safely go,
  Want and hunger never know;
  Soft green pastures He discloseth,
  Where His happy flock reposeth;
  When I faint or thirsty be,
  To the brook He leadeth me.

3 Should not I be glad all day
  In this blessèd fold to stay,
  By this holy Shepherd tended,
  Whose kind arms, when life is ended,
  Bear me to the world of light?
  Yes, O yes, my lot is bright.

Henrietta Louise von Hayn, 1778.

651. When He Cometh, When He Cometh.

When He cometh. 8 6, 8 5. With Refrain.

GEORGE FREDERICK ROOT, 1866.

1. When He com-eth, when He com-eth To make up His jew-els,

All His jew-els, pre-cious jew-els, His loved and His own,

REFRAIN:

Like the stars of the morn-ing, His bright crown a-dorn-ing,

They shall shine in their beau-ty, Bright gems for His crown. A-MEN.

Copyright by The John Church Co.

2 He will gather, He will gather
  The gems for His kingdom;
All the pure ones, all the bright ones,
  His loved and His own.

3 Little children, little children
  Who love their Redeemer
Are the jewels, precious jewels,
  His loved and His own.

William Orcutt Cushing, (1823—).

652. Praise the Lord of Heaven.

Pitts. 6 5, 6 5. D.   Composer Unknown.

1. Praise the Lord of heav - en, Praise Him in the height,

Praise Him, all ye an - gels, Praise Him, stars of light:

Praise Him, clouds and wa - [ters, Which a - bove the skies,

When His word com - mand - ed, Did es - tab-lished rise. A - MEN.

Or: David, No. 507.

2 Praise the Lord, ye fountains
   Of the deeps and seas,
Rocks, and hills, and mountains,
   Cedars, and all trees;
Praise Him, clouds and vapors,
   Snow and hail, and fire,
Stormy wind, fulfilling
   Only His desire.

3 Birds and beasts, O praise Him,
   Princes and all kings:
Praise Him, men and maidens,
   All created things:
For the Name of God is
   Excellent alone,
Over earth His footstool,
   Over heaven His throne.

Thomas Briarly Browne, 1844.

653. Around the Throne of God in Heaven.

Children's Praises. C. M. With Refrain.   Arranged by HENRY E. MATTHEWS, about 1853.

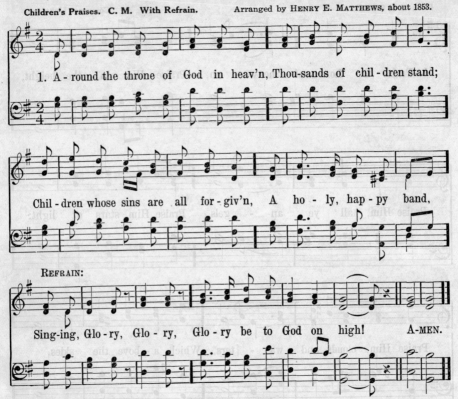

1. A-round the throne of God in heav'n, Thou-sands of chil-dren stand;

Chil-dren whose sins are all for-giv'n, A ho-ly, hap-py band,

REFRAIN:

Sing-ing, Glo-ry, Glo-ry, Glo-ry be to God on high!   A-MEN.

2 In flowing robes of spotless white
    See every one arrayed;
  Dwelling in everlasting light,
    And joys that never fade.

3 What brought them to that world above,
    That heaven so bright and fair,
  Where all is peace and joy and love;
    How came those children there?

4 Because the Saviour shed His blood
    To wash away their sin:
  Bathed in that pure and precious flood,
    Behold them white and clean!

5 On earth they sought the Saviour's grace,
    On earth they loved His Name;
  So now they see His blessèd face,
    And stand before the Lamb.

Anne Houlditch Shepherd, 1842.

654. Saviour, Teach Me Day by Day.

Ferrier. 7 7, 7 7.   JOHN BACCHUS DYKES, 1862.

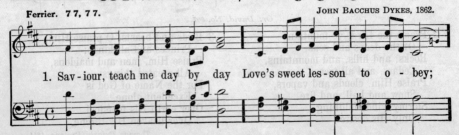

1. Sav-iour, teach me day by day Love's sweet les-son to o-bey;

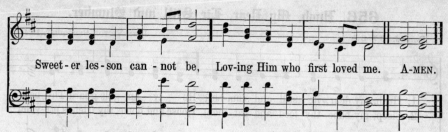

Sweet-er les-son can-not be, Lov-ing Him who first loved me. A-MEN.

2 With a childlike heart of love,
At Thy bidding may I move;
Prompt to serve and follow Thee,
Loving Him who first loved me.

3 Teach me all Thy steps to trace,
Strong to follow in Thy grace;
Learning how to love from Thee,
Loving Him who first loved me.

4 Love in loving finds employ,
In obedience all her joy;
Ever new that joy will be,
Loving Him who first loved me.

5 Thus may I rejoice to show
That I feel the love I owe;
Singing, till Thy face I see,
Of His love who first loved me.

Jane Elizabeth Leeson, 1842. a.

655. Take My Life, and Let It Be.

Mercy. 7 7, 7 7. Arranged from Louis Moreau Gottschalk, 1867.

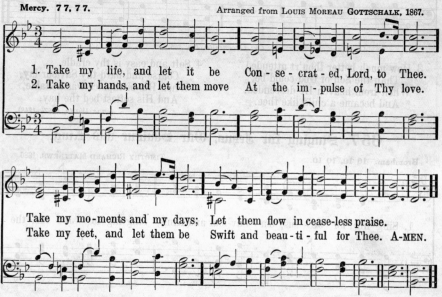

1. Take my life, and let it be Con-se-crat-ed, Lord, to Thee.
2. Take my hands, and let them move At the im-pulse of Thy love.

Take my mo-ments and my days; Let them flow in cease-less praise.
Take my feet, and let them be Swift and beau-ti-ful for Thee. A-MEN.

3 Take my voice, and let me sing,
Always, only, for my King.
Take my lips, and let them be
Filled with messages from Thee.

4 Take my silver and my gold;
Not a mite would I withhold.
Take my intellect, and use
Every power as Thou shalt choose.

5 Take my will, and make it Thine;
It shall be no longer mine.
Take my heart, it is Thine own;
It shall be Thy royal throne.

6 Take my love; my Lord, I pour
At Thy feet its treasure-store.
Take myself, and I will be
Ever, only, all for Thee.

Frances Ridley Havergal, 1874.

656. Hush, My Dear, Lie Still and Slumber.

Donald. 8 7, 8 7.

JOHN VICTOR BERGQUIST, 1924.

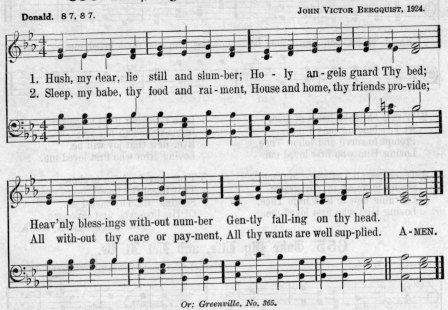

1. Hush, my dear, lie still and slum-ber; Ho - ly an-gels guard Thy bed;
2. Sleep, my babe, thy food and rai-ment, House and home, thy friends pro-vide;

Heav'nly bless-ings with-out num-ber Gen-tly fall-ing on thy head.
All with-out thy care or pay-ment, All thy wants are well sup-plied. A-MEN.

Or: Greenville, No. 365.

3 How much better thou'rt attended
  Than the Son of God could be,
When from heaven He descended,
  And became a child like thee.

4 Soft and easy is thy cradle,
  Coarse and hard thy Saviour lay,
When His birthplace was a stable,
  And His softest bed the hay.
                Isaac Watts, (1674-1748).

657. Singing for Jesus, Our Saviour and King.

Bromham. 10 10, 10 10.

TIMOTHY RICHARD MATTHEWS, 1886.

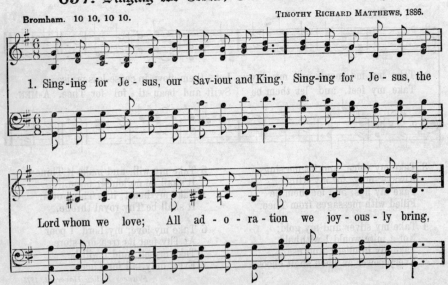

1. Sing-ing for Je - sus, our Sav-iour and King, Sing-ing for Je - sus, the

Lord whom we love; All ad - o - ra - tion we joy - ous-ly bring,

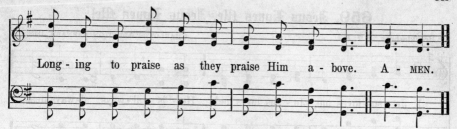

Long - ing to praise as they praise Him a - bove. A - MEN.

2 Singing for Jesus, and trying to win
Many to love Him, and join in the song;
Calling the weary and wandering in,
Rolling the chorus of gladness along.

3 Singing for Jesus, our Shepherd and Guide,
Singing for gladness of heart that He gives;
Singing for wonder and praise that He died,
Singing for blessing and joy that He lives.

4 Singing for Jesus—yes, singing for joy;
Thus will we praise Him, and tell out His love,
Till He shall call us to brighter employ,
Singing for Jesus, forever above.

Frances Ridley Havergal, (1836–1879).

658. Jesus, High in Glory.

Alle Jahre wieder. 6 5, 6 5.   JOHANN CHRISTIAN HEINRICH RINK, (1770-1846).

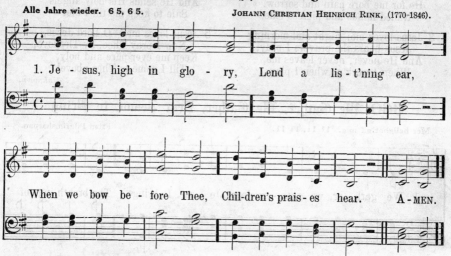

1. Je - sus, high in glo - ry, Lend a lis - t'ning ear,

When we bow be - fore Thee, Chil-dren's prais - es hear. A - MEN.

2 Though Thou art so holy,
Heaven's Almighty King,
Thou wilt stoop to listen,
When Thy praise we sing.

3 We are little children,
Weak and apt to stray;
Saviour, guide and keep us
In the heavenly way.

4 Save us, Lord, from sinning;
Watch us day by day;
Help us now to love Thee;
Take our sins away.

5 Then, when Jesus calls us
To our heavenly home,
We would gladly answer,
Saviour, Lord, we come.

Harriet Burn MacKeever, 1847.

659. Jesus Loves Me, Jesus Loves Me!

Brocklesbury. 8 7, 8 7.

CHARLOTTE ALINGTON BARNARD, 1868.

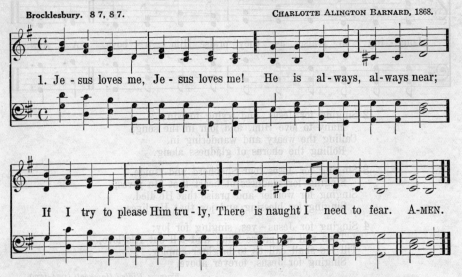

1. Je - sus loves me, Je - sus loves me! He is al - ways, al - ways near;

If I try to please Him tru - ly, There is naught I need to fear. A-MEN.

2 Jesus loves me; well I know it,
  For to save my soul He died;
  He for me bore pain and sorrow,
  Nailèd hands and piercèd side.

3 Jesus loves me; night and morning
  Jesus hears the prayers I pray;
  And He never, never leaves me,
  When I work or when I play.

4 Jesus loves me; and He watches
  Over me with loving eye,
  And He sends His holy angels
  Safe to keep me till I die.

5 Jesus loves me;—O Lord Jesus,
  Now I pray Thee, by Thy love,
  Keep me ever pure and holy,
  Till I come to Thee above!

Unknown.

660. We Gather, We Gather, Dear Jesus, to Bring.

Mer helighet gif mig. 11 11, 11 11.

From Pilgrimsharpan.

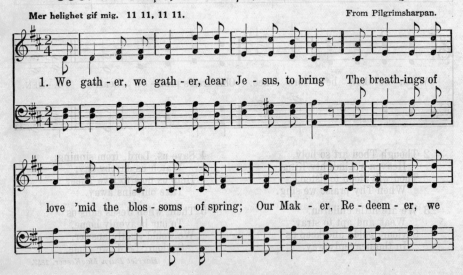

1. We gath - er, we gath - er, dear Je - sus, to bring The breath-ings of

love 'mid the blos - soms of spring; Our Mak - er, Re - deem - er, we

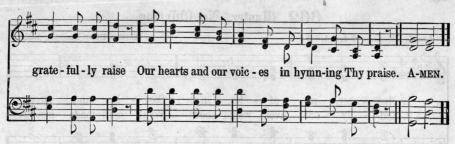

grate-ful-ly raise Our hearts and our voic-es in hymn-ing Thy praise. A-MEN.

2 When stooping to earth from the brightness of **heaven,**
Thy blood for our ransom so freely was given,
Thou deignedst to listen while children adored,
With joyful hosannas, the Blest of the Lord.

3 Those arms which embraced little children of **old**
Still love to encircle the lambs of the fold;
That grace which inviteth the wandering **home**
Hath never forbidden the youngest to come.

4 Hosanna! Hosanna! Great Teacher, we raise
Our hearts and our voices in hymning Thy **praise**
For precept and promise so graciously given,
For blessings of earth, and for glories of heaven.

J. N. Van Harlingen.

661. Jesus, Tender Shepherd, Hear Me.

Evening Prayer. 8 7, 8 7.   JOHN STAINER, 1898.

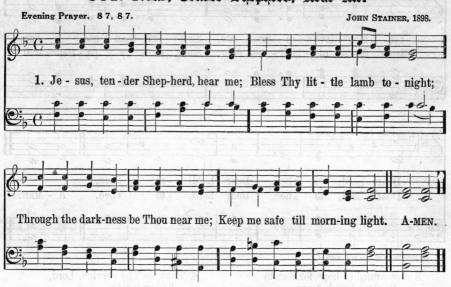

1. Je-sus, ten-der Shep-herd, hear me; Bless Thy lit-tle lamb to-night;

Through the dark-ness be Thou near me; Keep me safe till morn-ing light. A-MEN.

Or: Brocklesbury, No. 659.

2 All this day Thy hand has led me,
  And I thank Thee for Thy care;
Thou hast clothed me, warmed, and fed me,
  Listen to my evening prayer.

3 Let my sins be all forgiven;
  Bless the friends I love so well:
Take me, Lord, at last to heaven,
  Happy there with Thee to dwell.

Mary (Lundie) Duncan. 1839.

662. Master, No Offering.

Love's Offering. 6 4, 6 4, 6 6 4 4.   EDWIN POND PARKER, 1888.

1. Mas - ter, no of - fer - ing Cost - ly and sweet
2. Dai - ly our lives would show Weak - ness made strong,

May we, like Mag - da - lene, Lay at Thy feet;
Toil - some and gloom - y ways Bright - ened with song;

Yet may love's in - cense rise, Sweet - er than sac - ri - fice,
Some deeds of kind - ness done, Some souls by pa - tience won,

Dear Lord, to Thee, Dear Lord, to Thee.
Dear Lord, to Thee, Dear Lord, to Thee. A - MEN.

By permission of Edwin P. Parker.

3 Some word of hope for hearts
   Burdened with fears,
Some balm of peace for eyes
   Blinded with tears;
Some dews of mercy shed,
Some wayward footsteps led,
   Dear Lord, to Thee.

4 Thus, in Thy service, Lord,
   Till eventide
Closes the day of life,
   May we abide.
And when earth's labors cease,
Bid us depart in peace,
   Dear Lord, to Thee.

Edwin Pond Parker, 1888.

663. O Paradise! O Paradise!

Paradise. 8 6, 8 6, 6 6, 6 6.

JOSEPH BARNBY, 1866.

1. O Par - a - dise! O Par - a - dise! Who doth not crave for rest?

Who would not seek the hap - py land Where they that loved are blest;

REFRAIN:
Where loy - al hearts and true

Where loy - - - al hearts and true Stand ev - er in the light,

All rap - ture thro' and thro', In God's most ho - ly sight? A - MEN.

2 O Paradise! O Paradise!
The world is growing old;
Who would not be at rest and free
Where love is never cold?

3 O Paradise! O Paradise!
We long to sin no more;
We long to be as pure on earth
As on thy spotless shore.

4 O Paradise! O Paradise!
We shall not wait for long;
E'en now the loving ear may catch
Faint fragments of thy song.

5 Lord Jesus, King of Paradise,
O keep us in Thy love,
And guide us to that happy land
Of perfect rest above.

Frederick William Faber, 1862, a.

664. Praise God, from Whom All Blessings Flow.

LOUIS BOURGEOIS.
Genevan Psalter, 1551.

Old Hundredth. L. M.

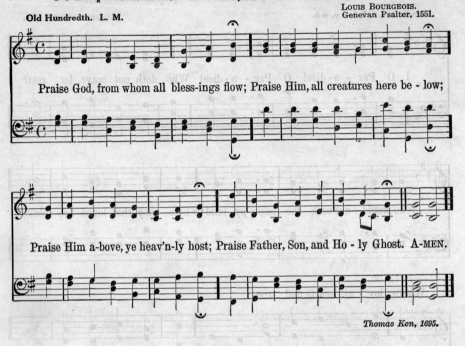

Praise God, from whom all bless-ings flow; Praise Him, all creatures here be - low;

Praise Him a-bove, ye heav'n-ly host; Praise Father, Son, and Ho - ly Ghost. A-MEN.

Thomas Ken, 1695.

665. To Father, Son, and Holy Ghost.

HART'S Psalter, 1615.

Dundee. C. M.

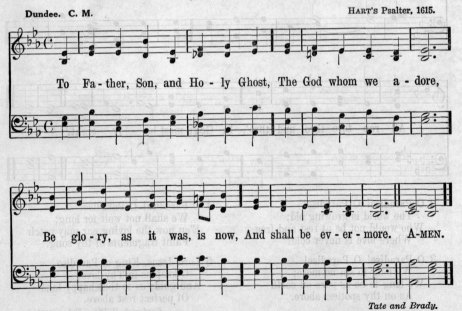

To Fa - ther, Son, and Ho - ly Ghost, The God whom we a - dore,

Be glo - ry, as it was, is now, And shall be ev - er - more. A-MEN.

Tate and Brady.

666. Glory Be to God the Father.

Hela världen fröjdes Herran.   8 7, 8 7, 7 7.   Swedish, 1689.

{Glo-ry be to God the Fa-ther, Glo-ry be to God the Son,}
{Glo-ry be to God the Spir-it, Ev-er-last-ing Three in One:}

Him let heav'n and earth a-dore, Now, hence-forth, and ev-er-more.   A-MEN.

667. To God the Father, Son.

St. Thomas.   S. M.   AARON WILLIAMS, 1770.

To God the Fa-ther, Son,   And Spir-it, One in Three,

Be glo-ry, as it was, is now, And shall for-ev-er be.   A-MEN.

John Wesley.

668. To God, the Ever-glorious.

Valet will ich dir geben. 7 6, 7 6. D.   MELCHIOR TESCHNER, 1613.

{To God, the Ev - er - glo - rious, The Fa - ther and the Son,}
{And Spir - it All - vic - to - rious, Thrice ho - ly Three in One;}

The God of our sal - va - tion, Whom earth and heav'n a - dore,

Praise, glo - ry, ad - o - ra - tion, Be now and ev - er - more. A - MEN.

Or: Missionary Hymn, No. 367.

669. Praise the God of All Creation.

Spanish Melody.
Autumn. 8 7, 8 7. D.   FRANCOIS HIPPOLITE BARTHELEMON? (1741-1808).

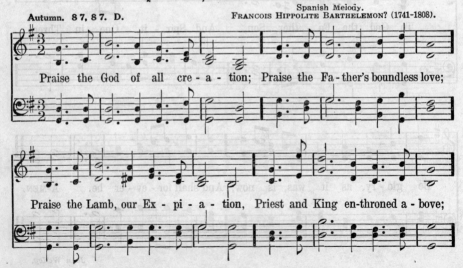

Praise the God of all cre - a - tion; Praise the Fa - ther's boundless love;

Praise the Lamb, our Ex - pi - a - tion, Priest and King en - throned a - bove;

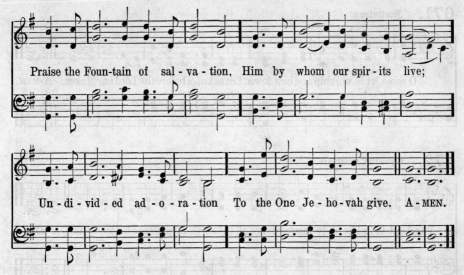

Praise the Foun-tain of sal - va - tion, Him by whom our spir - its live;

Un - di - vid - ed ad - o - ra - tion To the One Je - ho - vah give. A - MEN.

670. All Praise and Thanks to God.

Nun danket alle Gott. 6 7, 6 7, 6 6, 6 6. JOHANN CRÜGER, 1648.

{ All praise and thanks to God The Fa - ther, now be giv - en, }
{ The Son and Him who reigns With them in high - est heav - en; }

The One e - ter - nal God, Whom earth and heav'n a - dore;

For thus it was, is now, And shall be ev - er - more. A - MEN.

Martin Rinkart, 1630.

671. Invitatory.

O come, let us worship and bow down: Let us kneel before the Lord our Maker. A-MEN.

672. Opening Sentence.

The Lord is in His ho-ly tem-ple: Let all the earth keep silence before Him. A-MEN.

673. Opening Sentence.

GEORGE FREDERICK ROOT, (1820–1895).

The Lord is in His ho-ly tem-ple, The Lord is in His ho-ly tem-ple;

Let all the earth keep si-lence, Let all the earth keep si-lence be-

fore Him, Keep si-lence, Keep si-lence be-fore Him. A-MEN.

Used by permission of the John Church Co.

674. 𝕺𝖕𝖊𝖓𝖎𝖓𝖌 𝕾𝖊𝖓𝖙𝖊𝖓𝖈𝖊.

W. A. C. CRUICKSHANK.

Ho - ly, Ho - ly, Ho - ly, Lord God of hosts,

Heav'n and earth are full of Thy glo - ry: Glo - ry

be to Thee, O Lord Most High. A - - MEN.

675. *Invocation.*

Let the words of my mouth, And the med-i-ta-tion of my heart, Be ac-cept-a-ble in Thy sight, O Lord, my Strength and my Re-deem-er. A-MEN.

676. *Offertory.*

Arranged from LUDWIG VAN BEETHOVEN, (1770-1823).

All things come of Thee, O Lord: And of Thine own have we giv-en Thee. A-MEN.

677. *Offertory.*

EDWARD OSLER, 1836.   WILLIAM CROFT, 1708.

Do Thou, O Lord, our gifts ac-cept, And with Thy bless-ing speed;

Bless us in giv-ing; great-ly bless Our gifts to them that need. A-MEN.

678. *Offertory.*

All that is in the heav'n and earth is Thine, O Lord.

And of Thine own have we giv - en Thee. A - MEN.

679. *Response.*

JOHN STAINER, (1840–1901).

p

Lord, have mer - cy up - on us, And in - cline our hearts to

p

keep Thy law. Lord, have mer - cy up - on us, And

Slowly. *pp*

write all these Thy laws in our hearts, We be - seech Thee. A - MEN.

680. Response.

CLAUS AUGUST WENDELL, 1924.   Arranged from CHARLES FRANCOIS GOUNOD, (1818–1893).

Fa - ther in heav - en, hum-bly to Thee we pray, Keep us in ho - ly
still - ness, That we may hear Thy voice to - day. A - MEN.

681. Communion Response.

GERHARD THEODORE ALEXIS, 1924.

O Lamb of God,
O Lamb of God, That tak - est a - way the sin of the world, Have
mer - cy, have mer - cy up - on .... us. O Lamb of God,

O Lamb of God, That tak - est a - way the sin of the

world, Grant us, grant us, Grant us Thy peace.

682. Response.

Felix Mendelssohn, (1809-1847).
From Song of Praise.

All that hath life and breath, Sing to the Lord; All that hath life and breath,

Lord, ... Hal - le - lu - jah,

Sing to the Lord, Hal-le - lu - jah, Hal-le - lu - jah, Sing to the Lord.

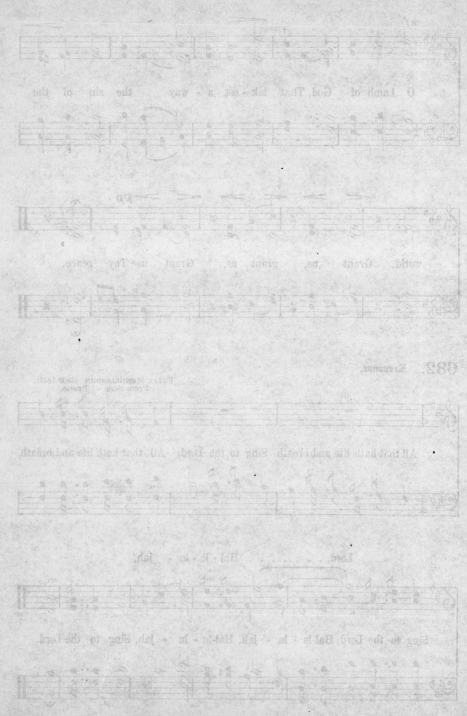

Order of Service

The Service

Morning

The Service shall begin with an appropriate **Hymn**. *During the singing the* **Minister** *shall proceed to the Altar and kneel in prayer. After the singing he shall rise, turn to the Congregation, and sing or say:**

Advent, Christmas, and Epiphany Seasons.   OSKAR LINDBERG.

Ho - ly, Ho - ly, Ho - - ly is the Lord . . . . of Hosts! The whole earth is full of His glo - - ry.

Lenten Season.   OSCAR BLOM.

Ho - ly, Ho - ly, Ho - ly is the Lord of Hosts! The whole earth is full of His glo - - ry.

* For the Introit which may be used at this place in the Service see pp. 581 to 593.

Easter and Pentecost Seasons.

HARALD FRYKLÖF.

Ho - ly, Ho - ly, Ho — ly is the Lord of Hosts!

The whole earth ... is full of His glo - - ry.

Trinity Season.*

Ho - ly, Ho - ly, Ho — ly is the Lord of Hosts!

The whole earth . . . is full of His glo - - ry.

* Melody and tenor may be sung as a duet.

Thereafter the **Minister** *shall say:*

The Lord is in His holy temple; His throne is in heaven. The Lord is nigh unto them that are of an humble and contrite spirit. He heareth the supplications of the penitent and inclineth to their prayers. Let us therefore draw near with boldness unto His throne of grace and confess our sins:

The Confession of Sins

The **Minister** *shall turn to the Altar, and with the* **Congregation** *unite in the following Confession of Sins:*

Holy and righteous God, merciful Father, we confess unto Thee that we are by nature sinful and unclean, and that we have sinned against Thee by thought, word, and deed. We have not loved Thee above all things, nor our neighbor as ourselves, and are worthy, therefore, to be cast away from Thy presence if Thou shouldst judge us according to our sins. But Thou hast promised, O heavenly Father, to receive with tender mercy all penitent sinners who turn unto Thee and with a living faith seek refuge in Thy Fatherly compassion and in the merits of the Saviour, Jesus Christ. Their transgressions Thou wilt not regard, nor impute unto them their sins. Relying upon Thy promise, we confidently beseech Thee to be merciful and gracious unto us and to forgive us all our sins, to the praise and glory of Thy Holy Name.

May the Almighty, Eternal God, in His infinite mercy and for the sake of our Saviour, Jesus Christ, forgive all our sins, and give us grace to amend our lives, and with Him obtain eternal life. Amen.

Or, the following may be used during Lent and on Holy Days:

Have mercy upon me, O God, according to Thy lovingkindness: according to the multitude of Thy tender mercies blot out my transgressions. Wash me thoroughly from mine iniquity, and cleanse me from my sin. For I know my transgressions; and my sin is ever before me. Against Thee, Thee only, have I sinned, and done that which is evil in Thy sight. Hide Thy face from my sins, and blot out all mine iniquities. Create in me a clean heart, O God; and renew a right spirit within me. Cast me not away from Thy presence; and take not Thy Holy Spirit from me.

Heavenly Father, hear my prayer for the sake of Thy Son, Jesus Christ. Amen.

Kyrie

The **Minister** *and the* **Congregation** *shall rise and sing:*

Adbent, Christmas, and Epiphany Seasons.

I.   Nürnberger Agende, 1639.

Lord, ... have mer - cy up - on us!

Christ, ... have mer - cy up - on us!

Lord, ... have mer - cy up - on us! . . . . *Modulation to Gloria in D, p. 568.*

II.   From FELTON.

Lord, have mer - cy up - on us! Christ, have mer - cy

up - on us! Lord, have mer - cy up - on us!

Lenten Season.

Bohemian Brethren, 1556.

Lord, ... have mer - cy up - on us! . . . .

Christ, ... have mer - cy up - on us! . . . .

Lord, ... have mer - cy up-on us! . . . .

Modulation to
Gloria in F, p. 568.

Easter and Pentecost Seasons.

Bjuråkers Handskrift, prior to 1550.

Lord, ... have mer - - cy up - on us!

Christ, .. have mer - - cy up - on us! ....

Lord, ... have mer - - - - cy up - - - on us!

Trinity Season. May also be used during *Lenten Season.*

I.

Bjuråkers Handskrift, prior to 1550.

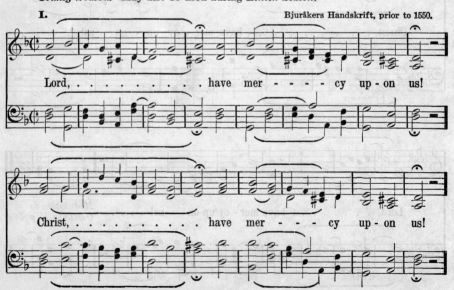

Lord, ... have mer - - - - cy up - on us!

Christ, ... have mer - - - cy up - on us!

Lord, ... have mer - - - - cy up-on us!   *Modulation to*
Gloria in F, p. 568.

II.   GERHARD THEODORE ALEXIS, 1925.

Lord, ... have mer - cy up - on us!   Christ, ... have

mer - cy up - on us! . . . . . .   Lord, . . . have mer - cy

up - on us! . . . . .   *Modulation to Gloria in F, p. 568.*

Gloria in Excelsis

The Minister, turning to the Congregation, shall sing or say:

Advent, Christmas, and Epiphany Seasons.

Adapted from
Bjuråkers Handskrift.

Glo - - - - ry be to God on high, and on earth.....

peace, good will . . . . toward men. *Modulation to F.*

Lenten and Trinity Seasons.

Bjuråkers Handskrift,
prior to 1550.

Glo - ry be to God on high, and on earth. . . . .

peace, good will . . . . toward men. *Modulation to F.*

Easter and Pentecost Seasons.

A. O.

Glo - ry be to God . . on high, and on earth peace, good will . . . toward men.

*The **Minister** shall turn to the Altar, and with the **Congregation** shall sing:*

NICOLAUS DECIUS ? 1539.

All glo-ry be to Thee, Most High, To Thee all ad-o-

ra-tion! In grace and truth Thou draw-est nigh To of-fer

us sal-va-tion. Thou show-est Thy good will to

men, And peace shall reign on earth a-gain; We praise Thy

Name for-ev-er. *Modulation to Bb.*

Modulation to G minor. (Lent.)

On Festival Days, or on any Sunday except during Lent, the following **(I. or II.)** *may be sung instead of "All glory be to Thee, Most High."*

I.

We praise Thee, we wor-ship Thee, We give thanks to Thee for Thy great glo-ry, O Lord God, Heav-en-ly King, God the Fa-ther Al-might-y! O Lord, the On-ly-be-got-ten Son, Je-sus Christ! Ho-ly Spir-it, Spir-it of grace and of truth and of peace! .. A-men, A-men, A------men.

Modulation to B♭.

The Salutation

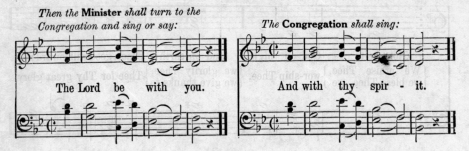

Then the **Minister** *shall turn to the Congregation and sing or say:*

The Lord be with you.

The **Congregation** *shall sing:*

And with thy spir - it.

Lenten Season

The **Minister:**

The Lord be with you.

The **Congregation:**

And with thy spir - it.

Then the **Minister** *shall say:*

Let us pray.

The Collect

The **Minister,** *turning to the Altar, shall read on Sundays and Festival Days the proper Collect. On special occasions one of the following may be used:*

O Lord God, Heavenly Father, Thou Who hast no pleasure in the death of the wicked, but that they turn from their way and live: we pray Thee that Thou wouldst mercifully avert the punishment that our sins deserve, for the sake of Jesus Christ, our Lord.

Or:

We beseech Thee, Almighty God, Heavenly Father, to grant us a true faith, a firm hope in Thy mercy, and a sincere love to our fellow men, through Jesus Christ, our Lord.

The **Congregation** *shall sing:*

A - - - men.

Lenten Season.

A - - - men.

The Epistle

*The **Minister** shall turn to the Congregation and say:*

The Epistle for (*here he shall name the Sunday or Festival Day*) is written in...........

*The Epistle ended, the **Minister** shall turn to the Altar, and the **Congregation** shall be seated.   A **Hymn** (**The Gradual**) shall then be sung.*

The Gospel

*The Hymn ended, the **Minister** shall turn to the Congregation and say:*

Lift up your hearts unto the Lord and hear the Gospel for the Day as it is written in......

*The **Congregation** shall arise, and the Gospel for the Day shall be read.   The Gospel ended, the **Minister** and the **Congregation** shall say*

The Apostles' Creed

I believe in God the Father Almighty, Maker of heaven and earth;

And in Jesus Christ His only Son, our Lord: Who was conceived by the Holy Spirit, Born of the Virgin Mary; Suffered under Pontius Pilate, Was crucified, dead and buried; He descended into hell; The third day He rose again from the dead; He ascended into heaven, And sitteth on the right hand of God the Father Almighty; From thence He shall come to judge the quick and the dead.

I believe in the Holy Spirit; The Holy Christian Church, the Communion of saints; The Forgiveness of sins; The Resurrection of the body; And the Life everlasting.   Amen.

Or:

The Nicene Creed

I believe in one God, the Father Almighty, Maker of heaven and earth, And of all things visible and invisible;

And in one Lord Jesus Christ, the Only-begotten Son of God, Begotten of His Father before all worlds, God of God, Light of Light, Very God of Very God, Begotten, not made, Being of one substance with the Father, By Whom all things were made; Who, for us men, and for our salvation, came down from heaven, and was incarnate by the Holy Spirit of the Virgin Mary, and was made man; and was crucified also for us under Pontius Pilate. He suffered and was buried; And the third day He rose again, according to the Scriptures; And ascended into heaven, and sitteth on the right hand of the Father; And He shall come again with glory to judge both the quick and the dead; Whose kingdom shall have no end.

And I believe in the Holy Spirit, the Lord and Giver of Life, Who proceedeth from the Father and the Son, Who with the Father and the Son together is worshiped and glorified, Who spake by the Prophets.

And I believe in one holy Christian and Apostolic Church.

I acknowledge one Baptism for the remission of sins; and I look for the resurrection of the dead; and the life of the world to come.   Amen.

*An **Anthem** in harmony with the lessons for the day may here be sung. Then shall follow one or more verses of a **Hymn** as an introduction to the Sermon.   In the meantime the* **Minister** *shall enter the Pulpit.*

The Sermon

The Sermon ended, the **Minister** *shall offer a prayer in his own words or the following:*

Praised be the Lord, and blessed forever, Who by His Word has comforted, taught, exhorted, and admonished us.   May His Holy Spirit confirm the Word in our hearts, that we be not forgetful hearers, but daily increase in faith, hope, love, and patience unto the end, and obtain salvation through Jesus Christ our Lord.   Amen.

Here may be used the prayer to be found in the lectionary of the pastor's altar book after the texts of each Sunday.

The **Church Notices** *may then be given.   The* **Announcement of a Death** *within the Congregation may be made as follows:*

We are again reminded that here we have no abiding city.   It has pleased the Lord in His infinite wisdom to call from our midst N. N. at the age of......

The Lord teach us so to consider our own departure, that when the hour is come we may be prepared for a blessed entrance into the heavenly kingdom.

When **Intercession for the Sick** *is requested, the* **Minister** *shall say:*

N. N. and N. N., who are sick, desire to be remembered in the prayers of the Congregation:

Almighty and Eternal God, Thou art the health and strength of them that trust in Thee.   We pray Thee that Thou wouldst look in mercy upon the sick and the needy, and especially upon Thy servants for whom we now invoke Thy mighty aid.   Turn their distress unto good, and if it be Thy will restore them to health.   But above all give them healing for the soul through Thy holy Word.   Help them by the remembrance of the bitter passion of Thy Son patiently to bear the affliction with which Thou hast visited them.   And finally, when their hour is come, deliver them from all evil and bring them safe to Thy heavenly kingdom; through Thy Son, Jesus Christ, our Lord.   Amen.

The Pulpit Office shall conclude with the following:

The grace of the Lord Jesus Christ, and the love of God, and the communion of the Holy Spirit, be with you all. Amen. (2 Cor. 13. 14.)

Or:

The God of all grace, Who called you unto His eternal glory in Christ, after that ye have suffered a little while, shall Himself perfect, establish, strengthen you. To Him be the dominion for ever and ever. Amen. (1 Pet. 5. 10, 11).

Easter and Pentecost Seasons.

Now the God of Peace, Who brought again from the dead the great Shepherd of the sheep with the blood of an eternal covenant, even our Lord Jesus, make you perfect in every good thing to do His will, working in us that which is well pleasing in His sight, through Jesus Christ; to whom be the glory for ever and ever. Amen. (Heb. 13. 20, 21.)

Trinity Season.

Now unto Him that is able to do exceeding abundantly above all that we ask or think, according to the power that worketh in us, unto Him be the glory in the Church and in Christ Jesus unto all generations for ever and ever. Amen. (Eph. 3. 20, 21).

At the End of the Church Year.

The God of peace Himself sanctify you wholly; and may your spirit and soul and body be preserved entire, without blame at the coming of our Lord Jesus Christ. Amen. (1 Th. 5. 23).

The Offering

Then shall an **Offertory** *be played, or an* **Anthem** *sung, during which the* **Offering** *shall be made. The* **Minister,** *having received the offering, shall place it upon the Altar and pray as follows:*

O God, Thou Giver of all good gifts, graciously receive and bless this offering which we Thy people place upon Thine Altar, for Jesus' sake. Amen.*

Then shall the **Congregation** *sing a* **Hymn,** *during which the* **Minister** *shall proceed to the Altar.*

The Salutation

The Minister shall turn to the Congregation and sing or say:

The Congregation shall sing:

The Lord be with you.

And with thy spir - it.

* A short offertory sentence may then be sung by the Choir. (See pp. 554, 555.)

Lenten Season

The Minister: *The* Congregation:

The Lord be with you.   And with thy spir - it.

The Minister *shall say:*

Let us pray.

Turning to the Altar, the Minister *shall offer*

The General Prayer *

Almighty and most Merciful God, the Father of our Lord Jesus Christ: We give Thee thanks for all Thy goodness and tender mercies. Be gracious unto us and remember not our sins. Sanctify and guide us through Thy Holy Spirit, and grant that we may walk in holiness of life according to Thy Word. Unite, strengthen, and preserve Thy Church through the Word and the Holy Sacraments. Have mercy, O Lord, on all the nations that walk in darkness and that dwell in the land of the shadow of death, and cause the saving and life-giving light of Thy Gospel to shine graciously upon them.

For Synodical and Conference Meetings. Bless those who are now assembled to deliberate concerning the welfare of Thy Church, that their counsels may further Thy glory and the upbuilding of Thy kingdom among us.

Be Thou the strength and stay of our land. Give it grace and honor. Grant health and prosperity to all in authority, especially to the President (and the Congress) of the United States, the Governor (and the Legislature) of this Commonwealth, and to all our Judges and Magistrates. Endue them with grace to rule after Thy good pleasure, to the maintenance of righteousness, and to the hindrance and punishment of wickedness, that we may lead a quiet and peaceable life in all godliness and honesty.

---

* On special Festival Days the prayers prescribed should precede the General Intercession. According to circumstances, those parts of the General Intercession referring to conditions that do not always prevail are omitted, such as the prayers for Church assemblies, for Confirmation Candidates, etc. Occasional prayers shall, when they occur, follow the General Prayer. During Lent and on special occasions the Litany may be used instead of the General Prayer.

Help us, O God, that we may live together in peace and concord, with true and Christian counsel in all that we undertake. Prosper every good work, and turn away from us all harm and evil. May Thy blessing rest upon the fruits of the earth, and give success to every lawful occupation on land and sea.

Let the light of Thy Word ever shine within our homes. Keep the children of the Church in the covenant which Thou hast made with them in Holy Baptism, and give all parents and teachers grace to nurture them in Thy truth, and fear. Bless, we pray Thee, the institutions of the Church: its colleges, its seminaries, and all its schools; that they may send forth men and women to serve Thee, in the Ministry of the Word, the Ministry of Mercy, and all the walks of life.

For Catechumens. Regard with special favor those who are being prepared for their first communion. Illumine their hearts and minds, and grant them unfeigned faith that they may ever walk as Thy disciples in the way of truth.

Help and comfort the sick and the poor, the oppressed and those who mourn, the afflicted and the dying. Graciously protect all widows and orphans. Support us in our last hour, and after this transitory life vouchsafe unto us eternal blessedness: through Jesus Christ, our Lord.

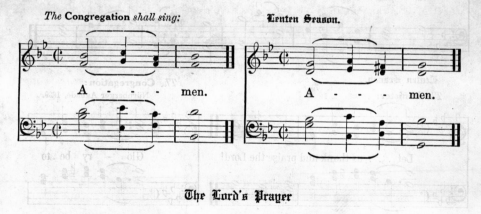

The **Congregation** *shall sing:*   **Lenten Season.**

A - - - men.   A - - - men.

The Lord's Prayer

The **Minister,** *together with the* **Congregation,** *shall continue:*

Our Father, Who art in heaven: Hallowed be Thy Name; Thy kingdom come; Thy will be done on earth, as it is in heaven; Give us this day our daily bread; And forgive us our trespasses, as we forgive those who trespass against us; And lead us not into temptation; but deliver us from evil; For Thine is the kingdom, and the power, and the glory, forever. Amen.

Benedicamus

Advent, Christmas, and Epiphany Seasons.

The Minister shall turn to the Congregation and sing or say:

Preussische Kirchenordnung, 1525.

Let   us   thank and   praise the   Lord!

The Congregation shall sing:

Glo-ry   be   to   Thee, O Lord! Hal - le-
lu - jah! Hal - le - lu - jah! Hal - le - lu - jah!

Lenten Season.

The Minister:

Let . . . us thank and praise the Lord!

The Congregation:

Nürnberger Agende, 1639.

Glo - ry be to
Thee, O Lord! Hal-le-lu-jah! Hal-le-lu-jah! Hal-le-lu-jah!

The Benediction

Then shall the **Minister** *say:*

Bow your hearts to God, and receive the Benediction.

The Lord bless thee, and keep thee.   The Lord make His face shine upon thee, and be gracious unto thee.   The Lord lift up His countenance upon thee, and give thee peace.

In the Name of the Father, and of the Son, and of the Holy Spirit. Amen.

The **Minister** *shall turn to the Altar, and the* **Congregation** *shall sing:*

The Service shall close with silent prayer, while the **Congregation** *remains standing and the* **Minister** *kneels before the Altar.*

The Introts

After the opening Hymn of the Service, where circumstances permit, the following Introits may be used.

First Sunday in Advent

The **Minister,** *turning to the Congregation, shall sing or say:*

GUSTAF HÄGG.

Be-hold, thy King com-eth un-to thee, just and hav-ing sal-va-tion.

The **Congregation** *shall sing:*

Bless-ed is He that com-eth in the Name of the Lord. Ho-san-na in the high - - - est.

The **Minister:**

Pre-pare ye the way of the Lord, a high-way for our God.

581

The **Congregation:**

For the glo - ry of the Lord shall be re - veal - - - ed.

Thus hath the mouth of the Lord spo - - - - ken.

The **Minister:**

Glo - ry be to the Fa - ther, and to the Son, and to the Ho - ly Spir - it.

The **Congregation:**

As it was in the be - gin - ning, is now, and ev - er

shall be, world . . . . with - out end. A - men.

Thereafter the **Minister** *shall say:*

The Lord is in His holy temple, etc.*

*See page 563.

Christmas Day

The **Minister,** *turning to the Congregation, shall sing or say:*

GUSTAF HÄGG.

Be-hold, I bring you good tidings of great joy. Hal-le - lu - - - jah!

The **Congregation** *shall sing:*

Which shall be to all the peo - ple. Hal-le - lu - - - - jah!

The **Minister:**

For there is born to you a Sav - iour. Hal-le - lu - - jah!

The **Congregation:**

He is Christ ... the Lord. Hal-le - lu - - - jah!

The **Minister:**

Glo - ry be to the Fa-ther, and to the Son, and to the Ho - ly Spir - it.

The **Congregation:**

As it was in the be - gin - ning, is now, and ev - er

shall be, world . . . . . with - out end. A - men.

Thereafter the **Minister** *shall say:*

The Lord is in His holy temple, etc.*

Easter Day

The **Minister,** *turning to the Congregation, shall sing or say:*

OSCAR BLOM.

The Lord . . . . . is ris - en. Hal - le - lu - jah!

*See page 563.

The **Congregation** *shall sing:*

He is ris - en in - deed. Hal - le - lu - jah!

The **Minister:**

Christ . . hath a - bol - ished death. Hal - - le - lu - jah!

The **Congregation:**

And brought life and im - mor - tal - i - ty to light. Hal - le - lu - - jah!

The **Minister:**

Glo - ry be to the Fa - ther, and to the Son, and to the Ho - ly Spir - it.

The **Congregation:**

As it was in the be-gin-ning, is now, and ev-er shall be, world . . . . . with-out end. A-men.

Thereafter the **Minister** *shall say:*

The Lord is in His holy temple, etc. *

Ascension Day

The **Minister,** *turning to the Congregation, shall sing or say:*

OSCAR BLOM.

Christ hath as-cend-ed un-to His Fa-ther and our Fa-ther, un-to His God and our God.

The **Congregation** *shall sing:*

His king-dom is an ev-er-last-ing king-dom, and His do-min-ion is from gen-er-a-tion to gen-er-a - - - tion.

*See page 563.

The **Minister:**

Our cit - i-zen-ship is in heav-en; whence al - so we wait for the Lord our Sav-iour.

The **Congregation:**

He shall de - liv - er us from ev - 'ry e - vil

work,   and shall save us un - to His heav'n-ly king - dom.

The **Minister:**

Glo - ry be   to the Fa-ther, and to the Son, and to the Ho - ly Spir - it.

The **Congregation:**

As it was in the be - gin - ning, is now, and ev - er shall be, world .... with - out end. A - men.

Thereafter the **Minister** *shall say:*

The Lord is in His holy temple, etc.*

Pentecost (Whitsunday)

The **Minister,** *turning to the Congregation, shall sing or say:*

OSCAR BLOM.

The Lord shall pour wa - ter up - on him that is thirst - y, and streams up - on the dry ground. Hal - le - lu - jah!

*See page 563.

The **Congregation** *shall sing:*

He shall pour out His Spir - it up - on all flesh. Hal - le - lu - - - jah!

The **Minister:**

With joy shall ye draw wa - ter out of the wells of sal - va - tion.

The **Congregation:**

I will take the cup of sal - va - tion, and call up - on the Name of the Lord.

The **Minister:**

Glo - ry be to the Fa - ther, and to the Son, and to the Ho - ly Spir - it.

The **Congregation:**

As it was in the be-gin-ning, is now, and ev-er

shall be, world .... with-out end. A-men.

Thereafter the **Minister** *shall say:*

The Lord is in His holy temple, etc.*

Trinity Sunday

The **Minister,** *turning to the Congregation, shall sing or say:*

HARALD FRYKLÖF,

Ho-ly, ho-ly, ho-ly is the Lord of hosts!

The **Congregation** *shall sing:*

The whole earth is full of His glo----ry.

*See page 563.

The **Minister:**

Of Him and thro' Him, and un-to Him are all things. Hal-le-lu - - jah!

The **Congregation:**

To Him be glo-ry for-ev - - er. Hal - - - le-lu - jah!

The **Minister:**

Glo-ry be to the Fa-ther, and to the Son, and to the Ho-ly Spir-it.

The **Congregation:**

As it was in the be-gin-ning, is now, and ev-er

shall be, world . . . . with-out end. A-men.

Thereafter the **Minister** *shall say:*

The Lord is in His holy temple, etc.*

*See page 563.

The Festival of the Reformation

The **Minister,** *turning to the Congregation, shall sing or say:*

HARALD FRYKLÖF.

God is our ref - uge and strength. Hal - le - lu - jah.

The **Congregation** *shall sing:*

A ver - y pres - ent help . . : in trou - ble. Hal - le - lu - jah.

The **Minister:**

For - ev - er, O Lord, Thy word is set - tled in heav - en.

The **Congregation:**

Thy faith-ful-ness is un-to all gen-er-a - - - tions.

The **Minister:**

Glo-ry be to the Fa-ther, and to the Son, and to the Ho-ly Spir-it.

The **Congregation:**

As it was in the be-gin-ning, is now, and ev-er

shall be, world .... with-out end. A-men.

Thereafter the **Minister** *shall say:*

The Lord is in His holy temple, etc.*

*See page 563.

The Holy Communion

With the Full Service

The Service *shall begin with an appropriate* **Hymn.** *During the singing the* **Minister** *shall proceed to the Altar and kneel in prayer. After the singing he shall rise, turn to the* Congregation *and say:*

In the Name of the Father, and of the Son, and of the Holy Spirit.

The Communion Sermon

Here shall follow a brief **Communion Sermon,** *after which the* **Minister** *shall turn to the* Altar, *kneel, and with the* **Congregation** *unite in the following* **Confession of Sins:**

The Confession of Sins

Holy and righteous God, merciful Father, we confess unto Thee that we are by nature sinful and unclean, and that we have sinned against Thee by thought, word, and deed. We have not loved Thee above all things, nor our neighbor as ourselves, and are worthy, therefore, to be cast away from Thy presence, if Thou shouldst judge us according to our sins. But Thou hast promised, O heavenly Father, to receive with tender mercy all penitent sinners who turn unto Thee and with a living faith seek refuge in Thy Fatherly compassion and in the merits of the Saviour, Jesus Christ. Their transgressions Thou wilt not regard, nor impute unto them their sins. Relying upon Thy promise, we confidently beseech Thee to be merciful and gracious unto us and to forgive us all our sins, to the praise and glory of Thy Holy Name.

The Absolution

The **Minister** *shall turn to the Congregation and pronounce the Absolution:*

If this be your sincere confession, and if with penitent hearts you earnestly desire the forgiveness of your sins for the sake of Jesus Christ, God, according to His promise, forgiveth you all your sins; and by the authority of God's Word and by the command of our Lord Jesus Christ, I declare unto you that God, through His grace, hath forgiven all your sins; in the Name of God the Father, and the Son, and the Holy Spirit. Amen.

Gloria in Excelsis

The Minister, still turned to the Congregation, shall sing or say:

Advent, Christmas, and Epiphany Seasons.

Adapted from Bjuråkers Handskrift.

Glo - - - - ry be to God on high, and on earth.....

peace, good will........... toward men.   *Modulation to F.*

Lenten and Trinity Seasons.

Bjuråkers Handskrift, prior to 1550.

Glo - ry be to God on high, and on earth.....

peace, good will.... toward men.   *Modulation to F.*

Easter and Pentecost Seasons.

A. O.

Glo - ry be to God.. on high, and on earth peace, good will... toward men.

The **Minister** *shall turn to the Altar, and with the* **Congregation** *shall sing:*

NICOLAUS DECIUS ? 1539.

All glo - ry be to Thee, Most High, To Thee all a - do-
ra - tion! In grace and truth Thou draw - est nigh To of - fer
us sal - va - tion. Thou show - est Thy good will to
men, And peace shall reign on earth a - gain; We praise Thy
Name for - ev - er. *Modulation to B♭.*

Modulation to G minor.(*Lent.*)

*On Festival days, or on any Sunday except during Lent, the following (**I.** or **II.**) may be sung instead of "All glory be to Thee, Most High."*

I.

We praise Thee, we wor-ship Thee, We give thanks to Thee for Thy great glo - ry, O Lord God, Heav-en-ly King, God the Fa-ther Al-might-y!

O Lord, the On-ly-be-got-ten Son, Je-sus Christ!

Ho-ly Spir-it, Spir-it of grace and of truth and of peace! . .

A-men, A-men, A - - - - - men. *Modulation to B♭.*

The Salutation

Then the **Minister** *shall turn to the Congregation and sing or say:*

The **Congregation** *shall sing:*

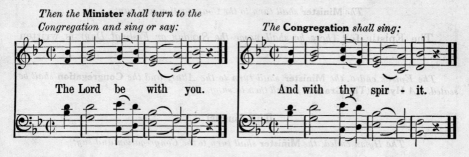

The Lord be with you.

And with thy spir - it.

Lenten Season

The **Minister:**

The **Congregation:**

The Lord be with you.

And with thy spir - it.

Then the **Minister** *shall say:*

Let us pray.

The Collect

The **Minister**, *turning to the Altar, shall read on Sundays and Festival Days the proper Collect. On special occasions one of the following may be used:*

O Lord God, Heavenly Father, Thou Who hast no pleasure in the death of the wicked, but that they turn from their way and live; we pray Thee that Thou wouldst mercifully avert the punishment that our sins deserve, for the sake of Jesus Christ, our Lord.

Or:

We beseech Thee, Almighty God, Heavenly Father, to grant us a true faith, a firm hope in Thy mercy, and a sincere love to our fellow-men, through Jesus Christ, our Lord.

The **Congregation** *shall sing:*

Lenten Season.

A - - - - men.

A - - - - men.

The Epistle

*The **Minister** shall turn to the Congregation and say:*

The Epistle for (*here he shall name the Sunday or Festival Day*) is written in............

*The Epistle ended, the **Minister** shall turn to the Altar, and the **Congregation** shall be seated. A **Hymn** (**The Gradual**) shall then be sung.*

The Gospel

*The Hymn ended, the **Minister** shall turn to the Congregation and say:*

Lift up your hearts unto the Lord and hear the Gospel for the Day as it is written in......

*The **Congregation** shall arise, and the Gospel for the Day shall be read. The Gospel ended, the **Minister** and the **Congregation** shall say*

The Apostles' Creed

I believe in God the Father Almighty, Maker of heaven and earth;

And in Jesus Christ His only Son, our Lord: Who was conceived by the Holy Spirit, Born of the Virgin Mary; Suffered under Pontius Pilate, Was crucified, dead and buried; He descended into hell; The third day He rose again from the dead; He ascended into heaven, And sitteth on the right hand of God the Father Almighty; From thence He shall come to judge the quick and the dead.

I believe in the Holy Spirit; The Holy Christian Church, the Communion of saints; The Forgiveness of sins; The Resurrection of the body; And the Life everlasting. Amen.

Or:

The Nicene Creed

I believe in one God, the Father Almighty, Maker of heaven and earth, And of all things visible and invisible;

And in one Lord Jesus Christ, the Only-begotten Son of God, Begotten of His Father before all worlds, God of God, Light of Light, Very God of Very God, Begotten, not made, Being of one substance with the Father, By Whom all things were made; Who, for us men, and for our salvation, came down from heaven, and was incarnate by the Holy Spirit of the Virgin Mary, and was made man; and was crucified also for us under Pontius Pilate. He suffered and was buried; And the third day He rose again, according to the Scriptures; And ascended into heaven, and sitteth on the right hand of the Father; And He shall come again with glory to judge both the quick and the dead; Whose kingdom shall have no end.

And I believe in the Holy Spirit, the Lord and Giver of Life, Who proceedeth from the Father and the Son, Who with the Father and the Son together is worshiped and glorified, Who spake by the Prophets.

And I believe in one holy Christian and Apostolic Church.

I acknowledge one Baptism for the remission of sins; and I look for the resurrection of the dead; and the life of the world to come. Amen.

An **Anthem** *in harmony with the lessons for the day may here be sung. Then shall follow one or more verses of a* **Hymn** *as an introduction to the Sermon. In the meantime the* **Minister** *shall enter the Pulpit.*

The Sermon

The Sermon ended, the **Minister** *shall offer a prayer in his own words or the following:*

Praised be the Lord, and blessed forever, Who by His Word has comforted, taught, exhorted, and admonished us. May His Holy Spirit confirm the Word in our hearts, that we be not forgetful hearers, but daily increase in faith, hope, love, and patience unto the end, and obtain salvation through Jesus Christ our Lord. Amen.

Here may be used the prayer to be found in the lectionary of the pastor's altar book after the texts of each Sunday.

The **Church Notices** *may then be given. The* **Announcement of a Death** *within the Congregation may be made as follows:*

We are again reminded that here we have no abiding city. It has pleased the Lord in His infinite wisdom to call from our midst N. N. at the age of......

The Lord teach us so to consider our own departure, that when the hour is come we may be prepared for a blessed entrance into the heavenly kingdom.

When **Intercession for the Sick** *is requested, the* **Minister** *shall say:*

N. N. and N. N., who are sick, desire to be remembered in the prayers of the Congregation:

Almighty and Eternal God, Thou art the health and strength of them that trust in Thee. We pray Thee that Thou wouldst look in mercy upon the sick and the needy, and especially upon Thy servants for whom we now invoke Thy mighty aid. Turn their distress unto good, and if it be Thy will restore them to health. But above all give them healing for the soul through Thy holy Word. Help them by the remembrance of the bitter passion of Thy Son patiently to bear the affliction with which Thou hast visited them. And finally, when their hour is come, deliver them from all evil and bring them safe to Thy heavenly kingdom; through Thy Son, Jesus Christ, our Lord. Amen.

The Pulpit Office shall conclude with the following:

The grace of the Lord Jesus Christ, and the love of God, and the communion of the Holy Spirit, be with you all.   Amen.   (2 Cor. 13. 14.)

Or:

The God of all grace, Who called you unto His eternal glory in Christ, after that ye have suffered a little while, shall Himself perfect, establish, strengthen you.   To Him be the dominion for ever and ever.   Amen.   (1 Pet. 5. 10, 11).

Easter and Pentecost Seasons.

Now the God of Peace, Who brought again from the dead the great Shepherd of the sheep with the blood of an eternal covenant, even our Lord Jesus, make you perfect in every good thing to do His will, working in us that which is well pleasing in His sight, through Jesus Christ; to whom be the glory for ever and ever.   Amen.   (Heb. 13. 20, 21.)

Trinity Season.

Now unto Him that is able to do exceeding abundantly above all that we ask or think, according to the power that worketh in us, unto Him be the glory in the Church and in Christ Jesus unto all generations for ever and ever. Amen.   (Eph. 3. 20, 21).

At the End of the Church Year.

The God of peace Himself sanctify you wholly; and may your spirit and soul and body be preserved entire, without blame at the coming of our Lord Jesus Christ.   Amen.   (1 Th. 5. 23).

The Offering

Then shall an **Offertory** *be played, or an* **Anthem** *sung, during which the* **Offering** *shall be made.   The* **Minister,** *having received the offering, shall place it upon the Altar and pray as follows:*

O God, Thou Giver of all good gifts, graciously receive and bless this offering which we Thy people place upon Thine Altar, for Jesus' sake. Amen.*

Then shall the **Congregation** *sing a Hymn, during which the* **Minister** *shall proceed to the Altar.*

The Salutation

The Minister shall turn to the Congregation and sing or say: *The Congregation shall sing:*

The Lord   be   with   you.   And with   thy   spir - it.

* A short offertory sentence may then be sung by the Choir. (See pp. 554, 555.)

Lenten Season

The **Minister:** The Lord be with you.

The **Congregation:** And with thy spir - it.

The **Minister** *shall say:*

Let us pray.

Turning to the Altar, the **Minister** *shall offer*

The General Prayer*

Almighty and most Merciful God, the Father of our Lord Jesus Christ: We give Thee thanks for all Thy goodness and tender mercies. Be gracious unto us and remember not our sins. Sanctify and guide us through Thy Holy Spirit, and grant that we may walk in holiness of life according to Thy Word. Unite, strengthen, and preserve Thy Church through the Word and the Holy Sacraments. Have mercy, O Lord, on all the nations that walk in darkness and that dwell in the land of the shadow of death, and cause the saving and life-giving light of Thy Gospel to shine graciously upon them.

For Synodical and Conference Meetings. Bless those who are now assembled to deliberate concerning the welfare of Thy Church, that their counsels may further Thy glory and the upbuilding of Thy kingdom among us.

Be Thou the strength and stay of our land. Give it grace and honor. Grant health and prosperity to all in authority, especially to the President (and the Congress) of the United States, the Governor (and the Legislature)

---

* On special **Festival Days** the prayers prescribed should precede the General Intercession. According to circumstances, those parts of the General Intercession referring to conditions that do not always prevail are omitted, such as the prayers for Church assemblies, for Confirmation Candidates, etc. Occasional prayers shall, when they occur, follow the General Prayer. During Lent and on special occasions the Litany may be used instead of the General Prayer.

of this Commonwealth, and to all our Judges and Magistrates. Endue them with grace to rule after Thy good pleasure, to the maintenance of righteousness, and to the hindrance and punishment of wickedness, that we may lead a quiet and peaceable life in all godliness and honesty.

Help us, O God, that we may live together in peace and concord, with true and Christian counsel in all that we undertake. Prosper every good work, and turn away from us all harm and evil. May Thy blessing rest upon the fruits of the earth, and give success to every lawful occupation on land and sea.

Let the light of Thy Word ever shine within our homes. Keep the children of the Church in the covenant which Thou hast made with them in Holy Baptism, and give all parents and teachers grace to nurture them in Thy truth and fear. Bless, we pray Thee, the institutions of the Church: its colleges, its seminaries, and all its schools; that they may send forth men and women to serve Thee, in the Ministry of the Word, the Ministry of Mercy, and all the walks of life.

For Catechumens. Regard with special favor those who are being prepared for their first communion. Illumine their hearts and minds, and grant them unfeigned faith that they may ever walk as Thy disciples in the way of truth.

Help and comfort the sick and the poor, the oppressed and those who mourn, the afflicted and the dying. Graciously protect all widows and orphans. Support us in our last hour, and after this transitory life vouchsafe unto us eternal blessedness: through Jesus Christ, our Lord.

The **Congregation** *shall sing:*   𝔏enten 𝔖eason.

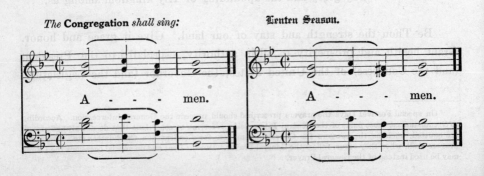

A - - - men.   A - - - men.

O Lamb of God, Most Holy

Then the **Congregation** *shall sing,* "**O Lamb of God, Most Holy,**" *while the* **Minister** *makes ready the elements of the Sacrament on the Altar.*

NIKOLAUS DECIUS, 1539.

O Lamb of God, most ho - ly, On Cal - va - ry an of - f'ring;

De - spis - ed, meek, and low - ly, Thou in Thy death and suf - f'ring

Our sins didst bear, our an - guish; The might of death didst van - quish;

Give us Thy peace, O Je - sus!   I. *Modulation to E♭.*   II. *Modulation to G minor.*

The Preface

I. * *The* **Minister** *shall turn to the Congregation and sing or say:*

Lift up your hearts unto God.

The **Congregation** *shall sing:*

We lift them up un-to the Lord our God.

II. *The* **Minister:**

Lift up your hearts un-to God.

The **Congregation:**

We lift them up unto the Lord our God.

I. *The* **Minister** *shall sing or say:*

Let us give thanks un-to the Lord.

The **Congregation** *shall sing:*

It is meet and right so to do.

II. *The* **Minister:**

Let us give thanks unto the Lord.

The **Congregation:**

It is meet and right so to do.

Vere Dignum

The **Minister** *shall turn to the Altar and say:*

It is truly meet, right, and salutary, that we should at all times, and in all places, give thanks unto Thee, O Lord, Holy Father, Almighty, Everlasting God, through Jesus Christ, our Lord. He is our Paschal Lamb, offered for us, the innocent Lamb of God, that taketh away the sin of the world. As He hath conquered death, is risen again, and liveth for evermore, even so all they who put their trust in Him shall through Him be victorious over sin and death, and inherit eternal life. And in order that we may keep in remembrance His unspeakable mercy, He hath instituted His Holy Supper.

---

* The setting chosen (I. or II.) shall be followed consistently throughout the service.

The Words of Institution

*Then shall the **Minister** say:*

Our Lord Jesus Christ, in the night in which He was betrayed, took bread; and when He had given thanks, He brake it and gave it to His disciples, saying, Take, eat; this is My Body, which is given for you; this do in remembrance of Me.

After the same manner, also, when He had supped, He took the cup, and when He had given thanks, He gave it to them, saying, Drink ye all of it; this Cup is the New Testament in My Blood, which is shed for you, and for many, for the remission of sins; this do, as oft as ye drink it, in remembrance of Me.

The Lord's Prayer

*The **Minister**, together with the **Congregation**, shall say:*

Our Father, Who art in heaven; Hallowed be Thy Name; Thy kingdom come; Thy will be done on earth, as it is in heaven; Give us this day our daily bread; And forgive us our trespasses, as we forgive those who trespass against us; And lead us not into temptation; But deliver us from evil; For Thine is the kingdom, and the power, and the glory, forever. Amen.

Sanctus

*Then shall the **Minister** and the **Congregation** together sing:*

Ho - ly, Ho - ly, Ho - - ly, Lord God Al-might-y; Heav'n and earth are full of Thy glo - - ry; Ho - san-na in the high - est. Bless-ed is He that com-eth in the Name of the Lord. Ho - san-na in the high - est.

II.

Ho - ly, Ho - ly, Ho - ly, Lord God Al - might - y;

Heav'n and earth are full of Thy glo - ry; Ho-

san - na in the high - est. Bless - ed is He that com - eth

in the Name of the Lord. Ho - san - na in the high - est.

Pax

The **Minister,** *turning to the Congregation, shall sing or say:*

I.

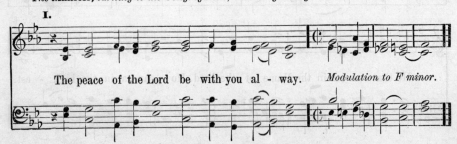

The peace of the Lord be with you al - way.   *Modulation to F minor.*

II.

The peace of the Lord be with you al - way.

Agnus Dei

The Communicants now come forward while the **Congregation** *sings:*

I.

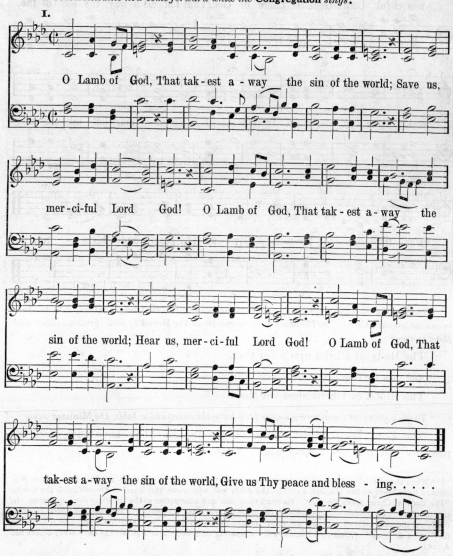

O Lamb of God, That tak - est a - way the sin of the world; Save us,

mer - ci - ful Lord God! O Lamb of God, That tak - est a - way the

sin of the world; Hear us, mer - ci - ful Lord God! O Lamb of God, That

tak - est a - way the sin of the world, Give us Thy peace and bless - ing. . . . .

II.

O Lamb of God, That tak-est a-way the sin of the world; Save us, mer-ci-ful Lord God! O Lamb of God, That tak-est a-way the sin of the world; Hear us, mer-ci-ful Lord God! O Lamb of God, That tak-est a-way the sin of the world, Give us Thy peace and bless-ing.

During the distribution, appropriate **Hymns** *are sung by the* **Congregation,** *with subdued organ accompaniment. The* **Minister** *first administers the* **Bread** *to each communicant with these words:**

The Body of Christ given for thee.

And then the **Cup** *with these words:*

The Blood of Christ shed for thee.

To each group of communicants, as they leave the communion table, the **Minister** *says:*

The Lord Jesus Christ, Whose Body and Blood ye have now received, preserve you unto everlasting life. Amen.

* When the officiating Pastor administers communion to himself he shall, when the first group of communicants have knelt at the chancel, kneel at the Altar and administer the bread to himself with the words: "The Body of Christ given for me." He shall then rise and administer to the kneeling communicants. In the distribution of the wine he proceeds in the same manner with the words: "The Blood of Christ shed for me." At the final salutation to this group of communicants the words "we" and "us" should be substituted for "ye" and "you." When two Ministers are officiating they may first administer to each other before the Altar.

Or else the **Minister** *shall say at the administration of the* **Bread:**

Jesus Christ, Whose Body thou now receivest, preserve thee unto everlasting life.

And at the administration of the **Cup:**

Jesus Christ, Whose Blood thou now receivest, preserve thee unto everlasting life.

In dismissing the communicants the **Minister** *shall say:*

The Grace and Peace of our Lord Jesus Christ be with you all.   Amen.

The Thanksgiving

When the distribution is ended, the **Minister** *shall say:*

Let us pray.

The **Congregation** *shall rise.   Turning to the Altar, the* **Minister** *shall say:*

We thank Thee, Almighty Father, Who, through Thy Son Jesus Christ, for our consolation and salvation hast instituted this Holy Supper: we pray Thee, grant us grace so to commemorate the death of Christ that we may be partakers of the great Supper in heaven.

Or:

We thank Thee, Almighty God, that through this gracious feast Thou hast refreshed and satisfied us, and we pray Thee that it may tend to the increase of our faith and to growth in godliness and all Christian virtues, through Thy Son, Jesus Christ, our Lord.

Or:

Lord Jesus Christ, Thou Who hast called us to this Holy Supper, we most heartily thank Thee for Thy mercy, that Thou hast nourished us with Thy Body and Blood, and that Thou hast filled and compassed us about with Thy goodness.   O Lord, abide with us; into Thy hands we commit ourselves, and put our trust in Thee.   Grant us to dwell with Thee forever.

The **Congregation** *shall sing:*

Advent, Christmas, and Epiphany Seasons.   Lenten Season.   Easter and Pentecost Seasons.   Trinity Season.

A-men.   A-men.   A-men.   A-men.

Benedicamus

Advent, Christmas, and Epiphany Seasons.

The **Minister** *shall turn to the Congregation and sing or say:*

Preussische Kirchenordnung, 1525.

Let us thank and praise the Lord!

The **Congregation** *shall sing:*

Glo - ry be to Thee, O Lord! Hal - le - lu - jah! Hal - le - lu - jah! Hal - le - lu - jah!

Lenten Season.

The **Minister:**

Let . . . us thank and praise the Lord!

The **Congregation:**

Nürnberger Agende, 1639.

Glo - ry be to Thee, O Lord! Hal-le-lu - jah! Hal-le-lu - jah! Hal-le-lu - jah!

The Benediction

Then shall the Minister say:

Bow your hearts to God, and receive the Benediction.

The Lord bless thee, and keep thee. The Lord make His face shine upon thee, and be gracious unto thee. The Lord lift up His countenance upon thee, and give thee peace.

In the Name of the Father, and of the Son, and of the Holy Spirit. Amen.

*The **Minister** shall turn to the Altar, and the **Congregation** shall sing:*

*The Service shall close with silent prayer, while the **Congregation** remains standing and the **Minister** kneels before the Altar.*

The Holy Communion
Without the Full Service

The Service shall begin with an appropriate **Hymn.** *During the singing the* **Minister** *shall proceed to the Altar and kneel in prayer. After the singing he shall rise, turn to the Congregation, and say:*

In the Name of the Father, and of the Son, and of the Holy Spirit.

The Communion Sermon

Here shall follow a brief **Communion Sermon,** *after which the* **Minister** *shall turn to the* **Altar,** *kneel, and with the* **Congregation** *unite in the following* **Confession of Sins:**

The Confession of Sins

Holy and righteous God, merciful Father, we confess unto Thee that we are by nature sinful and unclean, and that we have sinned against Thee by thought, word, and deed. We have not loved Thee above all things, nor our neighbor as ourselves, and are worthy, therefore, to be cast away from Thy presence, if Thou shouldst judge us according to our sins. But Thou hast promised, O heavenly Father, to receive with tender mercy all penitent sinners who turn unto Thee and with a living faith seek refuge in Thy fatherly compassion and in the merits of the Saviour, Jesus Christ. Their transgressions Thou wilt not regard, nor impute unto them their sins. Relying upon Thy promise, we confidently beseech Thee to be merciful and gracious unto us and to forgive us all our sins, to the praise and glory of Thy Holy Name.

The Absolution

The **Minister** *shall turn to the Congregation and pronounce the Absolution:*

If this be your sincere confession, and if with penitent hearts you earnestly desire the forgiveness of your sins for the sake of Jesus Christ, God, according to His promise, forgiveth you all your sins; and by the authority of God's Word and by the command of our Lord Jesus Christ, I declare unto you that God, through His grace, hath forgiven all your sins; in the Name of God the Father, and the Son, and the Holy Spirit. Amen.

Then the **Minister** *shall say:*

Let us give thanks and pray.

Turning to the Altar he shall pray:

Almighty, heavenly Father, we render unto Thee heartfelt thanks for this comforting absolution wherein Thou hast declared unto us forgiveness of our sins. We pray Thee so to prepare us through Thy Holy Spirit that we, in true penitence and faith, may receive the Sacrament of the Body and Blood of Thy Son Jesus Christ, and thereby be strengthened in Christian patience and in the hope of everlasting life, till Thou at last grant us a blessed departure; through Jesus Christ, our Saviour. Amen.

Here a suitable **Hymn** *shall be sung, following which the* **Announcements** *shall be made from the pulpit.   Then shall an* **Offertory** *be played, or an* **Anthem** *sung, during which the* **Offering** *shall be received.   The* **Minister,** *having received the offering, shall place it upon the Altar and pray as follows:*

O God, Thou Giver of all good gifts, graciously receive and bless this offering, which we Thy people place upon Thine Altar, for Jesus' sake. Amen.*

O Lamb of God, Most Holy

The **Congregation** *shall rise and sing,* "O Lamb of God, Most Holy," *while the* **Minister** *makes ready the elements of the Sacrament on the Altar.*

NIKOLAUS DECIUS, 1539.

O Lamb of God, most ho - ly, On Cal - va - ry an of - f'ring;

De - spis - ed, meek, and low - ly, Thou in Thy death and suf - f'ring

Our sins didst bear, our an - guish; The might of death didst van - quish;

Give us Thy peace, O Je - sus!   I. *Modulation to* E♭.   II. *Modulation to* G minor.

* A short offertory sentence may then be sung by the Choir.   (See pp. 554, 555.)

The Preface

I.* *The* **Minister** *shall turn to the Congregation and sing or say:*

Lift up your hearts unto God.

The **Congregation** *shall sing:*

We lift them up un-to the Lord our God.

II. *The* **Minister:**

Lift up your hearts un-to God.

The **Congregation:**

We lift them up unto the Lord our God.

I. *The* **Minister** *shall sing or say:*

Let us give thanks un-to the Lord.

The **Congregation** *shall sing:*

It is meet and right so to do.

II. *The* **Minister:**

Let us give thanks unto the Lord.

The **Congregation:**

It is meet and right so to do.

Vere Dignum

The **Minister** *shall turn to the Altar and say:*

It is truly meet, right, and salutary, that we should at all times, and in all places, give thanks unto Thee, O Lord, Holy Father, Almighty, Everlasting God, through Jesus Christ, our Lord. He is our Paschal Lamb, offered for us, the innocent Lamb of God, that taketh away the sin of the world. As He hath conquered death, is risen again, and liveth for evermore, even so all they who put their trust in Him shall through Him be victorious over sin and death, and inherit eternal life. And in order that we may keep in remembrance His unspeakable mercy, He hath instituted His Holy Supper.

*The setting chosen shall be followed throughout the service.

The Words of Institution

Then shall the **Minister** *say:*

Our Lord Jesus Christ, in the night in which He was betrayed, took bread; and when He had given thanks, He brake it and gave it to His disciples, saying, Take, eat; this is My Body, which is given for you; this do in remembrance of Me.

After the same manner, also, when He had supped, He took the cup, and when He had given thanks, He gave it to them, saying, Drink ye all of it; this Cup is the New Testament in My Blood, which is shed for you, and for many, for the remission of sins; this do, as oft as ye drink it, in remembrance of Me.

The Lord's Prayer

The **Minister,** *together with the* **Congregation,** *shall say:*

Our Father, Who art in heaven: Hallowed be Thy Name; Thy kingdom come; Thy will be done on earth, as it is in heaven; Give us this day our daily bread; And forgive us our trespasses, as we forgive those who trespass against us; And lead us not into temptation; But deliver us from evil; For Thine is the kingdom, and the power, and the glory, forever.   Amen.

Sanctus

Then shall the **Minister** *and the* **Congregation** *together sing:*

Ho - ly, Ho - ly, Ho - - ly, Lord God Al - might - y; Heav'n and earth are

full of Thy glo - - ry; Ho - san - na in the high - est. Bless - ed is

He that com - eth in the Name of the Lord. Ho - san - na in the high - est.

II.

Ho - ly, Ho - ly, Ho - ly, Lord God Al - might - y;

Heav'n and earth are full of Thy glo - ry; Ho-

san - na in the high - est. Bless - ed is He that com - eth

in the Name of the Lord. Ho - san-na in the high - est.

Pax

The **Minister,** *turning to the Congregation, shall sing or say:*

I.

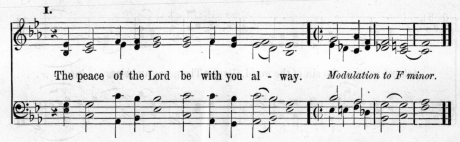

The peace of the Lord be with you al - way.   *Modulation to F minor.*

II.

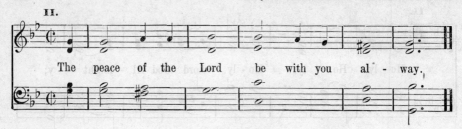

The peace of the Lord be with you al-way.

Agnus Dei

The Communicants now come forward while the **Congregation** *sings:*

I.

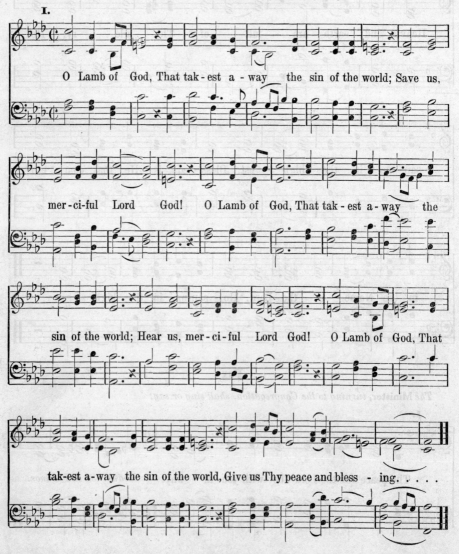

O Lamb of God, That tak-est a-way the sin of the world; Save us,

mer-ci-ful Lord God! O Lamb of God, That tak-est a-way the

sin of the world; Hear us, mer-ci-ful Lord God! O Lamb of God, That

tak-est a-way the sin of the world, Give us Thy peace and bless - ing. . . . .

II.

O Lamb of God, That tak-est a-way the sin of the world; Save us,

mer-ci-ful Lord God! O Lamb of God, That tak-est a-way the sin of the

world; Hear us, mer-ci-ful Lord God! O Lamb of God, That tak-est a-

way the sin of the world, Give us Thy peace and bless - ing.

During the distribution, appropriate **Hymns** *are sung by the* **Congregation,** *with subdued organ accompaniment. The* **Minister** *first administers the* **Bread** *to each communicant with these words:**

The Body of Christ given for thee.

And then the **Cup** *with these words:*

The Blood of Christ shed for thee.

To each group of communicants, as they leave the communion table, the **Minister** *says:*

The Lord Jesus Christ, Whose Body and Blood ye have now received, preserve you unto everlasting life. Amen.

---

* When the officiating Pastor administers communion to himself he shall, when the first group of communicants have knelt at the chancel, kneel at the Altar and administer the bread to himself with the words: "The Body of Christ given for me." He shall then rise and administer to the kneeling communicants. In the distribution of the wine he proceeds in the same manner with the words: "The Blood of Christ shed for me." At the final salutation to this group of communicants the words "we" and "us" should be substituted for "ye" and "you." When two Ministers are officiating they may first administer to each other before the Altar.

*Or else the **Minister** shall say at the administration of the **Bread**:*

Jesus Christ, Whose Body thou now receivest, preserve thee unto ever-lasting life.

*And at the administration of the **Cup**:*

Jesus Christ, Whose Blood thou now receivest, preserve thee unto ever-lasting life.

*In dismissing the communicants the **Minister** shall say:*

The Grace and Peace of our Lord Jesus Christ be with you all.   Amen.

The Thanksgiving

*When the distribution is ended, the **Minister** shall say:*

Let us pray.

*The **Congregation** shall rise.   Turning to the Altar, the **Minister** shall say:*

We thank Thee, Almighty Father, Who, through Thy Son Jesus Christ, for our consolation and salvation hast instituted this Holy Supper; we pray Thee, grant us grace so to commemorate the death of Christ that we may be partakers of the great Supper in heaven.

Or:

We thank Thee, Almighty God, that through this gracious feast Thou hast refreshed and satisfied us, and we pray Thee that it may tend to the increase of our faith and to growth in godliness and all Christian virtues, through Thy Son, Jesus Christ, our Lord.

Or:

Lord Jesus Christ, Thou Who hast called us to this Holy Supper, we most heartily thank Thee for Thy mercy, that Thou hast nourished us with Thy Body and Blood, and that Thou hast filled and compassed us about with Thy goodness.   O Lord, abide with us; into Thy hands we commit ourselves, and put our trust in Thee.   Grant us to dwell with Thee forever.

*The **Congregation** shall sing:*

Advent, Christmas, and Epiphany Seasons.   Lenten Season.   Easter and Pentecost Seasons.   Trinity Season.

A - men.   A - men.   A - men.   A - men.

Benedicamus

Advent, Christmas, and Epiphany Seasons.

*The **Minister** shall turn to the Congregation and sing or say:*

Preussische Kirchenordnung, 1525.

Let us thank and praise the Lord!

*The **Congregation** shall sing:*

Glo — ry be to Thee, O Lord! Hal — le —
lu — jah! Hal — le — lu — jah! Hal — le — lu — jah!

Lenten Season.

*The **Minister**:*

Let . . . us thank and praise the Lord!

*The **Congregation**:*

Nürnberger Agende, 1639.

Glo — ry be to
Thee, O Lord! Hal — le — lu — jah! Hal — le — lu — jah! Hal — le — lu — jah!

Easter and Pentecost Seasons.

The **Minister:**

Let us thank and praise the Lord!

The **Congregation:** SPANGENBERG, 1545.

Glo - ry be to Thee, O Lord!

Hal - le - lu - jah! Hal - le - lu - jah! Hal - le - lu - - - - - jah!

Trinity Season.

The **Minister:**

Let us thank and praise the Lord!   *Or:*

The **Minister:**

Let us thank and praise the Lord!

The **Congregation:**

Swedish.

Glo - ry be to Thee, O Lord! Hal - le - lu - -

jah! Hal - le - lu - - jah! Hal - le - lu - - jah!

The Benediction

Then shall the Minister say:

Bow your hearts to God, and receive the Benediction.

The Lord bless thee, and keep thee.   The Lord make His face shine upon thee, and be gracious unto thee.   The Lord lift up His countenance upon thee, and give thee peace.

In the Name of the Father, and of the Son, and of the Holy Spirit. Amen.

The Minister shall turn to the Altar, and the Congregation shall sing:

Advent, Christmas, and Epiphany Seasons.

A - men,   A - men,   A - - - - men.

Lenten Season.

A - men,   A - men,   A - - - - men.

Easter and Pentecost Seasons.

A - men,   A - men,   A - - - - men.

Trinity Season.

A - men,   A - men,   A - - - - - men.

The Service shall close with silent prayer, while the **Congregation** *remains standing and the* **Minister** *kneels before the Altar.*

Matins on Christmas Day

The Service shall begin with an appropriate **Hymn.** *During the singing the* **Minister** *shall proceed to the Altar and kneel in prayer. After the singing he shall rise, turn to the Congregation, and say:*

Grace be unto you and peace from God, our Father, and the **Lord** Jesus Christ. Amen.

Come, let us worship and bow down; let us kneel before **the Lord our** Maker, for He is our God.

The **Minister,** *turning to the Altar, shall kneel and pray:*

O God, Who hast made this most holy night to shine with the brightness of the true light: We praise Thy Holy Name. Above all things do we give thanks and praise to Thee, that Thou hast suffered Thine only begotten Son to become man for our salvation. We pray Thee, merciful Father, to keep us by Thy Spirit in a living knowledge of our Saviour, that we may ever be comforted by His incarnation and serve Thee as Thy children, till finally with all angels and the saints in light we may praise Thee forevermore; through Thy Son, Jesus Christ, our Lord. Amen.

The **Minister,** *rising, shall continue:*

Blessed be the Name of Jehovah from this time forth and forevermore. From the rising of the sun unto the going down of the same Jehovah's Name is to be praised. Jehovah is high above all nations, and His glory above the heavens. Who is like unto Jehovah our God, That hath His seat on high, That humbleth Himself to behold the things that are in heaven and in the earth! (Psalm 113. 2–6.)

Gloria Patri

The **Congregation** *shall rise, and with the* **Minister,** *still turned to the Altar, sing:*

Pfälzische Kirchenordnung, 1570.

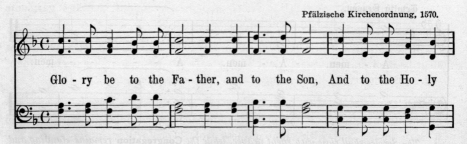

Glo - ry be to the Fa - ther, and to the Son, And to the Ho - ly

Spir - it; As it was in the be - gin - ning, Is now, and ev - er shall be, World.... with - out end. A - MEN.

The Scripture Lesson

After the singing, the **Minister** *shall turn to the Congregation and say:*

Hear the Word of God as it is recorded in the prophecy of Isaiah, the ninth chapter, beginning at the second verse:

The people that walked in darkness have seen a great light: they that dwelt in the land of the shadow of death, upon them hath the light shined.

Thou hast multiplied the nation, thou hast increased their joy: they joy before thee according to the joy in harvest, as men rejoice when they divide the spoil.

For the yoke of his burden, and the staff of his shoulder, the rod of his oppressor, thou hast broken as in the day of Midian.

For all the armor of the armed man in the tumult, and the garments rolled in blood, shall be for burning, for fuel of fire.

For unto us a Child is born, unto us a Son is given; and the government shall be upon his shoulder: and his name shall be called Wonderful, Counsellor, Mighty God, Everlasting Father, Prince of Peace.

Of the increase of his government and of peace there shall be no end, upon the throne of David, and upon his kingdom, to establish it, and to uphold it with justice and with righteousness from henceforth even for ever. The zeal of Jehovah of hosts will perform this. (Isaiah 9. 2-7.)

The Apostles' Creed

The **Minister** *and the* **Congregation** *shall then make the following Confession of Faith:*

I believe in God the Father Almighty, Maker of heaven and earth;

And in Jesus Christ, His only Son, our Lord: Who was conceived by the Holy Spirit, Born of the Virgin Mary; Suffered under Pontius Pilate, Was crucified, dead, and buried; He descended into hell; The third day He rose again from the dead; He ascended into heaven, And sitteth on the right hand of God the Father Almighty; From thence He shall come to judge the quick and the dead.

I believe in the Holy Spirit; The Holy Christian Church, the Communion of saints; The Forgiveness of sins; The Resurrection of the body; And the Life everlasting. Amen.

An **Anthem** *in harmony with the Day may here be sung. Then shall follow one or more verses of a* **Hymn** *as an introduction to the Sermon. In the meantime the* **Minister** *shall enter the Pulpit.*

The Sermon

The Sermon shall conclude with the following Prayer:

Lord God, our heavenly Father: Through Thy holy angels Thou didst announce to the shepherds in the field the birth of Thy Son, Jesus Christ, and didst bid them not to be fearful, but to rejoice that Christ the Saviour was born in the city of David. Remove, we pray Thee, through Thy Holy Spirit all fear from our hearts and grant us true and lasting joy. And though we be despised and suffer much in this present time, grant that with a firm faith we may embrace Thy Son Jesus Christ, Who for our sake became man to save us from death and all evil, and gain for us eternal salvation. Amen.

The **Church Notices** *may then be given. The Pulpit Office shall conclude with the following:*

The grace of the Lord Jesus Christ, and the love of God, and the communion of the Holy Spirit, be with you all. Amen.

Then shall an **Offertory** *be played, or an* **Anthem** *sung, during which the offering shall be made. The* **Minister,** *having received the offering, shall place it upon the Altar and pray as follows:*

O God, Thou Giver of all good gifts, graciously receive and bless this offering, which we Thy people place upon Thine Altar, for Jesus' sake. Amen.*

Then shall the **Congregation** *sing a Hymn, during which the* **Minister** *shall proceed to the Altar.*

---

*A short offertory sentence (see pp. 554, 555) may then be sung by the Choir.

The Salutation

The **Minister,** *turning to the Congregation, shall sing or say:*

The Lord be with you.

The **Congregation** *shall rise and sing:*

And with thy spir - it.

Then the **Minister** *shall say:*

Let us pray.

The Lord's Prayer

The **Minister** *shall turn to the Altar and with the* **Congregation** *shall pray:*

Our Father, Who art in heaven: Hallowed be Thy Name; Thy kingdom come; Thy will be done on earth, as it is in heaven; Give us this day our daily bread; And forgive us our trespasses, as we forgive those who trespass against us; And lead us not into temptation; But deliver us from evil; For Thine is the kingdom, and the power, and the glory, forever. Amen.

Benedicamus

The **Minister** *shall turn to the Congregation and sing or say:*

Preussische Kirchenordnung, 1525.

Let us thank and praise the Lord!

The **Congregation** *shall sing:*

Glo - ry be to Thee, O Lord! Hal - le - lu - jah! Hal - le - lu - jah! Hal - le - lu - jah!

Instead of the foregoing, **The Magnificat** *may be read:**

My soul doth magnify the Lord: and my spirit hath rejoiced in God my Saviour. For He hath regarded the low estate of His handmaiden. For behold, from henceforth all generations shall call me blessed. For He that is mighty hath done to me great things; and holy is His Name. And His mercy is on them that fear Him: from generation to generation. He hath showed strength with His arm; He hath scattered the proud in the imagination of their hearts. He hath put down the mighty from their seats, and exalted them of low degree. He hath filled the hungry with good things; and the rich He hath sent empty away. He hath holpen His servant Israel, in remembrance of His mercy: as He spake to our fathers, to Abraham, and to his seed for ever.

Glory be to the Father, and to the Son, and to the Holy Spirit: As it was in the beginning, is now, and ever shall be, world without end. Amen.

Then shall the **Minister** *say:*

Bow your hearts to God and receive the Benediction.

The Lord bless thee, and keep thee. The Lord make His face shine upon thee, and be gracious unto thee. The Lord lift up His countenance upon thee, and give thee peace.

In the Name of the Father, and of the Son, and of the Holy Spirit. Amen.

The **Minister** *shall turn to the Altar, and the* **Congregation** *shall sing:*

A - men,   A - men,   A - - - - - men.

The Service shall close with silent prayer, while the **Congregation** *remains standing and the* **Minister** *kneels before the Altar.*

---

* The Magnificat may be sung by the Choir. See p. 720.

Matins on Easter Sunday

The Service shall begin with an appropriate **Hymn.** *During the singing the* **Minister** *shall proceed to the Altar and kneel in prayer. After the singing he shall rise, turn to the Congregation, and say:*

Grace be unto you and peace from God, our Father, and from the Lord Jesus Christ. Amen.

Come, let us worship and bow down; let us kneel before the Lord our Maker, for He is our God.

The **Minister,** *turning to the Altar, shall kneel and pray:*

Almighty God, Heavenly Father, we thank Thee for the day in which life and immortality were brought to light through the resurrection of our blessed Lord from the dead. We thank Thee for the Word of life in Jesus Christ our Saviour, Who has overcome death and opened unto us the gate of eternal life. Grant that the glad Easter tidings may be abundantly blessed in our hearts. Awaken us by the power of Thy Holy Spirit that we may arise from the death of sin and walk in newness of life. May we live our lives upon the earth as those who look for the blessed hope and appearing of the glory of the risen Saviour. May the true light shine far this day, revealing and healing the sins of many hearts. Kindle within us heavenly desires, and grant that we may ever thirst for the Fountain of Life, Jesus Christ, Thy Son, our Lord. Amen.

The **Minister,** *rising, shall continue:*

Blessed be the Name of Jehovah from this time forth and forevermore. From the rising of the sun unto the going down of the same Jehovah's Name is to be praised. Jehovah is high above all nations, and His glory above the heavens. Who is like unto Jehovah our God, That hath His seat on high, That humbleth Himself to behold the things that are in heaven and in the earth! (Psalm 113. 2—6.)

Gloria Patri

The **Congregation** *shall rise, and with the* **Minister,** *still turned toward the Altar, sing:*

Pfälzische Kirchenordnung, 1550.

Glo - ry be to the Fa - ther, and to the Son, and to the Ho - ly

Spir - it; As it was in the be - gin - ning, Is

now, and ev - er shall be, World.... with - out end. A - men.

The Scripture Lesson

After the singing the **Minister** *shall turn to the Congregation and say:*

Hear the Word of God as it is recorded in the First Epistle of Peter, the first chapter, beginning at the third verse:

Blessed be the God and Father of our Lord Jesus Christ, Who according to His great mercy begat us again unto a living hope by the resurrection of Jesus Christ from the dead,

Unto an inheritance incorruptible, and undefiled, and that fadeth not away, reserved in heaven for you,

Who by the power of God are guarded through faith unto a salvation ready to be revealed in the last time.

Wherein ye greatly rejoice, though now for a little while, if need be, ye have been put to grief in manifold trials,

That the proof of your faith, being more precious than gold that perisheth though it is proved by fire, may be found unto praise and glory and honor at the revelation of Jesus Christ:

Whom not having seen ye love; on Whom, though now ye see Him not, yet believing, ye rejoice greatly with joy unspeakable and full of glory:

Receiving the end of your faith, even the salvation of your souls.

The Apostles' Creed

The **Minister** *and the* **Congregation** *shall then make the following Confession of Faith:*

I believe in God the Father Almighty, Maker of heaven and earth;

And in Jesus Christ, His only Son, our Lord: Who was conceived by the Holy Spirit, Born of the Virgin Mary; Suffered under Pontius Pilate, Was crucified, dead, and buried; He descended into hell; The third day He rose again from the dead; He ascended into heaven, And sitteth on the right hand of God the Father Almighty; From thence He shall come to judge the quick and the dead.

I believe in the Holy Spirit; The Holy Christian Church, the Communion of saints; The Forgiveness of sins; The Resurrection of the body; And the Life everlasting. Amen.

An **Anthem** *in harmony with the Day may here be sung. Then shall follow one or more verses of a* **Hymn** *as an introduction to the Sermon. In the meantime the* **Minister** *shall enter the Pulpit.*

The Sermon

The Sermon shall conclude with the following prayer:

Lord God, Heavenly Father! Thou hast delivered up Thy Son for our trespasses, and raised Him for our justification. We pray Thee, grant us Thy Holy Spirit, that through Him Thou mayest govern and direct us, keep us in the true faith and deliver us from sin, and finally at the last day raise us unto eternal life. Amen.

The **Church Notices** *may then be given. The Pulpit Office shall conclude with the following:*

The grace of the Lord Jesus Christ, and the love of God, and the communion of the Holy Spirit be with you all. Amen.

Then shall an **Offertory** *be played, or an* **Anthem** *sung, during which the offering shall be made. The* **Minister,** *having received the offering, shall place it upon the Altar and pray as follows:*

O God, Thou Giver of all good gifts, graciously receive and bless this offering, which we Thy people place upon Thine Altar, for Jesus' sake. Amen.*

Then shall the **Congregation** *sing a* **Hymn,** *during which the* **Minister** *shall proceed to the Altar.*

The Salutation

The **Minister** *shall turn to the Congregation and sing or say:*

The **Congregation** *shall rise and sing:*

The Lord be with you.

And with thy spir - it.

Then the **Minister** *shall say:*

Let us pray.

The **Minister** *shall then turn to the Altar and with the* **Congregation** *pray:*

Our Father, Who art in heaven: Hallowed be Thy Name; Thy kingdom come; Thy will be done on earth, as it is in heaven; Give us this day our daily bread; And forgive us our trespasses, as we forgive those who trespass against us; And lead us not into temptation; But deliver us from evil; For Thine is the kingdom, and the power, and the glory, forever. Amen.

Benedicamus

The **Minister** *shall turn to the Congregation and sing or say:*

The **Congregation** *shall sing:*

SPANGENBERG, 1545.

Let us thank and praise the Lord!

Glo - ry be to Thee, O Lord!

* A short offertory sentence (see pp. 554, 555) may then be sung by the Choir.

Hal - le - lu - jah! Hal - le - lu - jah! Hal - le - lu - - - - - - jah!

Instead of the Benedicamus the following may be sung or read:

Jehovah hath established His throne in the heavens; and His kingdom ruleth over all. Bless Jehovah, ye His angels, that are mighty in strength, that fulfil His Word, hearkening unto the voice of His Word. Bless Jehovah, all ye His hosts, ye ministers of His, that do His pleasure. Bless Jehovah, all ye His works, in all places of His dominion: Bless Jehovah, O my soul. (Psalm 103. 19—22.)

Then shall the **Minister** *say:*

Bow your hearts to God and receive the Benediction.

The Lord bless thee, and keep thee. The Lord make His face shine upon thee, and be gracious unto thee. The Lord lift up His countenance upon thee, and give thee peace.

In the Name of the Father, and of the Son, and of the Holy Spirit. Amen.

The **Minister** *shall turn to the Altar, and the* **Congregation** *shall sing:*

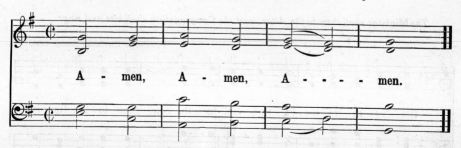

A - men, A - men, A - - - - men.

The Service shall close with silent prayer, while the **Congregation** *remains standing and the* **Minister** *kneels before the Altar.*

Vespers

The Service shall begin with an appropriate **Hymn.** *During the singing the* **Minister** *shall proceed to the Altar and kneel in prayer. After the singing he shall rise, turn to the Congregation, and say:*

Grace be unto you and peace from God, our Father, and the Lord Jesus Christ. Amen.

Come, let us worship and bow down; let us kneel before the Lord our Maker, for He is our God.

The Confession of Sins

The **Minister,** *turning to the Altar, shall kneel and pray:*

Merciful God, Heavenly Father, Whose grace endureth from generation to generation, Thou art patient and longsuffering and forgivest the sins and transgressions of all who truly repent. Look with compassion upon Thy people and hear their supplications. We have sinned against Thee. We are unworthy of Thy goodness and love. Remember not our transgressions; have mercy upon us; help us, O God, our Saviour. Grant us remission of all our sins and save us. Give us the grace of Thy Holy Spirit that we may amend our ways and with Thee obtain everlasting life; through Thy Son, Jesus Christ, our Lord. Amen.

The **Minister,** *rising and turning to the Congregation, shall say:*

If we walk in the light, as He is in the light, we have fellowship one with another, and the blood of Jesus His Son cleanseth us from all sin.

Gloria Patri

The **Minister** *shall turn to the Altar, and the* **Congregation** *shall rise and sing:*

Pfälzische Kirchenordnung, 1570.

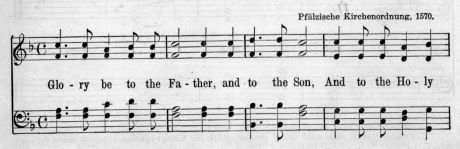

Glo - ry be to the Fa - ther, and to the Son, And to the Ho - ly

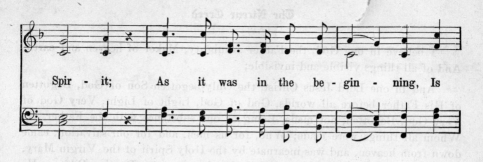

Spir - it; As it was in the be - gin - ning, Is

now, and ev - er shall be, World.... with - out end. A - MEN.

The Scripture Lesson

After the singing the **Minister** *shall turn to the Congregation and say:*

Hear the Word of God as it is recorded in the......

The **Minister** *and* **Congregation** *shall then make their Confession of Faith in the words of the Apostles' Creed or of the Nicene Creed.*

The Apostles' Creed

I believe in God the Father Almighty, Maker of heaven and earth;

And in Jesus Christ, His only Son, our Lord: Who was conceived by the Holy Spirit, Born of the Virgin Mary; Suffered under Pontius Pilate, Was crucified, dead, and buried; He descended into hell; The third day He rose again from the dead; He ascended into heaven, And sitteth on the right hand of God the Father Almighty; From thence He shall come to judge the quick and the dead.

I believe in the Holy Spirit; The Holy Christian Church, the Communion of saints; The Forgiveness of sins; The Resurrection of the body; And the Life everlasting. Amen.

The Nicene Creed

I believe in one God, the Father Almighty, Maker of heaven and earth, And of all things visible and invisible;

And in one Lord Jesus Christ, the Only-begotten Son of God, Begotten of His Father before all worlds, God of God, Light of Light, Very God of Very God, Begotten, not made, Being of one substance with the Father, By Whom all things were made; Who, for us men, and for our salvation, came down from heaven, and was incarnate by the Holy Spirit of the Virgin Mary, and was made man; and was crucified also for us under Pontius Pilate. He suffered and was buried; And the third day He rose again, according to the Scriptures; And ascended into heaven, and sitteth on the right hand of the Father; And He shall come again with glory to judge both the quick and the dead; Whose kingdom shall have no end.

And I believe in the Holy Spirit, the Lord and Giver of Life, Who proceedeth from the Father and the Son, Who with the Father and the Son together is worshiped and glorified, Who spake by the prophets.

And I believe one holy Christian and Apostolic Church.

I acknowledge one Baptism for the remission of sins; and I look for the resurrection of the dead and the life of the world to come.   Amen.

An **Anthem** *may here be sung.   Then shall follow one or more verses of a* **Hymn** *as an introduction to the Sermon.   In the meantime the* **Minister** *shall enter the Pulpit.*

The Sermon

The Sermon shall conclude with the following prayer:

We praise Thee, O God, that Thou hast permitted Thy Word to dwell richly among us to the salvation and building up of our souls on our most holy faith.   Heavenly Father, we thank Thee for the gift of Thy Son, Who was delivered up for our trespasses and raised for our justification.   We thank Thee that Thou hast permitted the message of this great salvation to come to us through the Gospel.   We pray Thee, grant us a living faith in Christ, a fervent love to Thee and to our fellow men, and a blessed hope through Jesus Christ, Thy Son, our Lord.   Amen.

The **Church Notices** *may then be given.   The Pulpit Office shall conclude with the following:*

The grace of the Lord Jesus Christ, and the love of God, and the communion of the Holy Spirit, be with you all.   Amen.

Then shall an **Offertory** *be played, or an* **Anthem** *sung, during which the offering shall be made.* *The* **Minister,** *having received the offering, shall place it upon the Altar and pray as follows:*

O God, Thou Giver of all good gifts, graciously receive and bless this offering, which we Thy people place upon Thine Altar, for Jesus' sake. Amen.*

Then shall the **Congregation** *sing a* **Hymn,** *during which the* **Minister** *shall proceed to the Altar.*

The Salutation

The **Minister** *shall turn to the Congregation and sing or say:*

The **Congregation** *shall rise and sing:*

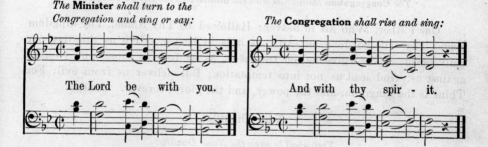

Lenten Season

The **Minister:**

The **Congregation:**

Then the **Minister** *shall say:*

Let us pray.

The **Minister** *shall turn to the Altar and pray:*

Watch over us, O Lord, our heavenly Father, and protect us from all evil, and grant that we may this night rest secure under Thy care. Preserve and bless Thy Church and our Government. Graciously remember the sick and those who are in need or in peril. Have mercy upon all men. And when our last evening shall come, grant us to fall asleep in Thy peace and to awake in Thy glory, through Jesus Christ, Thy Son, our Lord.

---

*A short offertory sentence (see pp. 554, 555) may then be sung by the Choir.

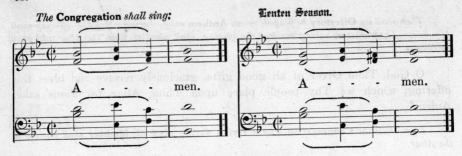

The **Congregation** *shall sing:*   **Lenten Season.**

A - - - men.   A - - - men.

The Lord's Prayer

The **Congregation** *shall unite with the* **Minister** *in the Lord's Prayer:*

Our Father, Who art in heaven: Hallowed be Thy Name; Thy kingdom come; Thy will be done on earth, as it is in heaven; Give us this day our daily bread; And forgive us our trespasses, as we forgive those who trespass against us; And lead us not into temptation; But deliver us from evil; For Thine is the kingdom, and the power, and the glory, forever. Amen.

Nunc Dimittis

Then shall be sung the Nunc Dimittis:

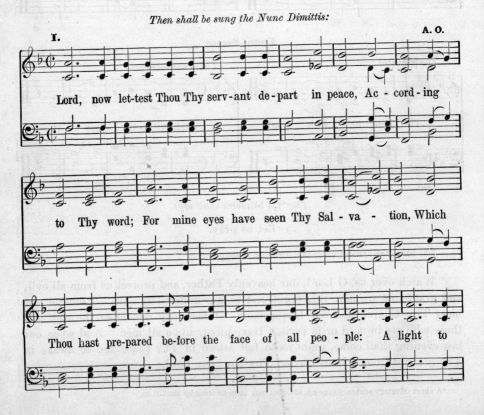

Lord, now let-test Thou Thy serv-ant de-part in peace, Ac-cord-ing

to Thy word; For mine eyes have seen Thy Sal-va-tion, Which

Thou hast pre-pared be-fore the face of all peo-ple: A light to

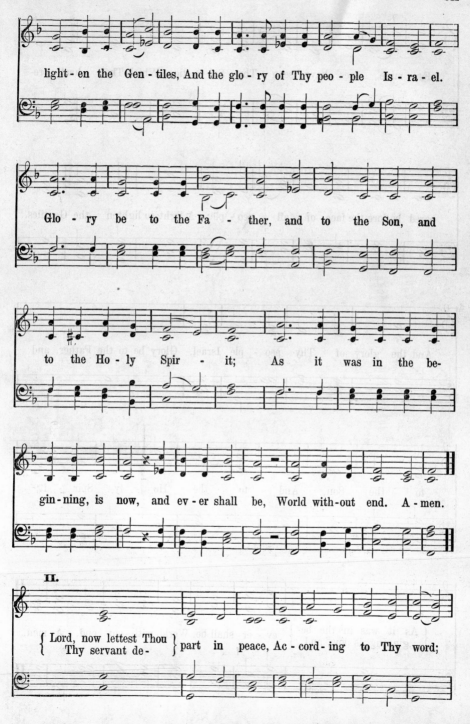

light-en the Gen-tiles, And the glo-ry of Thy peo-ple Is-ra-el.

Glo-ry be to the Fa-ther, and to the Son, and

to the Ho-ly Spir-it; As it was in the be-

gin-ning, is now, and ev-er shall be, World with-out end. A-men.

II.

{ Lord, now lettest Thou
Thy servant de- } part in peace, Ac-cord-ing to Thy word;

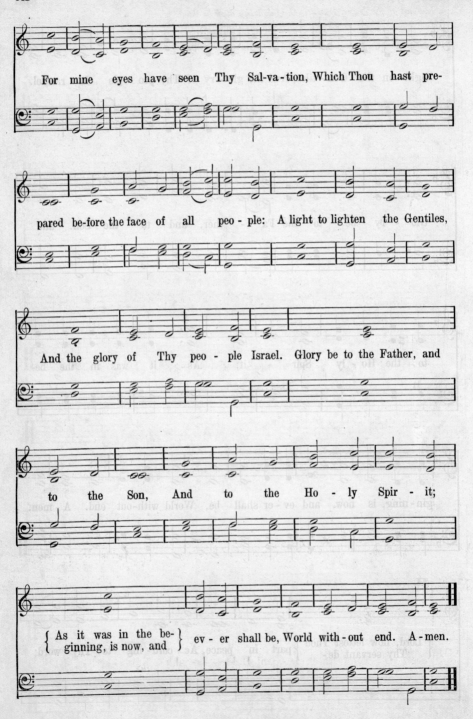

For mine eyes have seen Thy Sal-va-tion, Which Thou hast pre-

pared be-fore the face of all peo - ple: A light to lighten the Gentiles,

And the glory of Thy peo - ple Israel. Glory be to the Father, and

to the Son, And to the Ho - ly Spir - it;

{ As it was in the be- ginning, is now, and } ev - er shall be, World with - out end. A - men.

Instead of the Nunc Dimittis the following may be used:

Benedicamus

Advent, Christmas, and Epiphany Seasons.

The **Minister** *shall turn to the Congregation and sing or say:*

Preussische Kirchenordnung, 1525.

Let us thank and praise the Lord!

The **Congregation** *shall sing:*

Glo - ry be to Thee, O Lord! Hal - le - lu - jah! Hal - le - lu - jah! Hal - le - lu - jah!

Lenten Season.

The **Minister:**

Let . . . us thank and praise the Lord!

The **Congregation:**

Nürnberger Agende, 1639.

Glo - ry be to Thee, O Lord! Hal-le-lu - jah! Hal-le-lu-jah! Hal-le-lu - jah!

The Benediction

Then shall the **Minister** *say:*

Bow your hearts to God, and receive the Benediction.

The Lord bless thee, and keep thee. The Lord make His face shine upon thee, and be gracious unto thee. The Lord lift up His countenance upon thee, and give thee peace.

In the Name of the Father, and of the Son, and of the Holy Spirit. Amen.

The **Minister** *shall turn to the Altar, and the* **Congregation** *shall sing:*

Advent, Christmas, and Epiphany Seasons.

A - men, A - men, A - - - - - men.

Lenten Season.

A - men, A - men, A - - - - men.

Easter and Pentecost Seasons.

A - men, A - men, A - - - - men.

Trinity Season.

A - men, A - men, A - - - - men.

The Service shall close with silent prayer, while the **Congregation** *remains standing and the* **Minister** *kneels before the Altar.*

The Litany
and
Prayers on Special Occasions

Instead of the **General Prayer** *the* **Litany** *shall be used during* **Lent,** *on Sunday* **Rogate,** *and on special occasions.*

The **Minister** *shall turn to the Altar and say the following prayers. The* **Congregation,** *standing, shall sing or say the responses.*

From J. SPANGENBERG, 1545.

The Minister:

Lord, have mercy upon us.

The Congregation:

Lord, have mer - cy up - on us.

The Minister:

O Christ, hear us.

The Congregation:

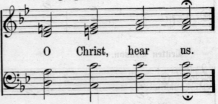

O Christ, hear us.

The Minister:

Christ, have mercy upon us.

The Congregation:

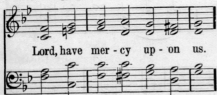

Christ, have mer - cy up - on us.

The Minister:

O God, the Father in heaven;

The Congregation:

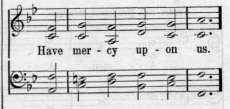

Have mer - cy up - on us.

The Minister:

Lord, have mercy upon us.

The Congregation:

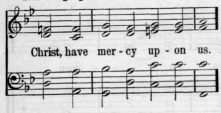

Lord, have mer - cy up - on us.

The Minister:

O God the Son, Redeemer of the world;

The Congregation:

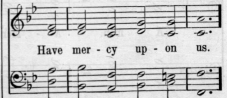

Have mer - cy up - on us.

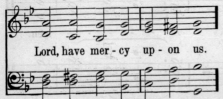

The **Minister:**

O God, the Holy Spirit;

The **Congregation:**

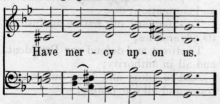

Have mer - cy up - on us.

The **Minister:**

Be gracious unto us.

The **Congregation:**

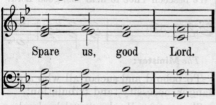

Spare us, good Lord.

The **Minister:**

Be gracious unto us.

The **Congregation:**

Help us, good Lord.

The **Minister:**

From all sin;
From all error;
From all evil:

The **Congregation:**

Good Lord, de - liv - er us.

The **Minister:**

From the crafts and assaults of the devil;
From sudden and evil death;
From pestilence and famine;
From war and bloodshed;
From sedition and rebellion;
From lightning and tempest;
From all calamity by fire and water;
And from everlasting death:

The **Congregation:**

Good Lord, de - liv - er us.

The **Minister:**

By the mystery of Thy holy Incarnation;
By Thy holy Nativity;
By Thy Baptism, Fasting, and Temptation;
By Thine Agony and Bloody Sweat;
By Thy Cross and Passion;
By Thy precious Death and Burial;
By Thy glorious Resurrection and Ascension;
And by the coming of the Holy Spirit, the Comforter:

The **Congregation:**

Help us, good Lord.

The **Minister:**

In all time of our tribulation;
In all time of our prosperity;
In the hour of our death;
And in the day of judgment:

The **Congregation:**

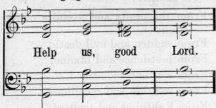

Help us, good Lord.

The **Minister:**

We poor sinners do beseech Thee;

The **Congregation:**

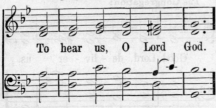

To hear us, O Lord God.

The **Minister:**

And to lead and govern Thy holy Christian Church in the right way;

To preserve all pastors and ministers of Thy Church in the true knowledge and understanding of Thy Word, and in holiness of life;

To put an end to all schisms and causes of offence;

To bring into the way of truth all such as have erred, and are deceived;

To beat down Satan under our feet;

To send faithful laborers into Thy harvest;

To accompany Thy Word with all Thy Spirit and grace;

To raise up them that fall, and to strengthen such as do stand;

And to comfort and help the weak-hearted and the distressed:

The **Congregation:**

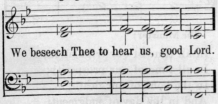

We beseech Thee to hear us, good Lord.

The **Minister:**

To give to all nations peace and concord;

To preserve our country from discord and contention;

To safeguard our nation against all its adversaries;

To direct and defend our President, and all in authority;

And to bless and keep our magistrates and all our people:

The **Congregation:**

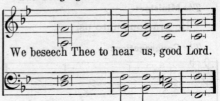

We beseech Thee to hear us, good Lord.

The **Minister:**

To behold and succor all who are in danger, necessity, and tribulation;

To protect all who travel by land or water;

To preserve all women in the perils of child-birth;

To strengthen and keep all sick persons and young children;

To set free all who are innocently imprisoned;

To defend and provide for all fatherless children and widows;

And to have mercy upon all men:

The **Congregation:**

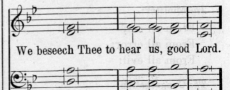

We beseech Thee to hear us, good Lord.

The **Minister:**

To forgive our enemies, persecutors, and slanderers, and to turn their hearts;

To give and preserve to our use the fruits of the earth;

And graciously to hear our prayers:

The **Congregation:**

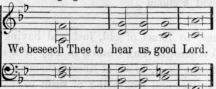

We beseech Thee to hear us, good Lord.

The **Minister:**

O Lord Jesus Christ, Son of God;

The **Congregation:**

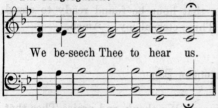

We be-seech Thee to hear us.

The **Minister:**

O Lamb of God, That takest away the sin of the world;

The **Congregation:**

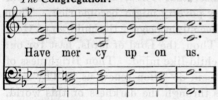

Have mer - cy up - on us.

The **Minister:**

O Lamb of God, That takest away the sin of the world;

The **Congregation:**

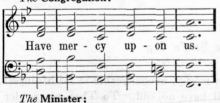

Have mer - cy up - on us.

The **Minister:**

O Lamb of God, That takest away the sin of the world;

The **Congregation:**

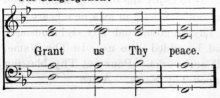

Grant us Thy peace.

The **Minister:**

O Christ, hear us.

The **Congregation:**

O Christ, hear us.

The **Minister:**

Lord, have mercy upon us.

The **Congregation:**

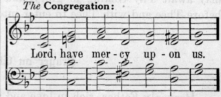

Lord, have mer - cy up - on us.

The **Minister:**

Christ, have mercy upon us.

The **Congregation:**

Christ, have mer - cy up - on us.

The **Minister:**

Lord, have mercy upon us.

The **Congregation:**

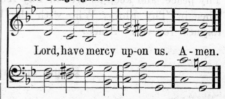

Lord, have mercy up-on us. A - men.

Then shall the **Minister,** *and the* **Congregation** *with him, say the Lord's Prayer:*

Our Father, Who art in heaven: Hallowed be Thy Name; Thy kingdom come; Thy will be done on earth, as it is in heaven; Give us this day our daily bread; And forgive us our trespasses, as we forgive those who trespass against us; And lead us not into temptation; But deliver us from evil; For Thine is the kingdom, and the power, and the glory, forever. Amen.

Prayer on Advent Sunday

Lord Jesus Christ, Thou Who camest to Israel of old, just and having salvation; We thank Thee that Thou still comest to Thy Church in Thy Word and Sacraments, to preach good tidings to the poor, to set at liberty them that are bruised, to proclaim release to the captives and recovering of sight to the blind. Grant us by Thy Holy Spirit to receive Thee with willing hearts and joyfully to hail Thee as our King. Strengthen us that we may fearlessly confess Thee before the world. Grant us grace that with watchfulness we may await Thy coming in glory, and in that hour be found ready to stand before Thee and with Thee to enter into Thine eternal joy. Amen.

Prayer on Christmas Day

Heavenly Father, rich in love and mercy! We thank and praise Thee that Thou hast graciously fulfilled the word of Thy promise to the fathers and suffered Thine only-begotten Son to become man for our salvation. Lord Jesus Christ, to Thee be everlasting praise, that Thou, being rich, for our sakes becamest poor that we through Thy poverty might become rich. Thou hast become our Brother that we with Thee might become the children of God. Be Thou born also in our hearts, and as Thou, the Lord of lords, hast for our sakes become a child, so give us a right child-like mind. Thou Brightness of the Father's glory and Image of His person, do Thou renew us in Thy holy likeness. Thou heavenly Light, light us through the darkness of this world. Thou eternal Life, give us life in Thee. Thou great Prince of peace, grant us Thy peace, and keep us ever in Thy Kingdom, that we may laud and magnify Thee in Thy glory, Who with the Father and the Holy Spirit livest and reignest forever. Amen.

Prayer on New Year's Day

Almighty and eternal God, great in mercy, unchangeable in faithfulness! Thou art the same and Thy years shall have no end. To Thee we render thanks and praise on this first day of the year for all the mercy which Thou hast so abundantly shown us in the days that are gone. We beseech Thee that Thou wilt ever henceforward grant us to enjoy the blessing which Thou hast prepared for us in Christ Jesus, Thy Son. Create in us a new heart with this New Year. Teach us to seek first Thy kingdom and Thy righteousness, and so shall all we need of earthly good be added unto us. In Thy Name, Lord Jesus, we would begin and end all our works. Pour out Thy blessing upon us, and upon all who with us call upon Thy Name. Amen.

Prayer during Lent

Lord Jesus, ineffably great was Thy love toward us, fallen men, that Thou didst become man and suffer shame, anguish, pain, and death for us sinners, who otherwise would have perished eternally. Give us grace that we may ever remember, and in faith receive, Thine atoning sacrifice; and that for this unspeakable mercy we may praise Thee and the Father and the Holy Spirit. Help us ever to live a Christian life, and in all need and adversity find comfort in the assurance that Thou art our Saviour, Who hast delivered us from the power of death and the devil, and Who finally wilt take us from this world of travail to Thyself in heaven, there to perfect Thy praise forever. Amen.

Prayer on Good Friday

Lord Jesus, Thou Lamb of God that takest away the sin of the world! We thank Thee for Thy great love toward us, miserable sinners, that Thou for our sake didst humble Thyself and become obedient unto death, even the death of the cross. Thou hast borne our griefs, and carried our sorrows. The chastisement of our peace was upon Thee, and with Thy stripes we are healed. Praised be Thy Holy Name! Cleanse us now from our sins by Thy blood, and grant us Thy peace. Help us by the power of Thy death to die unto sin and to take up the cross and follow Thee. Keep us in communion with Thee, that with all who have overcome by Thy blood we may finally thank and praise Thee forever. Amen.

Prayer on Easter Sunday

Almighty God, our heavenly Father! We enter into Thy presence with thanksgiving. We praise Thee that Thou, Who for our sins didst give Thine only-begotten Son, hast for our justification raised Him again and made Him the Conqueror of sin and death. Lord Jesus, Thou Prince of Life, grant us by Thy Holy Spirit that in the power of Thy Resurrection we may arise and walk in newness of life. Give us the comfort of a living hope. Come unto us as Thou didst come unto Thy first disciples, and give us Thy peace. Keep us in this peace even unto the end, and in the hour of death help us to hold fast to Thee, Who art the Resurrection and the Life. Raise at last our mortal bodies and fashion them like unto Thy glorified body, that with the Church triumphant we may finally sing: "Thanks be to God, Who giveth us the victory through our Lord Jesus Christ." Amen.

Prayer on Ascension Day

Holy and blessed Saviour! We praise Thee that Thou hast accomplished Thy work of redemption. Thou, King Eternal, art seated on the right hand of God, and the hosts of heaven do worship Thee. We, too, come before Thee with adoration, thanksgiving, and praise, that Thou hast redeemed us to God by Thy blood and opened unto us a way to heaven. We are but pilgrims and strangers in the earth; help us safely through the trials of this present time. Create in us a heavenly mind, that we may seek the things that are above, not the things that are upon the earth. Lord Jesus, Thou Who art the head of Thy Church, bestow upon Thy people the rich gifts of Thy Spirit, and exalt us with all Thy faithful unto the same place whither Thou art gone before, ever to behold Thy glory. Amen.

Prayer on the Day of Pentecost

O God, we praise Thee, that on the first day of Pentecost Thou didst pour forth Thy Holy Spirit upon Thy faithful people, and thereby didst found Thy Church upon the earth. We thank Thee that we, too, have been received into Thy Church. We thank Thee for Thy Word and Sacraments, by which Thou wouldst sanctify us through the power of Thy Holy Spirit. We beseech Thee, send forth Thy Holy Spirit upon us, upon our congregations, and upon our homes. Come, Holy Spirit, quicken our dull hearts; cleanse us from sin; increase our faith and kindle in us a fervent love one to another, that we may preserve the unity of the spirit in the bond of peace. Spirit of Truth, guide us in Thy truth, and grant us whatsoever is profitable for life and godliness, to Thy glory and our salvation. Amen.

Prayer on Trinity Sunday

Holy Triune God! We thank Thee that by Thy gracious revelation Thou hast made Thyself known to us as our God, and that in baptism Thou hast received us as Thy children of grace, born again unto eternal life. O Thou, Father of our Lord Jesus Christ, eternal Love and Mercy! Gracious Saviour, Lord Jesus Christ, our wisdom, our righteousness, our sanctification and our redemption! O Holy Spirit, Spirit of truth, of adoption, and of prayer! We praise Thee, we glorify Thee, we worship Thee, O Triune God. Come unto us, and make Thy abode with us. Create in us a true faith and a living hope. Grant us finally with Thy holy angels and all the elect to worship, praise, and serve Thee in Thy holy temple. Amen.

Prayer at Reformation Festivals

Almighty, ever-living God, we thank and praise Thee that in the time of our fathers Thou didst cause again the clear light of Thy gospel to shine forth, and that Thou didst give Thy servants grace fearlessly to confess Thy truth. We thank Thee that Thou hast granted us unto this day to hold fast Thy pure Word, unworthy though we be. Forbid, O God, that we should pervert Thy gospel and use our freedom for a cloak of wickedness. Mercifully keep us from error. May Thy Word and Thy Sacraments be transmitted pure to our posterity. Grant to the ministers of Thy Word to-day, as Thou didst to its first confessors, power and wisdom rightly to bear witness to Thee, and to overcome the adversaries of Thy gospel. Grant that Thy Church may be united more closely in truth and love; and be Thou, O God, our defense and stay against all the power of the enemy, that by Thy might we may be able to withstand in the evil day, and, having done all, to stand; to the praise and glory of Thy Name. Amen.

Prayer at Mission Festivals

Almighty God, loving Father, Thou Who gavest Thine only-begotten Son that the world might be saved through Him: We commend to Thy tender mercies all the nations that walk in darkness and that dwell in the land of the shadow of death. Kindle in our hearts a fervent love toward Thee, that we may be truly zealous for the extension of Thy kingdom upon the earth. The harvest indeed is plenteous, but the laborers are few. We pray Thee, O Lord, send forth laborers into Thy harvest. Strengthen and bless Thy servants in their labors. Grant that through the gospel Thy Name may be glorified in all the earth, and finally grant us with all the countless hosts of peoples and nations and tongues to serve and praise Thee in Thy glory forever. Amen.

Prayer on Thanksgiving Day

Heavenly Father, we thank Thee for the manifold gifts we have received from Thy bountiful hand. Thou hast permitted Thy Word to dwell abundantly among us, and Thou hast favored us with many earthly blessings. Lord, we are unworthy of Thy faithfulness and mercy; but we pray Thee, continue to be gracious toward us. Give us all things needful and wholesome, and grant us in all the vicissitudes of life to remain a people which trusts in Thy mighty aid, through Jesus Christ, our Lord. Amen.

Prayer for the Fruits of the Earth

Almighty God, merciful Father, Who of Thy great goodness dost replenish the earth with divers fruits to be the food of man and beast: We beseech Thee for Thy blessing that our land may yield us its fruits of increase. Grant seasonable weather for the harvest of the earth, and preserve it from all things harmful. Crown the year with Thy goodness. Preserve us, O God, from years of barrenness, from dearth and famine, and prosper us in Thy mercy. We confess our sins before Thee: be gracious unto Thy people and forsake us not; bless us with all that Thou hast ordained for our sustenance, and give us grace rightly to use the same to the praise and honor of Thy Holy Name; through Jesus Christ, our Lord. Amen.

Prayer for Those Who Are to Be Confirmed

Gracious Lord and loving Father! Through Holy Baptism Thou hast already received into Thy grace these Thy children who are now being prepared for their first communion. We beseech Thee, grant them a true knowledge of the grace which in the washing of regeneration Thou hast abundantly poured out upon them. Awaken and touch their hearts that in penitence and faith they may receive Thy salvation. And when they shall make their confession before Thee and before Thy Church, grant them the grace of Thy Holy Spirit worthily to commune at the Lord's table, and henceforth steadfastly to persevere unto the end in the confession and practice of their Christian faith; through Thy Son, Jesus Christ, our Lord. Amen.

Prayer in Time of War

O Lord, almighty God, eternal Father! Unto Thee do we cry; hear our prayer and manifest Thy grace unto us. We confess that in manifold ways we have sinfully misused the blessings of peace which Thou hast granted our land; forgive us, O Lord. Deliver us out of the distress with which war now threatens us. Protect, sustain, and help all who go forth to meet danger and death in defense of their country. Without Thy help, O Lord, wisdom and power avail nothing. Thou alone canst exalt the humble and lay the proud in the dust. In Thy Name we put our trust, and in Thy Name we raise our standard. Be our support, O Lord of hosts, and grant us deliverance out of the hand of our enemies, that we may in the tranquillity of peace render Thee praise for the fruits of peace. Hear us, merciful God and Father, for the sake of Thy Son, our Saviour. Amen.

Prayer in Times of Dearth and Famine

Almighty and gracious God, Who makest the earth to yield its increase for the sustenance and nourishment of man and beast: We have turned away from us Thy blessing through our sins, and the land is languishing from hunger. Lord God, look upon our need. O Lord, graciously lighten this punishment that we despair not. Make us patient and submissive. Bless our small provision. Bless the earth again with fruitfulness; grant seasonable weather; supply our need; and help us ever henceforth to use Thy gifts with thankfulness and moderation. Give us also with our daily bread nourishment for the soul, and we shall praise Thee now and throughout all eternity; through Thy Son, Jesus Christ, our Lord. Amen.

Prayer for the Sick

Almighty and eternal God, Thou art the health and strength of them that trust in Thee. We pray Thee that Thou wouldst look in mercy upon the sick and the needy. Turn their distress unto good, and if it be Thy will, restore them to health. But above all give them healing for the soul through Thy Holy Word. Help them by the remembrance of the bitter passion of Thy Son patiently to bear the affliction with which Thou hast visited them. And finally, when their hour is come, deliver them from all evil and bring them safe to Thy heavenly kingdom; through Thy Son, Jesus Christ, our Lord. Amen.

Prayer in Times of Plague

Eternal and righteous God! We bow before Thee and confess our sins with penitent hearts. We are deserving of the affliction of this plague with which Thou hast visited us. But we invoke Thy mercy; O Lord, be gracious unto us and spare us. Deal not with us after our sins, nor reward us after our iniquities. Save us from the visitation which is spreading terror, bereavement, and sorrow among us. Teach us to bear Thy discipline in patience and always to be ready for the summons to stand before Thy presence. Into Thy hands do we commit ourselves, for Thy mercy is great. Grant us the grace of Thy Holy Spirit, that neither death nor life may separate us from Thy love, which is in Christ Jesus, our Lord. Amen.

Prayer at the Laying of the Corner-stone for a New Church

Almighty and merciful God, graciously bless the work which we have now commenced in this place to Thy glory. Grant that the sanctuary to be raised upon this foundation may be a place wherein Thy people shall be gathered together to worship Thee, and where they may be fed with Thy living Word and Thy holy Sacraments. Take into Thy gracious protection all who shall work in this place, and grant unto them a spirit of godliness, that they may accomplish their task in a manner well pleasing to Thee. Let no adversity hinder the progress of their work. But as we pray Thee, O Lord, for Thy help in the building of this earthly temple, so we beseech Thee the more that Thou wouldst Thyself build up Thy Church into a spiritual house, to be a holy priesthood, to offer up spiritual sacrifices acceptable to Thee, through Jesus Christ, our Lord. Amen.

Prayer in a Congregation Where a Church is Being Erected

Lord Jesus Christ, Thou Who hast founded Thy Church, and through Thy servants still buildest up Thy spiritual Zion! Prosper, O Lord, our endeavor to build Thee a sanctuary in this place where Thy redeemed shall gather to hear Thy Word and partake of Thy Holy Sacraments, and to worship and praise Thy Holy Name. Establish Thou the work of our hands, for except Thou build the house, they labor in vain that build it. Preserve from harm and danger all that are here engaged. Bestow upon Thy Church unity of mind and will, and above all things grant that the temple of Thy Holy Spirit may be built and established in our hearts. Amen.

Prayer for Church Conventions

Almighty, eternal, and merciful God, Father of our Lord Jesus Christ! Thou hast set Thy Son to be the Head and Lord of Thy Church, and through Thy Holy Spirit gatherest together into Thy Church the children of God that are scattered abroad: We humbly beseech Thee to grant Thy Spirit to us (those) who are now assembled to take counsel for the affairs of Thy kingdom, that our (their) deliberations may tend to the glory of Thy Name and the enlargement of Thy kingdom. Do Thou govern us (them) by Thy Spirit, the Spirit of truth, and of peace, and of love, to the end that we (they) may faithfully perform the work entrusted to our (their) care; through Thy Son, Jesus Christ, our Lord. Amen.

Holy Baptism

In the Name of the Father, and of the Son, and of the Holy Spirit.

Beloved in the Lord! From the Word of God we learn that all men are born in sin, but also that Jesus Christ has come into the world to save sinners. Our Lord and Saviour has testified and said: "Except one be born of water and the Spirit, he cannot enter into the kingdom of God." (John 3. 5.) Therefore, according to His commandment,* we receive this child (these children) into the Christian Church through the washing of regeneration, and beseech our Lord and Saviour graciously to receive him (her, or them) and endue him (her, or them) with the power of the Holy Spirit unto a living faith and true godliness. To this end may God grant His blessing for the sake of Jesus Christ. Amen.

Lift up your hearts unto God!

Our Lord Jesus Christ Himself instituted Holy Baptism, when He said to His disciples:

"All authority hath been given unto Me in heaven and on earth. Go ye therefore, and make disciples of all the nations, baptizing them into the Name of the Father, and of the Son, and of the Holy Spirit: teaching them to observe all things whatsoever I commanded you: and lo, I am with you always, even unto the end of the world." (Mt. 28. 18–20.)

Hear also the holy and comforting Gospel according to St. Mark:

"They were bringing unto Him little children, that He should touch them: and the disciples rebuked them. But when Jesus saw it, He was moved with indignation, and said unto them, Suffer the little children to come unto Me; forbid them not: for to such belongeth the kingdom of God. Verily I say unto you, Whosoever shall not receive the kingdom of God as a little child, he shall in no wise enter therein. And He took them in His arms, and blessed them, laying His hands upon them." (Mk. 10. 13–16.)

---

* At a foundling's baptism insert here the words: "Since it is uncertain whether this child has received Holy Baptism."

Then the Minister shall place his hand upon the head of the Child and pray:

Our Father, Who art in heaven: Hallowed be Thy Name; Thy kingdom come; Thy will be done on earth, as it is in heaven; Give us this day our daily bread; And forgive us our trespasses, as we forgive those who trespass against us; And lead us not into temptation; But deliver us from evil; For Thine is the kingdom, and the power, and the glory, forever.   Amen.

The Merciful and Eternal God, Who alone saves from all evil; and Who has graciously called thee to be a partaker of the inheritance of the saints in light, through our Saviour Jesus Christ, deliver thee from the power of darkness and preserve thee in His truth and fear, now and forevermore.   Amen.

Let us hear the Christian faith, which we confess, and into which this child is (these children are) to be baptized.

I believe in God the Father Almighty, Maker of heaven and earth;

And in Jesus Christ His only Son, our Lord: Who was conceived by the Holy Spirit, Born of the Virgin Mary; Suffered under Pontius Pilate, Was crucified, dead, and buried; He descended into hell; The third day He rose again from the dead; He ascended into heaven, And sitteth on the right hand of God the Father Almighty; From thence He shall come to judge the quick and the dead.

I believe in the Holy Spirit; the Holy Christian Church, the Communion of saints; The Forgiveness of sins; The Resurrection of the body; And the Life everlasting.

The Minister shall continue:

Do you desire that this child (these children) shall upon this confession be baptized, and by baptism be received into the Communion of Christ and His Church?

The Parents or Sponsors answer:

Yes.

Then the Minister shall three times pour water upon the Child's head and say:

I baptize thee, N. N., into the Name of the Father, and of the Son, and of the Holy Spirit.   Amen.

Then shall the Minister say:

Let us give thanks and pray:

Almighty, Eternal God, our Heavenly Father, we give Thee hearty thanks that Thou dost continually preserve and increase Thy holy Christian Church, and that Thou hast now permitted this child (these children) to receive the washing of regeneration unto eternal life. We pray Thee to preserve him (her, or them) in the grace of baptism, so that he (she, or they) may grow up in Thy fear, and in the power of Christ's resurrection walk in newness of life, ever pleasing to Thee, and finally receive the inheritance of the saints in heaven; through the same, Thy Son, Jesus Christ, our Lord. Amen.

The Minister shall pronounce the Benediction upon the Child:

The Lord bless thee, and keep thee. The Lord make His face shine upon Thee, and be gracious unto thee. The Lord lift up His countenance upon thee, and give thee peace. In the Name of the Father, and of the Son, and of the Holy Spirit. Amen.

Thereupon the Minister shall admonish the Sponsors as follows:

Dearly Beloved! This child (these children), through the washing of regeneration, has (have) become a child (children) of God and joint-heir(s) with Jesus Christ. It becomes you who have witnessed this sacred act diligently to assist this child (these children) with Christian love and faithful prayers. Take solemnly to heart the obligation of the Church, especially in the event of the death of the parents before the child is (these children are) of age, to rear this child (these children) in the fear and admonition of the Lord, to the end that it (they) may faithfully keep the gifts of grace received in Holy Baptism.

The Minister shall continue:

Let us now hear the exhortation of God's Word to us who have received the grace of baptism:

"As therefore ye received Christ Jesus the Lord, so walk in Him, rooted and builded up in Him, and established in your faith, even as ye were taught, abounding in thanksgiving." (Col. 2. 6, 7.)

Glory be to the Father, and to the Son, and to the Holy Spirit; as it was in the beginning, is now, and ever shall be, world without end. Amen.

Then the Minister shall say to the Sponsors:

Depart in peace.

Emergency Baptism and Its Ratification

When the weak condition of the Child does not permit the delay involved in summoning a Minister, some other confirmed and Godfearing person, man or woman, may baptize the Child. When pure water has been procured, the Baptism is performed in the following manner:

Jesus said:

"All authority hath been given unto Me in heaven and on earth. Go ye therefore, and make disciples of all the nations, baptizing them into the Name of the Father, and of the Son, and of the Holy Spirit: teaching them to observe all things whatsoever I commanded you: and lo, I am with you always, even unto the end of the world." (Mt. 28. 18–20.)

He who performs the Baptism shall pour water on the Child's head three times and say:

I baptize thee, N. N., into the Name of the Father, and of the Son, and of the Holy Spirit. Amen.

Then shall he pray:

Our Father, Who art in heaven: Hallowed be Thy Name; Thy kingdom come; Thy will be done on earth, as it is in heaven; Give us this day our daily bread; And forgive us our trespasses, as we forgive those who trespass against us; And lead us not into temptation; But deliver us from evil; For Thine is the kingdom, and the power, and the glory, forever. Amen.

The Lord bless thee, and keep thee. The Lord make His face shine upon thee, and be gracious unto thee. The Lord lift up His countenance upon thee, and give thee peace. In the Name of the Father, and of the Son, and of the Holy Spirit. Amen.

Should the Child who received emergency baptism live, the Minister shall take care to ascertain exactly from those who were present, whether the Child was baptized according to the above-mentioned form. If he then finds that the baptism was not so performed, the Child is to be deemed unbaptized and shall be baptized according to the form prescribed for Infant Baptism. Otherwise the Baptism is to be ratified by the Minister in the following manner:

In the Name of the Father, and of the Son, and of the Holy Spirit. Amen.

Beloved in the Lord: Our Lord Jesus Christ expressly commanded His disciples: "Go ye therefore, and make disciples of all the nations, baptizing them into the Name of the Father, and of the Son, and of the Holy Spirit: teaching them to observe all things whatsoever I commanded you." Since now this child, N. N., according to the commandment of Jesus Christ, is baptized with water into the Name of the Father, and of the Son, and of the Holy Spirit, and we thus may be assured that he (she) has been received as a child of God and an heir of eternal life; therefore do I, a servant of Jesus Christ, approve and confirm this baptism in the Name of the Father, and of the Son, and of the Holy Spirit. Amen.

Hear the holy and comforting Gospel, according to St. Mark:

"They were bringing unto Him little children, that He should touch them: and the disciples rebuked them. But when Jesus saw it, He was moved with indignation, and said unto them, Suffer the little children to come unto Me; forbid them not: for to such belongeth the kingdom of God. Verily I say unto you, Whosoever shall not receive the kingdom of God as a little child, he shall in no wise enter therein. And He took them in His arms, and blessed them, laying His hands upon them." (Mk. 10. 13–16.)

Then the Minister shall place his hand upon the head of the Child and pray:

Our Father, Who art in heaven: Hallowed be Thy Name; Thy kingdom come; Thy will be done on earth, as it is in heaven; Give us this day our daily bread; And forgive us our trespasses, as we forgive those who trespass against us; And lead us not into temptation; But deliver us from evil; For Thine is the kingdom, and the power, and the glory, forever. Amen.

Let us hear the Christian faith, which we confess, and into which this child is baptized.

I believe in God the Father Almighty, Maker of heaven and earth;

And in Jesus Christ His only Son, our Lord: Who was conceived by the Holy Spirit, Born of the Virgin Mary; Suffered under Pontius Pilate, Was crucified, dead, and buried; He descended into hell; The third day He rose again from the dead; He ascended into heaven, And sitteth on the right hand of God the Father Almighty; From thence He shall come to judge the quick and the dead.

I believe in the Holy Spirit; The Holy Christian Church, the Communion of saints; The Forgiveness of sins; The Resurrection of the body; And the Life everlasting.

The Minister shall continue:

Let us pray!

Almighty, Eternal God, our Heavenly Father, we give Thee hearty thanks that Thou dost continually preserve and increase Thy holy Christian Church, and that Thou hast permitted this child to receive the washing of regeneration unto eternal life. We pray Thee to preserve him (her) in the grace of baptism, so that he (she) may grow up in Thy fear, and in the power of Christ's resurrection walk in newness of life, ever pleasing to Thee, and finally receive the inheritance of the saints in heaven; through the same, Thy Son, Jesus Christ, our Lord. Amen.

The Minister shall then pronounce the Benediction upon the Child:

The Lord bless thee, and keep thee. The Lord make His face shine upon thee, and be gracious unto thee. The Lord lift up His countenance upon thee, and give thee peace. In the Name of the Father, and of the Son, and of the Holy Spirit. Amen.

Finally the Minister shall say:

Depart in peace.

Baptism of an Adult Born of Christian Parents

The baptismal ceremony presupposes that the person who is to be baptized (the catechumen) has previously obtained requisite instruction. Witnesses should be present whether the baptism be performed in the presence of the congregation or not.

In the Name of the Father, and of the Son, and of the Holy Spirit.

Beloved in the Lord! Our Lord Jesus Christ has testified and said: "Except one be born of water and the Spirit, he cannot enter into the kingdom of God." (John 3. 5.) This youth (girl, man, woman), who has not previously received Holy Baptism, has declared that he (she) desires to be baptized. Let us therefore in Christian love pray for him (her):

Almighty God, dear heavenly Father: Our Saviour has said: "Ask, and it shall be given you; seek, and ye shall find; knock, and it shall be opened unto you." Open then to him (her) the door, that he (she) may be satisfied with the goodness of Thy house.

Lift up your hearts unto God!

Our Lord Jesus Christ Himself instituted Holy Baptism when He said to His disciples:

"All authority hath been given unto Me in heaven and on earth. Go ye therefore, and make disciples of all the nations, baptizing them into the Name of the Father, and of the Son, and of the Holy Spirit: teaching them to observe all things whatsoever I commanded you: and lo, I am with you always, even unto the end of the world." (Mt. 28. 18–20.)

The Catechumen shall then kneel, and the Minister shall place his hand upon his head and pray:

Our Father, Who art in heaven: Hallowed be Thy Name; Thy kingdom come; Thy will be done on earth, as it is in heaven; Give us this day our daily bread; And forgive us our trespasses, as we forgive those who trespass against us; And lead us not into temptation; But deliver us from evil; For Thine is the kingdom, and the power, and the glory, forever. Amen.

The Minister shall continue:

The Merciful and Eternal God, Who alone saves from all evil, and Who has graciously called thee to be a partaker of the inheritance of the saints in light, through our Saviour Jesus Christ, deliver thee from the power of darkness and preserve thee in His truth and fear, now and forevermore. Amen.

The Catechumen rising, the Minister shall continue: (*Or, the Catechumen shall himself make the Confession of Faith, saying: I believe, etc.*)

Do you believe in God the Father Almighty, Maker of heaven and earth?

Answer:

I do.

Do you believe in Jesus Christ His only Son, our Lord; Who was conceived by the Holy Spirit, Born of the Virgin Mary; Suffered under Pontius Pilate, Was crucified, dead, and buried; Descended into hell; The third day rose again from the dead; Ascended into heaven, And sitteth on the right hand of God the Father Almighty; Whence He shall come to judge the quick and the dead?

Answer:

I do.

Do you believe in the Holy Spirit; The Holy Christian Church, the Communion of Saints; The Forgiveness of sins; The Resurrection of the body; And the life everlasting?

Answer:

I do.

Then the Catechumen bows his head, and the Minister pours water three times thereon and says:

I baptize thee, N. N., into the Name of the Father, and of the Son, and of the Holy Spirit. Amen.

The Minister shall then pray:

Almighty, Eternal God, our Heavenly Father, we give Thee hearty thanks that Thou dost continually preserve and increase Thy holy Christian Church, and that Thou hast now permitted this youth (girl, man, woman) to receive the washing of regeneration unto eternal life. We pray thee to preserve him (her) in the grace of baptism, so that he (she) may grow in Thy fear, and in the power of Christ's resurrection walk in newness of life, ever pleasing to Thee, and finally receive the inheritance of the saints in heaven; through the same, Thy Son, Jesus Christ, our Lord. Amen.

Then shall the Minister address the baptized person in the following words:

Thou hast been baptized into Christ Jesus that like as He was raised from the dead through the glory of the Father, so thou also mayest walk in newness of life. The God of all grace would perfect, establish, and strengthen thee by His Word and the Holy Supper. Keep thyself, therefore, in fellowship with His Church in watchfulness and prayer. Fight the good fight of faith. The God of peace be with thee and help thee through all temptations and dangers, and save thee into His heavenly kingdom.

Then shall the baptized person kneel while the Minister pronounces the Benediction upon him:

The Lord bless thee, and keep thee. The Lord make His face shine upon thee, and be gracious unto thee. The Lord lift up His countenance upon thee, and give thee peace. In the Name of the Father, and of the Son, and of the Holy Spirit. Amen.

The Minister shall then admonish the Sponsors as follows:

Dearly Beloved: You who have witnessed the baptism of this youth (girl, man, woman) should be mindful of your duty to assist him (her) henceforth with Christian love and faithful prayers, that he (she) may faithfully keep the gifts of grace received in baptism. To this end may the Lord grant you His grace.

The Minister shall conclude with the following:

Let us now hear the exhortation of God's Word to us who have received the grace of baptism:

"As therefore ye received Christ Jesus the Lord, so walk in Him, rooted and builded up in Him, and established in your faith, even as ye were taught, abounding in thanksgiving." (Col. 2. 6, 7.)

Glory be to the Father, and to the Son, and to the Holy Spirit: as it was in the beginning, is now, and ever shall be, world without end. **Amen.**

Finally the Minister shall say:

Depart in peace.

Confirmation

When the Candidates for Confirmation are found to have the required Christian knowledge, as prescribed by the Synod and set forth in its accepted Catechism and Bible History, the Minister shall fix a day for their examination, which, in the presence of the congregation, shall precede the first Communion. Notice of this should be given from the pulpit to the effect that the Candidates for Confirmation will on a stated day be examined and make their vows. Moreover, the members of the congregation, especially the parents, foster parents or guardians, should be requested to be present, prayerfully to support the children on this solemn occasion and themselves be edified by this Christian rite. On the appointed day the Candidates assemble around the Altar, and the Service begins with the singing of a Hymn. At the close of the Hymn the Minister shall give a brief address* from the Altar, after which the examination begins. This should be so arranged that the essential parts of the doctrine of salvation are treated. Thereupon the Minister shall address the Candidates as follows:

Beloved in the Lord, you have now given a brief account of your knowledge in the doctrine which our Lord Jesus Christ has revealed to us in His Holy Word and which is preached and confessed in His Church. This is also the faith into which you have been baptized. I exhort you now before God and this Christian Church to confess your faith and make your vows:

Do you believe in God the Father Almighty?

Answer:

I believe in God the Father Almighty, Maker of heaven and earth.

Do you believe in Jesus Christ?

Answer:

I believe in Jesus Christ His only Son, our Lord; Who was conceived by the Holy Spirit, Born of the Virgin Mary; Suffered under Pontius Pilate; Was crucified, dead, and buried; He descended into hell; The third day He rose again from the dead; He ascended into heaven, And sitteth on the right hand of God the Father Almighty; From thence He shall come to judge the quick and the dead.

---

* When an Anthem is sung by the Choir it should follow the address.

Do you believe in the Holy Spirit?

Answer:

I believe in the Holy Spirit; The Holy Christian Church, the Communion of Saints; The Forgiveness of sins; The Resurrection of the body; And the Life everlasting.

Is it your earnest purpose, by virtue of the grace of baptism, to remain steadfast in this faith unto the end, and, as followers of Christ, to walk by faith in a new life, so as to love the Lord your God above all things and your neighbor as yourselves?

Answer:

Yes.

Will you, therefore, by the help of God, in watchfulness and prayer, diligently use the Word of God and faithfully seek your Saviour in His Holy Supper?

Answer:

Yes.

Will you also shun all false doctrines and be faithful to the Word of God according to our Evangelical Lutheran Confession?

Answer:

Yes.

Then shall the Minister say:

Dearly Beloved! You have now, before the omniscient and everpresent God, with your own lips confessed your faith and made your vows, and I hereby declare that you are admitted to the Holy Supper of the Lord, in the Name of the Father, and of the Son, and of the Holy Spirit.

The Lord grant you His grace to consecrate your whole life and all your powers to His will and service in Christ Jesus.

Here the Candidates are to kneel, and the Minister continues:

The Father of our Lord Jesus Christ grant you according to the riches of His glory, that you may be strengthened with power through His Spirit in the inward man, and be filled unto all the fulness of God.   Amen.

The Minister, still facing the Candidates, shall kneel and pray with them:

Our Father, Who art in Heaven: Hallowed be Thy Name; Thy kingdom come: Thy will be done on earth, as it is in heaven; Give us this day our daily bread; And forgive us our trespasses, as we forgive those who trespass against us; And lead us not into temptation; But deliver us from evil; For Thine is the kingdom, and the power, and the glory, forever.   Amen.

Then shall the Minister rise and say:

Let us unite in faithful prayer for these children (persons).

The Minister shall turn to the Altar and pray:

Almighty, Merciful God, Heavenly Father, Thou art the Author and Perfecter of all that is good within us. We pray Thee for these Thy servants who have been born again in baptism, and who through Thy Word are enabled to confess before this congregation Thy grace and love in Christ Jesus our Lord. Fulfill this good work which Thou hast begun in them. Teach their hearts more and more to know the preciousness of the salvation which Thine Only-Begotten Son hath secured for them. They are weak; do Thou strengthen them with Thy power. They are to pass through a world of danger; do Thou shield them with Thy might. They are exposed to temptations; do Thou help them to fight and to prevail. Give them the grace of Thy Holy Spirit for a blessed communion with Thee in Thy Holy Supper. Help them to confess Thy Name boldly before the world in word and in deed. Help them to watch and pray at all times, and, with Thy faithful people, confidently to await the coming of Thy dear Son, finally with Him to obtain eternal life. Amen.

If the laying on of hands is used, the Minister shall place his hand upon the head of each Candidate and pronounce a suitable Scriptural Benediction. Then the Minister, turning to the Congregation, shall say:

Bow your hearts to God and receive the Benediction.

The Lord bless thee, and keep thee. The Lord make His face shine upon thee, and be gracious unto thee. The Lord lift up His countenance upon thee, and give thee peace.

In the Name of the Father, and of the Son, and of the Holy Spirit. Amen.

The Minister shall turn to the Altar, and the Class shall stand, while the Congregation sings:

Amen. Amen. Amen.

The Service shall close with silent prayer, while the Congregation remains standing and the Minister kneels before the Altar.

The Solemnization of Marriage

The order as here given is to be followed when one ring is used. Instruction as to the procedure when two rings are used or when no ring is used will be found in the footnotes. When a marriage contracted before the civil authorities is to be sanctioned by the Church, this ceremony is used with the omission of the pledges and vows.

The Minister shall first give this exhortation:

In the Name of the Father, and of the Son, and of the Holy Spirit.

Dearly Beloved! Marriage is a holy estate instituted of God Himself for the preservation of the human family, and for the mutual help of those who enter into this sacred bond, to lighten the burdens of life, to alleviate its unavoidable cares, and by careful nurture to provide for the happiness of posterity. This is a holy institution; its obligations and objects are likewise holy.

It is the duty of the husband to love and honor his wife, and by careful consideration for her welfare ever seek to deepen her love for him. It is the duty of the wife to love her husband, share with him tenderly and faithfully the cares of the household, and at all times so conduct herself as to be his true help-meet. They should both carefully consider that they have entered into an estate in which their mutual happiness is dependent upon fidelity to their marriage vows; and, by due regard to their persons and their duties, they should seek to make themselves worthy of mutual esteem and love, and always set for each other a good example in a godly life. Wherefore it behooves them to pray earnestly for a virtuous helpmeet who appreciates the duties of the marriage estate as well as the blessedness which comes from fulfilling them. So shall the marriage begin and continue according to the will of God, and the highest happiness be thereby secured. To this end we pray Almighty God for His blessing on this Man and this Woman.

The Minister shall then say to the Man:

Before the omniscient God and in the presence of this Congregation (these witnesses), I ask thee, N. N., wilt thou have N. N., to be thy wedded wife, to love her in prosperity and in adversity?

Answer:

I will.

Then shall the Minister say to the Woman:

Before the omniscient God and in the presence of this Congregation (these witnesses), I ask thee, N. N., wilt thou have N. N., to be thy wedded husband, to love him in prosperity and in adversity?

Anwer:

I will.

668

The Minister shall then receive the ring from the Man (or, if two rings be used, the rings from the Man and from the Woman) and pray:

Almighty God, Who with a holy, wise and beneficent purpose hast instituted marriage: We pray Thee to let Thy blessing rest upon the solemn covenant which these Thy servants with this emblem (these emblems) seal* before Thee. Fulfill upon them the promises which Thou hast given to all who live according to Thy Word and who keep the obligations which Thou hast ordained for the welfare of mankind. Amen.

*The Man shall then receive the ring (which shall be held by both the Man and the Woman until the vows of both have been made), and the Man shall say: ***

I, N. N., take thee, N. N., to be my wedded wife, to love thee in prosperity and in adversity, and as a token thereof I give thee this ring.

The Woman shall say:

I, N. N., take thee, N. N., to be my wedded husband, to love thee in prosperity and in adversity, and as a token thereof I receive this ring.

The Man then places the ring on the fourth finger of the Woman's left hand, while the Minister says:

In the Name of the Father, and of the Son, and of the Holy Spirit. Amen.

Forasmuch as ye now have been joined in holy wedlock, I, as a servant of Jesus Christ, before God and this Christian Congregation (these witnesses) confirm your marriage covenant in the Name of the Father, and of the Son, and of the Holy Spirit. Amen.

---

*If the marriage ring has been given beforehand, the Minister shall say "have sealed." At the close of the prayer the Man shall place the ring on the fourth finger of the Woman's left hand. When the ring ceremony is not used, the words "with this emblem" ("these emblems") are omitted from the prayer.

**When two rings are used, the ceremony shall proceed as follows: The Minister shall instruct the Man and the Woman to hold the ring for the Woman. While they do this, the Man shall repeat the following words after the Minister:

I, N. N., take thee, N. N., to be my wedded wife, to love thee in prosperity and in adversity, and as an emblem thereof I give thee this ring.

The Man shall then place the ring on the fourth finger of the Woman's left hand.

Then the Minister shall instruct the Man and the Woman to hold the ring for the Man. While they do this, the Woman shall repeat the following words after the Minister:

I, N. N., take thee, N. N., to be my wedded husband, to love thee in prosperity and in adversity, and as an emblem thereof I give thee this ring.

The Woman shall then place the ring on the fourth finger of the Man's left hand.

When these vows have been made, the Man with his right hand shall take the Woman by her right hand, and the Minister shall say: In the Name of the Father, and of the Son, and of the Holy Spirit. Amen.

"Forasmuch as ye now have," etc. The ceremony shall then continue as above.

Note: When no ring is used the Minister shall cause the Man with his right hand to take the Woman by her right hand and they shall then repeat the marriage vows as above (without referring to the ring) while they hold each other's hands, after which the Minister shall say:

In the Name of the Father, and of the Son, and of the Holy Spirit. Amen.

"Forasmuch as ye now have," etc.

The ceremony shall then continue as above.

Our Saviour teaches us in the nineteenth chapter of the Gospel according to St. Matthew that marriage is a holy covenant, which cannot be set aside by men at will: "And there came unto Him Pharisees, trying Him, and saying, Is it lawful for a man to put away his wife for every cause? and He answered and said, Have ye not read, that He Who made them from the beginning made them male and female, and said, For this cause shall a man leave his father and mother, and shall cleave to his wife; and the two shall become one flesh? So that they are no more two, but one flesh. What therefore God hath joined together, let not man put asunder."

The Minister shall then say to the Man and the Woman:

Consider these words of the Lord Jesus Christ! Forget not that your marriage covenant, according to God's will, cannot be revoked, and receive with patience and thanksgiving all that may betide you in the providence of God.

The Minister shall then continue:

The Lord be with you and guide you in His truth and fear, now and forevermore.

The Man and the Woman shall kneel, and the Minister shall say:

Let us pray.

Almighty, Eternal God, unchangeable in grace and mercy: We pray Thee to fill the hearts of these Thy servants with Thy Holy Spirit, and graciously to bestow upon them every spiritual and temporal blessing. Bless the solemn covenant which they now have made before Thee, that loyalty and happiness may ever abide in their home, that unity and love may lighten their labors, (and that a virtuous posterity may cheer their declining years). Merciful God, hear their prayers, and be their very present help when they call upon Thee. Guide them with Thy counsel, that when their pilgrimage is ended they may be received into the Father's house of many mansions, through Thy Son, Jesus Christ, our Lord. Amen.

God Almighty send His light and truth to keep you all the days of your life. The hand of God protect you. His holy angels accompany you. God the Father, and the Son, and the Holy Spirit cause His grace to be mighty upon you. Amen.

Our Father, Who art in heaven: Hallowed be Thy Name; Thy kingdom come; Thy will be done on earth, as it is in heaven; Give us this day our daily bread; And forgive us our trespasses, as we forgive those who trespass against us; And lead us not into temptation; But deliver us from evil; For Thine is the kingdom, and the power, and the glory, forever. Amen.

The Lord bless you and keep you. The Lord make His face shine upon you, and be gracious unto you. The Lord lift up His countenance upon you, and give you peace.

In the Name of the Father, and of the Son, and of the Holy Spirit. Amen.

The Burial Service

I. Service at the House

When a brief service is held at the House before going to the Church or to the Grave, a Hymn may be sung, followed by a Prayer or a Collect.

II. Service at the Church

The Service shall begin with an appropriate **Hymn**.
Then shall be read from the Altar one or more of the following Scripture selections:

Psalm 130; Psalm 90; 1 Th. 4. 13—18; 1 Cor. 15. 12—26, 35—38; John 11. 21—27; Luke 7. 11—15; Matt. 9. 18, 19, 23—26.

Then the **Minister** *shall turn to the Altar and pray:*

Almighty and Everlasting God, Who by Thy Son hast promised us forgiveness of sin and deliverance from everlasting death: Strengthen us, we beseech Thee, by Thy Holy Spirit, that our trust in Thy grace in Christ Jesus may daily increase. Grant that with sure confidence we may hold fast the blessed hope that we shall not die, but only sleep, and at the last day be raised up unto eternal life, through the same Jesus Christ, Thy Son, our Lord. Amen.

Then shall be sung a **Hymn** *or an* **Anthem**, *after which shall follow the* **Sermon**.

The Sermon

After the Sermon the **Minister** *shall pray as follows:*

O Lord God, heavenly Father, Thou Who didst not spare Thine only-begotten Son, but hast given Him for us all: We most heartily thank Thee that through His burial our graves have been hallowed as places of rest. Grant us, we pray Thee, that He may so abide in our hearts that after the sufferings of this present time we may rest in peace, looking for a blessed resurrection: through the same Thy Son, Jesus Christ, our Lord. Amen.

The Church Service may close with a **Hymn**.

Or, it may conclude with the **Altar Service** *which follows.*

Or, when the Body is committed in the Church, the **Service at the Grave**, *as far as the Benediction, is read at this point, concluding with the Lord's Prayer.*

The Salutation

A short **Hymn** *is then sung, during which the* **Minister** *proceeds to the Altar. The singing ended, the* **Minister** *shall turn to the Congregation and sing or say:*

The Lord.... be with you.

The **Congregation** *shall sing:*

And with....... thy spir - it.

The **Minister** *shall turn to the Altar and say the following prayer:*

O Lord God, Who, on account of sin, turnest man to destruction, so teach us to number our days, that we may get us a heart of wisdom. Grant us a true faith in Thy Son, Jesus Christ, Who was delivered up for our trespasses, and was raised for our justification, and liveth forever. Give us grace to die daily from sin and so to live in accordance with Thy holy will, that in the hour of death we may be prepared for a blessed departure. Receive then our souls unto Thyself, and suffer our bodies, when they have rested in their graves, to rise on the last day to everlasting life. Amen.

Then, if it be convenient, one or two of the following burial Antiphons may be sung by the **Minister** *and the* **Congregation:**

Antiphon A

The **Minister:**

So...... teach us to num - ber our days,

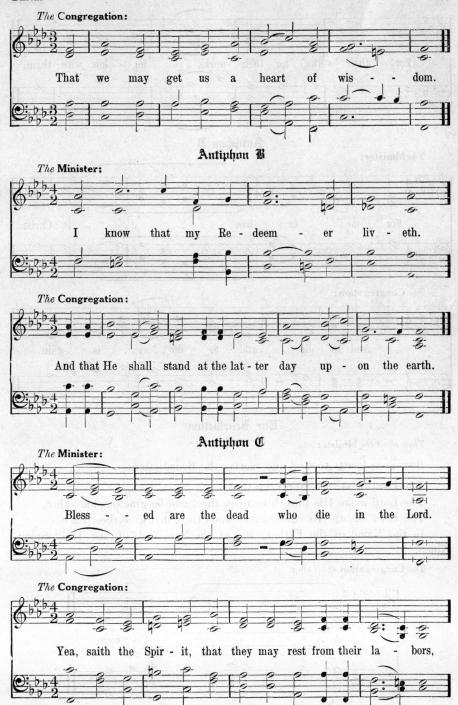

For their works, for their works.... fol - low with them.

Antiphon D

The **Minister:**

For me... to live............... is Christ.

The **Congregation:**

And to die, and to die..... is gain.

The Benediction

Then shall the **Minister** *say:*

Bow your hearts to God and receive the Benediction.

The Lord bless thee, and keep thee.
The Lord make His face shine upon thee, and be gracious unto thee.
The Lord lift up His countenance upon thee, and give thee peace.
In the Name of the Father, and of the Son, and of the Holy Spirit.
Amen.

The **Congregation** *shall sing:*

A -------------- men.

III. Service at the Grave

*The **Minister** shall throw earth upon the body three times while he says:*

Earth to earth, ashes to ashes, dust to dust; Jesus Christ, our Saviour, shall at the latter day raise thee from the dead.

Let us pray:

Almighty, Merciful, and Eternal God! Thou hast by reason of sin appointed unto men once to die; but, that we might not remain forever in the power of death, Thou hast given Thy Son Jesus Christ, who knew no sin, to suffer death for us, and through Him hast taken away the sting of death. Help us ever to remember that we also at Thy good pleasure shall be called hence and our bodies return to dust. Grant us grace to remember that we have not here an abiding city. Teach us to seek the things that are eternal, and so to walk in accordance with Thy Holy will that on the last day we may arise to everlasting life; through Thy Son, Jesus Christ, our Lord. Amen.

Or:*

O Lord God, Who, on account of sin, turnest man to destruction, so teach us to number our days that we may get us a heart of wisdom. Grant us a true faith in Thy Son, Jesus Christ, who was delivered up for our trespasses, and was raised for our justification, and liveth forever. Give us grace daily to die from sin and so to live in accordance with Thy holy will that in the hour of death we may be prepared for a blessed departure. Receive then our souls unto Thyself, and suffer our bodies, when they have rested in their graves, to rise on the last day to everlasting life. Amen.

Or:**

O Lord God, Father in heaven. O Lord, the Son of God, the Saviour of the world. O Lord, Thou Holy Spirit. Have mercy upon us. In the hour of death, and at the last judgment, help us, merciful Lord God. Amen.

Let us now hear the Word of God concerning death and the resurrection.

Then are read some suitable passages from Scripture, such as those quoted hereafter, as well as suitable hymns or stanzas from the Hymnal.

---

*This alternative may not be used if an altar service follows.

** Here a Hymn, or part of a Hymn, may be read.

Scripture Selections

✓ But we would not have you ignorant, brethren, concerning them that fall asleep; that ye sorrow not, even as the rest, who have no hope. For if we believe that Jesus died and rose again, even so them also that are fallen asleep in Jesus will God bring with Him.—1 Th. 4. 13, 14.

✓ Jesus said unto her, I am the resurrection, and the life: he that believeth on Me, though he die, yet shall he live; and whosoever liveth and believeth on Me shall never die.—Jn. 11. 25, 26.

Marvel not at this: for the hour cometh, in which all that are in the tombs shall hear His voice, and shall come forth; they that have done good, unto the resurrection of life; and they that have done evil, unto the resurrection of judgment.—Jn. 5. 28, 29.

Man, that is born of a woman, is of few days, and full of trouble. He cometh forth like a flower, and is cut down: he fleeth also as a shadow, and continueth not.—Job. 14. 1, 2.

Behold, Thou hast made my days as handbreadths; and my lifetime is as nothing before Thee: surely every man at his best estate is altogether vanity. Surely every man walketh in a vain show; surely they are disquieted in vain: he heapeth up riches, and knoweth not who shall gather them. And now, Lord, what wait I for? My hope is in Thee. Deliver me from all my transgressions: make me not the reproach of the foolish. I was dumb, I opened not my mouth; because Thou didst it.—Ps. 39. 5–9.

It is appointed unto men once to die, and after this cometh judgment.—Heb. 9. 27.

And I heard a voice from heaven saying, Write, Blessed are the dead who die in the Lord from henceforth: yea, saith the Spirit, that they may rest from their labors; for their works follow with them.—Rev. 14. 13.

Nevertheless I am continually with Thee: Thou hast holden my right hand. Thou wilt guide me with Thy counsel, and afterward receive me to glory. Whom have I in heaven but Thee? And there is none upon earth that I desire besides Thee. My flesh and my heart faileth; but God is the strength of my heart and my portion forever.—Ps. 73. 23–26.

Lord, Thou hast been our dwelling-place in all generations. Before the mountains were brought forth, or ever Thou hadst formed the earth and the world, even from everlasting to everlasting, Thou art God. Thou turnest man to destruction, and sayest, Return, ye children of men. For a thousand years in Thy sight are but as yesterday when it is past, and as a watch in the night. Thou carriest them away as with a flood; they are as a sleep: in the morning they are like grass which groweth up. In the morning it flourisheth, and groweth up; in the evening it is cut down, and withereth.—Ps. 90. 1–6.

For we are consumed in Thine anger, and in Thy wrath are we troubled. Thou hast set our iniquities before Thee, our secret sins in the light of Thy countenance. For all our days are passed away in Thy wrath: we bring our years to an end as a sigh.—Ps. 90. 7–9.

The days of our years are threescore years and ten, or even by reason of strength fourscore years; yet is their pride but labor and sorrow; for it is soon gone, and we fly away. Who knoweth the power of Thine anger, and Thy wrath according to the fear that is due unto Thee? So teach us to number our days, that we may get us a heart of wisdom.—Ps. 90. 10–12.

He entereth into peace; they rest in their beds, each one that walketh in His uprightness.—Is. 57. 2.

For to me to live is Christ, and to die is gain.—Phil. 1. 21.

Verily, verily, I say unto you, He that heareth My word, and believeth Him that sent Me, hath eternal life, and cometh not into judgment, but hath passed out of death into life. Verily, verily, I say unto you, The hour cometh, and now is, when the dead shall hear the voice of the Son of God; and they that hear shall live. For as the Father hath life in Himself, even so gave He to the Son also to have life in Himself.—Jn. 5. 24–26.

In My Father's house are many mansions; if it were not so, I would have told you; for I go to prepare a place for you. And if I go and prepare a place for you, I come again, and will receive you unto Myself; that where I am, there ye may be also.—Jn. 14. 2, 3.

Father, I desire that they also whom Thou hast given Me be with Me where I am, that they may behold My glory, which Thou hast given Me: for Thou lovedst Me before the foundation of the world.—Jn. 17. 24.

And if Christ is in you, the body is dead because of sin; but the spirit is life because of righteousness. But if the Spirit of Him that raised up Jesus from the dead dwelleth in you, He that raised up Christ Jesus from the dead shall give life also to your mortal bodies through His Spirit that dwelleth in you.—Rom. 8. 10, 11.

And if children, then heirs; heirs of God, and joint-heirs with Christ; if so be that we suffer with Him, that we may be also glorified with Him. For I reckon that the sufferings of this present time are not worthy to be compared with the glory which shall be revealed to us-ward.—Rom. 8. 17, 18.

For none of us liveth to himself, and none dieth to himself. For whether we live, we live unto the Lord; or whether we die, we die unto the Lord: whether we live therefore, or die, we are the Lord's. For to this end Christ died and lived again, that He might be Lord of both the dead and the living. —Rom. 14. 7-9.

If we have only hoped in Christ in this life, we are of all men most pitiable. But now hath Christ been raised from the dead, the firstfruits of them that are asleep. For since by man came death, by man came also the resurrection of the dead. For as in Adam all die, so also in Christ shall all be made alive. But each in his own order: Christ the firstfruits; then they that are Christ's, at His coming.—1 Cor. 15. 19-23.

Now this I say, brethren, that flesh and blood cannot inherit the kingdom of God; neither doth corruption inherit incorruption. For this corruptible must put on incorruption, and this mortal must put on immortality. But when this corruptible shall have put on incorruption, and this mortal shall have put on immortality, then shall come to pass the saying that is written, Death is swallowed up in victory. O death, where is thy victory? O death, where is thy sting? The sting of death is sin; and the power of sin is the law: but thanks be to God, Who giveth us the victory through our Lord Jesus Christ.—1 Cor. 15. 50, 53-57.

Hymnal Selections

For Infants and Young Persons: 599, 607, 608, 609.

For Older Persons and in General: 595, 598, 604, 606.

Thereupon the **Minister** *shall pray:*

Our Father, Who art in heaven: Hallowed be Thy Name; Thy kingdom come; Thy will be done on earth, as it is in heaven; Give us this day our daily bread; And forgive us our trespasses, as we forgive those who trespass against us; And lead us not into temptation; But deliver us from evil; For Thine is the kingdom, and the power, and the glory, forever. Amen.

The Lord bless thee, and keep thee. The Lord make His face shine upon thee, and be gracious unto thee. The Lord lift up His countenance upon thee, and give thee peace.

In the Name of the Father, and of the Son, and of the Holy Spirit. Amen.

General Morning and Evening Prayers

Morning Prayer

I give thanks unto Thee, Heavenly Father, through Jesus Christ, Thy dear Son, that Thou hast protected me through the night from all danger and harm. I beseech Thee to preserve and keep me this day also from all sin and evil, that in all my thoughts, words, and deeds, I may serve and please Thee. Into Thy hands I commend my body and soul and all that is mine. Let Thy holy angels have charge concerning me, that the wicked one have no power over me. Amen.   LUTHER.

Evening Prayer

I give thanks unto Thee, Heavenly Father, through Jesus Christ, Thy dear Son, that Thou hast this day so graciously protected me. I beseech Thee to forgive me all my sins and the wrong which I have done, and by Thy great mercy defend me from all the perils and dangers of this night. Into Thy hands I commend my body and soul and all that is mine. Let Thy holy angels have charge concerning me, that the wicked one have no power over me. Amen.   LUTHER.

Sunday

Almighty Father, enter into our midst to-day and fill us with Thyself. Say unto each one of us, "I am thy salvation." So speak to us that we fail not to hear. Show us Thyself and our need of Thee. Uphold Thy servants who to-day proclaim Thy word in Thy temple and with Thy people worship Thee. Touch the hearts of the hearers so that they may receive and serve Thee. Hear us, O Heavenly Father, for the sake of Thine only begotten Son. Amen.   AUGUSTINE.

Monday

Lord God, Heavenly Father, Thou whose will it is that we should love one another, give us grace to love every one we meet in our daily life. We pray Thee to be merciful to all men, but we pray especially for those whom Thy love hath given to us. Though our prayers be weak and faint, do Thou bestow upon them greater blessings than we know how to pray for. For Thy love surpasseth the love of men. Do unto them according to Thy will, that they may always and everywhere be under the shadow of Thy wing. Help them to love Thee, so that they may will and speak and do that which is pleasing in Thy sight. And may they at last attain unto life incorruptible. To Thee be all praise forever. Amen.   ANSELM.

Tuesday

Lord, Thou alone canst direct my course over life's troubled sea. Arise, O Lord, bid the storm within my heart be still, and make it calm, that I may look up to Thee and in Thee find rest and peace. Stay my wandering thoughts, and fix my mind on Thee alone. Let Thy Holy Spirit ever dwell within me, and make me Thy temple. O Thou, the Giver of every good and perfect gift, fill me with Thy fullness; so shall I have comfort and strength, joy and peace forevermore. Amen.   ARNDT.

Wednesday

O God, Thou art life and wisdom and blessedness; Thou alone art God, faithful and eternal. In Thee I have a never-failing source of joy. Teach me more and more to know Thee, that Thou mayest be more fully mine and that my joy in Thee may be full. And though my faith be unable in this present life so to receive Thee, grant that it may increase day by day until it be perfected in the life everlasting. My joy, while here, is the joy of hope; there it shall be the joy of perfect realization. Amen.   ANSELM.

Thursday

Almighty God, Thou carest for me as if Thou didst take thought of me alone, and Thou carest for all as if all were one. I see things of earth pass away, and I see other things come in their stead, but Thou abidest forever. Therefore, my God and Father, to Thee will I commend all that I have received from Thee. For so I can suffer no loss. Thou, O Lord, hast made me for Thyself, and my heart can find no rest till it rest in Thee. Amen.

AUGUSTINE.

Friday

Grant me, I beseech Thee, Almighty and most Merciful God, fervently to desire, wisely to search out, and perfectly to fulfil, all that is well-pleasing unto Thee. Order Thou my worldly condition to the glory of Thy name; and grant me the knowledge, desire, and ability to do that which Thou requirest of me, that so I may walk with Thee unto the perfect end.

Give me, O Lord, a steadfast heart which no unworthy affection may debase; give me an enduring heart which no tribulation can wear out; give me an upright heart which no unworthy purpose may tempt aside.

Bestow upon me also, O Lord my God, understanding to know Thee, diligence to seek Thee, wisdom to find Thee, and a faithfulness that may finally embrace Thee. Amen.   AQUINAS.

Saturday

I know, O Lord, and do with all humility acknowledge myself an object altogether unworthy of Thy love; but sure I am, Thou art an object altogether worthy of mine. Thou hast a right to my best service, yet in me there is no goodness to serve Thee. Do Thou, then, impart to me of that excellence which shall supply my want. Help me, according to Thy will, to cease from sin, that I may be capable of doing Thee service according to my duty. Enable me so to guard and govern myself, so to begin and finish my course, that when the race of life is run I may sleep in peace, and rest in Thee. Be with me unto the end, that my sleep may be rest indeed, my rest perfect security, and that security a blessed eternity. Amen.   AUGUSTINE.

Prayer before the Reading of the Word of God

Lord Jesus Christ, Thou hast commanded us to search the Scriptures and hast promised us that in them we shall find faith and eternal life. Thou alone art worthy to take the book and loose the seven seals thereof. Open Thou mine eyes, that I may behold wondrous things out of Thy law. Teach me the way of Thy statutes, and I shall keep it unto the end. Send me Thy Spirit from Thy holy heaven; and from the throne of Thy glory send Him to be with me and work with me, in order that I may realize what is well-pleasing unto Thee, that I may accomplish my work in Thy Name and to Thy glory, and that my heart may be filled with true faith, love, hope, humility, patience, meekness, piety, the fear of God, and blessedness in Him. Amen.

LOEHE.

Morning Prayer before Communion

Lord Jesus Christ, we thank Thee for the love in which Thou gavest Thyself a sacrifice for us, and we thank Thee for the love in which Thou givest us Thyself in Thy Holy Supper. We pray Thee this day to stand at the door of our heart and knock, that we may hear Thy voice and open wide the door. Enter, Lord Jesus, into our heart, and make us worthy guests as we approach Thy table to commune with Thee. So shalt Thou also permit us to sup with Thee in Thy heavenly kingdom. Grant us this, in order that the gracious work which Thou hast already done for us may not have been done in vain. Amen.   SCHARTAU.

Prayer Just before Communion

O loving Lord and Saviour, look upon me in mercy as Thou once didst look upon Peter when he had denied Thee, and upon the sinful woman in the house of the Pharisee, and upon the thief upon the cross. Give me grace to weep as did Peter bitterly over my sins, and as the sinful woman to love Thee with all my heart, and as the thief to be with Thee in Paradise. Amen.

Evening Prayer after Holy Communion

Dear God and Father, it is altogether true that I am not worthy that Thou shouldst come under my roof, but upon Thy own command and invitation have I sought Thee at Thy holy table. I fully and firmly believe that Thou of Thy mercy hast given me forgiveness of sins. I pray Thee to preserve me in the faith and in an unbroken communion with Thee. I doubt not Thy word of power. Thou hast fulfilled it in me, a poor, wretched sinner, to Thy glory. Amen.   LUTHER.

Prayer for Those in Anxiety for Their Souls

Have mercy upon me, O God, according to Thy lovingkindness; according to the multitude of Thy tender mercies, blot out my transgressions. With shame and sorrow I confess unto Thee that I have sinned against Thee and have done wickedly. My sin is great, and it is against Thee, O God, my Benefactor and my Saviour, that I have sinned. Thou hast showered upon me nothing but blessings, and Thou hast often forgiven me my sins.

And yet I have neglected to heed Thy word and warning. I have suffered the lust of my flesh and the temptations of the evil one to overpower me and to defile me. O my sin, O my folly! If Thou, Lord, shouldst mark iniquity, I could not stand before Thee. Have mercy upon me. Wash me thoroughly from mine iniquity and cleanse me from my sin. For I know my transgressions. Impute no sin to me, but grant me to rejoice in Thy merciful pardon. For Jesus' sake look graciously upon me and cast me not away from Thy presence. Create in me a clean heart, O God; and renew a right spirit within me. Then will I strive more earnestly to please Thee and will walk more carefully to avoid the snares of sin. Help me and be merciful unto me a sinner. Amen.

Prayer in Temptation

O Thou who knowest our hearts, and who seest our temptations and struggles, have pity upon us, and deliver us from the sins which war against our souls. Thou art all-powerful, we are weak and erring. Our trust is in Thee, O Thou good and faithful God. Guard us in peril, direct us in doubt, and save us from falling into sin. From the evil that is around and within us, graciously deliver us. Make the path of duty plain before us, and keep us therein unto the end. Amen.

Prayer for Mutual Forgiveness

To Thee, O Lord, I offer up my prayer for those who have in any wise caused me offense or grief, or have unjustly found fault with me, or have injured me. I pray also for those whom I at any time by word or deed, knowingly or unknowingly, have vexed or troubled or burdened or caused to stumble. Forgive us all our sins and our lack of charity one toward another.

Have mercy, O Lord, and make us so minded one toward another that we may be enabled to receive forgiveness and at last eternal life. Amen.

THOMAS À KEMPIS.

Prayer for a Dying Person

Almighty God, the Father of Jesus Christ, and our Father, Thou showest mercy at all times and in all places. Look with tender pity upon our poor, helpless brother whom Thou art now calling from this life. Grant him grace to remain firm and assured in his faith in Thee, that he may die as a true believer. Let him hear the words of Thy Son, our Saviour, "To-day shalt thou be with me in Paradise." Remember not his sins, but be mindful of the agony and bitter death which Thy Son hath suffered for him. Have compassion upon him and grant him a peaceful departure from this life. Give him a portion in the resurrection of the just, and let him dwell with Thee forever. Amen.

OLAVUS PETRI.

Prayers on a Birthday

Dear Heavenly Father, I thank Thee that Thou hast so graciously led and preserved me unto this day. Thou hast brought me to see the light of day and hast delivered me from the guilt of my first birth by giving me a second birth in holy Baptism. Thou art a faithful God, for Thou hast fulfilled all Thy precious promises to me. Forgive me, dear Lord, all my transgressions, pardon me, and grant me strength and wisdom to lead a life that is acceptable to Thee. As I advance in life, grant that I may ever grow in grace and in the knowledge of Thy will and in favor with Thee and with my fellow men. Grant that my years may not be spent in idleness or sin, but in labors useful to Thy Church and all men. And when my last hour is at hand, grant that it may be my birthday in heaven, so that the day of my death may be even better than the day of my birth. Into Thy hands I commend myself and my whole life. Forsake me never, dear Lord. Amen.

* * *

Lord, I know not what I ought to ask of Thee; Thou only knowest what I need; Thou lovest me better than I know how to love myself. O Father! give to Thy child that which he himself knows not how to ask. I dare not ask either for crosses or consolations; I simply present myself before Thee, I open my heart to Thee. Behold my needs which I know not myself; see and do according to Thy tender mercy. Smite, or heal; depress me, or raise me up; I adore all Thy purposes without knowing them; I am silent; I offer myself in sacrifice; I yield myself to Thee; I would have no other desire than to accomplish Thy will. Teach me to pray. Pray Thyself in me. Amen.

FÉNELON.

Prayer on a Wedding Anniversary

Lord, to Thee do we with confidence entrust our home and those whom Thou hast given us. We thank Thee for the comfort and love which Thou hast permitted us to enjoy. But earthly happiness is frail. We cannot care for ourselves, nor be a stay for others. Protect our loved ones. Thy will be done, O Lord. Thou alone knowest what is for our good. Do with us as seemeth best to Thee. Thou alone art our safety. Lead us all upon the plain path to the eternal goal. For the sake of Jesus Christ. Amen.

Order of Service for the Sunday School

I. Order for Opening

After singing an appropriate **Hymn**, *the School standing, the* **Superintendent** *shall say:*

In the Name of the Father, and of the Son, and of the Holy Spirit. Amen.

O come, let us worship and bow down; let us kneel before the Lord our Maker, for He is our God.

If we say that we have no sin, we deceive ourselves, and the truth is not in us.

If we confess our sins, He is faithful and righteous to forgive us our sins, and to cleanse us from all unrighteousness.

The Confession of Sins

Then the **Superintendent** *and the* **School** *shall say:*

Have mercy upon me, O God, according to Thy lovingkindness: According to the multitude of Thy tender mercies blot out my transgressions. Wash me thoroughly from mine iniquity, And cleanse me from my sin. For I know my transgressions; And my sin is ever before me. Against Thee, Thee only, have I sinned, And done that which is evil in Thy sight. Hide Thy face from my sins, And blot out all mine iniquities.

Create in me a clean heart, O God; And renew a right spirit within me. Cast me not away from Thy presence; And take not Thy Holy Spirit from me. (Ps. 51.)

Gloria Patri

The **School** *shall sing:*

Glo - ry be to the Fa - ther, and to the Son, And to the Ho - ly Spir - it; As it was in the be - gin - ning, Is

now, and ev - er shall be, World.... with - out end. A - MEN.

The Collect

Then the **Superintendent** *shall say the following, or some other Collect appropriate to the day:*

We beseech Thee, Almighty God, Heavenly Father, grant us a steadfast faith in Jesus Christ, a firm hope in Thy mercy, and a sincere love to Thee and to all our fellow men, through Jesus Christ our Lord.

The School shall sing: **Lenten Season.**

A - - - - - men.   A - - - - - - men.

The Scripture Lesson

Then the **Superintendent** *and the* **School** *shall read responsively the Scripture Lesson.*

The Apostles' Creed

After the reading of the Lesson, the **Superintendent** *and the* **School** *together shall say the Apostles' Creed.*

I believe in God the Father Almighty, Maker of heaven and earth;

And in Jesus Christ, His only Son, our Lord; Who was conceived by the Holy Spirit, Born of the Virgin Mary; Suffered under Pontius Pilate, Was crucified, dead, and buried; He descended into hell; The third day He rose again from the dead; He ascended into heaven, And sitteth on the right hand of God the Father Almighty; From thence He shall come to judge the quick and the dead.

I believe in the Holy Spirit; The Holy Christian Church, the Communion of Saints; The Forgiveness of sins; The Resurrection of the body; and the Life everlasting. Amen.

A **Hymn** *shall be sung, after which the* **Class Instruction** *shall begin.*

II. Order for Closing

The Class Instruction ended, and the School having been called to order, a **Lesson Review,** *or Questions on the* **Catechism** *may follow, after which* **Announcements** *shall be made.*
A **Hymn** *shall then be sung.*

The General Prayer

The hymn ended, the School shall stand while the **Superintendent** *shall say the following General Prayer (A free prayer may be offered):*

O Lord, most loving and merciful Saviour, Who didst call little children to come unto Thee, and didst lay Thy hands upon them, look upon us, we humbly beseech Thee, and bless us, Thy children, dedicated to Thy service in Holy Baptism. Bestow upon us Thy saving grace, and help us to remember our Creator in the days of our youth. Teach us that the fear of God is the beginning of wisdom.

Bless, O Lord, the instruction which we have received this hour, and grant that Thy precious Word may be so grafted into our hearts as to bring forth the fruits of righteousness, to the honor and glory of Thy name.

Teach us truly to believe in Thee, to love Thee with all our heart, to worship Thee and give Thee thanks, to obey Thy commandments, to reverence Thy holy Name and Word, and to serve Thee faithfully all the days of our lives.

Be gracious unto all of us. Preserve us from all danger. Deliver us from the power of the evil one and from the wickedness that is in the world. Defend us by day and by night. Unite us in the bonds of Christian love, and receive us at last unto Thyself in Thy heavenly kingdom. These and all things else necessary for us, and for the whole Church, we humbly beg in the Name of Jesus Christ our Lord, Who liveth and reigneth with Thee and the Holy Spirit, ever one God, world without end. Amen.

The Lord's Prayer

Then the **Superintendent** *and the* **School** *shall say:*

Our Father, Who art in heaven: Hallowed be Thy name; Thy kingdom come; Thy will be done on earth, as it is in heaven; Give us this day our daily bread; And forgive us our trespasses, as we forgive those who trespass against us; And lead us not into temptation; But deliver us from evil; for Thine is the kingdom, and the power, and the glory, forever. Amen.

Benedicamus

The **Superintendent** *shall say:*
Let us thank and praise the Lord.
The **School** *shall sing:*

Glo - ry be to Thee, O Lord! Hal - le - lu - -

jah! Hal - le - lu - - jah! Hal - le - lu - - jah!

Lenten Season.   Nürnberger Agende, 1639.

Glo - - - - ry be to Thee, O Lord!

Hal - le - lu - jah! Hal - le - lu - jah! Hal - le - lu - - jah!

The **Superintendent** *shall say:*

The grace of the Lord Jesus Christ,
And the love of God,
And the communion of the Holy Spirit
Be with you all.

The **School** *shall sing:*

A - men, A - men, A - - - - - - - men.

Lenten Season.

A - men, A - men, A - - - - men.

The Common Service

Used by permission of the Common Service Committee.

Morning

The **Congregation** *shall rise, and the* **Minister** *shall say:*

In the Name of the Father, and of the Son, and of the Holy Ghost.

The **Congregation** *shall sing or say:*

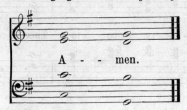

A - - men.

The Confession of Sins

The **Minister** *shall say:*

Beloved in the Lord! Let us draw near with a true heart, and confess our sins unto God our Father, beseeching Him, in the Name of our Lord Jesus Christ, to grant us forgiveness.

Versicle. Our help is in the Name of the Lord.

Response.

Who made *heaven* and earth.

V. I said, I will confess my transgressions unto the Lord.

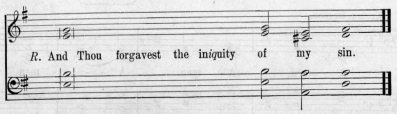

R. And Thou forgavest the in*iqui*ty of my sin.

688

Then shall the **Minister** *say:*

Almighty God, our Maker and Redeemer, we poor sinners confess unto Thee, that we are by nature sinful and unclean, and that we have sinned against Thee by thought, word, and deed. Wherefore we flee for refuge to Thine infinite mercy, seeking and imploring Thy grace, for the sake of our Lord Jesus Christ.

The **Congregation** *shall say with the* **Minister:**

O Most Merciful God, Who hast given Thine Only-begotten Son to die for us, have mercy upon us, and for His sake grant us remission of all our sins: and by Thy Holy Spirit increase in us true knowledge of Thee, and of Thy will, and true obedience to Thy Word, to the end that by Thy grace we may come to everlasting life; through Jesus Christ, our Lord. Amen.

Then shall the **Minister** *say:*

Almighty God, our Heavenly Father, hath had mercy upon us, and hath given His Only Son to die for us, and for His sake forgiveth us all our sins. To them that believe on His Name, He giveth power to become the sons of God, and bestoweth upon them His Holy Spirit. He that believeth, and is baptized, shall be saved. Grant this, O Lord, unto us all.

The **Congregation** *shall sing or say:*

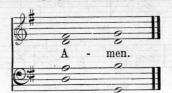

A - men.

The **Congregation** *shall stand until the close of the Collect.*

The Introit

The Introit for the Day (Pages 707-716) with the Gloria Patri shall be sung or said.

The Gloria Patri

I

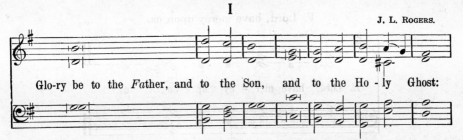

J. L. ROGERS.

Glo-ry be to the *Father,* and to the Son, and to the Ho - ly Ghost:

{ As it was in the be- }
{ ginning, is now, and } ev - er shall be, world with - out end. A-men.

For use in Lent.   Arranged by J. STAINER.

Glo - ry... be to the Fa - ther, and to the Son, and

to... the Ho - ly Ghost: As it { was in the be- } and
                                  { ginning, is now, }

ev - er shall be, world with - out end. A - - - men.

Then shall be sung or said the Kyrie.

The Kyrie

V. Lord, have mercy upon us.

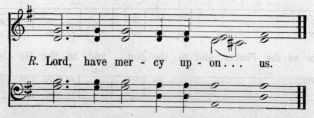

R. Lord, have mer - cy up - on... us.

V. Christ, have mercy upon us.　　　　*V.* Lord, have mercy upon us.

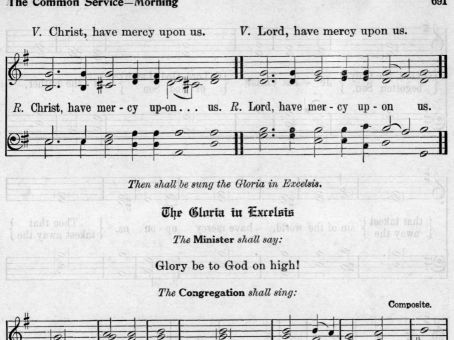

R. Christ, have mer - cy up-on... us.　*R.* Lord, have mer - cy up - on　us.

Then shall be sung the Gloria in Excelsis.

The Gloria in Excelsis

The **Minister** *shall say:*

Glory be to God on high!

The **Congregation** *shall sing:*

Composite.

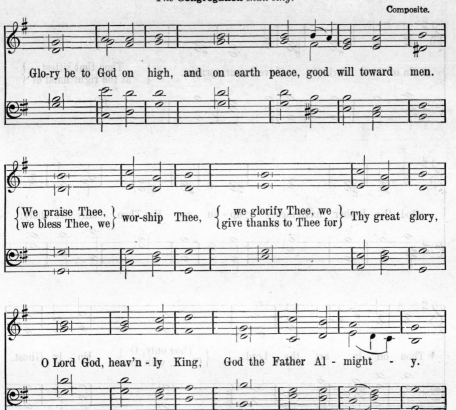

Glo-ry be to God on high, and on earth peace, good will toward men.

{We praise Thee, we bless Thee, we} wor-ship Thee, {we glorify Thee, we give thanks to Thee for} Thy great glory,

O Lord God, heav'n - ly King, God the Father Al - might - y.

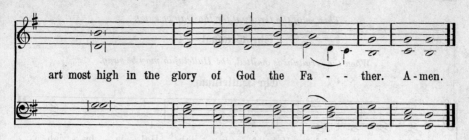

art most high in the glory of God the Fa - - ther. A - men.

Then shall the **Minister** *say:*

The Lord be with you.

The **Congregation** *shall sing or say:*

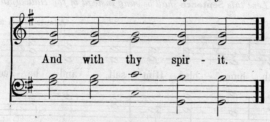

And with thy spir - it.

The **Minister** *shall say:*

Let us pray.

Then shall the **Minister** *say the Collect for the Day.*

The Collect

The Collect ended, the **Congregation** *shall sing or say:*

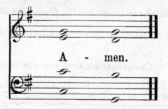

A - men.

Then shall the **Minister** *announce the Epistle for the Day, saying:*

The Epistle for (*here he shall name the Festival or Day*) is written in the——Chapter of——, beginning at the——Verse.

The Epistle

The Epistle ended, the **Minister** *shall say:*

Here endeth the Epistle for the Day.

Then may the Gradual for the Day be sung.

The Gradual

When the Gradual is omitted, the Hallelujah may be sung.

The Hallelujah

Hal - le - lu - jah,   Hal - le - lu - jah,   Hal - le - lu - jah.

In Lent this **Sentence** *shall be sung instead of the Hallelujah:*

Adapted from MERBECKE, 1550.

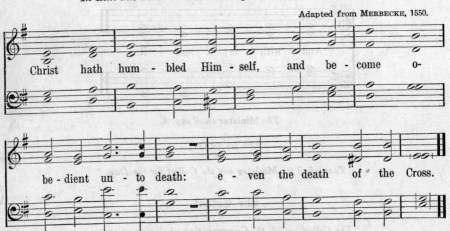

Christ   hath   hum - bled   Him - self,   and   be - come   o-

be - dient   un - to   death: e - ven   the   death   of   the   Cross.

Then shall the **Minister** *announce the Gospel for the Day, saying:*

The Holy Gospel is written in the——Chapter of St.——, beginning at the——Verse.

The **Congregation** *shall rise and sing:*

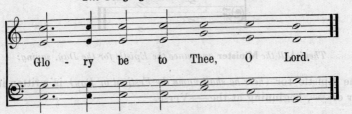

Glo - ry   be   to   Thee,   O   Lord.

Then shall the **Minister** *read the Gospel for the Day:*

The Gospel

The Gospel ended, the **Minister** *shall say:*

Here endeth the Gospel for the Day.

The **Congregation** *shall sing or say:*

Praise be to Thee, O Christ.

Then shall be said the Creed:

The Nicene Creed

I believe in one God, the Father Almighty, Maker of heaven and earth, And of all things visible and invisible;

And in one Lord Jesus Christ, the Only-begotten Son of God, Begotten of His Father before all worlds, God of God, Light of Light, Very God of very God, Begotten, not made, Being of one substance with the Father, By Whom all things were made; Who, for us men, and for our salvation, came down from heaven, and was incarnate by the Holy Ghost of the Virgin Mary, and was made man; And was crucified also for us under Pontius Pilate. He suffered and was buried; And the third day He rose again, according to the Scriptures; And ascended into heaven, and sitteth on the right hand of the Father; And He shall come again with glory to judge both the quick and the dead; Whose kingdom shall have no end.

And I believe in the Holy Ghost, The Lord and Giver of Life, Who proceedeth from the Father and the Son, Who with the Father and the Son together is worshiped and glorified, Who spake by the Prophets. And I believe one holy Christian and Apostolic Church. I acknowledge one Baptism for the remission of sins; And I look for the resurrection of the dead; and the life of the world to come. Amen.

The Apostles' Creed

I believe in God the Father Almighty, Maker of heaven and earth;

And in Jesus Christ His only Son, our Lord: Who was conceived by the Holy Ghost, Born of the Virgin Mary; Suffered under Pontius Pilate, Was crucified, dead, and buried; He descended into hell; The third day He rose again from the dead; He ascended into heaven, And sitteth on the right hand of God the Father Almighty; From thence He shall come to judge the quick and the dead.

I believe in the Holy Ghost; The Holy Christian Church, the Communion of saints; The Forgiveness of sins; The Resurrection of the body; And the Life everlasting. Amen.

Then shall be sung the Hymn.

The Hymn

Then shall follow the Sermon.

The Sermon

After the Sermon the **Congregation** *shall rise, and the* **Minister** *shall say:*

The Peace of God, which passeth all understanding, keep your hearts and minds through Christ Jesus.

Then shall the Offertory be sung, at the close of which the **Congregation** *shall be seated.*

One of the Offertories here following, or any other suitable Offertory, may be used.

The Offertory

TONUS REGIUS.

I

The sacrifices of *God* are a | broken | spirit:
    A broken and a contrite heart, O God, | Thou wilt | not de- | spise.
Do good in Thy good *plea*sure | unto | Zion:
    Build *Thou* the | walls · of Je- | rusa- | lem.
Then shalt Thou be pleased with the sacrifices of | righteous- | ness:
    With burnt-offering and | whole burnt- | offer- | ing.

II

Create in me a clean | heart, O | God:
    And re*new* a right | spirit · with- | in— | me.
Cast me not a*way* | from Thy | presence:
    And take not Thy | Holy | Spirit | from me.
Restore unto me the *joy* of | Thy sal- | vation:
    And up*hold* me with | Thy free | Spir- | it.

Or:

H. R. K.   From FREYLINGHAUSEN.

Cre-ate in me a clean heart, O God; and re-new a right spir-it with-in me. Cast me not a-way from Thy pres-ence; and take not Thy Ho-ly Spir-it from me. Re-store un-to me the joy of Thy sal-va - tion; and up-hold me with Thy free Spir-it.

*Then shall the Offering be received and placed by the **Minister** upon the Altar.*

The Offering

Then shall follow the General Prayer.

*At the end of each paragraph the **Congregation** may say:*

We beseech Thee to hear us, good Lord.

The General Prayer

Let us pray.

Almighty and most Merciful God, the Father of our Lord Jesus Christ: We give Thee thanks for all Thy goodness and tender mercies, especially for the gift of Thy dear Son, and for the revelation of Thy will and grace; and we beseech Thee so to implant Thy Word in us, that, in good and honest hearts, we may keep it, and bring forth fruit by patient continuance in well doing.

Most heartily we beseech Thee so to rule and govern Thy Church universal, that it may be preserved in the pure doctrine of Thy saving Word, whereby faith toward Thee may be strengthened, and charity increased in us toward all mankind.

Send forth Thy light and Thy truth unto the uttermost parts of the earth. Raise up faithful pastors and missionaries to preach the Gospel in our own land and to all nations; and guide, protect, and prosper them in all their labors.

Bless, we pray Thee, the institutions of the Church; its colleges, its seminaries, and all its schools; that they may send forth men and women to serve Thee, in the Ministry of the Word, the Ministry of Mercy, and all the walks of life.

Let the light of Thy Word ever shine within our homes. Keep the children of the Church in the covenant which Thou hast made with them in Holy Baptism; and grant all parents grace to bring them up in faith toward Thee and in obedience to Thy will.

Grant also health and prosperity to all that are in authority, especially to the President (and Congress) of the United States, the Governor (and Legislature) of this Commonwealth, and to all our Judges and Magistrates; and endue them with grace to rule after Thy good pleasure, to the maintenance of righteousness, and to the hindrance and punishment of wickedness, that we may lead a quiet and peaceable life, in all godliness and honesty.

All who are in trouble, want, sickness, anguish of labor, peril of death, or any other adversity, especially those who are in suffering for Thy Name and for Thy truth's sake, comfort, O God, with Thy Holy Spirit, that they may receive and acknowledge their afflictions as the manifestation of Thy fatherly will.

And although we have deserved Thy righteous wrath and manifold punishments, yet, we entreat Thee, O most Merciful Father, remember not the sins of our youth, nor our many transgressions; but out of Thine unspeakable goodness, grace, and mercy, defend us from all harm and danger of body and soul. Preserve us from false and pernicious doctrine, from war and bloodshed, from plague and pestilence, from all calamity by fire and water, from hail and tempest, from failure of harvest and from famine, from anguish of heart and despair of Thy mercy, and from an evil death. And in every time of trouble, show Thyself a very present Help, the Saviour of all men, and especially of them that believe.

Cause also the needful fruits of the earth to prosper, that we may enjoy them in due season. Give success to all lawful occupations on land and sea; to all pure arts and useful knowledge; and crown them with Thy blessing.

Here special Supplications, Intercessions, and Prayers may be made.

These, and whatsoever other things Thou wouldest have us ask of Thee, O God, vouchsafe unto us, for the sake of the bitter sufferings and death of Jesus Christ, Thine only Son, our Lord and Saviour, Who liveth and reigneth with Thee and the Holy Ghost, ever One God, world without end.

*Then shall the **Minister** and the **Congregation** say the Lord's Prayer.*

The Lord's Prayer

Our Father, Who art in heaven: Hallowed be Thy Name; Thy kingdom come; Thy will be done on earth, as it is in heaven; Give us this day our daily bread; And forgive us our trespasses, as we forgive those who trespass against us; And lead us not into temptation; But deliver us from evil; For Thine is the kingdom, and the power, and the glory, for ever and ever. Amen.

Then shall be sung a Hymn.

The Hymn

*If there be no Communion, the **Minister** standing at the Altar shall say the Benediction.*

The Benediction

The Lord bless thee, and keep thee.
The Lord make His face shine upon thee, and be gracious unto thee.
The Lord lift up His countenance upon thee, and give thee peace.

*The **Congregation** shall sing or say:*

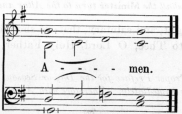

The Holy Communion

When there is a Communion, the **Minister** *shall go to the Altar during the singing of the* **Hymn.** *After Silent Prayer, he shall uncover the Vessels and reverently prepare for the Administration of the Holy Sacrament.*

The **Congregation** *shall rise and stand until the end of the* **Agnus Dei.**

The Preface

The **Minister** *shall say:*

The Lord be with you.

The **Congregation** *shall sing or say:*

And... with thy... spir - - it.

V. Lift up your hearts.

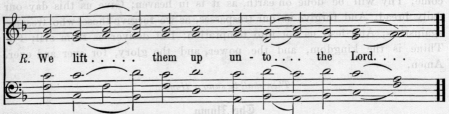

R. We lift..... them up un - to.... the Lord....

V. Let us give thanks unto the Lord our God.

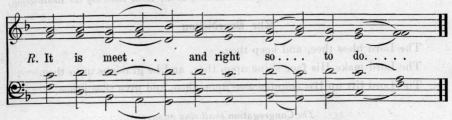

R. It is meet.... and right so.... to do....

Then shall the **Minister** *turn to the Altar and say:*

It is truly meet, right, and salutary, that we should at all times, and in all places, give thanks unto Thee, O Lord, Holy Father, Almighty Everlasting God.

Here shall follow the Proper Preface for the Day or Season. If there be none especially appointed, there shall follow immediately, "Therefore with Angels," etc.

Proper Prefaces

For Christmas.

For in the mystery of the Word made flesh, Thou hast given us a new revelation of Thy glory; that seeing Thee in the person of Thy Son, we may be drawn to the love of those things which are not seen. Therefore with Angels, etc.

For Epiphany.

And now do we praise Thee, that Thou didst send unto us Thine Only-begotten Son, and that in Him, being found in fashion as a man, Thou didst reveal the fullness of Thy Glory. Therefore with Angels, etc.

For Lent.

Who on the Tree of the Cross didst give salvation unto mankind; that whence death arose, thence life also might rise again: and that he who by a tree once overcame, might likewise by a Tree be overcome, through Christ our Lord; through Whom with Angels, etc.

For Easter.

But chiefly are we bound to praise Thee for the glorious Resurrection of Thy Son, Jesus Christ, our Lord: for He is the very Paschal Lamb, which was offered for us, and hath taken away the sin of the world; Who by His death hath destroyed death, and by His rising to life again, hath restored to us everlasting life. Therefore with Angels, etc.

For the Festival of the Ascension.

Through Jesus Christ our Lord, Who after His Resurrection appeared openly to all His disciples, and in their sight was taken up into Heaven, that He might make us partakers of His Divine Nature. Therefore with Angels, etc.

For the Festival of Pentecost.

Through Jesus Christ, Thy dear Son, our Lord and Saviour; Who ascending above the heavens and sitting at Thy right hand, poured out (on this day) the Holy Spirit, as He had promised, upon the chosen disciples; whereat the whole earth rejoices with exceeding joy. Therefore with Angels, etc.

For the Festival of the Holy Trinity.

Who with Thine Only-begotten Son, and the Holy Ghost, art One God, One Lord. And in the confession of the only true God, we worship the Trinity in Person, and the Unity in Substance, of Majesty Co-equal. Therefore with Angels, etc.

After the Preface shall follow immediately:

Therefore with Angels and Archangels, and with all the company of heaven, we laud and magnify Thy glorious Name; evermore praising Thee, and saying:

Then shall the Sanctus be sung or said.

The Sanctus

Ascribed to J. S. BACH.

Ho - ly, Ho - ly, Ho - - ly, Lord God of Sa - ba - oth;

Heaven and earth are full of Thy glo - ry; Ho - san - na

in the high - est. Bless - ed is He that com - eth in the

Name of the Lord. Ho - san - na in the high - est.

The Lord's Prayer

Then shall the **Minister** *say:*

Let us pray.

Our Father, Who art in heaven: Hallowed be Thy Name; Thy kingdom come; Thy will be done on earth, as it is in heaven; Give us this day our daily bread; And forgive us our trespasses, as we forgive those who trespass against us; And lead us not into temptation; But deliver us from evil; For Thine is the kingdom, and the power, and the glory, for ever and ever.

The **Congregation** *shall sing or say:*

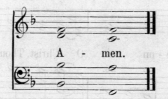

A - men.

Then shall the **Minister** *say the Words of Institution.*

The Words of Institution

Our Lord Jesus Christ, in the night in which He was betrayed,* took bread; and when He had given thanks, He brake it and gave it to His disciples, saying, Take, eat; this is My Body, which is given for you; this do in remembrance of Me.

Here he shall take the Paten, with the **Bread,** *in his hand.*

After the same manner also He** took the cup, when He had supped, and when He had given thanks, He gave it to them, saying, Drink ye all of it; this cup is the New Testament in My Blood, which is shed for you, and for many, for the remission of sins; this do, as oft as ye drink it, in remembrance of Me.

Here he shall take the* **Cup *in his hand.*

Then shall the **Minister** *turn to the Congregation and say:*

The Peace of the Lord be with you alway.

The **Congregation** *shall sing or say:*

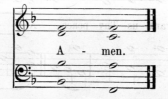

A - men.

Then shall be sung or said the Agnus Dei.

The Agnus Dei

BRAUNSCHWEIG, 1528.

O Christ, Thou Lamb of God, that tak-est a-way the sin of the world, have mer-cy up-on us. O Christ, Thou Lamb of God, that tak-est a-way the sin of the world, have mer-cy up-on us. O Christ, Thou Lamb of God, that tak-est a-way the sin of the world, grant us Thy peace. A - - - - - - men.

Then shall the **Communicants** *present themselves before the Altar and receive the Holy Sacrament.*

The Administration of the Holy Sacrament

When the **Minister** *giveth the* **Bread** *he shall say:*

Take and eat, this is the Body of Christ, given for thee.

When he giveth the **Cup** *he shall say:*

Take and drink, this is the Blood of the New Testament, shed for thy sins.

After he hath given the Bread and the Cup, the **Minister** *shall say:*

The Body of our Lord Jesus Christ and His precious Blood strengthen and preserve you in true faith unto everlasting life.

Then shall the **Congregation** *rise, and the Nunc Dimittis may be sung or said.*

The Nunc Dimittis

W. HINE.

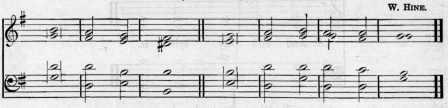

Lord, now lettest Thou Thy *servant* de- | part in | peace:
Ac- | cording | to Thy | word;
For mine eyes have *seen* | Thy sal- | vation:
Which Thou hast prepared before the *face* of | all | peo- | ple;
A *light* to | lighten · the | Gentiles:
And the *glory* of Thy | peo-ple | Isra- | el.

Glory be to the *Father,* and | to the | Son:
And | to the | Holy | Ghost;
As it was in the beginning, is now, and | ever | shall be:
World | without | end. A- | men.

Then shall be said the Thanksgiving.

The Thanksgiving

V. O give thanks unto the Lord, for He is good.

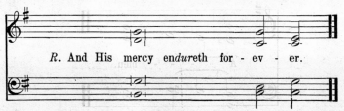

R. And His mercy en*dureth* for - ev - er.

We give thanks to Thee, Almighty God, that Thou hast refreshed us with this Thy salutary gift; and we beseech Thee, of Thy mercy, to strengthen us through the same in faith toward Thee, and in fervent love toward one another; through Jesus Christ, Thy dear Son, our Lord, Who liveth and reigneth with Thee and the Holy Ghost, ever One God, world without end.

The **Congregation** *shall sing or say:*

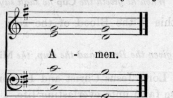

A - men.

Then may be sung or said the Salutation and the Benedicamus.

V. The Lord be with you.

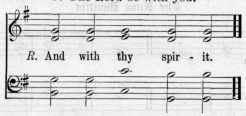

R. And with thy spir - it.

V. Bless we the Lord.

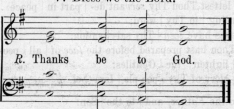

R. Thanks be to God.

Then shall the **Minister** *say the Benediction.*

The Benediction

The Lord bless thee, and keep thee.
The Lord make His face shine upon thee, and be gracious unto thee.
The Lord lift up His countenance upon thee, and give thee peace.

The **Congregation** *shall sing or say:*

A - - - - men.

The Introits

First Sunday in Advent.

Unto Thee, O Lord, do I lift up my soul : O my God, I trust in Thee;

Let me not be ashamed : let not mine enemies triumph over me;

Yea, let none that wait on Thee : be ashamed.

Psalm. Show me Thy ways, O Lord : teach me Thy paths.

Glory be to the Father, etc.

Second Sunday in Advent.

Daughter of Zion : behold thy salvation cometh. The Lord shall cause His glorious voice to be heard : and ye shall have gladness of heart.

Ps. Give ear, O Shepherd of Israel : Thou that leadest Joseph like a flock.

Glory be to the Father, etc.

Third Sunday in Advent.

Rejoice in the Lord alway : and again I say, Rejoice.

Let your moderation be known unto all men : the Lord is at hand.

Be careful for nothing : but in everything by prayer and supplication with thanksgiving let your requests be made known unto God.

Ps. Lord, Thou hast been favorable unto Thy land : Thou hast brought back the captivity of Jacob.

Glory be to the Father, etc.

Fourth Sunday in Advent.

Drop down, ye heavens, from above : and let the skies pour down righteousness. Let the earth open : and bring forth salvation.

Ps. The heavens declare the glory of God : and the firmament showeth His handiwork.

Glory be to the Father, etc.

Christmas Day.
The Nativity of Our Lord.

I. Early Service.

The Lord hath said unto Me, Thou art my Son : this day have I begotten Thee.

Ps. The Lord reigneth, He is clothed with majesty : the Lord is clothed with strength, wherewith He hath girded Himself.

Glory be to the Father, etc.

II. Later Service.

Unto us a Child is born, unto us a Son is given : and the government shall be upon His shoulder.

And His Name shall be called Wonderful, Counsellor, The Mighty God : The Everlasting Father, The Prince of Peace.

Ps. O sing unto the Lord a new song : for He hath done marvellous things.

Glory be to the Father, etc.

Second Christmas Day.

Introit *the same as for* CHRISTMAS DAY.

First Sunday after Christmas.

Thy testimonies are very sure : holiness becometh Thine house, O Lord, forever.

Thy throne is established of old : Thou art from everlasting.

Ps. The Lord reigneth, He is clothed with majesty : the Lord is clothed with strength, wherewith He hath girded Himself.

Glory be to the Father, etc.

New Year's Day. The Circumcision and the Name of Jesus.

O Lord, our Lord, how excellent is Thy Name in all the earth : Who hast set Thy glory above the heavens.

What is man that Thou art mindful of him : and the son of man that Thou visitest him?

Ps. Thou, O Lord, art our Father and our Redeemer : from everlasting is Thy Name.

Glory be to the Father, etc.

Sunday after New Year.

Introit *the same as for the* FIRST SUNDAY AFTER CHRISTMAS.

Epiphany of Our Lord.

Behold, the Lord, the Ruler, hath come : and the kingdom, and the power, and the glory are in His hand.

Ps. Give the King Thy judgments, O God : and Thy righteousness unto the King's Son.

Glory be to the Father, etc.

First Sunday after the Epiphany.

I saw also the Lord, sitting upon a throne : high and lifted up.

And I heard the voice of a great multitude, saying, Alleluia : for the Lord God Omnipotent reigneth.

Ps. Make a joyful noise unto the Lord, all ye lands : serve the Lord with gladness.

Glory be to the Father, etc.

Second Sunday after the Epiphany.

All the earth shall worship Thee : and shall sing unto Thee, O God.

They shall sing to Thy Name : O Thou Most Highest.

Ps. Make a joyful noise unto God, all ye lands : sing forth the honor of His Name, make His praise glorious.

Glory be to the Father, etc.

Third Sunday after the Epiphany.

Worship Him, all ye His angels : Zion heard and was glad.

The daughters of Judah rejoiced : because of Thy judgments, O Lord.

Ps. The Lord reigneth, let the earth rejoice : let the multitude of isles be glad thereof.

Glory be to the Father, etc.

Fourth Sunday after the Epiphany.

Introit *the same as for the* THIRD SUNDAY AFTER THE EPIPHANY.

Fifth Sunday after the Epiphany.

Introit *the same as for the* THIRD SUNDAY AFTER THE EPIPHANY.

Septuagesima Sunday.

The sorrows of death compassed me: the sorrows of hell compassed me about.

In my distress, I called upon the Lord : and He heard my voice out of His temple.

Ps. I will love Thee, O Lord my Strength : the Lord is my Rock and my Fortress.

Glory be to the Father, etc.

Sexagesima Sunday.

Awake, why sleepest Thou, O Lord : arise, cast us not off for ever.

Wherefore hidest Thou Thy face : and forgettest our affliction?

Our soul is bowed down to the dust : arise for our help and redeem us.

Ps. We have heard with our ears, O God : our fathers have told us what work Thou didst in their days.

Glory be to the Father, etc.

Quinquagesima Sunday.

Be Thou my strong Rock : for an house of defense to save me.

Thou art my Rock and my Fortress : therefore for Thy Name's sake lead me and guide me.

Ps. In Thee, O Lord, do I put my trust; let me never be ashamed : deliver me in Thy righteousness.

Glory be to the Father, etc.

Ash Wednesday.
First Day of Lent.

I will cry unto God Most High : unto God that performeth all things for me.

Yea, in the shadow of Thy wings will I make my refuge : until these calamities be overpast.

Ps. Be merciful unto me, O God, be merciful unto me : for my soul trusteth in Thee.

Glory be to the Father, etc.

Invocavit.
First Sunday in Lent.

He shall call upon Me, and I will answer him : I will deliver him and honor him.

With long life will I satisfy him : and show him My salvation.

Ps. He that dwelleth in the secret place of the Most High : shall abide under the shadow of the Almighty.

Glory be to the Father, etc.

Reminiscere.
Second Sunday in Lent.

Remember, O Lord, Thy tender mercies and Thy lovingkindnesses : for they have been ever of old.

Let not mine enemies triumph over me : God of Israel, deliver us out of all our troubles.

Ps. Unto Thee, O Lord, do I lift up my soul : O my God, I trust in Thee; let me not be ashamed.

Glory be to the Father, etc.

Oculi.
Third Sunday in Lent.

Mine eyes are ever toward the Lord : for He shall pluck my feet out of the net.

Turn Thee unto me, and have mercy upon me : for I am desolate and afflicted.

Ps. Unto Thee, O Lord, do I lift up my soul : O my God, I trust in Thee; let me not be ashamed.

Glory be to the Father, etc.

Laetare.
Fourth Sunday in Lent.

Rejoice, ye with Jerusalem, and be glad with her : all ye that love her.

Rejoice for joy with her : all ye that mourn for her.

Ps. I was glad when they said unto me : Let us go into the house of the Lord.

Glory be to the Father, etc.

Judica.
Fifth Sunday in Lent.

Judge me, O God : and plead my cause against an ungodly nation.

O deliver me from the deceitful and unjust man : for Thou art the God of my strength.

Ps. O send out Thy light and Thy truth : let them lead me; let them bring me unto Thy holy hill.

Glory be to the Father, etc.

Palmarum.
Sixth Sunday in Lent.

Be not Thou far from me, O Lord : O my strength, haste Thee to help me.

Save me from the lion's mouth : and deliver me from the horns of the unicorns.

Ps. My God, my God, why hast Thou forsaken me : why art Thou so far from helping me?

Glory be to the Father, etc.

Monday in Holy Week.

Plead my cause, O Lord, with them that strive with me : fight against them that fight against me.

Take hold of shield and buckler : and stand up for mine help.

Ps. Draw out also the spear, and stop the way against them that persecute me : say unto my soul, I am thy salvation.

Glory be to the Father, etc.

Tuesday in Holy Week.

God forbid that I should glory : save in the Cross of our Lord Jesus Christ.

In Him is salvation, life, and resurrection from the dead : by Him we are redeemed and set at liberty.

Ps. God be merciful unto us, and bless us : and cause His face to shine upon us.

Glory be to the Father, etc.

Wednesday in Holy Week.

At the Name of Jesus every knee shall bow : of things in heaven, and things in earth, and things under the earth.

For He became obedient unto death, even the death of the Cross : wherefore He is Lord, to the glory of God the Father.

Ps. Hear my prayer, O Lord : and let my cry come unto Thee.

Glory be to the Father, etc.

Thursday in Holy Week.

Introit *the same as for* TUESDAY IN HOLY WEEK.

Good Friday.

Introit *the same as for* TUESDAY IN HOLY WEEK; *or this:*

Surely He hath borne our griefs and carried our sorrows : He was wounded for our transgressions, He was bruised for our iniquities.

All we like sheep have gone astray : and the Lord hath laid on Him the iniquity of us all.

Ps. Hear my prayer, O Lord : and let my cry come unto Thee.

Glory be to the Father, etc.

Easter Day.
The Resurrection of Our Lord.

When I awake, I am still with Thee, Hallelujah : Thou hast laid Thine hand upon me. Hallelujah.

Such knowledge is too wonderful for me : it is high, I cannot attain unto it. Hallelujah. Hallelujah.

Ps. O Lord, Thou hast searched me and known me : Thou knowest my down-sitting and mine uprising.

Glory be to the Father, etc.

Or:

He is risen, Hallelujah : Why seek ye the Living among the dead? Hallelujah.

Remember how He spake unto you, Hallelujah : the Son of Man must be crucified, and the third day rise again. Hallelujah. Hallelujah.

Ps. Thou crownedst Him with glory and honor : Thou madest Him to have dominion over the works of Thy hands.
Glory be to the Father, etc.

Monday after Easter.

Introit and Collect *the same as for* EASTER DAY.

Quasi Modo Geniti.
First Sunday after Easter.

As newborn babes : desire the sincere milk of the Word.
Hear, O My people, and I will testify unto thee : O Israel, if thou wilt harken unto Me.
Ps. Sing aloud unto God our strength : make a joyful noise unto the God of Jacob.
Glory be to the Father, etc.

Misericordias Domini.
Second Sunday after Easter.

The earth is full of the goodness of the Lord : by the Word of the Lord were the heavens made.
Ps. Rejoice in the Lord, O ye righteous : for praise is comely for the upright.
Glory be to the Father, etc.

Jubilate.
Third Sunday after Easter.

Make a joyful noise unto God, all ye lands : sing forth the honor of His Name; make His praise glorious.
Ps. Say unto God, how terrible art Thou in Thy works : through the greatness of Thy power shall Thine enemies submit themselves unto Thee.
Glory be to the Father, etc.

Cantate.
Fourth Sunday after Easter.

O sing unto the Lord a new song : for He hath done marvellous things.

The Lord hath made known His salvation : His righteousness hath He openly showed in the sight of the heathen.
Ps. His right hand, and His holy arm : hath gotten Him the victory.
Glory be to the Father, etc.

Rogate.
Fifth Sunday after Easter.

With the voice of singing declare ye, and tell this : utter it even to the end of the earth. Hallelujah.
The Lord hath redeemed His servant Jacob : Hallelujah. Hallelujah.
Ps. Make a joyful noise unto God, all ye lands : sing forth the honor of His Name; make His praise glorious.
Glory be to the Father, etc.

The Ascension of Our Lord.

Ye men of Galilee, why stand ye gazing up into heaven? : Hallelujah.
This same Jesus which is taken up from you into heaven, shall so come in like manner as ye have seen Him go into heaven : Hallelujah. Hallelujah.
Ps. O clap your hands, all ye people : shout unto God with the voice of triumph.
Glory be to the Father, etc.

Exaudi.
Sixth Sunday after Easter.

Hear, O Lord, when I cry with my voice : Hallelujah.
When Thou saidst, Seek ye My face : my heart said unto Thee, Thy face, Lord, will I seek.
Hide not Thy face from me : Hallelujah. Hallelujah.
Ps. The Lord is my Light, and my Salvation : whom shall I fear?
Glory be to the Father, etc.

Festival of Pentecost. Whitsunday.

The Spirit of the Lord filleth the world : Hallelujah.

Let the righteous be glad; let them rejoice before God : yea, let them exceedingly rejoice. Hallelujah. Hallelujah.

Ps. Let God arise; let His enemies be scattered : let them also that hate Him flee before Him.

Glory be to the Father, etc.

Monday in Whitsun-week.

Introit *the same as for* WHITSUNDAY.

Festival of the Holy Trinity.

Blessed be the Holy Trinity, and the undivided Unity :

Let us give glory to Him because He hath shown His mercy to us.

Ps. O Lord, our Lord : how excellent is Thy Name in all the earth!

Glory be to the Father, etc.

First Sunday after Trinity.

O Lord, I have trusted in Thy mercy : my heart shall rejoice in Thy salvation.

I will sing unto the Lord : because He hath dealt bountifully with me.

Ps. How long wilt Thou forget me, O Lord : How long wilt Thou hide Thy face from me?

Glory be to the Father, etc.

Second Sunday after Trinity.

The Lord was my stay : He brought me forth also into a large place.

He delivered me : because He delighted in me.

Ps. I will love Thee, O Lord, my Strength : the Lord is my Rock, and my Fortress.

Glory be to the Father, etc.

Third Sunday after Trinity.

Turn Thee unto me, and have mercy upon me : for I am desolate and afflicted.

Look upon mine affliction and my pain : and forgive all my sins.

Ps. Unto Thee, O Lord, do I lift up my soul : O my God, I trust in Thee, let me not be ashamed.

Glory be to the Father, etc.

Fourth Sunday after Trinity.

The Lord is my Light and my Salvation; whom shall I fear :

The Lord is the Strength of my life; of whom shall I be afraid?

When the wicked, even mine enemies and my foes, came upon me : they stumbled and fell.

Ps. Though an host should encamp against me : my heart shall not fear.

Glory be to the Father, etc.

Fifth Sunday after Trinity.

Hear, O Lord, when I cry with my voice : Thou hast been my help.

Leave me not, neither forsake me : O God of my Salvation.

Ps. The Lord is my Light and my Salvation : whom shall I fear?

Glory be to the Father, etc.

Sixth Sunday after Trinity.

The Lord is the strength of His people : He is the saving strength of His anointed.

Save Thy people, and bless Thine inheritance : feed them also, and lift them up forever.

Ps. Unto Thee will I cry, O Lord, my Rock; be not silent unto me : lest if Thou be silent to me, I become like them that go down into the pit.

Glory be to the Father, etc.

Seventh Sunday after Trinity.

O clap your hands : all ye people.

Shout unto God : with the voice of triumph.

Ps. He shall subdue the people under us : and the nations under our feet.

Glory be to the Father, etc.

The Transfiguration of Our Lord.

The lightnings lightened the world : the earth trembled and shook.

Ps. How amiable are Thy tabernacles, O Lord of hosts : my soul longeth, yea, even fainteth for the courts of the Lord.

Glory be to the Father, etc.

Eighth Sunday after Trinity.

We have thought of Thy lovingkindness, O God : in the midst of Thy Temple.

According to Thy Name, O God, so is Thy praise unto the ends of the earth : Thy right hand is full of righteousness.

Ps. Great is the Lord, and greatly to be praised : in the city of our God, in the mountain of His holiness.

Glory be to the Father, etc.

Ninth Sunday after Trinity.

Behold, God is mine Helper : the Lord is with them that uphold my soul.

He shall reward evil unto mine enemies : cut them off in Thy truth, O Lord.

Ps. Save me, O God, by Thy Name : and judge me by Thy strength.

Glory be to the Father, etc.

Tenth Sunday after Trinity.

As for me, I will call upon God, and He shall hear my voice : He hath delivered my soul in peace from the battle that was against me.

God shall hear and afflict them, even He that abideth of old : Cast Thy burden upon the Lord, and He shall sustain thee.

Ps. Give ear to my prayer, O God : and hide not Thyself from my supplication.

Glory be to the Father, etc.

Eleventh Sunday after Trinity.

God is in His holy habitation : He is God Who setteth the solitary in families.

The God of Israel is He that giveth strength : and power unto His people.

Ps. Let God arise, let His enemies be scattered : let them also that hate Him flee before Him.

Glory be to the Father, etc.

Twelfth Sunday after Trinity.

Make haste, O God, to deliver me : make haste to help me, O Lord.

Let them be ashamed and confounded : that seek after my soul.

Ps. Let them be turned backward, and put to confusion : that desire my hurt.

Glory be to the Father, etc.

Thirteenth Sunday after Trinity.

Have respect, O Lord, unto Thy covenant : O let not the oppressed return ashamed.

Arise, O God, plead Thine own cause : and forget not the voice of Thine enemies.

Ps. O God, why hast Thou cast us off forever : Why doth Thine anger smoke against the sheep of Thy pasture?

Glory be to the Father, etc.

Fourteenth Sunday after Trinity.

Behold, O God our Shield : and look upon the face of Thine Anointed;

For a day in Thy courts : is better than a thousand.

Ps. How amiable are Thy tabernacles, O Lord of Hosts : my soul longeth, yea, even fainteth for the courts of the Lord.

Glory be to the Father, etc.

Fifteenth Sunday after Trinity.

Bow down Thine ear, O Lord, hear me : O Thou, my God, save Thy servant that trusteth in Thee.

Be merciful unto me, O Lord : for I cry unto Thee daily.

Ps. Rejoice the soul of Thy servant : for unto Thee, O Lord, do I lift up my soul.

Glory be to the Father, etc.

Sixteenth Sunday after Trinity.

Be merciful unto me, O Lord : for I cry unto Thee daily.

For Thou, Lord, art good, and ready to forgive : and plenteous in mercy unto all them that call upon Thee.

Ps. Bow down Thine ear, O Lord, hear me : for I am poor and needy.

Glory be to the Father, etc.

Seventeenth Sunday after Trinity.

Righteous art Thou, O Lord : and upright are Thy judgments.

Deal with Thy servant : according to Thy mercy.

Ps. Blessed are the undefiled in the way : who walk in the law of the Lord.

Glory be to the Father, etc.

Eighteenth Sunday after Trinity.

Reward them that wait for Thee, O Lord : and let Thy prophets be found faithful.

Hear the prayer of Thy servants : and of Thy people Israel.

Ps. I was glad when they said unto me : Let us go into the house of the Lord.

Glory be to the Father, etc.

Nineteenth Sunday after Trinity.

Say unto my soul, I am thy Salvation : the righteous cry, and the Lord heareth.

He delivereth them out of all their troubles : He is their God forever and ever.

Ps. Give ear, O My people, to My law : incline your ears to the words of My mouth.

Glory be to the Father, etc.

Twentieth Sunday after Trinity.

The Lord our God is righteous in all His works which He doeth : for we obeyed not His voice.

Give glory to Thy Name, O Lord : and deal with us according to the multitude of Thy mercies.

Ps. Great is the Lord, and greatly to be praised : in the city of our God, in the mountain of His holiness.

Glory be to the Father, etc.

Twenty-first Sunday after Trinity.

The whole world is in Thy power, O Lord, King Almighty : there is no man that can gainsay Thee.

For Thou hast made heaven and earth, and all the wondrous things under the heaven : Thou art Lord of all.

Ps. Blessed are the undefiled in the way : who walk in the law of the Lord.

Glory be to the Father, etc.

Twenty-second Sunday after Trinity.

If Thou, Lord, shouldest mark iniquities : O Lord, who shall stand?

But there is forgiveness with Thee : that Thou mayest be feared, O God of Israel.

Ps. Out of the depths have I cried unto Thee, O Lord : Lord, hear my voice.

Glory be to the Father, etc.

Twenty-third Sunday after Trinity.

I know the thoughts that I think toward you, saith the Lord : thoughts of peace, and not of evil.

Then shall ye call upon Me, and pray unto Me, and I will hearken unto you : and I will turn your captivity, and gather you from all nations and from all places.

Ps. Lord, Thou hast been favorable unto Thy land : Thou hast brought back the captivity of Jacob.

Glory be to the Father, etc.

Twenty-fourth Sunday after Trinity.

O come, let us worship and bow down : let us kneel before the Lord our Maker.

For He is our God : and we are the people of His pasture, and the sheep of His hand.

Ps. O come, let us sing unto the Lord : let us make a joyful noise to the Rock of our salvation.

Glory be to the Father, etc.

Twenty-fifth Sunday after Trinity.

Have mercy upon me, O Lord, for I am in trouble : deliver me from the hand of mine enemies, and from them that persecute me.

Let me not be ashamed, O Lord : for I have called upon Thee.

Ps. In Thee, O Lord, do I put my trust : let me never be ashamed.

Glory be to the Father, etc.

Twenty-sixth Sunday after Trinity.

Save me, O God, by Thy Name : and judge me by Thy strength.

Hear my prayer, O God : give ear to the words of my mouth.

Ps. He shall reward evil to mine enemies : cut them off in Thy truth.

Glory be to the Father, etc.

Twenty-seventh Sunday after Trinity.

The Introit here following shall be used the LAST SUNDAY AFTER TRINITY *of each year.*

I am Alpha and Omega, the beginning and the ending : which is, and which was, and which is to come, the Almighty.

Behold, the tabernacle of God is with men, and He will dwell with them : and they shall be His people, and God Himself shall be with them, and be their God.

Ps. Lift up your heads, O ye gates; and be ye lift up, ye everlasting doors : and the King of Glory shall come in.

Glory be to the Father, etc.

Minor Festivals of the Church Year.

The Day of the Presentation of Christ.

(Candlemas.)

We have thought of Thy loving-kindness, O God : in the midst of Thy temple.

According to Thy Name, O God, so is Thy praise unto the ends of the earth : Thy right hand is full of righteousness.

Ps. Great is the Lord, and greatly to be praised : in the city of our God, in the mountain of His holiness.

Glory be to the Father, etc.

The Annunciation.

March 25.

All the rich among the people shall entreat Thy favor : she shall be brought unto the King in raiment of needlework.

Her companions shall be brought unto Thee : with gladness and rejoicing.

Ps. My heart is inditing a good matter : I speak of the things which I have made touching the King.

Glory be to the Father, etc.

The Nativity of St. John, the Baptist.
June 24.

The voice of him that crieth in the wilderness : Prepare ye the way of the Lord, make straight in the desert a highway for our God.

And the glory of the Lord : shall be revealed.

Ps. It is a good thing to give thanks unto the Lord : and to sing praises unto Thy Name, O Most High.

Glory be to the Father, etc.

St. Michael and All Angels.

Bless the Lord, ye His angels, that excel in strength : that do His commandments, hearkening unto the voice of His word.

Bless ye the Lord, all ye His hosts : ye ministers of His that do His pleasure.

Ps. Bless the Lord, O my soul : and all that is within me bless His holy Name.

Glory be to the Father, etc.

The Festival of the Reformation.
October 31.

The Sunday preceding this Festival may be observed as REFORMATION SUNDAY, *except when October 31st fall on Saturday, in which event the following day may be observed as* REFORMATION SUNDAY.

The Lord of Hosts is with us : the God of Jacob is our Refuge.

Therefore will not we fear, though the earth be removed : and though the mountains be carried into the midst of the sea.

Ps. God is our Refuge and Strength: a very present help in trouble.

Glory be to the Father, etc.

All Saints' Day.
November 1.

These are they which have come out of great tribulation : and have washed their robes and made them white in the blood of the Lamb.

Therefore are they before the throne of God : and serve Him day and night in His temple.

Ps. Rejoice in the Lord, O ye righteous : for praise is comely for the upright.

Glory be to the Father, etc.

The Festival of Harvest.

O Lord, Thou crownest the year with Thy goodness : and Thy paths drop fatness.

Thou visitest the earth and waterest it : Thou blessest the springing thereof.

Ps. Praise waiteth for Thee, O God, in Zion : and unto Thee shall the vow be performed.

Glory be to the Father, etc.

A Day of Humiliation and Prayer.

Hear, O heavens, and give ear, O earth, for the Lord hath spoken : I have nourished and brought up children, and they have rebelled against Me.

They have forsaken the Lord, they have provoked the Holy One of Israel unto anger : they are gone away backward.

Ps. If Thou, Lord, shouldest mark iniquities : O Lord, who shall stand?

Glory be to the Father, etc.

A Day of General or Special Thanksgiving.

The proper Service for this Day is the Order for Matins; but when The Service is used the following Propria are appointed.

Let every thing that hath breath praise the Lord : Praise ye the Lord.

Praise Him for His mighty acts : Praise Him according to His excellent greatness.

Ps. Praise ye the Lord; praise God in His sanctuary : Praise Him in the firmament of His power.

Glory be to the Father, etc.

The Common Service
Vespers

The Versicles with the Gloria Patri shall be sung or said, the **Congregation** *standing until the end of the Psalm.*

The Hallelujah shall be omitted in Lent.

The Versicle.

O Lord, open Thou my lips.

TALLIS.

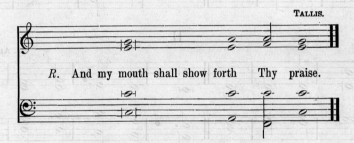

R.   And my mouth shall show forth   Thy   praise.

V.   Make haste, O God, to deliver me.

TALLIS.

R.   Make   haste   to   help   me,   O   Lord.

V.   Glory be to the Father, and to the Son, and to the Holy Ghost:

TALLIS.

R.   As it was in }
     the beginning, } is now, { and ever shall }
                              { be, world with- } out   end.   A-men.   Hal-le-lu-jah.

Then shall be said one or more Psalms.

The Psalm.

At the end of each Psalm the **Congregation** *shall sing or say the Gloria Patri.*

The Gloria Patri.

I

W. HAYES.

II

J. ALCOCK.

Glory be to the *Fa*ther, and | to the | Son:

And | to the | Holy | Ghost;

As it was in the beginning, is now, and | ever | shall be:

World | without | end.   A- | men.

III

For Lent.   Arranged by J. STAINER.

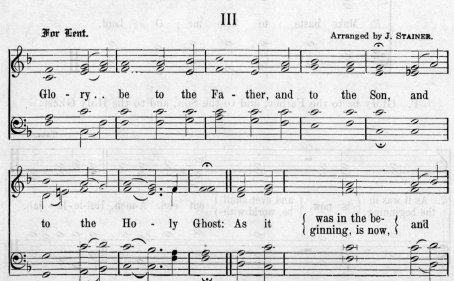

Glo - ry .. be to the Fa - ther, and to the Son, and

to the Ho - ly Ghost: As it { was in the be- } and
                                  { ginning, is now, }

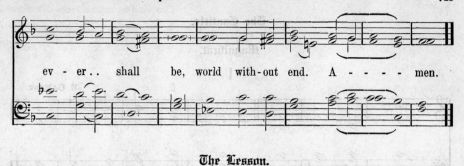

ev - er .. shall be, world with-out end. A - - - - men.

The Lesson.

The Scripture Lessons shall then be read. After each Lesson shall be sung or said the Response.

V. O Lord, have mercy upon us.

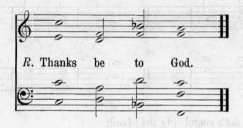

R. Thanks be to God.

*After the Lesson a **Responsory** or a **Hymn** may be sung.*

*A **Sermon** may then follow.*

*The **Offering** may then be received and placed upon the Altar.*

Then shall be sung the Hymn.

The Hymn.

*The **Congregation** shall rise and sing or say the Canticle.*

A Versicle shall be used with the Canticle.

V. Let my prayer be set forth before Thee as incense.

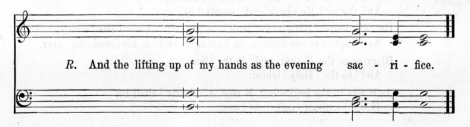

R. And the lifting up of my hands as the evening sac - ri - fice.

The Canticle.

Magnificat.

I

E. G. MONK.

II

ANON.

My soul doth *magni-* | fy the | Lord:
  And my spirit hath re- | joiced ˙ in | God my | Saviour.

For He | hath re- | garded:
  The low es- | tate of | His hand- | maiden.

For behold, | from hence- | forth:
  All gener- | ations ˙ shall | call me | blessed.

For He that is *might*y hath done to | me great | things:
  And | holy | is His | Name.

And His *mer*cy is on | them that | fear Him:
  From gener- | ation ˙ to | gener- | ation.

He hath showed *strength* | with His | arm:
  He hath scattered the *proud* in the imagi- | nation | of their | hearts.

He hath put down the *mighty* | from their | seats:
  And ex*alt*ed | them of | low de- | gree.

He hath filled the *hun*gry | with good | things:
  And the *rich* He | hath sent | empty ˙ a- | way.

He hath holpen His servant Israel, in re*mem*brance | of His | mercy:
  As he spake to our fathers, to Abraham, and | to his | seed, for | ever.

Glory be to the *Fa*ther, and | to the | Son:
  And | to the | Holy | Ghost;

As it was in the beginning, is now, and | ever | shall be:
  World | without | end.   A- | men.

Nunc Dimittis.

I

J. GOLDWIN.

II

J. MEDLEY.

Lord, now lettest Thou Thy *serv*ant de- | part in | peace:
Ac- | cording | to Thy | word;

For mine eyes have *seen* | Thy sal- | vation:
Which Thou hast prepared before the *face* of | all | peo- | ple;

A *light* to | lighten · the | Gentiles:
And the *glory* of Thy | peo-ple | Isra- | el.

Glory be to the *Father*, and | to the | Son:
And | to the | Holy | Ghost;

As it was in the beginning, is now, and | ever | shall be:
World | without | end.   A- | men.

The Prayer.

Then shall be said the Prayers.

The **Minister** *shall say:*

Lord, have mercy upon us.

The **Congregation** *shall sing or say:*

I

TALLIS.

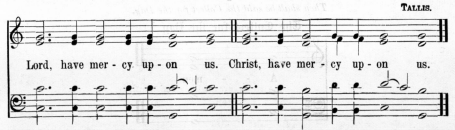

Lord, have mer - cy up - on   us.   Christ, have mer - cy up - on   us.

Lord, have mer - cy up - on..... us.

II

MERBECKE.

Lord, have mer - cy up - on us. Christ, have mer - cy up - on us.

Lord, have mer - - cy up - on..... us.

Then shall all say the **Lord's Prayer:**

Our Father, Who art in heaven: Hallowed be Thy Name; Thy kingdom come; Thy will be done on earth, as it is in heaven; Give us this day our daily bread; And forgive us our trespasses, as we forgive those who trespass against us; And lead us not into temptation; But deliver us from evil; For Thine is the kingdom, and the power, and the glory, for ever and ever. Amen.

Then may be sung or said:

V. The Lord be with you.

R. And with thy spir - it.

Let us pray.

Then shall be said the Collect for the Day.

The Collect for the Day.

A - - men.

Other Collects may then be said, and after them, this Collect for Peace with which a Versicle may be used.

   V. The Lord will give strength unto His people.

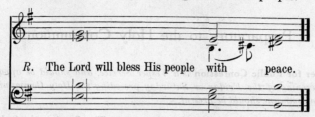

   R. The Lord will bless His people with peace.

The Collect for Peace

O God, from Whom all holy desires, all good counsels, and all just works do proceed: Give unto Thy servants that peace which the world cannot give; that our hearts may be set to obey Thy commandments, and also that by Thee, we, being defended from the fear of our enemies, may pass our time in rest and quietness; through the merits of Jesus Christ our Saviour, Who liveth and reigneth with Thee, and the Holy Ghost, ever One God, world without end.

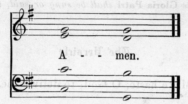

A - - men.

Then may be sung or said the **Benedicamus.**

   V. Bless we the Lord.

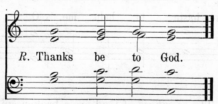

R. Thanks be to God.

Then shall the **Minister** *say the Benediction.*

  The Grace of our Lord Jesus Christ, and the Love of God, and the Communion of the Holy Ghost, be with you all.

A - men.

𝔒𝔯𝔡𝔢𝔯 𝔣𝔬𝔯 𝔓𝔲𝔟𝔩𝔦𝔠 𝔆𝔬𝔫𝔣𝔢𝔰𝔰𝔦𝔬𝔫

Preparatory to the Holy Communion

The Order for Public Confession *is a Vesper Service, and should be appointed for the afternoon or evening of the Friday or Saturday preceding the Holy Communion, when all who purpose to commune should be present.*

When the Confessional Service immediately precedes **The Service,** *the Order shall begin with the words:*

In the Name of the Father, and of the Son, and of the Holy Ghost.
R. Amen.

Then shall follow: The **Exhortation,** *the* **Confession,** *the* **Absolution,** *and the* **New Testament Benediction. The Service** *shall begin with the* **Introit for the Day.**

A **Hymn of Invocation of the Holy Ghost,** *or another suitable Hymn may be sung.*

The **Versicles** *with the* **Gloria Patri** *shall be sung or said, the Congregation standing until the end of the* **Psalm.**

𝔗𝔥𝔢 𝔙𝔢𝔯𝔰𝔦𝔠𝔩𝔢

Make haste, O God, to deliver me.

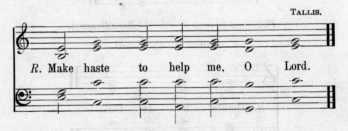

TALLIS.

R. Make haste to help me, O Lord.

V. The sacrifices of God are a broken spirit.

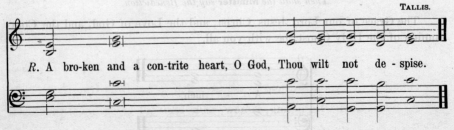

TALLIS.

R. A bro-ken and a con-trite heart, O God, Thou wilt not de - spise.

724

V. Glory be to the Father, and to the Son, and to the Holy Ghost:

TALLIS.

R. As it was in the beginning, is now, and ever shall be, world without end. A - men.

Then shall be sung or said this **Psalm:**

The Psalm

Have mercy upon me, O God, according to Thy loving kindness : according unto the multitude of Thy tender mercies, blot out my transgressions.

Wash me thoroughly from mine iniquity : and cleanse me from my sin.

For I acknowledge my transgressions : and my sin is ever before me.

Against Thee, Thee only, have I sinned, and done this evil in Thy sight: that Thou mightest be justified when Thou speakest, and be clear when Thou judgest.

Behold, I was shapen in iniquity : and in sin did my mother conceive me.

Behold, Thou desirest truth in the inward parts : and in the hidden part Thou shalt make me to know wisdom.

Purge me with hyssop, and I shall be clean : wash me, and I shall be white. than snow.

Make me to hear joy and gladness : that the bones which Thou hast broken may rejoice.

Hide Thy face from my sins : and blot out all mine iniquities.

Create in me a clean heart, O God : and renew a right spirit within me.

Cast me not away from Thy presence : and take not Thy Holy Spirit from me.

Restore unto me the joy of Thy salvation : and uphold me with Thy free Spirit.

Then will I teach transgressors Thy ways : and sinners shall be converted unto Thee.

O Lord, open Thou my lips : and my mouth shall show forth Thy praise.

Glory be to the Father, and to the Son, and to the Holy Ghost:

As it was in the beginning, is now, and ever shall be, world without end. Amen.

Then shall one or more of the following **Lessons of Holy Scripture** *be read.*

The Lesson

Exodus 20 : 1–17.	Matthew 11 : 25–30.
Daniel 9 : 4–9, 17–19.	Mark 12 : 28–31.
Isaiah 57 : 14–21.	Luke 13 : 1–9.
Isaiah 1 : 11–18.	Luke 15 : 1–2, 11–31.
1 John 1 : 5–9.	John 13 : 1–17.
1 Corinthians 11 : 23–29.	John 20 : 19–23.
Matthew 5 : 21–29.	

Then may follow an **Address** *or* **Sermon,** *after which shall be sung a* **Hymn.**

The Hymn

Then shall the Congregation stand, and the Minister shall say the following **Exhortation:**

The Exhortation

Dearly Beloved! Forasmuch as we purpose to come to the Holy Supper of our Lord Jesus Christ, it becometh us diligently to examine ourselves, as St. Paul exhorteth us. For this Holy Sacrament hath been instituted for the special comfort and strengthening of those who humbly confess their sins, and who hunger and thirst after righteousness.

But if we thus examine ourselves, we shall find in us nothing but sin and death, from which we can in no wise set ourselves free. Therefore our Lord Jesus Christ hath had mercy upon us, and hath taken upon Himself our nature, that so He might fulfill for us the whole will and law of God, and for us and for our deliverance suffer death and all that we by our sins have deserved. And to the end that we should the more confidently believe this, and be strengthened by our faith in cheerful obedience to His will, He hath instituted the Holy Sacrament of His Supper, in which He giveth us His Body to eat, and His Blood to drink.

Therefore whoso eateth of this Bread and drinketh of this Cup, firmly believing the words of Christ, dwelleth in Christ, and Christ in him, and hath eternal life.

We should also do this in remembrance of Him, showing His death, that He was delivered for our offenses, and raised again for our justification, and rendering unto Him most hearty thanks for the same, take up our cross and follow Him; and, according to His commandment, love one another even as He hath loved us. For we are all one body, even as we are all partakers of this one Bread, and drink of this one Cup.

Let us pray.

Almighty God, unto Whom all hearts are open, all desires known, and from Whom no secrets are hid: Cleanse the thoughts of our hearts by the inspiration of Thy Holy Spirit, that we may perfectly love Thee, and worthily magnify Thy holy Name; through Jesus Christ, Thy Son, our Lord. Amen.

Then shall the Minister begin the **Confession** *as here followeth:*

The Confession

I ask you in the presence of Almighty God, Who searcheth the heart:

Do you truly acknowledge, confess, and lament that you are by nature sinful, and that by omitting to do good and by doing evil you have in thought, word, and deed grieved and offended your God and Saviour, and thereby justly deserved His condemnation?

If this be the sincere confession of your hearts, declare it by saying: Yes.

Answer: Yes.

Do you truly believe that Jesus Christ came into the world to save sinners, and that all who believe on His Name receive the forgiveness of sins? Do you, therefore, earnestly desire to be delivered from all your sins, and are you confident that it is the gracious will of your Heavenly Father, for Christ's sake, to forgive your sins and to cleanse you from all unrighteousness?

If so, confess it by saying: Yes.

Answer: Yes.

Is it your earnest purpose, henceforth, to be obedient to the Holy Spirit, so as to hate and forsake all manner of sin, to live as in God's presence, and to strive daily after holiness of heart and life?

If so, answer: Yes.

Answer: Yes.

Let us humbly kneel, and make confession unto God, imploring His forgiveness through Jesus Christ our Lord.

Then shall all kneel, and say:

O God, our Heavenly Father, I confess unto Thee that I have grievously sinned against Thee in many ways; not only by outward transgression, but also by secret thoughts and desires, which I cannot fully understand, but which are all known unto Thee. I do earnestly repent, and am heartily sorry for these my offenses, and I beseech Thee of Thy great goodness to have mercy upon me, and for the sake of Thy dear Son Jesus Christ, our Lord, to forgive my sins, and graciously to help my infirmities. Amen.

Then shall the Minister rise and say the **Absolution.** *The Congregation shall remain kneeling until after the Benediction.*

The Absolution

Almighty God, our Heavenly Father, hath had mercy upon us, and for the sake of the sufferings, death, and resurrection of His dear Son Jesus Christ, our Lord, forgiveth us all our sins. As a Minister of the Church of Christ, and by His authority, I therefore declare unto you who do truly repent and believe in Him, the entire forgiveness of all your sins: In the Name of the Father, and of the Son, and of the Holy Ghost.

On the other hand, by the same authority, I declare unto the impenitent and unbelieving, that so long as they continue in their impenitence, God hath not forgiven their sins, and will assuredly visit their iniquities upon them, if they turn not from their evil ways, and come to true repentance and faith in Christ, ere the day of grace be ended.

Then shall the Minister kneel, and all shall say the **Lord's Prayer.**

The Prayer

Our Father, Who art in heaven: Hallowed be Thy Name; Thy kingdom come; Thy will be done on earth, as it is in heaven; Give us this day our daily bread; And forgive us our trespasses, as we forgive those who trespass against us; And lead us not into temptation; But deliver us from evil; For thine is the kingdom, and the power, and the glory, for ever and ever. Amen.

Then shall the Minister say the **Collect for the Day,** *except when* **The Service** *immediately follows this Order.*

(After the Collects.)

A - - men.

Then may other suitable Collects be said, and after them the **Collect for Peace.**

V. The Lord will give strength unto His people.

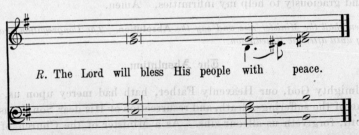

R. The Lord will bless His people with peace.

The Collect for Peace

O God, from Whom all holy desires, all good counsels, and all just works do proceed: Give unto Thy servants that peace which the world cannot give; that our hearts may be set to obey Thy commandments, and also that by Thee, we, being defended from the fear of our enemies, may pass our time in rest and quietness; through the merits of Jesus Christ, our Saviour, Who liveth and reigneth with Thee, and the Holy Ghost, ever One God, world without end.

A - - - men.

The Minister shall rise and say the **Benediction :**

The Grace of our Lord Jesus Christ, and the Love of God, and the Communion of the Holy Ghost, be with you all,

A - - - men.

Psalms
For Responsive Reading

PSALM 1.
The Righteous and the Wicked Contrasted.

BLESSED is the man that walketh not in the counsel of the wicked,
Nor standeth in the way of sinners,
Nor sitteth in the seat of scoffers:
But his delight is in the law of Jehovah;
And on his law doth he meditate day and night.
And he shall be like a tree planted by the streams of water,
That bringeth forth its fruit in its season,
Whose leaf also doth not wither;

And whatsoever he doeth shall prosper.
The wicked are not so,
But are like the chaff which the wind driveth away.
Therefore the wicked shall not stand in the judgment,
Nor sinners in the congregation of the righteous;
For Jehovah knoweth the way of the righteous;
But the way of the wicked shall perish.

PSALM 2.
The Reign of Jehovah's Anointed.

WHY do the nations rage,
And the peoples meditate a vain thing?
The kings of the earth set themselves,
And the rulers take counsel together,
Against Jehovah, and against his anointed, saying,
Let us break their bonds asunder,
And cast away their cords from us.
He that sitteth in the heavens will laugh:
The Lord will have them in derision.
Then will he speak unto them in his wrath,
And vex them in his sore displeasure:
Yet I have set my king
Upon my holy hill of Zion.
I will tell of the decree:
Jehovah said unto me, Thou art my son:

This day have I begotten thee.
Ask of me, and I will give thee the nations for thine inheritance,
And the uttermost parts of the earth for thy possession.
Thou shalt break them with a rod of iron;
Thou shalt dash them in pieces like a potter's vessel.
Now therefore be wise, O ye kings:
Be instructed, ye judges of the earth.
Serve Jehovah with fear,
And rejoice with trembling.
Kiss the son, lest he be angry, and ye perish in the way,
For his wrath will soon be kindled.
Blessed are all they that take refuge in him.

PSALM 8.
Jehovah's Glory and Man's Dignity.

O JEHOVAH, our Lord,
How excellent is thy name in all the earth,
Who hast set thy glory upon the heavens!
Out of the mouth of babes and sucklings hast thou established strength,
Because of thine adversaries,
That thou mightest still the enemy and the avenger.

When I consider thy heavens, the work of thy fingers,
The moon and the stars, which thou hast ordained;
What is man, that thou art mindful of him?
And the son of man, that thou visitest him?
For thou hast made him but little lower than God,

730

And crowned him with glory and honor.
Thou makest him to have dominion over
  the works of thy hands;
Thou hast put all things under his feet;
All sheep and oxen,
Yea, and the beasts of the field.

The birds of the heavens, and the fish of
  the sea,
*Whatsoever passeth through the paths of
  the seas.*
O Jehovah, our Lord,
*How excellent is thy name in all the
  earth!*

PSALM 9. 1, 2, 7–14.

A Psalm of Thanksgiving for God's Justice.

I WILL give thanks unto Jehovah with
  my whole heart;
*I will show forth all thy marvellous
  works.*
I will be glad and exult in thee;
*I will sing praise to thy name, O thou
  Most High.*
But Jehovah sitteth as king for ever:
*He hath prepared his throne for judg-
  ment;*
And he will judge the world in right-
  eousness.
*He will minister judgment to the peoples
  in uprightness.*
Jehovah also will be a high tower for the
  oppressed,
A high tower in times of trouble;

And they that know thy name will put
  their trust in thee;
*For thou, Jehovah, hast not forsaken them
  that seek thee.*
Sing praises to Jehovah, who dwelleth
  in Zion:
Declare among the people his doings.
For he that maketh inquisition for blood
  remembereth them;
He forgetteth not the cry of the poor.
Have mercy upon me, O Jehovah;
*Behold my affliction which I suffer of
  them that hate me,*
Thou that liftest me up from the gates
  of death;
That I may show forth all thy praise.
In the gates of the daughter of Zion
I will rejoice in thy salvation.

PSALM 19.

The Works and the Word of God.

THE heavens declare the glory of God;
  *And the firmament showeth his han-
  diwork.*
Day unto day uttereth speech,
And night unto night showeth knowledge.
There is no speech nor language;
Their voice is not heard.
Their line is gone out through all the
  earth,
And their words to the end of the world.
In them hath he set a tabernacle for the
  sun,
*Which is as a bridegroom coming out of
  his chamber,*
And rejoiceth as a strong man to run his
  course.
His going forth is from the end of the
  heavens,
And his circuit unto the ends of it;
*And there is nothing hid from the heat
  thereof.*
The law of Jehovah is perfect, restoring
  the soul:
*The testimony of Jehovah is sure, making
  wise the simple.*

The precepts of Jehovah are right, re-
  joicing the heart:
*The commandment of Jehovah is pure,
  enlightening the eyes.*
The fear of Jehovah is clean, enduring
  for ever:
*The ordinances of Jehovah are true, and
  righteous altogether.*
More to be desired are they than gold,
  yea, than much fine gold;
*Sweeter also than honey and the drop-
  pings of the honeycomb.*
Moreover by them is thy servant warned:
In keeping them there is great reward.
Who can discern his errors?
Clear thou me from hidden faults.
Keep back thy servant also from pre-
  sumptuous sins;
Let them not have dominion over me:
Then shall I be upright,
*And I shall be clear from great transgres-
  sion.*
Let the words of my mouth and the med-
  itation of my heart
Be acceptable in thy sight,
O Jehovah, my rock, and my redeemer.

PSALM 22. 22–31.

A Song of Praise.

I WILL declare thy name unto my breth-
ren:
*In the midst of the assembly will I
praise thee.*
Ye that fear Jehovah, praise him:
*And all ye the seed of Jacob, glorify him;
And stand in awe of him, all ye the seed
of Israel.*
For he hath not despised nor abhorred
the affliction of the afflicted;
*Neither hath he hid his face from him;
But when he cried unto him, he heard.*
Of thee cometh my praise in the great
assembly:
*I will pay my vows before them that fear
him.*
The meek shall eat and be satisfied;
*They shall praise Jehovah that seek after
him;*

Let your hearts live for ever.
All the ends of the earth shall remember
and turn unto Jehovah;
*And all the kindreds of the nations shall
worship before thee.*
For the kingdom is Jehovah's;
And he is the ruler over the nations.
All the fat ones of the earth shall eat
and worship:
*All they that go down to the dust shall
bow before him,*
Even he that cannot keep his soul alive.
A seed shall serve him;
*It shall be told of the Lord unto the next
generation.*
They shall come and shall declare his
righteousness
*Unto a people that shall be born, that he
hath done it.*

PSALM 24.

The King of Glory Entering Zion.

THE earth is Jehovah's, and the fulness
thereof;
The world, and they that dwell therein.
For he hath founded it upon the seas,
And established it upon the floods.
Who shall ascend into the hill of Jehovah?
And who shall stand in his holy place?
He that hath clean hands, and a pure
heart;
*Who hath not lifted up his soul unto
falsehood,*
And hath not sworn deceitfully.
He shall receive a blessing from Jehovah,
*And righteousness from the God of his
salvation.*

This is the generation of them that seek
after him,
That seek thy face, even Jacob.
Lift up your heads, O ye gates;
And be ye lifted up, ye everlasting doors:
And the King of glory will come in.
Who is the King of glory?
*Jehovah strong and mighty,
Jehovah mighty in battle.*
Lift up your heads, O ye gates;
Yea, lift them up, ye everlasting doors:
And the King of glory will come in.
Who is this King of glory?
*Jehovah of hosts,
He is the King of glory.*

PSALM 27.

A Psalm of Fearless Trust in God.

JEHOVAH is my light and my salva-
tion;
Whom shall I fear?
Jehovah is the strength of my life;
Of whom shall I be afraid?
When evil-doers came upon me to eat up
my flesh,
*Even mine adversaries and my foes, they
stumbled and fell.*
Though a host should encamp against
me,
My heart shall not fear:
Though war should rise against me,
Even then will I be confident.
One thing have I asked of Jehovah, that
will I seek after:

*That I may dwell in the house of Jeho-
vah, all the days of my life,*
To behold the beauty of Jehovah,
And to inquire in his temple.
For in the day of trouble he will keep
me secretly in his pavilion:
*In the covert of his tabernacle will he
hide me;*
He will lift me up upon a rock.
And now shall my head be lifted up
above mine enemies round about me;
And I will offer in his tabernacle sacri-
fices of joy;
*I will sing, yea, I will sing praises unto
Jehovah.*

Hear, O Jehovah, when I cry with my voice:
Have mercy also upon me, and answer me.
When thou saidst, Seek ye my face; my heart said unto thee,
Thy face, Jehovah, will I seek.
Hide not thy face from me;
Put not thy servant away in anger:
Thou hast been my help;
Cast me not off, neither forsake me, O God of my salvation.
When my father and my mother forsake me,
Then Jehovah will take me up.

Teach me thy way, O Jehovah;
And lead me in the plain path,
Because of mine enemies.
Deliver me not over unto the will of mine adversaries:
For false witnesses are risen up against me,
And such as breathe out cruelty.
I had fainted, unless I had believed to see the goodness of Jehovah
In the land of the living.
Wait for Jehovah:
Be strong, and let thy heart take courage;
Yea, wait thou for Jehovah.

PSALM 32.

Blessedness of Forgiveness and of Trust in God.

BLESSED is he whose transgression is forgiven,
Whose sin is covered.
Blessed is the man unto whom Jehovah imputeth not iniquity,
And in whose spirit there is no guile.
When I kept silence, my bones wasted away
Through my groaning all the day long.
For day and night thy hand was heavy upon me:
My moisture was changed as with the drought of summer.
I acknowledged my sin unto thee,
And mine iniquity did I not hide:
I said, I will confess my transgressions unto Jehovah;
And thou forgavest the iniquity of my sin.
For this let every one that is godly pray unto thee in a time when thou mayest be found:

Surely when the great waters overflow they shall not reach unto him.
Thou art my hiding-place; thou wilt preserve me from trouble;
Thou wilt compass me about with songs of deliverance.
I will instruct thee and teach thee in the way which thou shalt go:
I will counsel thee with mine eye upon thee.
Be ye not as the horse, or as the mule, which have no understanding;
Whose trappings must be bit and bridle to hold them in,
Else they will not come near unto thee.
Many sorrows shall be to the wicked;
But he that trusteth in Jehovah, loving-kindness shall compass him about.
Be glad in Jehovah, and rejoice, ye righteous;
And shout for joy, all ye that are upright in heart.

PSALM 34.

Jehovah a Provider and Deliverer.

I WILL bless Jehovah at all times:
His praise shall continually be in my mouth.
My soul shall make her boast in Jehovah:
The meek shall hear thereof, and be glad.
Oh magnify Jehovah with me,
And let us exalt his name together.
I sought Jehovah, and he answered me,
And delivered me from all my fears.
They looked unto him, and were radiant;
And their faces shall never be confounded.
This poor man cried, and Jehovah heard him,
And saved him out of all his troubles.

The angel of Jehovah encampeth round about them that fear him,
And delivereth them.
Oh taste and see that Jehovah is good:
Blessed is the man that taketh refuge in him.
Oh fear Jehovah, ye his saints;
For there is no want to them that fear him.
The young lions do lack and suffer hunger;
But they that seek Jehovah shall not want any good thing.
Come, ye children, hearken unto me:
I will teach you the fear of Jehovah.
What man is he that desireth life,

And loveth many days, that he may see good?
Keep thy tongue from evil,
And thy lips from speaking guile.
Depart from evil, and do good;
Seek peace, and pursue it.
The eyes of Jehovah are toward the righteous,
And his ears are open unto their cry.
The face of Jehovah is against them that do evil,
To cut off the remembrance of them from the earth.
The righteous cried, and Jehovah heard,
And delivered them out of all their troubles.

Jehovah is nigh unto them that are of a broken heart,
And saveth such as are of a contrite spirit.
Many are the afflictions of the righteous;
But Jehovah delivereth him out of them all.
He keepeth all his bones:
Not one of them is broken.
Evil shall slay the wicked;
And they that hate the righteous shall be condemned.
Jehovah redeemeth the soul of his servants;
And none of them that take refuge in him shall be condemned.

PSALM 42.

Thirsting for God in Trouble and Exile.

AS the hart panteth after the water brooks,
So panteth my soul after thee, O God.
My soul thirsteth for God, for the living God?
When shall I come and appear before God?
My tears have been my food day and night,
While they continually say unto me, Where is thy God?
These things I remember, and pour out my soul within me,
How I went with the throng, and led them to the house of God,
With the voice of joy and praise, a multitude keeping holyday.
Why art thou cast down, O my soul?
And why art thou disquieted within me?
Hope thou in God;
For I shall yet praise him
For the help of his countenance.
O my God, my soul is cast down within me:

Therefore do I remember thee from the land of the Jordan,
And the Hermons, from the hill Mizar.
Deep calleth unto deep at the noise of thy waterfalls:
All thy waves and thy billows are gone over me.
Yet Jehovah will command his lovingkindness in the daytime;
And in the night his song shall be with me,
Even a prayer unto the God of my life.
I will say unto God my rock, Why hast thou forgotten me?
Why go I mourning because of the oppression of the enemy?
As with a sword in my bones, mine adversaries reproach me,
While they continually say unto me, Where is thy God?
Why art thou cast down, O my soul?
And why art thou disquieted within me?
Hope thou in God;
For I shall yet praise him,
Who is the help of my countenance, and my God.

PSALM 46.

God the Refuge of His People.

GOD is our refuge and strength,
A very present help in trouble.
Therefore will we not fear, though the earth do change,
And though the mountains be shaken into the heart of the seas;
Though the waters thereof roar and be troubled,
Though the mountains tremble with the swelling thereof.
There is a river, the streams whereof make glad the city of God,
The holy place of the tabernacle of the Most High.

God is in the midst of her; she shall not be moved:
God will help her, and that right early.
The nations raged, the kingdoms were moved:
He uttered his voice, the earth melted.
Jehovah of hosts is with us;
The God of Jacob is our refuge.
Come, behold the works of Jehovah,
What desolations he hath made in the earth.
He maketh wars to cease unto the end of the earth;

He breaketh the bow, and cutteth the
  spear in sunder;
He burneth the chariots in the fire.
Be still, and know that I am God:

I will be exalted among the nations, I
  will be exalted in the earth.
Jehovah of hosts is with us;
The God of Jacob is our refuge.

PSALM 51. 1–17.

A Contrite Sinner's Prayer for Pardon.

HAVE mercy upon me, O God, according to thy lovingkindness:
According to the multitude of thy tender
  mercies blot out my transgressions.
Wash me thoroughly from mine iniquity,
And cleanse me from my sin.
For I know my transgressions;
And my sin is ever before me.
Against thee, thee only, have I sinned,
And done that which is evil in thy sight;
That thou mayest be justified when thou
  speakest,
And be clear when thou judgest.
Behold, I was brought forth in iniquity;
And in sin did my mother conceive me.
Behold, thou desirest truth in the inward
  parts;
And in the hidden part thou wilt make
  me to know wisdom.
Purify me with hyssop, and I shall be
  clean:
Wash me, and I shall be whiter than
  snow.
Make me to hear joy and gladness,
That the bones which thou hast broken
  may rejoice.

Hide thy face from my sins,
And blot out all mine iniquities.
Create in me a clean heart, O God;
And renew a right spirit within me.
Cast me not away from thy presence;
And take not thy Holy Spirit from me.
Restore unto me the joy of thy salvation;
And uphold me with a willing spirit.
Then will I teach transgressors thy
  ways;
And sinners shall be converted unto thee.
Deliver me from bloodguiltiness, O God,
  thou God of my salvation;
And my tongue shall sing aloud of thy
  righteousness.
O Lord, open thou my lips;
And my mouth shall show forth thy
  praise.
For thou delightest not in sacrifice; else
  would I give it:
Thou hast no pleasure in burnt-offering.
The sacrifices of God are a broken spirit:
A broken and a contrite heart, O God,
  thou wilt not despise.

PSALM 67.

The Nations Exhorted to Praise God.

GOD be merciful unto us, and bless us,
  And cause his face to shine upon us;
That thy way may be known upon earth.
Thy salvation among all nations.
Let the peoples praise thee, O God;
Let all the peoples praise thee.
Oh let the nations be glad and sing for joy;
For thou wilt judge the peoples with
  equity,

And govern the nations upon earth.
Let the peoples praise thee, O God;
Let all the peoples praise thee.
The earth hath yielded its increase:
God, even our own God, will bless us.
God will bless us;
And all the ends of the earth shall fear
  him.

PSALM 86. 1–12.

A Psalm of Supplication and Trust.

BOW down thine ear, O Jehovah, and
  answer me;
For I am poor and needy.
Preserve my soul; for I am godly:
O thou my God, save thy servant that
  trusteth in thee.
Be merciful unto me, O Lord;
For unto thee do I cry all the day long.
Rejoice the soul of thy servant:

For unto thee, O Lord, do I lift up my
  soul.
For thou, Lord, art good, and ready to
  forgive,
And abundant in lovingkindness unto all
  them that call upon thee.
Give ear, O Jehovah, unto my prayer;
And hearken unto the voice of my supplications.

In the day of my trouble I will call upon thee;
For thou wilt answer me.
There is none like unto thee among the gods, O Lord;
Neither are there any works like unto thy works.
All nations whom thou hast made shall come and worship before thee, O Lord;
And they shall glorify thy name.

For thou art great, and doest wondrous things:
Thou art God alone.
Teach me thy way, O Jehovah; I will walk in thy truth:
Unite my heart to fear thy name.
I will praise thee, O Lord my God, with my whole heart;
And I will glorify thy name for ever-more.

PSALM 98.

A Call to Praise Jehovah for His Righteousness.

OH sing unto Jehovah a new song;
For he hath done marvellous things:
His right hand, and his holy arm, hath wrought salvation for him.
Jehovah hath made known his salvation:
His righteousness hath he openly showed in the sight of the nations.
He hath remembered his loving-kindness and his faithfulness toward the house of Israel:
All the ends of the earth have seen the salvation of our God.
Make a joyful noise unto Jehovah, all the earth:
Break forth and sing for joy, yea, sing praises.

Sing praises unto Jehovah with the harp;
With the harp and the voice of melody.
With trumpets and sound of cornet
Make a joyful noise before the King, Je-hovah.
Let the sea roar, and the fulness thereof;
The world, and they that dwell therein;
Let the floods clap their hands;
Let the hills sing for joy together
Before Jehovah for he cometh to judge the earth:
He will judge the world with righteous-ness,
And the peoples with equity.

PSALM 111.

Jehovah Praised for His Goodness.

PRAISE ye Jehovah.
I will give thanks unto Jehovah with my whole heart,
In the council of the upright, and in the congregation.
The works of Jehovah are great,
Sought out of all them that have pleas-ure therein.
His work is honor and majesty;
And his righteousness endureth for ever.
He hath made his wonderful works to be remembered:
Jehovah is gracious and merciful.
He hath given food unto them that fear him:
He will ever be mindful of his covenant.
He hath showed his people the power of his works,

In giving them the heritage of the na-tions.
The works of his hands are truth and justice;
All his precepts are sure.
They are established for ever and ever;
They are done in truth and uprightness.
He hath sent redemption unto his peo-ple;
He hath commanded his covenant for ever:
Holy and reverend is his name.
The fear of Jehovah is the beginning of wisdom;
A good understanding have all they that do his commandments:
His praise endureth for ever

PSALM 119. 9-16.

Meditations and Prayers Relating to the Law of God.

WHEREWITH shall a young man cleanse his way?
By taking heed thereto according to thy word.
With my whole heart have I sought thee:

Oh let me not wander from thy com-mandments.
Thy word have I laid up in my heart,
That I might not sin against thee.
Blessed art thou, O Jehovah:

Teach me thy statutes.
With my lips have I declared
All the ordinances of thy mouth.
I have rejoiced in the way of thy testimonies,

As much as in all riches.
I will meditate on thy precepts,
And have respect unto thy ways.
I will delight myself in thy statutes:
I will not forget thy word.

PSALM 122.

Prayer for the Peace of Jerusalem.

I WAS glad when they said unto me,
Let us go unto the house of Jehovah.
Our feet are standing
Within thy gates, O Jerusalem,
Jerusalem, that art builded
As a city that is compact together;
Whither the tribes go up, even the tribes of Jehovah,
For an ordinance for Israel,
To give thanks unto the name of Jehovah.

For there are set thrones for judgment,
The thrones of the house of David.
Pray for the peace of Jerusalem:
They shall prosper that love thee.
Peace be within thy walls,
And prosperity within thy palaces.
For my brethren and companions' sakes,
I will now say, Peace be within thee.
For the sake of the house of Jehovah our God
I will seek thy good.

PSALM 145.

Jehovah Extolled for His Goodness and Power.

I WILL extol thee, my God, O King;
And I will bless thy name for ever and ever.
Every day will I bless thee;
And I will praise thy name for ever and ever.
Great is Jehovah, and greatly to be praised;
And his greatness is unsearchable.
One generation shall laud thy works to another,
And shall declare thy mighty acts.
Of the glorious majesty of thine honor,
And of thy wondrous works, will I meditate.
And men shall speak of the might of thy terrible acts;
And I will declare thy greatness.
They shall utter the memory of thy great goodness,
And shall sing of thy righteousness.
Jehovah is gracious, and merciful;
Slow to anger, and of great lovingkindness.
Jehovah is good to all;
And his tender mercies are over all his works.
All thy works shall give thanks unto thee, O Jehovah;
And thy saints shall bless thee.
They shall speak of the glory of thy kingdom,
And talk of thy power;

To make known to the sons of men his mighty acts,
And the glory of the majesty of his kingdom.
Thy kingdom is an everlasting kingdom,
And thy dominion endureth throughout all generations.
Jehovah upholdeth all that fall,
And raiseth up all those that are bowed down.
The eyes of all wait for thee;
And thou givest them their food in due season.
Thou openest thy hand,
And satisfiest the desire of every living thing.
Jehovah is righteous in all his ways,
And gracious in all his works.
Jehovah is nigh unto all them that call upon him,
To all that call upon him in truth.
He will fulfil the desire of them that fear him;
He also will hear their cry and will save them.
Jehovah preserveth all them that love him;
But all the wicked will he destroy.
My mouth shall speak the praise of Jehovah;
And let all flesh bless his holy name for ever and ever.

Lectionary

The Church Year

The Church Year begins on the First Sunday in Advent, about December first, and not, as the calendar year, January first.

The Church Year is divided into two parts, namely, from the First Sunday in Advent to Trinity Sunday, and from Trinity Sunday to the last Sunday after Trinity. The first part deals with the life of Christ, from His birth to His ascension and the descent of the Holy Spirit. The second part deals with the life of the Christian, from baptism to the day of judgment. The great theme of the first part is Christ *for* us, while that of the second part is Christ *in* us. The first part deals with all that *God has done* for our salvation through Christ. The second part is intended to show how the *Church may receive* the salvation of God through Christ and by daily sanctification be prepared for her Lord's second coming.

The three main festivals of the Church occur in the first part of the Church Year. They are Christmas, Easter, and Pentecost.

Christmas is preceded by the Advent season. Advent means "coming," and the texts of the four Advent Sundays treat of the coming of Jesus. Christmas celebrates His birth. The second day of Christmas commemorates the martyrs, suggested by Herod's murder of the Innocents. New Year's Day speaks of the Name of Jesus, which He received eight days after His birth. In this way we begin the secular year in the name of Jesus. Epiphany means "manifestation." It celebrates Christ's manifestation to the Wise Men and throughout the centuries to all the nations of the earth.

Easter, like Christmas, also has a period of preparation. This is known as the Lenten season. During this time the sermons dwell on the passion story of Christ, and the Church follows the Saviour in spirit on His way to the cross. The texts of Palm Sunday treat of His triumphal entry into Jerusalem, and of the Holy Supper instituted by Christ on the eve of His final sufferings. Good Friday commemorates the crucifixion, death, and burial of Jesus. Easter celebrates His resurrection.

Pentecost means "fiftieth," that is, fifty days after Easter. In the early Church this day was called Whitsunday, because the adult candidates for holy baptism who received the Sacrament on this day were robed in white. On Pentecost we commemorate the giving of the Holy Spirit and the founding of the Christian Church.

741

Besides these Main Festivals there are three Minor Festivals during the first part of the Church Year, namely, Candlemas, or the Day of the Presentation of Christ, when the child Jesus was presented in the Temple; the Day of the Annunciation, when His birth was announced by the angel to Mary, and Ascension Day, when He ascended into heaven.

During the second part of the Church Year there are four additional Minor Festivals, namely, the Day of John the Baptizer, the great herald of the Lord Jesus; the Festival of Christ's Transfiguration, when He was transfigured on the mount; St. Michael's Day, when special attention is given to the angels and the children; and All Saints' Day, to direct our thoughts to the redeemed in heaven. The last Sunday of the Church Year speaks of the Final Judgment.

In addition to the Festivals mentioned above, our Church observes four Prayer Days. The first is a day of general repentance, when we confess our sins as a Church and as a Nation before the Lord. The second is Reformation Day, when we thank God for the pure gospel doctrine. The third is Mission Day, when we unite in praying God for the conversion of the heathen. The fourth is Thanksgiving Day, when we praise God for the year's harvest and for all temporal and spiritual blessings.

Gospel and Epistle Texts for the Church Year

FIRST SUNDAY IN ADVENT.

The Coming of the Lord to His Church.

Collect. Stir up, we beseech Thee, Thy power, O Lord, and come, that by Thy protection we may be rescued from the threatening perils of our sins, and saved by Thy mighty deliverance; Who livest and reignest with the Father and the Holy Spirit, ever one God, world without end. AMEN.

I. EPISTLE, Romans 13. 11–14.
The New Day Calls for a New Life.

AND this, knowing the season, that already it is time for you to awake out of sleep: for now is salvation nearer to us than when we first believed. The night is far spent, and the day is at hand: let us therefore cast off the works of darkness, and let us put on the armor of light. Let us walk becomingly, as in the day; not in revelling and drunkenness, not in chambering and wantonness, not in strife and jealousy. But put ye on the Lord Jesus Christ, and make not provision for the flesh, to fulfil the lusts thereof.

I. GOSPEL, Matthew 21. 1–9.
Christ's Entry into Jerusalem.

AND when they drew nigh unto Jerusalem, and came unto Bethphage, unto the mount of Olives, then Jesus sent two disciples, saying unto them, Go into the village that is over against you, and straightway ye shall find an ass tied, and a colt with her: loose them, and bring them unto me. And if any one say aught unto you, ye shall say, The Lord hath need of them; and straightway he will send them.

Now this is come to pass, that it might be fulfilled which was spoken through the prophet, saying,

Tell ye the daughter of Zion,
Behold, thy King cometh unto thee,
Meek, and riding upon an ass,
And upon a colt the foal of an ass.

And the disciples went, and did even as Jesus appointed them, and brought the ass, and the colt, and put on them their garments; and he sat thereon. And the most part of the multitude spread their garments in the way; and others cut branches from the trees, and spread them in the way. And the multitudes that went before him, and that followed, cried, saying, Hosanna to the son of David: Blessed is he that cometh in the name of the Lord; Hosanna in the highest.

II. EPISTLE, Psalm 24.
Preparing the King's Highway.

A Psalm of David.

THE earth is Jehovah's and the fulness thereof;
The world, and they that dwell therein.
For he hath founded it upon the seas,
And established it upon the floods.
Who shall ascend into the hill of Jehovah,
And who shall stand in his holy place?
He that hath clean hands, and a pure heart;
Who hath not lifted up his soul unto falsehood,
And hath not sworn deceitfully.
He shall receive a blessing from Jehovah,
And righteousness from the God of his salvation.
This is the generation of them that seek after him,
That seek thy face, even Jacob.
Lift up your heads, O ye gates;
And be ye lifted up, ye everlasting doors:
And the King of glory will come in.
Who is the King of glory?
Jehovah strong and mighty,
Jehovah mighty in battle.
Lift up your heads, O ye gates;
Yea, lift them up, ye everlasting doors:
And the King of glory will come in.
Who is this King of glory?
Jehovah of hosts,
He is the King of glory.

743

II. Gospel, John 18. 36, 37.
The King of Truth.

JESUS answered, My kingdom is not of this world: if my kingdom were of this world, then would my servants fight, that I should not be delivered to the Jews: but now is my kingdom not from hence.

Pilate therefore said unto him, Art thou a king then?

Jesus answered, Thou sayest that I am a king. To this end have I been born, and to this end am I come into the world, that I should bear witness unto the truth. Every one that is of the truth heareth my voice.

III. Epistle, Isaiah 62. 10–12.
Raising Aloft the Banner of God.

Thus saith the Prophet of the Lord:

GO through, go through the gates; prepare ye the way of the people; cast up, cast up the highway; gather out the stones; lift up an ensign for the peoples. Behold, Jehovah hath proclaimed unto the end of the earth, Say ye to the daughter of Zion, Behold, thy salvation cometh; behold, his reward is with him, and his recompense before him. And they shall call them The holy people, The redeemed of Jehovah: and thou shalt be called Sought out, A city not forsaken.

III. Gospel, Luke 4. 16–22.
Jesus in the Synagogue of Nazareth.

AND he came to Nazareth, where he had been brought up: and he entered, as his custom was, into the synagogue on the sabbath day, and stood up to read. And there was delivered unto him the book of the prophet Isaiah. And he opened the book, and found the place where it was written,

The Spirit of the Lord is upon me,
Because he anointed me to preach good tidings to the poor:
He hath sent me to proclaim release to the captives,
And recovering of sight to the blind,
To set at liberty them that are bruised,
To proclaim the acceptable year of the Lord.

And he closed the book, and gave it back to the attendant, and sat down: and the eyes of all in the synagogue were fastened on him. And he began to say unto them, To-day hath this scripture been fulfilled in your ears.

And all bare him witness, and wondered at the words of grace which proceeded out of his mouth.

SECOND SUNDAY IN ADVENT.
Waiting for the Day of the Lord.

Collect. Stir up our hearts, O Lord, to make ready the way of Thine only-begotten Son, so that by His coming we may be enabled to serve Thee with pure minds; Who liveth and reigneth with Thee and the Holy Spirit, ever one God, world without end. Amen.

I. Epistle, Romans 15. 4–13.
The Patient Endurance of Hope.

WHATSOEVER things were written aforetime were written for our learning, that through patience and through comfort of the scriptures we might have hope.

Now the God of patience and of comfort grant you to be of the same mind one with another according to Christ Jesus: that with one accord ye may with one mouth glorify the God and Father of our Lord Jesus Christ. Wherefore receive ye one another, even as Christ also received you, to the glory of God.

For I say that Christ hath been made a minister of the circumcision for the truth of God, that he might confirm the promises given unto the fathers, and that the Gentiles might glorify God for his mercy; as it is written,

Therefore will I give praise unto thee among the Gentiles,
And sing unto thy name.
And again he saith,
Rejoice, ye Gentiles, with his people.
And again,
Praise the Lord, all ye Gentiles;
And let all the peoples praise him.
And again, Isaiah saith,
There shall be the root of Jesse,
And he that ariseth to rule over the Gentiles;
On him shall the Gentiles hope.

Now the God of hope fill you with all joy and peace in believing, that ye may abound in hope, in the power of the Holy Spirit.

I. Gospel, Luke 21. 25–36.
Signs of the Coming of the Lord.

THERE shall be signs in sun and moon and stars; and upon the earth distress of nations, in perplexity for the roaring of the sea and the billows; men fainting for fear, and for expectation of the things which are coming on the world: for the powers of the heavens shall be shaken. And then shall they see the Son of man coming in a cloud with power and great glory. But when these things begin to come to pass, look up, and lift up your heads; because your redemption draweth nigh.

And he spake unto them a parable: Behold the fig tree, and all the trees: when they now shoot forth, ye see it and know of your own selves that the summer is now nigh. Even so ye also, when ye see these things coming to pass, know ye that the kingdom of God is nigh. Verily I say unto you, This generation shall not pass away, till all things be accomplished. Heaven and earth shall pass away: but my words shall not pass away.

But take heed to yourselves, lest haply your hearts be overcharged with surfeiting, and drunkenness, and cares of this life, and that day come on you suddenly as a snare: for so shall it come upon all them that dwell on the face of all the earth. But watch ye at every season, making supplication, that ye may prevail to escape all these things that shall come to pass, and to stand before the Son of man.

II. EPISTLE, Hebrews 10. 35–39.
Perseverance in Hope.

CAST not away therefore your boldness, which hath great recompense of reward. For ye have need of patience, that, having done the will of God, ye may receive the promise.

For yet a very little while,

He that cometh shall come, and shall not tarry.

But my righteous one shall live by faith:

And if he shrink back, my soul hath no pleasure in him.

But we are not of them that shrink back unto perdition; but of them that have faith unto the saving of the soul.

II. GOSPEL, Luke 12. 35–40.
Servants Looking for Their Lord.

LET your loins be girded about, and your lamps burning; and be ye yourselves like unto men looking for their lord, when he shall return from the marriage feast; that, when he cometh and knocketh, they may straightway open unto him.

Blessed are those servants, whom the lord when he cometh shall find watching: verily I say unto you, that he shall gird himself, and make them sit down to meat, and shall come and serve them. And if he shall come in the second watch, and if in the third, and find them so, blessed are those servants.

But know this, that if the master of the house had known in what hour the thief was coming, he would have watched, and not have left his house to be broken through. Be ye also ready: for in an hour that ye think not the Son of man cometh.

III. EPISTLE, James 5. 7–10.
Awaiting the Coming of the Lord.

BE patient therefore, brethren, until the coming of the Lord. Behold, the husbandman waiteth for the precious fruit of the earth, being patient over it, until it receive the early and latter rain. Be ye also patient; establish your hearts: for the coming of the Lord is at hand. Murmur not, brethren, one against another, that ye be not judged: behold, the judge standeth before the doors. Take, brethren, for an example of suffering and of patience, the prophets who spake in the name of the Lord.

III. GOSPEL, Luke 17. 20–30.
The Coming of the Kingdom.

AND being asked by the Pharisees, when the kingdom of God cometh, he answered them and said, The kingdom of God cometh not with observation: neither shall they say, Lo, here! or, There! for lo, the kingdom of God is within you.

And he said unto the disciples, The days will come, when ye shall desire to see one of the days of the Son of man, and ye shall not see it. And they shall say to you, Lo, there! Lo, here! go not away, nor follow after them: for as the lightning, when it lighteneth out of the one part under the heaven, shineth unto the other part under heaven; so shall the Son of man be in his day. But first must he suffer many things and be rejected of this generation.

And as it came to pass in the days of Noah, even so shall it be also in the days of the Son of man. They ate, they drank, they married, they were given in marriage, until the day that Noah entered into the ark, and the flood came, and destroyed them all. Likewise even as it came to pass in the days of Lot; they ate, they drank, they bought, they sold, they planted, they builded; but in the day that Lot went out from Sodom it rained fire and brimstone from heaven, and destroyed them all: after the same manner shall it be in the day that the Son of man is revealed.

THIRD SUNDAY IN ADVENT.

The Forerunner of the Lord.

Collect. O Lord God, we beseech Thee, give ear to our prayers, and lighten the darkness of our hearts by Thy gracious visitation, through Jesus Christ, Thy Son, our Lord. AMEN.

I. EPISTLE, 1 Corinthians 4. 1–5.
Appeal to the Judgment of God.

LET a man so account of us, as of ministers of Christ, and stewards of the mysteries of God. Here, moreover, it is required in stewards, that a man be found faithful.

But with me it is a very small thing that I should be judged of you, or of man's judgment: yea, I judge not mine own self. For I know nothing against myself; yet am I not hereby justified: but he that judgeth me is the Lord. Wherefore judge nothing before the time, until the Lord come, who will both bring to light the hidden things of darkness, and make manifest the counsels of the hearts; and then shall each man have his praise from God.

I. GOSPEL, Matthew 11. 2–10.
John's Message to Jesus.

NOW when John heard in the prison the works of the Christ, he sent by his disciples and said unto him, Art thou he that cometh, or look we for another? And Jesus answered and said unto them, Go and tell John the things which ye hear and see: the blind receive their sight, and the lame walk, the lepers are cleansed, and the deaf hear, and the dead are raised up, and the poor have good tidings preached to them. And blessed is he, whosoever shall find no occasion of stumbling in me.

And as these went their way, Jesus began to say unto the multitudes concerning John, What went ye out into the wilderness to behold? a reed shaken with the wind? But what went ye out to see? a man clothed in soft raiment? Behold, they that wear soft raiment are in kings' houses. But wherefore went ye out? to see a prophet? Yea, I say unto you, and much more than a prophet. This is he of whom it is written,

Behold, I send my messenger before thy face,

Who shall prepare thy way before thee.

II. EPISTLE, 2 Peter 1. 19–21.
The Light of the Prophetic Word.

WE have the word of prophecy made more sure; whereunto ye do well that ye take heed, as unto a lamp shining in a dark place, until the day dawn, and the day-star arise in your hearts: knowing this first, that no prophecy of scripture is of private interpretation. For no prophecy ever came by the will of man: but men spake from God, being moved by the Holy Spirit.

II. GOSPEL, Matthew 11. 11–19.
The Testimony of Jesus to John.

VERILY I say unto you, Among them that are born of women there hath not arisen a greater than John the Baptist: yet he that is but little in the kingdom of heaven is greater than he. And from the days of John the Baptist until now the kingdom of heaven suffereth violence, and men of violence take it by force. For all the prophets and the law prophesied until John. And if ye are willing to receive it, this is Elijah, that is to come. He that hath ears to hear, let him hear.

But whereunto shall I liken this generation? It is like unto children sitting in the marketplaces, who call unto their fellows and say, We piped unto you, and ye did not dance; we wailed, and ye did not mourn. For John came neither eating nor drinking, and they say, He hath a demon. The Son of man came eating and drinking, and they say, Behold, a gluttonous man and a winebibber, a friend of publicans and sinners! And wisdom is justified by her works.

III. EPISTLE, 1 Peter 1. 8–13.
Salvation Foretold by the Prophets.

JESUS CHRIST: whom not having seen ye love; on whom, though now ye see him not, yet believing, ye rejoice greatly with joy unspeakable and full of glory: receiving the end of your faith, even the salvation of your souls.

Concerning which salvation the prophets sought and searched diligently, who prophesied of the grace that should come unto you: searching what time or what manner of time the Spirit of Christ which was in them did point unto, when it testified beforehand the sufferings of Christ, and the glories that should follow them. To whom it was revealed, that not unto themselves, but unto you, did they minister these things, which now have been announced unto you through them that preached the gospel unto you by the Holy Spirit sent forth from heaven; which things angels desire to look into.

Wherefore girding up the loins of your mind, be sober and set your hope perfectly on the grace that is to be brought unto you at the revelation of Jesus Christ.

III. Gospel, Luke 3. 1–14.
John Preaches Repentance.

NOW in the fifteenth year of the reign of Tiberius Cæsar, Pontius Pilate, being governor of Judæa, and Herod being tetrarch of Galilee, and his brother Philip tetrarch of the region of Ituræa and Trachonitis, and Lysanias tetrarch of Abilene, in the highpriesthood of Annas and Caiaphas, the word of God came unto John the son of Zacharias in the wilderness.

And he came into all the region round about the Jordan, preaching the baptism of repentance unto remission of sins; as it is written in the book of the words of Isaiah the prophet,
The voice of one crying in the wilderness,
Make ye ready the way of the Lord,
Make his paths straight.
Every valley shall be filled,
And every mountain and hill shall be brought low;
And the crooked shall become straight,
And the rough ways smooth;
And all flesh shall see the salvation of God.

He said therefore to the multitudes that went out to be baptized of him, Ye offspring of vipers, who warned you to flee from the wrath to come? Bring forth therefore fruits worthy of repentance, and begin not to say within yourselves, We have Abraham to our father: for I say unto you, that God is able of these stones to raise up children unto Abraham. And even now the axe also lieth at the root of the trees; every tree therefore that bringeth not forth good fruit is hewn down, and cast into the fire.

And the multitudes asked him, saying, What then must we do? And he answered and said unto them, He that hath two coats, let him impart to him that hath none; and he that hath food, let him do likewise. And there came also publicans to be baptized, and they said unto him, Teacher, what must we do? And he said unto them, Extort no more than that which is appointed you. And soldiers also asked him, saying, And we, what must we do? And he said unto them, Extort from no man by violence, neither accuse any one wrongfully; and be content with your wages.

FOURTH SUNDAY IN ADVENT.
The Lord Is at Hand.

Collect. O Lord, stir up, we beseech Thee, Thy power, and come among us; help us with Thy great might, that by Thy grace that which is hindered by our sins may be speedily accomplished by Thy bountiful mercy; through Jesus Christ, Thy Son, our Lord. Amen.

I. Epistle, Philippians 4. 4–7.
The Presence of the Lord Gives Joy.

REJOICE in the Lord always: again I will say, Rejoice. Let your forbearance be known unto all men. The Lord is at hand. In nothing be anxious; but in everything by prayer and supplication with thanksgiving let your requests be made known unto God. And the peace of God, which passeth all understanding, shall guard your hearts and your thoughts in Christ Jesus.

I. Gospel, John 1, 19–28.
The Testimony of John.

THIS is the witness of John, when the Jews sent unto him from Jerusalem priests and Levites to ask him, Who art thou? And he confessed, and denied not; and he confessed, I am not the Christ. And they asked him, What then? Art thou Elijah? And he saith, I am not. Art thou the prophet? And he answered, No. They said therefore unto him, Who art thou? that we may give an answer to them that sent us? What sayest thou of thyself? He said, I am the voice of one crying in the wilderness, Make straight the way of the Lord, as said Isaiah the prophet.

And they had been sent from the Pharisees. And they asked him, and said unto him, Why then baptizest thou, if thou art not the Christ, neither Elijah, neither the prophet? John answered them, saying, I baptize in water: in the midst of you standeth one whom ye know not, even he that cometh after me, the latchet of whose shoe I am not worthy to unloose.

These things were done in Bethany beyond the Jordan, where John was baptizing.

II. Epistle, Isaiah 40. 9–11.
The Power and Mercy of the Coming Lord.

O THOU that tellest good tidings to Zion, get thee up on a high mountain; O thou that tellest good tidings to Jerusalem, lift up thy voice with strength; lift it up, be not afraid; say unto the cities of Judah, Behold, your God!

Behold, the Lord Jehovah will come as a mighty one, and his arm will rule for him: Behold, his reward is with him, and his recompense before him. He will feed his flock like a shepherd, he will gather the lambs in his arm, and carry them in his bosòm, and will gently lead those that have their young.

II. Gospel, John 3. 22–36.
The Friend of the Bridegroom.

AFTER these things came Jesus and his disciples into the land of Judæa; and there he tarried with them, and baptized.

And John also was baptizing in Ænon near to Salim, because there was much water there: and they came, and were baptized. For John was not yet cast into prison.

There arose therefore a questioning on the part of John's disciples with a Jew about purifying. And they came unto John, and said to him, Rabbi, he that was with thee beyond the Jordan, to whom thou hast borne witness, behold, the same baptizeth, and all men come to him.

John answered and said, A man can receive nothing, except it have been given him from heaven. Ye yourselves bear me witness, that I said, I am not the Christ, but, that I am sent before him. He that hath the bride is the bridegroom: but the friend of the bridegroom, that standeth and heareth him, rejoiceth greatly because of the bridegroom's voice: this my joy therefore is made full. He must increase, but I must decrease.

He that cometh from above is above all: he that is of the earth is of the earth, and of the earth he speaketh: he that cometh from heaven is above all. What he hath seen and heard, of that he beareth witness; and no man receiveth his witness. He that hath received his witness hath set his seal to this, that God is true. For he whom God hath sent speaketh the words of God: for he giveth

not the Spirit by measure. The Father loveth the Son, and hath given all things into his hand. He that believeth on the Son hath eternal life; but he that obeyeth not the Son shall not see life, but the wrath of God abideth on him.

III. Epistle, Isaiah 51. 3–5.
The Coming Lord a Righteous Saviour.

JEHOVAH hath comforted Zion; he hath comforted all her waste places, and hath made her wilderness like Eden, and her desert like the garden of Jehovah; joy and gladness shall be found therein, thanksgiving, and the voice of melody.

Attend unto me, O my people; and give ear unto me, O my nation: for a law shall go forth from me, and I will establish my justice for a light of the peoples. My righteousness is near, my salvation is gone forth, and mine arms shall judge the peoples; the isles shall wait for me, and on mine arm shall they trust.

III. Gospel, John 5. 31–39.
The Father Bears Witness of the Son.

IF I bear witness of myself, my witness is not true. It is another that beareth witness of me; and I know that the witness which he witnesseth of me is true. Ye have sent unto John, and he hath borne witness unto the truth. But the witness which I receive is not from man; howbeit I say these things, that ye may be saved. He was the lamp that burneth and shineth; and ye were willing to rejoice for a season in his light. But the witness which I have is greater than that of John; for the works which the Father hath given me to accomplish, the very works that I do, bear witness of me, that the Father hath sent me. And the Father that sent me, he hath borne witness of me. Ye have neither heard his voice at any time, nor seen his form. And ye have not his word abiding in you: for whom he sent, him ye believe not. Ye search the scriptures, because ye think that in them ye have eternal life; and these are they which bear witness of me.

CHRISTMAS DAY.
The Nativity.

Collect. (Early Service.) O God, who hast made this most holy night to shine with the brightness of the true Light; grant, we beseech Thee, that as we have known on earth the mysteries of that Light, we may also come to the fullness of its joys in heaven; through the same our Lord Jesus Christ, who liveth and

reigneth with Thee and the Holy Spirit, ever one God, world without end. Amen.

Collect. O Lord God, Thou who hast blessed and comforted the world through the birth of Thy Son Jesus Christ, we humbly pray Thee that, as we now rejoice over His coming in the flesh, we may also receive Him with joy at His coming to final judgment; through the same Thy Son, Jesus Christ, our Lord. AMEN.

I. EPISTLE, Isaiah 9. 2–7.
The Prince of Peace.

THE people that walked in darkness have seen a great light: they that dwelt in the land of the shadow of death, upon them hath the light shined.

Thou hast multiplied the nation, thou hast increased their joy: they joy before thee according to the joy in harvest, as men rejoice when they divide the spoil.

For the yoke of his burden, and the staff of his shoulder, the rod of his oppressor, thou hast broken as in the day of Midian. For all the armor of the armed man in the tumult, and the garments rolled in blood, shall be for burning, for fuel of fire.

For unto us a child is born, unto us a son is given; and the government shall be upon his shoulder: and his name shall be called Wonderful, Counsellor, Mighty God, Everlasting Father, Prince of Peace.

Of the increase of his government and of peace there shall be no end, upon the throne of David, and upon his kingdom, to establish it, and to uphold it with justice and with righteousness from henceforth even for ever. The zeal of Jehovah of hosts will perform this.

I. GOSPEL, Luke 2. 1–20.
The Birth of Jesus.

NOW it came to pass in those days, there went out a decree from Cæsar Augustus, that all the world should be enrolled. This was the first enrolment made when Quirinius was governor of Syria. And all went to enrol themselves, every one to his own city.

And Joseph also went up from Galilee, out of the city of Nazareth, into Judæa, to the city of David, which is called Bethlehem, because he was of the house and family of David; to enrol himself with Mary, who was betrothed to him, being great with child.

And it came to pass, while they were there, the days were fulfilled that she should be delivered. And she brought forth her firstborn son; and she wrapped him in swaddling clothes, and laid him in a manger, because there was no room for them in the inn.

And there were shepherds in the same country abiding in the field, and keeping watch by night over their flock. And an angel of the Lord stood by them, and the glory of the Lord shone round about them: and they were sore afraid. And the angel said unto them, Be not afraid; for behold, I bring you good tidings of great joy which shall be to all the people: for there is born to you this day in the city of David a Saviour, who is Christ the Lord. And this is the sign unto you: Ye shall find a babe wrapped in swaddling clothes, and lying in a manger. And suddenly there was with the angel a multitude of the heavenly host praising God, and saying,

Glory to God in the highest,
And on earth peace among men in whom he is well pleased.

And it came to pass, when the angels went away from them into heaven, the shepherds said one to another, Let us now go even unto Bethlehem, and see this thing that is come to pass, which the Lord hath made known unto us. And they came with haste, and found both Mary and Joseph, and the babe lying in the manger. And when they saw it, they made known concerning the saying which was spoken to them about this child. And all that heard it wondered at the things which were spoken unto them by the shepherds. But Mary kept all these sayings, pondering them in her heart.

And the shepherds returned, glorifying and praising God for all the things that they had heard and seen, even as it was spoken unto them.

II. EPISTLE, Hebrews 1. 1–3.
Christ the Image of God.

GOD, having of old time spoken unto the fathers in the prophets by divers portions and in divers manners, hath at the end of these days spoken unto us in his Son, whom he appointed heir of all things, through whom also he made the worlds; who being the effulgence of his glory, and the very image of his substance, and upholding all things by the word of his power, when he had made purification of sins, sat down on the right hand of the Majesty on high.

II. GOSPEL, John 1. 1–14.
The Word Became Flesh.

IN the beginning was the Word, and the Word was with God, and the Word was God.

The same was in the beginning with God. All things were made through him; and without him was not anything made that hath been made. In him was life; and the life was the light of men. And the light shineth in the darkness; and the darkness apprehended it not.

There came a man, sent from God, whose name was John. The same came for witness, that he might bear witness of the light, that all might believe through him. He was not the light, but came that he might bear witness of the light. There was the true light, even the light which lighteth every man, coming into the world.

He was in the world, and the world was made through him, and the world knew him not. He came unto his own, and they that were his own received him not. But as many as received him, to them gave he the right to become children of God, even to them that believe on his name: who were born, not of blood, nor of the will of the flesh, nor of the will of man, but of God.

And the Word became flesh, and dwelt among us (and we beheld his glory, glory as of the only begotten from the Father), full of grace and truth.

III. EPISTLE, Titus 2. 11–14.
God Gives Life to the World.

THE grace of God hath appeared, bringing salvation to all men, instructing us, to the intent that, denying ungodliness and worldly lusts, we should live soberly and righteously and godly in this present world; looking for the blessed hope and appearing of the glory of the great God and our Saviour Jesus Christ; who gave himself for us, that he might redeem us from all iniquity, and purify unto himself a people for his own possession, zealous of good works.

III. GOSPEL, Matthew 1. 18–24.
Immanuel.

NOW the birth of Jesus Christ was on this wise: When his mother Mary had been betrothed to Joseph, before they came together she was found with child of the Holy Spirit. And Joseph her husband, being a righteous man, and not willing to make her a public example, was minded to put her away privily.

But when he thought on these things, behold, an angel of the Lord appeared unto him in a dream, saying, Joseph, thou son of David, fear not to take unto thee Mary thy wife: for that which is conceived in her is of the Holy Spirit. And she shall bring forth a son; and thou shalt call his name JESUS; for it is he that shall save his people from their sins.

Now all this is come to pass, that it might be fulfilled which was spoken by the Lord through the prophet, saying,

Behold, the virgin shall be with child, and shall bring forth a son,
And they shall call his name Immanuel;
Which is, being interpreted, God with us.

And Joseph arose from his sleep, and did as the angel of the Lord commanded him.

SECOND DAY OF CHRISTMAS.
The Martyrs.

Collect. O Lord, most merciful God, Who didst give the holy martyrs the Spirit of Power to confess Thy Son, our Saviour, and to seal that confession with their blood: we pray Thee, give us grace to follow in their footsteps and to remain steadfast in the true faith unto the end; through the same Jesus Christ, Thy Son, our Lord. AMEN.

I. EPISTLE, Acts 6. 8–15; 7. 54–60.
The First Martyr Bears Witness to Christ.

AND Stephen, full of grace and power, wrought great wonders and signs among the people.

But there arose certain of them that were of the synagogue called the synagogue of the Libertines, and of the Cyrenians, and of the Alexandrians, and of them of Cilicia and Asia, disputing with Stephen. And they were not able to withstand the wisdom and the Spirit by which he spake. Then they suborned men, who said, We have heard him speak blasphemous words against Moses, and against God. And they stirred up the people, and the elders, and the scribes, and came upon him, and seized him, and brought him into the council, and set up false witnesses, who said, This man ceaseth not to speak words against this holy place, and the law: for we have heard him say, that this Jesus of Nazareth shall destroy this place, and shall change the customs which Moses delivered unto us.

And all that sat in the council, fastening their eyes on him, saw his face as it had been the face of an angel.

Now when they heard these things, they were cut to the heart, and they gnashed on him with their teeth.

But he, being full of the Holy Spirit, looked up stedfastly into heaven, and saw the glory of God, and Jesus standing on the right hand of God, and said, Behold,

I see the heavens opened, and the Son of man standing on the right hand of God.

But they cried out with a loud voice, and stopped their ears, and rushed upon him with one accord; and they cast him out of the city, and stoned him; and the witnesses laid down their garments at the feet of a young man named Saul. And they stoned Stephen, calling upon the Lord, and saying, Lord Jesus, receive my spirit. And he kneeled down, and cried with a loud voice, Lord, lay not this sin to their charge. And when he had said this, he fell asleep.

I. Gospel, Matthew 23. 34–39.
God's Judgment upon Persecutors.

BEHOLD, I send unto you prophets, and wise men, and scribes: some of them shall ye kill and crucify; and some of them shall ye scourge in your synagogues, and persecute from city to city: that upon you may come all the righteous blood shed on the earth, from the blood of Abel the righteous unto the blood of Zachariah son of Barachiah, whom ye slew between the sanctuary and the altar. Verily I say unto you, All these things shall come upon this generation.

O Jerusalem, Jerusalem, that killeth the prophets, and stoneth them that are sent unto her! how often would I have gathered thy children together, even as a hen gathereth her chickens under her wings, and ye would not! Behold, your house is left unto you desolate. For I say unto you, Ye shall not see me henceforth, till ye shall say, Blessed is he that cometh in the name of the Lord.

II. Epistle, 1 Peter 4. 12–19.
The Purging Fires of Persecution.

BELOVED, think it not strange concerning the fiery trial among you, which cometh upon you to prove you, as though a strange thing happened unto you: but insomuch as ye are partakers of Christ's sufferings, rejoice; that at the revelation of his glory also ye may rejoice with exceeding joy.

If ye are reproached for the name of Christ, blessed are ye; because the Spirit of glory and the Spirit of God resteth upon you. For let none of you suffer as a murderer, or a thief, or an evil-doer, or as a meddler in other men's matters: but if a man suffer as a Christian, let him not be ashamed; but let him glorify God in this name.

For the time is come for judgment to begin at the house of God: and if it begin first at us, what shall be the end of them that obey not the gospel of God? And if the righteous is scarcely saved, where shall the ungodly and sinner appear? Wherefore let them also that suffer according to the will of God commit their souls in well-doing unto a faithful Creator.

II. Gospel, Matthew 10. 32–39.
The Unavoidable Conflict.

EVERY one therefore who shall confess me before men, him will I also confess before my Father who is in heaven. But whosoever shall deny me before men, him will I also deny before my Father who is in heaven.

Think not that I came to send peace on the earth: I came not to send peace, but a sword. For I came to set a man at variance against his father, and the daughter against her mother, and the daughter in law against her mother in law: and a man's foes shall be they of his own household. He that loveth father or mother more than me is not worthy of me; and he that loveth son or daughter more than me is not worthy of me. And he that doth not take his cross and follow after me, is not worthy of me. He that findeth his life shall lose it; and he that loseth his life for my sake shall find it.

III. Epistle, 2 Timothy 2. 3–9.
The Soldier of Christ Endures Hardship.

SUFFER hardship with me, as a good soldier of Christ Jesus. No soldier on service entangleth himself in the affairs of this life; that he may please him who enrolled him as a soldier.

And if also a man contend in the games, he is not crowned, except he have contended lawfully. The husbandman that laboreth must be the first to partake of the fruits.

Consider what I say; for the Lord shall give thee understanding in all things. Remember Jesus Christ, risen from the dead, of the seed of David, according to my gospel: wherein I suffer hardships unto bonds, as a malefactor; but the word of God is not bound.

III. Gospel, Luke 12. 49–53.
The Baptism of Fire.

I CAME to cast fire upon the earth; and what do I desire, if it is already kindled? But I have a baptism to be baptized with; and how am I straitened till it be accomplished? Think ye that I am come to give peace in the earth? I tell you, Nay; but rather division: for there shall be from henceforth five in one house divided, three against two, and two against three. They shall be divided, father against son, and son against father; mother against daughter, and daughter against her mother; mother in law against her daughter in law, and daughter in law against her mother in law.

SUNDAY AFTER CHRISTMAS.

The Childhood of Jesus.

Collect. Almighty and eternal God, direct our actions according to Thy good pleasure, that in the name of Thy beloved Son we may be made to abound in good works; through the same Jesus Christ our Lord, who liveth and reigneth with Thee and the Holy Spirit, ever one God, world without end. AMEN.

I. EPISTLE, Galatians 4. 1–7.
Christ Makes Us Children of God.

SO long as the heir is a child, he differeth nothing from a bondservant though he is lord of all; but is under guardians and stewards until the day appointed of the father. So we also, when we were children, were held in bondage under the rudiments of the world: but when the fulness of the time came, God sent forth his Son, born of a woman, born under the law, that he might redeem them that were under the law, that we might receive the adoption of sons. And because ye are sons, God sent forth the Spirit of his Son into our hearts, crying, Abba, Father. So that thou art no longer a bondservant, but a son; and if a son, then an heir through God.

I. GOSPEL, Luke 2. 33–40.
The Consolation of Israel.

AND his father and his mother were marvelling at the things which were spoken concerning him; and Simeon blessed them, and said unto Mary his mother, Behold, this child is set for the falling and the rising of many in Israel; and for a sign which is spoken against; yea and a sword shall pierce through thine own soul; that thoughts out of many hearts may be revealed.

And there was one Anna, a prophetess, the daughter of Phanuel, of the tribe of Asher (she was of a great age, having lived with a husband seven years from her virginity, and she had been a widow even unto fourscore and four years), who departed not from the temple, worshipping with fastings and supplications night and day. And coming up at that very hour she gave thanks unto God, and spake of him to all them that were looking for the redemption of Jerusalem.

And when they had accomplished all things that were according to the law of the Lord, they returned into Galilee, to their own city Nazareth.

And the child grew, and waxed strong, filled with wisdom: and the grace of God was upon him.

II. EPISTLE, Isaiah 40. 26–31.
The Lord Gives Strength to the Weary.

LIFT up your eyes on high, and see who hath created these, that bringeth out their host by number; he calleth them all by name; by the greatness of his might, and for that he is strong in power, not one is lacking.

Why sayest thou, O Jacob, and speakest, O Israel, My way is hid from Jehovah, and the justice due to me is passed away from my God? Hast thou not known? hast thou not heard? The everlasting God, Jehovah, the Creator of the ends of the earth, fainteth not, neither is weary; there is no searching of his understanding. He giveth power to the faint; and to him that hath no might he increaseth strength. Even the youths shall faint and be weary, and the young men shall utterly fail: but they that wait for Jehovah shall renew their strength; they shall mount up with wings as eagles; they shall run, and not be weary; they shall walk, and not faint.

II. GOSPEL, Luke 12. 32.
The Little Flock.

FEAR not, little flock; for it is your Father's good pleasure to give you the kingdom.

III. EPISTLE, Psalm 62. 5–8.
God Is Our Refuge.

MY soul, wait thou in silence for God only;
For my expectation is from him.
He only is my rock and my salvation:
He is my high tower; I shall not be moved.
With God is my salvation and my glory:
The rock of my strength, and my refuge, is in God.
Trust in him at all times, ye people;
Pour out your heart before him:
God is a refuge for us.

III. GOSPEL, Matthew 2. 13–23.

The Protecting Hand of God.

NOW when they were departed, behold, an angel of the Lord appeareth to Joseph in a dream, saying, Arise and take the young child and his mother, and flee into Egypt, and be thou there until I tell thee: for Herod will seek the young child to destroy him.

And he arose and took the young child and his mother by night, and departed into Egypt; and was there until the death of Herod: that it might be fulfilled which was spoken by the Lord through the prophet, saying, Out of Egypt did I call my son.

Then Herod, when he saw that he was mocked of the Wise-men, was exceeding wroth, and sent forth, and slew all the male children that were in Bethlehem, and in all the borders thereof, from two years old and under, according to the time which he had exactly learned of the Wise-men. Then was fulfilled that which was spoken through Jeremiah the prophet, saying,

A voice was heard in Ramah,
Weeping and great mourning,
Rachel weeping for her children;
And she would not be comforted, because they are not.

But when Herod was dead, behold, an angel of the Lord appeareth in a dream to Joseph in Egypt, saying, Arise and take the young child and his mother, and go into the land of Israel: for they are dead that sought the young child's life.

And he arose and took the young child and his mother, and came into the land of Israel. But when he heard that Archelaus was reigning over Judæa in the room of his father Herod, he was afraid to go thither; and being warned of God in a dream, he withdrew into the parts of Galilee, and came and dwelt in a city called Nazareth; that it might be fulfilled which was spoken through the prophets, that he should be called a Nazarene.

NEW YEAR'S DAY.

The Childhood of Jesus.

Collect. O Lord God, who for our sake hast sent Thine only-begotten Son into this uncertain world, grant us Thy grace, that through Him our hearts may be made free from all fear and that our deeds may be pleasing in Thy sight; through the same Thy Son, Jesus Christ, our Lord. AMEN.

I. EPISTLE (a), Titus 3. 4–7.

Baptism Reveals the Goodness of God.

BUT when the kindness of God our Saviour, and his love toward man, appeared, not by works done in righteousness, which we did ourselves, but according to his mercy he saved us, through the washing of regeneration and renewing of the Holy Spirit, which he poured out upon us richly, through Jesus Christ our Saviour; that, being justified by his grace, we might be made heirs according to the hope of eternal life.

I. EPISTLE (b), Lamentations 3. 22–26.

The Grace of God New Every Morning.

IT is of Jehovah's lovingkindnesses that we are not consumed, because his compassions fail not.
They are new every morning; great is thy faithfulness.

Jehovah is my portion, saith my soul; therefore will I hope in him.
Jehovah is good unto them that wait for him, to the soul that seeketh him.
It is good that a man should hope and quietly wait for the salvation of Jehovah.

I. GOSPEL, Luke 2. 21.

The Name of Jesus.

WHEN eight days were fulfilled for circumcising him, his name was called Jesus, which was so called by the angel before he was conceived in the womb.

II. EPISTLE, Psalm 121.

Jehovah Our Keeper.

I WILL lift up mine eyes unto the mountains:
From whence shall my help come?
My help cometh from Jehovah,
Who made heaven and earth.
He will not suffer thy foot to be moved:
He that keepeth thee will not slumber.
Behold, he that keepeth Israel
Will neither slumber nor sleep.
Jehovah is thy keeper:
Jehovah is thy shade upon thy right hand.
The sun shall not smite thee by day,
Nor the moon by night.
Jehovah will keep thee from all evil;
He will keep thy soul.

Jehovah will keep thy going out and thy coming in
From this time forth and for evermore.

II. GOSPEL, John 14. 13.
Prayer in the Name of Jesus.

WHATSOEVER ye shall ask in my name, that will I do, that the Father may be glorified in the Son.

III. EPISTLE, Revelation 2. 1–5.
We Shall All Give Account for the Day of Grace.

THESE things saith he that holdeth the seven stars in his right hand, he that walketh in the midst of the seven golden candlesticks:

I know thy works, and thy toil and patience, and that thou canst not bear evil men, and didst try them that call themselves apostles, and they are not, and didst find them false; and thou hast patience and didst bear for my name's sake, and hast not grown weary.

But I have this against thee, that thou didst leave thy first love. Remember therefore whence thou art fallen, and repent and do the first works; or else I come to thee, and will move thy candlestick out of its place, except thou repent.

III. GOSPEL, Luke 13. 6–9.
Intercession for the Barren Fig Tree.

AND he spake this parable: A certain man had a fig tree planted in his vineyard; and he came seeking fruit thereon, and found none. And he said unto the vinedresser, Behold, these three years I come seeking fruit on this fig tree, and find none: cut it down; why doth it also cumber the ground? And he answering saith unto him, Lord, let it alone this year also, till I shall dig about it, and dung it: and if it bear fruit thenceforth, well; but if not, thou shalt cut it down.

SUNDAY AFTER NEW YEAR.
Holy Baptism.

Collect. O Lord God, who art the strength of them that call upon Thy name, graciously hear our prayer; and, because human frailty can do nothing without Thee, help us by Thy grace to keep Thy commandments and in word and deed to be acceptable in Thy sight; through Thy Son, Jesus Christ, our Lord. AMEN.

I. EPISTLE (a), Romans 6. 3–11.
Baptism Consecrates to a New Life.

ARE ye ignorant that all we who were baptized into Christ Jesus were baptized into his death?

We were buried therefore with him through baptism into death: that like as Christ was raised from the dead through the glory of the Father, so we also might walk in newness of life. For if we have become united with him in the likeness of his death, we shall be also in the likeness of his resurrection; knowing this, that our old man was crucified with him, that the body of sin might be done away, that so we should no longer be in bondage to sin; for he that hath died is justified from sin.

But if we died with Christ, we believe that we shall also live with him; knowing that Christ being raised from the dead dieth no more; death no more hath dominion over him. For the death that he died, he died unto sin once: but the life that he liveth, he liveth unto God. Even so reckon ye also yourselves to be dead unto sin, but alive unto God in Christ Jesus.

I. EPISTLE (b), Titus 3. 4–7.
The Goodness of God Revealed in Holy Baptism.

BUT when the kindness of God our Saviour, and his love toward man, appeared, not by works done in righteousness, which we did ourselves, but according to his mercy he saved us, through the washing of regeneration and renewing of the Holy Spirit, which he poured out upon us richly, through Jesus Christ our Saviour; that, being justified by his grace, we might be made heirs according to the hope of eternal life.

I. GOSPEL, Matthew 3. 13–17.
The Baptism of Jesus.

THEN cometh Jesus from Galilee to the Jordan unto John, to be baptized of him. But John would have hindered him, saying, I have need to be baptized of thee, and comest thou to me? But Jesus answering said unto him, Suffer it now: for thus it becometh us to fulfil all righteousness. Then he suffereth him.

And Jesus, when he was baptized, went up straightway from the water: and lo, the heavens were opened unto him, and he saw the Spirit of God descending as a dove, and coming upon him; and lo, a voice out of the heavens, saying, This is my beloved Son, in whom I am well pleased.

II. EPISTLE, Colossians 2. 9–15.

Baptism Means Communion with Christ.

IN him dwelleth all the fulness of the Godhead bodily, and in him ye are made full, who is the head of all principality and power: in whom ye were also circumcised with a circumcision not made with hands, in the putting off of the body of the flesh, in the circumcision of Christ; having been buried with him in baptism, wherein ye were also raised with him through faith in the working of God, who raised him from the dead.

And you, being dead through your trespasses and the uncircumcision of your flesh, you, I say, did he make alive together with him, having forgiven us all our trespasses; having blotted out the bond written in ordinances that was against us, which was contrary to us: and he hath taken it out of the way, nailing it to the cross; having despoiled the principalities and the powers, he made a show of them openly, triumphing over them in it.

II. GOSPEL, John 1. 29–34.

John's Testimony on the Baptism of Jesus.

ON the morrow he seeth Jesus coming unto him, and saith, Behold, the Lamb of God, that taketh away the sin of the world! This is he of whom I said, After me cometh a man who is become before me: for he was before me. And I knew him not; but that he snould be made manifest t Israel, for this cause came I baptizing in water.

And John bare witness, saying, I have beheld the Spirit descending as a dove out of heaven; and it ¿bode upon him. And I knew him not: but he that sent me to baptize in water, he said unto me, Upon whomsoever thou shalt see the Spirit descending, and abiding upon him, the same is he that baptizeth in the Holy Spirit. And I have seen, and have borne witness that this is the Son of God.

III. EPISTLE, Acts 8. 26–39.

The Baptism of the Ethiopian.

AN angel of the Lord spake unto Philip, saying, Arise, and go toward the south unto the way that goeth down from Jerusalem unto Gaza: the same is desert.

And he arose and went: and behold, a man of Ethiopia, a eunuch of great authority under Candace, queen of the Ethiopians, who was over all her treasure, who had come to Jerusalem to worship; and he was returning and sitting in his chariot, and was reading the prophet Isaiah.

And the Spirit said unto Philip, Go near, and join thyself to this chariot. And Philip ran to him, and heard him reading Isaiah the prophet, and said, Understandest thou what thou readest? And he said, How can I, except some one shall guide me? And he besought Philip to come up and sit with him.

Now the passage of the scripture which he was reading was this,

He was led as a she¿p to the slaughter;
And as a lamb before his shearer is dumb,
So he openeth not his mouth:
In his humiliation his judgment was taken away:
His generation who shall declare?
For his life is taken from the earth.

And the eunuch answered Philip, and said, I pray thee, of whom speaketh the prophet this? of himself, or of some other? And Philip opened his mouth, and beginning from this scripture, preached unto him Jesus.

And as they went on the way, they came unto a certain water; and the eunuch saith, Behold, here is water; what doth hinder me to be baptized? And he commanded the chariot to stand still: and they both went down into the water, both Philip and the eunuch; and he baptized him.

And when they came up out of the water, the Spirit of the Lord caught away Philip; and the eunuch saw him no more, for he went on his way rejoicing.

III. GOSPEL, Matthew 3. 11, 12.

Jesus Baptizes with the Holy Spirit and with Fire.

I INDEED baptize you in water unto repentance: but he that cometh after me is mightier than I, whose shoes I am not worthy to bear: he shall baptize you in the Holy Spirit and in fire: whose fan is in his hand, and he will thoroughly cleanse his threshing-floor; and he will gather his wheat into the garner, but the chaff he will burn up with unquenchable fire.

EPIPHANY.
The Dawn of a New Day.

Collect. O God, who by a star didst lead the Gentiles to Thine only-begotten Son, mercifully grant that we who know Thee now by faith may be guided through life to behold Thy glory in heaven; through the same Thy Son, Jesus Christ, our Lord. AMEN.

I. EPISTLE, Isaiah 60. 1–6.
The Glory of the Lord Rises upon Zion.

ARISE, shine; for thy light is come, and the glory of Jehovah is risen upon thee.

For, behold, darkness shall cover the earth, and gross darkness the peoples; but Jehovah will arise upon thee, and his glory shall be seen upon thee. And nations shall come to thy light, and kings to the brightness of thy rising.

Lift up thine eyes round about, and see: they all gather themselves together, they come to thee; thy sons shall come from far, and thy daughters shall be carried in the arms. Then thou shalt see and be radiant, and thy heart shall thrill and be enlarged; because the abundance of the sea shall be turned unto thee, and the wealth of the nations shall come unto thee.

The multitude of camels shall cover thee, the dromedaries of Midian and Ephah; all they from Sheba shall come; they shall bring gold and frankincense, and shall proclaim the praises of Jehovah.

I. GOSPEL, Matthew 2. 1–12.
The Wise-men.

NOW when Jesus was born in Bethlehem of Judæa in the days of Herod the king, behold, Wise-men from the east came to Jerusalem, saying, Where is he that is born King of the Jews? for we saw his star in the east, and are come to worship him.

And when Herod the king heard it, he was troubled, and all Jerusalem with him. And gathering together all the chief priests and scribes of the people, he inquired of them where the Christ should be born.

And they said unto him, In Bethlehem of Judæa: for thus it is written through the prophet,

And thou Bethlehem, land of Judah,
Art in no wise least among the princes of Judah:
For out of thee shall come forth a governor,
Who shall be shepherd of my people Israel.

Then Herod privily called the Wise-men, and learned of them exactly what time the star appeared. And he sent them to Bethlehem, and said, Go and search out exactly concerning the young child; and when ye have found him, bring me word, that I also may come and worship him.

And they, having heard the king, went their way; and lo, the star, which they saw in the east, went before them, till it came and stood over where the young child was. And when they saw the star, they rejoiced with exceeding great joy.

And they came into the house and saw the young child with Mary his mother; and they fell down and worshipped him; and opening their treasures they offered unto him gifts, gold and frankincense and myrrh.

And being warned of God in a dream that they should not return to Herod, they departed into their own country another way.

II. EPISTLE, 2 Corinthians 4. 3–6.
The Glory of God in the Face of Jesus Christ.

EVEN if our gospel is veiled, it is veiled in them that perish: in whom the god of this world hath blinded the minds of the unbelieving, that the light of the gospel of the glory of Christ, who is the image of God, should not dawn upon them.

For we preach not ourselves, but Christ Jesus as Lord, and ourselves as your servants for Jesus' sake. Seeing it is God, that said, Light shall shine out of darkness, who shined in our hearts, to give the light of the knowledge of the glory of God in the face of Jesus Christ.

II. GOSPEL, John 8. 12.
Jesus the Light of the World.

JESUS spake unto them, saying, I am the light of the world: he that followeth me shall not walk in the darkness, but shall have the light of life.

III. EPISTLE, Isaiah 2. 2–5.
The Nations Shall Come to Zion.

IT shall come to pass in the latter days, that the mountain of Jehovah's house shall be established on the top of the mountains, and shall be exalted above the hills; and all nations shall flow unto it. And many peoples shall go and say, Come ye, and let us go up to the mountain of Jehovah, to the house of the God of Jacob; and he will teach us of his ways, and we will walk in his paths: for out of Zion shall go forth the law, and the word of Jehovah from Jerusalem. And he will judge between the nations, and will decide concerning many peoples; and they shall beat their swords into plowshares, and their spears into pruning-hooks; nation shall not lift up sword against nation, neither shall they learn war any more.

O house of Jacob, come ye, and let us walk in the light of Jehovah.

III. GOSPEL, Matthew 12. 15–21.
Jesus the Desire of All Nations.

AND Jesus...withdrew from thence: and many followed him; and he healed them all, and charged them that they should not make him known: that it might be fulfilled which was spoken through Isaiah the prophet, saying,

Behold, my servant whom I have chosen;
My beloved in whom my soul is well pleased:
I will put my Spirit upon him,
And he shall declare judgment to the Gentiles.
He shall not strive, nor cry aloud;
Neither shall any one hear his voice in the streets.
A bruised reed shall he not break,
And smoking flax shall he not quench,
Till he send forth judgment unto victory.
And in his name shall the Gentiles hope.

FIRST SUNDAY AFTER EPIPHANY.
Jesus As Disciple and Teacher.

Collect. O Lord, we beseech Thee mercifully to receive the prayers of Thy people who call upon Thee; and grant that they may both perceive and know what things they ought to do, and also that they may have grace and power faithfully to fulfill the same through Jesus Christ, Thy Son, our Lord, who liveth and reigneth with Thee and the Holy Spirit, ever one God, world without end. AMEN.

I. EPISTLE, Romans 12. 1–5.
The Spiritual Service of the Christian.

I BESEECH you therefore, brethren, by the mercies of God, to present your bodies a living sacrifice, holy, acceptable to God, which is your spiritual service. And be not fashioned according to this world: but be ye transformed by the renewing of your mind, that ye may prove what is the good and acceptable and perfect will of God.

For I say through the grace that was given me, to every man that is among you, not to think of himself more highly than he ought to think; but so to think as to think soberly, according as God hath dealt to each man a measure of faith. For even as we have many members in one body, and all the members have not the same office: so we, who are many, are one body in Christ, and severally members one of another.

I. GOSPEL, Luke 2. 42–52.
Jesus in the Temple at the Age of Twelve.

WHEN he was twelve years old, they went up after the custom of the feast; and when they had fulfilled the days, as they were returning, the boy Jesus tarried behind in Jerusalem; and his parents knew it not; but supposing him to be in the company, they went a day's journey; and they sought for him among their kinsfolk and acquaintance: and when they found him not, they returned to Jerusalem, seeking for him.

And it came to pass, after three days they found him in the temple, sitting in the midst of the teachers, both hearing them, and asking them questions: and all that heard him were amazed at his understanding and his answers. And when they saw him, they were astonished; and his mother said unto him, Son, why hast thou thus dealt with us? behold, thy father and I sought thee sorrowing. And he said unto them, How is it that ye sought me? knew ye not that I must be in my Father's house? And they understood not the saying which he spake unto them.

And he went down with them, and came to Nazareth; and he was subject unto them: and his mother kept all these sayings in her heart.

And Jesus advanced in wisdom and stature, and in favor with God and men.

II. Epistle, Psalm 84.

Faith Longs for the Tabernacles of God.

HOW amiable are thy tabernacles,
O Jehovah of hosts!
My soul longeth, yea, even fainteth for
the courts of Jehovah;
My heart and my flesh cry out unto
the living God.
Yea, the sparrow hath found her a
house,
And the swallow a nest for herself,
where she may lay her young,
Even thine altars, O Jehovah of hosts,
my King, and my God.
Blessed are they that dwell in thy
house:
They will be still praising thee.
Blessed is the man whose strength is
in thee;
In whose heart are the highways to
Zion.
Passing through the valley of Weeping
they make it a place of springs;
Yea, the early rain covereth it with
blessings.
They go from strength to strength;
Every one of them appeareth before
God in Zion.
O Jehovah God of hosts, hear my
prayer;
Give ear, O God of Jacob.
Behold, O God our shield,
And look upon the face of thine
anointed.
For a day in thy courts is better than
a thousand.
I had rather be a doorkeeper in the
house of my God,
Than to dwell in the tents of wicked-
ness.
For Jehovah God is a sun and a shield:
Jehovah will give grace and glory;
No good thing will be withheld from
them that walk uprightly.
O Jehovah of hosts,
Blessed is the man that trusteth in
thee.

II. Gospel, John 7. 14–18.

The Teaching of Jesus Is from God.

WHEN it was now the midst of the
feast Jesus went up into the temple,
and taught. The Jews therefore marvelled, saying, How knoweth this man
letters, having never learned?

Jesus therefore answered them, and
said, My teaching is not mine, but his
that sent me. If any man willeth to do
his will, he shall know of the teaching,
whether it is of God, or whether I speak
from myself. He that speaketh from
himself seeketh his own glory: but he
that seeketh the glory of him that sent
him, the same is true, and no unrighteousness is in him.

III. Epistle, Hebrews 2. 11–16.

Jesus Calls His Followers Brethren.

BOTH he that sanctifieth and they that
are sanctified are all of one: for which
cause he is not ashamed to call them
brethren, saying,
I will declare thy name unto my brethren,
In the midst of the congregation will
I sing thy praise.
And again, I will put my trust in him.
And again, Behold, I and the children
whom God hath given me.

Since then the children are sharers in
flesh and blood, he also himself in like
manner partook of the same; that
through death he might bring to nought
him that had the power of death, that is,
the devil; and might deliver all them
who through fear of death were all their
lifetime subject to bondage. For verily
not to angels doth he give help, but he
giveth help to the seed of Abraham.

III. Gospel, Matthew 12. 46–50.

The Kindred of Jesus.

WHILE he was yet speaking to the
multitude, behold, his mother and his
brethren stood without, seeking to speak
to him.
And one said unto him, Behold, thy
mother and thy brethren stand without,
seeking to speak to thee.
But he answered and said unto him
that told him, Who is my mother? and
who are my brethren? And he stretched
forth his hand towards his disciples, and
said, Behold, my mother and my brethren! For whosoever shall do the will of
my Father who is in heaven, he is my
brother, and sister, and mother.

SECOND SUNDAY AFTER EPIPHANY.

The Presence of Jesus Hallows the Home.

Collect. Almighty and eternal God, who dost govern all things in heaven and earth; mercifully hear the supplications of Thy people, and grant us Thy peace all the days of our life; through Thy Son, Jesus Christ our Lord. AMEN.

I. EPISTLE, Romans 12. 6–16.
Faith and Love in Our Social Relations.

HAVING gifts differing according to the grace that was given to us, whether prophecy, let us prophesy according to the proportion of our faith; or ministry, let us give ourselves to our ministry; or he that teacheth, to his teaching; or he that exhorteth, to his exhorting: he that giveth, let him do it with liberality; he that ruleth, with diligence; he that showeth mercy, with cheerfulness.

Let love be without hypocrisy. Abhor that which is evil; cleave to that which is good. In love of the brethren be tenderly affectioned one to another; in honor preferring one another; in diligence not slothful; fervent in spirit; serving the Lord; rejoicing in hope; patient in tribulation; continuing stedfastly in prayer; communicating to the necessities of the saints; given to hospitality. Bless them that persecute you; bless, and curse not. Rejoice with them that rejoice; weep with them that weep. Be of the same mind one toward another. Set not your mind on high things, but condescend to things that are lowly.

I. GOSPEL, John 2. 1–11.
The Wedding in Cana.

THE third day there was a marriage in Cana of Galilee: and the mother of Jesus was there: and Jesus also was bidden, and his disciples, to the marriage.

And when the wine failed, the mother of Jesus saith unto him, They have no wine. And Jesus saith unto her, Woman, what have I to do with thee? mine hour is not yet come. His mother saith unto the servants, Whatsoever he saith unto you, do it.

Now there were six waterpots of stone set there after the Jews' manner of purifying, containing two or three firkins apiece. Jesus saith unto them, Fill the waterpots with water. And they filled them up to the brim. And he saith unto them, Draw out now, and bear unto the ruler of the feast. And they bare it.

And when the ruler of the feast tasted the water now become wine, and knew not whence it was (but the servants that had drawn the water knew), the ruler of the feast calleth the bridegroom, and saith unto him, Every man setteth on first the good wine; and when men have drunk freely, then that which is worse: thou hast kept the good wine until now.

This beginning of his signs did Jesus in Cana of Galilee, and manifested his glory; and his disciples believed on him.

II. EPISTLE, 2 Timothy 1. 3–5.
The Christian Home a Blessing to the Children.

I THANK God, whom I serve from my forefathers in a pure conscience, how unceasing is my remembrance of thee in my supplications, night and day longing to see thee, remembering thy tears, that I may be filled with joy; having been reminded of the unfeigned faith that is in thee; which dwelt first in thy grandmother Lois, and thy mother Eunice; and, I am persuaded, in thee also.

II. GOSPEL, John 4. 5–26.
The Samaritan Woman.

SO he cometh to a city of Samaria called Sychar, near to the parcel of ground that Jacob gave to his son Joseph: and Jacob's well was there. Jesus therefore, being wearied with his journey, sat thus by the well. It was about the sixth hour.

There cometh a woman of Samaria to draw water: Jesus saith unto her, Give me to drink. For his disciples were gone away into the city to buy food.

The Samaritan woman therefore saith unto him, How is it that thou, being a Jew, askest drink of me, who am a Samaritan woman? (For Jews have no dealings with Samaritans.)

Jesus answered and said unto her, If thou knewest the gift of God, and who it is that saith to thee, Give me to drink, thou wouldest have asked of him, and he would have given thee living water.

The woman saith unto him, Sir, thou hast nothing to draw with, and the well is deep: whence then hast thou that living water? Art thou greater than our father Jacob, who gave us the well, and drank thereof himself, and his sons, and his cattle?

Jesus answered and said unto her, Every one that drinketh of this water shall thirst again: but whosoever drinketh of the water that I shall give him shall never thirst; but the water that I shall give him shall become in him a well of water springing up unto eternal life.

The woman saith unto him, Sir, give me this water, that I thirst not, neither come all the way hither to draw.

Jesus saith unto her, Go, call thy husband, and come hither. The woman answered and said unto him, I have no husband. Jesus saith unto her, Thou saidst well, I have no husband: for thou hast had five, husbands; and he whom thou now hast is not thy husband: this hast thou said truly.

The woman saith unto him, Sir, I perceive that thou art a prophet. Our fathers worshipped in this mountain; and ye say, that in Jerusalem is the place where men ought to worship.

Jesus saith unto her, Woman, believe me, the hour cometh, when neither in this mountain, nor in Jerusalem, shall ye worship the Father. Ye worship that which ye know not: we worship that which we know; for salvation is from the Jews. But the hour cometh, and now is, when the true worshippers shall worship the Father in spirit and truth: for such doth the Father seek to be his worshippers. God is a Spirit: and they that worship him must worship in spirit and truth.

The woman saith unto him, I know that Messiah cometh (he that is called Christ): when he is come, he will declare unto us all things. Jesus saith unto her, I that speak unto thee am he.

III. Epistle, Ephesians 6. 1–4.
The Lord's Care for Parents and Children.

CHILDREN, obey your parents in the Lord: for this is right. Honor thy father and mother (which is the first com-

mandment with promise), that it may be well with thee, and thou mayest live long on the earth.

And, ye fathers, provoke not your children to wrath: but nurture them in the chastening and admonition of the Lord.

III. Gospel, Luke 19. 1–10.
Jesus in the Home of Zacchæus.

AND he entered and was passing through Jericho.

And behold, a man called by name Zacchæus; and he was a chief publican, and he was rich. And he sought to see Jesus who he was; and could not for the crowd, because he was little of stature. And he ran on before, and climbed up into a sycomore tree to see him: for he was to pass that way.

And when Jesus came to the place, he looked up, and said unto him, Zacchæus, make haste, and come down; for to-day I must abide at thy house.

And he made haste, and came down, and received him joyfully. And when they saw it, they all murmured, saying, He is gone in to lodge with a man that is a sinner.

And Zacchæus stood, and said unto the Lord, Behold, Lord, the half of my goods I give to the poor; and if I have wrongfully exacted aught of any man, I restore fourfold.

And Jesus said unto him, To-day is salvation come to this house, forasmuch as he also is a son of Abraham. For the Son of man came to seek and to save that which was lost.

THIRD SUNDAY AFTER EPIPHANY.
Jesus the Creator of Faith.

Collect. Almighty and eternal God, look with mercy upon our infirmities, and in all our dangers stretch forth the right hand of Thy majesty to help and defend us; through Jesus Christ, our Lord. Amen.

I. Epistle, Romans 12. 16–21.
Evil Overcome with Good.

BE not wise in your own conceits. Render to no man evil for evil. Take thought for things honorable in the sight of all men. If it be possible, as much as in you lieth, be at peace with all men. Avenge not yourselves, beloved, but give

place unto the wrath of God: for it is written, Vengeance belongeth unto me; I will recompense, saith the Lord. But if thine enemy hunger, feed him; if he thirst, give him to drink: for in so doing thou shalt heap coals of fire upon his head. Be not overcome of evil, but overcome evil with good.

I. Gospel, Matthew 8. 1–13.
Jesus Heals the Servant of the Nobleman.

WHEN he was come down from the mountain, great multitudes followed him. And behold, there came to him a leper and worshipped him, saying, Lord, if thou wilt, thou canst make me clean. And he stretched forth his hand, and touched him, saying, I will; be thou made clean. And straightway his leprosy was cleansed. And Jesus saith unto him, See thou tell no man; but go, show thyself to the priest, and offer the gift that Moses commanded, for a testimony unto them.

And when he was entered into Capernaum, there came unto him a centurion, beseeching him, and saying, Lord, my servant lieth in the house sick of the palsy, grievously tormented. And he saith unto him, I will come and heal him. And the centurion answered and said, Lord, I am not worthy that thou shouldest come under my roof; but only say the word, and my servant shall be healed. For I also am a man under authority, having under myself soldiers: and I say to this one, Go, and he goeth; and to another, Come, and he cometh; and to my servant, Do this, and he doeth it.

And when Jesus heard it, he marvelled, and said to them that followed, Verily I say unto you, I have not found so great faith, no, not in Israel. And I say unto you, that many shall come from the east and the west, and shall sit down with Abraham, and Isaac, and Jacob, in the kingdom of heaven: but the sons of the kingdom shall be cast forth into the outer darkness: there shall be the weeping and the gnashing of teeth.

And Jesus said unto the centurion, Go thy way; as thou hast believed, so be it done unto thee. And the servant was healed in that hour.

II. EPISTLE, Hebrews 11. 1–22.

Faith Is Assurance and Conviction.

FAITH is assurance of things hoped for, a conviction of things not seen. For therein the elders had witness borne to them.

By faith we understand that the worlds have been framed by the word of God, so that what is seen hath not been made out of things which appear.

By faith Abel offered unto God a more excellent sacrifice than Cain, through which he had witness borne to him that he was righteous, God bearing witness in respect of his gifts: and through it he being dead yet speaketh.

By faith Enoch was translated that he should not see death; and he was not found, because God translated him: for he hath had witness borne to him that before his translation he had been well-pleasing unto God: and without faith it is impossible to be well-pleasing unto him; for he that cometh to God must believe that he is, and that he is a rewarder of them that seek after him.

By faith Noah, being warned of God concerning things not seen as yet, moved with godly fear, prepared an ark to the saving of his house; through which he condemned the world, and became heir of the righteousness which is according to faith.

By faith Abraham, when he was called, obeyed to go out unto a place which he was to receive for an inheritance; and he went out, not knowing whither he went. By faith he became a sojourner in the land of promise, as in a land not his own, dwelling in tents, with Isaac and Jacob, the heirs with him of the same promise: for he looked for the city which hath the foundations, whose builder and maker is God.

By faith even Sarah herself received power to conceive seed when she was past age, since she counted him faithful who had promised: wherefore also there sprang of one, and him as good as dead, so many as the stars of heaven in multitude, and as the sand, which is by the sea-shore, innumerable.

These all died in faith, not having received the promises, but having seen them and greeted them from afar, and having confessed that they were strangers and pilgrims on the earth. For they that say such things make it manifest that they are seeking after a country of their own. And if indeed they had been mindful of that country from which they went out, they would have had opportunity to return. But now they desire a better country, that is, a heavenly: wherefore God is not ashamed of them, to be called their God; for he hath prepared for them a city.

By faith Abraham, being tried, offered up Isaac: yea, he that had gladly received the promises was offering up his only begotten son; even he to whom it was said, In Isaac shall thy seed be called: accounting that God is able to raise up, even from the dead; from whence he did also in a figure receive him back. By faith Isaac blessed Jacob and Esau, even concerning things to come. By faith Jacob, when he was dying, blessed each of the sons of Joseph; and worshipped, leaning upon the top of his staff. By faith Joseph, when his end was nigh, made mention of the departure of the children of Israel; and gave commandment concerning his bones.

II. Gospel, John 4. 27–42.

Samaritans Believe in Jesus.

AND upon this came his disciples; and they marvelled that he was speaking with a woman; yet no man said, What seekest thou? or, Why speakest thou with her?

So the woman left her waterpot, and went away into the city, and saith to the people, Come, see a man, who told me all things that ever I did: can this be the Christ? They went out of the city, and were coming to him.

In the mean while the disciples prayed him, saying, Rabbi, eat. But he said unto them, I have meat to eat that ye know not. The disciples therefore said one to another, Hath any man brought him aught to eat? Jesus saith unto them, My meat is to do the will of him that sent me, and to accomplish his work. Say not ye, There are yet four months, and then cometh the harvest? behold, I say unto you, Lift up your eyes, and look on the fields, that they are white already unto harvest. He that reapeth receiveth wages, and gathereth fruit unto life eternal; that he that soweth and he that reapeth may rejoice together. For herein is the saying true, One soweth, and another reapeth. I sent you to reap that whereon ye have not labored: others have labored, and ye are entered into their labor.

And from that city many of the Samaritans believed on him because of the word of the woman, who testified, He told me all things that ever I did. So when the Samaritans came unto him, they besought him to abide with them: and he abode there two days. And many more believed because of his word; and they said to the woman, Now we believe, not because of thy speaking: for we have heard for ourselves, and know that this is indeed the Saviour of the world.

III. Epistle, 2 Thessalonians 2. 13–17.

God Gives Comfort and Hope.

WE are bound to give thanks to God always for you, brethren beloved of the Lord, for that God chose you from the beginning unto salvation in sanctification of the Spirit and belief of the truth; whereunto he called you through our gospel, to the obtaining of the glory of our Lord Jesus Christ. So then, brethren, stand fast, and hold the traditions which ye were taught, whether by word, or by epistle of ours.

Now our Lord Jesus Christ himself, and God our Father who loved us and gave us eternal comfort and good hope through grace, comfort your hearts and establish them in every good work and word.

III. Gospel, Matthew 8. 14–17.

Jesus the Great Physician.

WHEN Jesus was come into Peter's house, he saw his wife's mother lying sick of a fever. And he touched her hand, and the fever left her; and she arose, and ministered unto him.

And when even was come, they brought unto him many possessed with demons: and he cast out the spirits with a word, and healed all that were sick: that it might be fulfilled which was spoken through Isaiah the prophet, saying, Himself took our infirmities, and bare our diseases.

FOURTH SUNDAY AFTER EPIPHANY.

Jesus Delivers from Danger and Despair.

Collect. O Lord, our heavenly Father, who knowest us to be set in the midst of so many and great dangers that by reason of the frailty of our nature we cannot always stand upright: grant us such strength and protection as will support us in all dangers, and carry us through all temptations; through Jesus Christ, Thy Son, our Lord. Amen.

I. Epistle, Romans 13. 8–10.

Love Is the Fulfillment of the Law.

OWE no man anything, save to love one another: for he that loveth his neighbor hath fulfilled the law. For this, Thou shalt not commit adultery, Thou shalt not kill, Thou shalt not steal, Thou shalt not covet, and if there be any other commandment, it is summed up in this word, namely, Thou shalt love thy neighbor as thyself. Love worketh no ill to his neighbor: love therefore is the fulfilment of the law.

I. Gospel, Matthew 8. 23–27.

Jesus Stills the Tempest.

WHEN he was entered into a boat, his disciples followed him. And behold, there arose a great tempest in the sea, insomuch that the boat was covered with the waves: but he was asleep.

And they came to him, and awoke him,

saying, Save, Lord; we perish. And he saith unto them, Why are ye fearful, O ye of little faith? Then he arose, and rebuked the winds and the sea; and there was a great calm.

And the men marvelled, saying, What manner of man is this, that even the winds and the sea obey him?

II. Epistle, Hebrews 11. 23–40.
Faith Creates Men of Power.

BY faith Moses, when he was born, was hid three months by his parents, because they saw he was a goodly child; and they were not afraid of the king's commandment.

By faith Moses, when he was grown up, refused to be called the son of Pharaoh's daughter; choosing rather to share ill treatment with the people of God, than to enjoy the pleasures of sin for a season; accounting the reproach of Christ greater riches than the treasures of Egypt: for he looked unto the recompense of reward. By faith he forsook Egypt, not fearing the wrath of the king: for he endured, as seeing him who is invisible. By faith he kept the passover, and the sprinkling of the blood, that the destroyer of the firstborn should not touch them.

By faith they passed through the Red sea as by dry land: which the Egyptians assaying to do were swallowed up.

By faith the walls of Jericho fell down, after they had been compassed about for seven days. By faith Rahab the harlot perished not with them that were disobedient, having received the spies with peace.

And what shall I more say? for the time will fail me if I tell of Gideon, Barak, Samson, Jephthah; of David and Samuel and the prophets: who through faith subdued kingdoms, wrought righteousness, obtained promises, stopped the mouths of lions, quenched the power of fire, escaped the edge of the sword, from weakness were made strong, waxed mighty in war, turned to flight armies of aliens. Women received their dead by a resurrection: and others were tortured, not accepting their deliverance; that they might obtain a better resurrection: and others had trial of mockings and scourgings, yea, moreover of bonds and imprisonment: they were stoned, they were sawn asunder, they were tempted, they were slain with the sword: they went about in sheepskins, in goatskins; being destitute, afflicted, ill-treated (of whom the world was not worthy), wandering in deserts and mountains and caves, and the holes of the earth. And these all, having had witness borne to them through their faith, received not the promise, God having provided some better thing concerning us, that apart from us they should not be made perfect.

II. Gospel, John 6. 66–69.
The Twelve Remaining Faithful to Jesus.

UPON this many of his disciples went back, and walked no more with him. Jesus said therefore unto the twelve, Would ye also go away? Simon Peter answered him, Lord, to whom shall we go? thou hast the words of eternal life. And we have believed and know that thou art the Holy One of God.

III. Epistle, 2 Timothy 1. 7–10.
Jesus Gives Power, Not Fearfulness.

GOD gave us not a spirit of fearfulness; but of power and love and discipline. Be not ashamed therefore of the testimony of our Lord, nor of me his prisoner: but suffer hardship with the gospel according to the power of God; who saved us, and called us with a holy calling, not according to our works, but according to his own purpose and grace, which was given us in Christ Jesus before times eternal, but hath now been manifested by the appearing of our Saviour Christ Jesus, who abolished death, and brought life and immortality to light through the gospel.

III. Gospel, Matthew 14. 22–33.
Jesus Walks on the Sea.

AND straightway he constrained the disciples to enter into the boat, and to go before him unto the other side, till he should send the multitudes away.

And after he had sent the multitudes away, he went up into the mountain apart to pray: and when even was come, he was there alone. But the boat was now in the midst of the sea, distressed by the waves; for the wind was contrary. And in the fourth watch of the night he came unto them, walking upon the sea. And when the disciples saw him walking on the sea, they were troubled, saying, It is a ghost; and they cried out for fear. But straightway Jesus spake unto them, saying, Be of good cheer; it is I; be not afraid. And Peter answered him and said, Lord, if it be thou, bid me come unto thee upon the waters. And he said, Come. And Peter went down from the boat, and walked upon the waters to come to Jesus. But when he saw the wind, he was afraid;

and beginning to sink, he cried out, saying, Lord, save me. And immediately Jesus stretched forth his hand, and took hold of him, and saith unto him, O thou of little faith, wherefore didst thou

doubt? And when they were gone up into the boat, the wind ceased. And they that were in the boat worshipped him, saying, Of a truth thou art the Son of God.

FIFTH SUNDAY AFTER EPIPHANY.

The Power of Jesus to Keep His Own.

Collect. O Lord, we beseech Thee, keep Thy Church and household continually in the true faith, that they who lean upon the hope of eternal life may evermore be defended by Thy mighty hand, through Jesus Christ, Thy Son, our Lord. AMEN.

I. EPISTLE, Colossians 3. 12–17.

Love Is the Bond of Union.

PUT on therefore, as God's elect, holy and beloved, a heart of compassion, kindness, lowliness, meekness, longsuffering; forbearing one another, and forgiving each other, if any man have a complaint against any; even as the Lord forgave you, so also do ye: and above all these things put on love, which is the bond of perfectness.

And let the peace of Christ rule in your hearts, to the which also ye were called in one body; and be ye thankful.

Let the word of Christ dwell in you richly; in all wisdom teaching and admonishing one another with psalms and hymns and spiritual songs, singing with grace in your hearts unto God.

And whatsoever ye do, in word or in deed, do all in the name of the Lord Jesus, giving thanks to God the Father through him.

I. GOSPEL, Matthew 13. 24–30.

The Wheat and the Tares.

ANOTHER parable set he before them, saying, The kingdom of heaven is likened unto a man that sowed good seed in his field: but while men slept, his enemy came and sowed tares also among the wheat, and went away.

But when the blade sprang up and brought forth fruit, then appeared the tares also.

And the servants of the householder came and said unto him, Sir, didst thou not sow good seed in thy field? whence then hath it tares? And he said unto them, An enemy hath done this. And the servants say unto him, Wilt thou then that we go and gather them up? But he saith, Nay; lest haply while ye gather up the tares, ye root up the wheat with them. Let both grow together until

the harvest: and in the time of the harvest I will say to the reapers, Gather up first the tares, and bind them in bundles to burn them; but gather the wheat into my barn.

II. EPISTLE, 1 Corinthians 1. 9–18.

Unity in the Church of Christ.

GOD is faithful, through whom ye were called into the fellowship of his Son Jesus Christ our Lord.

Now I beseech you, brethren, through the name of our Lord Jesus Christ, that ye all speak the same thing, and that there be no divisions among you; but that ye be perfected together in the same mind and in the same judgment.

For it hath been signified unto me concerning you, my brethren, by them that are of the household of Chloe, that there are contentions among you. Now this I mean, that each one of you saith, I am of Paul; and I of Apollos; and I of Cephas; and I of Christ. Is Christ divided? was Paul crucified for you? or were ye baptized into the name of Paul?

I thank God that I baptized none of you, save Crispus and Gaius; lest any man should say that ye were baptized into my name. And I baptized also the household of Stephanas: besides, I know not whether I baptized any other. For Christ sent me not to baptize, but to preach the gospel: not in wisdom of words, lest the cross of Christ should be made void.

For the word of the cross is to them that perish foolishness; but unto us who are saved it is the power of God.

II. GOSPEL, Mark 9. 38–41.

Jesus Teaches Tolerance.

JOHN said unto him, Teacher, we saw one casting out demons in thy name; and we forbade him, because he followed not us.

But Jesus said, Forbid him not: for there is no man who shall do a mighty work in my name, and be able quickly to speak evil of me. For he that is not against us is for us. For whosoever shall give you a cup of water to drink, because ye are Christ's, verily I say unto you, he shall in no wise lose his reward.

III. EPISTLE, Ephesians 4. 14–16.

Union with Christ Gives Stability.

WE may be no longer children, tossed to and fro and carried about with every wind of doctrine, by the sleight of men, in craftiness, after the wiles of error; but speaking truth in love, may grow up in all things into him, who is the head, even Christ; from whom all the body fitly framed and knit together through that which every joint supplieth, according to the working in due measure

of each several part, maketh the increase of the body unto the building up of itself in love.

III. GOSPEL, Mark 4. 26–29.

The Seed Growing Secretly.

AND he said, So is the kingdom of God, as if a man should cast seed upon the earth; and should sleep and rise night and day, and the seed should spring up and grow, he knoweth not how. The earth beareth fruit of herself; first the blade, then the ear, then the full grain in the ear. But when the fruit is ripe, straightway he putteth forth the sickle, because the harvest is come.

SIXTH SUNDAY AFTER EPIPHANY.

(Same as Twenty-Sixth after Trinity).

SEPTUAGESIMA SUNDAY.

By Grace Alone.

Collect. O Lord, we beseech Thee to hear the prayers of Thy people: that we, who are justly punished for our offences, may be mercifully delivered by Thy goodness, to the glory of Thy name; through Jesus Christ, Thy Son, our Lord. AMEN.

I. EPISTLE, 1 Corinthians 9. 24–27.

The Incorruptible Crown of Victory.

KNOW ye not that they that run in a race run all, but one receiveth the prize? Even so run; that ye may attain. And every man that striveth in the games exerciseth self-control in all things. Now they do it to receive a corruptible crown; but we an incorruptible. I therefore so run, as not uncertainly; so fight I, as not beating the air: but I buffet my body, and bring it into bondage: lest by any means, after that I have preached to others, I myself should be rejected.

I. GOSPEL, Matthew 20. 1–16.

The Laborers in the Vineyard.

THE kingdom of heaven is like unto a man that was a householder, who went out early in the morning to hire laborers into his vineyard. And when he had agreed with the laborers for a shilling a day, he sent them into his vineyard. And he went out about the third hour, and saw others standing in the marketplace idle; and to them he said, Go ye also into the vineyard, and whatsoever

is right I will give you. And they went their way.

Again he went out about the sixth and the ninth hour, and did likewise.

And about the eleventh hour he went out, and found others standing; and he saith unto them, Why stand ye here all the day idle? They say unto him, Because no man hath hired us. He saith unto them, Go ye also into the vineyard.

And when even was come, the lord of the vineyard saith unto his steward, Call the laborers, and pay them their hire, beginning from the last unto the first. And when they came that were hired about the eleventh hour, they received every man a shilling. And when the first came, they supposed that they would receive more; and they likewise received every man a shilling. And when they received it, they murmured against the householder, saying, These last have spent but one hour, and thou hast made them equal unto us, who have borne the burden of the day and the scorching heat.

But he answered and said to one of them, Friend, I do thee no wrong: didst not thou agree with me for a shilling? Take up that which is thine, and go thy way; it is my will to give unto this last, even as unto thee. Is it not lawful for me to do what I will with mine own? or is thine eye evil, because I am good?

So the last shall be first, and the first last.

II. EPISTLE, 1 Corinthians 3. 7–23.

The Humility of God's Fellow-workers.

SO then neither is he that planteth anything, neither he that watereth; but God that giveth the increase. Now he that planteth and he that watereth are one: but each shall receive his own reward according to his own labor. For we are God's fellow-workers: ye are God's husbandry, God's building.

According to the grace of God which was given unto me, as a wise masterbuilder I laid a foundation; and another buildeth thereon. But let each man take heed how he buildeth thereon. For other foundation can no man lay than that which is laid, which is Jesus Christ. But if any man buildeth on the foundation gold, silver, costly stones, wood, hay, stubble; each man's work shall be made manifest: for the day shall declare it, because it is revealed in fire; and the fire itself shall prove each man's work of what sort it is. If any man's work shall abide which he built thereon, he shall receive a reward. If any man's work shall be burned, he shall suffer loss: but he himself shall be saved; yet so as through fire.

Know ye not that ye are a temple of God, and that the Spirit of God dwelleth in you? If any man destroyeth the temple of God, him shall God destroy; for the temple of God is holy, and such are ye.

Let no man deceive himself. If any man thinketh that he is wise among you in this world, let him become a fool, that he may become wise. For the wisdom of this world is foolishness with God. For it is written, He that taketh the wise in their craftiness: and again, The Lord knoweth the reasonings of the wise, that they are vain. Wherefore let no one glory in men. For all things are yours; whether Paul, or Apollos, or Cephas, or the world, or life, or death, or things present, or things to come; all are yours; and ye are Christ's; and Christ is God's.

II. GOSPEL, Matthew 19. 27–30.

The Reward of Following Christ.

THEN answered Peter and said unto him, Lo, we have left all, and followed thee; what then shall we have?

And Jesus said unto them, Verily I say unto you, that ye who have followed me, in the regeneration when the Son of man shall sit on the throne of his glory, ye also shall sit upon twelve thrones, judging the twelve tribes of Israel. And every one that hath left houses, or brethren, or sisters, or father, or mother, or children, or lands, for my name's sake, shall receive a hundredfold, and shall inherit eternal life. But many shall be last that are first; and first that are last.

III. EPISTLE, Philippians 3. 7–14.

Loss for Christ's Sake Is Gain.

WHAT things were gain to me, these have I counted loss for Christ. Yea verily, and I count all things to be loss for the excellency of the knowledge of Christ Jesus my lord: for whom I suffered the loss of all things, and do count them but refuse, that I may gain Christ, and be found in him, not having a righteousness of mine own, even that which is of the law, but that which is through faith in Christ, the righteousness which is from God by faith: that I may know him, and the power of his resurrection, and the fellowship of his sufferings, becoming conformed unto his death; if by any means I may attain unto the resurrection from the dead.

Not that I have already obtained, or am already made perfect: but I press on, if so be that I may lay hold on that for which also I was laid hold on by Christ Jesus. Brethren, I count not myself yet to have laid hold: but one thing I do, forgetting the things which are behind, and stretching forward to the things which are before, I press on toward the goal unto the prize of the high calling of God in Christ Jesus.

III. GOSPEL, Luke 17. 7–10.

Service without Thought of Reward.

WHO is there of you, having a servant plowing or keeping sheep, that will say unto him, when he is come in from the field, Come straightway and sit down to meat; and will not rather say unto him, Make ready wherewith I may sup, and gird thyself, and serve me, till I have eaten and drunken; and afterward thou shalt eat and drink? Doth he thank the servant because he did the things that were commanded? Even so ye also, when ye shall have done all the things that are commanded you, say, We are unprofitable servants; we have done that which it was our duty to do.

SEXAGESIMA SUNDAY.

The Word of God.

Collect. O God, who seest that we put not our trust in anything that we do, mercifully grant that by the power of Thy Son, the Teacher of nations, we may be defended against all adversity; through the same, our Lord Jesus Christ, who liveth and reigneth with Thee and the Holy Spirit, ever one God, world without end. AMEN.

I. EPISTLE, 2 Corinthians 11. 19–31.

Servants of the Word Must Expect Hardship and Danger.

YE bear with the foolish gladly, being wise yourselves. For ye bear with a man, if he bringeth you into bondage, if he devoureth you, if he taketh you captive, if he exalteth himself, if he smiteth you on the face.

I speak by way of disparagement, as though we had been weak. Yet whereinsoever any is bold (I speak in foolishness), I am bold also. Are they Hebrews? so am I. Are they Israelites? so am I. Are they the seed of Abraham? so am I. Are they ministers of Christ? (I speak as one beside himself) I more; in labors more abundantly, in prisons more abundantly, in stripes above measure, in deaths oft. Of the Jews five times received I forty stripes save one. Thrice was I beaten with rods, once was I stoned, thrice I suffered shipwreck, a night and a day have I been in the deep; in journeyings often, in perils of rivers, in perils of robbers, in perils from my countrymen, in perils from the Gentiles, in perils in the city, in perils in the wilderness, in perils in the sea, in perils among false brethren; in labor and travail, in watchings often, in hunger and thirst, in fastings often, in cold and nakedness.

Besides those things that are without, there is that which presseth upon me daily, anxiety for all the churches. Who is weak, and I am not weak? who is caused to stumble, and I burn not? If I must needs glory, I will glory of the things that concern my weakness. The God and Father of the Lord Jesus, he who is blessed for evermore knoweth that I lie not.

I. GOSPEL, Luke 8. 4–15.

The Parable of the Sower.

WHEN a great multitude came together, and they of every city resorted unto him, he spake by a parable:

The sower went forth to sow his seed: and as he sowed, some fell by the way side; and it was trodden under foot, and the birds of the heaven devoured it. And other fell on the rock; and as soon as it grew, it withered away, because it had no moisture. And other fell amidst the thorns; and the thorns grew with it, and choked it. And other fell into the good ground, and grew, and brought forth fruit a hundredfold.

As he said these things, he cried, He that hath ears to hear, let him hear.

And his disciples asked him what this parable might be. And he said, Unto you it is given to know the mysteries of the kingdom of God: but to the rest in parables; that seeing they may not see, and hearing they may not understand. Now the parable is this: The seed is the word of God. And those by the way side are they that have heard; then cometh the devil, and taketh away the word from their heart, that they may not believe and be saved. And those on the rock are they who, when they have heard, receive the word with joy; and these have no root, who for a while believe, and in time of temptation fall away. And that which fell among the thorns, these are they that have heard, and as they go on their way they are choked with cares and riches and pleasures of this life, and bring no fruit to perfection. And that in the good ground, these are such as in an honest and good heart, having heard the word, hold it fast, and bring forth fruit with patience.

II. EPISTLE, Isaiah 55. 6–11.

The Word of God Shall Not Return Void.

SEEK ye Jehovah while he may be found; call ye upon him while he is near: let the wicked forsake his way, and the unrighteous man his thoughts; and let him return unto Jehovah, and he will have mercy upon him; and to our God, for he will abundantly pardon.

For my thoughts are not your thoughts, neither are your ways my ways, saith Jehovah. For as the heavens are higher than the earth, so are my ways higher than your ways, and my thoughts than your thoughts.

For as the rain cometh down and the snow from heaven, and returneth not thither, but watereth the earth, and maketh it bring forth and bud, and giveth seed to the sower and bread to the eater; so shall my word be that goeth forth out of my mouth: it shall not return unto me void, but it shall accomplish that which I please, and it shall prosper in the thing whereto I sent it.

II. Gospel, John 12. 35–38.

Jesus Exhorts Us to Walk by the Light.

JESUS therefore said unto them, Yet a little while is the light among you. Walk while ye have the light, that darkness overtake you not: and he that walketh in the darkness knoweth not whither he goeth. While ye have the light, believe on the light, that ye may become sons of light.

These things spake Jesus, and he departed and hid himself from them. But though he had done so many signs before them, yet they believed not on him: that the word of Isaiah the prophet might be fulfilled, which he spake,

Lord, who hath believed our report? And to whom hath the arm of the Lord been revealed?

III. Epistle, 2 Timothy 3. 10—4. 5.

Preaching the Word in Season and Out of Season.

THOU didst follow my teaching, conduct, purpose, faith, longsuffering, love, patience, persecutions, sufferings; what things befell me at Antioch, at Iconium, at Lystra; what persecutions I endured: and out of them all the Lord delivered me.

Yea, and all that would live godly in Christ Jesus shall suffer persecution. But evil men and impostors shall wax worse and worse, deceiving and being deceived. But abide thou in the things which thou hast learned and hast been assured of, knowing of whom thou hast learned them; and that from a babe thou hast known the sacred writings which are able to make thee wise unto salvation through faith which is in Christ Jesus.

Every scripture inspired of God is also profitable for teaching, for reproof, for correction, for instruction which is in righteousness: that the man of God may be complete, furnished completely unto every good work.

I charge thee in the sight of God, and of Christ Jesus, who shall judge the living and the dead, and by his appearing and his kingdom: preach the word; be urgent in season, out of season; reprove, rebuke, exhort, with all longsuffering and teaching. For the time will come when they will not endure the sound doctrine; but, having itching ears, will heap to themselves teachers after their own lusts; and will turn away their ears from the truth, and turn aside unto fables. But be thou sober in all things, suffer hardship, do the work of an evangelist, fulfil thy ministry.

III. Gospel, Matthew 10. 2–16.

Jesus Commissions the Twelve.

NOW the names of the twelve apostles are these: The first, Simon, who is called Peter, and Andrew his brother; James the son of Zebedee, and John his brother; Philip, and Bartholomew; Thomas, and Matthew the publican; James the son of Alphæus, and Thaddæus; Simon the Canænan, and Judas Iscariot, who also betrayed him.

These twelve Jesus sent forth, and charged them, saying, Go not into any way of the Gentiles, and enter not into any city of the Samaritans: but go rather to the lost sheep of the house of Israel. And as ye go, preach, saying, The kingdom of heaven is at hand. Heal the sick, raise the dead, cleanse the lepers, cast out demons: freely ye received, freely give.

Get you no gold, nor silver, nor brass in your purses; no wallet for your journey, neither two coats, nor shoes, nor staff: for the laborer is worthy of his food.

And into whatsoever city or village ye shall enter, search out who in it is worthy; and there abide till ye go forth. And as ye enter into the house, salute it. And if the house be worthy, let your peace come upon it: but if it be not worthy, let your peace return to you. And whosoever shall not receive you, nor hear your words, as ye go forth out of that house or that city, shake off the dust of your feet. Verily I say unto you, It shall be more tolerable for the land of Sodom and Gomorrah in the day of judgment, than for that city.

Behold, I send you forth as sheep in the midst of wolves: be ye therefore wise as serpents, and harmless as doves.

QUINQUAGESIMA SUNDAY.

The Path of Suffering.

Collect. O Lord, we beseech Thee, mercifully hear our prayers, and having set us free from the bonds of sin, deliver us from all evil; through Jesus Christ, Thy Son, our Lord. AMEN.

I. EPISTLE, 1 Corinthians 13. 1–13.

The Greatest of These Is Love.

IF I speak with the tongues of men and of angels, but have not love, I am become sounding brass or a clanging cymbal. And if I have the gift of prophecy, and know all mysteries and all knowledge; and if I have all faith, so as to remove mountains, but have not love, I am nothing. And if I bestow all my goods to feed the poor, and if I give my body to be burned, but have not love, it profiteth me nothing.

Love suffereth long, and is kind; love envieth not; love vaunteth not itself, is not puffed up, doth not behave itself unseemly, seeketh not its own, is not provoked, taketh not account of evil; rejoiceth not in unrighteousness, but rejoiceth with the truth; beareth all things, believeth all things, hopeth all things, endureth all things.

Love never faileth: but whether there be prophecies, they shall be done away; whether there be tongues, they shall cease; whether there be knowledge, it shall be done away. For we know in part, and we prophesy in part; but when that which is perfect is come, that which is in part shall be done away.

When I was a child, I spake as a child, I felt as a child, I thought as a child; now that I am become a man, I have put away childish things. For now we see in a mirror, darkly; but then face to face: now I know in part; but then shall I know fully even as also I was fully known.

But now abideth faith, hope, love, these three; and the greatest of these is love.

I. GOSPEL, Luke 18. 31–43.

Jesus Goes Up to Jerusalem.

AND he took unto him the twelve, and said unto them, Behold, we go up to Jerusalem, and all the things that are written through the prophets shall be accomplished unto the Son of man. For he shall be delivered up unto the Gentiles, and shall be mocked, and shamefully treated, and spit upon: and they shall scourge and kill him: and the third day he shall rise again.

And they understood none of these things; and this saying was hid from them, and they perceived not the things that were said.

And it came to pass, as he drew nigh unto Jericho, a certain blind man sat by the way side begging: and hearing a multitude going by, he inquired what this meant. And they told him, that Jesus of Nazareth passeth by. And he cried, saying, Jesus, thou son of David, have mercy on me. And they that went before rebuked him, that he should hold his peace: but he cried out the more a great deal, Thou son of David, have mercy on me. And Jesus stood, and commanded him to be brought unto him: and when he was come near, he asked him, What wilt thou that I should do unto thee? And he said, Lord, that I may receive my sight. And Jesus said unto him, Receive thy sight: thy faith hath made thee whole. And immediately he received his sight, and followed him, glorifying God: and all the people, when they saw it, gave praise unto God.

II. EPISTLE, Psalm 40, 7–9.

The Joy of Obedience to God.

LO, I am come; In the roll of the book it is written of me:
I delight to do thy will, O my God;
Yea, thy law is within my heart.
I have proclaimed glad tidings of righteousness in the great assembly.
Lo, I will not refrain my lips,
O Jehovah, thou knowest.

II. GOSPEL, John 12. 20–33.

The Grain of Wheat Must Die.

NOW there were certain Greeks among those that went up to worship at the feast: these therefore came to Philip, who was of Bethsaida of Galilee, and asked him, saying, Sir, we would see Jesus. Philip cometh and telleth Andrew: Andrew cometh, and Philip, and they tell Jesus.

And Jesus answereth them, saying, The hour is come, that the Son of man should be glorified. Verily, verily, I say unto you, Except a grain of wheat fall into the earth and die, it abideth by itself alone; but if it die, it beareth much fruit. He that loveth his life loseth it; and he that hateth his life in this world shall keep it unto life eternal.

If any man serve me, let him follow me, and where I am, there shall also my servant be: if any man serve me, him will the Father honor.

Now is my soul troubled; and what shall I say? Father, save me from this hour. But for this cause came I unto this hour. Father, glorify thy name.

There came therefore a voice out of heaven, saying, I have both glorified it, and will glorify it again.

The multitude, therefore, that stood by, and heard it, said that it had thundered: others said, An angel hath spoken to him. Jesus answered and said, This voice hath not come for my sake, but for your sakes. Now is the judgment of this world: now shall the prince of this world be cast out. And I, if I be lifted up from the earth, will draw all men unto myself.

But this he said, signifying by what manner of death he should die.

III. Epistle, 1 Corinthians 1. 20–25.
Christ the Power of God.

WHERE is the wise? where is the scribe? where is the disputer of this world? hath not God made foolish the wisdom of the world? For seeing that in the wisdom of God the world through its wisdom knew not God, it was God's good pleasure through the foolishness of the preaching to save them that believe. Seeing that Jews ask for signs, and Greeks seek after wisdom: but we preach Christ crucified, unto Jews a stumblingblock, and unto Gentiles foolishness; but unto them that are called, both Jews and Greeks, Christ the power of God, and the wisdom of God. Because the foolishness of God is wiser than men; and the weakness of God is stronger than men.

III. Gospel, Mark 10. 32–45.
Through Suffering to Glory.

AND they were on the way, going up to Jerusalem; and Jesus was going before them: and they were amazed; and they that followed were afraid.

And he took again the twelve, and began to tell them the things that were to happen unto him, saying, Behold, we go up to Jerusalem; and the Son of man shall be delivered unto the chief priests and the scribes; and they shall condemn him to death, and shall deliver him unto the Gentiles: and they shall mock him, and shall spit upon him, and shall scourge him, and shall kill him: and after three days he shall rise again.

And there come near unto him James and John, the sons of Zebedee, saying unto him, Teacher, we would that thou shouldest do for us whatsoever we shall ask of thee. And he said unto them, What would ye that I should do for you? And they said unto him, Grant unto us that we may sit, one on thy right hand, and one on thy left hand, in thy glory. But Jesus said unto them, Ye know not what ye ask. Are ye able to drink the cup that I drink? or to be baptized with the baptism that I am baptized with? And they said unto him, We are able. And Jesus said unto them, The cup that I drink ye shall drink; and with the baptism that I am baptized withal shall ye be baptized: but to sit on my right hand or on my left hand is not mine to give; but it is for them for whom it hath been prepared.

And when the ten heard it, they began to be moved with indignation concerning James and John.

And Jesus called them to him, and saith unto them, Ye know that they who are accounted to rule over the Gentiles lord it over them; and their great ones exercise authority over them. But it is not so among you: but whosoever would become great among you, shall be your minister; and whosoever would be first among you, shall be servant of all. For the Son of man also came not to be ministered unto, but to minister, and to give his life a ransom for many.

FIRST SUNDAY IN LENT.
Temptation.

Collect. O Lord God, stretch forth the right hand of Thy majesty to defend us from them that rise up against us; and grant peace and joy to Thy Church, through Jesus Christ, Thy Son, our Lord. Amen.

I. Epistle, 2 Corinthians 6. 1–10.
God Gives Patience to His Servants.

WORKING together with him we entreat also that ye receive not the grace of God in vain (for he saith,

At an acceptable time I hearkened unto thee,

And in a day of salvation did I succor thee:

behold, now is the acceptable time; behold, now is the day of salvation): giving no occasion of stumbling in anything, that our ministration be not blamed; but in everything commending ourselves, as ministers of God, in much patience, in afflictions, in necessities, in distresses, in stripes, in imprisonments, in tumults, in labors, in watchings, in fastings; in pureness, in knowledge, in longsuffering, in kindness, in the Holy Spirit, in love unfeigned, in the word of truth, in the power of God; by the armor of righteousness on the right hand and on the left, by glory and dishonor, by evil report and good report; as deceivers, and yet true; as unknown, and yet well known; as dying, and behold, we live; as chastened, and not killed; as sorrowful, yet always rejoicing; as poor, yet making many rich; as having nothing, and yet possessing all things.

I. Gospel, Matthew 4. 1–11.
The Temptation of Jesus in the Wilderness.

THEN was Jesus led up of the Spirit into the wilderness to be tempted of the devil.

And when he had fasted forty days and forty nights, he afterward hungered. And the tempter came and said unto him, If thou art the Son of God, command that these stones become bread. But he answered and said, It is written, Man shall not live by bread alone, but by every word that proceedeth out of the mouth of God.

Then the devil taketh him into the holy city; and he set him on the pinnacle of the temple, and saith unto him, If thou art the Son of God, cast thyself down: for it is written,

He shall give his angels charge concerning thee:

and,

On their hands they shall bear thee up, Lest haply thou dash thy foot against a stone.

Jesus said unto him, Again it is written, Thou shalt not make trial of the Lord thy God.

Again, the devil taketh him unto an exceeding high mountain, and showeth him all the kingdoms of the world, and the glory of them; and he said unto him, All these things will I give thee, if thou wilt fall down and worship me. Then saith Jesus unto him, Get thee hence, Satan: for it is written, Thou shalt worship the Lord thy God, and him only shalt thou serve.

Then the devil leaveth him; and behold, angels came and ministered unto him.

II. Epistle, James 1. 12–15.
God Tempts No Man.

BLESSED is the man that endureth temptation; for when he hath been approved, he shall receive the crown of life, which the Lord promised to them that love him. Let no man say when he is tempted, I am tempted of God; for God cannot be tempted with evil, and he himself tempteth no man: but each man is tempted, when he is drawn away by his own lust, and enticed. Then the lust, when it hath conceived, beareth sin: and the sin, when it is fullgrown, bringeth forth death.

II. Gospel, Matthew 16. 21–23.
Jesus Refuses to Flee from Suffering.

FROM that time began Jesus to show unto his disciples, that he must go unto Jerusalem, and suffer many things of the elders and chief priests and scribes, and be killed, and the third day be raised up.

And Peter took him, and began to rebuke him, saying, Be it far from thee, Lord: this shall never be unto thee. But he turned, and said unto Peter, Get thee behind me, Satan: thou art a stumblingblock unto me: for thou mindest not the things of God, but the things of men.

III. Epistle, Hebrews 4. 15, 16.
Jesus Gives Power to Conquer Temptation.

WE have not a high priest that cannot be touched with the feeling of our infirmities; but one that hath been in all points tempted like as we are, yet without sin. Let us therefore draw near with boldness unto the throne of grace, that we may receive mercy, and may find grace to help us in time of need.

III. Gospel, Luke 10. 17–20.
The Source of True Joy.

AND the seventy returned with joy, saying, Lord, even the demons are subject unto us in thy name.

And he said unto them, I beheld Satan fallen as lightning from heaven. Behold, I have given you authority to tread upon serpents and scorpions, and over all the power of the enemy: and nothing shall in any wise hurt you. Nevertheless in this rejoice not, that the spirits are subject unto you; but rejoice that your names are written in heaven.

SECOND SUNDAY IN LENT.

Victorious Faith.

Collect. O God, who seest that of ourselves we have no power for good, keep us both outwardly and inwardly, that we may be protected against all bodily evils, and that our hearts may be purged of all impure thoughts; through Jesus Christ, Thy Son, our Lord. AMEN.

I. EPISTLE, 1 Thessalonians 4. 1–7.

God's Call to Holiness.

BRETHREN, we beseech and exhort you in the Lord Jesus, that, as ye received of us how ye ought to walk and to please God, even as ye do walk,—that ye abound more and more. For ye know what charge we gave you through the Lord Jesus.

For this is the will of God, even your sanctification, that ye abstain from fornication; that each one of you know how to possess himself of his own vessel in sanctification and honor, not in the passion of lust, even as the Gentiles who know not God; that no man transgress, and wrong his brother in the matter: because the Lord is an avenger in all these things, as also we forwarned you and testified. For God called us not for uncleanness, but in sanctification.

I. GOSPEL, Matthew 15. 21–28.

The Canaanitish Woman.

AND Jesus went out thence and withdrew into the parts of Tyre and Sidon.

And behold, a Canaanitish woman came out from those borders, and cried, saying, Have mercy on me, O Lord, thou son of David; my daughter is grievously vexed with a demon. But he answered her not a word.

And his disciples came and besought him, saying, Send her away; for she crieth after us. But he answered and said, I was not sent but unto the lost sheep of the house of Israel.

But she came and worshipped him, saying, Lord, help me. And he answered and said, It is not meet to take the children's bread and cast it to the dogs. But she said, Yes, Lord: for even the dogs eat of the crumbs which fall from their master's table.

Then Jesus answered and said unto her, O woman, great is thy faith: be it done unto thee even as thou wilt. And here daughter was healed from that hour.

II. EPISTLE, Genesis 32. 24–29.

Jacob Wrestles with God in Prayer.

AND Jacob was left alone; and there wrestled a man with him until the breaking of the day. And when he saw that he prevailed not against him, he touched the hollow of his thigh; and the hollow of Jacob's thigh was strained, as he wrestled with him. And he said, Let me go, for the day breaketh. And he said, I will not let thee go, except thou bless me. And he said unto him, What is thy name? And he said, Jacob. And he said, Thy name shall be called no more Jacob, but Israel: for thou hast striven with God and with men, and hast prevailed. And Jacob asked him, and said, Tell me, I pray thee, thy name. And he said, Wherefore is it that thou dost ask after my name?

And he blessed him there.

II. GOSPEL, Luke 7. 36–50.

The Sinful Woman in the House of Simon.

AND one of the Pharisees desired him that he would eat with him. And he entered into the Pharisee's home and sat down to meat.

And behold, a woman who was in the city, a sinner; and when she knew that he was sitting at meat in the Pharisee's house, she brought an alabaster cruse of ointment, and standing behind at his feet, weeping, she began to wet his feet with her tears, and wiped them with the hair of her head, and kissed his feet, and anointed them with the ointment.

Now when the Pharisee that had bidden him saw it, he spake within himself, saying, This man, if he were a prophet, would have perceived who and what manner of woman this is that toucheth him, that she is a sinner.

And Jesus answering said unto him, Simon, I have somewhat to say unto thee. And he saith, Teacher, say on. A certain lender had two debtors: the one owed five hundred shillings, and the other fifty. When they had not wherewith to pay, he forgave them both. Which of them therefore will love him most?

Simon answered and said, He, I suppose, to whom he forgave the most.

And he said unto him, Thou hast rightly judged. And turning to the woman, he said unto Simon, Seest thou this woman? I entered into thy house, thou gavest me no water for my feet: but she hath wetted my feet with her tears, and wiped them with her hair. Thou gavest me no kiss: but she, since the time I came in, hath not ceased to kiss my feet. My head with oil thou didst not anoint: but she hath anointed my feet with ointment. Wherefore I say unto thee, Her sins, which are many, are forgiven; for she loved much: but to whom little is forgiven, the same loveth little.

And he said unto her, Thy sins are forgiven.

And they that sat at meat with him began to say within themselves, Who is this that even forgiveth sins?

And he said unto the woman, Thy faith hath saved thee; go in peace.

III. EPISTLE, Hebrews 5. 7–9.

Suffering Teaches Obedience.

CHRIST also...who in the days of his flesh, having offered up prayers and supplications with strong crying and tears unto him that was able to save him from death, and having been heard for his godly fear, though he was a Son, yet learned obedience by the things which he suffered; and having been made perfect, he became unto all them that obey him the author of eternal salvation.

III. GOSPEL, Mark 9. 14–32.

Jesus and the Man of Feeble Faith.

AND when they came to the disciples, they saw a great multitude about them, and scribes questioning with them. And straightway all the multitude, when they saw him, were greatly amazed, and running to him saluted him.

And he asked them, What question ye with them?

And one of the multitude answered him, Teacher, I brought unto thee my son, who hath a dumb spirit; and wheresoever it taketh him, it dasheth him down: and he foameth, and grindeth his teeth, and pineth away: and I spake to thy disciples

that they should cast it out; and they were not able.

And he answereth them and saith, O faithless generation, how long shall I be with you? how long shall I bear with you? bring him unto me.

And they brought him unto him: and when he saw him, straightway the spirit tare him grievously; and he fell on the ground, and wallowed foaming. And he asked his father, How long time is it since this hath come unto him? And he said, From a child. And oft-times it hath cast him both into the fire and into the waters, to destroy him: and if thou canst do anything, have compassion on us, and help us.

And Jesus said unto him, If thou canst! All things are possible to him that believeth.

Straightway the father of the child cried out, and said, I believe; help thou mine unbelief.

And when Jesus saw that a multitude came running together, he rebuked the unclean spirit, saying unto him, Thou dumb and deaf spirit, I command thee, come out of him, and enter no more into him. And having cried out, and torn him much, he came out: and the boy became as one dead; insomuch that the more part said, He is dead. But Jesus took him by the hand, and raised him up; and he arose.

And when he was come into the house, his disciples asked him privately, How is it that we could not cast it out? And he said unto them, This kind can come out by nothing, save by prayer.

And they went forth from thence, and passed through Galilee; and he would not that any man should know it. For he taught his disciples, and said unto them, The Son of man is delivered up into the hands of men, and they shall kill him; and when he is killed, after three days he shall rise again. But they understood not the saying, and were afraid to ask him.

THIRD SUNDAY IN LENT.

The Parting.

Collect. We beseech Thee, Almighty God, look upon the hearty desires of Thy humble servants, and protect us by Thy mighty hand, through Jesus Christ, Thy Son, our Lord. AMEN.

I. EPISTLE, Ephesians 5. 1–9.

The Children of Light Walk in the Light.

BE ye therefore imitators of God, as beloved children; and walk in love, even as Christ also loved you, and gave

himself up for us, an offering and a sacrifice to God for an odor of a sweet smell.

But fornication, and all uncleanness, or covetousness, let it not even be named among you, as becometh saints; nor filthiness, nor foolish talking, or jesting, which are not befitting: but rather giving of thanks. For this we know of a surety, that no fornicator, nor unclean person, nor covetous man, who is an idolater, hath any inheritance in the kingdom of Christ and God.

Let no man deceive you with empty words: for because of these things cometh the wrath of God upon the sons of disobedience. Be not ye therefore partakers with them; for ye were once darkness, but are now light in the Lord: walk as children of light (for the fruit of the light is in all goodness and righteousness and truth.)

I. GOSPEL (a), Luke 11. 14–28.

Jesus Reveals the Power of Evil.

AND he was casting out a demon that was dumb. And it came to pass, when the demon was gone out, the dumb man spake; and the multitudes marvelled.

But some of them said, By Beelzebub the prince of the demons casteth he out demons. And others, trying him, sought of him a sign from heaven.

But he, knowing their thoughts, said unto them, Every kingdom divided against itself is brought to desolation; and a house divided against a house falleth. And if Satan also is divided against himself, how shall his kingdom stand? because ye say that I cast out demons by Beelzebub. And if I by Beelzebub cast out demons, by whom do your sons cast them out? therefore shall they be your judges. But if I by the finger of God cast out demons, then is the kingdom of God come upon you.

When the strong man fully armed guardeth his own court, his goods are in peace: but when a stronger than he shall come upon him, and overcome him, he taketh from him his whole armor wherein he trusted, and divideth his spoils. He that is not with me is against me; and he that gathereth not with me scattereth.

The unclean spirit when he is gone out of the man, passeth through waterless places, seeking rest, and finding none, he saith, I will turn back unto my house whence I came out. And when he is come, he findeth it swept and garnished. Then goeth he, and taketh to him seven other spirits more evil than himself; and they enter in and dwell there: and the last state of that man becometh worse than the first.

And it came to pass, as he said these things, a certain woman out of the multitude lifted up her voice, and said unto him, Blessed is the womb that bare thee, and the breasts which thou didst suck. But he said, Yea rather, blessed are they that hear the word of God, and keep it.

I. GOSPEL (b), Matthew 26. 36–46.

Jesus with His Disciples in Gethsemane.

THEN cometh Jesus with them unto a place called Gethsemane, and saith unto his disciples, Sit ye here, while I go yonder and pray.

And he took with him Peter and the two sons of Zebedee, and began to be sorrowful and sore troubled. Then saith he unto them, My soul is exceeding sorrowful, even unto death: abide ye here, and watch with me.

And he went forward a little, and fell on his face, and prayed, saying, My Father, if it be possible, let this cup pass away from me: nevertheless, not as I will, but as thou wilt.

And he cometh unto the disciples, and findeth them sleeping, and saith unto Peter, What, could ye not watch with me one hour? Watch and pray, that ye enter not into temptation: the spirit indeed is willing, but the flesh is weak.

Again a second time he went away, and prayed, saying, My Father, if this cannot pass away, except I drink it, thy will be done.

And he came again and found them sleeping, for their eyes were heavy. And he left them again, and went away, and prayed a third time, saying again the same words.

Then cometh he to the disciples, and saith unto them, Sleep on now, and take your rest: behold, the hour is at hand, and the Son of man is betrayed into the hands of sinners. Arise, let us be going: behold, he is at hand that betrayeth me.

II. EPISTLE, Psalm 116. 1–9.

God Delivers Out of Distress.

I love Jehovah, because he heareth my voice and my supplications.
Because he hath inclined his ear unto me,
Therefore will I call upon him as long as I live.
The cords of death compassed me,
And the pains of Sheol gat hold upon me:
I found trouble and sorrow.
Then called I upon the name of Jehovah:
O Jehovah, I beseech thee, deliver my soul.
Gracious is Jehovah, and righteous;
Yea, our God is merciful.
Jehovah preserveth the simple:
I was brought low, and he saved me.
Return unto thy rest, O my soul;
For Jehovah hath dealt bountifully with thee.

For thou hast delivered my soul from
death,
Mine eyes from tears,
And my feet from falling.
I will walk before Jehovah
In the land of the living.

II. GOSPEL (a), John 7. 19–31.

*The Jews Question the Authority of
Jesus.*

Jesus said unto the Jews:

DID not Moses give you the law, and
yet none of you doeth the law? Why
seek ye to kill me?

The multitude answered, Thou hast a
demon: who seeketh to kill thee?

Jesus answered and said unto them, I
did one work, and ye all marvel because
thereof. Moses hath given you circumcision (not that it is of Moses, but of the
fathers); and on the sabbath ye circumcise a man. If a man receiveth circumcision on the sabbath, that the law of Moses
may not be broken; are ye wroth with
me, because I made a man every whit
whole on the sabbath? Judge not according to appearance, but judge righteous
judgment.

Some therefore of them of Jerusalem
said, Is not this he whom they seek to
kill? And lo, he speaketh openly, and
they say nothing unto him. Can it be
that the rulers indeed know that this is
the Christ? Howbeit we know this man
whence he is: b.t when the Christ cometh, no one knoweth whence he is.

Jesus therefore cried in the temple,
teaching and saying, Ye both know me,
and know whence I am; and I am not
come of myself, but he that sent me is
true, whom ye know not. I know him;
because I am from him, and he sent me.

They sought therefore to take him: and
no man laid his hand on him, because his
hour was not yet come. But of the multitude many believed on him; and they
said, When the Christ shall come, will he
do more signs than those which this man
hath done?

II. GOSPEL (b), Luke 22. 31–38.

*Parting Words of Warning and
Instruction.*

Jesus said:

SIMON, Simon, behold, Satan asked to
have you, that he might sift you as
wheat: but I made supplication for thee,
that thy faith fail not; and do thou,
when once thou hast turned again, establish thy brethren.

And he said unto him, Lord, with thee
I am ready to go both to prison and to
death.

And he said, I tell thee, Peter, the cock
shall not crow this day, until thou shalt
thrice deny that thou knowest me.

And he said unto them, When I sent
you forth without purse, and wallet, and
shoes, lacked ye anything? And they
said, Nothing. And he said unto them,
But now, he that hath a purse, let him
take it, and likewise a wallet; and he
that hath none, let him sell his cloak,
and buy a sword. For I say unto you,
that this which is written must be fulfilled in me, And he was reckoned with
transgressors: for that which concerneth
me hath fulfilment. And they said, Lord,
behold, here are two swords. And he said
unto them, It is enough.

III. EPISTLE, Colossians 1. 24–29.

*The Joy of Sharing the Sufferings of
Christ.*

I REJOICE in my sufferings for your
sake, and fill up on my part that which
is lacking of the afflictions of Christ in
my flesh for his body's sake, which is the
church; whereof I was made a minister,
according to the dispensation of God
which was given to you-ward, to fulfil
the word of God, even the mystery which
hath been hid for ages and generations:
but now hath it been manifested to his
saints, to whom God was pleased to make
known what is the riches of the glory of
this mystery among the Gentiles, which
is Christ in you the hope of glory: whom
we proclaim, admonishing every man and
teaching every man in all wisdom, that
we may present every man perfect in
Christ; whereunto I labor also, striving
according to his working, which worketh
in me mightily.

III. GOSPEL (a), Luke 4. 31–37.

The Power and Authority of Jesus.

AND he came down to Capernaum, a
city of Galilee. And he was teaching
them on the sabbath day: and they were
astonished at his teaching; for his word
was with authority.

And in the synagogue there was a man,
that had a spirit of an unclean demon;
and he cried out with a loud voice, Ah!
what have we to do with thee, Jesus thou
Nazarene? art thou come to destroy us?
I know thee who thou art, the Holy One
of God. And Jesus rebuked him, saying,
Hold thy peace, and come out of him.
And when the demon had thrown him
down in the midst, he came out of him,
having done him no hurt.

And amazement came upon all, and they
spake together, one with another, saying,
What is this word? for with authority

and power he commandeth the unclean spirits, and they come out. And there went forth a rumor concerning him into every place of the region round about.

III. GOSPEL (b), John 13. 31–38.

Jesus on the Last Stage of His Journey.

WHEN therefore he was gone out, Jesus saith, Now is the Son of man glorified, and God is glorified in him; and God shall glorify him in himself, and straightway shall he glorify him. Little children, yet a little while I am with you. Ye shall seek me: and as I said unto the Jews, Whither I go, ye cannot come; so now I say unto you. A new commandment I give unto you, that ye love one another; even as I have loved you, that ye also love one another. By this shall all men know that ye are my disciples, if ye have love one to another.

Simon Peter saith unto him, Lord, whither goest thou? Jesus answered, Whither I go, thou canst not follow me now; but thou shalt follow afterwards. Peter saith unto him, Lord, why cannot I follow thee even now? I will lay down my life for thee. Jesus answereth, Wilt thou lay down thy life for me? Verily, verily, I say unto thee, The cock shall not crow, till thou hast denied me thrice.

FOURTH SUNDAY IN LENT.

Bread for the Hungry.—Jesus Is Arrested and Tried.

Collect. Grant, we beseech Thee, Almighty God, that we, who for our evil deeds deserve to be punished, may by the comfort of Thy grace mercifully be relieved; through Jesus Christ, Thy Son, our Lord. AMEN.

I. EPISTLE (a), Galatians 4. 22–31.

The Two Covenants.

IT is written, that Abraham had two sons, one by the handmaid, and one by the freewoman. Howbeit the son by the handmaid is born after the flesh; but the son of the freewoman is born through promise.

Which things contain an allegory: for these women are two covenants; one from mount Sinai, bearing children unto bondage, which is Hagar. Now this Hagar is mount Sinai in Arabia, and answereth to the Jerusalem that now is: for she is in bondage with her children. But the Jerusalem that is above is free, which is our mother. For it is written,

Rejoice, thou barren that bearest not;
Break forth and cry, thou that travailest not:
For more are the children of the desolate than of her that hath the husband.

Now we, brethren, as Isaac was, are children of promise. But as then he that was born after the flesh persecuted him that was born after the Spirit, so also it is now. Howbeit what saith the scripture? Cast out the handmaid and her son: for the son of the handmaid shall not inherit with the son of the freewoman. Wherefore, brethren, we are not children of a handmaid, but of the freewoman.

I. EPISTLE (b), Romans 6. 19–23.

The Christian a Servant of Righteousness·

AS ye presented your members as servants to uncleanness and to iniquity unto iniquity, even so now present your members as servants to righteousness unto sanctification.

For when ye were servants of sin, ye were free in regard of righteousness. What fruit then had ye at that time in the things whereof ye are now ashamed? for the end of those things is death.

But now being made free from sin and become servants to God, ye have your fruit unto sanctification, and the end eternal life. For the wages of sin is death; but the free gift of God is eternal life in Christ Jesus our Lord.

I. GOSPEL (a), John 6. 1–15.

Jesus Feeds the Five Thousand Men.

JESUS went away to the other side of the sea of Galilee, which is the sea of Tiberias. And a great multitude followed him, because they beheld the signs which he did on them that were sick. And Jesus went up into the mountain, and there he sat with his disciples.

Now the passover, the feast of the Jews, was at hand.

Jesus therefore lifting up his eyes, and seeing that a great multitude cometh unto him, saith unto Philip, Whence are we to buy bread, that these may eat? And this he said to prove him: for he himself knew what he would do.

Philip answered him, Two hundred shillings' worth of bread is not sufficient for them, that every one may take a little. One of his disciples, Andrew, Simon Peter's brother, saith unto him, There is a lad here, who hath five barley loaves, and two fishes: but what are these among so many?

Jesus said, Make the people sit down. Now there was much grass in the place. So the men sat down, in number about five thousand.

Jesus therefore took the loaves; and having given thanks, he distributed to them that were set down; likewise also of the fishes as much as they would.

And when they were filled, he saith unto his disciples, Gather up the broken pieces which remain over, that nothing be lost. So they gathered them up, and filled twelve baskets with broken pieces from the five barley loaves, which remained over unto them that had eaten. When therefore the people saw the sign which he did, they said, This is of a truth the prophet that cometh into the world.

Jesus therefore perceiving that they were about to come and take him by force, to make him king, withdrew again into the mountain himself alone.

I. GOSPEL (b), Matthew 26. 59–66.
Jesus on Trial before the Council.

NOW the chief priests and the whole council sought false witness against Jesus, that they might put him to death; and they found it not, though many false witnesses came.

But afterward came two, and said, This man said, I am able to destroy the temple of God, and to build it in three days.

And the high priest stood up, and said unto him, Answerest thou nothing? what is it which these witness against thee?

But Jesus held his peace.

And the high priest said unto him, I adjure thee by the living God, that thou tell us whether thou art the Christ, the Son of God.

Jesus saith unto him, Thou hast said: nevertheless I say unto you, Henceforth ye shall see the Son of man sitting at the right hand of Power, and coming on the clouds of heaven.

Then the high priest rent his garments, saying, He hath spoken blasphemy: what further need have we of witnesses? behold, now ye have heard the blasphemy: what think ye? They answered and said, He is worthy of death.

II. EPISTLE, Psalm 42.
God Quenches the Soul's Thirst.

AS the hart panteth after the water brooks,
So panteth my soul after thee, O God.
My soul thirsteth for God, for the living God:

When shall I come and appear before God?
My tears have been my food day and night,
While they continually say unto me, Where is thy God?
These things I remember, and pour out my soul within me,
How I went with the throng, and led them to the house of God,
With the voice of joy and praise, a multitude keeping holyday.
Why art thou cast down, O my soul?
And why art thou disquieted within me?
Hope thou in God; for I shall yet praise him
For the help of his countenance.
O my God, my soul is cast down within me:
Therefore do I remember thee from the land of the Jordan,
And the Hermons, from the hill Mizar.
Deep calleth unto deep at the noise of thy waterfalls:
All thy waves and thy billows are gone over me.
Yet Jehovah will command his lovingkindness in the day-time;
And in the night his song shall be with me,
Even a prayer unto the God of my life.
I will say unto God my rock, Why hast thou forgotten me?
Why go I mourning because of the oppression of the enemy?
As with a sword in my bones, mine adversaries reproach me,
While they continually say unto me, Where is thy God?
Why art thou cast down, O my soul?
And why art thou disquieted within me?
Hope thou in God; for I shall yet praise him,
Who is the help of my countenance, and my God.

II. GOSPEL (a), John 6. 24–36.
The Bread of Life.

WHEN the multitude therefore saw that Jesus was not there, neither his disciples, they themselves got into the boats, and came to Capernaum, seeking Jesus. And when they found him on the other side of the sea, they said unto him, Rabbi, when camest thou hither?

Jesus answered them and said, Verily, verily, I say unto you, Ye seek me, not because ye saw signs, but because ye ate of the loaves, and were filled. Work not for the food which perisheth, but for the food which abideth unto eternal life, which the Son of man shall give unto you: for him the Father, even God, hath sealed.

They said therefore unto him, What must we do, that we may work the works of God?

Jesus answered and said unto them, This is the work of God, that ye believe on him whom he hath sent.

They said therefore unto him, What then doest thou for a sign, that we may see, and believe thee? what workest thou? Our fathers ate the manna in the wilderness; as it is written, He gave them bread out of heaven to eat.

Jesus therefore said unto them, Verily, verily, I say unto you, It was not Moses that gave you the bread out of heaven; but my Father giveth you the true bread out of heaven. For the bread of God is that which cometh down out of heaven, and giveth life unto the world.

They said therefore unto him, Lord, evermore give us this bread.

Jesus said unto them, I am the bread of life: he that cometh to me shall not hunger, and he that believeth on me shall never thirst. But I said unto you, that ye have seen me, and yet believe not.

II. Gospel (b), Mark 14. 43–50.
Jesus Meets the Traitor.

AND straightway, while he yet spake, cometh Judas, one of the twelve, and with him a multitude with swords and staves, from the chief priests and the scribes and the elders.

Now he that betrayed him had given them a token, saying, Whomsoever I shall kiss, that is he; take him, and lead him away safely. And when he was come, straightway he came to him, and saith, Rabbi; and kissed him. And they laid hands on him, and took him.

But a certain one of them that stood by drew his sword, and smote the servant of the high priest, and struck off his ear. And Jesus answered and said unto them, Are ye come out, as against a robber, with swords and staves to seize me? I was daily with you in the temple teaching, and ye took me not: but this is done that the scriptures might be fulfilled.

And they all left him, and fled.

III. Epistle, Jeremiah 20. 7–11.
Steadfastness in Trials.

O JEHOVAH, thou hast persuaded me, and I was persuaded; thou art stronger than I, and hast prevailed; I am become a laughing-stock all the day, every one mocketh me.

For as often as I speak, I cry out; I cry, Violence and destruction! because the word of Jehovah is made a reproach unto me, and a derision, all the day.

And if I say, I will not make mention of him, nor speak any more in his name, then there is in my heart as it were a burning fire shut up in my bones, and I am weary with forbearing, and I cannot contain.

For I have heard the defaming of many, terror on every side. Denounce, and we will denounce him, say all my familiar friends, they that watch for my fall; peradventure he will be persuaded, and we shall prevail against him, and we shall take our revenge on him.

But Jehovah is with me as a mighty one and a terrible: therefore my persecutors shall stumble and they shall not prevail; they shall be utterly put to shame, because they have not dealt wisely, even with an everlasting dishonor which shall never be forgotten.

III. Gospel (a), John 6. 52–66.
The True Food of the Soul.

THE Jews therefore strove one with another, saying, How can this man give us his flesh to eat?

Jesus therefore said unto them, Verily, verily, I say unto you, Except ye eat the flesh of the Son of man and drink his blood, ye have not life in yourselves. He that eateth my flesh and drinketh my blood hath eternal life; and I will raise him up at the last day. For my flesh is meat indeed, and my blood is drink indeed. He that eateth my flesh and drinketh my blood abideth in me, and I in him. As the living Father sent me, and I live because of the Father; so he that eateth me, he also shall live because of me. This is the bread which came down out of heaven: not as the fathers ate, and died; he that eateth this bread shall live for ever.

These things said he in the synagogue, as he taught in Capernaum.

Many therefore of his disciples, when they heard this, said, This is a hard saying; who can hear it?

But Jesus knowing in himself that his disciples murmured at this, said unto them, Doth this cause you to stumble? What then if ye should behold the Son of man ascending where he was before? It is the spirit that giveth life; the flesh profiteth nothing: the words that I have spoken unto you are spirit, and are life. But there are some of you that believe not.

For Jesus knew from the beginning who they were that believed not, and who it was that should betray him.

And he said, For this cause have I said unto you, that no man can come unto me, except it be given unto him of the Father.

Upon this many of his disciples went back, and walked no more with him.

III. GOSPEL (b), John 18. 15–27.

Peter's Denial.

AND Simon Peter followed Jesus, and so did another disciple. Now that disciple was known unto the high priest, and entered in with Jesus into the court of the high priest; but Peter was standing at the door without. So the other disciple, who was known unto the high priest, went out and spake unto her that kept the door, and brought in Peter. The maid therefore that kept the door saith unto Peter, Art thou also one of this man's disciples? He saith, I am not. Now the servants and the officers were standing there, having made a fire of coals; for it was cold; and they were warming themselves: and Peter also was with them, standing and warming himself.

The high priest therefore asked Jesus of his disciples, and of his teaching. Jesus answered him, I have spoken openly to the world; I ever taught in synagogues, and in the temple, where all the Jews come together; and in secret spake I nothing. Why askest thou me? ask them that have heard me, what I spake unto them: behold, these know the things which I said. And when he had said this, one of the officers standing by struck Jesus with his hand, saying, Answerest thou the high priest so? Jesus answered him, If I have spoken evil, bear witness of the evil: but if well, why smitest thou me? Annas therefore sent him bound unto Caiaphas the high priest.

Now Simon Peter was standing and warming himself. They said therefore unto him, Art thou also one of his disciples? He denied, and said, I am not. One of the servants of the high priest, being a kinsman of him whose ear Peter cut off, saith, Did not I see thee in the garden with him? Peter therefore denied again: and straightway the cock crew.

FIFTH SUNDAY IN LENT.

Hatred Increasing.—Jesus Condemned to Death.

Collect. We beseech Thee, Almighty God, mercifully to look upon Thy people, that by Thy great goodness they may be governed and preserved evermore, both in body and soul; through Jesus Christ, Thy Son, our Lord. AMEN.

I. EPISTLE, Hebrews 9. 11–15.

The Death of Christ Cleansing the Conscience.

CHRIST having come a high priest of the good things to come, through the greater and more perfect tabernacle, not made wih hands, that is to say, not of this creation, nor yet through the blood of goats and calves, but through his own blood, entered in once for all into the holy place, having obtained eternal redemption.

For if the blood of goats and bulls, and the ashes of a heifer sprinkling them that have been defiled, sanctify unto the cleanness of the flesh: how much more shall the blood of Christ, who through the eternal Spirit offered himself without blemish unto God, cleanse your conscience from dead works to serve the living God?

And for this cause he is the mediator

of a new covenant, that a death having taken place for the redemption of the transgressions that were under the first covenant, they that have been called may receive the promise of the eternal inheritance.

I. GOSPEL (a), John 8. 46–59.

The Hatred of the Jews against Jesus.

Jesus said unto the Jews:

WHICH of you convicteth me of sin? If I say truth, why do ye not believe me? He that is of God heareth the words of God: for this cause ye hear them not, because ye are not of God.

The Jews answered and said unto him. Say we not well that thou art a Samaritan, and hast a demon?

Jesus answered, I have not a demon; but I honor my Father, and ye dishonor me. But I seek not mine own glory: there is one that seeketh and judgeth. Verily, verily, I say unto you, If a man keep my word, he shall never see death.

The Jews said unto him, Now we know that thou hast a demon. Abraham died, and the prophets: and thou sayest, If a man keep my word, he shall never taste of death. Art thou greater than our father Abraham, who died? and the prophets died: whom makest thou thyself?

Jesus answered, If I glorify myself, my glory is nothing: it is my father that glorifieth me; of whom ye say, that he is your God; and ye have not known him: but I know him; and if I should say, I know him not, I shall be like unto you, a liar: but I know him, and keep his word. Your father Abraham rejoiced to see my day; and he saw it, and was glad.

The Jews therefore said unto him, Thou art not yet fifty years old, and hast thou seen Abraham? Jesus said unto them, Verily, verily, I say unto you, Before Abraham was born, I am.

They took up stones therefore to cast at him: but Jesus hid himself, and went out of the temple.

I. Gospel (b), Matthew 27. 15–26.

Barabbas or Jesus.

NOW at the feast the governor was wont to release unto the multitude one prisoner, whom they would. And they had then a notable prisoner, called Barabbas. When therefore they were gathered together, Pilate said unto them, Whom will ye that I release unto you? Barabbas, or Jesus who is called Christ? For he knew that for envy they had delivered him up.

And while he was sitting on the judgment-seat, his wife sent unto him, saying, Have thou nothing to do with that righteous man; for I have suffered many things this day in a dream because of him.

Now the chief priests and the elders persuaded the multitudes that they should ask for Barabbas, and destroy Jesus. But the governor answered and said unto them, Which of the two will ye that I release unto you? And they said, Barabbas. Pilate saith unto them, What then shall I do unto Jesus who is called Christ? They all say, Let him be crucified. And he said, Why, what evil hath he done? But they cried out exceedingly, saying, Let him be crucified.

So when Pilate saw that he prevailed nothing, but rather that a tumult was arising, he took water, and washed his hands before the multitude, saying, I am innocent of the blood of this righteous man; see ye to it. And all the people answered and said, His blood be on us, and on our children.

Then released he unto them Barabbas; but Jesus he scourged and delivered to be crucified.

II. Epistle, Psalm 69. 6–16.

The Distressed Soul Crying unto God.

LET not them that wait for thee be put to shame through me, O Lord Jehovah of hosts:
Let not those that seek thee be brought to dishonor through me, O God of Israel.
Because for thy sake I have borne reproach;
Shame hath covered my face.
I am become a stranger unto my brethren,
And an alien unto my mother's children.
For the zeal of thy house hath eaten me up;
And the reproaches of them that reproach thee are fallen upon me.
When I wept, and chastened my soul with fasting,
That was to my reproach.
When I made sackcloth my clothing,
I became a byword unto them.
They that sit in the gate talk of me;
And I am the song of the drunkards.
But as for me. my prayer is unto thee, O Jehovah, in an acceptable time:
O God, in the abundance of thy lovingkindness,
Answer me in the truth of thy salvation.
Deliver me out of the mire, and let me not sink:
Let me be delivered from them that hate me, and out of the deep waters.
Let not the waterflood overwhelm me, Neither let the deep swallow me up;
And let not the pit shut its mouth upon me.
Answer me, O Jehovah; for thy lovingkindness is good:
According to the multitude of thy tender mercies turn thou unto me.

II. Gospel (a), John 11. 47–57.

Caiaphas Urging the Death of Jesus.

THE chief priests therefore and the Pharisees gathered a council, and said, What do we? for this man doeth many signs. If we let him thus alone, all men will believe on him: and the Romans will come and take away both our place and our nation.

But a certain one of them, Caiaphas, being high priest that year, said unto them, Ye know nothing at all, nor do ye take account that it is expedient for you that one man should die for the people, and that the whole nation perish not.

Now this he said not of himself: but being high priest that year, he prophesied that Jesus should die for the nation;

and not for the nation only, but that he might also gather together into one the children of God that are scattered abroad.

So from that day forth they took counsel that they might put him to death.

Jesus therefore walked no more openly among the Jews, but departed thence into the country near to the wilderness, into a city called Ephraim; and there he tarried with the disciples.

Now the passover of the Jews was at hand: and many went up to Jerusalem out of the country before the passover, to purify themselves. They sought therefore for Jesus, and spake one with another, as they stood in the temple, What think ye? That he will not come to the feast? Now the chief priests and the Pharisees had given commandment, that, if any man knew where he was, he should show it, that they might take him.

II. Gospel (b), Luke 23. 1–12.

Christ before Pilate and Herod.

AND the whole company of them rose up, and brought him before Pilate. And they began to accuse him, saying, We found this man perverting our nation, and forbidding to give tribute to Cæsar, and saying that he himself is Christ a king.

And Pilate asked him, saying, Art thou the King of the Jews? And he answered him and said, Thou sayest.

And Pilate said unto the chief priests and the multitudes, I find no fault in this man. But they were the more urgent, saying, He stirreth up the people, teaching throughout all Judæa, and beginning from Galilee even unto this place. But when Pilate heard it, he asked whether the man were a Galilæan. And when he knew that he was of Herod's jurisdiction, he sent him unto Herod, who himself also was at Jerusalem in these days.

Now when Herod saw Jesus, he was exceeding glad: for he was of a long time desirous to see him because he had heard concerning him, and he hoped to see some miracle done by him. And he questioned him in many words; but he answered him nothing. And the chief priests and the scribes stood, vehemently accusing him. And Herod with his soldiers set him at nought, and mocked him, and arraying him in gorgeous apparel sent him back to Pilate. And Herod and Pilate became friends with each other that very day: for before they were at enmity between themselves.

III. Epistle, 2 Corinthians 1. 3–7.

God Comforting the Suffering Soul.

BLESSED be the God and Father of our Lord Jesus Christ, the Father of mercies and God of all comfort; who comforteth us in all our affliction, that we may be able to comfort them that are in any affliction, through the comfort wherewith we ourselves are comforted of God. For as the sufferings of Christ abound unto us, even so our comfort also aboundeth through Christ. But whether we are afflicted, it is for your comfort and salvation; or whether we are comforted, it is for your comfort, which worketh in the patient enduring of the same suffering which we also suffer: and our hope for you is stedfast; knowing that, as ye are partakers of the sufferings, so also are ye of the comfort.

III. Gospel (a), John 8. 31–45.

Jesus Exposes the Plot of the Jews.

JESUS therefore said to those Jews that had believed him, If ye abide in my word, then are ye truly my disciples; and ye shall know the truth, and the truth shall make you free.

They answered unto him, We are Abraham's seed, and have never yet been in bondage to any man: how sayest thou, Ye shall be made free?

Jesus answered them, Verily, verily, I say unto you, Every one that committeth sin is the bondservant of sin. And the bondservant abideth not in the house for ever: the son abideth for ever. If therefore the Son shall make you free, ye shall be free indeed. I know that ye are Abraham's seed; yet ye seek to kill me, because my word hath not free course in you. I speak the things which I have seen with my Father: and ye also do the things which ye heard from your father.

They answered and said unto him, Our father is Abraham.

Jesus saith unto them, If ye were Abraham's children, ye would do the works of Abraham. But now ye seek to kill me, a man that hath told you the truth, which I heard from God: this did not Abraham. Ye do the works of your father.

They said unto him, We were not born of fornication; we have one Father, even God.

Jesus said unto them, If God were your Father, ye would love me: for I came forth and am come from God; for neither have I come of myself, but he sent me. Why do ye not understand my speech? Even because ye cannot hear my word. Ye are of your father the devil, and the lusts of your father it is your will to do. He was a murderer from the beginning, and standeth not in the truth, because there is no truth in him. When he speaketh a lie, he speaketh of his own: for he is a liar, and the father thereof. But because I say the truth, ye believe me not.

III. GOSPEL (b), John 19. 1–11.

Jesus Crowned with Thorns.

PILATE therefore took Jesus, and scourged him. And the soldiers platted a crown of thorns, and put it on his head, and arrayed him in a purple garment; and they came unto him and said, Hail, King of the Jews! and they struck him with their hands.

And Pilate went out again, and saith unto them, Behold, I bring him out to you, that ye may know that I find no crime in him. Jesus therefore came out, wearing the crown of thorns and the purple garment. And Pilate saith unto them, Behold, the man! When therefore the chief priests and the officers saw him, they cried out, saying, Crucify him, crucify him! Pilate saith unto them, Take him yourselves, and crucify him: for I find no crime in him. The Jews answered him, We have a law, and by that law he ought to die, because he made himself the Son of God.

When Pilate therefore heard this saying he was the more afraid; and he entered into the Prætorium again, and saith unto Jesus, Whence art thou? But Jesus gave him no answer. Pilate therefore said unto him, Speakest thou not unto me? knowest thou not that I have power to release thee, and have power to crucify thee? Jesus answered him, Thou wouldest have no power against me, except it were given thee from above: therefore he that delivered me unto thee hath greater sin.

PALM SUNDAY.

The Last Farewell.

Collect. Almighty and eternal God, who hast sent Thy Son, our Saviour Jesus Christ, to take upon Him our flesh, and to suffer death upon the cross: mercifully grant that we may follow the example of His patience, and obey Thy holy will; through the same Jesus Christ, Thy Son, our Lord. AMEN.

I. EPISTLE, Philippians 2. 5–11.

The Self-humiliation and Exaltation of Christ.

HAVE this mind in you, which was also in Christ Jesus: who existing in the form of God, counted not the being on an equality with God a thing to be grasped, but emptied himself, taking the form of a servant, being made in the likeness of men; and being found in fashion as a man, he humbled himself, becoming obedient even unto death, yea, the death of the cross. Wherefore God also highly exalted him, and gave unto him the name which is above every name; that in the name of Jesus every knee should bow, of things in heaven and things on earth and things under the earth, and that every tongue should confess that Jesus Christ is Lord, to the glory of God the Father.

I. GOSPEL, John 12. 1–16.

The Departure of Jesus from Bethany.

JESUS therefore six days before the passover came to Bethany, where Lazarus was, whom Jesus raised from the dead. So they made him a supper there: and Martha served; but Lazarus was one of them that sat at meat with him.

Mary therefore took a pound of ointment of pure nard, very precious, and anointed the feet of Jesus, and wiped his feet with her hair: and the house was filled with the odor of the ointment.

But Judas Iscariot, one of his disciples, that should betray him, saith, Why was not this ointment sold for three hundred shillings, and given to the poor? Now this he said, not because he cared for the poor; but because he was a thief, and having the bag took away what was put therein. Jesus therefore said, Suffer her to keep it against the day of my burying. For the poor ye have always with you; but me ye have not always.

The common people therefore of the Jews learned that he was there: and they came, not for Jesus' sake only, but that they might see Lazarus also, whom he had raised from the dead. But the chief priests took counsel that they might put Lazarus also to death; because that by reason of him many of the Jews went away, and believed on Jesus.

On the morrow a great multitude that had come to the feast, when they heard that Jesus was coming to Jerusalem, took the branches of the palm trees, and went forth to meet him, and cried out, Hosanna: blessed is he that cometh in the name of the Lord, even the King of

Israel. And Jesus, having found a young ass, sat thereon; as it is written, Fear not, daughter of Zion: behold, thy King cometh, sitting on an ass's colt. These things understood not his disciples at the first: but when Jesus was glorified, then remembered they that these things were written of him, and that they had done these things unto him.

II. EPISTLE, John 6. 32–35.

Jesus the Bread of Life.

JESUS therefore said unto them, Verily, verily, I say unto you, It was not Moses that gave you the bread out of heaven; but my Father giveth you the true bread out of heaven. For the bread of God is that which cometh down out of heaven, and giveth life unto the world.

They said therefore unto him, Lord, evermore give us this bread.

Jesus said unto them, I am the bread of life: he that cometh to me shall not hunger, and he that believeth on me shall never thirst.

II. GOSPEL, 1 Corinthians 11. 23–29.

The Lord's Supper.

I RECEIVED of the Lord that which also I delivered unto you, that the Lord Jesus in the night in which he was betrayed took bread; and when he had given thanks, he brake it, and said, This is my body, which is for you: this do in remembrance of me.

In like manner also the cup, after supper, saying, This cup is the new covenant in my blood: this do as often as ye drink it, in remembrance of me.

For as often as ye eat this bread, and drink the cup, ye proclaim the Lord's death till he come. Wherefore whosoever shall eat the bread or drink the cup of the Lord in an unworthy manner, shall be guilty of the body and the blood of the Lord. But let a man prove himself, and so let him eat of the bread, and drink of the cup. For he that eateth and drinketh, eateth and drinketh judgment unto himself, if he discern not the body.

III. EPISTLE, Hebrews 8. 8–12.

The New Covenant.

BEHOLD, the days come, saith the Lord,
That I will make a new covenant with the house of Israel and with the house of Judah;

Not according to the covenant that I made with their fathers
In the day that I took them by the hand to lead them forth out of the land of Egypt;
For they continued not in my covenant,
And I regarded them not, saith the Lord.
For this is the covenant that I will make with the house of Israel
After those days, saith the Lord;
I will put my laws into their mind,
And on their heart also will I write them:
And I will be to them a God,
And they shall be to me a people:
And they shall not teach every man his fellow-citizen,
And every man his brother, saying, Know the Lord:
For all shall know me,
From the least to the greatest of them.
For I will be merciful to their iniquities,
And their sins will I remember no more.

III. GOSPEL, Luke 22. 14–22.

The First Communion.

AND when the hour was come, he sat down, and the apostles with him. And he said unto them, With desire I have desired to eat this passover with you before I suffer: for I say unto you, I shall not eat it, until it be fulfilled in the kingdom of God.

And he received a cup, and when he had given thanks, he said, Take this, and divide it among yourselves: for I say unto you, I shall not drink from henceforth of the fruit of the vine, until the kingdom of God shall come.

And he took bread, and when he had given thanks, he brake it, and gave to them, saying, This is my body which is given for you: this do in remembrance of me.

And the cup in like manner after supper, saying, This cup is the new covenant in my blood, even that which is poured out for you. But behold, the hand of him that betrayeth me is with me on the table. For the Son of man indeed goeth, as it hath been determined: but woe unto that man through whom he is betrayed!

GOOD FRIDAY.

The Crucifixion.

Collect. O Lord God, Heavenly Father, who hast not spared Thine only Son, but delivered Him up for us all, that He might bear our sins upon the cross: grant that our hearts may be so fixed with steadfast faith in Him, that we may obtain remission of sin and redemption from eternal death; through the same our Lord Jesus Christ. AMEN.

I. EPISTLE (a). Philippians 2. 5–11.

Christ's Self-humiliation and Exaltation.

HAVE this mind in you which was also in Christ Jesus: who, existing in the form of God, counted not the being on an equality with God a thing to be grasped, but emptied himself, taking the form of a servant, being made in the likeness of men; and being found in fashion as a man, he humbled himself, becoming obedient even unto death, yea, the death of the cross. Wherefore also God highly exalted him, and gave unto him the name which is above every name; that in the name of Jesus every knee should bow, of things in heaven and things on earth and things under the earth, and that every tongue should confess that Jesus Christ is Lord, to the glory of God the Father.

I. EPISTLE (b), Isaiah 52. 13,—53. 12.

The Suffering Servant of Jehovah.

BEHOLD, my servant shall deal wisely, he shall be exalted and lifted up, and shall be very high. Like as many were astonished at thee (his visage was so marred more than any man, and his form more than the sons of men), so shall he sprinkle many nations; kings shall shut their mouths at him: for that which had not been told them shall they see; and that which they had not heard shall they understand.

Who hath believed our message? and to whom hath the arm of Jehovah been revealed? For he grew up before him as a tender plant, and as a root out of a dry ground: he hath no form nor comeliness; and when we see him, there is no beauty that we should desire him. He was despised, and rejected of men; a man of sorrows, and acquainted with grief: and as one from whom men hide their face he was despised; and we esteemed him not.

Surely he hath borne our griefs, and carried our sorrows; yet we did esteem him stricken, smitten of God, and afflicted. But he was wounded for our transgressions, he was bruised for our iniquities; the chastisement of our peace was upon him; and with his stripes we are healed. All we like sheep have gone astray; we have turned every one to his own way; and Jehovah hath laid on him the iniquity of us all.

He was oppressed, yet when he was afflicted he opened not his mouth; as a lamb that is led to the slaughter, and as a sheep that before its shearers is dumb, so he opened not his mouth. By oppression and judgment he was taken away; and as for his generation, who among them considered that he was cut off out of the land of the living for the transgression of my people to whom the stroke was due? And they made his grave with the wicked, and with a rich man in his death; although he had done no violence, neither was any deceit in his mouth.

Yet it pleased Jehovah to bruise him; he hath put him to grief: when thou shalt make his soul an offering for sin, he shall see his seed, he shall prolong his days, and the pleasure of Jehovah shall prosper in his hand. He shall see of the travail of his soul, and shall be satisfied: by the knowledge of himself shall my righteous servant justify many; and he shall bear their iniquities. Therefore will I divide him a portion with the great, and he shall divide the spoil with the strong; because he poured out his soul unto death, and was numbered with the transgressors: yet he bare the sin of many, and made intercession for the transgressors.

I. GOSPEL, Luke 23. 32–43*

Christ on the Cross.

AND there were also two others, malefactors, led with him to be put to death.

And when they came unto the place which is called The skull, there they crucified him, and the malefactors, one on the right hand and the other on the left.

And Jesus said, Father, forgive them; for they know not what they do.

And parting his garments among them, they cast lots. And the people stood beholding. And the rulers also scoffed at him, saying, He saved others; let him save himself, if this be the Christ of God, his chosen. And the rulers also mocked

*The Fifth Part of the Passion History should be used as the text for the morning sermon on Good Friday, and the Sixth Part for the evening sermon.

him, coming to him, offering him vinegar, and saying, If thou art the King of the Jews, save thyself. And there was also a superscription over him, THIS IS THE KING OF THE JEWS.

And one of the malefactors that were hanged railed on him, saying, Art not thou the Christ? save thyself and us. But the other answered, and rebuking him said, Dost thou not even fear God, seeing thou art in the same condemnation? And we indeed justly; for we receive the due reward of our deeds: but this man hath done nothing amiss. And he said, Jesus, remember me when thou comest in thy kingdom. And he said unto him, Verily I say unto thee, To-day shalt thou be with me in Paradise.

EASTER DAY.

The Resurrection of Christ.

Collect. [EARLY SERVICE.] Almighty God, who through Thine only-begotten Son, Jesus Christ, hast overcome death, and opened unto us the gate of everlasting life: we humbly beseech Thee, that we who celebrate the solemnities of His Resurrection may by the renewal of the Holy Spirit rise again from the death of the soul; through Jesus Christ, our Lord, who liveth and reigneth with Thee and the Holy Spirit, ever one God, world without end. AMEN.

Collect. Almighty and eternal God, Thou Who didst deliver Thy people out of Egypt by the hand of Thy servant Moses, and didst command them to observe the Passover and eat the paschal lamb: bring us also, O heavenly Father, out of the spiritual Egypt, and make us partakers of the true Paschal Lamb, Jesus Christ, our Lord, who this day hath conquered death, and opened the way to eternal life, and now liveth and reigneth with Thee and the Holy Spirit, ever one God, world without end. AMEN.

I. EPISTLE (a), 1 Corinthians 5. 7, 8.

Preparing for the Passover.

PURGE out the old leaven, that ye may be a new lump, even as ye are unleavened. For our passover also hath been sacrificed, even Christ: wherefore let us keep the feast, not with old leaven, neither with the leaven of malice and wickedness, but with the unleavened bread of sincerity and truth.

I. EPISTLE (b), 1 Corinthians 15. 53–58.

God Hath Given the Victory.

THIS corruptible must put on incorruption, and this mortal must put on immortality. But when this corruptible shall have put on incorruption, and this mortal shall have put on immortality, then shall come to pass the saying that is written, Death is swallowed up in victory.

O death, where is thy victory? O death, where is thy sting? The sting of death is sin; and the power of sin is the law: but thanks be to God, who giveth us the victory through our Lord Jesus Christ.

Wherefore, my beloved brethren, be ye stedfast, unmovable, always abounding in the work of the Lord, forasmuch as ye know that your labor is not vain in the Lord.

I. GOSPEL, Mark 16. 1–8.

The Resurrection.

AND when the sabbath was past, Mary Magdalene, and Mary the mother of James, and Salome, bought spices, that they might come and anoint him. And very early on the first day of the week, they come to the tomb when the sun was risen.

And they were saying among themselves, Who shall roll us away the stone from the door of the tomb? and looking up, they see that the stone is rolled back: for it was exceeding great.

And entering into the tomb, they saw a young man sitting on the right side, arrayed in a white robe; and they were amazed. And he saith unto them, Be not amazed: ye seek Jesus, the Nazarene, who hath been crucified: he is risen; he is not here: behold, the place where they laid him! But go, tell his disciples and Peter, He goeth before you into Galilee: there shall ye see him, as he said unto you.

And they went out, and fled from the tomb; for trembling and astonishment had come upon them: and they said nothing to any one; for they were afraid.

II. EPISTLE, 1 Corinthians 15. 12–21.

Christ the Earnest of Our Resurrection.

NOW if Christ is preached that he hath been raised from the dead, how say some among you that there is no resurrection of the dead? But if there is no resurrection of the dead, neither hath Christ been raised: and if Christ hath not been raised, then is our preaching vain, your faith also is vain. Yea, and we are found false witnesses of God; because we witnessed of God that he raised up Christ: whom he raised not up, if so be that the dead are not raised. For if the dead are not raised, neither hath Christ been raised: and if Christ hath not been raised, your faith is vain; ye are yet in your sins. Then they also that are fallen asleep in Christ have perished. If we have only hoped in Christ in this life, we are of all men most pitiable.

But now hath Christ been raised from the dead, the firstfruits of them that are asleep. For since by man came death, by man came also the resurrection of the dead.

II. GOSPEL, John 20. 10–18.
The First Meeting with the Risen Saviour.

SO the disciples went away again unto their own home.

But Mary was standing without at the tomb weeping: so, as she wept, she stooped and looked into the tomb; and she beholdeth two angels in white sitting, one at the head, and one at the feet, where the body of Jesus had lain. And they say unto her, Woman, why weepest thou? She saith unto them, Because they have taken away my Lord, and I know not where they have laid him.

When she had thus said, she turned herself back, and beholdeth Jesus standing, and knew not that it was Jesus. Jesus saith unto her, Woman, why weepest thou? whom seekest thou? She, supposing him to be the gardner, saith unto him, Sir, if thou hast borne him hence, tell me where thou hast laid him, and I will take him away. Jesus saith unto her, Mary. She turneth herself, and saith unto him in Hebrew, Rabboni; which is to say, Teacher. Jesus saith to her, Touch me not; for I am not yet ascended unto the Father: but go unto my brethren, and say to them, I ascend unto my Father and your Father, and my God and your God.

Mary Magdalene cometh and telleth the disciples, I have seen the Lord; and that he had said these things unto her.

III. EPISTLE, Ephesians 1. 15–23.
The Resurrection of Christ Revealing the Power of God.

FOR this cause I also, having heard of the faith in the Lord Jesus which is among you, and the love which ye show toward all the saints, cease not to give thanks for you, making mention of you in my prayers; that the God of our Lord Jesus Christ, the Father of glory, may give unto you a spirit of wisdom and revelation in the knowledge of him; having the eyes of your heart enlightened, that ye may know what is the hope of his calling, what the riches of the glory of his inheritance in the saints, and what the exceeding greatness of his power to usward who believe, according to that working of the strength of his might which he wrought in Christ, when he raised him from the dead, and made him to sit at his right hand in the heavenly places, far above all rule, and authority, and power, and dominion, and every name that is named, not only in this world, but also in that which is to come: and he put all things in subjection under his feet, and gave him to be head over all things to the church, which is his body, the fulness of him that filleth all in all.

III. GOSPEL, Matthew 28. 1–8.
The Message of the Resurrection.

NOW late on the sabbath day, as it began to dawn toward the first day of the week, came Mary Magdalene and the other Mary to see the sepulchre.

And behold, there was a great earthquake; for an angel of the Lord descended from heaven, and came and rolled away the stone, and sat upon it. His appearance was as lightning, and his raiment white as snow: and for fear of him the watchers did quake, and became as dead men.

And the angel answered and said unto the women, Fear not ye; for I know that ye seek Jesus, who hath been crucified. He is not here; for he is risen, even as he said. Come, see the place where the Lord lay. And go quickly, and tell his disciples, He is risen from the dead; and lo, he goeth before you into Galilee; there shall ye see him: lo, I have told you.

And they departed quickly from the tomb with fear and great joy, and ran to bring his disciples word.

EASTER MONDAY.

The Witnesses of the Resurrection.

Collect. O God, who didst grant Thy Son Jesus Christ eternal victory over death, and who through Him didst open unto us the way of life: grant fulfillment, we pray Thee, to the longing for life and immortality which Thou hast kindled in our hearts; through the same Thy Son, Jesus Christ, our Lord. AMEN.

I. EPISTLE, Acts 10. 34–43.

The Risen Christ Proclaimed to the Gentiles.

AND Peter opened his mouth, and said, Of a truth I perceive that God is no respecter of persons: but in every nation he that feareth him, and worketh righteousness, is acceptable to him. The word which he sent unto the children of Israel, preaching good tidings of peace by Jesus Christ (he is Lord of all)—that saying ye yourselves know, which was published throughout all Judæa, beginning from Galilee, after the baptism which John preached; even Jesus of Nazareth, how God anointed him with the Holy Spirit and with power: who went about doing good, and healing all that were oppressed of the devil; for God was with him.

And we are witnesses of all things which he did both in the country of the Jews, and in Jerusalem; whom also they slew, hanging him on a tree. Him God raised up the third day, and gave him to be made manifest, not to all the people, but unto witnesses that were chosen before of God, even to us, who ate and drank with him after he rose from the dead. And he charged us to preach unto the people, and to testify that this is he who is ordained of God to be the Judge of the living and the dead. To him bear all the prophets witness, that through his name every one that believeth on him shall receive remission of sins.

I. GOSPEL, Luke 24. 13–35.

The Disciples in Emmaus.

AND behold, two of them were going that very day to a village named Emmaus, which was threescore furlongs from Jerusalem. And they communed with each other of all these things which had happened.

And it came to pass, while they communed together and questioned together, that Jesus himself drew near, and went with them. But their eyes were holden that they should not know him. And he said unto them, What communications are these that ye have one with another, as ye walk?

And they stood still, looking sad. And one of them, named Cleopas, answering said unto him, Dost thou alone sojourn in Jerusalem and not know the things which are come to pass there in these days?

And he said unto them, What things? And they said unto him, The things concerning Jesus the Nazarene, who was a prophet mighty in deed and word before God and all the people: and how the chief priests and our rulers delivered him up to be condemned to death, and crucified him. But we hoped that it was he who should redeem Israel. Yea and besides all this, it is now the third day since these things came to pass. Moreover certain women of our company amazed us, having been early at the tomb; and when they found not his body, they came, saying, that they had also seen a vision of angels, who said that he was alive. And certain of them that were with us went to the tomb, and found it even so as the women had said: but him they saw not.

And he said unto them, O foolish men, and slow of heart to believe in all that the prophets have spoken? Behooved it not the Christ to suffer these things, and to enter into his glory? And beginning from Moses and from all the prophets, he interpreted to them in all the scriptures the things concerning himself.

And they drew nigh unto the village, whither they were going: and he made as though he would go further. And they constrained him, saying, Abide with us; for it is toward evening, and the day is now far spent. And he went in to abide with them. And it came to pass, when he had sat down with them to meat, he took the bread and blessed; and breaking it he gave to them. And their eyes were opened, and they knew him; and he vanished out of their sight.

And they said one to another, Was not our heart burning within us, while he spake to us in the way, while he opened to us the scriptures?

And they rose up that very hour, and returned to Jerusalem, and found the eleven gathered together, and them that were with them, saying, The Lord is risen indeed, and hath appeared to Simon. And they rehearsed the things that happened in the way, and how he was known of them in the breaking of the bread.

II. Epistle, 2 Corinthians 5. 14–21.

The Believer a New Creature.

THE love of Christ constraineth us; because we thus judge, that one died for all, therefore all died; and he died for all, that they that live should no longer live unto themselves, but unto him who for their sakes died and rose again. Wherefore we henceforth know no man after the flesh: even though we have known Christ after the flesh, yet now we know him so no more.

Wherefore if any man is in Christ, he is a new creature: the old things are passed away; behold, they are become new. But all things are of God, who reconciled us to himself through Christ, and gave unto us the ministry of reconciliation; to wit, that God was in Christ reconciling the world unto himself, not reckoning unto them their trespasses, and having committed unto us the word of reconciliation.

We are ambassadors therefore on behalf of Christ, as though God were entreating by us: we beseech you on behalf of Christ, be ye reconciled to God. Him who knew no sin he made to be sin on our behalf; that we might become the righteousness of God in him.

II. Gospel, John 20. 1–10.

The Disciples at the Tomb.

NOW on the first day of the week cometh Mary Magdalene early, while it was yet dark, unto the tomb, and seeth the stone taken away from the tomb.

She runneth therefore, and cometh to Simon Peter, and to the other disciple whom Jesus loved, and saith unto them, They have taken away the Lord out of the tomb, and we know not where they have laid him.

Peter therefore went forth, and the other disciple, and they went toward the tomb. And they ran both together: and the other disciple outran Peter, and came first to the tomb; and stooping and looking in, he seeth the linen cloths lying; yet entered he not in.

Simon Peter therefore also cometh, following him, and entered into the tomb; and he beholdeth the linen cloths lying, and the napkin, that was upon his head, not lying with the linen cloths, but rolled up in a place by itself. Then entered in therefore the other disciple also, who came first to the tomb, and he saw, and believed. For as yet they knew not the scripture, that he must rise again from the dead.

So the disciples went away again unto their own home.

III. Epistle, 1 Peter 1. 18–23.

The Resurrection of Christ Begets a Living Hope.

YE were redeemed, not with corruptible things, with silver or gold, from your vain manner of life handed down from your fathers; but with precious blood, as of a lamb without blemish and without spot, even the blood of Christ: who was foreknown indeed before the foundation of the world, but was manifested at the end of the times for your sake, who through him are believers in God, that raised him from the dead, and gave him glory; so that your faith and hope might be in God. Seeing ye have purified your souls in your obedience to the truth unto unfeigned love of the brethren, love one another from the heart fervently: having been begotten again, not of corruptible seed, but of incorruptible, through the word of God, which liveth and abideth.

III. Gospel, Matthew 28. 8–15.

The Guards of the Tomb.

AND they departed quickly from the tomb with fear and great joy, and ran to bring his disciples word. And behold, Jesus met them, saying, All hail. And they came and took hold of his feet, and worshipped him. Then saith Jesus unto them, Fear not: go tell my brethren that they depart into Galilee, and there shall they see me.

Now while they were going, behold, some of the guard came into the city, and told unto the chief priests all the things that were come to pass.

And when they were assembled with the elders, and had taken counsel, they gave much money unto the soldiers, saying, Say ye, His disciples came by night, and stole him away while we slept. And if this come to the governor's ears, we will persuade him, and rid you of care.

So they took the money, and did as they were taught: and this saying was spread abroad among the Jews, and continueth until this day.

FIRST SUNDAY AFTER EASTER.

The Lord Liveth.

Collect. Grant, we beseech Thee, almighty God, that we, who have celebrated the solemnities of the Lord's Resurrection, may keep in our hearts Thy gracious gift, so that we may die daily unto sin and arise unto newness of life; through Thy Son, Jesus Christ, our Lord. AMEN.

I. EPISTLE, 1 John 5. 4–10.

Faith in the Risen Lord Overcometh the World.

WHATSOEVER is begotten of God overcometh the world: and this is the victory that hath overcome the world, even our faith. And who is he that overcometh the world, but he that believeth that Jesus is the Son of God?

This is he that came by water and blood, even Jesus Christ; not with the water only, but with the water and with the blood. And it is the Spirit that beareth witness, because the Spirit is the truth. For there are three who bear witness, the Spirit, and the water, and the blood: and the three agree in one.

If we receive the witness of men, the witness of God is greater: for the witness of God is this, that he hath borne witness concerning his Son. He that believeth on the Son of God hath the witness in him: he that believeth not God hath made him a liar; because he hath not believed in the witness that God hath borne concerning his Son.

I. GOSPEL, John 20. 19–31.

Jesus and Thomas.

WHEN therefore it was evening, on that day, the first day of the week, and when the doors were shut where the disciples were, for fear of the Jews, Jesus came and stood in the midst, and saith unto them, Peace be unto you. And when he had said this, he showed unto them his hands and his side. The disciples therefore were glad, when they saw the Lord.

Jesus therefore said to them again, Peace be with you: as the Father hath sent me, even so send I you. And when he had said this, he breathed on them, and saith unto them, Receive ye the Holy Spirit: whose soever sins ye forgive, they are forgiven unto them; whose soever sins ye retain, they are retained.

But Thomas, one of the twelve, called Didymus, was not with them when Jesus came. The other disciples therefore said unto him, We have seen the Lord. But he said unto them, Except I shall see in his hands the print of the nails, and put my finger into the print of the nails, and put my hand into his side, I will not believe.

And after eight days again his disciples were within, and Thomas with them. Jesus cometh, the doors being shut, and stood in the midst, and said, Peace be unto you. Then saith he to Thomas, Reach hither thy finger, and see my hands; and reach hither thy hand, and put it into my side: and be not faithless, but believing. Thomas answered and said unto him, My Lord and my God. Jesus saith unto him, Because thou hast seen me, thou hast believed: blessed are they that have not seen, and yet have believed.

Many other signs therefore did Jesus in the presence of the disciples, which are not written in this book: but these are written, that ye may believe that Jesus is the Christ, the Son of God; and that believing ye may have life in his name.

II. EPISTLE, Acts 3. 12–20.

Peter Preaching the Risen Christ.

WHEN Peter saw it, he answered unto the people, Ye men of Israel, why marvel ye at this man? or why fasten ye your eyes on us, as though by our own power or godliness we had made him to walk? The God of Abraham, and of Isaac, and of Jacob, the God of our fathers, hath glorified his Servant Jesus; whom ye delivered up, and denied before the face of Pilate, when he had determined to release him. But ye denied the Holy and Righteous One, and asked for a murderer to be granted unto you, and killed the Prince of life; whom God raised from the dead; whereof we are witnesses. And by faith in his name hath his name made this man strong, whom ye behold and know: yea, the faith which is through him hath given him this perfect soundness in the presence of you all.

And now, brethren, I know that in ignorance ye did it, as did also the rulers. But the things which God foreshowed by the mouth of all the prophets, that his Christ should suffer, he thus fulfilled. Repent ye therefore, and turn again, that your sins may be blotted out, that so there may come seasons of refreshing from the presence of the Lord; and that he may send the Christ who hath been appointed for you, even Jesus.

II. GOSPEL, John 21. 1–14.

The Risen Saviour at the Sea of Tiberias.

JESUS manifested himself again to the disciples at the sea of Tiberias; and he manifested himself on this wise. There were together Simon Peter, and Thomas called Didymus, and Nathanael of Cana in Galilee, and the sons of Zebedee, and two other of his disciples.

Simon Peter saith unto them, I go a fishing. They say unto him, We also come with thee. They went forth and entered into the boat; and that night they took nothing.

But when day was now breaking, Jesus stood on the beach: yet the disciples knew not that it was Jesus. Jesus therefore saith unto them, Children, have ye aught to eat? They answered him, No. And he said unto them, Cast the net on the right side of the boat, and ye shall find. They cast therefore, and now they were not able to draw it for the multitude of fishes.

That disciple therefore whom Jesus loved saith unto Peter, It is the Lord. So when Simon Peter heard that it was the Lord, he girt his coat about him (for he was naked), and cast himself into the sea. But the other disciples came in the little boat (for they were not far from the land, but about two hundred cubits off), dragging the net full of fishes.

So when they got out upon the land, they see a fire of coals there, and fish laid thereon, and bread. Jesus saith unto them, Bring of the fish which ye have now taken. Simon Peter therefore went up, and drew the net to land, full of great fishes, a hundred and fifty and three: and for all there were so many, the net was not rent. Jesus saith unto them, Come and break your fast. And none of the disciples durst inquire of him, Who art thou? knowing that it was the Lord. Jesus cometh, and taketh the bread, and giveth them, and the fish likewise.

This is now the third time that Jesus was manifested to the disciples, after that he was risen from the dead.

III. EPISTLE, Acts 13. 32–41.

Paul Preaching the Risen Christ.

WE bring you good tidings of the promise made unto the fathers, that God hath fulfilled the same unto our children, in that he raised up Jesus; as also it is written in the second psalm, Thou art my Son, this day have I begotten thee. And as concerning that he raised him up from the dead, now no more to return to corruption, he hath spoken on this wise, I will give you the holy and sure blessings of David. Because he saith also in another psalm, Thou wilt not give thy Holy One to see corruption.

For David, after he had in his own generation served the counsel of God, fell asleep, and was laid unto his fathers, and saw corruption: but he whom God raised up saw no corruption.

Be it known unto you therefore, brethren, that through this man is proclaimed unto you remission of sins: and by him every one that believeth is justified from all things, from which ye could not be justified by the law of Moses. Beware therefore, lest that come upon you which is spoken in the prophets:

Behold, ye despisers, and wonder, and perish;

For I work a work in your days,

A work which ye shall in no wise believe, if one declare it unto you.

III. GOSPEL, John 21. 15–23.

"Lovest Thou Me?"

JESUS saith to Simon Peter, Simon, son of John, lovest thou me more than these? He saith unto him, Yea, Lord; thou knowest that I love thee. He saith unto him, Feed my lambs. He saith to him again a second time, Simon, son of John, lovest thou me? He saith unto him, Yea, Lord; thou knowest that I love thee. He saith unto him, Tend my sheep. He saith unto him the third time, Simon, son of John, lovest thou me? Peter was grieved because he said unto him the third time, Lovest thou me? And he said unto him, Lord, thou knowest all things; thou knowest that I love thee. Jesus saith unto him, Feed my sheep.

Verily, verily, I say unto thee, When thou wast young, thou girdedst thyself, and walkedst whither thou wouldest: but when thou shalt be old, thou shalt stretch forth thy hands, and another shall gird thee, and carry thee whither thou wouldest not. Now this he spake, signifying by what manner of death he should glorify God.

And when he had spoken this, he saith unto him, Follow me. Peter, turning about, seeth the disciple whom Jesus loved following; who also leaned back on his breast at the supper, and said, Lord, who is he that betrayeth thee? Peter therefore seeing him saith to Jesus, Lord, and what shall this man do? Jesus saith unto him, If I will that he tarry till I come, what is that to thee? follow thou me.

This saying therefore went forth among the brethren, that that disciple should not die: yet Jesus said not unto him, that he should not die; but, If I will that he tarry till I come, what is that to thee?

SECOND SUNDAY AFTER EASTER.

The Shepherd and the Sheep.

Collect. O God, who, by the humiliation of Thy Son, didst raise the fallen world: grant unto Thy faithful ones perpetual gladness, and those whom Thou hast delivered from the danger of everlasting death do Thou make partakers of eternal joys; through the same Jesus Christ, Thy Son, our Lord. AMEN.

I. EPISTLE, 1 Peter 2. 21–25.
In the Footsteps of Christ.

HEREUNTO were ye called: because Christ also suffered for you, leaving you an example, that ye should follow his steps: who did no sin, neither was guile found in his mouth: who, when he was reviled, reviled not again; when he suffered, threatened not; but committed himself to him that judgeth righteously: who his own self bare our sins in his body upon the tree, that we, having died unto sins, might live unto righteousness; by whose stripes ye were healed. For ye were going astray like sheep; but are now returned unto the Shepherd and Bishop of your souls.

I. GOSPEL, John 10. 11–16.
The Good Shepherd.

I AM the good shepherd: the good shepherd layeth down his life for the sheep.

He that is a hireling, and not a shepherd, whose own the sheep are not, beholdeth the wolf coming, and leaveth the sheep, and fleeth, and the wolf snatcheth them, and scattereth them: he fleeth because he is a hireling, and careth not for the sheep.

I am the good shepherd; and I know mine own, and mine own know me, even as the Father knoweth me, and I know the Father; and I lay down my life for the sheep.

And other sheep I have, which are not of this fold: them also I must bring, and they shall hear my voice; and they shall become one flock, one shepherd.

II. EPISTLE, Hebrews 13. 20, 21.
The Great Shepherd of the Sheep.

NOW the God of peace, who brought again from the dead the great shepherd of the sheep with the blood of an eternal covenant, even our Lord Jesus, make you perfect in every good thing to do his will, working in us that which is well-pleasing in his sight, through Jesus Christ; to whom be the glory for ever and ever. Amen.

II. GOSPEL, Matthew 9. 36–38.
Sheep without a Shepherd.

WHEN he saw the multitudes, he was moved with compassion for them, because they were distressed and scattered, as sheep not having a shepherd.

Then saith he unto his disciples, The harvest indeed is plenteous, but the laborers are few. Pray ye therefore the Lord of the harvest, that he send forth laborers into his harvest.

III. EPISTLE, Psalm 23.
The Lord Is My Shepherd.

JEHOVAH is my shepherd; I shall not want.

He maketh me to lie down in green pastures;
He leadeth me beside still waters.
He restoreth my soul:
He guideth me in the paths of righteousness for his name's sake.
Yea, though I walk through the valley of the shadow of death,
I will fear no evil; for thou art with me;
Thy rod and thy staff, they comfort me.
Thou preparest a table before me in the presence of mine enemies:
Thou hast anointed my head with oil;
My cup runneth over.
Surely goodness and lovingkindness shall follow me all the days of my life;
And I shall dwell in the house of Jehovah for ever.

III. GOSPEL, John 10. 1–10.
True Shepherd and True Sheep.

VERILY, verily, I say unto you, He that entereth not by the door into the fold of the sheep, but climbeth up some other way, the same is a thief and a robber. But he that entereth in by the door is the shepherd of the sheep. To him the porter openeth; and the sheep hear his voice: and he calleth his own sheep by name, and leadeth them out. When he hath put forth all his own, he goeth before them, and the sheep follow him: for they know his voice. And a stranger will they not follow, but will flee from him: for they know not the voice of strangers.

This parable spake Jesus unto them: but they understood not what things they were which he spake unto them.

Jesus therefore said unto them again,

Verily, verily, I say unto you, I am the door of the sheep. All that came before me are thieves and robbers: but the sheep did not hear them. I am the door; by me if any man enter in, he shall be saved, and shall go in and go out, and shall find pasture. The thief cometh not, but that he may steal, and kill, and destroy; I came that they may have life, and may have it abundantly.

THIRD SUNDAY AFTER EASTER.

Homeward Bound.

Collect. O God, who showest to them that are in error the light of Thy truth, to the intent that they may return into the way of righteousness: grant unto all those who confess the name of Christ that they may avoid those things that are contrary to their profession, and follow all such things as are agreeable to the same; through Jesus Christ, Thy Son, our Lord. AMEN.

EPISTLE, 1 Peter 2. 11–20.
The Christian a Stranger and a Pilgrim.

BELOVED, I beseech you as sojourners and pilgrims, to abstain from fleshly lusts, which war against the soul; having your behavior seemly among the Gentiles; that, wherein they speak against you as evil-doers, they may by your good works, which they behold, glorify God in the day of visitation.

Be subect to every ordinance of man for the Lord's sake: whether to the king, as supreme; or unto governors, as sent by him for vengeance on evil-doers and for praise to them that do well. For so is the will of God, that by well-doing ye should put to silence the ignorance of foolish men: as free, and not using your freedom for a cloak of wickedness, but as bondservants of God. Honor all men. Love the brotherhood. Fear God. Honor the king.

Servants, be in subjection to your masters with all fear; not only to the good and gentle, but also to the froward. For this is acceptable, if for conscience toward God a man endureth griefs, suffering wrongfully. For what glory is it, if, when ye sin, and are buffeted for it, ye shall take it patiently? But if, when ye do well, and suffer for it, ye shall take it patiently, this is acceptable with God.

I. GOSPEL, John 16. 16–22.
The Tribulation of the Christian Is Brief.

A LITTLE while, and ye behold me no more; and again a little while, and ye shall see me.

Some of his disciples therefore said one to another, What is this that he saith unto us, A little while, and ye behold me not; and again a little while, and ye shall see me: and, Because I go to the Father? They said therefore, What is this that he saith, A little while? We know not what he saith.

Jesus perceived that they were desirous to ask him, and he said unto them, Do ye inquire among yourselves concerning this, that I said, A little while, and ye behold me not, and again a little while, and ye shall see me? Verily, verily, I say unto you, that ye shall weep and lament, but the world shall rejoice: ye shall be sorrowful, but your sorrow shall be turned into joy. A woman when she is in travail hath sorrow, because her hour is come: but when she is delivered of the child, she remembereth no more the anguish, for the joy that a man is born into the world. And ye therefore now have sorrow: but I will see you again, and your heart shall rejoice, and your joy no one taketh away from you.

II. EPISTLE, 2 Corinthians 4. 16–18.
Tribulation Leads to Glory.

WHEREFORE we faint not; but though our outward man is decaying, yet our inward man is renewed day by day.

For our light affliction, which is for the moment, worketh for us more and more exceedingly an eternal weight of glory; while we look not at the things which are seen, but at the things which are not seen: for the things which are seen are temporal; but the things which are not seen are eternal.

II. GOSPEL, John 17. 1–8.
Jesus Prays for Eternal Life for His Followers.

THESE things spake Jesus; and lifting up his eyes to heaven, he said,

Father, the hour is come; glorify thy Son, that the Son may glorify thee: even as thou gavest him authority over all flesh, that to all whom thou hast given him, he should give eternal life. And this is life eternal, that they should know thee the only true God, and him whom thou didst send, even Jesus Christ.

I glorified thee on the earth, having accomplished the work which thou hast given me to do. And now, Father, glorify thou me with thine own self with the glory which I had with thee before the world was.

I manifested thy name unto the men whom thou gavest me out of the world: thine they were, and thou gavest them to me; and they have kept thy word. Now they know that all things whatsoever thou hast given me are from thee: for the words which thou gavest me I have given unto them; and they received them, and knew of a truth that I came forth from thee, and they believed that thou didst send me.

III. EPISTLE, 1 Peter 1. 3–8.
The Incorruptible Inheritance in Heaven.

BLESSED be the God and Father of our Lord Jesus Christ, who according to his great mercy begat us again unto a living hope by the resurrection of Jesus Christ from the dead, unto an inheritance incorruptible, and undefiled, and that fadeth not away, reserved in heaven for you, who by the power of God are guarded through faith unto a salvation ready to be revealed in the last time. Wherein ye greatly rejoice, though now for a little while, if need be, ye have been put to grief in manifold trials, that the proof of your faith, being more precious than gold that perisheth though it is proved by fire, may be found unto praise and glory and honor at the revelation of Jesus Christ; whom not having seen ye love; on whom, though now ye see him not, yet believing, ye rejoice greatly with joy unspeakable and full of glory.

III. GOSPEL, John 14. 1–12.
The Way to the Father's House.

LET not your heart be troubled: believe in God, believe also in me. In my Father's house are many mansions; if it were not so, I would have told you; for I go to prepare a place for you. And if I go and prepare a place for you, I come again, and will receive you unto myself; that where I am, there ye may be also. And whither I go, ye know the way.

Thomas saith unto him, Lord, we know not whither thou goest; how know we the way? Jesus saith unto him, I am the way, and the truth, and the life: no one cometh unto the Father, but by me. If ye had known me, ye would have known my Father also: from henceforth ye know him, and have seen him.

Philip saith unto him, Lord, show us the Father, and it sufficeth us. Jesus saith unto him, Have I been so long time with you, and dost thou not know me, Philip? he that hath seen me hath seen the Father; how sayest thou, Show us the Father? Believest thou not that I am in the Father, and the Father in me? the words that I say unto you I speak not from myself: but the Father abiding in me doeth his works. Believe me that I am in the Father, and the Father in me: or else believe me for the very works' sake. Verily, verily, I say unto you, He that believeth on me, the works that I do shall he do also; and greater works than these shall he do; because I go unto the Father.

FOURTH SUNDAY AFTER EASTER.
The Blessing of Christ's Absence.

Collect. O God, who makest the faithful to be of one mind: grant unto Thy people that they may love to do what Thou commandest, and desire what Thou dost promise, that among the manifold changes of this world our hearts may there be fixed where true joys are to be found; through Jesus Christ, our Lord. AMEN.

I. EPISTLE, James 1. 17–21.
Good and Perfect Gifts from Above.

EVERY good gift and every perfect gift is from above, coming down from the Father of lights, with whom can be no variation, neither shadow that is cast by turning. Of his own will he brought us forth by the word of truth, that we should be a kind of firstfruits of his creatures.

Ye know this, my beloved brethren. But let every man be swift to hear, slow to speak, slow to wrath: for the wrath of man worketh not the righteousness of God. Wherefore putting away all filthiness and overflowing of wickedness, receive with meekness the implanted word, which is able to save your souls.

I. GOSPEL, John 16. 5–15.
Growth in the Truth.

Jesus said unto His disciples:

NOW I go unto him that sent me; and none of you asketh me, Whither goest thou? But because I have spoken these things unto you, sorrow hath filled your heart. Nevertheless I tell you the truth: It is expedient for you that I go away; for if I go not away, the Comforter will not come unto you; but if I go, I will send him unto you.

And he, when he is come, will convict the world in respect of sin, and of righteousness, and of judgment: of sin, because they believed not on me; of righteousness, because I go to the Father, and ye behold me no more; of judgment, because the prince of this world hath been judged.

I have yet many things to say unto you, but ye cannot bear them now. Howbeit when he, the Spirit of truth, is come, he shall guide you into all the truth: for he shall not speak from himself; but what things soever he shall hear, these shall he speak: and he shall declare unto you the things that are to come. He shall glorify me: for he shall take of mine, and shall declare it unto you. All things whatsoever the Father hath are mine: therefore said I, that he taketh of mine, and shall declare it unto you.

II. Epistle, Hebrews 13. 12–16.

Following Jesus Means Separation from the World.

JESUS also, that he might sanctify the people through his own blood, suffered without the gate. Let us therefore go forth unto him without the camp, bearing his reproach. For we have not here an abiding city, but we seek after the city which is to come. Through him then let us offer up a sacrifice of praise to God continually, that is, the fruit of lips which make confession to his name. But to do good and to communicate forget not: for with such sacrifices God is well pleased.

II. Gospel, John 17. 9–17.

Jesus Praying for His Disciples in the World.

I PRAY for them: I pray not for the world, but for those whom thou hast given me; for they are thine: and all things that are mine are thine, and thine are mine: and I am glorified in them. And I am no more in the world, and these are in the world, and I come to thee. Holy Father, keep them in thy name which thou hast given me, that they may be one, even as we are. While I was with them, I kept them in thy name which thou hast given me: and I guarded them, and not one of them perished, but the son of perdition; that the scripture might be fulfilled. But now I come to thee; and these things I speak in the world, that they may have my joy made full in themselves. I have given them thy word; and the world hated them, because they are not of the world, even as I am not of the world. I pray not that thou shouldest take them from the world, but that thou shouldest keep them from the evil one. They are not of the world, even as I am not of the world. Sanctify them in the truth: thy word is truth.

III. Epistle, 1 John 3. 18–24.

God Is Greater Than Our Heart.

MY little children, let us not love in word, neither with the tongue; but in deed and truth. Hereby shall we know that we are of the truth, and shall assure our heart before him: because if our heart condemn us, God is greater than our heart, and knoweth all things.

Beloved, if our heart condemn us not, we have boldness toward God; and whatsoever we ask we receive of him, because we keep his commandments and do the things that are pleasing in his sight.

And this is his commandment, that we should believe in the name of his Son Jesus Christ, and love one another, even as he gave us commandment. And he that keepeth his commandments abideth in him, and he in him. And hereby we know that he abideth in us, by the Spirit which he gave us.

III. Gospel, John 15. 10–17.

The Intercourse of the Friends of Jesus.

IF ye keep my commandments, ye shall abide in my love; even as I have kept my Father's commandments, and abide in his love.

These things have I spoken unto you, that my joy may be in you, and that your joy may be made full. This is my commandment, that ye love one another, even as I have loved you. Greater love hath no man than this, that a man lay down his life for his friends. Ye are my friends, if ye do the things which I command you. No longer do I call you servants; for the servant knoweth not what his lord doeth: but I have called you friends; for all things that I heard from my Father I have made known unto you.

Ye did not choose me, but I chose you, and appointed you, that ye should go and bear fruit, and that your fruit should abide: that whatsoever ye shall ask of the Father in my name, he may give it you.

These things I command you, that ye may love one another.

FIFTH SUNDAY AFTER EASTER.

Prayer.

Collect. O Lord, from whom all good things come, grant to us Thy humble servants, that by Thy holy inspiration we may think those things that are good, and by Thy merciful guiding may perform the same; through Jesus Christ, Thy Son, our Lord. AMEN.

I. EPISTLE, James 1. 22–27.

Hearers and Doers of the Word.

BE ye doers of the word, and not hearers only, deluding your own selves. For if any one is a hearer of the word and not a doer, he is like unto a man beholding his natural face in a mirror: for he beholdeth himself, and goeth away, and straightway forgetteth what manner of man he was. But he that looketh into the perfect law, the law of liberty, and so continueth, being not a hearer that forgetteth but a doer that worketh, this man shall be blessed in his doing.

If any man thinketh himself to be religious, while he bridleth not his tongue but deceiveth his heart, this man's religion is vain. Pure religion and undefiled before our God and Father is this, to visit the fatherless and widows in their affliction, and to keep oneself unspotted from the world.

I. GOSPEL, John 16. 23–33.

Prayer in the Name of Jesus.

VERILY, verily, I say unto you, If ye shall ask anything of the Father, he will give it you in my name. Hitherto have ye asked nothing in my name: ask, and ye shall receive, that your joy may be made full.

These things have I spoken unto you in dark sayings: the hour cometh, when I shall no more speak unto you in dark sayings, but shall tell you plainly of the Father. In that day ye shall ask in my name: and I say not unto you, that I will pray the Father for you; for the Father himself loveth you, because ye have loved me, and have believed that I came forth from the Father. I came out from the Father, and am come into the world: again, I leave the world, and go unto the Father.

His disciples say, Lo, now speakest thou plainly, and speakest no dark saying. Now know we that thou knowest all things, and needest not that any man should ask thee: by this we believe that thou camest forth from God.

Jesus answered them, Do ye now believe? Behold, the hour cometh, yea, is come, that ye shall be scattered, every man to his own, and shall leave me alone: and yet I am not alone, because the Father is with me. These things have I spoken unto you, that in me ye may have peace. In the world ye have tribulation: but be of good cheer; I have overcome the world.

II. EPISTLE, Hebrews 7. 23–27.

The Unchangeable Priesthood of Christ.

AND they indeed have been made priests many in number, because that by death they are hindered from continuing: but he, because he abideth for ever, hath his priesthood unchangeable. Wherefore also he is able to save to the uttermost them that draw near unto God through him, seeing he ever liveth to make intercession for them.

For such a high priest became us, holy, guileless, undefiled, separated from sinners, and made higher than the heavens; who needeth not daily, like those high priests, to offer up sacrifices, first for his own sins, and then for the sins of the people: for this he did once for all, when he offered up himself.

II. GOSPEL, John 17. 18–23.

Jesus Praying for the Unity of His Disciples.

AS thou didst send me into the world, even so sent I them into the world. And for their sakes I sanctify myself, that they themselves also may be sanctified in truth.

Neither for these only do I pray, but for them also that believe on me through their word; that they may all be one; even as thou, Father, art in me, and I in thee, that they also may be in us: that the world may believe that thou didst send me.

And the glory which thou hast given me I have given unto them; that they may be one, even as we are one; I in them, and thou in me, that they may be perfected into one; that the world may know that thou didst send me, and lovedst them, even as thou lovedst me.

III. EPISTLE, Numbers 6. 22–27.

The Lord Blessing His People.

AND Jehovah spake unto Moses, saying, Speak unto Aaron and unto his sons, saying, On this wise ye shall bless the children of Israel: ye shall say unto them,

Jehovah bless thee, and keep thee:

Jehovah make his face to shine upon thee, and be gracious unto thee:

Jehovah lift up his countenance upon thee, and give thee peace.

So shall they put my name upon the children of Israel; and I will bless them.

III. Gospel, Luke 11. 1–13.

Jesus Teaching His Disciples to Pray.

AND it came to pass, as he was praying in a certain place, that when he ceased, one of his disciples said unto him, Lord, teach us to pray, even as John also taught his disciples.

And he said unto them, When ye pray say, Father, Hallowed be thy name. Thy kingdom come. Give us day by day our daily bread. And forgive us our sins; for we ourselves also forgive every one that is indebted to us. And bring us not into temptation.

And he said unto them, Which of you shall have a friend, and shall go unto him at midnight, and say to him, Friend, lend me three loaves; for a friend of mine is come to me from a journey, and I have nothing to set before him; and he from within shall answer and say, Trouble me not: the door is now shut, and my children are with me in bed; I cannot rise and give thee? I say unto you, Though he will not rise and give him because he is his friend, yet because of his importunity he will arise and give him as many as he needeth.

And I say unto you, Ask, and it shall be given you; seek, and ye shall find; knock, and it shall be opened unto you. For every one that asketh receiveth; and he that seeketh findeth; and to him that knocketh it shall be opened.

And of which of you that is a father shall his son ask a loaf, and he give him a stone? or a fish, and he for a fish give him a serpent? Or if he shall ask an egg, will he give him a scorpion? If ye then, being evil, know how to give good gifts unto your children, how much more shall your heavenly Father give the Holy Spirit to them that ask him?

ASCENSION DAY.

From Humiliation to Exaltation.

Collect. Grant, we beseech Thee, Almighty God, that like as we do believe Thy only-begotten Son, our Lord Jesus Christ, to have ascended into the heavens, so we may also in heart and mind thither ascend, and with him continually dwell, Who liveth and reigneth with Thee and the Holy Spirit, ever one God, world without end. Amen.

I. Epistle, Acts 1. 1–11.

Jesus Promising the Kingdom.

THE former treatise I made, O Theophilus, concerning all that Jesus began both to do and to teach, until the day in which he was received up, after that he had given commandment through the Holy Spirit unto the apostles whom he had chosen: to whom he also showed himself alive after his passion by many proofs, appearing unto them by the space of forty days, and speaking the things concerning the kingdom of God: and being assembled together with them, he charged them not to depart from Jerusalem, but to wait for the promise of the Father, which, said he, ye heard from me: for John indeed baptized with water; but ye shall be baptized in the Holy Spirit not many days hence.

They therefore, when they were come together, asked him, saying, Lord, dost thou at this time restore the kingdom to Israel?

And he said unto them, It is not for you to know times or seasons, which the Father hath set within his own authority. But ye shall receive power, when the Holy Spirit is come upon you: and ye shall be my witnesses both in Jerusalem, and in all Judæa and Samaria, and unto the uttermost part of the earth.

And when he had said these things, as they were looking, he was taken up; and a cloud received him out of their sight.

And while they were looking stedfastly into heaven as he went, behold, two men stood by them in white apparel; who also said, Ye men of Galilee, why stand ye looking into heaven? this Jesus, who was received up from you into heaven, shall so come in like manner as ye beheld him going into heaven.

I. Gospel, Mark 16. 14–20.

The Commission of Christ, and His Ascension.

AND afterward he was manifested unto the eleven themselves as they sat at meat; and he upbraided them with their unbelief and hardness of heart, because they believed not them that had seen him after he was risen.

And he said unto them, Go ye into all the world, and preach the gospel to the whole creation. He that believeth and is baptized shall be saved; but he that disbelieveth shall be condemned.

And these signs shall accompany them that believe: in my name shall they cast out demons; they shall speak with new tongues; they shall take up serpents, and if they drink any deadly thing, it shail in no wise hurt them; they shall lay hands on the sick, and they shall recover.

So then the Lord Jesus, after he had spoken unto them, was received up into heaven, and sat down at the right hand of God. And they went forth and preached everywhere, the Lord working with them, and confirming the word by the signs that followed. Amen.

II. EPISTLE, Psalm 110. 1–3.
The King Ascending His Throne.

JEHOVAH saith unto my Lord, Sit thou at my right hand,
Until I make thine enemies thy footstool.
Jehovah will send forth the rod of thy strength out of Zion:
Rule thou in the midst of thine enemies.
Thy people offer themselves willingly
In the day of thy power, in holy array:
Out of the womb of the morning
Thou hast the dew of thy youth.

II. GOSPEL, John 17. 24–26.
Jesus Praying for the Perfecting of His Followers.

FATHER, I desire that they also whom thou hast given me be with me where I am, that they may behold my glory, which thou hast given me: for thou lovedst me before the foundation of the world. O righteous Father, the world knew thee not, but I knew thee; and these knew that thou didst send me; and I made known unto them thy name, and will make it known; that the love where-with thou lovedst me may be in them, and I in them.

III. EPISTLE, Romans 8. 34–39.
Nothing Can Separate Us from Christ.

WHO is he that condemneth? It is Christ Jesus that died, yea rather, that was raised from the dead, who is at the right hand of God, who also maketh intercession for us.

Who shall separate us from the love of Christ? shall tribulation, or anguish, or persecution, or famine, or nakedness, or peril, or sword? · Even as it is written,
For thy sake we are killed all the day long;
We were accounted as sheep for the slaughter.
Nay, in all these things we are more than conquerors through him that loved us.

For I am persuaded that neither death, nor life, nor angels, nor principalities, nor things present, nor things to come, nor powers, nor height, nor depth, nor any other creature, shall be able to separate us from the love of God, which is in Christ Jesus our Lord.

III. GOSPEL, Luke 24. 49–53.
Jesus Blessing His Disciples and Ascending into Heaven.

BEHOLD, I send forth the promise of my Father upon you: but tarry ye in the city, until ye be clothed with power from on high.

And he led them out until they were over against Bethany: and he lifted up his hands, and blessed them. And it came to pass, while he blessed them, he parted from them, and was carried up into heaven. And they worshipped him, and returned to Jerusalem with great joy: and were continually in the temple, blessing God.

SIXTH SUNDAY AFTER EASTER.
Waiting for the Promise of the Father.

Collect. Almighty, eternal God, grant us, we pray Thee, a true love for Thee, that we may desire that which Thou dost command and with all our heart and all our powers serve Thee; through Thy Son, Jesus Christ, our Lord AMEN.

I. EPISTLE, 1 Peter 4. 7–11.
The Time of Expectation to Be Filled with Labor.

THE end of all things is at hand: be ye therefore of sound mind, and be sober unto prayer: above all things being fervent in your love among yourselves; for love covereth a multitude of sins: using hospitality one to another without murmuring: according as each hath received a gift, ministering it among yourselves, as good stewards of the manifold grace of God; if any man speaketh, speaking as it were oracles of God; if any man ministereth, ministering as of the strength which God supplieth: that in all things God may be glorified through Jesus Christ, whose is the glory and the dominion for ever and ever. Amen.

I. Gospel, John 15. 26—16. 4.
Jesus Promising the Gift of the Holy Spirit.

WHEN the Comforter is come, whom I will send unto you from the Father, even the Spirit of truth, which proceedeth from the Father, he shall bear witness of me: and ye also bear witness, because ye have been with me from the beginning.

These things have I spoken unto you, that ye should not be caused to stumble. They shall put you out of the synagogues: yea, the hour cometh, that whosoever killeth you shall think that he offereth service unto God. And these things will they do, because they have not known the Father, nor me. But these things have I spoken unto you, that when their hour is come, ye may remember them, how that I told you. And these things I said not unto you from the beginning, because I was with you.

II. Epistle, Colossians 3. 1-10.
Seeking the Things That Are Above.

IF then ye were raised together with Christ, seek the things that are above, where Christ is, seated on the right hand of God.

Set your mind on the things that are above, not on the things that are upon the earth. For ye died, and your life is hid with Christ in God.

When Christ, who is our life, shall be manifested, then shall ye also with him be manifested in glory.

Put to death therefore your members which are upon the earth: fornication, uncleanness, passion, evil desire, and covetousness, which is idolatry; for which things' sake cometh the wrath of God upon the sons of disobedience: wherein ye also once walked, when ye lived in these things; but now do ye also put them all away: anger, wrath, malice, railing, shameful speaking out of your mouth: lie not one to another; seeing that ye have put off the old man with his doings, and have put on the new man, that is being renewed unto knowledge after the image of him that created him.

II. Gospel, Matthew 10. 24-31.
The Spirit of Courage and Confidence.

A DISCIPLE is not above his teacher, nor a servant above his lord. It is enough for the disciple that he be as his teacher, and the servant as his lord. If they have called the master of the house Beelzebub, how much more them of his household!

Fear them not therefore: for there is nothing covered, that shall not be revealed; and hid, that shall not be known. What I tell you in the darkness, speak ye in the light; and what ye hear in the ear, proclaim upon the house-tops.

And be not afraid of them that kill the body, but are not able to kill the soul: but rather fear him who is able to destroy both soul and body in hell. Are not two sparrows sold for a penny? and not one of them shall fall on the ground without your Father: but the very hairs of your head are all numbered. Fear not therefore: ye are of more value than many sparrows.

III. Epistle, Romans 8. 26-28.
The Holy Spirit Helping Our Infirmity.

THE Spirit also helpeth our infirmity: for we know not how to pray as we ought; but the Spirit himself maketh intercession for us with groanings which cannot be uttered; and he that searcheth the hearts knoweth what is the mind of the Spirit, because he maketh intercession for the saints according to the will of God.

And we know that to them that love God all things work together for good, even to them that are called according to his purpose.

III. Gospel, John 15. 18-25.
The Spirit of This World.

IF the world hateth you, ye know that it hath hated me before it hated you. If ye were of the world, the world would love its own: but because ye are not of the world, but I chose you out of the world, therefore the world hateth you.

Remember the word that I said unto you, A servant is not greater than his lord. If they persecuted me, they will also persecute you; if they kept my word, they will keep yours also.

But all these things will they do unto you for my name's sake, because they know not him that sent me.

If I had not come and spoken unto them, they had not had sin: but now they have no excuse for their sin. He that hateth me hateth my Father also. If I had not done among them the works which none other did, they had not had sin: but now have they both seen and hated both me and my Father. But this cometh to pass, that the word may be fulfilled that is written in their law, They hated me without a cause.

WHITSUNDAY.
(Pentecost.)
The Gift of the Holy Spirit.

Collect. O God, who didst teach the hearts of Thy faithful people, by sending them the light of Thy Holy Spirit: grant us by the same Spirit to have a right judgment in all things, and evermore to rejoice in His holy comfort; through our Lord Jesus Christ, Thy Son, who liveth and reigneth with Thee and the Holy Spirit, ever one God, world without end. AMEN.

I. EPISTLE, Acts 2. 1–18.
The Spirit Poured Forth upon the Disciples.

WHEN the day of Pentecost was now come, they were all together in one place. And suddenly there came from heaven a sound as of the rushing of a mighty wind, and it filled all the house where they were sitting. And there appeared unto them tongues parting asunder, like as of fire; and it sat upon each one of them. And they were all filled with the Holy Spirit, and began to speak with other tongues, as the Spirit gave them utterance.

Now there were dwelling at Jerusalem Jews, devout men, from every nation under heaven. And when this sound was heard, the multitude came together, and were confounded, because that every man heard them speaking in his own language. And they were all amazed and marvelled, saying, Behold, are not all these that speak Galilæans? And how hear we, every man in our own language wherein we were born? Parthians and Medes and Elamites, and the dwellers in Mesopotamia, in Judæa and Cappadocia, in Pontus and Asia, in Phrygia and Pamphylia, in Egypt and the parts of Libya about Cyrene, and sojourners from Rome, both Jews and proselytes, Cretans and Arabians, we hear them speaking in our tongues the mighty works of God. And they were all amazed, and were perplexed, saying one to another, What meaneth this? But others mocking said, They are filled with new wine.

But Peter, standing up with the eleven, lifted up his voice, and spake forth unto them, saying, Ye men of Judæa, and all ye that dwell at Jerusalem, be this known unto you, and give ear unto my words. For these are not drunken, as ye suppose; seeing it is but the third hour of the day; but this is that which hath been spoken through the prophet Joel:

And it shall be in the last days, saith God,
I will pour forth of my Spirit upon all flesh:
And your sons and your daughters shall prophesy,
And your young men shall see visions, And your old men shall dream dreams:
Yea and on my servants and on my handmaidens in those days
Will I pour forth of my Spirit; and they shall prophesy.

I. GOSPEL, John 14. 23–31.
The Guidance of the Holy Spirit.

IF a man love me, he will keep my word: and my Father will love him, and we will come unto him, and make our abode with him. He that loveth me not keepeth not my words: and the word which ye hear is not mine, but the Father's who sent me.

These things have I spoken unto you, while yet abiding with you. But the Comforter, even the Holy Spirit, whom the Father will send in my name, he shall teach you all things, and bring to your remembrance all that I said unto you.

Peace I leave with you; my peace I give unto you: not as the world giveth, give I unto you. Let not your heart be troubled, neither let it be fearful.

Ye heard how I said to you, I go away, and I come unto you. If ye loved me, ye would have rejoiced, because I go unto the Father: for the Father is greater than I. And now I have told you before it come to pass, that, when it is come to pass, ye may believe.

I will no more speak much with you, for the prince of the world cometh: and he hath nothing in me; but that the world may know that I love the Father, and as the Father gave me commandment, even so I do.

II. EPISTLE, Ephesians 2. 17–22.
The Holy Spirit Makes Us Fellow-citizens with the Saints.

HE came and preached peace to you that were far off, and peace to them that were nigh: for through him we both have our access in one Spirit unto the Father.

So then ye are no more strangers and sojourners, but ye are fellow-citizens with the saints, and of the household of God, being built upon the foundation of the apostles and prophets, Christ Jesus himself being the chief corner stone; in whom each several building, fitly framed together, groweth into a holy temple in the Lord; in whom ye also are builded together for a habitation of God in the Spirit.

II. GOSPEL, John 7. 37–39.
The Living Water of the Spirit.

NOW on the last day, the great day of the feast, Jesus stood and cried, saying, If any man thirst, let him come unto me and drink.

He that believeth on me, as the scripture hath said, from within him shall flow rivers of living water.

But this spake he of the Spirit, which they that believed on him were to receive: for the Spirit was not yet given; because Jesus was not yet glorified.

III. EPISTLE, Acts 2. 37–47.
The Increase of the Church.

NOW when they heard this, they were pricked in their heart, and said unto Peter and the rest of the apostles, Brethren, what shall we do?

And Peter said unto them, Repent ye, and be baptized every one of you in the name of Jesus Christ unto the remission of your sins, and ye shall receive the gift of the Holy Spirit. For to you is the promise, and to your children, and to all that are afar off, even as many as the Lord our God shall call unto him.

And with many other words he testified, and exhorted them, saying, Save yourselves from this crooked generation.

They then that received his word were baptized: and there were added unto them in that day about three thousand souls. And they continued stedfastly in the apostles' teaching and fellowship, in the breaking of bread and the prayers.

And fear came upon every soul: and many wonders and signs were done through the apostles.

And all that believed were together, and had all things common; and they sold their possessions and goods, and parted them to all, according as any man had need.

And day by day, continuing stedfastly with one accord in the temple, and breaking bread at home, they took their food with gladness and singleness of heart, praising God, and having favor with all the people. And the Lord added to them day by day those that were saved.

III. GOSPEL, John 14. 15–21.
The Promise of Another Comforter.

IF ye love me, ye will keep my commandments. And I will pray the Father, and he shall give you another Comforter, that he may be with you for ever, even the Spirit of truth: whom the world cannot receive; for it beholdeth him not, neither knoweth him: ye know him; for he abideth with you, and shall be in you.

I will not leave you desolate: I come unto you. Yet a little while, and the world beholdeth me no more; but ye behold me: because I live, ye shall live also.

In that day ye shall know that I am in my Father, and ye in me, and I in you. He that hath my commandments, and keepeth them, he it is that loveth me: and he that loveth me shall be loved of my Father, and I will love him, and will manifest myself unto him.

WHITMONDAY.
The Progress of the Spirit.

Collect. O Lord God, who didst shed abroad Thy Holy Spirit upon the first disciples: grant Thy Church that which we pray for in the name of the same Holy Spirit; and as Thou hast given us the true faith, keep us, we beseech Thee, in Thy peace; through Thy Son, Jesus Christ, our Lord. AMEN.

I. EPISTLE, Acts 10. 42–48.
The Spirit Shed Abroad upon the Gentiles.

HE charged us to preach unto the people, and to testify that this is he who is ordained of God to be the Judge of the living and the dead.

To him bear all the prophets witness, that through his name every one that believeth on him shall receive remission of sins.

While Peter yet spake these words, the Holy Spirit fell on all them that heard the word. And they of the circumcision that believed were amazed, as many as came with Peter, because that on the Gentiles also was poured out the gift of the Holy Spirit. For they heard them speak with tongues, and magnify God.

Then answered Peter, Can any man forbid the water, that these should not be baptized, who have received the Holy Spirit as well as we? And he commanded them to be baptized in the name of Jesus Christ.

I. GOSPEL, John 3. 16–21.

The Giving of the Only Begotten Son.

FOR God so loved the world, that he gave his only begotten Son, that whosoever believeth on him should not perish, but have eternal life.

For God sent not the Son into the world to judge the world; but that the world should be saved through him.

He that believeth on him is not judged: he that believeth not hath been judged already, because he hath not believed on the name of the only begotten Son of God.

And this is the judgment, that the light is come into the world, and men loved the darkness rather than the light; for their works were evil. For every one that doeth evil hateth the light, and cometh not to the light, lest his works should be reproved. But he that doeth the truth cometh to the light, that his works may be made manifest, that they have been wrought in God.

II. EPISTLE, 1 Corinthians 12. 12–30.

The Church As the Body of Christ.

AS the body is one, and hath many members, and all the members of the body being many, are one body; so also is Christ. For in one Spirit were we all baptized into one body, whether Jews or Greeks, whether bond or free; and were all made to drink of one Spirit.

For the body is not one member, but many. If the foot shall say, Because I am not the hand, I am not of the body; it is not therefore not of the body. And if the ear shall say, Because I am not the eye, I am not of the body; it is not therefore not of the body. If the whole body were an eye, where were the hearing? If the whole were hearing, where were the smelling?

But now hath God set the members each one of them in the body, even as it pleased him. And if they were all one member, where were the body? But now they are many members, but one body. And the eye cannot say to the hand, I have no need of thee: or again the head to the feet, I have no need of you.

Nay, much rather, those members of the body which seem to be more feeble are necessary: and those parts of the body, which we think to be less honorable, upon these we bestow more abundant honor; and our uncomely parts have more abundant comeliness; whereas our comely parts have no need: but God tempered the body together, giving more abundant honor to that part which

lacked; that there should be no schism in the body; but that the members should have the same care one for another.

And whether one member suffereth, all the members suffer with it; or one member is honored, all the members rejoice with it.

Now ye are the body of Christ, and severally members thereof. And God hath set some in the church, first apostles, secondly prophets, thirdly teachers, then miracles, then gifts of healings, helps, governments, divers kinds of tongues. Are all apostles? are all prophets? are all teachers? are all workers of miracles? have all gifts of healings? do all speak with tongues? do all interpret?

II. GOSPEL, John 6. 44–47.

The Father Draws Men to the Son.

NO man can come to me, except the Father that sent me draw him: and I will raise him up in the last day.

It is written in the prophets, And they shall all be taught of God. Every one that hath heard from the Father, and hath learned, cometh unto me.

Not that any man hath seen the Father, save he that is from God, he hath seen the Father. Verily, verily, I say unto you, He that believeth hath eternal life.

III. EPISTLE, Acts 11. 19–26.

The First Church of Gentile Christians.

THEY therefore that were scattered abroad upon the tribulation that arose about Stephen travelled as far as Phœnicia, and Cyprus, and Antioch, speaking the word to none save only to Jews.

But there were some of them, men of Cyprus and Cyrene, who, when they were come to Antioch, spake unto the Greeks also, preaching the Lord Jesus. And the hand of the Lord was with them: and a great number that believed turned unto the Lord. And the report concerning them came to the ears of the church which was in Jerusalem: and they sent forth Barnabas as far as Antioch: who, when he was come, and had seen the grace of God, was glad; and he exhorted them all, that with purpose of heart they would cleave unto the Lord: for he was a good man, and full of the Holy Spirit and of faith: and much people was added unto the Lord.

And he went forth to Tarsus to seek for Saul; and when he had found him, he brought him unto Antioch. And it came to pass, that even for a whole year they were gathered together with the church, and taught much people; and that the disciples were called Christians first in Antioch.

III. GOSPEL, John 12. 44–50.
Increased Responsibility.

JESUS cried and said, He that believeth on me, believeth not on me, but on him that sent me. And he that beholdeth me beholdeth him that sent me. I am come a light into the world, that whosoever believeth on me may not abide in the darkness. And if any man hear my sayings, and keep them not, I judge him not: for I came not to judge the world, but to save the world. He that rejecteth me, and receiveth not my sayings, hath one that judgeth him: the word that I spake, the same shall judge him in the last day. For I spake not from myself; but the Father that sent me, he hath given me a commandment, what I should say, and what I should speak. And I know that his commandment is life eternal; the things therefore which I speak, even as the Father hath said unto me, so I speak.

TRINITY SUNDAY.
The Spirit and the New Life.

Collect. Almighty and eternal God, who hast given unto us, Thy servants, the true faith to know Thee, our heavenly Father, and Thy Son, and the Holy Spirit, and to worship Thee, the only true God: keep us steadfast in this faith and defend us from all danger and adversity; Thou that livest and reignest, ever one God, world without end. AMEN.

I. EPISTLE, Romans 11. 33–36.
The Glory of God.

O THE depth of the riches both of the wisdom and the knowledge of God! how unsearchable are his judgments, and his ways past tracing out! For who hath known the mind of the Lord? or who hath been his counsellor? or who hath first given to him, and it shall be recompensed unto him again? For of him, and through him, and unto him, are all things. To him be the glory for ever. Amen.

I. GOSPEL, John 3. 1–15.
Jesus and Nicodemus.

NOW there was a man of the Pharisees, named Nicodemus, a ruler of the Jews: the same came unto Jesus by night, and said to him, Rabbi, we know that thou art a teacher come from God; for no one can do these signs that thou doest, except God be with him. Jesus answered and said unto him, Verily, verily, I say unto thee, Except one be born anew, he cannot see the kingdom of God. Nicodemus saith unto him, How can a man be born when he is old? can he enter a second time into his mother's womb, and be born? Jesus answered, Verily, verily, I say unto thee, Except one be born of water and the Spirit, he cannot enter into the kingdom of God. That which is born of the flesh is flesh; and that which is born of the Spirit is spirit. Marvel not that I said unto thee, Ye must be born anew. The wind bloweth where it will, and thou hearest the voice thereof, but knowest not whence it cometh, and whither it goeth: so is every one that is born of the Spirit.

Nicodemus answered and said unto him, How can these things be? Jesus answered and said unto him, Art thou the teacher of Israel, and understandest not these things? Verily, verily, I say unto thee, We speak that which we know, and bear witness of that which we have seen; and ye receive not our witness. If I told you earthly things and ye believe not, how shall ye believe if I tell you heavenly things? And no one hath ascended into heaven, but he that descended out of heaven, even the Son of man, who is in heaven. And as Moses lifted up the serpent in the wilderness, even so must the Son of man be lifted up; that whosoever believeth may in him have eternal life.

II. EPISTLE, 1 John 3. 1–9.
The Children of God.

BEHOLD what manner of love the Father hath bestowed upon us, that we should be called children of God; and such we are. For this cause the world knoweth us not, because it knew him not.

Beloved, now are we children of God, and it is not yet made manifest what we shall be. We know that, if he shall be manifested, we shall be like him; for we shall see him even as he is. And every one that hath this hope set on him purifieth himself, even as he is pure. Every one that doeth sin doeth also lawlessness; and sin is lawlessness. And ye know that he was manifested to take away sins, and in him is no sin. Whosoever abideth in him sinneth not: whosoever sinneth hath not seen him, neither knoweth him.

My little children, let no man lead you astray: he that doeth righteousness is righteous, even as he is righteous: he that doeth sin is of the devil; for the devil sinneth from the beginning. To this end was the Son of God manifested, that he might destroy the works of the devil.

Whosoever is begotten of God doeth no sin, because his seed abideth in him: and he cannot sin, because he is begotten of God.

II. GOSPEL, John 15. 1–9.

The Vine and the Branches.

I AM the true vine, and my Father is the husbandman.

Every branch in me that beareth not fruit, he taketh it away: and every branch that beareth fruit, he cleanseth it, that it may bear more fruit. Already ye are clean because of the word which I have spoken unto you.

Abide in me, and I in you. As the branch cannot bear fruit of itself, except it abide in the vine; so neither can ye, except ye abide in me.

I am the vine, ye are the branches: he that abideth in me, and I in him, the same beareth much fruit: for apart from me ye can do nothing.

If a man abide not in me, he is cast forth as a branch, and is withered; and they gather them, and cast them into the fire, and they are burned.

If ye abide in me, and my words abide in you, ask whatsoever ye will, and it shall be done unto you. Herein is my Father glorified, that ye bear much fruit; and so shall ye be my disciples. Even as the Father hath loved me, I also have loved you: abide ye in my love.

III. EPISTLE, Colossians 1. 9–23.

Christ the Head of the Church.

FOR this cause we also, since the day we heard it, do not cease to pray and make request for you, that ye may be filled with the knowledge of his will in all spiritual wisdom and understanding, to walk worthily of the Lord unto all pleasing, bearing fruit in every good work, and increasing in the knowledge of God; strengthened with all power, ac-cording to the might of his glory, unto all patience and longsuffering with joy; giving thanks unto the Father, who made us meet to be partakers of the inheritance of the saints in light; who delivered us out of the power of darkness, and translated us into the kingdom of the Son of his love; in whom we have our redemption, the forgiveness of our sins: who is the image of the invisible God, the firstborn of all creation; for in him were all things created, in the heavens and upon the earth, things visible and things invisible, whether thrones or dominions or principalities or powers; all things have been created through him, and unto him; and he is before all things, and in him all things consist.

And he is the head of the body, the church: who is the beginning, the firstborn from the dead; that in all things he might have the preëminence. For it was the good pleasure of the Father that in him should all the fulness dwell; and through him to reconcile all things unto himself, having made peace through the blood of his cross; through him, I say, whether things upon the earth, or things in the heavens.

And you, being in time past alienated and enemies in your mind in your evil works, yet now hath he reconciled in the body of his flesh through death, to present you holy and without blemish and unreprovable before him: if so be that ye continue in the faith, grounded and stedfast, and not moved away from the hope of the gospel which ye heard, which was preached in all creation under heaven; whereof I Paul was made a minister.

III. GOSPEL, Matthew 28. 18–20.

All Nations to Be Made Disciples of Christ.

AND Jesus came to them and spake unto them, saying, All authority hath been given unto me in heaven and on earth. Go ye therefore, and make disciples of all the nations, baptizing them into the name of the Father and of the Son and of the Holy Spirit: teaching them to observe all things whatsoever I commanded you: and lo, I am with you always, even unto the end of the world.

FIRST SUNDAY AFTER TRINITY.

Priceless Values.

Collect. O God, the strength of all those who put their trust in Thee: mercifully accept our prayers; and because, through the weakness of our mortal nature, we can do no good thing without Thee, grant us the help of Thy grace, that in keeping Thy commandments we may please Thee, both in will and in deed; through Jesus Christ, Thy Son, our Lord. Amen.

I. Epistle, 1 John 4. 16–21.
Perfect Love Casteth Out Fear.

GOD is love; and he that abideth in love abideth in God, and God abideth in him.

Herein is love made perfect with us, that we may have boldness in the day of judgment; because as he is, even so are we in this world.

There is no fear in love: but perfect love casteth out fear, because fear hath punishment; and he that feareth is not made perfect in love.

We love, because he first loved us.

If a man say, I love God, and hateth his brother, he is a liar: for he that loveth not his brother whom he hath seen, cannot love God whom he hath not seen. And this commandment have we from him, that he who loveth God love his brother also.

I. Gospel, Luke 16. 19–31.
The Rich Man and Lazarus.

NOW there was a certain rich man, and he was clothed in purple and fine linen, faring sumptuously every day: and a certain beggar named Lazarus was laid at his gate, full of sores, and desiring to be fed with the crumbs that fell from the rich man's table; yea, even the dogs came and licked his sores.

And it came to pass, that the beggar died, and that he was carried away by the angels into Abraham's bosom: and the rich man also died, and was buried.

And in Hades he lifted up his eyes, being in torments, and seeth Abraham afar off, and Lazarus in his bosom. And he cried and said, Father Abraham, have mercy on me, and send Lazarus, that he may dip the tip of his finger in water, and cool my tongue; for I am in anguish in this flame.

But Abraham said, Son, remember that thou in thy lifetime receivedst thy good things, and Lazarus in like manner evil things: but now here he is comforted, and thou art in anguish. And besides all this, between us and you there is a great gulf fixed, that they that would pass from hence to you may not be able, and that none may cross over from thence to us.

And he said, I pray thee therefore, father, that thou wouldest send him to my father's house; for I have five brethren; that he may testify unto them, lest they also come into this place of torment. But Abraham saith, They have Moses and the prophets; let them hear them. And he said, Nay, father Abraham: but if one go to them from the dead, they will repent. And he said unto him, If they hear not Moses and the prophets, neither will they be persuaded, if one rise from the dead.

II. Epistle, James 4. 13–16.
Our Life Is Not Our Own.

COME now, ye that say, To-day or to-morrow we will go into this city and spend a year there, and trade, and get gain: whereas ye know not what shall be on the morrow. What is your life? For ye are a vapor that appeareth for a little time, and then vanisheth away. For that ye ought to say, If the Lord will, we shall both live, and do this or that. But now ye glory in your vauntings: all such glorying is evil.

II. Gospel, Luke 12. 13–21.
The Rich Fool.

AND one out of the multitude said unto him, Teacher, bid my brother divide the inheritance with me.

But he said unto him, Man, who made me a judge or a divider over you?

And he said unto them, Take heed, and keep yourselves from all covetousness: for a man's life consisteth not in the abundance of the things which he possesseth.

And he spake a parable unto them, saying, The ground of a certain rich man brought forth plentifully: and he reasoned within himself, saying, What shall I do, because I have not where to bestow my fruits? And he said, This will I do: I will pull down my barns, and build greater; and there will I bestow all my grain and my goods. And I will say to my soul, Soul, thou hast much goods laid up for many years; take thine ease, eat, drink, be merry. But God said unto him, Thou foolish one, this night is thy soul required of thee; and the things which thou hast prepared, whose shall they be?

So is he that layeth up treasure for himself, and is not rich toward God.

III. EPISTLE, 1 Timothy 6. 6–19.
The Fear of God Is Better Than Wealth.

GODLINESS with contentment is great gain: for we brought nothing into the world, for neither can we carry anything out; but having food and covering we shall be therewith content. But they that are minded to be rich fall into a temptation and a snare and many foolish and hurtful lusts, such as drown men in destruction and perdition. For the love of money is a root of all kinds of evil: which some reaching after have been led astray from the faith, and have pierced themselves through with many sorrows. But thou, O man of God, flee these things; and follow after righteousness, godliness, faith, love, patience, meekness. Fight the good fight of the faith, lay hold on the life eternal, whereunto thou wast called, and didst confess the good confession in the sight of many witnesses. I charge thee in the sight of God, who giveth life to all things, and of Christ Jesus, who before Pontius Pilate witnessed the good confession; that thou keep the commandment, without spot, without reproach, until the appearing of our Lord Jesus Christ: which in its own times he shall show, who is the blessed and only Potentate, the King of kings, and Lord of lords; who only hath immortality, dwelling in light unapproachable; whom no man hath seen, nor can see: to whom be honor and power eternal. Amen. Charge them that are rich in this present world, that they be not highminded, nor have their hope set on the uncertainty of riches, but on God, who giveth us richly all things to enjoy; that they do good, that they be rich in good works, that they be ready to distribute, willing to communicate; laying up in store for themselves a good foundation against the time to come, that they may lay hold on the life which is life indeed.

III. GOSPEL, Matthew 16. 24–27.
The Value of a Human Soul.

THEN said Jesus unto his disciples, If any man would come after me, let him deny himself, and take up his cross, and follow me. For whosoever would save his life shall lose it: and whosoever shall lose his life for my sake shall find it. For what shall a man be profited, if he shall gain the whole world, and forfeit his life? or what shall a man give in exchange for his life? For the Son of man shall come in the glory of his Father with his angels; and then shall he render unto every man according to his deeds.

SECOND SUNDAY AFTER TRINITY.
The Call to the Kingdom of God.

Collect. O Lord God, who never failest to help and govern those whom Thou dost bring up in Thy steadfast fear and love: make us to have a perpetual fear and love of Thy holy Name; through Jesus Christ, Thy Son, our Lord. AMEN.

I. EPISTLE, 1 John 3. 13–18.
He That Loves Has Passed from Death to Life.

MARVEL not, brethren, if the world hateth you. We know that we have passed out of death into life, because we love the brethren. He that loveth not abideth in death. Whosoever hateth his brother is a murderer: and ye know that no murderer hath eternal life abiding in him. Hereby know we love, because he laid down his life for us: and we ought to lay down our lives for the brethren. But whoso hath the world's goods, and beholdeth his brother in need, and shutteth up his compassion from him, how doth the love of God abide in him? My little children, let us not love in word, neither with the tongue; but in deed and truth.

I. GOSPEL, Luke 14. 16–24.
The Great Supper.

A CERTAIN man made a great supper; and he bade many; and he sent forth his servant at supper time to say to them that were bidden, Come; for all things are now ready.

And they all with one consent began to make excuse. The first said unto him, I have bought a field, and I must needs go out and see it; I pray thee have me excused. And another said, I have bought five yoke of oxen, and I go to prove them; I pray thee have me excused. And another said, I have married a wife, and therefore I cannot come.

And the servant came, and told his lord these things. Then the master of the house being angry said to his servant, Go out quickly into the streets and lanes of the city, and bring in hither the poor and maimed and blind and lame.

And the servant said, Lord, what thou didst command is done, and yet there is room.

And the lord said unto the servant, Go out into the highways and hedges, and constrain them to come in, that my house may be filled. For I say unto you, that none of those men that were bidden shall taste of my supper.

II. EPISTLE, 1 Corinthians 1. 26–31.
The Wise Put to Shame.

BEHOLD your calling, brethren, that not many wise after the flesh, not many mighty, not many noble, are called: but God chose the foolish things of the world, that he might put to shame them that are wise; and God chose the weak things of the world, that he might put to shame the things that are strong; and the base things of the world, and the things that are despised, did God choose, yea and the things that are not, that he might bring to nought the things that are: that no flesh should glory before God. But of him are ye in Christ Jesus, who was made unto us wisdom from God, and righteousness and sanctification, and redemption: that, according as it is written, He that glorieth, let him glory in the Lord.

II. GOSPEL, Luke 14. 25–35.
The Cost of Discipleship.

NOW there went with him great multitudes: and he turned, and said unto them, If any man cometh unto me, and hateth not his own father, and mother, and wife, and children, and brethren, and sisters, yea, and his own life also, he cannot be my disciple. Whosoever doth not bear his own cross, and come after me, cannot be my disciple.

For which of you, desiring to build a tower, doth not first sit down and count the cost, whether he have wherewith to complete it? Lest haply, when he hath laid a foundation, and is not able to finish, all that behold begin to mock him, saying, This man began to build, and was not able to finish.

Or what king, as he goeth to encounter another king in war, will not sit down first and take counsel whether he is able with ten thousand to meet him that cometh against him with twenty thousand? Or else, while the other is yet a great way off, he sendeth an ambassage, and asketh conditions of peace.

So therefore whosoever he be of you that renounceth not all that he hath, he cannot be my disciple. Salt therefore is good: but if even the salt have lost its savor, wherewith shall it be seasoned? It is fit neither for the land nor for the dunghill: men cast it out. He that hath ears to hear, let him hear.

III. EPISTLE, Hosea 11. 1–7.
The Disappointed Love of God.

WHEN Israel was a child, then I loved him, and called my son out of Egypt. The more the prophets called them, the more they went from them: they sacrificed unto the Baalim, and burned incense to graven images. Yet I taught Ephraim to walk; I took them on my arms; but they knew not that I healed them. I drew them with cords of a man, with bands of love; and I was to them as they that lift up the yoke on their jaws; and I laid food before them.

They shall not return into the land of Egypt; but the Assyrian shall be their king, because they refused to return to me. And the sword shall fall upon their cities, and shall consume their bars, and devour them, because of their own counsels. And my people are bent on backsliding from me: though they call them to him that is on high, none at all will exalt him.

III. GOSPEL, Luke 9. 51–62.
Complete Surrender to Jesus.

AND it came to pass, when the days were well-nigh come that he should be received up, he stedfastly set his face to go to Jerusalem, and sent messengers before his face: and they went, and entered into a village of the Samaritans, to make ready for him. And they did not receive him, because his face was as though he were going to Jerusalem. And when his disciples James and John saw this, they said, Lord, wilt thou that we bid fire to come down from heaven, and consume them? But he turned and rebuked them. And they went to another village.

And as they went on the way, a certain man said unto him, I will follow thee whithersoever thou goest. And Jesus said unto him, The foxes have holes, and the birds of the heaven have nests; but the Son of man hath not where to lay his head.

And he said unto another, Follow me. But he said, Lord, suffer me first to go and bury my father. But he said unto him, Leave the dead to bury their own dead; but go thou and publish abroad the kingdom of God.

And another also said, I will follow thee, Lord; but first suffer me to bid farewell to them that are at my house. But Jesus said unto him, No man, having put his hand to the plow, and looking back, is fit for the kingdom of God.

THIRD SUNDAY AFTER TRINITY.
The Prevenient Grace of God.

Collect. O Lord God, the Protector of all that trust in Thee, without Whom nothing is strong, nothing is holy: increase and multiply upon us Thy mercy; that, Thou being our Ruler and Guide, we may so pass through things temporal that we finally lose not the things eternal; through Jesus Christ, Thy Son, our Lord. AMEN.

I. EPISTLE, 1 Peter 5. 6–11.
God Calls and Perfects.

HUMBLE yourselves therefore under the mighty hand of God, that he may exalt you in due time; casting all your anxiety upon him, because he careth for you.

Be sober, be watchful: your adversary the devil, as a roaring lion, walketh about, seeking whom he may devour: whom withstand stedfast in your faith, knowing that the same sufferings are accomplished in your brethren who are in the world.

And the God of all grace, who called you unto his eternal glory in Christ, after that ye have suffered a little while, shall himself perfect, establish, strengthen you. To him be the dominion for ever and ever. Amen.

I. GOSPEL, Luke 15. 1–10.
The Lost Sheep and the Lost Coin.

NOW all the publicans and sinners were drawing near unto him to hear him. And both the Pharisees and the scribes murmured, saying, This man receiveth sinners, and eateth with them.

And he spake unto them this parable, saying, What man of you, having a hundred sheep, and having lost one of them, doth not leave the ninety and nine in the wilderness, and go after that which is lost, until he find it? And when he hath found it, he layeth it on his shoulders, rejoicing. And when he cometh home, he calleth together his friends and his neighbors, saying unto them, Rejoice with me, for I have found my sheep which was lost. I say unto you, that even so there shall be joy in heaven over one sinner that repenteth, more than over ninety and nine righteous persons, who need no repentance.

Or what woman having ten pieces of silver, if she lose one piece, doth not light a lamp, and sweep the house, and seek diligently until she find it? And when she hath found it, she calleth together her friends and neighbors, saying, Rejoice with me, for I have found the piece which I had lost. Even so, I say unto you, there is joy in the presence of the angels of God over one sinner that repenteth.

II. EPISTLE, Romans 4. 1–8.
Righteousness a Free Gift of Grace.

WHAT then shall we say that Abraham, our forefather, hath found according to the flesh? For if Abraham was justified by works, he hath whereof to glory; but not toward God? For what saith the scripture? And Abraham believed God, and it was reckoned unto him for righteousness. Now to him that worketh, the reward is not reckoned as of grace, but as of debt. But to him that worketh not, but believeth on him that justifieth the ungodly, his faith is reckoned for righteousness. Even as David also pronounceth blessing upon the man, unto whom God reckoneth righteousness apart from works, saying,

Blessed are they whose iniquities are forgiven,

And whose sins are covered.

Blessed is the man to whom the Lord will not reckon sin.

II. GOSPEL, Luke 15. 11–32.
The Prodigal Son.

AND he said, A certain man had two sons: and the younger of them said to his father, Father, give me the portion of thy substance that falleth to me. And he divided unto them his living.

And not many days after, the younger son gathered all together and took his journey into a far country; and there he wasted his substance with riotous living.

And when he had spent all, there arose a mighty famine in that country; and he began to be in want. And he went and joined himself to one of the citizens of that country; and he sent him into his fields to feed swine. And he would fain have filled his belly with the husks that the swine did eat: and no man gave unto him.

But when he came to himself he said, How many hired servants of my father's have bread enough and to spare, and I perish here with hunger! I will arise and go to my father, and will say unto him, Father, I have sinned against heaven, and in thy sight: I am no more worthy to be called thy son: make me as one of thy hired servants.

And he arose, and came to his father. But while he was yet afar off, his father saw him, and was moved with compassion, and ran, and fell on his neck, and kissed him. And the son said unto him, Father, I have sinned against heaven, and in thy sight: I am no more worthy to be called thy son. But the father said to his servants, Bring forth quickly the best robe, and put it on him; and put a ring on his hand, and shoes on his feet: and bring the fatted calf, and kill it, and let us eat, and make merry: for this my son was dead, and is alive again; he was lost, and is found. And they began to be merry.

Now his elder son was in the field: and as he came and drew nigh to the house, he heard music and dancing. And he called to him one of the servants, and inquired what these things might be. And he said unto him, Thy brother is come; and thy father hath killed the fatted calf, because he hath received him safe and sound. But he was angry, and would not go in: and his father came out, and entreated him. But he answered and said to his father, Lo, these many years do I serve thee, and I never transgressed a commandment of thine; and yet thou never gavest me a kid, that I might make merry with my friends: but when this thy son came, who hath devoured thy living with harlots, thou killedst for him the fatted calf. And he said unto him, Son, thou art ever with me, and all that is mine is thine. But it was meet to make merry and be glad: for this thy brother was dead, and is alive again; and was lost, and is found.

III. EPISTLE, Ephesians 2. 1–10.
Salvation a Gift of God.

YOU did he make alive, when ye were dead through your trespasses and sins, wherein ye once walked according to the course of this world, according to the prince of the powers of the air, of the spirit that now worketh in the sons of disobedience; among whom we also all once lived in the lusts of our flesh, doing the desires of the flesh, and of the mind, and were by nature children of wrath, even as the rest:—but God, being rich in mercy, for his great love wherewith he loved us, even when we were dead through our trespasses, made us alive together with Christ (by grace have ye been saved), and raised us up with him, and made us to sit with him in the heavenly places, in Christ Jesus: that in the ages to come he might show the exceeding riches of his grace in kindness toward us in Christ Jesus: for by grace have ye been saved through faith; and that not of yourselves, it is the gift of God; not of works, that no man should glory. For we are his workmanship, created in Christ Jesus for good works.

III. GOSPEL, Matthew 9. 9–13.
Jesus Eating with Publicans and Sinners.

AND as Jesus passed by from thence, he saw a man, called Matthew, sitting at the place of toll: and he saith unto him, Follow me. And he arose, and followed him.

And it came to pass, as he sat at meat in the house, behold, many publicans and sinners came and sat down with Jesus and his disciples.

And when the Pharisees saw it, they said unto his disciples, Why eateth your Teacher with the publicans and sinners? But when he heard it, he said, They that are whole have no need of a physician, but they that are sick. But go ye and learn what this meaneth, I desire mercy, and not sacrifice: for I came not to call the righteous, but sinners.

FOURTH SUNDAY AFTER TRINITY.
The Judgments of Men and of God.

Collect. Grant, O Lord, we beseech Thee, that the course of this world may be so peaceably ordered by Thy governance, that Thy Church may joyfully serve Thee in all godly quietness; through Jesus Christ, Thy Son, our Lord. AMEN.

I. EPISTLE, Romans 8. 18–23.
Creation Longing for Deliverance.

I RECKON that the sufferings of this present time are not worthy to be compared with the glory which shall be revealed to us-ward. For the earnest expectation of the creation waiteth for the revealing of the sons of God. For the creation was subjected to vanity, not of its own will, but by reason of him who subjected it, in hope that the creation itself also shall be delivered from the bondage of corruption into the liberty of the glory of the children of God. For we know that the whole creation groaneth and travaileth in pain together until now. And not only so, but ourselves also, who have the first-fruits of the

Spirit, even we ourselves groan within ourselves, waiting for our adoption, to wit, the redemption of our body.

I. Gospel, Luke 6. 36–42.
The Mote and the Beam.

BE ye merciful, even as your Father is merciful. And judge not, and ye shall not be judged: and condemn not, and ye shall not be condemned: release, and ye shall be released: give, and it shall be given unto you; good measure, pressed down, shaken together, running over, shall they give into your bosom. For with what measure ye mete it shall be measured to you again.

And he spake also a parable unto them, Can the blind guide the blind? shall they not both fall into a pit? The disciple is not above his teacher: but every one when he is perfected shall be as his teacher. And why beholdest thou the mote that is in thy brother's eye, but considerest not the beam that is in thine own eye? Or how canst thou say to thy brother, Brother, let me cast out the mote that is in thine eye, when thou thyself beholdest not the beam that is in thine own eye? Thou hypocrite, cast out first the beam out of thine own eye, and then shalt thou see clearly to cast out the mote that is in thy brother's eye.

II. Epistle, Romans 2. 1–13.
The Just Judgment of God.

THOU art without excuse, O man, whosoever thou art that judgest: for wherein thou judgest another, thou condemnest thyself; for thou that judgest dost practise the same things. And we know that the judgment of God is according to truth against them that practise such things.

And reckonest thou this, O man, who judgest them that practise such things, and doest the same, that thou shalt escape the judgment of God? Or despisest thou the riches of his goodness and forbearance and longsuffering, not knowing that the goodness of God leadeth thee to repentance? but after thy hardness and impenitent heart treasurest up for thyself wrath in the day of wrath and revelation of the righteous judgment of God; who will render to every man according to his works: to them that by patience in well-doing seek for glory and honor and incorruption, eternal life: but unto them that are factious, and obey not the truth, but obey unrighteousness, shall be wrath and indignation, tribulation and anguish, upon every soul of man that worketh evil, of the Jew first, and also

of the Greek: but glory and honor and peace to every man that worketh good, to the Jew first, and also to the Greek: for there is no respect of persons with God. For as many as have sinned without the law shall also perish without the law: and as many as have sinned under the law shall be judged by the law; for not the hearers of the law are just before God, but the doers of the law shall be justified.

II. Gospel, John 8. 1–11.
The Woman Taken in Adultery.

JESUS went unto the mount of Olives. And early in the morning he came again into the temple, and all the people came unto him; and he sat down, and taught them.

And the scribes and the Pharisees bring a woman taken in adultery; and having set her in the midst, they say unto him, Teacher, this woman hath been taken in adultery, in the very act. Now in the law Moses commanded us to stone such: what then sayest thou of her? And this they said, trying him, that they might have whereof to accuse him. But Jesus stooped down, and with his finger, wrote on the ground.

But when they continued asking him, he lifted up himself, and said unto them, He that is without sin among you, let him first cast a stone at her. And again he stooped down, and with is finger wrote on the ground.

And they, when they heard it, went out one by one, beginning from the eldest, even unto the last; and Jesus was left alone, and the woman, where she was, in the midst. And Jesus lifted up himself, and said unto her, Woman, where are they? did no man condemn thee? And she said, No man, Lord. And Jesus said, Neither do I condemn thee: go thy way; from henceforth sin no more.

III. Epistle, Romans 14. 1–18.
Lenience in Judgment.

HIM that is weak in faith receive ye, yet not for decision of scruples. One man hath faith to eat all things: but he that is weak eateth herbs. Let not him that eateth set at nought him that eateth not; and let not him that eateth not judge him that eateth: for God hath received him. Who art thou that judgest the servant of another? to his own lord he standeth or falleth. Yea, he shall be made to stand; for the Lord hath power to make him stand.

One man esteemeth one day above another: another esteemeth every day alike. Let each man be fully assured in his own mind. He that regardeth the day, regardeth it unto the Lord: and he that eateth, eateth unto the Lord, for he giveth God thanks; and he that eateth not, unto the Lord he eateth not, and giveth God thanks. For none of us liveth to himself, and none dieth to himself. For whether we live, we live unto the Lord; or whether we die, we die unto the Lord: whether we live therefore, or die, we are the Lord's. For to this end Christ died and lived again, that he might be Lord of both the dead and the living. But thou, why dost thou judge thy brother? or thou again, why dost thou set at nought thy brother? for we shall all stand before the judgment-se ˙ of God. For it is written,

As I live, saith the Lord, to me every
knee shall bow,
And every tongue shall confess to God.

So then each one of us shall give account of himself to God.

Let us not therefore judge one another any more: but judge ye this rather, that no man put a stumblingblock in his brother's way, or an occasion of falling. I know, and am persuaded in the Lord Jesus, that nothing is unclean of itself: save that to him who accounteth anything to be unclean, to him it is unclean. For if because of meat thy brother is grieved, thou walkest no longer in love. Destroy not with thy meat him for whom Christ died. Let not then your good be evil spoken of: for the kingdom of God is not eating and drinking, but righteousness and peace and joy in the Holy Spirit. For he that herein serveth Christ is well-pleasing to God, and approved of men.

III. GOSPEL, Luke 13. 1–5.

Exhortation to Repentance.

NOW there were some present at that very season who told him of the Galilæans, whose blood Pilate had mingled with their sacrifices.

And he answered and said unto them, Think ye that these Galilæans were sinners above all the Galilæans, because they have suffered these things? I tell you, Nay: but, except ye repent, ye shall all in like manner perish.

Or those eighteen, upon whom the tower in Siloam fell, and killed them, think ye that they were offenders above all the men that dwell in Jerusalem? I tell you, Nay: but, except ye repent, ye shall all likewise perish.

FIFTH SUNDAY AFTER TRINITY.
Discipleship.

Collect. O God, who hast prepared for those who love Thee such good things as pass man's understanding: pour into our hearts such love toward Thee, that we, loving Thee above all things, may obtain Thy promises, which exceed all that we can desire; through Jesus Christ, Thy Son, our Lord. AMEN.

I. EPISTLE, 1 Peter 3. 8–15.

The Christian Is Called to Inherit a Blessing.

BE ye all likeminded, compassionate, loving as brethren, tenderhearted, humbleminded: not rendering evil for evil or reviling for reviling; but contrariwise blessing; for hereunto were ye called, that ye should inherit a blessing. For,

He that would love life,
And see good days,
Let him refrain his tongue from evil,
And his lips that they speak no guile:
And let him turn away from evil, and
do good;
Let him seek peace, and pursue it.

For the eyes of the Lord are upon the
righteous,
And his ears unto their supplications:
But the face of the Lord is upon them
that do evil.

And who is he that will harm you, if ye be zealous of that which is good? But even if ye should suffer for righteousness' sake, blessed are ye: and fear not their fear, neither be troubled; but sanctify in your hearts Christ as Lord.

I. GOSPEL, Luke 5. 1–11.

The Draught of Fishes.

NOW it came to pass, while the multitude pressed upon him and heard the word of God, that he was standing by the lake of Gennesaret; and he saw two boats standing by the lake: but the fishermen had gone out of them, and were washing their nets.

And he entered into one of the boats, which was Simon's, and asked him to put out a little from the land. And he sat down and taught the multitudes out of the boat.

And when he had left speaking, he said unto Simon, Put out into the deep, and let down your nets for a draught. And Simon answered and said, Master, we toiled all night, and took nothing: but at thy word I will let down the nets.

And when they had done this, they inclosed a great multitude of fishes; and their nets were breaking; and they beckoned unto their partners in the other boat, that they should come and help them. And they came, and filled both the boats, so that they began to sink.

But Simon Peter, when he saw it, fell down at Jesus' knees, saying, Depart from me; for I am a sinful man, O Lord. For he was amazed, and all that were with him, at the draught of the fishes which they had taken; and so were also James and John, sons of Zebedee, who were partners with Simon.

And Jesus said unto Simon, Fear not; from henceforth thou shalt catch men. And when they had brought their boats to land, they left all, and followed him.

II. EPISTLE, Genesis 12. 1–4.
The Call of Abraham.

NOW Jehovah said unto Abram, Get thee out of thy country, and from thy kindred, and from thy father's house, unto the land that I will show thee: and I will make of thee a great nation, and I will bless thee, and make thy name great; and be thou a blessing: and I will bless them that bless thee, and him that curseth thee will I curse: and in thee shall all the families of the earth be blessed.

So Abram went, as Jehovah had spoken unto him.

II. GOSPEL, John 1. 35–51.
The First Disciples.

AGAIN on the morrow John was standing, and two of his disciples; and he looked upon Jesus as he walked, and saith, Behold, the Lamb of God!

And the two disciples heard him speak, and they followed Jesus. And Jesus turned, and beheld them following, and saith unto them, What seek ye? And they said unto him, Rabbi (which is to say, being interpreted, Teacher), where abidest thou? He saith unto them, Come, and ye shall see. They came therefore and saw where he abode; and they abode with him that day: it was about the tenth hour.

One of the two that heard John speak and followed him, was Andrew, Simon Peter's brother. He findeth first his own brother Simon, and saith unto him, We have found the Messiah (which is, being interpreted, Christ). He brought him unto Jesus. Jesus looked upon him, and said, Thou art Simon the son of John: thou shalt be called Cephas (which is by interpretation, Peter).

On the morrow he was minded to go forth into Galilee, and he findeth Philip: and Jesus saith unto him, Follow me. Now Philip was from Bethsaida, of the city of Andrew and Peter.

Philip findeth Nathanael, and saith unto him, We have found him, of whom Moses in the law, and the prophets, wrote, Jesus of Nazareth, the son of Joseph. And Nathanael said unto him, Can any good thing come out of Nazareth? Philip saith unto him, Come and see.

Jesus saw Nathanael coming to him, and saith of him, Behold, an Israelite indeed, in whom is no guile! Nathanael saith unto him, Whence knowest thou me? Jesus answered and said unto him, Before Philip called thee, when thou wast under the fig tree, I saw thee. Nathanael answered him, Rabbi, thou art the Son of God; thou art King of Israel. Jesus answered and said unto him, Because I said unto thee, I saw thee underneath the fig tree, believest thou? thou shalt see greater things than these. And he saith unto him, Verily, verily, I say unto you, Ye shall see the heaven opened, and the angels of God ascending and descending upon the Son of man.

III. EPISTLE, Acts 26. 1–29.
Paul's Call to the Apostleship.

AND Agrippa said unto Paul, Thou art permitted to speak for thyself. Then Paul stretched forth his hand, and made his defence:

I think myself happy, king Agrippa, that I am to make my defense before thee this day touching all the things whereof I am accused by the Jews: especially because thou art expert in all customs and questions which are among the Jews: wherefore I beseech thee to hear me patiently.

My manner of life then from my youth up, which was from the beginning among mine own nation and at Jerusalem, know all the Jews; having knowledge of me from the first, if they be willing to testify, that after the straitest sect of our religion I lived a Pharisee. And now I stand here to be judged for the hope of the promise made of God unto our fathers; unto which promise our twelve tribes, earnestly serving God night and day, hope to attain. And concerning this hope I am accused by the Jews, O king!

Why is it judged incredible with you, if God doth raise the dead?

I verily thought with myself that I ought to do many things contrary to the name of Jesus of Nazareth. And this I also did in Jerusalem: and I both shut up many of the saints in prisons, having received authority from the chief priests, and when they were put to death I gave my vote against them. And punishing them oftentimes in all the synagogues, I strove to make them blaspheme; and being exceedingly mad against them, I persecuted them even unto foreign cities. Whereupon as I journeyed to Damascus with the authority and commission of the chief priests, at midday, O king, I saw on the way a light from heaven, above the brightness of the sun, shining round about me and them that journeyed with me. And when we were all fallen to the earth, I heard a voice saying unto me in the Hebrew language, Saul, Saul, why persecutest thou me? it is hard for thee to kick against the goad. And I said, Who art thou, Lord? And the Lord said, I am Jesus whom thou persecutest. But arise, and stand upon thy feet; for to this end have I appeared unto thee, to appoint thee a minister and a witness both of the things wherein thou hast seen me, and of the things wherein I will appear unto thee; delivering thee from the people, and from the Gentiles, unto whom I send thee, to open their eyes, that they may turn from darkness to light and from the power of Satan unto God, that they may receive remission of sins and an inheritance among them that are sanctified by faith in me.

Wherefore, O king Agrippa, I was not disobedient unto the heavenly vision: but declared both to them of Damascus first, and at Jerusalem, and throughout all the country of Judæa, and also to the Gentiles, that they should repent and turn to God, doing works worthy of repentance. For this cause the Jews seized me in the temple, and assayed to kill me. Having therefore obtained the help that is from God, I stand unto this day testifying both to small and great, saying nothing but what the prophets and Moses did say should come; how that the Christ

must suffer, and how that he first by the resurrection of the dead should proclaim light both to the people and to the Gentiles.

And as he thus made his defence, Festus saith with a loud voice, Paul, thou art mad; thy much learning is turning thee mad.

But Paul saith, I am not mad, most excellent Festus; but speak forth words of truth and soberness. For the king knoweth of these things, unto whom also I speak freely: for I am persuaded that none of these things is hidden from him; for this hath not been done in a corner. King Agrippa, believest thou the prophets? I know that thou believest.

And Agrippa said unto Paul, With but little persuasion thou wouldest fain make me a Christian.

And Paul said, I would to God, that whether with little or with much, not thou only, but also all that hear me this day, might become such as I am, except these bonds.

III. Gospel, Matthew 16. 13–20.

The Confession of the Disciples.

NOW when Jesus came into the parts of Cæsarea Philippi, he asked his disciples, saying, Who do men say that the Son of man is? And they said, Some say John the Baptist; some Elijah; and others, Jeremiah, or one of the prophets.

He saith unto them, But who say ye that I am? And Simon Peter answered and said, Thou art the Christ, the Son of the living God.

And Jesus answered and said unto him, Blessed art thou, Simon Bar-Jonah: for flesh and blood hath not revealed it unto thee, but my Father who is in heaven. And I also say unto thee, that thou art Peter, and upon this rock I will build my church; and the gates of Hades shall not prevail against it. I will give unto thee the keys of the kingdom of heaven: and whatsoever thou shalt bind on earth shall be bound in heaven; and whatsoever thou shalt loose on earth shall be loosed in heaven.

Then charged he the disciples that they should tell no man that he was the Christ.

SIXTH SUNDAY AFTER TRINITY.

The Law of God.

Collect. Lord of all power and might, Who art the Author and Giver of all good things: graft in our hearts the love of Thy Name, increase in us true faith, nourish us with all goodness, and of Thy great mercy keep us in the same; through Jesus Christ, Thy Son, our Lord. AMEN.

I. EPISTLE, Romans 6. 3–11.
Crucified with Christ.

ARE ye ignorant that all we who were baptized into Christ Jesus were baptized into his death?

We were buried therefore with him through baptism into death: that like as Christ was raised from the dead through the glory of the Father, so we also might walk in newness of life. For if we have become united with him in the likeness of his death, we shall be also in the likeness of his resurrection; knowing this, that our old man was crucified with him, that the body of sin might be done away, that so we should no longer be in bondage to sin; for he that hath died is justified from sin.

But if we died with Christ, we believe that we shall also live with him; knowing that Christ being raised from the dead dieth no more; death no more hath dominion over him. For the death that he died, he died unto sin once: but the life that he liveth, he liveth unto God. Even so reckon ye also yourselves to be dead unto sin, but alive unto God in Christ Jesus.

I. GOSPEL, Matthew 5. 20–26.
The Higher Righteousness Required by Christ.

FOR I say unto you, that except your righteousness shall exceed the righteousness of the scribes and Pharisees, ye shall in no wise enter into the kingdom of heaven.

Ye have heard that it was said to them of old time, Thou shalt not kill; and whosoever shall kill shall be in danger of the judgment: but I say unto you, that every one who is angry with his brother shall be in danger of the judgment; and whosoever shall say to his brother, Raca, shall be in danger of the council; and whosoever shall say, Thou fool, shall be in danger of the hell of fire.

If therefore thou art offering thy gift at the altar, and there rememberest that thy brother hath aught against thee, leave there thy gift before the altar, and go thy way, first be reconciled to thy brother, and then come and offer thy gift.

Agree with thine adversary quickly, while thou art with him in the way; lest haply the adversary deliver thee to the judge, and the judge deliver thee to the officer, and thou be cast into prison. Verily I say unto thee, Thou shalt by no means come out thence, till thou have paid the last farthing.

II. EPISTLE, Isaiah 5. 8–16.
God's Judgment of the Oppressor.

WOE unto them that join house to house, that lay field to field, till there be no room, and ye be made to dwell alone in the midst of the land!

In mine ears saith Jehovah of hosts, Of a truth many houses shall be desolate, even great and fair, without inhabitant. For ten acres of vineyard shall yield one bath, and a homer of seed shall yield but an ephah.

Woe unto them that rise up early in the morning, that they may follow strong drink; that tarry late into the night, till wine inflame them! And the harp and the lute, the tabret and the pipe, and wine, are in their feasts; but they regard not the work of Jehovah, neither have they considered the operation of his hands.

Therefore my people are gone into captivity for lack of knowledge; and their honorable men are famished, and their multitude are parched with thirst. Therefore Sheol hath enlarged its desire, and opened its mouth without measure; and their glory, and their multitude, and their pomp, and he that rejoiceth among them, descend into it. And the mean man is bowed down, and the great man is humbled, and the eyes of the lofty are humbled: but Jehovah of hosts is exalted in justice, and God the Holy One is sanctified in righteousness.

II. GOSPEL, Matthew 5. 17–19.
The Majesty of the Law.

THINK not that I came to destroy the law or the prophets: I came not to destroy, but to fulfil. For verily I say unto you, Till heaven and earth pass away, one jot or one tittle shall in no wise pass away from the law, till all things be accomplished.

Whosoever therefore shall break one of these least commandments, and shall teach men so, shall be called least in the kingdom of heaven: but whosoever shall do and teach them, he shall be called great in the kingdom of heaven.

III. EPISTLE, James 2. 8–17.
Faith Apart from Works Is Dead.

IF ye fulfil the royal law, according to the scripture, Thou shalt love thy neighbor as thyself, ye do well: but if ye have respect of persons, ye commit sin, being convicted by the law as transgressors. For whosoever shall keep the whole law, and yet stumble in one point, he is become guilty of all. For he that said, Do not commit adultery, said also, Do not kill. Now if thou dost not commit adultery, but killest, thou art become a transgressor of the law.

So speak ye, and so do, as men that are to be judged by a law of liberty. For judgment is without mercy to him that hath showed no mercy: mercy glorieth against judgment.

What doth it profit, my brethren, if a man say he hath faith, but have not works? can that faith save him? If a brother or sister be naked and in lack of daily food, and one of you say unto them, Go in peace, be ye warmed and filled; and yet ye give them not the things needful to the body; what doth it profit? Even so faith, if it have not works, is dead in itself.

III. GOSPEL, Matthew 5. 38–42.
The Law of Love and the Law of Retaliation.

YE have heard that it was said, An eye for an eye, and a tooth for a tooth: but I say unto you, Resist not him that is evil: but whosoever smiteth thee on thy right cheek, turn to him the other also. And if any man would go to law with thee, and take away thy coat, let him have thy cloak also. And whosoever shall compel thee to go one mile, go with him two. Give to him that asketh thee, and from him that would borrow of thee turn not thou away.

THE TRANSFIGURATION OF CHRIST.
On the Mount of Transfiguration.

Collect. O Lord God, whose only begotten Son was transfigured with the patriarchs on the holy mount, let Thy Word be our light through the darkness of the present world, and grant that we may behold Thy glory in the world to come; through the same Thy Son, Jesus Christ, our Lord. AMEN.

I. EPISTLE, 2 Peter 1. 16–18.
Christ's Glory and Honor.

WE did not follow cunningly devised fables, when we made known unto you the power and coming of our Lord Jesus Christ, but we were eyewitnesses of his majesty. For he received from God the Father honor and glory, when there was borne such a voice to him by the Majestic Glory, This is my beloved Son, in whom I am well pleased: and this voice we ourselves heard borne out of heaven, when we were with him in the holy mount.

I. GOSPEL, Matthew 17. 1–8.
The Transfiguration of Christ.

AFTER six days Jesus taketh with him Peter and James, and John his brother, and bringeth them up into a high mountain apart: and he was transfigured before them; and his face did shine as the sun, and his garments became white as the light. And behold, there appeared unto them Moses and Elijah talking with him.

And Peter answered, and said unto Jesus, Lord, it is good for us to be here: if thou wilt, I will make here three tabernacles; one for thee, and one for Moses, and one for Elijah.

While he was yet speaking, behold, a bright cloud overshadowed them: and behold, a voice out of the cloud, saying, This is my beloved Son, in whom I am well pleased; hear ye him. And when the disciples heard it, they fell on their face, and were sore afraid. And Jesus came and touched them and said, Arise and be not afraid. And lifting up their eyes, they saw no one, save Jesus only.

II. EPISTLE, 2 Corinthians 12. 2–9.
The Revelations of Paul.

I KNOW a man in Christ, fourteen years ago (whether in the body, I know not; or whether out of the body, I know not; God knoweth), such a one caught up even to the third heaven. And I know such a man (whether in the body, or apart from the body, I know not; God knoweth), how that he was caught up into Paradise, and heard unspeakable words, which it is not lawful for a man to utter.

On behalf of such a one will I glory: but on mine own behalf I will not glory, save in my weaknesses. For if I should desire to glory, I shall not be foolish; for I shall speak the truth: but I forbear, lest any man should account of me above that which he seeth me to be, or heareth from me.

And by reason of the exceeding greatness of the revelations, that I should not be exalted overmuch, there was given to me a thorn in the flesh, a messenger of Satan to buffet me, that I should not be exalted overmuch. Concerning this thing I besought the Lord thrice, that it might depart from me. And he hath said unto me, My grace is sufficient for thee: for my power is made perfect in weakness. Most gladly therefore will I rather glory in my weaknesses, that the power of Christ may rest upon me.

II. GOSPEL, John 13. 31, 32.
The Glory of the Son of Man.

JESUS saith, Now is the Son of man glorified, and God is glorified in him; and God shall glorify him in himself, and straightway shall he glorify him.

III. EPISTLE, Revelation 1. 9–18.
John's Vision on Patmos.

I JOHN, your brother and partaker with you in the tribulation and kingdom and patience which are in Jesus, was in the isle that is called Patmos, for the word of God and the testimony of Jesus.

I was in the Spirit on the Lord's day, and I heard behind me a great voice, as of a trumpet saying, What thou seest, write in a book and send it to the seven churches: unto Ephesus, and unto Smyrna, and unto Pergamum, and unto Thyatira, and unto Sardis, and unto Philadelphia, and unto Laodicea.

And I turned to see the voice that spake with me. And having turned I saw seven golden candlesticks; and in the midst of the candlesticks one like unto a son of man, clothed with a garment down to the foot, and girt about at the breasts with a golden girdle. And his head and his hair were white as white wool, white as snow; and his eyes were as a flame of fire; and his feet like unto burnished brass, as if it had been refined in a furnace; and his voice as the voice of many waters. And he had in his right hand seven stars: and out of his mouth proceeded a sharp two-edged sword: and his countenance was as the sun shineth in his strength.

And when I saw him, I fell at his feet as one dead. And he laid his right hand upon me, saying, Fear not; I am the first and the last, and the Living one; and I was dead, and behold, I am alive for evermore, and I have the keys of death and of Hades.

III. GOSPEL, Matthew 17. 9–13.
The Descent from the Mount of Transfiguration.

AS they were coming down from the mountain, Jesus commanded them, saying, Tell the vision to no man, until the Son of man be risen from the dead.

And his disciples asked him, saying, Why then say the scribes that Elijah must first come?

And he answered and said, Elijah indeed cometh, and shall restore all things: but I say unto you, that Elijah is come already, and they knew him not, but did unto him whatsoever they would. Even so shall the Son of man also suffer of them.

Then understood the disciples that he spake unto them of John the Baptist.

EIGHTH SUNDAY AFTER TRINITY.
Error.

Collect. Grant us, Lord, we beseech Thee, the Spirit to think and to do always such things as are right, that we, who cannot do anything that is good without Thee, may by Thee be enabled to live according to Thy will; through Jesus Christ, Thy Son, our Lord. AMEN.

I. EPISTLE, Romans 8. 12–17.
The Spirit's Testimony of Our Adoption.

BRETHREN, we are debtors, not to the flesh, to live after the flesh: for if ye live after the flesh, ye must die; but if by the Spirit ye put to death the deeds of the body, ye shall live.

For as many as are led by the Spirit of God, these are sons of God. For ye received not the spirit of bondage again unto fear; but ye received the spirit of adoption, whereby we cry, Abba, Father.

The Spirit himself beareth witness with our spirit, that we are children of God: and if children, then heirs; heirs of God, and joint-heirs with Christ; if so be that we suffer with him, that we may be also glorified with him.

I. Gospel, Matthew 7. 15–21.
False Prophets.

BEWARE of false prophets, who come to you in sheep's clothing, but inwardly are ravening wolves.

By their fruits ye shall know them. Do men gather grapes of thorns, or figs of thistles? Even so every good tree bringeth forth good fruit; but the corrupt tree bringeth forth evil fruit. A good tree cannot bring forth evil fruit, neither can a corrupt tree bring forth good fruit. Every tree that bringeth not forth good fruit is hewn down, and cast into the fire. Therefore by their fruits ye shall know them.

Not every one that saith unto me, Lord, Lord, shall enter into the kingdom of heaven; but he that doeth the will of my Father who is in heaven.

II. Epistle, Galatians 3. 1–4.
The Folly of Apostasy.

O FOOLISH GALATIANS, who did bewitch you, before whose eyes Jesus Christ was openly set forth crucified? This only would I learn from you, Received ye the Spirit by the works of the law, or by the hearing of faith? Are ye so foolish? having begun in the Spirit, are ye now perfected in the flesh? Did ye suffer so many things in vain? if it be indeed in vain.

II. Gospel, Matthew 7. 13, 14.
The Two Ways.

ENTER ye in by the narrow gate: for wide is the gate and broad is the way, that leadeth to destruction, and many are they that enter in thereby. For narrow is the gate, and straitened the way, that leadeth unto life, and few are they that find it.

III. Epistle, 1 John 4. 1–6.
Proving the Spirits.

BELOVED, believe not every spirit, but prove the spirits, whether they are of God; because many false prophets are gone out into the world.

Hereby know ye the Spirit of God: every spirit that confesseth that Jesus Christ is come in the flesh is of God: and every spirit that confesseth not Jesus is not of God: and this is the spirit of the antichrist, whereof ye have heard that it cometh; and now it is in the world already.

Ye are of God, my little children, and have overcome them: because greater is he that is in you than he that is in the world. They are of the world, therefore speak they as of the world, and the world heareth them. We are of God: he that knoweth God heareth us; he who is not of God heareth us not. By this we know the spirit of truth, and the spirit of error.

III. Gospel, Matthew 7. 22–29.
The House on the Rock.

MANY will say to me in that day, Lord, Lord, did we not prophesy by thy name, and by thy name cast out demons, and by thy name do many mighty works? And then will I profess unto them, I never knew you: depart from me. ye that work iniquity.

Every one therefore that heareth these words of mine, and doeth them, shall be likened unto a wise man, who built his house upon the rock: and the rain descended, and the floods came, and the winds blew, and beat upon that house; and it fell not: for it was founded upon the rock. And every one that heareth these words of mine, and doeth them not, shall be likened unto a foolish man, who built his house upon the sand: and the rain descended, and the floods came, and the winds blew, and smote upon that house; and it fell: and great was the fall thereof.

And it came to pass, when Jesus had finished these words, the multitudes were astonished at his teaching: for he taught them as one having authority, and not as their scribes.

NINTH SUNDAY AFTER TRINITY.
The Responsibility of Stewardship.

Collect. Let Thy merciful ears, O Lord, be open to the prayers of Thy humble servants; and, that they may obtain their petitions, make them to ask such things as shall please Thee; through Jesus Christ, Thy Son, our Lord. Amen.

I. Epistle, 1 Corinthians 10. 6–13.
Godlessness Leads to Destruction.

NOW these things were our examples, to the intent we should not lust after evil things, as they also lusted. Neither be ye idolaters, as were some of them;

as it is written, The people sat down to eat and drink, and rose up to play. Neither let us commit fornication, as some of them committed, and fell in one day three and twenty thousand. Neither let us make trial of the Lord, as some of them made trial, and perished by the serpents. Neither murmur ye, as some of them murmured, and perished by the destroyer.

Now these things happened unto them by way of example; and they were written for our admonition, upon whom the ends of the ages are come. Wherefore let him that thinketh he standeth take heed lest he fall. There hath no temptation taken you but such as man can bear: but God is faithful, who will not suffer you to be tempted above that ye are able; but will with the temptation make also the way of escape, that ye may be able to endure it.

I. Gospel, Luke 16. 1–9.

The Unrighteous Steward.

AND he said also unto the disciples, There was a certain rich man, who had a steward; and the same was accused unto him that he was wasting his goods. And he called him, and said unto him, What is this that I hear of thee? render the account of thy stewardship; for thou canst be no longer steward.

And the steward said within himself, What shall I do, seeing that my lord taketh away the stewardship from me? I have not strength to dig; to beg I am ashamed.

I am resolved what to do, that, when I am put out of the stewardship, they may receive me into their houses. And calling to him each one of his lord's debtors, he said to the first, How much owest thou unto my lord? And he said, A hundred measures of oil. And he said unto him, Take thy bond, and sit down quickly and write fifty. Then said he to another, And how much owest thou? And he said, A hundred measures of wheat. He saith unto him, Take thy bond, and write fourscore.

And his lord commended the unrighteous steward because he had done wisely, for the sons of this world are for their own generation wiser than the sons of the light. And I say unto you, Make to yourselves friends by means of the mammon of unrighteousness; that, when it shall fail, they may receive you into the eternal tabernacles.

II. Epistle, Proverbs 6. 6–11.

Idleness Brings Misfortune.

GO to the ant, thou sluggard;
Consider her ways, and be wise:
Which having no chief,
Overseer, or ruler,
Provideth her bread in the summer,
And gathereth her food in the harvest.
How long wilt thou sleep, O sluggard?
When wilt thou arise out of thy sleep?
Yet a little sleep, a little slumber,
A little folding of the hands to sleep:
So shall thy poverty come as a robber,
And thy want as an armed man.

II. Gospel, Luke 12. 42–48.

The Householder, the Steward, and the Household.

AND the Lord said, Who then is the faithful and wise steward, whom his lord shall set over his household, to give them their portion of food in due season? Blessed is that servant, whom his lord when he cometh shall find so doing. Of a truth I say unto you, that he will set him over all that he hath.

But if that servant shall say in his heart, My lord delayeth his coming; and shall begin to beat the menservants and the maidservants, and to eat and drink, and to be drunken; the lord of that servant shall come in a day when he expecteth not, and in an hour when he knoweth not, and shall cut him asunder, and appoint his portion with the unfaithful.

And that servant, who knew his lord's will, and made not ready, nor did according to his will, shall be beaten with many stripes; but he that knew not, and did things worthy of stripes, shall be beaten with few stripes. And to whomsoever much is given, of him shall much be required: and to whom they commit much, of him will they ask the more.

III. Epistle, 2 Thessalonians 3. 10–13.

Christians Are Good Workers.

EVEN when we were with you, this we commanded you, If any will not work, neither let him eat. For we hear of some that walk among you disorderly, that work not at all, but are busybodies. Now them that are such we command and exhort in the Lord Jesus Christ, that with quietness they work, and eat their own bread. But ye, brethren, be not weary in well-doing.

III. GOSPEL, Luke 16. 10–15.

Faithfulness in Little Things.

HE that is faithful in a very little is faithful also in much: and he that is unrighteous in a very little is unrighteous also in much.

If therefore ye have not been faithful in the unrighteous mammon, who will commit to your trust the true riches?

And if ye have not been faithful in that which is another's, who will give you that which is your own?

No servant can serve two masters: for either he will hate the one, and love the other; or else he will hold to one, and despise the other. Ye cannot serve God and mammon.

And the Pharisees, who were lovers of money, heard all these things; and they scoffed at him. And he said unto them, Ye are they that justify yourselves in the sight of men; but God knoweth your hearts: for that which is exalted among men is an abomination in the sight of God.

TENTH SUNDAY AFTER TRINITY.

Wasted Opportunities.

Collect. O God, who declarest Thy almighty power chiefly in showing mercy and pity: mercifully grant unto us such a measure of Thy grace that we, running the way of Thy commandments, may obtain Thy gracious promises, and be made partakers of Thy heavenly treasure; through Jesus Christ, Thy Son, our Lord. AMEN.

I. EPISTLE, 1 Corinthians 12. 2–11.

The Manifold Gifts of Grace.

YE know that when ye were Gentiles ye were led away unto those dumb idols, howsoever ye might be led. Wherefore I make known unto you, that no man speaking in the Spirit of God saith, Jesus is anathema; and no man can say, Jesus is Lord, but in the Holy Spirit.

Now there are diversities of gifts, but the same Spirit. And there are diversities of ministrations, and the same Lord. And there are diversities of workings, but the same God, who worketh all things in all.

But to each one is given the manifestation of the Spirit to profit withal. For to one is given through the Spirit the word of wisdom; and to another the word of knowledge, according to the same Spirit: to another faith, in the same Spirit; and to another gifts of healings, in the one Spirit; and to another workings of miracles; and to another prophecy; and to another discernings of spirits; to another divers kinds of tongues; and to another the interpretation of tongues: but all these worketh the one and the same Spirit, dividing to each one severally even as he will.

I. GOSPEL, Luke 19. 41–47.

Jesus Weeping over Jerusalem.

AND when he drew nigh, he saw the city and wept over it, saying, If thou hadst known in this day, even thou, the things which belong unto peace! but now they are hid from thine eyes. For the days shall come upon thee, when thine enemies shall cast up a bank about thee, and compass thee round, and keep thee in on every side, and shall dash thee to the ground, and thy children within thee; and they shall not leave in thee one stone upon another; because thou knowest not the time of thy visitation.

And he entered into the temple, and began to cast out them that sold, saying unto them, It is written, And my house shall be a house of prayer: but ye have made it a den of robbers.

And he was teaching daily in the temple.

II. EPISTLE, Romans 11. 17–24.

The Goodness and the Severity of God.

IF some of the branches were broken off, and thou, being a wild olive, wast grafted in among them, and didst become partaker with them of the root of the fatness of the olive tree; glory not over the branches: but if thou gloriest, it is not thou that bearest the root, but the root thee.

Thou wilt say then, Branches were broken off, that I might be grafted in. Well; by their unbelief they were broken off, and thou standest by thy faith. Be not highminded, but fear: for if God spared not the natural branches, neither will he spare thee.

Behold then the goodness and severity of God: toward them that fell, severity; but toward thee, God's goodness, if thou continue in his goodness: otherwise thou also shalt be cut off. And they also, if they continue not in their unbelief, shall be grafted in: for God is able to graft them in again. For if thou wast cut out of that which is by nature a wild olive tree, and wast grafted contrary to nature into a good olive tree; how much more shall these, which are the natural branches, be grafted into their own olive tree?

II. GOSPEL, Luke 4. 23-30.
Jesus Rejected at Nazareth.

AND he said unto them, Doubtless ye will say unto me this parable, Physician, heal thyself: whatsoever we have heard done at Capernaum, do also here in thine own country.

And he said, Verily I say unto you, No prophet is acceptable in his own country. But of a truth I say unto you, There were many widows in Israel in the days of Elijah, when the heaven was shut up three years and six months, when there came a great famine over all the land; and unto none of them was Elijah sent, but only to Zarephath, in the land of Sidon, unto a woman that was a widow.

And there were many lepers in Israel in the time of Elisha the prophet; and none of them was cleansed, but only Naaman the Syrian.

And they were all filled with wrath in the synagogue, as they heard these things; and they rose up, and cast him forth out of the city, and led him unto the brow of the hill whereon their city was built, that they might throw him down headlong. But he passing through the midst of them went his way.

III. EPISTLE, Hebrews 3. 12-19.
Disobedience Hardens the Heart.

TAKE heed, brethren, lest haply there shall be in any one of you an evil heart of unbelief, in falling away from the living God: but exhort one another day by day, so long as it is cálled To-day; lest any one of you be hardened by the deceitfulness of sin: for we are become partakers of Christ, if we hold fast the beginning of our confidence firm unto the end: while it is said,

To-day if ye shall hear his voice, Harden not your hearts, as in the provocation.

For who, when they heard, did provoke? nay, did not all they that came out of Egypt by Moses? And with whom was he displeased forty years? was it not with them that sinned, whose bodies fell in the wilderness? And to whom sware he that they should not enter into his rest, but to them that were disobedient? And we see that they were not able to enter in because of unbelief.

III. GOSPEL, Matthew 11. 20-24.
The Unrepentant Cities.

THEN began he to upbraid the cities wherein most of his mighty works were done, because they repented not.

Woe unto thee, Chorazin! woe unto thee, Bethsaida! for if the mighty works had been done in Tyre and Sidon which were done in you, they would have repented long ago in sackcloth and ashes. But I say unto you, it shall be more tolerable for Tyre and Sidon in the day of judgment, than for you.

And thou, Capernaum, shalt thou be exalted unto heaven? thou shalt go down unto Hades: for if the mighty works had been done in Sodom which were done in thee, it would have remained until this day. But I say unto you that it shall be more tolerable for the land of Sodom in the day of judgment, than for thee.

ELEVENTH SUNDAY AFTER TRINITY.
True and False Righteousness.

Collect. Almighty and eternal God, Who art always more ready to hear than we to pray, and art wont to give more than either we desire or deserve: pour down upon us the abundance of Thy mercy, forgiving us our shortcomings, and giving us those good things which we are not worthy to ask, but through the merits and mediation of Jesus Christ, Thy Son, our Lord. AMEN.

I. EPISTLE, 1 Corinthians 15. 1-10.
Grace Makes Us Humble and Strong.

NOW I make known unto you, brethren, the gospel which I preached unto you, which also ye received, wherein also ye stand, by which also ye are saved, if ye hold fast the word which I preached unto you, except ye believed in vain.

For I delivered unto you first of all that which also I received: that Christ died for our sins according to the scriptures; and that he was buried; and that he hath been raised on the third day according to the scriptures; and that he appeared to Cephas; then to the twelve; then he appeared to above five hundred brethren at once, of whom the greater part remain until now, but some are fallen asleep; then he appeared to James; then to all the apostles; and last of all, as to the child untimely born, he appeared to me also.

For I am the least of the apostles, that am not meet to be called an apostle, because I persecuted the church of God. But by the grace of God I am what I am: and his grace which was bestowed upon me was not found vain; but I labored more abundantly than they all: yet not I, but the grace of God which was with me.

I. Gospel, Luke 18. 9–14.
The Pharisee and the Publican.

A ND he spake also this parable unto certain who trusted in themselves that they were righteous, and set all others at nought:

Two men went up into the temple to pray; the one a Pharisee, and the other a publican. The Pharisee stood and prayed thus with himself, God, I thank thee, that I am not as the rest of men, extortioners, unjust, adulterers, or even as this publican. I fast twice in the week; I give tithes of all that I get. But the publican, standing afar off, would not lift up so much as his eyes unto heaven, but smote his breast, saying, God, be thou merciful to me, a sinner.

I say unto you, This man went down to his house justified rather than the other: for every one that exalteth himself shall be humbled; but he that humbleth himself shall be exalted.

II. Epistle, Romans 3. 21–31.
Righteousness by Faith Excludes Boasting.

B UT now apart from the law a righteousness of God hath been manifested, being witnessed by the law and the prophets; even the righteousness of God through faith in Jesus Christ unto all them that believe; for there is no distinction; for all have sinned, and fall short of the glory of God; being justified freely by his grace through the redemption that is in Christ Jesus: whom God set forth to be a propitiation, through faith, in his blood, to show his righteousness because of the passing over of the sins done aforetime, in the forbearance of God; for the showing, I say, of his

righteousness at this present season: that he might himself be just, and the justifier of him that hath faith in Jesus.

Where then is the glorying? It is excluded. By what manner of law? of works? Nay: but by a law of faith. We reckon therefore that a man is justified by faith apart from the works of the law. Or is God the God of Jews only? is he not the God of Gentiles also? Yea, of Gentiles also: if so be that God is one, and he shall justify the circumcision by faith, and the uncircumcision through faith.

Do we then make the law of none effect through faith? God forbid: nay, we establish the law.

II. Gospel, Matthew 21. 28–31.
The Two Sons Sent into the Vineyard.

A MAN had two sons; and he came to the first, and said, Son, go work today in the vineyard. And he answered and said, I will not: but afterward he repented himself, and went. And he came to the second, and said likewise. And he answered and said, I go, sir: and went not.

Which of the two did the will of his father? They say, the first. Jesus saith unto them, Verily I say unto you, that the publicans and harlots go into the kingdom of God before you.

III. Epistle, 1 John 1. 8—2. 2.
Self-examination Leads to Confession of Sin.

I F we say that we have no sin, we deceive ourselves, and the truth is not in us. If we confess our sins, he is faithful and righteous to forgive us our sins, and to cleanse us from all unrighteousness. If we say that we have not sinned, we make him a liar, and his word is not in us.

My little children, these things write I unto you that ye may not sin. And if any man sin, we have an Advocate with the Father, Jesus Christ the righteous: and he is the propitiation for our sins; and not for ours only, but also for the whole world.

III. Gospel, Matthew 23. 1–12.
Scribes and Pharisees in the Seat of Moses.

T HEN spake Jesus to the multitudes and to his disciples, saying, The scribes and the Pharisees sit on Moses' seat: all things therefore whatsoever they bid you, these do and observe: but do not ye after their works; for they say, and do not. Yea, they bind heavy burdens and grievous to be borne, and lay them on men's shoulders; but they themselves will not move them with their finger. But all their works they do to be seen of men: for they make broad their phylacteries, and enlarge the borders of their garments, and love the chief place at feasts, and the chief seats in the synagogues, and the salutations in the marketplaces, and to be called of men, Rabbi. But be not ye called Rabbi: for one is your teacher, and all ye are brethren. And call no man your father on the earth: for one is your Father, even he who is in heaven. Neither be ye called masters: for one is your master, even the Christ. But he that is greatest among you shall be your servant, And whosoever shall exalt himself shall be humbled; and whosoever shall humble himself shall be exalted.

TWELFTH SUNDAY AFTER TRINITY.

The Use of the Tongue.

Collect. Almighty and merciful God, of whose gift it cometh that Thy faithful people do unto Thee true and laudable service: grant, we beseech Thee, that we may so faithfully serve Thee in this life, that we fail not finally to attain Thy heavenly promises; through Jesus Christ, Thy Son, our Lord. AMEN.

I. EPISTLE, 2 Corinthians 3. 4–18.

The Letter Killeth, the Spirit Giveth Life.

SUCH confidence have we through Christ to God-ward: not that we are sufficient of ourselves, to account anything as from ourselves; but our sufficiency is from God; who also made us sufficient as ministers of a new covenant; not of the letter, but of the Spirit: for the letter killeth, but the spirit giveth life. But if the ministration of death, written, and engraven on stones, came with glory, so that the children of Israel could not look stedfastly upon the face of Moses for the glory of his face; which glory was passing away: how shall not rather the ministration of the spirit be with glory? For if the ministration of condemnation hath glory, much rather doth the ministration of righteousness exceed in glory. For verily that which hath been made glorious hath not been made glorious in this respect by reason of the glory that surpasseth. For if that which passeth away was with glory, much more that which remaineth is in glory. Having therefore such a hope, we use great boldness of speech, and are not as Moses, who put a veil upon his face, that the children of Israel should not look stedfastly on the end of that which was passing away: but their minds were hardened: for until this very day at the reading of the old covenant the same veil remaineth, it not being revealed to them that it is done away in Christ. But unto this day, whensoever Moses is read, a veil lieth upon their heart. But whensoever it shall turn to the Lord, the veil is taken away.

Now the Lord is the Spirit: and where the Spirit of the Lord is, there is liberty. But we all, with unveiled face beholding as in a mirror the glory of the Lord, are transformed into the same image from glory to glory, even as from the Lord the Spirit.

I. GOSPEL, Mark 7. 31–37.

Jesus Heals the Deafmute.

AND again he went out from the borders of Tyre, and came through Sidon unto the sea of Galilee, through the midst of the borders of Decapolis.

And they bring unto him one that was deaf, and had an impediment in his speech; and they beseech him to lay his hand upon him. And he took him aside from the multitude privately, and put his fingers into his ears, and he spat, and touched his tongue; and looking up to heaven, he sighed, and saith unto him, Ephphatha, that is, Be opened. And his ears were opened, and the bond of his tongue was loosed, and he spake plain.

And he charged them that they should tell no man: but the more he charged them, so much the more a great deal they published it. And they were beyond measure astonished, saying, He hath done all things well; he maketh even the deaf to hear, and the dumb to speak.

II. EPISTLE, James 3. 8–12.

The Taming of the Tongue.

THE tongue can no man tame; it is a restless evil, it is full of deadly poison. Therewith bless we the Lord and Father; and therewith curse we men, who are made after the likeness of God: out of the same mouth cometh forth blessing and cursing. My brethren, these things ought not so to be. Doth the fountain send forth from the same opening sweet water and bitter? can a fig tree, my brethren, yield olives, or a vine figs? neither can salt water yield sweet.

II. GOSPEL, Matthew 12. 33–37.
Idle Words.

EITHER make the tree good, and its fruit good; or make the tree corrupt, and its fruit corrupt; for the tree is known by its fruit.

Ye offspring of vipers, how can ye, being evil, speak good things? for out of the abundance of the heart the mouth speaketh. The good man out of his good treasure bringeth forth good things: and the evil man out of his evil treasure bringeth forth evil things.

And I say unto you, that every idle word that men shall speak, they shall give account thereof in the day of judgment. For by thy words thou shalt be justified, and by thy words thou shalt be condemned.

III. EPISTLE, 1 Corinthians 2. 9–16.
Spiritual Things Spiritually Discerned.

IT is written,
  Things which eye saw not, and ear heard not,
And which entered not into the heart of man,
Whatsoever things God prepared for them that love him.
But unto us God revealed them through the Spirit: for the Spirit searcheth all

things, yea, the deep things of God. For who among men knoweth the things of a man, save the spirit of the man, which is in him? even so the things of God none knoweth, save the Spirit of God.

But we received, not the spirit of the world, but the spirit which is from God; that we might know the things that were freely given to us of God. Which things also we speak, not in words which man's wisdom teacheth, but which the Spirit teacheth; combining spiritual things with spiritual words.

Now the natural man receiveth not the things of the Spirit of God: for they are foolishness unto him; and he cannot know them, because they are spiritually judged. But he that is spiritual judgeth all things, and he himself is judged of no man. For who hath known the mind of the Lord, that he should instruct him? But we have the mind of Christ.

III. GOSPEL, Matthew 5. 33–37.
Sincerity in Speech.

AGAIN, ye have heard that it was said of them of old time, Thou shalt not forswear thyself, but shalt perform unto the Lord thine oaths: but I say unto you, Swear not at all; neither by the heaven, for it is the throne of God; nor by the earth, for it is the footstool of his feet; nor by Jerusalem, for it is the city of the great King. Neither shalt thou swear by thy head, for thou canst not make one hair white or black. But let your speech be, Yea, yea; Nay, nay: and whatsoever is more than these is of the evil one.

THIRTEENTH SUNDAY AFTER TRINITY.
Mercy.

Collect. Almighty and eternal God, give unto us the increase of faith, hope, and charity; and, that we may obtain that which Thou dost promise, make us to love that which Thou dost command; through Jesus Christ, Thy Son, our Lord. AMEN.

I. EPISTLE (a), Galatians 3. 16–22.
The Promise Is Older Than the Law.

NOW to Abraham were the promises spoken, and to his seed. He saith not, And to seeds, as of many; but as of one, And to thy seed, which is Christ. Now this I say: A covenant confirmed beforehand by God, the law, which came four hundred and thirty years after, doth not disannul so as to make the promise

of none effect. For if the inheritance is of the law, it is no more of promise: but God hath granted it to Abraham by promise.

What then is the law? It was added because of transgressions, till the seed should come to whom the promise hath been made; and it was ordained through angels by the hand of a mediator. Now a mediator is not a mediator of one; but God is one. Is the law then against the promises of God? God forbid: for if there had been a law given which could make alive, verily righteousness would have been of the law. But the scripture shut up all things under sin, that the promise by faith in Jesus Christ might be given to them that believe.

I. EPISTLE (b), Galatians 3. 21–28.
Faith Liberates and Unites.

IS the law then against the promises of God? God forbid: for if there had been a law given which could make alive, verily righteousness would have been of the law. But the scripture shut up all things under sin, that the promise by faith in Jesus Christ might be given to them that believe.

But before faith came, we were kept in ward under the law, shut up unto the faith which should afterwards be revealed. So that the law is become our tutor to bring us unto Christ, that we might be justified by faith. But now that faith is come, we are no longer under a tutor. For ye are all sons of God, through faith, in Christ Jesus. For as many of you as were baptized into Christ did put on Christ. There can be neither Jew nor Greek, there can be neither bond nor free, there can be no male and female; for ye all are one man in Christ Jesus.

I. GOSPEL, Luke 10. 23–37.
The Good Samaritan.

AND turning to the disciples, he said privately, Blessed are the eyes which see the things that ye see: for I say unto you, that many prophets and kings desired to see the things which ye see, and saw them not; and to hear the things which ye hear, and heard them not.

And behold, a certain lawyer stood up and made trial of him, saying, Teacher, what shall I do to inherit eternal life? And he said unto him, What is written in the law? how readest thou? And he answering said, Thou shalt love the Lord thy God with all thy heart, and with all thy soul, and with all thy strength, and with all thy mind; and thy neighbor as thyself. And he said unto him, Thou hast answered right: this do, and thou shalt live. But he, desiring to justify himself, said unto Jesus, And who is my neighbor?

Jesus made answer and said, A certain man was going down from Jerusalem to Jericho; and he fell among robbers, who both stripped him and beat him, and departed, leaving him half dead.

And by chance a certain priest was going down that way: and when he saw him he passed by on the other side.

And in like manner a Levite also, when he came to the place, and saw him, passed by on the other side.

But a certain Samaritan, as he journeyed, came where he was: and when he saw him, he was moved with compassion, and came to him, and bound up his wounds, pouring on them oil and wine; and he set him on his own beast, and brought him to an inn, and took care of him. And on the morrow he took out two shillings, and gave them to the host, and said, Take care of him; and whatsoever thou spendest more, I, when I come back again, will repay thee.

Which of these three, thinkest thou, proved neighbor unto him that fell among robbers? And he said, He that showed mercy on him. And Jesus said unto him, Go, and do thou likewise.

II. EPISTLE, 1 John 4. 7–10.
Love Is of God.

BELOVED, let us love one another: for love is of God; and every one that loveth is begotten of God, and knoweth God. He that loveth not knoweth not God; for God is love.

Herein was the love of God manifested in us, that God hath sent his only begotten Son into the world that we might live through him. Herein is love, not that we loved God, but that he loved us, and sent his son to be the propitiation for our sins.

II. GOSPEL, Matthew 5. 43—6. 4.
Jesus Teaches Brotherly Love.

YE have heard that it was said, Thou shalt love thy neighbor, and hate thine enemy: but I say unto you, Love your enemies, and pray for them that persecute you; that ye may be sons of your Father who is in heaven: for he maketh his sun to rise on the evil and the good, and sendeth rain on the just and the unjust.

For if ye love them that love you, what reward have ye? do not even the publicans the same? And if ye salute your brethren only, what do ye more than others? do not even the Gentiles the same? Ye therefore shall be perfect, as your heavenly Father is perfect.

Take heed that ye do not your righteousness before men, to be seen of them: else ye have no reward with your Father who is in heaven.

When therefore thou doest alms, sound not a trumpet before thee, as the hypocrites do in the synagogues and in the streets, that they may have glory of men. Verily I say unto you, They have received their reward. But when thou doest alms, let not thy left hand know what thy right hand doeth: that thine alms may be in secret: and thy Father who seeth in secret shall recompense thee.

III. EPISTLE. 2 Corinthians 9. 6–10.

Bountiful Seed and Bountiful Harvest.

HE that soweth sparingly shall reap also sparingly; and he that soweth bountifully shall reap also bountifully. Let each man do according as he hath purposed in his heart: not grudgingly, or of necessity: for God loveth a cheerful giver. And God is able to make all grace abound unto you; that ye, having always all sufficiency in everything, may abound unto every good work: as it is written,

He hath scattered abroad, he hath given to the poor;

His righteousness abideth for ever.

And he that supplieth seed to the sower, and bread for food, shall supply and multiply your seed for sowing, and increase the fruits of your righteousness.

III. GOSPEL, Mark 12. 41–44.

The Widow's Mite.

AND he sat down over against the treasury, and beheld how the multitude cast money into the treasury: and many that were rich cast in much. And there came a poor widow, and she cast in two mites, which make a farthing. And he called unto him his disciples, and said unto them, Verily I say unto you, This poor widow cast in more than all they that are casting into the treasury: for they all did cast in of their superfluity; but she of her want did cast in all that she had, even all her living.

FOURTEENTH SUNDAY AFTER TRINITY.

Gratitude.

Collect. Keep, we beseech Thee, O Lord, Thy Church, with Thy perpetual mercy; and, because the frailty of man without Thee cannot but fall, keep us ever by Thy help from all things hurtful, and lead us to all things profitable to our salvation; through Jesus Christ our Lord. AMEN.

I. EPISTLE, Galatians 5. 16–24.

The Flesh Lusteth against the Spirit.

WALK by the Spirit, and ye shall not fulfil the lust of the flesh. For the flesh lusteth against the Spirit, and the Spirit against the flesh; for these are contrary the one to the other; that ye may not do the things that ye would. But if ye are led by the Spirit, ye are not under the law.

Now the works of the flesh are manifest, which are these: fornication, uncleanness, lasciviousness, idolatry, sorcery, enmities, strife, jealousies, wraths, factions, divisions, parties, envyings, drunkenness, revellings, and such like; of which I forewarn you, even as I did forewarn you, that they who practise such things shall not inherit the kingdom of God.

But the fruit of the Spirit is love, joy, peace, longsuffering, kindness, goodness, faithfulness, meekness, self-control; against such there is no law. And they that are of Christ Jesus have crucified the flesh with the passions and the lusts thereof.

I. GOSPEL, Luke 17. 11–19.

The Ten Lepers.

AND it came to pass, as they were on the way to Jerusalem, that he was passing along the borders of Samaria and Galilee.

And as he entered into a certain village, there met him ten men that were lepers, who stood afar off: and they lifted up their voices, saying, Jesus, Master, have mercy on us. And when he saw them, he said unto them, Go and show yourselves unto the priests. And it came to pass, as they went, they were cleansed.

And one of them, when he saw that he was healed, turned back, with a loud voice glorifying God; and he fell upon his face at his feet, giving him thanks; and he was a Samaritan. And Jesus answering said, Were not the ten cleansed? but where are the nine? Were there none found that returned to give glory to God, save this stranger? And he said unto him, Arise, and go thy way: thy faith hath made thee whole.

II. EPISTLE, Psalm 147. 1–11.

It Is Good to Praise the Lord.

PRAISE ye Jehovah;

For it is good to sing praises unto our God;

For it is pleasant, and praise is comely. Jehovah doth build up Jerusalem;

He gathereth together the outcasts of Israel.

He healeth the broken in heart,

And bindeth up their wounds.

He counteth the number of the stars;
He calleth them all by their names.
Great is our Lord, and mighty in
power;
His understanding is infinite.
Jehovah upholdeth the meek:
He bringeth the wicked down to the
ground.
Sing unto Jehovah with thanksgiving;
Sing praises upon the harp unto our
God,
Who covereth the heavens with clouds,
Who prepareth rain for the earth,
Who maketh grass to grow upon the
mountains.
He giveth to the beast his food,
And to the young ravens which cry.
He delighteth not in the strength of
the horse:
He taketh no pleasure in the legs of a
man.
Jehovah taketh pleasure in them that
fear him,
In those that hope in his lovingkind-
ness.

II. GOSPEL, John 5. 1–14.

The Man at Bethesda.

AFTER these things there was a feast
of the Jews; and Jesus went up to
Jerusalem.

Now there is in Jerusalem by the
sheep gate a pool, which is called in Hebrew Bethesda, having five porches. In
these lay a multitude of them that were
sick, blind, halt, withered.

And a certain man was there, who had
been thirty and eight years in his infirmity. When Jesus saw him lying, and
knew that he had been now a long time
in that case, he saith unto him, Wouldest thou be made whole? The sick man
answered him, Sir, I have no man, when
the water is troubled, to put me into the
pool: but while I am coming, another
steppeth down before me. Jesus saith
unto him, Arise, take up thy bed, and
walk. And straightway the man was
made whole, and took up his bed and
walked.

Now it was the sabbath on that day.
So the Jews said unto him that was
cured, It is the sabbath, and it is not
lawful for thee to take up thy bed. But
he answered them, He that made me
whole, the same said unto me, Take up
thy bed and walk. They asked him, Who
is the man that said unto thee, Take up
thy bed, and walk? But he that was

healed knew not who it was; for Jesus
had conveyed himself away, a multitude
being in the place.

Afterward Jesus findeth him in the
temple, and said unto him, Behold, thou
art made whole: sin no more, lest a
worse thing befall thee.

III. EPISTLE, 1 Timothy 1. 12–17.

The Mercy of God Begets Gratitude.

I THANK him that enabled me, even
Christ Jesus our Lord, for that he
counted me faithful, appointing me to
his service; though I was before a blas-
phemer, and a persecutor, and injurious:
howbeit I obtained mercy, because I did
it ignorantly in unbelief; and the grace
of our Lord abounded exceedingly with
faith and love which is in Christ Jesus.
Faithful is the saying, and worthy of all
acceptation, that Christ Jesus came into
the world to save sinners; of whom I am
chief: howbeit for this cause I obtained
mercy, that in me as chief might Jesus
Christ show forth all his longsuffering,
for an ensample of them that should
thereafter believe on him unto eternal
life.

Now unto the King eternal, immortal,
invisible, the only God, be honor and
glory for ever and ever. Amen.

III. GOSPEL, Matthew 11. 25–30.

Jesus Gives Thanks to His Father.

AT that season Jesus answered and
said, I thank thee, O Father, Lord of
heaven and earth, that thou didst hide
these things from the wise and understanding, and didst reveal them unto
babes: yea, Father, for so it was well-
pleasing in thy sight.

All things have been delivered unto me
of my Father: and no one knoweth the
Son, save the Father; neither doth any
know the Father, save the Son, and he
to whomsoever the Son willeth to reveal
him.

Come unto me, all ye that labor and
are heavy laden, and I will give you
rest. Take my yoke upon you, and learn
of me; for I am meek and lowly in heart:
and ye shall find rest unto your souls.
For my yoke is easy, and my burden is
light.

FIFTEENTH SUNDAY AFTER TRINITY.
Our Daily Bread.

Collect. O Lord God, who ever carest for us in Thy providence and never failest in Thy dispensations: we pray Thee, remove from us those things that may injure us, and grant us whatever may be for our profit; through Jesus Christ, Thy Son, our Lord. AMEN.

I. EPISTLE, Galatians 5. 25—6. 10.
Chistians Bearing One Another's Burdens.

IF we live in the Spirit, by the Spirit let us also walk. Let us not become vainglorious, provoking one another, envying one another.

Brethren, even if a man be overtaken in any trespass, ye who are spiritual, restore such a one in a spirit of gentleness; looking to thyself lest thou also be tempted.

Bear ye one another's burdens, and so fulfil the law of Christ. For if a man thinketh himself to be something when he is nothing, he deceiveth himself. But let each man prove his own work, and then shall he have his glorying in regard of himself alone, and not of his neighbor. For each man shall bear his own burden.

But let him that is taught in the word communicate unto him that teacheth in all good things.

Be not deceived; God is not mocked: for whatsoever a man soweth that shall he also reap. For he that soweth unto his own flesh shall of the flesh reap corruption; but he that soweth unto the Spirit shall of the Spirit reap eternal life. And let us not be weary in well-doing: for in due season we shall reap, if we faint not.

So then, as we have opportunity, let us work that which is good toward all men, and especially toward them that are of the household of the faith.

I. GOSPEL, Matthew 6. 24–34.
Our Chief Concern.

NO man can serve two masters: for either he will hate the one, and love the other; or else he will hold to one, and despise the other. Ye cannot serve God and mammon.

Therefore I say unto you, Be not anxious for your life, what ye shall eat, or what ye shall drink; nor yet for your body, what ye shall put on. Is not the life more than the food, and the body than the raiment.

Behold the birds of the heaven, that they sow not, neither do they reap, nor gather into barns; and your heavenly Father feedeth them. Are not ye of much more value than they? And which of you by being anxious can add one cubit unto the measure of his life?

And why are ye anxious concerning raiment? Consider the lilies of the field, how they grow; they toil not, neither do they spin; yet I say unto you, that even Solomon in all his glory was not arrayed like one of these. But if God doth so clothe the grass of the field, which to-day is, and to-morrow is cast into the oven, shall he not much more clothe you, O ye of little faith?

Be not therefore anxious, saying, What shall we eat? or, What shall we drink? or, Wherewithal shall we be clothed? For after all these things do the Gentiles seek; for your heavenly Father knoweth that ye have need of all these things. But seek ye first his kingdom, and his righteousness; and all these things shall be added unto you. Be not therefore anxious for the morrow: for the morrow will be anxious for itself. Sufficient unto the day is the evil thereof.

II. EPISTLE, Acts 20. 32–35.
It is More Blessed to Give Than to Receive.

AND now I commend you to God, and to the word of his grace, which is able to build you up, and to give you the inheritance among all them that are sanctified.

I coveted no man's silver, or gold, or apparel. Ye yourselves know that these hands ministered unto my necessities, and to them that were with me. In all things I gave you an example, that so laboring ye ought to help the weak, and to remember the words of the Lord Jesus, that he himself said, It is more blessed to give than to receive.

II. GOSPEL, Luke 10. 38–42.
Martha and Mary.

NOW as they went on their way, he entered into a certain village: and a certain woman named Martha received him into her house.

And she had a sister called Mary, who also sat at the Lord's feet, and heard his word. But Martha was cumbered about much serving; and she came up to him. and said, Lord, dost not thou care that my sister did leave me to serve alone? bid her therefore that she help me.

And the Lord answered and said unto her, Martha, Martha, thou art anxious and troubled about many things: but one thing is needful: for Mary hath chosen the good part, which shall not be taken away from her.

III. EPISTLE, 1 Corinthians 7. 29–31.
The Independence of the Christian.

BUT this I say, brethren, the time is shortened, that henceforth both those that have wives may be as though they had none; and those that weep, as though they wept not; and those that rejoice, as though they rejoiced not; and those that buy, as though they possessed not; and those that use the world, as not using it to the full: for the fashion of this world passeth away.

III. GOSPEL, Matthew 6. 19–23.
The Uncertainty of Temporal Possessions.

LAY not up for yourselves treasures upon the earth, where moth and rust consume, and where thieves break through and steal: but lay up for yourselves treasures in heaven, where neither moth nor rust doth consume, and where thieves do not break through nor steal: for where thy treasure is, there will thy heart be also.

The lamp of the body is the eye: if therefore thine eye be single, thy whole body shall be full of light. But if thine eye be evil, thy whole body shall be full of darkness. If therefore the light that is in thee be darkness. how great is the darkness!

SIXTEENTH SUNDAY AFTER TRINITY.

The Shadow of Death.

Collect. Dear Lord, we pray Thee, make us willing to obey and serve Thee, and forasmuch as we are distressed by our enemy death, and without Thee cannot prevail, quicken us to call upon Thee for help; through Thy Son, Jesus Christ, our Lord. AMEN.

I. EPISTLE, Ephesians 3. 13–21.
Strength to the Inner Man.

WHEREFORE I ask that ye may not faint at my tribulations for you, which are your glory.

For this cause I bow my knees unto the Father, from whom every family in heaven and on earth is named, that he would grant you, according to the riches of his glory, that ye may be strengthened with power through his Spirit in the inward man; that Christ may dwell in your hearts through faith; to the end that ye, being rooted and grounded in love, may be strong to apprehend with all the saints what is the breadth and length and height and depth, and to know the love of Christ which passeth knowledge, that ye may be filled unto all the fulness of God.

Now unto him that is able to do exceeding abundantly above all that we ask or think, according to the power that worketh in us, unto him be the glory in the church and in Christ Jesus unto all generations for ever and ever. Amen.

I. GOSPEL, Luke 7. 11–17.
The Widow of Nain's Son.

AND it came to pass soon afterwards, that he went to a city called Nain; and his disciples went with him, and a great multitude.

Now when he drew near to the gate of the city, behold, there was carried out one that was dead, the only son of his mother, and she was a widow; and much people of the city was with her.

And when the Lord saw her, he had compassion on her, and said unto her, Weep not. And he came nigh and touched the bier: and the bearers stood still. And he said, Young man, I say unto thee, Arise. And he that was dead sat up, and began to speak. And he gave him to his mother. And fear took hold on all: and they glorified God, saying, A great prophet is arisen among us: and, God hath visited his people.

And this report went forth concerning him in the whole of Judæa, and all the region round about.

II. EPISTLE, 2 Corinthians 4. 7–14.
Life Victorious over Death.

BUT we have this treasure in earthen vessels, that the exceeding greatness of the power may be of God, and not from ourselves; we are pressed on every side, yet not straitened; perplexed, yet not unto despair; pursued, yet not forsaken; smitten down, yet not destroyed; always bearing about in the body the dying of

Jesus, that the life also of Jesus may be manifested in our body.

For we who live are always delivered unto death for Jesus' sake, that the life also of Jesus may be manifested in our mortal flesh. So then death worketh in us, but life in you. But having the same spirit of faith, according to that which is written, I believed, and therefore did I speak; we also believe, and therefore also we speak; knowing that he that raised up the Lord Jesus shall raise up us also with Jesus, and shall present us with you.

II. GOSPEL, John 11. 1–44.

Jesus Raising Lazarus.

NOW a certain man was sick, Lazarus of Bethany, of the village of Mary and her sister Martha. And it was that Mary who anointed the Lord with ointment, and wiped his feet with her hair, whose brother Lazarus was sick.

The sisters therefore sent unto him, saying, Lord, behold, he whom thou lovest is sick. But when Jesus heard it, he said, This sickness is not unto death, but for the glory of God, that the Son of God may be glorified thereby.

Now Jesus loved Martha, and her sister, and Lazarus. When therefore he heard that he was sick, he abode at that time two days in the place where he was. Then after this he saith to the disciples, Let us go into Judæa again. The disciples say unto him, Rabbi, the Jews were but now seeking to stone thee; and goest thou thither again? Jesus answered, Are there not twelve hours in the day? If a man walk in the day, he stumbleth not, because he seeth the light of this world. But if a man walk in the night, he stumbleth because the light is not in him.

These things spake he: and after this he saith unto them, Our friend Lazarus is fallen asleep; but I go, that I may awake him out of sleep. The disciples therefore said unto him, Lord, if he is fallen asleep, he will recover. Now Jesus had spoken of his death: but they thought that he spake of taking rest in sleep. Then Jesus therefore said unto them plainly, Lazarus is dead. And I am glad for your sakes that I was not there, to the intent ye may believe; nevertheless let us go unto him. Thomas therefore, who is called Didymus, said unto his fellow-disciples, Let us also go, that we may die with him.

So when Jesus came, he found that he had been in the tomb four days already. Now Bethany was nigh unto Jerusalem, about fifteen furlongs off; and many of the Jews had come to Martha and Mary, to console them concerning their brother.

Martha therefore, when she heard that Jesus was coming, went and met him: but Mary still sat in the house. Martha therefore said unto Jesus, Lord, if thou hadst been here, my brother had not died. And even now I know that, whatsoever thou shalt ask of God, God will give thee. Jesus saith unto her, Thy brother shall rise again. Martha saith unto him, I know that he shall rise again in the resurrection at the last day. Jesus said unto her, I am the resurrection and the life: he that believeth on me, though he die, yet shall he live; and whosoever liveth and believeth on me shall never die. Believest thou this? She saith unto him, Yea, Lord: I have believed that thou art the Christ, the Son of God, even he that cometh into the world.

And when she had said this, she went away, and calleth Mary her sister secretly, saying, The Teacher is here, and calleth thee. And she, when she heard it, arose quickly, and went unto him. (Now Jesus was not yet come into the village, but was still in the place where Martha met him.) The Jews then who were with her in the house, and were consoling her, when they saw Mary, that she rose up quickly and went out, followed her, supposing that she was going unto the tomb to weep there. Mary therefore, when she came where Jesus was, and saw him, fell down at his feet, saying unto him, Lord, if Thou hadst been here, my brother had not died.

When Jesus therefore saw her weeping, and the Jews also weeping who came. with her, he groaned in the spirit, and was troubled, and said, Where have ye laid him? They say unto him, Lord, come and see. Jesus wept. The Jews therefore said, Behold how he loved him! But some of them said, Could not this man, who opened the eyes of him that was blind, have caused that this man also should not die? Jesus therefore again groaning in himself cometh to the tomb.

Now it was a cave, and a stone lay against it. Jesus saith, Take ye away the stone. Martha, the sister of him that was dead, saith unto him, Lord, by this time the body decayeth; for he hath been dead four days. Jesus saith unto her, Said I not unto thee, that, if thou believedst, thou shouldest see the glory of God? So they took away the stone. And Jesus lifted up his eyes, and said, Father, I thank thee that thou heardest me. And I knew that thou hearest me always: but because of the multitude that standeth around I said it, that they may believe that thou didst send me. And when he had thus spoken, he cried with a loud voice, Lazarus, come forth. He that was dead came forth, bound hand and foot with grave-clothes; and his face was bound about with a napkin. Jesus saith unto them, Loose him, and let him go.

III. Epistle, Philippians 1. 19–26.
Courage to Live and to Die.

I KNOW that this shall turn out to my salvation, through your supplication and the supply of the Spirit of Jesus Christ, according to my earnest expectation and hope, that in nothing shall I be put to shame, but that with all boldness, as always, so now also Christ shall be magnified in my body, whether by life, or by death.

For to me to live is Christ, and to die is gain. But to live in the flesh,—if this shall bring fruit from my work, then what I shall choose I know not. But I am in a strait betwixt the two, having

the desire to depart and be with Christ; for it is very far better: yet to abide in the flesh is more needful for your sake.

And having this confidence, I know that I shall abide, yea, and abide with you all, for your progress and joy in the faith; that your glorying may abound in Christ Jesus in me through my presence with you again.

III. Gospel, John 5. 19–21.
The Power of Jesus to Give Life.

JESUS therefore answered and said unto them, Verily, verily, I say unto you, The Son can do nothing of himself, but what he seeth the Father doing: for what things soever he doeth, these the Son also doeth in like manner. For the Father loveth the Son, and showeth him all things that himself doeth: and greater works than these will he show him, that ye may marvel. For as the Father raiseth the dead and giveth them life, even so the Son also giveth life to whom he will.

SEVENTEENTH SUNDAY AFTER TRINITY.
The Liberty of the Christian.

Collect. Lord, we beseech Thee, grant Thy people grace to withstand the temptation of the world, the flesh, and the devil, and with pure hearts and minds to follow Thee, the only God; through Jesus Christ, Thy Son, our Lord. Amen.

I. Epistle, Ephesians 4. 1–6.
Keeping the Unity of the Spirit.

I THEREFORE, the prisoner in the Lord, beseech you to walk worthily of the calling wherewith ye were called, with all lowliness and meekness, with longsuffering, forbearing one another in love; giving diligence to keep the unity of the Spirit in the bond of peace. There is one body, and one Spirit, even as also ye were called in one hope of your calling; one Lord, one faith, one baptism, one God and Father of all, who is over all, and through all, and in all.

I. Gospel, Luke 14. 1–11.
Jesus a Guest in the House of a Pharisee.

AND it came to pass, when he went into the house of one of the rulers of the Pharisees on a sabbath to eat bread, that they were watching him.

And behold, there was before him a certain man that had the dropsy. And Jesus answering spake unto the lawyers and Pharisees, saying, Is it lawful to heal on the sabbath, or not? But they held their peace. And he took him, and healed him, and let him go.

And he said unto them, Which of you shall have an ass or an ox fallen into a well, and will not straightway draw him up on a sabbath day? And they could not answer again unto these things.

And he spake a parable unto those that were bidden, when he marked how they chose out the chief seats; saying unto them, When thou art bidden of any man to a marriage feast, sit not down in the chief seat; lest haply a more honorable man than thou be bidden of him, and he that bade thee and him shall come and say to thee, Give this man place; and then thou shalt begin with shame to take the lowest place. But when thou art bidden, go and sit down in the lowest place; that when he that hath bidden thee cometh, he may say to thee, Friend, go up higher: then shalt thou have glory in the presence of all that sit at meat with thee. For every one that exalteth himself shall be humbled; and he that humbleth himself shall be exalted.

II. EPISTLE, Colossians 2. 16–23.
Conscience and the Commandments of Men.

LET no man therefore judge you in meat, or in drink, or in respect of a feast day or a new moon or a sabbath day: which are a shadow of the things to come; but the body is Christ's.

Let no man rob you of your prize by a voluntary humility and worshipping of the angels, dwelling in the things which he hath seen, vainly puffed up by his fleshly mind, and not holding fast the Head, from whom all the body, being supplied and knit together through the joints and bands, increaseth with the increase of God.

If ye died with Christ from the rudiments of the world, why, as though living in the world, do ye subject yourselves to ordinances, Handle not, nor taste, nor touch (all which things are to perish with the using), after the precepts and doctrines of men? Which things have indeed a show of wisdom in will-worship, and humility, and severity to the body; but are not of any value against the indulgence of the flesh.

II. GOSPEL, Mark 2. 23—3. 5.
The True Observance of the Sabbath.

AND it came to pass, that he was going on the sabbath day through the grain fields; and his disciples began, as they went, to pluck the ears.

And the Pharisees said unto him, Behold, why do they on the sabbath day that which is not lawful?

And he said unto them, Did ye never read what David did, when he had need, and was hungry, he, and they that were with him? How he entered into the house of God when Abiathar was high priest, and ate the showbread, which it is not lawful to eat save for the priests, and gave also to them that were with him? And he said unto them, The sabbath was made for man, and not man for the sabbath: so that the Son of man is lord even of the sabbath.

And he entered again into the synagogue; and there was a man there who had his hand withered. And they watched him, whether he would heal him on the sabbath day; that they might accuse him. And he saith unto the man that had his hand withered, Stand forth. And he saith unto them, Is it lawful on the sabbath day to do good, or to do harm? to save a life, or to kill? But they held their peace. And when he had looked round about on them with anger, being grieved at the hardening of their heart, he saith unto the man, Stretch

forth thy hand. And he stretched it forth; and his hand was restored.

III. EPISTLE, Galatians 5. 1–14.
Freedom to Serve.

FOR freedom did Christ set us free: stand fast therefore, and be not entangled again in a yoke of bondage.

Behold, I Paul say unto you, that, if ye receive circumcision, Christ will profit you nothing. Yea, I testify again to every man that receiveth circumcision, that he is a debtor to do the whole law. Ye are severed from Christ, ye who would be justified by the law; ye are fallen away from grace. For we through the Spirit by faith wait for the hope of righteousness. For in Christ Jesus neither circumcision availeth anything, nor uncircumcision; but faith working through love.

Ye were running well; who hindered you that ye should not obey the truth? This persuasion came not of him that calleth you. A little leaven leaveneth the whole lump. I have confidence to you-ward in the Lord, that ye will be none otherwise minded: but he that troubleth you shall bear his judgment, whosoever he be.

But I, brethren, if I still preach circumcision, why am I still persecuted? then hath the stumblingblock of the cross been done away. I would that they that unsettle you would even go beyond circumcision.

For ye, brethren, were called for freedom; only use not your freedom for an occasion to the flesh, but through love be servants one to another. For the whole law is fulfilled in one word, even in this: Thou shalt love thy neighbor as thyself.

III. GOSPEL, John 8. 31–36.
"The Truth Shall Make You Free."

JESUS therefore said to those Jews that had believed him, If ye abide in my word, then are ye truly my disciples: and ye shall know the truth, and the truth shall make you free.

They answered unto him, We are Abraham's seed, and have never yet been in bondage to any man: how sayest thou, Ye shall be made free?

Jesus answered them, Verily, verily, I say unto you, Every one that committeth sin is the bondservant of sin. And the bondservant abideth not in the house for ever: the son abideth for ever. If therefore the Son shall make you free, ye shall be free indeed.

EIGHTEENTH SUNDAY AFTER TRINITY.

The Way of Perfection.

Collect. O God, forasmuch as without Thee we are not able to please Thee: mercifully grant that Thy Holy Spirit may in all things direct and rule our hearts; through Jesus Christ, Thy Son, our Lord. AMEN.

I. EPISTLE, 1 Corinthians 1. 4-8.

Christ Shall Establish Us unto the End.

I THANK my God always concerning you, for the grace of God which was given you in Christ Jesus; that in everything ye were enriched in him, in all utterance and all knowledge; even as the testimony of Christ was confirmed in you: so that ye come behind in no gift; waiting for the revelation of our Lord Jesus Christ; who shall also confirm you unto the end, that ye be unreprovable in the day of our Lord Jesus Christ.

I. GOSPEL, Matthew 22. 34-46.

The Chief Commandment of the Law.

THE Pharisees, when they heard that he had put the Sadducees to silence, gathered themselves together. And one of them, a lawyer, asked him a question, trying him: Teacher, which is the great commandment in the law?

And he said unto them, Thou shalt love the Lord thy God with all thy heart, and with all thy soul, and with all thy mind. This is the great and first commandment. And a second like unto it is this, Thou shalt love thy neighbor as thyself. On these two commandments the whole law hangeth, and the prophets.

Now while the Pharisees were gathered together, Jesus asked them a question, saying, What think ye of the Christ? whose son is he?

They say unto him, The son of David. He saith unto them, How then doth David in the Spirit call him Lord, saying,

The Lord said unto my Lord,
Sit thou on my right hand,
Till I put thine enemies underneath thy feet?

If David then calleth him Lord, how is he his son?

And no one was able to answer him a word, neither durst any man from that day forth ask him any more questions.

II. EPISTLE, Romans 10. 1-13.

True Zeal for Righteousness Leading to Christ.

BRETHREN, my heart's desire and my supplication to God is for them, that they may be saved.

For I bear them witness that they have a zeal for God, but not according to knowledge. For being ignorant of God's righteousness, and seeking to establish their own, they did not subject themselves to the righteousness of God.

For Christ is the end of the law unto righteousness to every one that believeth. For Moses writeth that the man that doeth the righteousness which is of the law shall live thereby. But the righteousness which is of faith saith thus, Say not in thy heart, Who shall ascend into heaven? (that is, to bring Christ down:) or, Who shall descend into the abyss? (that is, to bring Christ up from the dead.) But what saith it? The word is nigh thee, in thy mouth, and in thy heart: that is, the word of faith, which we preach: because if thou shalt confess with thy mouth Jesus as Lord, and shalt believe in thy heart that God raised him from the dead, thou shalt be saved: for with the heart man believeth unto righteousness; and with the mouth confession is made unto salvation. For the scripture saith, Whosoever believeth on him shall not be put to shame.

For there is no distinction between Jew and Greek: for the same Lord is Lord of all, and is rich unto all that call upon him: for, Whosoever shall call upon the name of the Lord shall be saved.

II. GOSPEL, Matthew 13. 44-46.
The Treasure and the Pearl.

THE kingdom of heaven is like unto a treasure hidden in the field; which a man found, and hid; and in his joy he goeth and selleth all that he hath, and buyeth that field.

Again, the kingdom of heaven is like unto a man that is a merchant seeking goodly pearls: and having found one pearl of great price, he went and sold all that he had, and bought it.

III. EPISTLE, 1 John 2. 7-17.
The Commandment of Christ Shedding Light upon the Way.

BELOVED, no new commandment write I unto you, but an old commandment which ye had from the beginning: the old commandment is the word which ye heard.

Again, a new commandment write I unto you, which thing is true in him and in you; because the darkness is passing away, and the true light already shineth.

He that saith he is in the light and hateth his brother is in the darkness even until now. He that loveth his brother abideth in the light, and there is no occasion of stumbling in him. But he that hateth his brother is in the darkness, and walketh in the darkness, and knoweth not whither he goeth, because the darkness hath blinded his eyes.

I write unto you, my little children, because your sins are forgiven you for his name's sake. I write unto you, fathers, because ye know him who is from the beginning. I write unto you, young men, because ye have overcome the evil one.

I have written unto you, little children, because ye know the Father. I have written unto you, fathers, because ye know him who is from the beginning. I have written unto you, young men, because ye are strong, and the word of God abideth in you, and ye have overcome the evil one.

Love not the world, neither the things that are in the world. If any man love the world, the love of the Father is not in him. For all that is in the world, the lust of the flesh and the lust of the eyes and the vainglory of life, is not of the Father, but is of the world. And the world passeth away, and the lust thereof: but he that doeth the will of God abideth for ever.

III. GOSPEL, Mark 10. 17–27.
The Rich Young Ruler.

AND as he was going forth into the way, there ran one to him, and kneeled to him, and asked him, Good Teacher, what shall I do that I may inherit eternal life?

And Jesus said unto him, Why callest thou me good? none is good save one, even God. Thou knowest the commandments, Do not kill, Do not commit adultery, Do not steal, Do not bear false witness, Do not defraud, Honor thy father and mother.

And he said unto him, Teacher, all these things have I observed from my youth.

And Jesus looking upon him loved him, and said unto him, One thing thou lackest: go, sell whatsoever thou hast, and give to the poor, and thou shalt have treasure in heaven: and come, follow me.

And his countenance fell at the saying, and he went away sorrowful: for he was one that had great possessions.

And Jesus looked round about, and saith unto his disciples, How hardly shall they that have riches enter into the kingdom of God!

And the disciples were amazed at his words. But Jesus answereth again, and saith unto them, Children, how hard is it for them that trust in riches to enter into the kingdom of God! It is easier for a camel to go through a needle's eye, than for a rich man to enter into the kingdom of God.

And they were astonished exceedingly, saying unto him, Then who can be saved? Jesus looking upon them saith, With men it is impossible, but not with God: for all things are possible with God.

NINETEENTH SUNDAY AFTER TRINITY.
The Narrow Way of Faith.

Collect. O Lord God, graciously hear our prayers, and as Thou dost grant us the desire and the will to pray, grant also, we beseech Thee, the fulfillment of our prayers, according to Thy holy will; through Thy Son, Jesus Christ, our Lord. AMEN.

I. EPISTLE, Ephesians 4. 17, 20–28.

Be Renewed in the Spirit of Your Mind.

THIS I say therefore, and testify in the Lord, that ye no longer walk as the Gentiles also walk, in the vanity of their mind. . . .

Ye did not so learn Christ; if so be that ye heard him, and were taught in

him, even as truth is in Jesus: that ye put away, as concerning your former manner of life, the old man, that waxeth corrupt after the lusts of deceit; and that ye be renewed in the spirit of your mind, and put on the new man, that after God hath been created in righteousness and holiness of truth.

Wherefore, putting away falsehood, speak ye truth each one with his neighbor: for we are members one of another.

Be ye angry, and sin not: let not the sun go down upon your wrath: neither give place to the devil.

Let him that stole steal no more: but rather let him labor, working with his hands the thing that is good, that he may have whereof to give to him that hath need.

I. GOSPEL, Matthew 9. 1–8.

Jesus Healing the Man Sick of the Palsy.

AND he entered into a boat, and crossed over, and came into his own city.

And behold, they brought to him a man sick of the palsy, lying on a bed: and Jesus seeing their faith said unto the sick of the palsy, Son, be of good cheer; thy sins are forgiven.

And behold, certain of the scribes said within themselves, This man blasphemeth.

And Jesus knowing their thoughts said, Wherefore think ye evil in your hearts? For which is easier, to say, Thy sins are forgiven; or to say, Arise, and walk? But that ye may know that the Son of man hath authority on earth to forgive sins (then saith he to the sick of the palsy), Arise, and take up thy bed, and go unto thy house. And he arose, and departed to his house.

But when the multitudes saw it, they were afraid, and glorified God, who had given such authority unto men.

II. EPISTLE, Psalm 73. 1–5, 22–28.

The Problems of Life Driving Us Nearer to God.

SURELY God is good to Israel,
Even to such as are pure in heart.
But as for me, my feet were almost gone;
My steps had well nigh slipped.
For I was envious at the arrogant,
When I saw the prosperity of the wicked.
For there are no pangs in their death:
But their strength is firm.
They are not in trouble as other men;
Neither are they plagued like other men.
So brutish was I, and ignorant;
I was as a beast before thee.
Nevertheless I am continually with thee:
Thou hast holden my right hand.
Thou wilt guide me with thy counsel,
And afterward receive me to glory.
Whom have I in heaven but thee?
And there is none upon earth that I desire besides thee.
My flesh and my heart faileth;
But God is the strength of my heart and my portion for ever.
For, lo, they that are far from thee shall perish:
Thou hast destroyed all them that play the harlot, departing from thee.

But it is good for me to draw near unto God:
I have made the Lord Jehovah my refuge,
That I may tell of all thy works.

II. GOSPEL, John 9. 1–41.

The Man Born Blind.

AND as he passed by, he saw a man blind from his birth. And his disciples asked him, saying, Rabbi, who sinned, this man, or his parents, that he should be born blind?

Jesus answered, Neither did this man sin nor his parents: but that the works of God should be made manifest in him. We must work the works of him that sent me, while it is day: the night cometh, when no man can work. When I am in the world, I am the light of the world.

When he had thus spoken, he spat on the ground, and made clay of the spittle, and anointed his eyes with the clay, and said unto him, Go, wash in the pool of Siloam (which is by interpretation, Sent). He went away, therefore, and washed, and came seeing.

The neighbors therefore, and they that saw him aforetime, that he was a beggar, said, Is not this he that sat and begged? Others said, It is he: others said, No, but he is like him. He said, I am he.

They said therefore unto him, How then were thine eyes opened? He answered, The man that is called Jesus made clay, and anointed mine eyes, and said unto me, Go to Siloam, and wash: so I went away and washed, and I received sight. And they said unto him, Where is he? He saith, I know not.

They bring to the Pharisees him that aforetime was blind. Now it was the sabbath on the day when Jesus made the clay, and opened his eyes. Again therefore the Pharisees also asked him how he received his sight. And he said unto them, He put clay upon mine eyes, and I washed, and I see. Some therefore of the Pharisees said, This man is not from God, because he keepeth not the sabbath. But others said, How can a man that is a sinner do such signs? And there was a division among them. They say therefore unto the blind man again, What sayest thou of him, in that he opened thine eyes? And he said, He is a prophet.

The Jews therefore did not believe concerning him, that he had been blind, and had received his sight, until they called the parents of him that had received his sight, and asked them, saying, Is this your son, who ye say was born blind? how then doth he now see? His parents answered and said, We know that this is our son, and that he was born blind: but how he now seeth, we know not; or who opened his eyes we know not: ask him; he is of age; he shall speak for himself. These things said his parents, because they feared the Jews: for the Jews had agreed already, that if any man should confess him to be Christ, he should be put out of the synagogue. Therefore said his parents, He is of age; ask him.

So. they called a second time the man that was blind, and said unto him, Give glory to God: we know that this man is a sinner. He therefore answered, Whether he is a sinner, I know not: one thing I know, that, whereas I was blind, now I see. They said therefore unto him, What did he to thee? how opened he thine eyes? He answered them, I told you even now, and ye did not hear; wherefore would ye hear it again? would ye also become his disciples? And they reviled him, and said, Thou art his disciple; but we are disciples of Moses. We know that God hath spoken unto Moses: but as for this man, we know not whence he is. The man answered and said unto them, Why, herein is the marvel, that ye know not whence he is, and yet he opened mine eyes. We know that God heareth not sinners: but if any man be a worshipper of God, and do his will, him he heareth. Since the world began it was never heard that any one opened the eyes of a man born blind. If this man were not from God, he could do nothing. They answered and said unto him, Thou wast altogether born in sins, and dost thou teach us? And they cast him out. Jesus heard that they had cast him out; and finding him, he said, Dost thou believe on the Son of God? He answered and said, And who is he, Lord, that I may believe on him. Jesus said unto him, Thou hast both seen him, and he it is that speaketh with thee. And he said, Lord, I believe. And he worshipped him, And Jesus said, For judgment came I into this world, that they that see not may see; and that they that see may become blind.

Those of the Pharisees who were with him heard these things, and said unto him, Are we also blind? Jesus said unto them, If ye were blind, ye would have no sin: but now ye say, We see: your sin remaineth.

III. Epistle, Romans 7. 14–25.
The Conflict between the Spiritual Man and the Natural Man.

WE know that the law is spiritual: but I am carnal, sold under sin. For that which I do I know not: for not what I would, that do I practise; but what I hate, that I do.

But if what I would not, that I do, I consent unto the law that it is good. So now it is no more I that do it, but sin which dwelleth in me. For I know that in me, that is, in my flesh, dwelleth no good thing: for to will is present with me, but to do that which is good is not. For the good which I would I do not: but the evil which I would not, that I practise. But if what I would not, that I do, it is no more I that do it, but sin which dwelleth in me.

I find then the law, that, to me who would do good, evil is present. For I delight in the law of God after the inward man: but I see a different law in my members, warring against the law of my mind, and bringing me into captivity under the law of sin which is in my members.

Wretched man that I am! who shall deliver me out of the body of this death? I thank God through Jesus Christ our Lord. So then I of myself with the mind, indeed, serve the law of God; but with the flesh the law of sin.

III. Gospel, John 7. 40–52.
Jesus Contradicted and Defended.

SOME of the multitude therefore, when they heard these words, said, This is of a truth the prophet. Others said, This is the Christ. But some said, What, doth the Christ come out of Galilee? Hath not the scripture said that the Christ cometh of the seed of David, and from Bethlehem, the village where David was?

So there arose a division in the multitude because of him. And some of them would have taken him; but no man laid hands on him.

The officers therefore came to the chief priests and Pharisees; and they said unto them, Why did ye not bring him? The officers answered, Never man so spake. The Pharisees therefore answered them, Are ye also led astray? Hath any of the rulers believed on him, or of the Pharisees? But this multitude that knoweth not the law are accursed.

Nicodemus saith unto them (he that came to him before, being one of them), Doth our law judge a man, except it first hear from himself and know what he doeth? They answered and said unto him, Art thou also of Galilee? Search, and see that out of Galilee ariseth no prophet.

TWENTIETH SUNDAY AFTER TRINITY.

Spiritual Indifference.

Collect. Grant, we beseech Thee, merciful Lord, to Thy faithful people pardon and peace, that they may be cleansed from all their sins, and serve Thee with a quiet mind; through Jesus Christ, Thy Son, our Lord. AMEN.

I. EPISTLE, Ephesians 5. 15–20.
The Careful Use of Time.

LOOK therefore carefully how ye walk, not as unwise, but as wise; redeeming the time, because the days are evil. Wherefore be ye not foolish, but understand what the will of the Lord is. And be not drunken with wine, wherein is riot, but be filled with the Spirit; speaking one to another in psalms and hymns and spiritual songs, singing and making melody with your heart to the Lord; giving thanks always for all things in the name of our Lord Jesus Christ to God, even the Father.

I. GOSPEL, Matthew 22. 1–14.
The Man without a Wedding Garment.

AND Jesus answered and spake again in parables unto them, saying, The kingdom of heaven is likened unto a certain king, who made a marriage feast for his son, and sent forth his servants to call them that were bidden to the marriage feast; and they would not come. Again he sent forth other servants, saying, Tell them that are bidden, Behold, I have made ready my dinner, my oxen and my fatlings are killed, and all things are ready: come to the marriage feast. But they made light of it, and went their ways, one to his own farm, another to his merchandise; and the rest laid hold on his servants, and treated them shamefully, and killed them. But the king was wroth; and he sent his armies, and destroyed those murderers, and burned their city. Then saith he to his servants, The wedding is ready, but they that were bidden were not worthy. Go ye therefore unto the partings of the highways, and as many as ye shall find, bid to the marriage feast. And those servants went out into the highways, and gathered together all as many as they found, both bad and good: and the wedding was filled with guests. But when the king came in to behold the guests, he saw there a man who had not on a wedding-garment: and he saith unto him, Friend, how camest thou in hither not having a wedding-garment?

And he was speechless. Then the king said to the servants, Bind him hand and foot, and cast him out into the outer darkness; there shall be the weeping and the gnashing of teeth. For many are called, but few chosen.

II. EPISTLE, Hebrews 10. 19–31.
Holding Fast the Confession of Hope.

HAVING therefore, brethren, boldness to enter into the holy place by the blood of Jesus, by the way which he dedicated for us, a new and living way, through the veil, that is to say, his flesh; and having a great priest over the house of God; let us draw near with a true heart in fulness of faith, having our hearts sprinkled from an evil conscience: and having our body washed with pure water, let us hold fast the confession of our hope that it waver not; for he is faithful that promised: and let us consider one another to provoke unto love and good works; not forsaking our own assembling together, as the custom of some is, but exhorting one another; and so much the more, as ye see the day drawing nigh.

For if we sin wilfully after that we have received the knowledge of the truth, there remaineth no more a sacrifice for sins, but a certain fearful expectation of judgment, and a fierceness of fire which shall devour the adversaries. A man that hath set at nought Moses' law dieth without compassion on the word of two or three witnesses: of how much sorer punishment, think ye, shall he be judged worthy, who hath trodden under foot the Son of God, and hath counted the blood of the covenant wherewith he was sanctified an unholy thing, and hath done despite unto the Spirit of grace? For we know him that said, Vengeance belongeth unto me, I will recompense. And again, The Lord shall judge his people. It is a fearful thing to fall into the hands of the living God.

II. GOSPEL, Matthew 25. 14–30.
The Entrusted Talents.

FOR it is as when a man, going into another country, called his own servants, and delivered unto them his goods. And unto one he gave five talents, to another two, to another one; to each according to his several ability; and he went on his journey.

Straightway he that received the five talents went and traded with them, and made other five talents. In like manner he also that received the two gained other two. But he that received the one went away and digged in the earth, and hid his lord's money.

Now after a long time the lord of those servants cometh, and maketh a reckoning with them.

And he that received the five talents came and brought other five talents, saying, Lord, thou deliveredst unto me five talents: lo, I have gained other five talents. His lord said unto him, Well done, good and faithful servant: thou hast been faithful over a few things, I will set thee over many things; enter thou into the joy of thy lord.

And he also that received the two talents came and said, Lord, thou deliveredst unto me two talents: lo, I have gained other two talents. His lord said unto him, Well done, good and faithful servant: thou hast been faithful over a few things, I will set thee over many things; enter thou into the joy of thy lord.

And he also that had received the one talent came and said, Lord, I knew thee that thou art a hard man, reaping where thou didst not sow, and gathering where thou didst not scatter; and I was afraid, and went away and hid thy talent in the earth: lo, thou hast thine own.

But his lord answered and said unto him, Thou wicked and slothful servant, thou knewest that I reap where I sowed not, and gather where I did not scatter; thou oughtest therefore to have put my money to the bankers, and at my coming I should have received back mine own with interest. Take ye away therefore the talent from him, and give it unto him that hath the ten talents. For unto every one that hath shall be given, and he shall have abundance: but from him that hath not, even that which he hath shall be taken away. And cast ye out the unprofitable servant into the outer darkness: there shall be the weeping and the gnashing of teeth.

III. Epistle, 1 Peter 2. 3–9.
Christ a Stumbling-block to the Unbeliever.

THE Lord is gracious: unto whom coming, a living stone, rejected indeed of men, but with God elect, precious, ye also, as living stones, are built up a spiritual house, to be a holy priesthood, to offer up spiritual sacrifices, acceptable to God through Jesus Christ. Because it is contained in scripture,

Behold, I lay in Zion a chief corner stone, elect, precious:
And he that believeth on him shall not be put to shame.
For you therefore that believe is the preciousness: but for such as disbelieve,
The stone which the builders rejected,
The same was made the head of the corner;
and,
A stone of stumbling, and a rock of offence;
for they stumble at the word, being disobedient: whereunto also they were appointed. But ye are an elect race, a royal priesthood, a holy nation, a people for God's own possession, that ye may show forth the excellencies of him who called you out of darkness into his marvelous light.

III. Gospel, Matthew 21. 33–46.
The Wicked Husbandmen.

HEAR another parable: There was a man that was a householder, who planted a vineyard, and set a hedge about it, and digged a winepress in it, and built a tower, and let it out to husbandmen, and went into another country.

And when the season of the fruits drew near, he sent his servants to the husbandmen, to receive his fruits. And the husbandmen took his servants, and beat one, and killed another, and stoned another.

Again, he sent other servants more than the first: and they did unto them in like manner.

But afterward he sent unto them his son, saying, They will reverence my son. But the husbandmen, when they saw the son, said among themselves, This is the heir; come, let us kill him, and take his inheritance. And they took him, and cast him forth out of the vineyard, and killed him.

When therefore the lord of the vineyard shall come, what will he do unto those husbandmen?

They say unto him, He will miserably destroy those miserable men, and will let out the vineyard unto other husbandmen, who shall render him the fruits in their seasons.

Jesus saith unto them, Did ye never read in the scriptures,
The stone which the builders rejected,
The same was made the head of the corner;
This was from the Lord,
And it is marvellous in our eyes?
Therefore say I unto you, The kingdom of God shall be taken away from you, and shall be given to a nation bringing

forth the fruits thereof. And he that falleth on this stone shall be broken to pieces: but on whomsoever it shall fall, it will scatter him as dust.

And when the chief priests and the Pharisees heard his parables, they perceived that he spake of them. And when they sought to lay hold on him, they feared the multitudes, because they took him for a prophet.

TWENTY-FIRST SUNDAY AFTER TRINITY.
The Foundation of Faith.

Collect. Lord, we beseech Thee to keep us in continual godliness; that through Thy protection we may be free from all adversities, and devoutly given to serve Thee in good works, to the glory of Thy name; through Jesus Christ, Thy Son, our Lord. AMEN.

I. EPISTLE, Ephesians 6. 10–18.
The Whole Armor of God.

BE strong in the Lord, and in the strength of his might. Put on the whole armor of God, that ye may be able to stand against the wiles of the devil.

For our wrestling is not against flesh and blood, but against the principalities, against the powers, against the world-rulers of this darkness, against the spiritual hosts of wickedness in the heavenly places.

Wherefore take up the whole armor of God, that ye may be able to withstand in the evil day, and, having done all, to stand. Stand therefore, having girded your loins with truth, and having put on the breastplate of righteousness, and having shod your feet with the preparation of the gospel of peace; withal taking up the shield of faith, wherewith ye shall be able to quench all the fiery darts of the evil one. And take the helmet of salvation, and the sword of the Spirit, which is the word of God: with all prayer and supplication praying at all seasons in the Spirit, and watching thereunto in all perseverance and supplication for all the saints.

I. GOSPEL, John 4. 46–53.
The Nobleman's Son.

THERE was a certain nobleman, whose son was sick at Capernaum. When he heard that Jesus was come out of Judæa into Galilee, he went unto him, and besought him that he would come down, and heal his son; for he was at the point of death.

Jesus therefore said unto him, Except ye see signs and wonders, ye will in no wise believe. The nobleman saith unto him, Sir, come down ere my child die. Jesus saith unto him, Go thy way; thy son liveth. The man believed the word that Jesus spake unto him, and he went his way.

And as he was now going down, his servants met him, saying, that his son lived. So he inquired of them the hour when he began to amend. They said therefore unto him, Yesterday at the seventh hour the fever left him. So the father knew that it was at that hour in which Jesus said unto him, Thy son liveth: and himself believed, and his whole house.

II. EPISTLE, Hebrews 11. 24–27.
Faith Looking to the Invisible Reward.

BY faith Moses, when he was grown up, refused to be called the son of Pharaoh's daughter; choosing rather to share ill treatment with the people of God, than to enjoy the pleasures of sin for a season; accounting the reproach of Christ greater riches than the treasures of Egypt: for he looked unto the recompense of reward. By faith he forsook Egypt, not fearing the wrath of the king: for he endured, as seeing him who is invisible.

II. GOSPEL, Matthew 16. 1–4.
The Signs of the Times.

AND the Pharisees and Sadducees came, and trying him asked him to show them a sign from heaven.

But he answered and said unto them, When it is evening, ye say, It will be fair weather: for the heaven is red. And in the morning, It will be foul weather to-day: for the heaven is red and lowering. Ye know how to discern the face of the heaven; but ye cannot discern the signs of the times. An evil and adulterous generation seeketh after a sign; and there shall no sign be given unto it, but the sign of Jonah. And he left them, and departed.

III. EPISTLE, Romans 5. 1–8.
The Love of God in Christ Making Faith Certain.

BEING therefore justified by faith, we have peace with God through our Lord Jesus Christ; through whom also we have had our access by faith into this grace wherein we stand; and we rejoice in hope of the glory of God.

And not only so, but we also rejoice in our tribulations: knowing that tribulation worketh stedfastness; and stedfastness, approvedness; and approvedness, hope: and hope putteth not to shame; because the love of God hath been shed abroad in our hearts through the Holy Spirit which was given unto us. For while we were yet weak, in due season Christ died for the ungodly. For scarcely for a righteous man will one die: for peradventure for the good man some one would even dare to die. But God commendeth his own love toward us, in that, while we were yet sinners, Christ died for us.

III. GOSPEL, John 10. 22–30.
Jesus Showing How Faith Arrives at Certainty.

AND it was the feast of the dedication at Jerusalem: it was winter; and Jesus was walking in the temple in Solomon's porch.

The Jews therefore came round about him, and said unto him, How long dost thou hold us in suspense? If thou art the Christ, tell us plainly.

Jesus answered them, I told you, and ye believe not: the works that I do in my Father's name, these bear witness of me. But ye believe not, because ye are not of my sheep. My sheep hear my voice, and I know them, and they follow me: and I give unto them eternal life; and they shall never perish, and no one shall snatch them out of my hand. My Father, who hath given them unto me, is greater than all; and no one is able to snatch them out of the Father's hand. I and the Father are one.

TWENTY-SECOND SUNDAY AFTER TRINITY.
Mutual Forgiveness.

Collect. O God, our Refuge and Strength, Who art the Author of all godliness: be ready, we beseech Thee, to hear the devout prayers of Thy Church; and grant that those things which we ask faithfully we may obtain effectually; through Jesus Christ, Thy Son, our Lord. AMEN.

I. EPISTLE, Philippians 1. 3–11.
Abounding Love Making Us Strong in the Lord.

I THANK my God upon all my remembrance of you, always in every supplication of mine on behalf of you all making my supplication with joy, for your fellowship in furtherance of the gospel from the first day until now; being confident of this very thing, that he who began a good work in you will perfect it until the day of Jesus Christ: even as it is right for me to be thus minded on behalf of you all, because I have you in my heart, inasmuch as, both in my bonds and in the defence and confirmation of the gospel, ye all are partakers with me of grace. For God is my witness, how I long after you all in the tender mercies of Christ Jesus.

And this I pray, that your love may abound yet more and more in knowledge and all discernment; so that ye may approve the things that are excellent; that ye may be sincere and void of offence unto the day of Christ; being filled with the fruits of righteousness, which are through Jesus Christ, unto the glory and praise of God.

I. GOSPEL, Matthew 18. 23–35.
The Unmerciful Servant.

THEREFORE is the kingdom of heaven likened unto a certain king, who would make a reckoning with his servants.

And when he had begun to reckon, one was brought unto him, that owed him ten thousand talents. But forasmuch as he had not wherewith to pay, his lord commanded him to be sold, and his wife, and children, and all that he had, and payment to be made. The servant therefore fell down and worshipped him, saying, Lord, have patience with me, and I will pay thee all. And the lord of the servant, being moved with compassion, released him, and forgave him the debt.

But that servant went out, and found one of his fellow-servants, who owed him a hundred shillings: and he laid hold on him, and took him by the throat, saying, Pay what thou owest. So his fellow-servant fell down and besought him, saying, Have patience with me, and I will pay thee. And he would not: but went and cast him into prison, till he should pay that which was due.

So when his fellow-servants saw what was done, they were exceeding sorry, and came and told unto their lord all that was done. Then his lord called him unto him, and saith to him, Thou wicked servant, I forgave thee all that debt, because thou besoughtest me: shouldest not thou also have had mercy on thy fellow-servant, even as I had mercy on thee? And his lord was wroth, and delivered him to the tormentors, till he should pay all that was due.

So shall also my heavenly Father do unto you, if ye forgive not every one his brother from your hearts.

II. EPISTLE, Ephesians 4. 30–32.
Forgiving As God Forgave.

GRIEVE not the Holy Spirit of God, in whom ye were sealed unto the day of redemption. Let all bitterness, and wrath, and anger, and clamor, and railing, be put away from you, with all malice: and be ye kind one to another, tenderhearted, forgiving each other, even as God also in Christ forgave you.

II. GOSPEL, Matthew 18. 15–22.
Forgiveness without Measure.

IF thy brother sin against thee, go, show him his fault between thee and him alone: if he hear thee, thou hast gained thy brother. But if he hear thee not, take with thee one or two more, that at the mouth of two witnesses or three every word may be established. And if he refuse to hear them, tell it unto the church: and if he refuse to hear the church also, let him be unto thee as the Gentile and the publican. Verily I say unto you, What things soever ye shall bind on earth shall be bound in heaven; and what things soever ye shall loose on earth shall be loosed in heaven.

Again I say unto you, that if two of you shall agree on earth as touching anything that they shall ask, it shall be done for them of my Father who is in heaven. For where two or three are gathered together in my name, there am I in the midst of them.

Then came Peter and said to him, Lord, how oft shall my brother sin against me, and I forgive him? until seven times? Jesus saith unto him, I say not unto thee, Until seven times; but, Until seventy times seven.

III. EPISTLE, 1 Thessalonians 5. 14–23.
The Goal of Perfect Holiness.

WE exhort you, brethren, admonish the disorderly, encourage the fainthearted; support the weak, be longsuffering toward all.

See that none render unto any one evil for evil; but always follow after that which is good, one toward another, and toward all.

Rejoice always; pray without ceasing; in everything give thanks: for this is the will of God in Christ Jesus to you-ward.

Quench not the Spirit; despise not prophesyings; prove all things; hold fast that which is good; abstain from every form of evil.

And the God of peace himself sanctify you wholly; and may your spirit and soul and body be preserved entire, without blame at the coming of our Lord Jesus Christ.

III. GOSPEL, Mark 4. 21–25.
Love Abounding.

AND he said unto them, Is the lamp brought to be put under the bushel, or under the bed, and not to be put on the stand? For there is nothing hid, save that it should be manifested; neither was anything made secret, but that it should come to light. If any man hath ears to hear, let him hear.

And he said unto them, Take heed what ye hear: with what measure ye mete it shall be measured unto you; and more shall be given unto you. For he that hath, to him shall be given: and he that hath not, from him shall be taken away even that which he hath.

TWENTY-THIRD SUNDAY AFTER TRINITY.
Christian Patriotism.

Collect. O Lord, we beseech Thee, absolve Thy people from their offences; that through Thy bountiful goodness we may all be delivered from the bonds of our sins, which by our frailty we have committed. Grant this, O heavenly Father, through Jesus Christ, Thy Son, our Lord, AMEN.

I. EPISTLE, Philippians 3. 17—4. 3.
Our Citizenship in Heaven.

BRETHREN, be ye imitators together of me, and mark them that so walk even as ye have us for an ensample.

For many walk, of whom I told you often, and now tell you even weeping, that they are the enemies of the cross of Christ: whose end is perdition, whose god is the belly, and whose glory is in their shame, who mind earthly things.

For our citizenship is in heaven; whence also we wait for a Saviour, the Lord Jesus Christ: who shall fashion anew the body of our humiliation, that it may be conformed to the body of his glory, according to the working whereby he is able even to subject all things unto himself.

Wherefore, my brethren beloved and longed for, my joy and crown, so stand fast in the Lord, my beloved.

I exhort Euodia, and I exhort Syntyche, to be of the same mind in the Lord. Yea, I beseech thee also, true yokefellow, help these women, for they labored with me in the gospel, with Clement also, and the rest of my fellow-workers, whose names are in the book of life.

I. Gospel, Matthew 22. 15–22.

The Tribute to Cæsar and to God.

THEN went the Pharisees, and took counsel how they might ensnare him in his talk. And they send to him their disciples, with the Herodians, saying, Teacher, we know that thou art true, and teachest the way of God in truth, and carest not for any one: for thou regardest not the person of men. Tell us therefore, What thinkest thou? Is it lawful to give tribute unto Cæsar, or not?

But Jesus perceived their wickedness, and said, Why make ye trial of me, ye hypocrites? Show me the tribute money. And they brought unto him a denarius. And he saith unto them, Whose is this image and superscription? They say unto him, Cæsar's. Then saith he unto them, Render therefore unto Cæsar the things that are Cæsar's; and unto God the things that are God's.

And when they heard it, they marvelled, and left him, and went away.

II. Epistle, 1 Timothy 2. 1–6.

Exhortation to Prayer for All.

I EXHORT therefore, first of all, that supplications, prayers, intercessions, thanksgivings, be made for all men; for kings and all that are in high place; that we may lead a tranquil and quiet life in all godliness and gravity. This is good and acceptable in the sight of God our Saviour; who would have all men to be saved, and come to the knowledge of the truth. For there is one God, one mediator also between God and men, himself

man, Christ Jesus, who gave himself a ransom for all; the testimony to be borne in its own times.

II. Gospel, Matthew 7. 12.

The Golden Rule.

ALL things therefore whatsoever ye would that men should do unto you, even so do ye also unto them: for this is the law and the prophets.

III. Epistle, Romans 13. 1–7.

The Christian's Relation to Civil Authority.

LET every soul be in subjection to the higher powers: for there is no power but of God; and the powers that be are ordained of God. Therefore he that resisteth the power, withstandeth the ordinance of God: and they that withstand shall receive to themselves judgment. For rulers are not a terror to the good work, but to the evil. And wouldest thou have no fear of the power? do that which is good, and thou shalt have praise from the same: for he is a minister of God to thee for good. But if thou do that which is evil, be afraid; for he beareth not the sword in vain: for he is a minister of God, an avenger for wrath to him that doeth evil. Wherefore ye must needs be in subjection, not only because of the wrath, but also for conscience' sake. For for this cause ye pay tribute also; for they are ministers of God's service, attending continually upon this very thing. Render to all their dues: tribute to whom tribute is due; custom to whom custom; fear to whom fear; honor to whom honor.

III. Gospel, Matthew 17. 24–27.

Jesus Paying the Temple Tribute.

AND when they were come to Capernaum, they that received the half shekel came to Peter, and said, Doth not your teacher pay the half-shekel? He saith, Yea.

And when he came into the house, Jesus spake first to him, saying, What thinkest thou, Simon? the kings of the earth, from whom do they receive toll or tribute? from their sons, or from strangers? And when he said, From strangers, Jesus said unto him, Therefore the sons are free. But, lest we cause them to stumble, go thou to the sea, and cast a hook, and take up the fish that first cometh up; and when thou hast opened his mouth, thou shalt find a shekel: that take, and give unto them for me and thee.

TWENTY-FOURTH SUNDAY AFTER TRINITY.

The Life That Never Dies.

Collect. Almighty and eternal God, we beseech Thee, show Thy mercy unto Thy humble servants, that we who put no trust in our own merits may not be dealt with after the severity of Thy judgment, but according to Thy mercy; through Jesus Christ, Thy Son, our Lord. AMEN.

I. EPISTLE, Colossians 1. 9–12.

The Inheritance of the Saints in Light.

FOR this cause we also, since the day we heard it, do not cease to pray and make request for you, that ye may be filled with the knowledge of his will in all spiritual wisdom and understanding, to walk worthily of the Lord unto all pleasing, bearing fruit in every good work, and increasing in the knowledge of God; strengthened with all power, according to the might of his glory, unto all patience and longsuffering with joy; giving thanks unto the Father, who made us meet to be partakers of the inheritance of the saints in light.

I. GOSPEL, Matthew 9. 18–26.

The Daughter of Jairus.

WHILE he spake these things unto them, behold, there came a ruler, and worshipped him, saying, My daughter is even now dead: but come and lay thy hand upon her, and she shall live. And Jesus rose, and followed him, and so did his disciples.

And behold, a woman, who had an issue of blood twelve years, came behind him, and touched the border of his garment: for she said within herself, If I do but touch his garment, I shall be made whole. But Jesus turning and seeing her said, Daughter, be of good cheer; thy faith hath made thee whole. And the woman was made whole from that hour.

And when Jesus came unto the ruler's house, and saw the flute-players, and the crowd making a tumult, he said, Give place: for the damsel is not dead, but sleepeth. And they laughed him to scorn. But when the crowd was put forth, he entered in, and took her by the hand; and the damsel arose.

And the fame hereof went forth into all that land.

II. EPISTLE, 1 Corinthians 15. 35–49.

Sown in Corruption, Raised in Incorruption.

BUT some one will say, How are the dead raised? and with what manner of body do they come?

Thou foolish one, that which thou thyself sowest is not quickened except it die: and that which thou sowest, thou sowest not the body that shall be, but a bare grain, it may chance of wheat, or of some other kind; but God giveth it a body even as it pleased him, and to each seed a body of its own.

All flesh is not the same flesh: but there is one flesh of men, and another flesh of beasts, and another flesh of birds, and another of fishes. There are also celestial bodies, and bodies terrestrial: but the glory of the celestial is one, and the glory of the terrestrial is another. There is one glory of the sun, and another glory of the moon, and another glory of the stars; for one star differeth from another star in glory.

So also is the resurrection of the dead. It is sown in corruption; it is raised in incorruption: it is sown in dishonor; it is raised in glory: it is sown in weakness; it is raised in power: it is sown a natural body; it is raised a spiritual body. If there is a natural body, there is also a spiritual body. So also it is written, The first man Adam became a living soul. The last Adam became a life-giving spirit.

Howbeit that is not first which is spiritual, but that which is natural; then that which is spiritual. The first man is of the earth, earthy: the second man is of heaven. As is the earthy, such are they also that are earthy: and as is the heavenly, such are they also that are heavenly. And as we have borne the image of the earthy, we shall also bear the image of the heavenly.

II. GOSPEL, John 6. 37–40.

Jesus Permits None of His Own to Perish.

ALL that which the Father giveth me shall come unto me; and him that cometh to me I will in no wise cast out.

For I am come down from heaven, not to do mine own will, but the will of him that sent me. And this is the will of him that sent me, that of all that which he hath given me I should lose nothing, but should raise it up at the last day.

For this is the will of my Father, that every one that beholdeth the Son, and believeth on him, should have eternal life; and I will raise him up at the last day.

III. Epistle, 2 Corinthians 5. 1–10.

The Christian's Translation to His Heavenly Home.

WE know that if the earthly house of our tabernacle be dissolved, we have a building from God, a house not made with hands, eternal, in the heavens. For verily in this we groan, longing to be clothed upon with our habitation which is from heaven: if so be that being clothed we shall not be found naked. For indeed we that are in this tabernacle do groan, being burdened; not for that we would be unclothed, but that we would be clothed upon, that what is mortal may be swallowed up of life.

Now he that wrought us for this very thing is God, who gave unto us the earnest of the Spirit. Being therefore always of good courage, and knowing that, whilst we are at home in the body, we are absent from the Lord (for we walk by faith, not by sight); we are of good courage, I say, and are willing rather to be absent from the body, and to be at home with the Lord.

Wherefore also we make it our aim, whether at home or absent, to be well-pleasing unto him. For we must all be made manifest before the judgment-seat of Christ; that each one may receive the things done in the body, according to what he hath done, whether it be good or bad.

III. Gospel, Luke 20. 27–40.

The Resurrection of the Dead.

AND there came to him certain of the Sadducees, they that say that there is no resurrection; and they asked him, saying, Teacher, Moses wrote unto us, that if a man's brother die, having a wife, and he be childless, his brother should take the wife, and raise up seed unto his brother. There were therefore seven brethren: and the first took a wife, and died childless; and the second; and the third took her; and likewise the seven also left no children, and died. Afterward the woman also died. In the resurrection therefore whose wife of them shall she be? for the seven had her to wife.

And Jesus said unto them, The sons of this world marry, and are given in marriage: but they that are accounted worthy to attain to that world, and the resurrection from the dead, neither marry, nor are given in marriage: for neither can they die any more: for they are equal unto the angels; and are sons of God, being sons of the resurrection. But that the dead are raised, even Moses showed, in the place concerning the Bush, when he calleth the Lord the God of Abraham, and the God of Isaac, and the God of Jacob. Now he is not the God of the dead, but of the living: for all live unto him.

And certain of the scribes answering said, Teacher, thou hast well said. For they durst not any more ask him any question.

TWENTY-FIFTH SUNDAY AFTER TRINITY.

The Last Times.

Collect. Stir up, we beseech Thee, O Lord, the hearts of Thy faithful people, that they may always bring forth the fruit of good works, and of Thee be graciously rewarded; through Jesus Christ, Thy Son, our Lord. Amen.

I. Epistle, 1 Thessalonians 4. 13–18.

The Faithful Resurrected and Transformed.

WE would not have you ignorant, brethren, concerning them that fall asleep; that ye sorrow not, even as the rest, who have no hope. For if we believe that Jesus died and rose again, even so them also that are fallen asleep in Jesus will God bring with him.

For this we say unto you by the word of the Lord, that we that are alive, that

are left unto the coming of the Lord, shall in no wise precede them that are fallen asleep. For the Lord Himself shall descend from heaven, with a shout, with the voice of the archangel, and with the trump of God: and the dead in Christ shall rise first; then we that are alive, that are left, shall together with them be caught up in the clouds, to meet the Lord in the air: and so shall we ever be with the Lord. Wherefore comfort one another with these words.

I. Gospel, Matthew 24. 15–28.

The Abomination of Desolation.

WHEN therefore ye see the abomination of desolation, which was spoken of through Daniel the prophet, standing in the holy place (let him that readeth understand), then let them that are in Judæa flee unto the mountains: let him that is on the housetop not go down to take out the things that are in his house: and let him that is in the field not return back to take his cloak.

But woe unto them that are with child and to them that give suck in those days!

And pray ye that your flight be not in the winter, neither on a sabbath: for then shall be great tribulation, such as hath not been from the beginning of the world until now, no, nor ever shall be. And except those days had been shortened, no flesh would have been saved: but for the elect's sake those days shall be shortened.

Then if any man shall say unto you, Lo, here is the Christ, or Here; believe it not. For there shall arise false Christs, and false prophets, and shall show great signs and wonders; so as to lead astray, if possible, even the elect. Behold, I have told you beforehand. If therefore they shall say unto you, Behold, he is in the wilderness; go not forth: Behold, he is in the inner chambers; believe it not. For as the lightning cometh forth from the east, and is seen even unto the west; so shall be the coming of the Son of man. Wheresoever the carcase is, there will the eagles be gathered together.

II. Epistle, 2 Thessalonians 2. 1–12.
Faith Self-possessed unto the End.

NOW we beseech you, brethren, touching the coming of our Lord Jesus Christ, and our gathering together unto him; to the end that ye be not quickly shaken from your mind, nor yet be troubled, either by spirit, or by word, or by epistle as from us, as that the day of the Lord is just at hand; let no man beguile you in any wise: for it will not be, except the falling away come first, and the man of sin be revealed, the son of perdition, he that opposeth and exalteth himself against all that is called God or that is worshipped; so that he sitteth in the temple of God, setting himself forth as God. Remember ye not, that, when I was yet with you, I told you these things? And now ye know that which remaineth, to the end that he may be revealed in his own season. For the mystery of lawlessness doth already work: only there is one that restraineth now, until he be taken out of the way. And then shall be revealed the lawless one, whom the Lord Jesus shall slay with the breath of his mouth, and bring to nought by the manifestation of his coming; even he, whose coming is according to the working of Satan with all power and signs

and lying wonders, and with all deceit of unrighteousness for them that perish; because they received not the love of the truth, that they might be saved. And for this cause God sendeth them a working of error, that they should believe a lie: that they all might be judged who believed not the truth, but had pleasure in unrighteousness.

II. Gospel, Luke 13. 22–29.
Jesus Warning Against False Security.

AND he went on his way through cities and villages, teaching, and journeying on unto Jerusalem.

And one said unto him, Lord, are they few that are saved?

And he said unto them, Strive to enter in by the narrow door: for many, I say unto you, shall seek to enter in, and shall not be able. When once the master of the house is risen up, and hath shut to the door, and ye begin to stand without, and to knock at the door, saying, Lord, open to us; and he shall answer and say to you, I know not whence ye are; then shall ye begin to say, We did eat and drink in thy presence, and thou didst teach in our streets; and he shall say, I tell you, I know not whence ye are; depart from me, all ye workers of iniquity. There shall be the weeping and the gnashing of teeth, when ye shall see Abraham, and Isaac, and Jacob, and all the prophets, in the kingdom of God, and yourselves cast forth without. And they shall come from the east and west, and from the north and south, and shall sit down in the kingdom of God.

III. Epistle, 1 Thessalonians 5. 2–10.
The Coming of the Day of the Lord.

YOURSELVES know perfectly that the day of the Lord so cometh as a thief in the night. When they are saying, Peace and safety, then sudden destruction cometh upon them, as travail upon a woman with child; and they shall in no wise escape.

But ye, brethren, are not in darkness, that that day should overtake you as a thief: for ye are all sons of light, and sons of the day: we are not of the night, nor of darkness; so then let us not sleep, as do the rest, but let us watch and be sober. For they that sleep sleep in the night; and they that are drunken are drunken in the night.

But let us, since we are of the day, be sober, putting on the breastplate of faith and love; and for a helmet, the hope of salvation. For God appointed us not unto wrath, but unto the obtaining of salvation through our Lord Jesus Christ, who died for us, that, whether we wake or sleep, we should live together with him.

III. Gospel, Matthew 24. 1–14.
The Tribulation of the Last Times.

AND Jesus went out from the temple, and was going on his way; and his disciples came to him to show him the buildings of the temple. But he answered and said unto them, See ye not all these things? verily I say unto you, There shall not be left here one stone upon another, that shall not be thrown down.

And as he sat on the mount of Olives, the disciples came unto him privately, saying, Tell us, when shall these things be? and what shall be the sign of thy coming, and of the end of the world?

And Jesus answered and said unto them, Take heed that no man lead you astray. For many shall come in my name, saying, I am the Christ, and shall lead many astray.

And ye shall hear of wars and rumors of wars; see that ye be not troubled: for these things must needs come to pass; but the end is not yet. For nation shall rise against nation, and kingdom against kingdom; and there shall be famines and earthquakes in divers places.

But all these things are the beginning of travail. Then shall they deliver you up unto tribulation, and shall kill you: and ye shall be hated of all the nations for my name's sake. And then shall many stumble, and shall deliver up one another, and shall hate one another. And many false prophets shall arise, and shall lead many astray. And because iniquity shall be multiplied, the love of the many shall wax cold. But he that endureth to the end, the same shall be saved.

And this gospel of the kingdom shall be preached in the whole world for a testimony unto all the nations; and then shall the end come.

TWENTY-SIXTH SUNDAY AFTER TRINITY.
(Also Sixth after Epiphany)
Watchfulness.

Collect. O Lord God, so rule and govern our hearts and minds by Thy Holy Spirit, that, being ever mindful of the end of all things, and of Thy righteous judgment, we may be stirred up to holiness of living here in order that we may dwell with Thee forever hereafter; through Jesus Christ, Thy Son, our Lord. Amen.

I. Epistle, 2 Peter 3. 3–13.
The Lord Will Return.

IN the last days mockers shall come with mockery, walking after their own lusts, and saying, Where is the promise of his coming? for, from the day that the fathers fell asleep, all things continue as they were from the beginning of the creation.

For this they willfully forget, that there were heavens from of old, and an earth compacted out of water and amidst water, by the word of God; by which means the world that then was, being overflowed with water, perished: but the heavens that now are, and the earth, by the same word have been stored up for fire, being reserved against the day of judgment and destruction of ungodly men.

But forget not this one thing, beloved, that one day is with the Lord as a thousand years, and a thousand years as one day. The Lord is not slack concerning his promise, as some count slackness;

but is longsuffering to you-ward, not wishing that any should perish, but that all should come to repentance.

But the day of the Lord will come as a thief; in the which the heavens shall pass away with a great noise, and the elements shall be dissolved with fervent heat, and the earth and the works that are therein shall be burned up.

Seeing that these things are thus all to be dissolved, what manner of persons ought ye to be in all holy living and godliness, looking for and earnestly desiring the coming of the day of God, by reason of which the heavens being on fire shall be dissolved, and the elements shall melt with fervent heat? But according to his promise, we look for new heavens and a new earth, wherein dwelleth righteousness.

I. Gospel, Matthew 25. 1–13.
The Ten Virgins.

THEN shall the kingdom of heaven be likened unto ten virgins, who took their lamps, and went forth to meet the bridegroom. And five of them were foolish, and five were wise. For the foolish, when they took their lamps, took no oil with them: but the wise took oil in their vessels with their lamps.

Now while the bridegroom tarried, they all slumbered and slept. But at midnight there is a cry, Behold, the bridegroom! Come ye forth to meet him.

Then all those virgins arose, and trimmed their lamps. And the foolish said unto the wise, Give us of your oil; for our lamps are going out. But the wise answered, saying, Peradventure there will not be enough for us and you: go ye rather to them that sell, and buy for yourselves.

And while they went away to buy, the bridegroom came; and they that were ready went in with him to the marriage feast: and the door was shut. Afterward came also the other virgins, saying, Lord, open to us. But he answered and said, Verily I say unto you, I know you not.

Watch therefore, for ye know not the day nor the hour.

II. Epistle, Psalm 139. 1–12, 23, 24.

God's Knowledge of the Ways of Men.

O JEHOVAH, thou hast searched me, and known me.
Thou knowest my downsitting and mine uprising;
Thou understandest my thought afar off.
Thou searchest out my path and my lying down,
And art acquainted with all my ways.
For there is not a word in my tongue,
But, lo, O Jehovah, thou knowest it altogether.
Thou hast beset me behind and before,
And laid thy hand upon me.
Such knowledge is too wonderful for me;
It is high, I cannot attain unto it.
Whither shall I go from thy Spirit?
Or whither shall I flee from thy presence?
If I ascend up into heaven, thou art there:
If I make my bed in Sheol, behold, thou art there.
If I take the wings of the morning,
And dwell in the uttermost parts of the sea;
Even there shall thy hand lead me,
And thy right hand shall hold me.
If I say, Surely the darkness shall overwhelm me,
And the light about me shall be night;
Even the darkness hideth not from thee,
But the night shineth as the day:
The darkness and the light are both alike to thee.
Search me, O God, and know my heart:
Try me and know my thoughts;
And see if there be any wicked way in me,
And lead me in the way everlasting.

II. Gospel, Mark 13. 31–37.

Admonition to Watchfulness.

HEAVEN and earth shall pass away: but my words shall not pass away.

But of that day or that hour knoweth no one, not even the angels in heaven, neither the Son, but the Father.

Take ye heed, watch and pray: for ye know not when the time is. It is as when a man, sojourning in another country, having left his house, and given authority to his servants, to each one his work, commanded also the porter to watch. Watch therefore: for ye know not when the lord of the house cometh, whether at even, or at midnight, or at cockcrowing, or in the morning; lest coming suddenly he find you sleeping. And what I say unto you I say unto all, Watch.

III. Epistle, Revelation 22. 10–17, 20.

Faith Longing for the Appearing of the Lord.

AND he saith unto me, Seal not up the words of the prophecy of this book; for the time is at hand. He that is unrighteous, let him do unrighteousness still: and he that is filthy, let him be made filthy still; and he that is righteous, let him do righteousness still: and he that is holy, let him be made holy still.

Behold, I come quickly; and my reward is with me, to render to each man according as his work is. I am the Alpha and the Omega, the first and the last, the beginning and the end.

Blessed are they that wash their robes, that they may have the right to come to the tree of life, and may enter in by the gates into the city. Without are the dogs, and the sorcerers, and the fornicators, and the murderers, and the idolaters, and every one that loveth and maketh a lie.

I Jesus have sent mine angel to testify unto you these things for the churches. . I am the root and the offspring of David, the bright, the morning star.

And the Spirit and the bride say, Come. And he that heareth, let him say, Come. And he that is athirst, let him come: he that will, let him take the water of life freely.

He who testifieth these things saith, Yea: I come quickly. Amen: come, Lord Jesus.

III. Gospel, Matthew 24. 35–44.

The Unexpected Coming of the Son of Man.

HEAVEN and earth shall pass away, but my words shall not pass away.
But of that day and hour knoweth no

one, not even the angels of heaven, neither the Son, but the Father only.

And as were the days of Noah, so shall be the coming of the Son of man. For as in those days which were before the flood they were eating and drinking, marrying and giving in marriage, until the day that Noah entered into the ark, and they knew not until the flood came, and took them all away; so shall be the coming of the Son of man. Then shall two men be in the field; one is taken, and one is left: two women shall be grinding at the mill; one is taken, and one is left.

Watch, therefore: for ye know not on what day your Lord cometh. But know this, that if the master of the house had known in what watch the thief was coming, he would have watched, and would not have suffered his house to be broken through. Therefore be ye also ready; for in an hour that ye think not the Son of man cometh.

TWENTY-SEVENTH SUNDAY AFTER TRINITY.
The Last Judgment.

Collect. Grant, O Lord God, that we may not, like the foolish virgins, fall asleep in our sins, but always watch and pray, and be ready to enter into Thine eternal glory; through Jesus Christ, Thy Son, our Lord. AMEN.

I. EPISTLE, 2 Thessalonians 1, 3–10.
God's Righteous Judgment.

WE are bound to give thanks to God always for you, brethren, even as it is meet, for that your faith groweth exceedingly, and the love of each one of you all toward one another aboundeth; so that we ourselves glory in you in the churches of God for your patience and faith in all your persecutions and in the afflictions which ye endure; which is a manifest token of the righteous judgment of God; to the end that ye may be counted worthy of the kingdom of God, for which ye also suffer: if so be that it is a righteous thing with God to recompense affliction to them that afflict you, and to you that are afflicted rest with us, at the revelation of the Lord Jesus from heaven with the angels of his power in flaming fire, rendering vengeance to them that know not God, and to them that obey not the gospel of our Lord Jesus: who shall suffer punishment, even eternal destruction from the face of the Lord and from the glory of his might, when he shall come to be glorified in his saints, and to be marvelled at in all them that believed (because our testimony unto you was believed) in that day.

I. GOSPEL, Matthew 25. 31–46.
The Son of Man on His Throne of Glory.

WHEN the Son of man shall come in his glory, and all the angels with him, then shall he sit on the throne of his glory: and before him shall be gathered all the nations: and he shall separate them one from another, as the shepherd separateth the sheep from the goats; and he shall set the sheep on his right hand, but the goats on the left.

Then shall the King say unto them on his right hand, Come, ye blessed of my Father, inherit the kingdom prepared for you from the foundation of the world: for I was hungry, and ye gave me to eat; I was thirsty, and ye gave me drink; I was a stranger, and ye took me in; naked, and ye clothed me; I was sick, and ye visited me; I was in prison, and ye came unto me.

Then shall the righteous answer him, saying, Lord, when saw we thee hungry, and fed thee? or athirst, and gave thee drink? And when saw we thee a stranger, and took thee in? or naked, and clothed thee? And when saw we thee sick, or in prison, and came unto thee?

And the King shall answer and say unto them, Verily I say unto you, Inasmuch as ye did it unto one of these my brethren, even these least, ye did it unto me.

Then shall he say also unto them on the left hand, Depart from me, ye cursed, into the eternal fire which is prepared for the devil and his angels: for I was hungry, and ye did not give me to eat; I was thirsty, and ye gave me no drink; I was a stranger, and ye took me not in; naked, and ye clothed me not; sick, and in prison, and ye visited me not.

Then shall they also answer, saying, Lord, when saw we thee hungry, or athirst, or a stranger, or naked, or sick, or in prison, and did not minister unto thee?

Then shall he answer them, saying, Verily I say unto you, Inasmuch as ye did it not unto one of these least, ye did it not unto me.

And these shall go away into eternal punishment: but the righteous into eternal life.

II. Epistle, 1 Corinthians 15. 22–28.

All Things to Be Put in Subjection to God.

AS in Adam all die, so also in Christ shall all be made alive. But each in his own order: Christ the firstfruits; then they that are Christ's at his coming.

Then cometh the end, when he shall deliver up the kingdom to God, even the Father; when he shall have abolished all rule and all authority and power. For he must reign, till he hath put all his enemies under his feet. The last enemy that shall be abolished is death. For, He put all things in subjection under his feet.

But when he saith, All things are put in subjection, it is evident that he is excepted who did subject all things unto him. And when all things have been subjected unto him, then shall the Son also himself be subjected to him that did subject all things unto him, that God may be all in all.

II. Gospel, John 5. 22–29.

Resurrection to Life or to Judgment.

FOR neither doth the Father judge any man, but he hath given all judgment unto the Son; that all may honor the Son, even as they honor the Father. He that honored not the Son honoreth not the Father that sent him.

Verily, verily, I say unto you, He that heareth my word, and believeth him that sent me, hath eternal life, and cometh not into judgment, but hath passed out of death into life.

Verily, verily, I say unto you, The hour cometh, and now is, when the dead shall hear the voice of the Son of God; and they that hear shall live. For as the Father hath life in himself, even so gave he to the Son also to have life in himself; and he gave him authority to execute judgment, because he is a son of man.

Marvel not at this: for the hour cometh, in which all that are in the tombs shall hear his voice, and shall come forth; they that have done good, unto the resurrection of life; and they that have done evil, unto the resurrection of judgment.

III. Epistle, Revelation 20. 11—21. 7.

New Heavens and a New Earth.

AND I saw a great white throne, and him that sat upon it, from whose face the earth and the heaven fled away; and there was found no place for them. And I saw the dead, the great and the small, standing before the throne; and books were opened: and another book was opened, which is the book of life: and the dead were judged out of the things which were written in the books, according to their works.

And the sea gave up the dead that were in it; and death and Hades gave up the dead that were in them: and they were judged every man according to their works.

And death and Hades were cast into the lake of fire. This is the second death, even the lake of fire. And if any was not found written in the book of life, he was cast into the lake of fire.

And I saw a new heaven and a new earth: for the first heaven and the first earth are passed away; and the sea is no more.

And I saw the holy city, new Jerusalem, coming down out of heaven from God, made ready as a bride adorned for her husband. And I heard a great voice out of the throne saying, Behold, the tabernacle of God is with men, and he shall dwell with them, and they shall be his peoples, and God himself shall be with them, and be their God: and he shall wipe away every tear from their eyes; and death shall be no more; neither shall there be mourning, nor crying, nor pain, any more: the first things are passed away.

And he that sitteth on the throne said, Behold, I make all things new. And he saith, Write: for these words are faithful and true.

And he said unto me, They are come to pass. I am the Alpha and the Omega, the beginning and the end. I will give unto him that is athirst of the fountain of the water of life freely. He that overcometh shall inherit these things; and I will be his God, and he shall be my son.

III. Gospel, Matthew 13. 47–50.

The Parable of the Net.

AGAIN, the kingdom of heaven is like unto a net, that was cast into the sea, and gathered of every kind: which, when it was filled, they drew up on the beach; and they sat down, and gathered the good into vessels, but the bad they cast away.

So shall it be in the end of the world: the angels shall come forth, and sever the wicked from among the righteous, and shall cast them into the furnace of fire: there shall be the weeping and the gnashing of teeth.

Minor Festivals of the Church Year

THE DAY OF THE PRESENTATION OF CHRIST.

(Candlemas.)

The Revelation.

Collect. Almighty and everliving God, we humbly beseech Thy Majesty, that as Thine only-begotten Son was this day presented in the temple in substance of our flesh, so we may be presented unto Thee with pure and clean hearts, by the same Thy Son, Jesus Christ, our Lord, Who liveth and reigneth with Thee and the Holy Spirit, ever one God, world without end. AMEN.

I. EPISTLE, Malachi 3. 1–4.

The Promised One Arrives.

BEHOLD, I send my messenger, and he shall prepare the way before me: and the Lord, whom ye seek, will suddenly come to his temple; and the messenger of the covenant, whom ye desire, behold, he cometh, saith Jehovah of hosts.

But who can abide the day of his coming? and who shall stand when he appeareth? for he is like a refiner's fire, and like fullers' soap: and he will sit as a refiner and purifier of silver, and he will purify the sons of Levi, and refine them as gold and silver; and they shall offer unto Jehovah offerings in righteousness. Then shall the offering of Judah and Jerusalem be pleasant unto Jehovah, as in the days of old, and as in ancient years.

I. GOSPEL, Luke 2. 22–32.

The Song of Simeon.

AND when the days of their purification according to the law of Moses were fulfilled, they brought him up to Jerusalem, to present him to the Lord (as it is written in the law of the Lord, Every male that openeth the womb shall be called holy to the Lord), and to offer a sacrifice according to that which is said in the law of the Lord, A pair of turtledoves, or two young pigeons.

And behold, there was a man in Jerusalem, whose name was Simeon; and this man was righteous and devout, looking for the consolation of Israel: and the Holy Spirit was upon him. And it had been revealed unto him by the Holy Spirit, that he should not see death, before he had seen the Lord's Christ. And he came in the Spirit into the temple: and when the parents brought in the child Jesus, that they might do concerning him after the custom of the law, then he received him into his arms, and blessed God, and said,

Now lettest thou thy servant depart, Lord,
According to thy word, in peace;
For mine eyes have seen thy salvation,
Which thou hast prepared before the face of all peoples;
A light for revelation to the Gentiles,
And the glory of thy people Israel.

EPISTLE, Psalm 100. 1–5.

Praise to Jehovah.

MAKE a joyful noise unto Jehovah, all ye lands,
Serve Jehovah with gladness:
Come before his presence with singing.
Know ye that Jehovah, he is God:
It is he that hath made us, and we are his;
We are his people, and the sheep of his pasture.
Enter into his gates with thanksgiving,
And into his courts with praise:
Give thanks unto him, and bless his name.
For Jehovah is good: his lovingkindness endureth for ever,
And his faithfulness unto all generations.

II. GOSPEL, John 1. 16–18.

Grace and Truth through Jesus Christ.

OF his fulness we all received, and grace for grace. For the law was given through Moses; grace and truth came through Jesus Christ. No man hath seen God at any time; the only begotten Son, who is in the bosom of the Father, he hath declared him.

III. EPISTLE, 1 John 1. 1-7.

Christ's Message from God.

THAT which was from the beginning, that which we have heard, that which we have seen with our eyes, that which we beheld, and our hands handled, concerning the Word of life (and the life was manifested, and we have seen, and bear witness, and declare unto you the life, the eternal life, which was with the Father, and was manifested unto us); that which we have seen and heard declare we unto you also, that ye also may have fellowship with us: yea, and our fellowship is with the Father, and with his Son Jesus Christ: and these things we write, that our joy may be made full.

And this is the message which we have heard from him and announce unto you, that God is light, and in him is no darkness at all. If we say that we have fellowship with him and walk in the dark-ness, we lie, and do not the truth: but if we walk in the light, as he is in the light, we have fellowship one with another, and the blood of Jesus his Son cleanseth us from all sin.

III. GOSPEL, Matthew 13. 31-33.

The Mustard Seed and the Leaven.

ANOTHER parable set he before them, saying, The kingdom of heaven is like unto a grain of mustard seed, which a man took, and sowed in his field: which indeed is less than all seeds; but when it is grown, it is greater than the herbs, and becometh a tree, so that the birds of the heaven come and lodge in the branches thereof.

Another parable spake he unto them: The kingdom of heaven is like unto leaven, which a woman took, and hid in three measures of meal, till it was all leavened.

THE DAY OF ANNUNCIATION.

The Annunciation.

Collect. O God, who by Thy mercy didst send Thine only-begotten Son to be born here on earth for our salvation, as announced by the message of an angel: grant us, heavenly Father, to be grateful to Thee for Thy great mercy, and ever to love Thy holy will; through the same Thy Son, Jesus Christ, our Lord. AMEN.

I. EPISTLE, Isaiah 7. 10-15.

Immanuel Promised.

AND Jehovah spake again unto Ahaz, saying, Ask thee a sign of Jehovah thy God; ask it either in the depth, or in the height above.

But Ahaz said, I will not ask, neither will I tempt Jehovah.

And he said, Hear ye now, O house of David: Is it a small thing for you to weary men, that ye will weary my God also? Therefore the Lord himself will give you a sign: behold, a virgin shall conceive, and bear a son, and shall call his name Immanuel. Butter and honey shall he eat, when he knoweth to refuse the evil, and choose the good.

I. GOSPEL, Luke 1. 26-38.

The Angel's Message to Mary.

NOW in the sixth month the angel Gabriel was sent from God unto a city of Galilee, named Nazareth, to a virgin betrothed to a man whose name was Joseph, of the house of David; and the virgin's name was Mary. And he came in unto her, and said, Hail, thou that art highly favored, the Lord is with thee.

But she was greatly troubled at the saying, and cast in her mind what manner of salutation this might be.

And the angel said unto her, Fear not, Mary: for thou hast found favor with God. And behold, thou shalt conceive in thy womb, and bring forth a son, and shalt call his name JESUS. He shall be great, and shall be called the Son of the Most High: and the Lord God shall give unto him the throne of his father David: and he shall reign over the house of Jacob for ever; and of his kingdom there shall be no end.

And Mary said unto the angel, How shall this be, seeing I know not a man?

And the angel answered and said unto her, The Holy Spirit shall come upon thee, and the power of the Most High shall overshadow thee: wherefore also the holy thing which is begotten shall be called the Son of God. And behold, Elisabeth thy kinswoman, she also hath conceived a son in her old age; and this is the sixth month with her that was called barren. For no word from God shall be void of power.

And Mary said, Behold, the handmaid of the Lord; be it unto me according to thy word.

And the angel departed from her.

II. Epistle, Isaiah 49. 5, 6.
The Coming of the Lord.

AND now saith Jehovah that formed me from the womb to be his servant, to bring Jacob again to him, and that Israel be gathered unto him (for I am honorable in the eyes of Jehovah, and my God is become my strength); yea, he saith, It is too light a thing that thou shouldest be my servant to raise up the tribes of Jacob, and to restore the preserved of Israel: I will also give thee for a light to the Gentiles, that thou mayest be my salvation unto the end of the earth.

II. Gospel, Luke 1. 39–45.
Mary and Elisabeth.

AND Mary arose in these days and went into the hill country with haste, into a city of Judah; and entered into the house of Zacharias and saluted Elisabeth.

And it came to pass, when Elisabeth heard the salutation of Mary, the babe leaped in her womb; and Elisabeth was filled with the Holy Spirit; and she lifted up her voice with a loud cry, and said,

Blessed art thou among women, and blessed is the fruit of thy womb. And whence is this to me, that the mother of my Lord should come unto me? For behold, when the voice of thy salutation came into mine ears, the babe leaped in my womb for joy. And blessed is she that believed; for there shall be a fulfilment of the things which have been spoken to her from the Lord.

III. Epistle, Jeremiah 33. 14–16.
The Branch of Righteousness.

BEHOLD, the days come, saith Jehovah, that I will perform that good word which I have spoken concerning the house of Israel and concerning the house of Judah.

In those days, and at that time, will I cause a Branch of righteousness to grow up unto David; and he shall execute justice and righteousness in the land.

In those days shall Judah be saved, and Jerusalem shall dwell safely; and this is the name whereby she shall be called: Jehovah our righteousness.

III. Gospel, Luke 1. 46–55.
The Song of Mary.

AND Mary said,
My soul doth magnify the Lord,
And my spirit hath rejoiced in God my Saviour.
For he hath looked upon the low estate of his handmaid:
For behold, from henceforth all generations shall call me blessed.
For he that is mighty hath done to me great things;
And holy is his name.
And his mercy is unto generations and generations
On them that fear him.
He hath showed strength with his arm;
He hath scattered the proud in the imagination of their heart.
He hath put down princes from their thrones,
And hath exalted them of low degree.
The hungry he hath filled with good things;
And the rich he hath sent empty away.
He hath given help to Israel his servant,
That he might remember mercy
(As he spake unto our fathers)
Toward Abraham and his seed for ever.

THE DAY OF JOHN THE BAPTIST.
Heaven and Earth.

Collect. Almighty God, who didst send Thy chosen servant, John the Baptist, that he through his preaching and baptism should prepare the way for Thy Son, Jesus Christ: grant us Thy grace that we according to his word may amend our sinful lives, and steadfastly follow Him of whom John bare witness; through Thy Son, Jesus Christ, our Lord. Amen.

I. Epistle, Isaiah 40. 1–8.
The Herald Preaching Comfort.

COMFORT ye, comfort ye my people, saith your God. Speak ye comfortably to Jerusalem; and cry unto her, that her warfare is accomplished, that her iniquity is pardoned, that she hath received of Jehovah's hand double for all her sins.

The voice of one that crieth, Prepare ye in the wilderness the way of Jehovah; make level in the desert a highway for our God. Every valley shall be exalted, and every mountain and hill shall be made low; and the uneven shall be made level, and the rough places a plain: and the glory of Jehovah shall be revealed, and all flesh shall see it together; for the mouth of Jehovah hath spoken it.

The voice of one saying, Cry. And one said, What shall I cry? All flesh is grass, and all the goodliness thereof is as the flower of the field. The grass withereth, the flower fadeth, because the breath of Jehovah bloweth upon it; surely the people is grass. The grass withereth, the flower fadeth; but the word of our God shall stand forever.

I. Gospel, Luke 1. 57–80.
The Birth of John the Baptist.

NOW Elisabeth's time was fulfilled that she should be delivered; and she brought forth a son. And her neighbors and her kinsfolk heard that the Lord had magnified his mercy towards her; and they rejoiced with her.

And it came to pass on the eighth day, that they came to circumcise the child; and they would have called him Zacharias, after the name of his father. And his mother answered and said, Not so; but he shall be called John. And they said unto her, There is none of thy kindred that is called by this name.

And they made signs to his father, what he would have him called. And he asked for a writing tablet, and wrote, saying, His name is John. And they marvelled all. And his mouth was opened immediately, and his tongue loosed, and he spake, blessing God.

And fear came on all that dwelt round about them: and all these sayings were noised abroad throughout all the hill country of Judæa. And all that heard them laid them up in their heart, saying, What then shall this child be? For the hand of the Lord was with him.

And his father Zacharias was filled with the Holy Spirit, and prophesied, saying,

Blessed be the Lord, the God of Israel;
For he hath visited and wrought redemption for his people,
And hath raised up a horn of salvation for us
In the house of his servant David
(As he spake by the mouth of his holy prophets that have been from of old),
Salvation from our enemies, and from the hand of all that hate us;
To show mercy towards our fathers,
And to remember his holy covenant;
The oath which he sware unto Abraham our father,
To grant unto us that we being delivered out of the hand of our enemies
Should serve him without fear,
In holiness and righteousness before him all our days.
Yea and thou, child, shalt be called the prophet of the Most High:
For thou shalt go before the face of the Lord to make ready his ways;

To give knowledge of salvation unto his people
In the remission of their sins,
Because of the tender mercy of our God,
Whereby the dayspring from on high shall visit us,
To shine upon them that sit in darkness and the shadow of death;
To guide our feet into the way of peace.
And the child grew, and waxed strong in spirit, and was in the deserts till the day of his showing unto Israel.

II. Epistle, Acts 17. 22–31.
God the Creator and Lord of All Things.

AND Paul stood in the midst of the Areopagus, and said,

Ye men of Athens, in all things I perceive that ye are very religious. For as I passed along, and observed the objects of your worship, I found also an altar with this inscription, To an Unknown God. What therefore ye worship in ignorance, this I set forth unto you. The God that made the world and all things therein, he, being Lord of heaven and earth, dwelleth not in temples made with hands; neither is he served by men's hands, as though he needed anything, seeing he himself giveth to all life, and breath, and all things; and he made of one every nation of men to dwell on all the face of the earth, having determined their appointed seasons, and the bounds of their habitation; that they should seek God, if haply they might feel after him and find him, though he is not far from each one of us: for in him we live, and move, and have our being; as certain even of your own poets have said,

For we are also his offspring.
Being then the offspring of God, we ought not to think that the Godhead is like unto gold, or silver, or stone, graven by art and device of man. The times of ignorance therefore God overlooked; but now he commanded men that they should all everywhere repent: inasmuch as he hath appointed a day in which he will judge the world in righteousness by the man whom he hath ordained; whereof he hath given assurance unto all men, in that he hath raised him from the dead.

II. Gospel, Luke 1. 5–25.
The Message of the Angel to Zacharias.

THERE was in the days of Herod, king of Judæa, a certain priest named Zacharias, of the course of Abijah: and he had a wife of the daughters of Aaron, and her name was Elisabeth. And they were both righteous before God, walking in all the commandments and ordinances of the Lord blameless. And they had no child, because that Elisabeth was barren, and they both were now well stricken in years.

Now it came to pass, while he executed the priest's office before God in the order of his course, according to the custom of the priest's office, his lot was to enter into the temple of the Lord and burn incense. And the whole multitude of the people were praying without at the hour of incense. And there appeared unto him an angel of the Lord standing on the right side of the altar of incense. And Zacharias was troubled when he saw him, and fear fell upon him.

But the angel said unto him, Fear not, Zacharias, because thy supplication is heard, and thy wife Elisabeth shall bear thee a son, and thou shalt call his name John. And thou shalt have joy and gladness; and many shall rejoice at his birth. For he shall be great in the sight of the Lord, and he shall drink no wine nor strong drink; and he shall be filled with the Holy Spirit, even from his mother's womb. And many of the children of Israel shall he turn unto the Lord their God. And he shall go before his face in the spirit and power of Elijah, to turn the hearts of the fathers to the children, and the disobedient to walk in the wisdom of the just; to make ready for the Lord a people prepared for him.

And Zacharias said unto the angel, Whereby shall I know this? for I am an old man, and my wife well stricken in years.

And the angel answering said unto him, I am Gabriel, that stand in the presence of God; and I was sent to speak unto thee, and to bring thee these good tidings. And behold, thou shalt be silent and not able to speak, until the day that these things shall come to pass, because thou believedst not my words, which shall be fulfilled in their season.

And the people were waiting for Zacharias, and they marvelled while he tarried in the temple. And when he came out, he could not speak unto them: and they perceived that he had seen a vision in the temple: and he continued making signs unto them, and remained dumb.

And it came to pass, when the days of his ministration were fulfilled, he departed unto his house.

And after these days Elisabeth his wife conceived; and she hid herself five months, saying, Thus hath the Lord done unto me in the days wherein he looked upon me, to take away my reproach among men.

III. Epistle, Psalm 103. 8–18.
The Greatness of God's Mercy.

JEHOVAH is merciful and gracious,
Slow to anger, and abundant in lovingkindness.
He will not always chide;
Neither will he keep his anger for ever.
He hath not dealt with us after our sins,
Nor rewarded us after our iniquities.
For as the heavens are high above the earth,
So great is his lovingkindness toward them that fear him.
As far as the east is from the west,
So far hath he removed our transgressions from us.
Like as a father pitieth his children,
So Jehovah pitieth them that fear him.
For he knoweth our frame;
He remembereth that we are dust.
As for man, his days are as grass;
As a flower of the field, so he flourisheth.
For the wind passeth over it, and it is gone;
And the place thereof shall know it no more.
But the lovingkindness of Jehovah is from everlasting to everlasting upon them that fear him,
And his righteousness unto children's children;
To such as keep his covenant,
And to those that remember his precepts to do them.

III. Gospel, Mark 6. 14–29.
The Death of John the Baptist.

AND king Herod heard thereof; for his name had become known: and he said, John the Baptizer is risen from the dead, and therefore do these powers work in him. But others said, It is Elijah. And others said, It is a prophet, even as one of the prophets. But Herod, when he heard thereof, said, John, whom I beheaded, he is risen.

For Herod himself had sent forth and laid hold upon John, and bound him in prison for the sake of Herodias, his brother Philip's wife; for he had married her. For John said unto Herod, It is not lawful for thee to have thy brother's wife. And Herodias set herself against him, and desired to kill him; and she could not; for Herod feared John, knowing that he was a righteous and holy man, and kept him safe. And when he heard him, he was much perplexed; and he heard him gladly.

And when a convenient day was come, that Herod on his birthday made a supper to his lords, and the high captains, and the chief men of Galilee; and when the daughter of Herodias herself came in and danced, she pleased Herod and them that sat at meat with him; and the king said unto the damsel, Ask of me whatsoever thou wilt, and I will give it thee. And he sware unto her, Whatsoever thou shalt ask of me, I will give it thee, unto the half of my kingdom. And she went out, and said unto her mother, What shall I ask? And she said, The head of John the Baptizer. And she came in straightway with haste unto the king, and asked, saying, I will that thou forthwith give me on a platter the head of John the Baptist. And the king was exceeding sorry; but for the sake of his oaths, and of them that sat at meat, he would not reject her.

And straightway the king sent forth a soldier of his guard, and commanded to bring his head: and he went and beheaded him in the prison, and brought his head on a platter, and gave it to the damsel; and the damsel gave it to her mother.

And when his disciples heard thereof, they came and took up his corpse, and laid it in a tomb.

ST. MICHAEL'S DAY.

Greatness and Lowliness.

Collect. O God, who in Thy divine wisdom hast sent Thy holy angels to serve them that shall inherit salvation: grant us grace, O heavenly Father, to resist the enemy of our souls and by Thy help to gain the victory over all evil; through Thy Son, Jesus Christ, our Lord. AMEN.

I. EPISTLE, Revelation 12. 7–12.
Michael Contending against the Dragon.

AND there was war in heaven: Michael and his angels going forth to war with the dragon; and the dragon warred and his angels; and they prevailed not; neither was their place found any more in heaven. And the great dragon was cast down, the old serpent, he that is called the Devil and Satan, the deceiver of the whole world; he was cast down to the earth, and his angels were cast down with him. And I heard a great voice in heaven, saying,

Now is come the salvation, and the power, and the kingdom of our God, and the authority of his Christ: for the accuser of our brethren is cast down, who accuseth them before our God day and night. And they overcame him because of the blood of the Lamb, and because of the word of their testimony; and they loved not their life even unto death. Therefore rejoice, O heavens, and ye that dwell in them. Woe for the earth and for the sea: because the devil is gone down unto you, having great wrath, knowing that he hath but a short time.

I. GOSPEL, Matthew 18. 1–10.
The Greatest in the Kingdom of Heaven.

IN that hour came the disciples unto Jesus, saying, Who then is greatest in the kingdom of heaven? And he called to him a little child, and set him in the midst of them, and said, Verily I say unto you, Except ye turn, and become as little children, ye shall in no wise enter into the kingdom of heaven. Whosoever therefore shall humble himself as this little child, the same is the greatest in the kingdom of heaven. And whoso shall receive one such little child in my name receiveth me: but whoso shall cause one of these little ones that believe on me to stumble, it is profitable for him that a great millstone should be hanged about his neck, and that he should be sunk in the depth of the sea. Woe unto the world because of occasions of stumbling! for it must needs be that the occasions come; but woe to that man through whom the occasion cometh! And if thy hand or thy foot causeth thee to stumble, cut it off, and cast it from thee: it is good for thee to enter into life maimed or halt, rather than having two hands or two feet to be cast into the eternal fire. And if thine eye causeth thee to stumble, pluck it out, and cast it from thee: it is good for thee to enter life with one eye, rather than having two eyes to be cast into the hell of fire. See that ye despise not one of these little ones: for I say unto you, that in heaven their angels do always behold the face of my Father who is in heaven.

II. EPISTLE, Psalm 113. 1–7.
No One Like unto God.

PRAISE ye Jehovah,
Praise, O ye servants of Jehovah,
Praise the name of Jehovah.
Blessed be the name of Jehovah
From this time forth and for evermore.

From the rising of the sun unto the
going down of the same
Jehovah's name is to be praised.
Jehovah is high above all nations,
And his glory above the heavens.
Who is like unto Jehovah our God,
That hath his seat on high,
That humbleth himself to behold
The things that are in heaven and in
the earth?
He raiseth up the poor out of the dust,
And lifteth up the needy from the
dunghill.

II. GOSPEL, Mark 10. 13–16.

Jesus and the Children.

AND they were bringing unto him little
children, that he should touch them:
and the disciples rebuked them. But
when Jesus saw it, he was moved with
indignation, and said unto them,

Suffer the little children to come unto
me; forbid them not: for to such belongeth the kingdom of God. Verily I
say unto you, Whosoever shall not receive the kingdom of God as a little
child, he shall in no wise enter therein.

And he took them in his arms, and
blessed them, laying his hands upon
them.

III. EPISTLE, Genesis 28. 10–17.

Jacob's Ladder.

AND Jacob went out from Beer-sheba,
and went toward Haran.

And he lighted upon a certain place,
and tarried there all night, because the
sun was set; and he took one of the
stones of the place, and put it under his
head, and lay down in that place to sleep.

And he dreamed: and, behold, a ladder
set up on the earth, and the top of it

reached to heaven; and, behold, the angels of God ascending and descending
on it.

And, behold, Jehovah stood above it,
and said, I am Jehovah, the God of Abraham thy father, and the God of Isaac:
the land whereon thou liest, to thee will
I give it, and to thy seed; and thy seed
shall be as the dust of the earth, and
thou shalt spread abroad to the west, and
to the east, and to the north, and to the
south: and in thee and in thy seed shall
all the families of the earth be blessed.
And, behold, I am with thee, and will
keep thee whithersoever thou goest, and
will bring thee again into this land; for
I will not leave thee, until I have done
that which I have spoken to thee of.

And Jacob awaked out of his sleep, and
he said, Surely Jehovah is in this place;
and I knew it not. And he was afraid,
and said, How dreadful is this place! this
is none other than the house of God, and
this is the gate of heaven.

III. GOSPEL, Matthew 21. 14–17.

The Children in the Temple.

AND the blind and the lame came to
him in the temple; and he healed
them.

But when the chief priests and the
scribes saw the wonderful things that he
did, and the children that were crying
in the temple and saying, Hosanna to the
son of David; they were moved with indignation, and said unto him, Hearest
thou what these are saying?

And Jesus saith unto them, Yea: did
ye never read, Out of the mouth of babes
and sucklings thou hast perfected praise?

And he left them, and went forth out
of the city to Bethany, and lodged there.

ALL SAINTS' DAY.

The Saints.

Collect. Almighty God, grant, we beseech Thee, that the example of Thy
saints may inspire us to holy living; and
as we commemorate their lives, give us
Thy grace to follow them in faith and
good works; through Thy Son, Jesus
Christ, our Lord. AMEN.

I. EPISTLE (a), Revelation 7. 2–4, 9–12.

The Great Multitude Praising God.

AND I saw another angel ascend from
the sunrising, having the seal of the
living God: and he cried with a great
voice to the four angels to whom it was

given to hurt the earth and the sea, saying, Hurt not the earth, neither the sea,
nor the trees, till we shall have sealed
the servants of our God on their foreheads.

And I heard the number of them that
were sealed, a hundred and forty and
four thousand, sealed out of every tribe
of the children of Israel.

After these things I saw, and behold,
a great multitude, which no man could
number, out of every nation and of all
tribes and peoples and tongues, standing
before the throne and before the Lamb,
arrayed in white robes, and palms in

their hands; and they cry with a great voice, saying,

Salvation unto our God who sitteth on the throne, and unto the Lamb.

And all the angels were standing round about the throne, and about the elders and the four living creatures; and they fell before the throne on their faces, and worshipped God, saying,

Amen: Blessing, and glory, and wisdom, and thanksgiving, and honor, and power, and might, be unto our God for ever and ever. Amen.

I. Epistle (b), Revelation 7. 9–17.
The Innumerable Multitude before the Throne.

AFTER these things I saw, and behold, a great multitude, which no man could number, out of every nation and of all tribes and peoples and tongues, standing before the throne and before the Lamb, arrayed in white robes, and palms in their hands; and they cry with a great voice, saying,

Salvation unto our God who sitteth on the throne, and unto the Lamb.

And all the angels were standing round about the throne, and about the elders and the four living creatures; and they fell before the throne on their faces, and worshipped God, saying,

Amen: Blessing, and glory, and wisdom, and thanksgiving, and honor, and power, and might, be unto our God for ever and ever. Amen.

And one of the elders answered, saying unto me, These that are arrayed in the white robes, who are they, and whence came they?

And I say unto him, My lord, thou knowest.

And he said to me, These are they that come out of the great tribulation, and they washed their robes, and made them white in the blood of the Lamb. Therefore are they before the throne of God; and they serve him day and night in his temple: and he that sitteth on the throne shall spread his tabernacle over them. They shall hunger no more, neither thirst any more; neither shall the sun strike upon them, nor any heat: for the Lamb that is in the midst of the throne shall be their shepherd, and shall guide them unto fountains of waters of life: and God shall wipe away every tear from their eyes.

I. Gospel, Matthew 5. 1–12.
The Beatitudes.

AND seeing the multitudes, he went up into the mountain: and when he had sat down, his disciples came unto him:

and he opened his mouth and taught them, saying,

Blessed are the poor in spirit: for theirs is the kingdom of heaven.

Blessed are they that mourn: for they shall be comforted.

Blessed are the meek: for they shall inherit the earth.

Blessed are they that hunger and thirst after righteousness: for they shall be filled.

Blessed are the merciful: for they shall obtain mercy.

Blessed are the pure in heart: for they shall see God.

Blessed are the peacemakers: for they shall be called sons of God.

Blessed are they that have been persecuted for righteousness' sake: for theirs is the kingdom of heaven. Blessed are ye when men shall reproach you, and persecute you, and say all manner of evil against you falsely, for my sake. Rejoice, and be exceeding glad: for great is your reward in heaven: for so persecuted they the prophets that were before you.

II. Epistle, Hebrews 12. 1–3.
The Cloud of Witnesses.

THEREFORE let us also, seeing we are compassed about with so great a cloud of witnesses, lay aside every weight, and the sin which doth so easily beset us, and let us run with patience the race that is set before us, looking unto Jesus the author and perfecter of our faith, who for the joy that was set before him endured the cross, despising shame, and hath sat down at the right hand of the throne of God. For consider him that hath endured such gainsaying of sinners against himself, that ye wax not weary, fainting in your souls.

II. Gospel, Matthew 5. 13–16.
The Salt of the Earth and the Light of the World.

YE are the salt of the earth: but if the salt have lost its savor, wherewith shall it be salted? it is thenceforth good for nothing, but to be cast out and trodden under foot of men.

Ye are the light of the world. A city set on a hill cannot be hid. Neither do men light a lamp, and put it under the bushel, but on the stand; and it shineth unto all that are in the house. Even so let your light shine before men; that they may see your good works, and glorify your Father who is in heaven.

III. EPISTLE, Revelation 14. 1-3.

The Saints Serving God before the Throne.

AND I saw, and behold, the Lamb standing on the mount Zion, and with him a hundred and forty and four thousand, having his name, and the name of his Father, written on their foreheads.

And I heard a voice from heaven, as the voice of many waters, and as the voice of a great thunder: and the voice which I heard was as the voice of harpers harping with their harps: and they sing as it were a new song before the throne, and before the four living creatures and the elders: and no man could learn the song save the hundred and forty and four thousand, even they that had been purchased out of the earth.

III. GOSPEL, Luke 6. 20-26.

Blessings and Woes.

AND he lifted up his eyes on his disciples, and said, Blessed are ye poor: for yours is the kingdom of God. Blessed are ye that hunger now: for ye shall be filled. Blessed are ye that weep now: for ye shall laugh. Blessed are ye, when men shall hate you, and when they shall separate you from their company, and reproach you, and cast out your name as evil, for the Son of man's sake. Rejoice in that day, and leap for joy: for behold, your reward is great in heaven; for in the same manner did their fathers unto the prophets.

But woe unto you that are rich! for ye have received your consolation. Woe unto you, ye that are full now! for ye shall hunger. Woe unto you, ye that laugh now! for ye shall mourn and weep. Woe unto you, when all men shall speak well of you! for in the same manner did their fathers to the false prophets.

FIRST DAY OF PRAYER.

Repentance.

Collect. O Lord God, who hast no pleasure in the death of the wicked, but that the wicked turn from his evil way, and live: save us from the just punishment of our sins and make us a people that fear and serve Thee; through Thy Son, Jesus Christ, our Lord. AMEN.

EPISTLE, Psalm 130. 1-8.

The Penitent Crying unto the Lord.

OUT of the depths have I cried unto thee, O Jehovah.
Lord, hear my voice:
Let thine ears be attentive
To the voice of my supplications.
If thou, Jehovah, shouldest mark iniquities,
O Lord, who could stand?
But there is forgiveness with thee,
That thou mayest be feared.
I wait for Jehovah, my soul doth wait,
And in his word do I hope.
My soul waiteth for the Lord
More than watchmen wait for the morning;
Yea, more than watchmen for the morning.

O Israel, hope in Jehovah;
For with Jehovah there is lovingkindness,
And with him is plenteous redemption.
And he will redeem Israel
From all his iniquities.

GOSPEL, Matthew 11. 20-24.

Woes Pronounced upon the Impenitent.

THEN began he to upbraid the cities wherein most of his mighty works were done, because they repented not.

Woe unto thee, Chorazin! woe unto thee, Bethsaida! for if the mighty works had been done in Tyre and Sidon which were done in you, they would have repented long ago in sackcloth and ashes. But I say unto you, it shall be more tolerable for Tyre and Sidon in the day of judgment, than for you.

And thou, Capernaum, shalt thou be exalted unto heaven? thou shalt go down unto Hades: for if the mighty works had been done in Sodom which were done in thee, it would have remained until this day. But I say unto you that it shall be more tolerable for the land of Sodom in the day of judgment, than for thee.

SECOND DAY OF PRAYER.

The Reformation.

Collect. O Lord God, our heavenly Father, Thou who hast revealed to us the way of salvation: preserve to us Thy gospel, and let Thy Word be proclaimed in purity and power, so that Thy Church may trust only in Thy grace and be kept in holiness of life; through Thy Son, Jesus Christ, our Lord, who liveth and reigneth with Thee and the Holy Spirit, world without end. AMEN.

EPISTLE, Romans 1. 16, 17.

The Righteous Shall Live by Faith.

I AM not ashamed of the gospel: for it is the power of God unto salvation to every one that believeth; to the Jew first, and also to the Greek. For therein is revealed a righteousness of God from faith unto faith: as it is written, But the righteous shall live by faith.

GOSPEL, Matthew 11. 25–30.

The Way of God.

AT that season Jesus answered and said, I thank thee, O Father, Lord of heaven and earth, that thou didst hide these things from the wise and understanding, and didst reveal them unto babes: yea, Father, for so it was well-pleasing in thy sight.

All things have been delivered unto me of my Father: and no one knoweth the Son, save the Father; neither doth any know the Father, save the Son, and he to whomsoever the Son willeth to reveal him.

Come unto me, all ye that labor and are heavy laden, and I will give you rest. Take my yoke upon you, and learn of me; for I am meek and lowly in heart: and ye shall find rest unto your souls. For my yoke is easy, and my burden is light.

THIRD DAY OF PRAYER.

Missions.

Collect. Almighty God, we pray Thee, quicken Thy Church to serve Thee and to extend Thy Kingdom throughout the earth, so that all peoples may see Thy salvation and Thy name may be glorified from the rising of the sun even unto the going down thereof; through Thy Son, Jesus Christ, our Lord, who liveth and reigneth with Thee and the Holy Spirit, world without end. AMEN.

EPISTLE, Psalm 96. 1–10.

The Lord Is King of the Nations.

OH sing unto Jehovah a new song:
Sing unto Jehovah, all the earth.
Sing unto Jehovah, bless his name;
Show forth his salvation from day to day.
Declare his glory among the nations,
His marvellous works among all the peoples.
For great is Jehovah, and greatly to be praised:
He is to be feared above all gods.
For all the gods of the peoples are idols;
But Jehovah made the heavens.
Honor and majesty are before him:
Strength and beauty are in his sanctuary.

Ascribe unto Jehovah, ye kindreds of the peoples,
Ascribe unto Jehovah glory and strength.
Ascribe unto Jehovah the glory due unto his name:
Bring an offering, and come into his courts.
Oh worship Jehovah in holy array:
Tremble before him, all the earth.
Say among the nations, Jehovah reigneth:
The world also is established that it cannot be moved:
He will judge the peoples with equity.

GOSPEL, Matthew 28. 18–20.

The Gospel Coming to All Peoples.

AND Jesus came to them and spake unto them, saying, All authority hath been given unto me in heaven and on earth. Go ye therefore, and make disciples of all the nations, baptizing them into the name of the Father and of the Son and of the Holy Spirit: teaching them to observe all things whatsoever I commanded you: and lo, I am with you always, even unto the end of the world.

FOURTH DAY OF PRAYER.

Thanksgiving.

Collect. Almighty God, our heavenly Father, Thou who ever givest good gifts unto men and dost protect us daily from all harm and danger: grant us grace to acknowledge Thy goodness, and quicken us to give praise and thanks to Thee; through Thy Son, Jesus Christ, our Lord, who liveth and reigneth with Thee and the Holy Spirit, world without end. AMEN.

EPISTLE, Psalm 103. 1–5.

Praise to God for All Things.

BLESS Jehovah, O my soul;
And all that is within me, bless his holy name.
Bless Jehovah, O my soul,
And forget not all his benefits:
Who forgiveth all thine iniquities;
Who healeth all thy diseases;

Who redeemeth thy life from destruction;
Who crowneth thee with lovingkindness and tender mercies;
Who satisfieth thy desire with good things,
So that thy youth is renewed like the eagle.

GOSPEL, Romans 11. 33–36.

The Unsearchable Wisdom of God.

O THE depth of the riches both of the wisdom and the knowledge of God! how unsearchable are his judgments, and his ways past tracing out! For who hath known the mind of the Lord? or who hath been his counsellor? or who hath first given to him, and it shall be recompensed unto him again? For of him, and through him, and unto him, are all things. To him be the glory for ever. Amen.

The Passion of Our Lord
As Recorded by the Four Evangelists

FIRST PART.

Jesus among His Disciples at Jerusalem Prior to His Suffering and Death.

1. *Preparation for the Passover.*

NOW THE FEAST of unleavened bread drew nigh, and Jesus said unto his disciples, Ye know that after two days the feast of the Passover cometh; and the Son of man is delivered up to be crucified.

Then were gathered together the chief priests and the scribes, and the elders of the people, unto the court of the high priest, who was called Caiaphas, and they took counsel together that they might take Jesus by subtlety, and put him to death. But they said, Not during the feast, lest a tumult arise among the people; for they feared the people.

And Satan entered into Judas who was called Iscariot, he that was one of the twelve. And he went away, and communed with the chief priests and captains, how he might deliver him unto them. And they when they heard it, were glad, and promised and covenanted to give him money. He consented, and they weighed unto him thirty pieces of silver. And from that time he sought opportunity how he might conveniently deliver him unto them in the absence of the multitude.

Now on the first day of unleavened bread, on which the passover must be sacrificed, the disciples came to Jesus, saying unto him, Where wilt thou that we go and make ready for thee to eat the passover? And he sent two of his disciples, Peter and John, saying, Go and make ready for us the passover, that we may eat. Go into the city, and behold, there shall meet you a man bearing a pitcher of water; follow him into the house whereinto he goeth. And ye shall say unto the master of the house, The Teacher saith unto thee, My time is at hand; I keep the Passover at thy house with my disciples. Where is the guest-chamber, where I shall eat the passover with them? And he will show you a large upper room furnished: there make ready for us. The disciples went forth, and came into the city, and did as Jesus appointed them; and they made ready the passover.

2. *The Passover Celebrated and the Lord's Supper Instituted.*

WHEN it was evening and the hour was come, he sat down at meat with the twelve disciples; and as they were eating, he said unto them, With desire I have desired to eat this passover with you before I suffer: for I say unto you, I shall not eat it, until it be fulfilled in the kingdom of God. And he received a cup, and when he had given thanks, he said, Take this, and divide it among yourselves: for I say unto you, I shall not drink from henceforth of the fruit of the vine, until the kingdom of God shall come.

And as they were eating, Jesus took bread, and blessed, and when he had given thanks he brake it; and he gave to the disciples, and said, Take, eat; this is my body, which is given for you; this do in remembrance of me. And he took a cup in like manner after supper, and when he had given thanks, he gave to them, saying, Drink ye all of it; for this cup is the new covenant in my blood, even that which is poured out for you; this do, as often as ye drink it, in remembrance of me. And they all drank of it.

3. *Jesus Washes the Feet of His Disciples.*

THERE arose also a contention among the disciples, which of them was accounted to be greatest. Jesus, knowing that the Father had given all things into his hands, and that he came forth from God, and goeth unto God, riseth from supper, and layeth aside his garments; and he took a towel, and girded himself. Then he poured water into the basin, and began to wash the disciples' feet, and to wipe them with the towel wherewith he was girded. So he cometh to Simon Peter. He saith unto him, Lord, dost thou wash my feet? Jesus answered and said unto him, What I do thou knowest not now; but thou shalt understand hereafter. Peter saith unto him, Thou shalt never wash my feet. Jesus answered him, If I wash thee not, thou hast no part with me. Simon Peter saith unto him, Lord, not my feet only, but also my hands and my head. Jesus saith to him, He that is bathed needeth not save to wash his feet, but is clean every whit: and ye are clean, but not all. For he knew him that should betray him; therefore said he, Ye are not all clean.

So when he had washed their feet, and taken his garments, and sat down again, he said unto them, Know ye what I have done to you? Ye call me Teacher, and Lord: and ye say well; for so I am. If I then, the Lord and the Teacher, have washed your feet, ye also ought to wash one another's feet. For I have given you an example, that ye also should do as I have done to you. The kings of the Gentiles have lordship over them; and they that have authority over them are called Benefactors. But ye shall not be so: but he that is the greater among you, let him become as the younger; and he that is chief, as he that doth serve. For which is greater, he that sitteth at meat, or he that serveth? is not he that sitteth at meat? But I am in the midst of you as he that serveth. Verily, verily, I say unto you, A servant is not greater than his lord; neither one that is sent greater than he that sent him. If ye know these things, blessed are ye if ye do them.

4. *The Traitor Warned.*

AS THEY were eating, Jesus said, Verily I say unto you, that one of you shall betray me. The Son of man goeth, even as it is written of him: but woe unto that man through whom the Son of man is betrayed! good were it for that man if he had not been born. The disciples looked one on another, doubting of whom he spake. They were exceeding sorrowful, and began to say unto him every one, Is it I, Lord? There was at the table reclining in Jesus' bosom one of his disciples, whom Jesus loved. Simon Peter therefore beckoned to him, and said, Tell us who it is of whom he speaketh. He leaning back, as he was, on Jesus' breast saith unto him, Lord, who is it? Jesus therefore answereth, He it is, for whom I shall dip the sop, and give it him. So when he had dipped the sop, he taketh and giveth it to Judas, the son of Simon Iscariot. And Judas, who betrayed him, answered and said, Is it I, Rabbi? He saith unto him, Thou hast said. And after the sop, then entered Satan into him. Jesus therefore saith unto him, What thou doest, do quickly. Now no man at the table knew for what intent he spake this unto him. For some thought, because Judas had the bag, that Jesus said unto him, Buy what things we have need of for the feast; or, that he should give something to the poor. He then having received the sop went out straightway: and it was night.

5. *The Parting Words of Jesus.*

WHEN he was gone out, Jesus saith, Now is the Son of man glorified, and God is glorified in him, and straightway shall glorify him.

Little children, yet a little while I am with you. Ye shall seek me: and as I said unto the Jews, Whither I go, ye cannot come; so now I say unto you. A new commandment I give unto you, that ye love one another; even as I have loved you, that ye also love one another. By this shall all men know that ye are my disciples, if ye have love to one another.

But ye are they that have continued with me in my temptation; and I appoint unto you a kingdom, even as my Father appointed unto me, that ye may eat and drink at my table in my kingdom; and ye shall sit on thrones judging the twelve tribes of Israel.

Simon Peter saith unto him, Lord, whither goest thou? Jesus answered, Whither I go, thou canst not follow me now; but thou shalt follow afterwards. Peter saith unto him, Lord, why cannot I follow thee even now? I will lay down my life for thee. Jesus answereth, Wilt thou lay down thy life for me? Verily, I say unto thee, that thou to-day, even this night, before the cock crow twice, shalt deny me thrice. But he spake exceeding vehemently, If I must die with thee, I will not deny thee. And in like manner also said they all.

When they had sung a hymn, they went out into the mount of Olives. Then saith Jesus unto them, All ye shall be offended in me this night: for it is written, I will smite the shepherd, and the sheep of the flock shall be scattered abroad. But after I am raised up, I will go before you into

Galilee. But Peter answered and said unto him, If all be offended in thee, I will never be offended. Jesus said unto him, Simon, Simon, behold, Satan asked to have you, that he might sift you as wheat: but I made supplication for thee, that thy faith fail not; and do thou, when once thou hast turned again, establish thy brethren.

And he said unto them, When I sent you forth without purse, and wallet, and shoes, lacked ye anything? And they said, Nothing. And he said unto them, But now, he that hath a purse, let him take it, and likewise a wallet; and he that hath none, let him sell his cloak, and buy a sword. For I say unto you, that this which is written must be fulfilled in me, And he was reckoned with transgressors: for that which concerneth me hath fulfilment. And they said, Lord, behold, here are two swords. And he said unto them, It is enough.

SECOND PART.

Christ's Agony in Gethsemane.

JESUS went forth over the brook Kidron unto the mount of Olives, and the disciples followed him. And they came unto a place which was named Gethsemane, where was a garden, into which he entered, himself and his disciples. Now Judas also, who betrayed him, knew the place: for Jesus ofttimes resorted thither with his disciples.

And when he was at the place he said unto them, Sit ye here, while I go yonder and pray. And he took with him Peter and the two sons of Zebedee, James and John, and began to be sorrowful and sore troubled. Then saith he unto them, My soul is exceeding sorrowful, even unto death: abide ye here, and watch with me. And he went forward a little, and was parted from them about a stone's cast; and he kneeled down, and fell on his face on the ground, and prayed, that, if it were possible, the hour might pass away from him. And he said, My Father, if it be possible, let this cup pass away from me: nevertheless not my will, but thine, be done. When he rose up from his prayer, he came unto his disciples, and found them sleeping, and said unto Peter, Simon, sleepest thou?

couldest thou not watch one hour? and unto them all, What, could ye not watch with me one hour? Why sleep ye? rise, watch and pray, that ye enter not into temptation: the spirit indeed is willing, but the flesh is weak. And a second time he went away, and prayed, saying the same words, My Father, if this cannot pass away, except I drink it, thy will be done. And he came again and found them sleeping, for their eyes were very heavy; and they knew not what to answer him. And he left them again, and went away, and prayed a third time, saying again the same words. And there appeared unto him an angel from heaven, strengthening him. And being in an agony he prayed more earnestly; and his sweat became as it were great drops of blood falling down upon the ground. Then cometh he the third time to his disciples, and saith unto them, Sleep on now, and take your rest.

It is enough: Behold, the hour is at hand, and the Son of man is betrayed into the hands of sinners. Arise, let us be going: behold, he that betrayeth me is at hand.

THIRD PART.

Christ before Annas and Caiaphas.

1. *Jesus Betrayed and Made Prisoner.*

WHILE Jesus yet spake, lo, Judas, one of the twelve, having received the band of soldiers and officers from the chief priests and the Pharisees, and the scribes, and the elders of the people, cometh thither, and with him a great multitude with swords and staves, with lanterns and torches. Now he that betrayed him had given them a token, saying, Whomsoever I shall kiss, that is he; take him, and lead him away safely. Jesus therefore, knowing all the things that were coming upon him, went forth, and saith unto them, Whom seek ye? They answered him, Jesus of Nazareth. Jesus saith unto them, I am he. When therefore he said unto them, I am he, they went backward, and fell to the ground. Again therefore he asked them, Whom seek ye? And they said, Jesus of Nazareth. Jesus answered, I told you that I am he; if therefore ye seek me, let these go their way: that the word might be fulfilled which he spake, Of those whom thou hast given me I lost not one. And when Judas was come, straightway he came to Jesus, and saith, Hail, Rabbi; and kissed him. And Jesus said unto him, Judas, betrayest thou the Son of man with a kiss? Friend, do that for which thou art come. Then they came and laid hands on Jesus, and took him. And when they that were about him saw what would follow, they said, Lord, shall we smite with the sword? And behold, Simon Peter stretched out his hand, and drew his sword, and smote the servant of the high priest, and struck off his right ear. Now the servant's name was Malchus. Jesus therefore said unto Peter, Put up the sword into the sheath: for all they that take the sword shall perish with the sword. Or thinkest thou that I cannot beseech my Father, and he shall even now send me more than twelve legions of angels? How then should the scriptures be fulfilled, that thus it must be? The cup which the Father hath given me, shall I not drink it? And he touched the servant's ear, and healed him.

And Jesus said unto the chief priests, and captains of the temple, and elders, and to the multitudes that were come against him, Are ye come out, as against a robber, with swords and staves to seize me? When I sat daily with you in the temple teaching, ye stretched not forth your hands against me: but this is your hour, and the power of darkness. But this is come to pass, that the scripture of the prophets might be fulfilled.

Then all the disciples left him, and fled. And a certain young man followed with him, having a linen cloth cast about him, over his naked body: and they laid hold on him; but he left the linen cloth, and fled naked. So the band and the chief captain, and the officers of the Jews, seized Jesus and bound him, and led him to Annas first; for he was father-in-law to Caiaphas, who was high priest that year. Annas therefore sent him bound unto Caiaphas the high priest. Now Caiaphas was he that gave counsel to the Jews, that it was expedient that one man should die for the people. And there all the chief priests and the elders and the scribes were gathered together.

2. Peter's Denials.

SIMON PETER followed Jesus afar off to see the end, and so did another disciple. Now that disciple was known unto the high priest, and entered with Jesus into the court of the high priest; but Peter was standing at the door without. So the other disciple, who was known to the high priest, went out and spake unto her that kept the door, and brought in Peter. The maid therefore that kept the door saith unto Peter, Art thou also one of this man's disciples? He saith, Woman, I know him not. Now the servants and the officers were standing there, having made a fire of coals; for it was cold; and they were warming themselves; and Peter also was with them, standing and warming himself. One of the servants of the high priest, being a kinsman of him whose ear Peter cut off, saith, Did not I see thee in the garden with him? But Peter said, Man, I know not what thou sayest. And straightway the cock crew. And after a little while they that stood by came and said to Peter, Of a truth thou also art one of them; for thy speech maketh thee known. Then began he to curse and to swear, I know not this man of whom you speak. And immediately, while he yet spake, the second time the cock crew. And the Lord turned, and looked upon Peter. And Peter remembered the word of the Lord, how that he said unto him, Before the cock crow twice this day thou shalt deny me thrice. And he went out and wept bitterly.

3. Christ before Caiaphas and the Sanhedrin.

THE HIGH PRIEST asked Jesus of his disciples, and of his teaching. Jesus answered him, I have spoken openly to the world; I ever taught in the synagogue, and in the temple, where all the Jews come together; and in secret spake I nothing. Why askest thou me? Ask them that have heard me, what I spake unto them: behold, these know the things which I said. And when he had said this, one of the officers standing by struck Jesus with his hand, saying, Answerest thou the high priest so? Jesus answered him, If I have spoken evil, bear witness of the evil: but if well, why smitest thou me?

Now the chief priests and the whole council sought false witness against Jesus, that they might put him to death; and they found it not, though many false witnesses came. For many bore false witness against him, and their witness agreed not together. But afterward came two, and said, We heard him say, I will destroy this temple that is made with hands, and in three days I will build another made without hands. And not even so did their witness agree together.

And the high priest stood up in the midst, and asked Jesus, saying, Answerest thou nothing? What is it which these witness against thee? But he held his peace, and answered nothing. Again the high priest asked him, and saith unto him, I adjure thee by the living God, that thou tell us whether thou art the Christ, the Son of God. And Jesus said, I am: henceforth ye shall see the Son of man sitting at the right hand of the power of God, and coming with the clouds of heaven. And the high priest rent his clothes, and saith, What further need have we of witnesses? Ye have heard the blasphemy: what think ye? And they all condemned him, and said, He is worthy of death. And some began to spit on him, and to cover his face, and to buffet him, and to say unto him, Prophesy unto us, thou Christ: who is he that struck thee? And the officers received him with blows of their hands. And many other things spake they against him, reviling him.

Now when morning was come, all the chief priests and the elders of the people took counsel against Jesus to put him to death.

4. Remorse and Death of Judas.

THEN Judas, who betrayed him, when he saw that he was condemned, repented himself, and brought back the thirty pieces of silver to the chief priests and elders, saying, I have sinned in that I betrayed innocent blood. But they said, What is that to us? see thou to it. And he cast down the pieces of silver into the sanctuary, and departed; and he went away and hanged himself. And the chief priests took the pieces of silver, and said, It is not lawful to put them into the treasury, since it is the price of blood. And they took counsel, and bought with them the potter's field, to bury strangers in. Wherefore the field was called the field of blood unto this day. Then was fulfilled that which was spoken through Jeremiah the prophet, saying, And they took the thirty pieces of silver, the price of him that was priced, whom certain of the children of Israel did price; and they gave them for the potter's field, as the Lord appointed me.

FOURTH PART.

The Trial of Christ before Pilate and Herod.

1. Jesus Examined before Pilate.

THEY led Jesus from Caiaphas into the Prætorium, and delivered him up to Pilate the governor; and it was early; and they themselves entered not into the Prætorium, that they might not be defiled, but might eat the passover. Pilate therefore went out to them, and saith, What accusation bring ye against this man? They answered and said unto him, If this man were not an evil-doer, we should not have delivered him unto thee. Pilate said unto them, Take him yourselves, and judge him according to your law. The Jews said unto him, It is not lawful for us to put any man to death: that the word of Jesus might be fulfilled, which he spake, signifying by what manner of death he should die.

And they began to accuse him, saying, We found this man perverting our nation, and forbidding to give tribute to Cæsar, and saying that he himself is Christ a King. And when he was accused by the chief priests and elders, he answered nothing. Then saith Pilate unto him, Hearest thou not how many things they witness against thee? And he gave him no answer, not even to one word: insomuch that the governor marvelled greatly.

Pilate therefore entered again into the Prætorium, and called Jesus, and said unto him, Art thou the King of the Jews? Jesus answered, Sayest thou this of thyself, or did others tell it thee concerning me? Pilate answered, Am I a Jew? Thine own nation and the chief priests delivered thee unto me: what hast thou done? Jesus answered, My kingdom is not of this world: if my kingdom were of this world, then would my servants fight, that I should not be delivered to the Jews: but now is my kingdom not from hence. Pilate therefore said unto him, Art thou a king then? Jesus answered, Thou sayest that I am a king. To this end have I been born, and to this end am I come into the world, that I should bear witness unto the truth. Every one that is of the truth heareth my voice. Pilate saith unto him, What is truth? And when he had said this, he went out again unto the Jews, and saith unto them, I find no crime in him.

2. *Jesus Accused before Herod.*

PILATE said unto the chief priests and the multitudes, I find no fault in this man. But they were the more urgent, saying, He stirreth up the people, teaching throughout all Judæa, and beginning from Galilee even unto this place. But when Pilate heard it, he asked whether the man were a Galilæan. And when he knew that he was of Herod's jurisdiction, he sent him unto Herod, who himself also was at Jerusalem in these days.

Now when Herod saw Jesus, he was exceeding glad: for he was of a long time desirous to see him, because he had heard concerning him; and he hoped to see some miracle done by him. And he questioned him in many words; but he answered him nothing. And the chief priests and the scribes stood vehemently accusing him. And Herod and his soldiers set him at nought, and mocked him, and arraying him in gorgeous apparel sent him back to Pilate. And Herod and Pilate became friends with each other that very day: for before they were at enmity between themselves.

And Pilate called together the chief priests and the rulers and the people, and said unto them, Ye brought unto me this man, as one that perverteth the people: and behold, I, having examined him before you, found no fault in this man touching those things whereof ye accuse him: no, nor yet Herod: for he sent him back unto us; and behold, nothing worthy of death hath been done by him. I will therefore chastise him, and release him.

3. *Barabbas Released and Jesus Scourged.*

NOW AT THE FEAST the governor was wont to release unto the multitude one prisoner, whom they would. And they had then a noted prisoner, called Barabbas, a robber, who for a certain insurrection made in the city, and for murder, was cast into prison. And the multitude went up and began to ask him to do as he was wont to do unto them. And Pilate answered them, saying, Will ye that I release unto you the King of the Jews? For he perceived that for envy the chief priests had delivered him up. And while he was sitting on the judgment-seat, his wife sent unto him, saying, Have thou nothing to do with that righteous man; for I have suffered many things this day in a dream because of him.

Now the chief priests and the elders persuaded the multitudes that they should ask for Barabbas, that he should rather release him unto them, and destroy Jesus. But the governor, desiring to release Jesus, answered and said unto them, Which of the two will ye that I release unto you? And they said, Barabbas. Pilate said unto them, What then shall I do unto Jesus who is called Christ? And they cried out again, Crucify him. And Pilate said unto them the third time, Why, what evil hath this man done? I have found no cause of death in him. I will therefore chastise him, and release him. But they were urgent with loud voices, asking that he might be crucified. And their voices prevailed. And Pilate, wishing to content the multitude, released unto them Barabbas, but Jesus he scourged and delivered up to their will.

4. *Jesus Crowned with Thorns and Condemned to Death.*

THEN the soldiers of the governor took Jesus into the Prætorium, and gathered unto him the whole band. And they stripped him, and put on him a scarlet robe. And they platted a crown of thorns and put it upon his head, and a reed in his right hand; and they kneeled down before him, and mocked him, saying, Hail, King of the Jews! And they spat upon him, and took the reed and smote him on the head.

And Pilate went out again, and said unto them, Behold, I bring him out to you, that ye may know that I find no crime in him. Jesus therefore came out, wearing the crown of thorns and the purple garment. And Pilate said unto them, Behold the man! When the chief priests and the officers saw him, they cried out, Crucify him, crucify him! Pilate saith unto them, Take him yourselves, and crucify him: for I find no crime in him. The Jews answered him, We have a law, and by that law he ought to die, because he made himself the Son of God.

When Pilate therefore heard this saying, he was the more afraid; and he entered into the Prætorium again, and saith to Jesus, Whence art thou? But Jesus gave him no answer. Pilate therefore saith unto him, Speakest thou not unto me? Knowest thou not that I have power to release thee, and have power to crucify thee? Jesus answered him, Thou wouldest have no power against me, except it were given thee from above: therefore he that delivered me unto thee hath greater sin.

Upon this Pilate sought to release him: but the Jews cried out, saying, If thou release this man, thou art not Cæsar's friend: every one that maketh himself a king speaketh against Cæsar. When Pilate therefore heard these words, he brought Jesus out, and sat down on the judgment-seat at a place called The Pavement, but in Hebrew, Gabbatha. And he said unto the Jews, Behold, your king! They therefore cried out, Away with him; away with him, crucify him! Pilate saith unto them, Shall I crucify your King? The chief priests answered, We have no king but Cæsar.

So when Pilate saw that he prevailed nothing, but rather that a tumult was arising, he took water, and washed his hands before the multitude, saying, I am innocent of the blood of this righteous man; see ye to it. And all the people answered and said, His blood be on us, and on our children.

And Pilate gave sentence that what they asked for should be done. Then therefore he delivered him unto them to be crucified.

FIFTH PART.

The Suffering of Our Lord on Golgotha and His Last Words on the Cross.

1. *Jesus on His Way to Calvary.*

AND WHEN THEY had mocked him, they took off from him the purple robe, and put on him his garments. And they led him out to crucify him. And he went out unto the place which is called Golgotha, bearing the cross for himself. And when they came out, they compelled one passing by, Simon of Cyrene, coming from the country, the father of Alexander and Rufus, to go with them, and laid on him the cross, to bear it after Jesus.

And there followed him a great multitude of people, and of women who bewailed and lamented him. But Jesus turning unto them said, Daughters of Jerusalem, weep not for me, but weep for yourselves, and for your children. For behold, the days are coming, in which they shall say, Blessed are the barren, and the wombs that never bare, and the breasts that never gave suck. Then shall they begin to say to the mountains, Fall on us; and to the hills, Cover us. For if they do these things in the green tree, what shall be done in the dry?

And there were also two others, malefactors, led with him to be put to death. And when they came unto the place called The Skull, they offered him wine mingled with gall: and when he had tasted it, he would not drink.

2. *Jesus Crucified.*

AND THERE they crucified him, and the malefactors, one on the right hand and the other on the left, and Jesus in the midst. And it was the third hour. And Jesus said, *Father, forgive them; for they know not what they do.* And Pilate wrote a title also, and they set up over his head on the cross his accusation; and there was written, JESUS OF NAZARETH, THE KING OF THE JEWS. This title therefore read many of the Jews, for the place where Jesus was crucified was nigh to the city; and it was written in Hebrew, and in Latin, and in Greek. The chief priests of the Jews therefore said to Pilate, Write not, The King of the Jews; but, that he said, I am King of the Jews. Pilate answered, What I have written I have written.

And the soldiers, when they had crucified Jesus, took his garments and made four parts, to every soldier a part; and also the coat; now the coat was without seam, woven from the top throughout. They said therefore one to another, Let us not rend it, but cast lots for it, whose it shall be: that the scripture might be fulfilled, which saith,
They parted my garments among them,
And upon my vesture did they cast lots.

These things therefore the soldiers did; and they sat and watched him there.

But there were standing by the cross of Jesus his mother, and his mother's sister, Mary the wife of Clopas, and Mary Magdalene. When Jesus therefore saw his mother, and the disciple standing by whom he loved, he said unto his mother, *Woman, behold thy son!* Then saith he to the disciple, *Behold, thy mother!* And from that hour the disciple took her unto his own home.

And the people stood beholding. And they that passed by railed on him, wagging their heads, and saying, Ha! thou that destroyest the temple, and buildest it in three days, save thyself; if thou art the Son of God, come down from the cross. In like manner the chief priests mocking him among themselves, with the scribes and elders, said, He saved others; himself he cannot save. He is the King of Israel; let him now come down from the cross, and we will believe on him. He trusteth on God; let him deliver him now, if he desireth him: for he said, I am the Son of God. And the robbers also that were crucified with him cast upon him the same reproach. And the soldiers also mocked him, coming to him, offering him vinegar, and saying, If thou art the King of the Jews, save thyself.

And one of the malefactors that were hanged railed on him, saying, Art not thou the Christ? save thyself and us. But the other answered, and rebuking him said, Dost thou not even fear God, seeing thou art in the same condemnation? And we indeed justly; for we receive the due reward of our deeds: but this man hath done nothing amiss. And he said, Jesus, remember me when thou comest in thy kingdom. And he said unto him, *Verily, I say unto thee, To-day shalt thou be with me in Paradise.*

3. The Death of Jesus on the Cross.

WHEN the sixth hour was come, there was darkness over the whole land until the ninth hour, the sun's light failing. And at the ninth hour Jesus cried with a loud voice, saying, Eli, Eli, lama sabachthani, that is, *My God, my God, why hast thou forsaken me?* And some of them that stood there, when they heard it, said, This man calleth Elijah.

After this Jesus, knowing that all things are now finished, that the scripture might be accomplished, said, *I thirst.* There was set there a vessel full of vinegar. And straightway one of them ran, and took a sponge, and filled it with vinegar, and put it on a reed, and gave him to drink. And the rest said, Let be; let us see whether Elijah cometh to save him.

And when Jesus therefore had received the vinegar, he said, *It is finished.* And crying with a loud voice, he said,

Father, into thy hands I commend my spirit: and having said this, he bowed his head and yielded up his spirit.

And behold, the veil of the temple was rent in two from the top to the bottom; and the earth did quake, and the rocks were rent, and the tombs were opened; and many bodies of the saints that had fallen asleep were raised; and coming forth out of the tombs after his resurrection they entered into the holy city and appeared unto many.

Now the centurion, and they that were with him watching Jesus, when they saw the earthquake, and the things that were done, feared exceedingly, saying, Certainly this was a righteous man. And many women were there beholding from afar, who had followed Jesus from Galilee, ministering unto him: among whom was Mary Magdalene, and Mary the mother of James and Joses, and Salome, the mother of the sons of Zebedee; and many other women that came up with him unto Jerusalem. And all the multitude that came together to this sight, when they beheld the things that were done, returned smiting their breasts.

The Jews therefore, because it was the Preparation, that the bodies should not remain on the cross upon the sabbath (for the day of that sabbath was a high day), asked of Pilate that their legs might be broken, and that they might be taken away. The soldiers therefore came, and brake the legs of the first, and of the other that was crucified with him: but when they came to Jesus, and saw that he was dead already, they brake not his legs: howbeit one of the soldiers with a spear pierced his side, and straightway there came out blood and water.

And he that hath seen hath borne witness, and his witness is true: and he knoweth that he saith true, that ye also may believe. For these things came to pass, that the scripture might be fulfilled, A bone of him shall not be broken. And again another scripture saith, They shall look on him whom they pierced.

SIXTH PART.

The Burial of Jesus.

IT was the Preparation, that is, the day before the sabbath. And when even was now come, there came a rich man from Arimathæa, named Joseph, a good and righteous man, who was looking for the kingdom of God, being a disciple of Jesus, but secretly, for fear of the Jews. He had not consented to their counsel

and deed. This man went to Pilate and asked for the body of Jesus. And Pilate marvelled if he were already dead: and calling unto him the centurion, he asked him whether he had been any while dead. And when he learned it of the centurion, he granted the corpse to Joseph. He came therefore, and took away his body.

And there came also Nicodemus, he who at the first came to him by night, bringing a mixture of myrrh and aloes, about a hundred pounds. So they took the body of Jesus, and bound it in linen cloths with the spices, as the custom of the Jews is to bury.

Now in the place where he was crucified there was a garden; and in the garden a new tomb, which Joseph had hewn out in the rock, wherein never man had yet lain. There then because of the Jews' Preparation (for the tomb was nigh at hand) they laid Jesus. And they rolled a great stone against the door of the tomb, and departed. And Mary Magdalene was there, and Mary the mother of Joses, sitting over against the sepulchre, and beheld the tomb, and how his body was laid. And they returned, and prepared spices and ointments. And on the sabbath they rested according to the commandment.

Now on the morrow, which is the day after the Preparation, the chief priests and the Pharisees were gathered together unto Pilate, saying, Sir, we remember that that deceiver said while he was yet alive, After three days I rise again. Command therefore that the sepulchre be made sure until the third day, lest haply his disciples come, and steal him away, and say unto the people, He is risen from the dead: and the last error will be worse than the first. Pilate said unto them, Ye have a guard: go, make it as sure as ye can. So they went, and made the sepulchre sure, sealing the stone, the guard being with them.

prepared spices and ointments. And on the sabbath they rested according to the commandment.

Now on the morrow, which is the day after the Preparation, the chief priests and the Pharisees were gathered together unto Pilate, saying, Sir, we remember that that deceiver said while he was yet alive, After three days I rise again. Command therefore that the sepulchre be made sure until the third day, lest haply his disciples come, and steal him away, and say unto the people, He is risen from the dead: and the last error will be worse than the first. Pilate said unto them, Ye have a guard: go, make it as sure as ye can. So they went, and made the sepulchre sure, sealing the stone, the guard being with them.

And there came also Nicodemus, he who at the first came to him by night, bringing a mixture of myrrh and aloes, about a hundred pounds. So they took the body of Jesus, and bound it in linen cloths with the spices, as the custom of the Jews is to bury.

Now in the place where he was crucified there was a garden; and in the garden a new tomb, wherein Joseph had hewn out in the rock, wherein never man had yet lain. There then because of the Jews' Preparation (for the tomb was nigh at hand) they laid Jesus. And they rolled a great stone against the door of the tomb, and departed. And Mary Magdalene was there, and Mary the mother of Joses, sitting over against the sepulchre, and beheld the tomb, and how his body was laid. And they returned, and

Indexes

Indexes

Scripture Themes for the Church Year

FIRST SUNDAY IN ADVENT.
The Coming of the Lord to His Church.

The new day calls for a new life. Rom. 13. 11–14.
Christ's entry into Jerusalem. Mt. 21. 1–9.
Preparing the King's highway. Ps. 24.
The King of Truth. Jn. 18. 36, 37.
Raising aloft the banner of God. Is. 62. 10–12.
Jesus in the synagogue of Nazareth. Lk. 4. 16–22.

SECOND SUNDAY IN ADVENT.
Waiting for the Day of the Lord.

The patient endurance of hope. Rom. 15. 4–13.
Signs of the coming of the Lord Lk. 21. 25–36.
Perseverance in hope. Heb. 10. 35–39.
Servants looking for their Lord. Lk. 12. 35–40.
Awaiting the coming of the Lord. Jas. 5. 7–10.
The coming of the kingdom. Lk. 17. 20–30.

THIRD SUNDAY IN ADVENT.
The Forerunner of the Lord.

Appeal to the judgment of God. 1 Cor. 4. 1–5.
John's message to Jesus. Mt. 11. 2–10.
The Light of the prophetic word. 2 Pet. 1. 19–21.
The testimony of Jesus to John. Mt. 11. 11–19.
Salvation foretold by the prophets. 1 Pet. 1. 7–13.
John preaches repentance. Lk. 3. 1–14.

FOURTH SUNDAY IN ADVENT.
The Lord is at Hand.

The presence of the Lord gives joy. Phil. 4. 4–7.
The testimony of John. Jn. 1. 19–28.
The power and mercy of the coming Lord. Is. 40. 9–11.
The friend of the Bridegroom. Jn. 3. 22–36.
The coming Lord a righteous Saviour. Is. 51. 3–5.
The Father bears witness of the Son. Jn. 5. 31–39.

CHRISTMAS DAY.
The Nativity.

The Prince of Peace. Is. 9. 2–7.
The birth of Jesus. Lk. 2. 1–20.
Christ the image of God. Heb. 1. 1–3.
The Word became flesh. Jn. 1. 1–14.
God gives life to the world. Tit. 2. 11–14.
Immanuel. Mt. 1. 18–24.

SECOND DAY OF CHRISTMAS.
The Martyrs.

The first martyr bears witness to Christ. Acts 6. 8 –15; 7. 54–60.
God's judgment upon persecutors. Mt. 23. 34–39.

The purging fires of persecution. 1 Pet. 4. 12–19.
The unavoidable conflict. Mt. 10. 32–39.
The soldier of Christ endures hardship. 2 Tim. 2. 3–9.
The baptism of fire. Lk. 12. 49–53.

SUNDAY AFTER CHRISTMAS.
The Childhood of Jesus.

Christ makes us children of God. Gal. 4. 1–7.
The consolation of Israel. Lk. 2. 33–40.
The Lord gives strength to the weary. Is. 40. 26–31.
The little flock. Lk. 12. 32.
God is our refuge. Ps. 62. 5–8.
The protecting hand of God. Mt. 2. 13–23.

NEW YEAR'S DAY.
The Childhood of Jesus.

The grace of God new every morning. Lam. 3. 22–26.
Baptism reveals the goodness of God. Tit. 3. 4–7.
The name of Jesus. Lk. 2. 21.
Jehovah our keeper. Ps. 121. 1–8.
Prayer in the name of Jesus. Jn. 14. 13.
We shall all give account for the day of grace. Rev. 2. 1–5.
Intercession for the barren fig tree. Lk. 13. 6–9.

SUNDAY AFTER NEW YEAR.
Holy Baptism.

Baptism consecrates to a new life. Rom. 6. 3–11.
The goodness of God revealed in Holy Baptism. Tit. 3. 4–7.
The baptism of Jesus. Mt. 3. 13–17.
Baptism means communion with Christ. Col. 2. 9–15.
John's testimony on the baptism of Jesus. Jn. 1. 29–34.
The baptism of the Ethiopian. Acts 8. 26–39.
Jesus baptizes in the Holy Spirit and in fire. Mt. 3. 11, 12.

EPIPHANY.
The Dawn of a New Day.

The glory of the Lord rises upon Zion. Is. 60. 1–6.
The Wise-men. Mt. 2. 1–12.
The glory of God in the face of Jesus Christ. 2 Cor. 4. 3–6.
Jesus the Light of the world. Jn. 8. 12.
The nations shall come to Zion. Is. 2. 2–5.
Jesus the desire of all nations. Mt. 12. 15–21.

FIRST SUNDAY AFTER EPIPHANY.
Jesus As Disciple and Teacher.

The spiritual service of the Christian. Rom. 12. 1–5.
Jesus in the temple at the age of twelve. Lk. 2. 42–52.

God quenches the soul's thirst. Ps. 42. 1–11.
The bread of life. Jn. 6. 24–36.
Jesus meets the traitor. Mk. 14. 43–50.
Steadfastness in trials. Jer. 20. 7–11.
The true food of the soul. Jn. 6. 52–66.
Peter's denial. Jn. 18. 15–27.

FIFTH SUNDAY IN LENT.
Hatred Increasing. — Jesus Condemned to Death.

The death of Christ cleansing the conscience. Heb. 9. 11–15.
The hatred of the Jews against Jesus. Jn. 8. 46–50.
Barabbas or Jesus. Mt. 27. 15–26.
The distressed soul crying unto God. Ps. 69. 6–16.
Caiaphas urges the death of Jesus. Jn. 11. 47–57.
Christ before Pilate and Herod. Lk. 23. 1–12.
God comforting the suffering soul. 2 Cor. 1. 3–7.
Jesus exposes the plot of the Jews. Jn. 8. 31–45.
Jesus crowned with thorns. Jn. 19. 1–11.

PALM SUNDAY.
The Last Farewell.

The self-humiliation and exaltation of Christ. Phil. 2. 5–11.
The departure of Jesus from Bethany. Jn. 12. 1–16.
Jesus the bread of life. Jn. 6. 32–35.
The Lord's Supper. 1 Cor. 11. 23–29.
The new covenant. Heb. 8. 8–12.
The first communion. Lk. 22. 14–22.

GOOD FRIDAY.
The Crucifixion.

The suffering servant of Jehovah. Is. 52. 13—53. 12.
Christ's self-humiliation and exaltation. Phil. 2. 5–11.
Christ on the cross. Lk. 23. 32–43.

EASTER DAY.
The Resurrection of Christ.

Preparing for the Passover. 1 Cor. 5. 7, 8.
God hath given the victory. 1 Cor. 15. 53–58.
The Resurrection. Mk. 16. 1–8.
Christ the earnest of our resurrection. 1 Cor. 15. 12–21.
The first meeting with the risen Saviour. Jn. 20. 10–18.
The Resurrection of Christ revealing the power of God. Eph. 1. 15–23.
The message of the Resurrection. Mt. 28. 1–8.

EASTER MONDAY.
The Witnesses of the Resurrection.

The risen Christ proclaimed to the Gentiles. Acts 10. 34–43.
The disciples in Emmaus. Lk. 24. 13–35.
The believer a new creature. 2 Cor. 5. 14–21.
The disciples at the tomb. Jn. 20. 1–10.
The Resurrection of Christ begets a living hope. 1 Pet. 1. 18–23.
The guard at the tomb. Mt. 28. 9–15.

FIRST SUNDAY AFTER EASTER.
The Lord Liveth.

Faith in the risen Lord overcometh the world. 1 Jn. 5. 4–10.
Jesus and Thomas. Jn. 20. 19–31.
Peter preaching the risen Christ. Acts 3. 12–20.
The risen Saviour at the sea of Tiberias. Jn. 21. 1–14.
Paul preaching the risen Christ. Acts 13. 32–41.
"Lovest thou me?" Jn. 21. 15–23.

SECOND SUNDAY AFTER EASTER.
The Shepherd and the Sheep.

In the footsteps of Christ. 1 Pet. 2. 21–25.
The Good Shepherd. Jn. 10. 11–16.
The Great Shepherd of the sheep. Heb. 13. 20, 21.
Sheep without a Shepherd. Mt. 9. 36–38.
The Lord is my Shepherd. Ps. 23. 1–6.
True Shepherd and true sheep. Jn. 10. 1–10.

THIRD SUNDAY AFTER EASTER.
Homeward Bound.

The Christian a stranger and a pilgrim. 1 Pet. 2. 11–20.
The tribulation of the Christian is brief. Jn. 16. 16–22.
Tribulation leads to glory. 2 Cor. 4. 16–18.
Jesus prays for eternal life for His followers. Jn. 17. 1–8.
The incorruptible inheritance in heaven. 1 Pet. 1. 3–8.
The way to the Father's house. Jn. 14. 1–12.

FOURTH SUNDAY AFTER EASTER.
The Blessing of Christ's Absence.

Good and perfect gifts from above. Jas. 1. 17–21.
Growth in the truth. Jn. 16. 5–15.
Following Jesus means separation from the world. Heb. 13. 12–16.
Jesus praying for His disciples in the world. Jn. 17. 9–17.
God is greater than our heart. 1 Jn. 3. 18–24.
The intercourse of the friends of Jesus. Jn. 15. 10–17.

FIFTH SUNDAY AFTER EASTER.
Prayer.

Hearers and doers of the Word. Jas. 1. 22–27.
Prayer in the name of Jesus. Jn. 16. 23–33.
The unchangeable priesthood of Christ. Heb. 7. 23–27.
Jesus praying for the unity of His disciples. Jn. 17. 18–23.
The Lord blessing His people. Num. 6. 22–27.
Jesus teaching His disciples to pray. Lk. 11. 1–13.

ASCENSION DAY.
From Humiliation to Exaltation.

Jesus promising the kingdom. Acts 1. 1–11.
The commission of Christ, and His ascension. Mk. 16. 14–20.
The King ascending His throne. Ps. 110. 1–3.

Jesus praying for the perfecting of His followers.
Jn. 17. 24–26.
Nothing can separate us from Christ. Rom. 8. 34–39.
Jesus blessing His disciples and ascending into heaven.
Lk. 24. 49–53.

SIXTH SUNDAY AFTER EASTER.
Waiting for the Promise of the Father.
The time of expectation to be filled with labor. 1
Pet. 4. 7–11.
Jesus promising the gift of the Holy Spirit. Jn. 15.
26—16. 4.
Seeking the things that are above. Col. 3. 1–10.
The spirit of courage and confidence. Mt. 10. 24–31.
The Holy Spirit helping our infirmity. Rom. 8. 26
–28.
The spirit of this world. Jn. 15. 18–25.

WHITSUNDAY.
(Pentecost.)
The Gift of the Holy Spirit.
The Spirit poured forth upon the disciples. Acts 2.
1–18.
The guidance of the Holy Spirit. Jn. 14. 23–31.
The Holy Spirit makes us fellow-citizens with the
saints. Eph. 2. 17–22.
The living water of the Spirit. Jn. 7. 37–39.
The increase of the Church. Acts 2. 37–47.
The promise of another comforter. Jn. 14. 15–21.

WHITMONDAY.
The Progress of the Spirit.
The Spirit shed abroad upon the Gentiles. Acts 10.
42–48.
The giving of the only-begotten Son. Jn. 3. 16–21.
The Church as the body of Christ. 1 Cor. 12. 12–30.
The Father draws men to the Son. Jn. 6. 44–47.
The first church of Gentile Christians. Acts 11. 19–26.
Increased responsibility. Jn. 12. 44–50.

TRINITY SUNDAY.
The Spirit and the New Life.
The glory of God. Rom. 11. 33–36.
Jesus and Nicodemus. Jn. 3. 1–15.
The children of God. 1 Jn. 3. 1–9.
The vine and the branches. Jn. 15. 1–9.
Christ the head of the Church. Col. 1. 9–23.
All nations to be made disciples of Christ. Mt. 28.
18–20.

FIRST SUNDAY AFTER TRINITY.
Priceless Values.
Perfect love casteth out fear. 1 Jn. 4. 16–21.
The rich man and Lazarus. Lk. 16. 19–31.
Our life is not our own. Jas. 4. 13–16.
The rich fool. Lk. 12. 13–21.
The fear of God is better than wealth. 1 Tim. 6.
6–19.
The value of a human soul. Mt. 16. 24–27.

SECOND SUNDAY AFTER TRINITY.
The Call to the Kingdom of God.
He that loves has passed from death to life. 1 Jn.
3. 13–18.
The Great Supper. Lk. 14. 16–24.

The wise put to shame. 1 Cor. 1. 26–31.
The cost of discipleship. Lk. 14. 25–35.
The disappointed love of God. Hos. 11. 1–7.
Complete surrender to Jesus. Lk. 9. 51–62.

THIRD SUNDAY AFTER TRINITY.
The Prevenient Grace of God.
God calls and perfects. 1 Pet. 5. 6–11.
The lost sheep and the lost coin. Lk. 15. 1–10.
Righteousness a free gift of grace. Rom. 4. 1–8.
The prodigal son. Lk. 15. 11–32.
Salvation a gift of God. Eph. 2. 1–10.
Jesus eating with publicans and sinners. Mt. 9. 9
–13.

FOURTH SUNDAY AFTER TRINITY.
The Judgment of Men and of God.
Creation longing for deliverance. Rom. 8. 18–23.
The mote and the beam. Lk. 6. 36–42.
The just judgment of God. Rom. 2. 1–13.
The woman taken in adultery. Jn. 8. 1–11.
Lenience in judgment. Rom. 14. 1–18.
Exhortation to repentance. Lk. 13. 1–5.

FIFTH SUNDAY AFTER TRINITY.
Discipleship.
The Christian is called to inherit a blessing. 1 Pet.
3. 8–15.
The draught of fishes. Lk. 5. 1–11.
The call of Abraham. Gen. 12. 1–4.
The first disciples. Jn. 1. 35–51.
Paul's call to the apostleship. Acts 26. 1–29.
The confession of the disciples. Mt. 16. 13–20.

SIXTH SUNDAY AFTER TRINITY.
The Law of God.
Crucified with Christ. Rom. 6. 3–11.
The higher righteousness required by Christ. Mt. 5.
20–26.
God's judgment of the oppressor. Is. 5. 8–16.
The majesty of the law. Mt. 5. 17–19.
Faith apart from works is dead. Jas. 2. 8–17.
The law of love and the law of retaliation. Mt. 5.
38–42.

THE TRANSFIGURATION OF CHRIST.
On the Mount of Transfiguration.
Christ's glory and honor. 2 Pet. 1. 16–18.
The transfiguration of Christ. Mt. 17. 1–8.
The revelations given to Paul. 2 Cor. 12. 2–9.
The glory of the Son of Man. Jn. 13. 31, 32.
John's vision on Patmos. Rev. 1. 9–18.
The descent from the Mount of Transfiguration. Mt.
17. 9–13.

EIGHTH SUNDAY AFTER TRINITY.
Error.
The Spirit's testimony of our adoption. Rom. 8.
12–17.
False prophets. Mt. 7. 15–21.
The folly of apostasy. Gal. 3. 1–4.
The two ways. Mt. 7. 13, 14.
Proving the Spirit. 1 Jn. 4. 1–6.
The house on the rock. Mt. 7. 22–29.

NINTH SUNDAY AFTER TRINITY.
The Responsibility of Stewardship.
Godlessness leads to destruction. 1 Cor. 10. 6–13.
The unrighteous steward. Lk. 16. 1–9.
Idleness brings misfortune. Prov. 6. 6–11.
The householder, the steward, and the household. Lk. 12. 42–48.
Christians are good workers. 2 Th. 3. 10–13.
Faithfulness in little things. Lk. 16. 10–15.

TENTH SUNDAY AFTER TRINITY.
Wasted Opportunities.
The manifold gifts of grace. 1 Cor. 12. 2–11.
Jesus weeping over Jerusalem. Lk. 19. 41–47.
The goodness and the severity of God. Rom. 11. 17–24.
Jesus rejected at Nazareth. Lk. 4. 23–30.
Disobedience hardens the heart. Heb. 3. 12–19.
The unrepentant cities. Mt. 11. 20–24.

ELEVENTH SUNDAY AFTER TRINITY.
True and False Righteousness.
Grace makes us humble and strong. 1 Cor. 15. 1–10.
The Pharisee and the publican. Lk. 18. 9–14.
Righteousness by faith excludes boasting. Rom. 3. 21–31.
The two sons sent into the vineyard. Mt. 21. 28–31.
Self-examination leads to confession of sin. 1 Jn. 1. 8—2. 2.
Scribes and Pharisees in the seat of Moses. Mt. 23. 1–12.

TWELFTH SUNDAY AFTER TRINITY.
The Use of the Tongue.
The letter killeth, the spirit giveth life. 2 Cor. 3. 4–18.
Jesus heals the deafmute. Mk. 7. 31–37.
The taming of the tongue. Jas. 3. 8–12.
Idle words. Mt. 12. 33–37.
Spiritual things spiritually discerned. 1 Cor. 2. 9 –16.
Sincerity in speech. Mt. 5. 33–37.

THIRTEENTH SUNDAY AFTER TRINITY.
Mercy.
Faith liberates and unites. Gal. 3. 21–28.
The promise is older than the law. Gal. 3. 16–22.
The good Samaritan. Lk. 10. 23–37.
Love is of God. 1 Jn. 4. 7–10.
Jesus teaches brotherly love. Mt. 5. 43—6. 4.
Bountiful seed and bountiful harvest. 2 Cor. 9. 6–10.
The widow's mite. Mk. 12. 41–44.

FOURTEENTH SUNDAY AFTER TRINITY.
Gratitude.
The flesh lusteth against the spirit. Gal. 5. 16–24.
The ten lepers. Lk. 17. 11–19.
It is good to praise the Lord. Ps. 147. 1–11.
The man at Bethesda. Jn. 5. 1–14.
The mercy of God begets gratitude. 1 Tim. 1. 12–17.
Jesus gives thanks to His Father. Mt. 11. 25–30.

FIFTEENTH SUNDAY AFTER TRINITY.
Our Daily Bread.
Christians bearing one another's burdens. Gal. 5. 25 —6. 10.
Our chief concern. Mt. 6. 24–34.
It is more blessed to give than to receive. Acts 20. 32–35.
Martha and Mary. Lk. 10. 38–42.
The independence of the Christian. 1 Cor. 7. 29–31.
The uncertainty of temporal possessions. Mt. 6. 19 –23.

SIXTEENTH SUNDAY AFTER TRINITY.
The Shadow of Death.
Strength to the inner man. Eph. 3. 13–21.
The widow of Nain's son. Lk. 7. 11–17.
Life victorious over death. 2 Cor. 4. 7–14.
Jesus raising Lazarus. Jn. 11. 1–44.
Courage to live and to die. Phil. 1. 19–26.
The power of Jesus to give life. Jn. 5. 19–21.

SEVENTEENTH SUNDAY AFTER TRINITY.
The Liberty of the Christian.
Keeping the unity of the Spirit. Eph. 4. 1–6.
Jesus a guest in the house of the Pharisee. Lk. 14. 1–11.
Conscience and the commandments of men. Col. 2. 16–23.
The true observance of the Sabbath. Mk. 2. 23 –3. 5
Freedom to serve. Gal. 5. 1–14.
"The truth shall make you free." Jn. 8. 31–36.

EIGHTEENTH SUNDAY AFTER TRINITY.
The Way of Perfection.
Christ shall establish us unto the end. 1 Cor. 1. 4–8.
The chief commandment of the law. Mt. 22. 34–46.
True zeal for righteousness leading to Christ. Rom. 10. 1–13.
The treasure and the pearl. Mt. 13. 34–46.
The commandment of Christ shedding light upon the way. 1 Jn. 2. 7–17.
The rich young ruler. Mk. 10. 17–27.

NINETEENTH SUNDAY AFTER TRINITY.
The Narrow Way of Faith.
Be renewed in the spirit of your mind. Eph. 4. 17–28.
Jesus healing the man sick of the palsy. Mt. 9. 1–8.
The problems of life driving us nearer to God. Ps. 73. 1–5, 22–28.
The man born blind. Jn. 9. 1–41.
The conflict between the spiritual man and the natural man. Rom. 7. 14–25.
Jesus contradicted and defended. Jn. 7. 40–52.

TWENTIETH SUNDAY AFTER TRINITY.
Spiritual Indifference.
The careful use of time. Eph. 5. 15–20.
The man without a wedding garment. Mt. 22. 1–14.
Holding fast the confession of hope. Heb. 10. 19–31.
The entrusted talents. Mt. 25. 14–30.

Christ a stumbling-block to the unbeliever. **1 Pet. 2.** 3–9.
The wicked husbandmen. **Mt. 21.** 33–46.

TWENTY-FIRST SUNDAY AFTER TRINITY.
The Foundation of Faith.

The whole armor of God. **Eph. 6.** 10–18.
The Nobleman's Son. **Jn. 4.** 46–53.
Faith looking to the invisible reward. **Heb. 11.** 24 –27.
The signs of the times. **Mt. 16.** 1–4.
The love of God in Christ making faith certain. **Rom. 5.** 1–8.
Jesus showing how faith arrives at certainty. **Jn. 10.** 22–30.

TWENTY-SECOND SUNDAY AFTER TRINITY.
Mutual Forgiveness.

Abounding love making us strong in the Lord. **Phil. 1.** 3–11.
The unmerciful servant. **Mt. 18.** 23–35.
Forgiving as God forgave. **Eph. 4.** 30–32.
Forgiveness without measure. **Mt. 18.** 15–22.
The goal of perfect holiness. **1 Th. 5.** 14–23.
Love abounding. **Mk. 4.** 21–25.

TWENTY-THIRD SUNDAY AFTER TRINITY.
Christian Patriotism.

Our citizenship in heaven. **Phil. 3.** 17—4. 3.
The tribute to Cæsar and to God. **Mt. 22.** 15–22.
Exhortation to prayer for all. **1 Tim. 2.** 1–6.
The golden rule. **Mt. 7.** 12.
The Christian's relation to civic authority. **Rom. 13.** 1–7.
Jesus paying the temple tribute. **Mt. 17.** 24–27.

TWENTY-FOURTH SUNDAY AFTER TRINITY.
The Life That Never Dies.

The inheritance of the saints in light. **Col. 1.** 9–12.
The daughter of Jairus. **Mt. 9.** 18–26.

Sown in corruption, raised in incorruption. **1 Cor. 15.** 35–49.
Jesus permits none of His own to perish. **Jn. 6.** 37–40.
The Christian's translation to his heavenly home. **2 Cor. 5.** 1–10.
The resurrection of the dead. **Lk. 20.** 27–40.

TWENTY-FIFTH SUNDAY AFTER TRINITY.
The Last Times.

The faithful resurrected and transformed. **1 Th. 4.** 13–18.
The abomination of desolation. **Mt. 24.** 15–28.
Faith self-possessed unto the end. **2 Th. 2.** 1–12.
Jesus warning against false security. **Lk. 13.** 22–29.
The coming of the Day of the Lord. **1 Th. 5.** 1–10.
The tribulation of the last times. **Mt. 24.** 1–14.

TWENTY-SIXTH SUNDAY AFTER TRINITY.
Watchfulness.

The Lord will return. **2 Pet. 3.** 3–13.
The ten virgins. **Mt. 25.** 1–13.
God's knowledge of the ways of men. **Ps. 139.** 1–12, 23, 24.
Admonition to watchfulness. **Mk. 13.** 31–37.
Faith longing for the appearing of the Lord. **Rev. 22.** 10–17, 20.
The unexpected coming of the Son of Man. **Mt. 24.** 35–44.

TWENTY-SEVENTH SUNDAY AFTER TRINITY.
The Last Judgment.

God's righteous judgment. **2 Th. 1.** 3–10.
The Son of Man on His throne of glory. **Mt. 25.** 31–46.
All things to be put in subjection to God. **1 Cor. 15.** 22–28.
Resurrection to life or to judgment. **Jn. 5.** 22–29.
New heavens and a new earth. **Rev. 20.** 11—21. 7.
The parable of the net. **Mt. 13.** 47–50.

MINOR FESTIVALS OF THE CHURCH YEAR

THE DAY OF THE PRESENTATION OF CHRIST.
(Candlemas.)
The Revelation.

The promised One arrives. **Mal. 3.** 1–4.
The song of Simeon. **Lk. 2.** 22–32.
Praise to Jehovah. **Ps. 100.** 1–5.
Grace and truth through Jesus Christ. **Jn. 1.** 16–18.
Christ's message from God. **1 Jn. 1.** 1–7.
The mustard seed and the leaven. **Mt. 13.** 31–33.

THE DAY OF ANNUNCIATION.
The Annunciation.

Immanuel promised. **Is. 7.** 10–15.
The angel's message to Mary. **Lk. 1.** 26–38.
The coming of the Lord. **Is. 49.** 5, 6.
Mary and Elisabeth. **Lk. 1.** 39–45.
The branch of righteousness. **Jer. 33.** 14–16.
The song of Mary. **Lk. 1.** 46–55.

THE DAY OF JOHN THE BAPTIST.
Heaven and Earth.

The herald preaching comfort. **Is. 40.** 1–8.
The birth of John the Baptist. **Lk. 1.** 57–80.
God the Creator and Lord of all things. **Acts 17.** 22–31.
The message of the angel to Zacharias. **Lk. 1.** 5–25.
The greatness of God's mercy. **Ps. 103.** 8–18.
The death of John the Baptist. **Mk. 6.** 14–29.

ST. MICHAEL'S DAY.
Greatness and Lowliness.

Michael contending against the dragon. **Rev. 12.** 7–12.
The greatest in the kingdom of heaven. **Mt. 18.** 1–10.
No one like unto God. **Ps. 113.** 1–7.
Jesus and the children. **Mk. 10.** 13–16.
Jacob's ladder. **Gen. 28.** 10–17.
The children in the temple. **Mt. 21.** 14–17.

ALL SAINTS' DAY.

The Saints.

The innumerable multitude before the throne. **Rev.** 7. 9–17.

The great multitude praising God. Rev. 7. 2–4, 9–12.

The beatitudes. Mt. 5. 1–12.

The cloud of witnesses. Heb. 12. 1–3.

The salt of the earth and the light of the world. Mt. 5. 13–16.

The saints serving God before the throne. Rev. 14. 1–3.

Blessings and woes. Lk. 6. 20–26.

FIRST DAY OF PRAYER.

Repentance.

The penitent crying unto the Lord. Ps. 130. 1–8.

Woes pronounced upon the impenitent. Mt. 11. 20 –24.

SECOND DAY OF PRAYER.

The Reformation.

The righteous shall live by faith. Rom. 1. 16, 17.

The way to God. Mt. 11. 25–30.

THIRD DAY OF PRAYER.

Missions.

The Lord is king of the nations. Ps. 96. 1–10.

The gospel coming to all peoples. Mt. 28. 18–20.

FOURTH DAY OF PRAYER.

Thanksgiving.

Praise to God for all things. Ps. 103. 1–5.

The unsearchable wisdom of God. Rom. 11. 33–36.

Psalms

Those marked * are used as pericopes.

Authors, Translators, and Sources of Hymns

Composers and Sources of Tunes

Composers and Sources of Tunes

𝔗𝔲𝔫𝔢𝔰

Metres

Subjects

Advent of Christ, 1—23.
Angels, 208; 318.
Anniversaries, 299; 295; 579.
Ascension of Christ, 145—153.
Atonement, 118: 4; 145: 2; 149:
2; 190: 3; 237: 2. See also
Work of Christ.
Baptism, 59; 225—233; 258: 1,
2, 3.
Bible. See *Word of God.*
Blindness, Spiritual, 67: 2; 68:
2; 72: 4–7; 158: 1, 2; 159:
1, 3; ⁻⁻⁰: 5; 173: 1; 249: 6;
302: 2; 347: 3; 370: 2.
Blood of Christ, 97: 105: 1; 106;
107; 108: 3–5; 109: 1, 2;
111; 113; 114; 145: 1–3; 193:
3; 207: 1; 237; 420—424;
426; 427; 441: 3.
Born again. See *Regeneration.*
Charities. See *Missions, Inner.*
Chastening, 411: 4–6. See also
Trials and *Resignation.*
Children—
Prayers for the, 534—536.
Prayers for the use of, 537—
542.
Hymns for, 632—663.
Death of, 607—609.
Christ, Ascension of. See *Ascension.*
Christ, Birth of. See *Christmas.*
Christ, Divinity of, 14: 1, 3; 50:
2; 317. See also *Christ—God.*
Christ dwelling in us. See *Mystical Union.*
Christ glorified, 147; 150: 1, 2.
See also *Ascension Hymns.*
Christ, Incarnation of, 4: 4; 6:
3; 23: 1–3; 24: 3; 33: 2, 4;
34: 2, 3; 37: 2; 40: 1, 2; 61:
2; 76; 115: 4.
Christ, Longing for, 47; 58: 5;
72: 5, 6; 73: 2; 74: 6, 7;
88; 139; 198; 241; 243; 259;
352; 416; 448; 449; 450;
462; 482; 485; 493; 494;
602; 608.
Christ, Passion of, 52: 2, 3; 83:
1, 2; 84; 85; 90—121; 149:
1, 2; 237; 239; 240: 1, 3, 4;
420; 421; 422; 423.
Christ, Presence of, 196.
Christ, Resurrection of, 122—137.
Christ, Second advent of, 7; 8;
9; 10: 2; 11; 12: 4; 17; 19;
20; 47: 5; 73: 3; 76: 3; 137:
4; 143: 5; 146: 5, 6; 151: 4;
187; 197: 3; 198. See also

hymns on *Resurrection* and
Judgment.
Christ, Temptation of, 84; 85.
Christ, Transfiguration of, 203;
204; 205.
Christ, True Man and true God,
50: 2.
Christ, Virgin birth of, 23; 33;
42; 46: 1.
Christ, Work of, 16; 21; 87;
90; 91, 92; 93; 95: 1; 98;
99; 100; 101: 1; 102; 104:
2; 105; 106; 117; 118; 119;
120; 125; 126; 128; 1; 130;
132; 135; 137; 143; 173;
489; 602.
Christ, Names and offices of—
Advocate, 332: 3.
Anointed, 16: 1; 28: 4; 117:
2; 145: 4.
Author of Life, 122: 3.
Beloved, 121: 2.
Branch, 76: 1.
Bread, 134: 4; 169: 1; 236:
1, 2; 238: 1; 239: 2; 240:
3; 241: 3; 242: 1; 246: 7;
249: 1; 250: 1; 452: 1; 477.
Bridegroom, 6: 5; 17: 1, 2;
73: 3; 199: 1, 2; 460: 2.
Brother, 25: 2; 166: 3; 468: 2.
Changeless One, 556: 1.
Conqueror, 147: 1, 2; 434: 5.
Comforter, 4: 5; 88: 1, 2;
465: 1.
Counsellor, 40: 2; 41: 5.
Corner-stone, 273: 1; 274; 5;
275: 2; 276: 1.
Creator, 122: 1.
Crown, 317: 1; 469.
Crucified, 112: 5; 113: 1; 194:
2; 212: 2.
David's Seed, 200: 3.
Day, 556: 1.
Dayspring, 7: 3; 38: 2; 68: 1,
3; 69: 1; 200: 1; 548: 1.
Daystar, 590: 3.
Defender, 434: 3.
Desire of Nations, 22: 1; 34:
3; of hearts, 144: 1.
Expectation, Hope and, 17: 4;
130: 3; 139: 3; 144: 1;
256: 1.
First-begotten, 126: 3.
First-born, 130: 3.
Firstfruits, 123: 4.
Foundation, 264: 1; 273: 1;
279: 1.
Fount, 250: 3; 320: 1.

Fount of Grace, 75: 1; 97:
113: 3, 5.
Fount of Life, 241: 1; 452: 2.
Fountain in desert, 95: 1.
Friend, 88; 116: 4; 120: 2;
143: 4; 193: 2; 245: 3;
252: 3; 259: 1, 4; 261: 5;
343; 430; 468; 470.
Glory, 139: 5; 200: 4.
God, 144: 1; 151: 1; 338: 4;
374: 4; 469: 4.
God of armies, 147: 2.
Guard, 251: 2; 252: 3; 259:
3; 587: 1.
Guide, 136: 4; 210: 6; 252: 5;
259: 1; 434: 6; 464.
Head, 213: 2, 3; 273: 1.
Health, 122: 2.
Hope and Expectation. See *Expectation.*
Immanuel, 7: 1; 34: 2; 40: 5;
42: 3; 149: 4.
Intercessor, 145; 149: 3; 191:
2.
Joy, 134: 3; 144: 5; 150: 3;
241: 1; 469; 491; 521: 3.
Judge, 611.
Key of David, 7: 4.
King, 1; 2; 5; 6: 1, 4; 18;
20; 22; 40; 42: 1; 43: 3;
47: 1, 2; 60: 3, 5; 62: 2;
71: 1; 121: 3; 130: 3; 132:
4; 147; 149: 1; 150: 1, 2;
151; 152: 4, 5; 153; 200:
3, 4; 201; 317; 341; 522;
615: 1; 642.
Lamb, 71; 73: 3; 74: 7; 90;
117: 3; 125: 4; 130: 1; 134:
2; (Paschal), 148: 1; 149:
2; 152: 2, 3; 176: 2; 199:
3; 206; 209: 1, 3; 239: 4;
336: 4; 425: 1; 427; 456;
461: 3.
Leader, 622: 3.
Life, 122: 2; 252: 2; 276: 3;
336: 4; 428; 429; 491: 3.
See also *Author* and *Prince.*
Light, 4: 1; 11; 12; 34: 2;
36: 1; 41: 1; 61: 1; 65: 1,
3; 67; 68; 69; 70; 71; 75;
123: 2; 168: 2; 199: 2;
200: 4; 241: 1; 321; 325;
336: 4; 347: 1, 2; 361;
370: 2; 432: 3; 518; 521;
556.
Lord, 206; 213: 3; 244: 4;
615: 1.
Lord of all, 153.

Scripture References

Hymns for Church Seasons and Special Services

Third Sunday in Lent.

No.

Thou camest down from heaven on high........ 87
Lord, Thy death and passion give............. 92
Crushed by my sin, O Lord, to Thee..........237
Lord, teach us how to pray aright............303

Graduals:

Jesus, in my walk and living.................475
My Jesus, as Thou wilt.................490: 1–3

Fourth Sunday in Lent.

Friend of the weary, O refresh us............. 88
O Bread of life from heaven..................169
O Jesus, Joy of loving hearts.................241
Guide me, O Thou great Jehovah.............452

Graduals:

Lord, Thy death and passion give.........92: 1, 2
Jesus, Thy blood and righteousness.......426: 1–3

Fifth Sunday in Lent.

Blessing, and honor, and glory, and power......336
Not all the blood of beasts...................423
Thou art the Truth, the Way, the Life.........428
Thou art the Way: to Thee alone.............429
Jesus is my Joy, my All.....................491

Graduals:

Christ, the Life of all the living...........91: 2, 3
Lord, Thy death and passion give..........92: 1, 2

Other hymns for Lent: 52, 83, 90–97, 108, 109, 111, 191, 420–423, 426, 451, 461, 472, 504.

Palm Sunday.

O Zion, He approacheth....................1: 2–6
Jerusalem, lift up thy voice.................... 5
Rise, arise! Rise, arise....................... 6
According to Thy gracious word...............239
O Jesus, Joy of loving hearts.................241
O Jesus Christ, Thou Bread of life............249

Graduals:

Ride on, ride on in majesty.................. 98
O Bread of life from heaven..................169

Holy Thursday.

Suffering Son of Man, be near me............. 93
'Tis midnight, and on Olive's brow...........100
Over Kedron Jesus treadeth..................101
Go to dark Gethsemane.................102: 1, 2
My crucified Saviour, despised and contemned...114

Good Friday.

O Lamb of God, most holy.................... 90
Christ, the Life of all the living............. 91
There is a fountain filled with blood........... 97
Near the cross was Mary weeping..............104
When I survey the wondrous cross.............107
There is a green hill far away................108
'Tis finished! So the Saviour cried...........110

No.

Sinful world, behold the anguish.............112
Ah, holy Jesus, how hast Thou offended........115
Thine agony, O Lord, is o'er.................119
Mute are the pleading lips of Him.............120
Our sins, our sorrows, Lord, were laid on Thee..121
Lord Jesus Christ, true man and God.........594

Graduals:

Suffering Son of Man, be near me............. 93
Thy cross, O Jesus, Thou didst bear...........105

Other hymns for Holy Week: 89, 92–96, 99–103, 106, 109, 111, 113, 114, 116–118.

Easter.

Welcome, happy morning! age to age shall say..122
The Saviour is risen..........................123
I know that my Redeemer lives................124
Blest Easter day, what joy is thine............125
Come, see the place where Jesus lay...........126
The day of Resurrection!.....................128
Day of wonder, day of gladness................129
Christ the Lord is risen to-day................130
Come, ye faithful, raise the strain.............131
Christ the Lord is risen to-day................132
Morning breaks upon the tomb................133
In death's strong grasp the Saviour lay........134
Praise the Saviour...........................135

Graduals:

Welcome, Thou Victor in the strife............127
Thou art the Way: to Thee alone.........429: 3, 4

First Sunday after Easter.

I know that my Redeemer lives................124
Come, ye faithful, raise the strain.........131: 2, 3
In triumph our Redeemer.....................137
My hope is built on nothing less..........424: 1, 4
I know in Whom I trust......................434
How firm a foundation, ye saints of the Lord....439
Vanish doubt and hesitation..................440
Behold, by sovereign grace alone..............444

Graduals:

Welcome, Thou Victor in the strife............127
Jesus, Thy blood and righteousness......426: 1, 2, 4

Second Sunday after Easter.

The Saviour is risen....................123: 3, 4
O dear Redeemer crucified...................138
Though we all in sinful blindness.............173
We hail Thee, Lord, Thy Church's Rock........213
With God and His mercy, His Spirit, and Word..272
The Lord my Shepherd is.....................480

Graduals:

Jesus, I my cross have taken.............446: 1, 2
Thine forever! God of love..............252: 4, 5

Third Sunday after Easter.

In the holy Father's keeping..................140
The little while I linger here..................457

DAILY PRAYER.

Morning.

Evening.

The Lord's Day.

(See also hymns for opening and closing of services.)

First Words of Stanzas

First Lines of Hymns

First Lines of Hymns

Pericopes and Other Scripture Passages Contained in the Hymnal

(The composite text of The Passion of Our Lord is necessarily omitted.)

Pericopes

		PAGE
	....	818
	....	801
	....	769
	1–10	819
15.	12–21	785
15.	22–28	847
15.	35–49	841
15.	53–58	785

II CORINTHIANS.
1.	3–7	781
3.	4–18	821
4.	3–6	756
4.	7–14	827
4.	16–18	792
5.	1–10	842
5.	14–21	788
6.	1–10	770
9.	6–10	824
11.	19–31	767
12.	2–9	814

GALATIANS.
3.	1–4	816
3.	16–22	822
3.	21–28	823
4.	1–7	752
4.	22–31	776
5.	1–14	830
5.	16–24	824
5.	25—6. 10	826

EPHESIANS.
1.	15–23	786
2.	1–10	808
2.	17–22	799
3.	13–21	827
4.	1–6	829
4.	14–16	765
4.	17, 20–28	832
4.	30–32	839
5.	1–9	773
5.	15–20	835
6.	1–4	760
6.	10–18	837

PHILIPPIANS.
1.	3–11	838
1.	19–26	829
2.	5–11	782, 784
3.	7–14	766

3.	17—4. 3	839
4.	4–7	747

COLOSSIANS.
1.	9–12	841
1.	9–23	803
1.	24–29	775
2.	9–15	755
2.	16–23	830
3.	1–10	798
3.	12–17	764

I THESSALONIANS.
4.	1–7	772
4.	13–18	842
5.	2–10	843
5.	14–23	839

II THESSALONIANS.
1.	3–10	846
2.	1–12	843
2.	13–17	762
3.	10–13	817

I TIMOTHY.
1.	12–17	825
2.	1–6	840
6.	6–19	805

II TIMOTHY.
1.	3–5	759
1.	7–10	763
2.	3–9	751
3.	10—4. 5	768

TITUS.
2.	11–14	750
3.	4–7	753, 754

HEBREWS.
1.	1–3	749
2.	11–16	758
3.	12–19	819
4.	15, 16	771
5.	7–9	773
7.	23–27	795
8.	8–12	783
9.	11–15	779
10.	19–31	835
10.	35–39	745
11.	1–22	761
11.	23–40	763

		PAGE
11.	24–27	837
12.	1–3	855
13.	12–16	794
13.	20, 21	791

JAMES.
1.	12–15	771
1.	17–21	793
1.	22–27	795
2.	8–17	814
3.	8–12	821
4.	13–16	804
5.	7–10	745

I PETER.
1.	3–8	793
1.	8–13	746
1.	18–23	788
2.	3–9	836
2.	11–20	792
2.	21–25	791
3.	8–15	819
4.	7–11	797
4.	12–19	751
5.	6–11	807

II PETER.
1.	16–18	814
1.	19–21	746
3.	3–13	844

I JOHN.
1.	1–7	849
1.	8—2. 2	820
2.	7–17	831
3.	1–9	802
3.	13–18	805
3.	18–24	794
4.	1–6	816
4.	7–10	823
4.	16–21	804
5.	4–10	789

REVELATION.
1.	9–18	815
2.	1–5	754
7.	2–4, 9–12	854
7.	9–17	855
12.	7–12	853
14.	1–3	856
20.	11—21. 7	847
22.	10–17, 20	845